Transformations of the Word

Transformations of the

Transformations
of the
Word

Spenser, Herbert, Vaughan

JOHN N. WALL

The University of Georgia Press
Athens and London

© 1988 by the University of Georgia Press

Athens, Georgia 30602

All rights reserved

Set in Linotron Garamond No. 3

The paper in this book meets the guidelines for permanence and durability of the
Committee on Production Guidelines for Book Longevity of the Council on Library
Resources.

Printed in the United States of America

92 91 90 89 88   5 4 3 2 1

Library of Congress Cataloging in Publication Data

Wall, John N.

Transformations of the Word.

Bibliography: p.

Includes index.

1. English poetry—Early modern, 1500–1700—History
and criticism. 2. Christian poetry, English—Early
modern, 1500–1700—History and criticism. 3. Church
of England—History. 4. Church of England. Book of
common prayer. 5. Spenser, Edmund, 1552?–1599—Religion.
6. Herbert, George, 1593–1633—Religion. 7. Vaughan,
Henry, 1622–1695—Religion. 8. Religion and literature—
England. I. Title.

PR535.R4W35   1988   821'.3'09382   86-24969

ISBN 0-8203-0930-3 (alk. paper)

British Library Cataloging in Publication Data available

For Harvey and John, and for Herschel and Gwynne—
"The harbingers are come. See, see their mark."

Vides ut in Christo noventur omnia et rerum vocabula permutentur.
ERASMUS
Enchiridion militis christiani

(You see how in Christ all is made new and the names of
things are completely transformed.)

Be thou *Verbum* too, a Word, as God was; a Speaking, and a
Doing Word, to his glory, and the edification of others.
JOHN DONNE
Sermon for Trinity Sunday 1627

Contents

Acknowledgments

This study began, as much as anything which involves experience and reflection over a number of years can be said to begin at a specific time and place, in the fall of 1970 in the Church of the Advent on Brimmer Street in Boston one Sunday morning during the 11:00 Mass. It was an auspicious time for me to begin to consider the relationships between religion and literature. I was studying for orals in my graduate program in English at Harvard University and I was also working through my middler year at the Episcopal Theological School. While I was reviewing and enriching my knowledge of Renaissance literature, I was also enrolled in Harvey Guthrie's course in prayer and the spiritual life, in which I was learning the importance for Anglicanism of its emphasis on the centrality of corporate worship. Two years before at Harvard I had taken Herschel Baker's seminar Religion and Literature from More to Milton, which had confirmed for me an interest in the literature and culture of the English Renaissance initiated earlier in undergraduate classes with O. B. Hardison, Stephen Baxter, and Samuel Hill of the University of North Carolina at Chapel Hill. The previous year I had taken a seminar at Harvard with Alan Heimert on British and American Puritanism, a seminar at the Episcopal Theological School with John Booty on the theological controversies of the sixteenth and seventeenth centuries in England, a year-long study of liturgy and the arts with Dwight Walsh of the Boston University School of Theology, and another year-long study of the history of Christian theology with Harry Bumpus, S.J., of Weston College.

This was also a time in which the consequences of several generations of research and reflection were beginning to produce changes in the language and ceremonial of worship. Prayer Book revision was very much on people's minds. It was said frequently that the changes coming about were the greatest and most far-reaching since the Reformation. As a result, as I took part that Sunday in the worship of a parish of the Episcopal church, I was attuned to the importance of worship, especially changes in worship, for the church's understanding of itself. I was very aware of the opportunities and the costs of liturgical change, of the ways in which theology and worship can interact, and of the significance of the nonverbal as well as the verbal in the performance of the liturgy.

I was also aware that seminary senior thesis and graduate school dissertation loomed ahead, and that I needed to decide soon what I would write about if I were to complete both degree programs in any reasonable period of time. With all that in mind on that Sunday, during a choral part of the Advent's rich Anglo-Catholic ceremonial of the Mass, I happened to turn to the back of the Prayer Book and glance through the Thirty-nine Articles of Religion, noting especially Article XXXV with its reference to the first "Book of Homilies, which were set forth in the time of Edward the Sixth" and its claim that this book, along with the second Book of Homilies of Elizabeth's reign, "doth contain a godly and wholesome Doctrine, and necessary for these times . . . and therefore we judge them to be read in Churches by the Ministers, diligently and distinctly, that they may be understanded of the people." Remembering that the Book of Common Prayer, the use of which I was then participating in, was also in large measure a product of the reign of Edward VI and also intended to be "understanded of the people," I began to wonder what the Book of Homilies and, perhaps, other founding texts of the Church of England, now relegated to passing reference in the back of the Prayer Book, might tell me about the intentions of Thomas Cranmer and his fellow Reformers as they set out to transform a medieval Latin church into a reformed vernacular one. Later, when I found out that Cranmer intended the twelve sermons in that first Book of Homilies to be read over and over during the use of the Prayer Book in every church in England in "suche ordre as they stande in the boke," I also began to wonder about the cultural situation and the pedagogical theory which would lead Cranmer to adopt such a (seemingly) unpromising method of Christian education.

These questions formed the origins of my study. I have rehearsed this narrative of origins to make clear that as this study explores the consequences of occasions of worship long past for poets long dead, it also represents yet another work that comes after, and responds to, the interactions among reading, preaching, prayer, and Communion that Cranmer made possible in English with his Prayer Books of 1549 and 1552. What I have experienced now has thus been a constant reminder of what happened then and how that might have been experienced and understood and what might have happened as a result. There is much about the past we cannot know, but there is much we can know if we take the time to reconstruct it. Thus, one All Saints' Day's use of the Great Litany several years ago reminded me that this was Cranmer's first effort at corporate prayer in English and thus represents an embryonic form of the whole Prayer Book. After we started doing baptisms on Sunday mornings as part of the main service and stopped doing them on Saturday afternoons with only the family and godparents present, I found that Cranmer sought a similar practice in the 1550s.

My sense that what we were discovering in working with the new Prayer Book enlightened the experience of the early English Reformers and my growing awareness that the documents of Cranmer's Reformation comprised a definite program for church reform sustained me through my seminary thesis, graciously overseen by William Wolf and Lloyd Patterson of the Episcopal Theological School faculty, and through my Harvard dissertation, supervised with unfailing support and encouragement by Gwynne Blakemore Evans and John Booty.

Toward the end, Gwynne wanted to know how we might talk about the ways in which the public worship of the Church of England influenced the major writers of the Elizabethan and Jacobean eras. Here, after all, were texts so integral to the life of Renaissance England that we could determine from them what prayers and biblical passages were read and, with a lesser degree of certainty, what sermons were preached in churches all over England day by day, Sunday by Sunday, year after year, throughout this age. We also know that it is the habitual in experience that often determines whether other things will seem commonplace or strikingly new; we know that the habitual by virtue of constant repetition is more determinative of understanding than the occasional.

Yet coming to answer Gwynne's question—to understand and articulate how writers of the English Renaissance were influenced by the fact that their primary source of knowledge about Christianity was the ongoing worship of the Church of England—has proven to be a difficult and so far impossible question to answer. What I provide here is a preliminary report on only one aspect of the issue—the relationship between the Church of England and three major writers who clearly (or so I believe) supported, encouraged, and promoted involvement in the goals and methods of the Reformers who created the Church of England through the documents that enabled its corporate worship. I complete it, appropriately enough, on the day appointed on the calendar of the Episcopal church for 1986 to observe the inaugural use of the first Book of Common Prayer on the Feast of Pentecost, June 9, 1549. This day the Episcopal church calls on its members to remember "Thomas Cranmer, [who,] with others, restored the language of the people in the prayers of [the] Church" and to be "thankful for this heritage." Cranmer's heritage has been a rich one indeed; to describe its influence is one task of this study.

I also complete it as a member and sometimes convener of an Episcopal parish very different from the one in which I began it. St. Mark's Episcopal Church in Raleigh is as eucharistically centered as the Church of the Advent in Boston, but its language of worship is contemporary and its ceremonial is direct and straightforward. I would not be without either in my experience, and both have taught me much that is in this book. Both in different ways have enabled me to experience and not just imagine the ways in which the practice of worship affects the understanding of doctrine. Both have made clear how Cranmer's tradition is one in which what is important is what happens and not just what one believes about what happens when a people gather to break bread and share one cup.

The Episcopal church in the last two decades has been through another Reformation. It has again had its Cranmers and Latimers and Jewels and Hookers; it has also had its Gardiners and Bonners. The results of change are not always predictable, but its patterns and actors often are. We have discovered again the difficulty of change and the depth of resistance to it, yet we have also reexperienced Cranmer's vision of worship in the language "understanded of the people" that brings the faithful together to perform their ministries at one table. Spenser envisioned what such a community might accomplish in an often hostile and uncomprehending society; Herbert tended that community and Vaughan sustained it in its darkest hour. My own recent experience has helped to illumine their situations for me.

In getting from that day of beginning at the Church of the Advent in Boston and at Harvard to this day of completion at St. Mark's in Raleigh and at North Carolina State University, I have incurred many debts. The dedication inscribes my special gratitude to Herschel Baker, whose seminar opened this field for me, and to Gwynne Evans, who saw me through the dissertation and who has continued to read and speak encouragingly about the various forms this study has taken over the years. It also records my special thanksgiving for John Booty, who taught me about the English Reformation and who also continues to encourage and support my work, and for Harvey Guthrie, dean of the Episcopal Theological School, my tutor and instructor in biblical studies, prayer, and liturgy, who more than anyone has helped me understand the ethos of Anglicanism.

Since coming to North Carolina State University I have had the good fortune to have in Larry Champion and John Bassett two supportive department heads who have helped me find time for research. Charlene Turner has typed or supervised production of the various drafts and versions of this manuscript in her always splendid way. Among my colleagues at NCSU, Tom Hester has enriched my understanding of Renaissance literature and Tony Harrison has cared to know how the work was going. They and others have made NCSU a good place to practice this profession.

Grants from the Mellon Foundation and the National Endowment for the Humanities have made possible postdoctoral years at Duke University and at the National Humanities Center. At Duke, Leigh DeNeef invited me to take part in his graduate seminars in Renaissance literature and helped me greatly at a crucial time. The community of scholars at the National Humanities Center in 1980–81 heard about this study and made it better by their comments as I prepared the first full draft. I am especially grateful to D. W. Robertson, Paul Ricoeur, Thomas Cripps, Judith Ferster, and Stephen Marcus. Kent Mulligan and all the staff of the National Humanities Center made me feel welcomed and made possible more productive work than I had any right to expect to get done in a year.

My wife and my daughters know how much I appreciate their parts in my life and my part in theirs, including their support of me during this undertaking.

An early version of the section on Book I of Spenser's *Faerie Queene* was published as "The English Reformation and the Recovery of Christian Community in Spenser's *The Faerie Queene*," in *Studies in Philology* 80 (1983): 161–162. I am grateful to the editor for permitting me to use that material again here. Drafts of other sections were read at meetings of the Modern Language Association, the South Atlantic Modern Language Association, and the Southeastern Renaissance Conference.

My readers for the University of Georgia Press—S. K. Heninger, Ira Clark, and Coburn Freer—gave the manuscript their time and attention and made its final versions better by their astute sense of its weaknesses as well as its strengths. For the Press, Debra Winter and Mary Hill helped me make matters of style and format into as much of an asset as I am capable. As always, credit for what is helpful here must belong in large measure to this cloud of witnesses; I will take responsibility for what is not.

John Donne should be a part of the group of writers I treat here. But he turned out to need his own book.

Raleigh, North Carolina
The Feast of the Book of Common Prayer
May 22, 1986

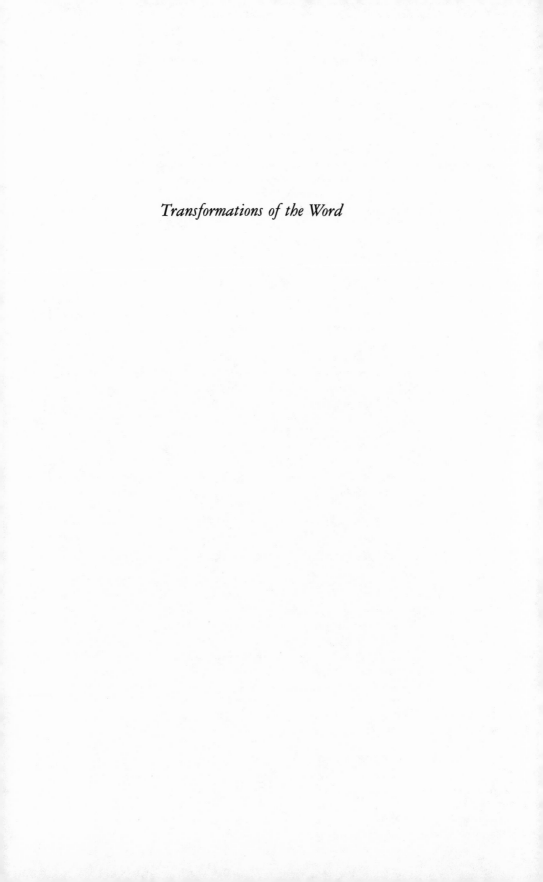

Transformations of the Word

Prologue: Poetry and Reformation in Renaissance England

And may not I presume a little further, to show the reasonableness of this word *vates,* and say that the holy David's Psalms are a divine poem? If I do, I shall not do it without the testimony of great learned men, both ancient and modern. But even the name of Psalms will speak for me, which being interpreted, is nothing but songs. . . . But truly now having named him, I fear me I seem to profane that holy name, applying it to poetry, which is among us thrown down to so ridiculous an estimation. But they that with quiet judgments will look a little deeper into it, shall find the end and working of it such as, being rightly applied, deserveth not to be scourged out of the Church of God. —Sir Philip Sidney[1]

My argument is that the poems of Spenser, Herbert, and Vaughan are best seen in the context of the "Church of God," which for them in the sixteenth and seventeenth centuries was the Church of England.[2] Since all Englishfolk during the reigns of Elizabeth, James, and Charles were required by law to be baptized and to take part regularly in the worship of the Church of England, this may seem an unexceptional claim. It is not. Most studies of literature and religion bring the literary text into relationship with a prior body of theological discourse which is used to inform and explain the "meaning" of the poem or fictional work under consideration. Because the post-Reformation Church of England "defied all efforts to categorize it confessionally,"[3] it is therefore less amenable than other Reformation traditions to the kind of definition usually found in studies relating religion and literature. As a result, its distinctive articulations of Christianity have been obscured, confused with other traditions, or denied significance for the writers of the age.

Opinion about the religious orientation of English Renaissance writers is now divided between those who posit continuity between medieval religious writing and its sixteenth-century inheritors and those who see these writers' primary orientation in the direction of one or another tradition of continental Protestantism. In each case, interpreters assume the availability of fixed, widely held formulations of the faith intelligible apart from the day-to-day lives of institutions and individuals. They also place theological formulations on a level different from the literary texts they seek to interpret in reference to theological discourse. Thus, the writings of Calvin or Luther are used to explain the poems of Spenser or Herbert when these poets seem to be using the language or concepts of, say, justification by faith or predestination. Such approaches ignore the common heritage of texts and religious traditions shared by all sixteenth-century European Christians. They also privilege theological writing in its relationship to religious poetry, making the theological discourse prior to and informing of the poetic discourse.[4] Finally, they do not allow for the possibility that the Church of England could be both reformed and distinct from continental reformed traditions, that, starting from a shared critique of medieval Christianity, it could have gone its own way to establish a tradition of Christian orientation and interpretation different in style, content, and emphasis from the traditions evolved by continental Protestants.

I will acknowledge that the Church of England was Protestant in that it differentiated itself in fundamental ways from the medieval church at the time of its Reformation. I will also agree that the Church of England shared certain concerns with the continental Reformations, especially in advocating vernacular worship and Scripture, in recovering the preaching office (but not apart from the Eucharist), in demystifying the priesthood and restoring the Eucharist to the people, and in rejecting medieval definitions of the Christian life, especially in the destruction of the monastic model and its attendant complex of contemplative devotions. What follows is, therefore, not a reading of religious literature from an "Anglo-Catholic" perspective. I do not accept the claims of some church historians that the Prayer Book of 1549, with its use of the word "Mass" for the Eucharist or Holy Communion, represents an ideal moment in the history of Anglicanism from which later developments represent a decline. There were certainly those among the English in the 1530s and 1540s who were prepared to accept what would essentially be a medieval church independent of papal authority, and they are available to be claimed as progenitors by anyone today, but Cranmer was not among them.

Nor is this, however, another reading from the perspective of a "Protestant poetics," as Barbara Lewalski and others have popularized the term.[5] The Anglican tradition among Christian bodies is now a distinctive "third stream" within Western Christendom alongside Roman Catholicism and the reformed church traditions; the origins of its distinctiveness are already in place in the documents of the Edwardian Reformation (1547–1553) and the shape of the Elizabethan Settlement of Religion (1559). I believe, therefore, that the English Reformation possessed a distinctive character which affected the religious writing of the age in profound ways and which prevents us from importing continental writing wholesale to explain it. That distinctive character inheres in the fact that the English Reformation was primarily a liturgical reformation, achieved through changing the religious behavior of England as a nation rather than by exchanging one theological formulary for another. This kind of reformation, no less far-reaching in its significance than any other, makes it possible for us to see formal theological discourse and religious poetic discourse as mutually informing efforts to reach the common end of enriching and furthering the religious life intended by the liturgical documents of the English Reformation. Or, at least it was possible for poets like Sidney to claim, ranking poetry from the point of view of its "end and working," that their art was worthy not to be "scourged out of the Church of God."

This is not to deny that the writings of continental Reformers were important and influential in England, to some more than others. But the writings of all European Christians in the sixteenth and seventeenth centuries should be seen as reinterpretations of the texts received and common to all (the Bible itself, and interpretations of Christian belief from the age of the Fathers); thus the writings of the continental Reformers should be seen not as determining English belief but, in constellation with the writings both in prose and poetry of the English Reformers, as mutually informing but also often contradictory examples of the ways in which various Christian traditions which shared in their common desire to differentiate themselves from both the medieval church and the contemporary Roman Catholic church reinterpreted the received theological tradition, especially the formulations of Paul and Augustine.

To establish a place for the Church of England within the parameters of scholarly discourse about religious literature, I must discuss briefly how recent studies of religion and literature in the Renaissance articulate the historical context for their interaction. Having done this, I plan to shift the ground of discussion away from what I will identify as received assumptions and toward something at once more concrete and more elusive. I will be concerned here with religion as it functions in a society, rather than with religion as a code of belief or as a personal and interior experience, although obviously both will have their roles to play.[6] Among the many ways in which a religious tradition can affect a society, two at least seem to me central; they may appear contradictory and are often articulated in opposing terms, but they can be linked in that one must precede the other. Religion to be functional in a society must first enable the members of that society to feel a sense of continuity, dependability, and predictability about their lives and therefore experience a sense of reassurance and security. Christianity in its origins is rich in "comfortable words" ("I am with you always . . . I will send a comforter . . . whatever you ask in my name will be granted you"), but the late medieval church experienced a crisis in its ability to communicate assurance successfully. Thus, we may characterize responses to this crisis among the separating traditions after the Reformation in terms of their assertion of assurance and its sources. The reassertion of papal authority and Thomistic formularies, the claims to authority for the Bible and of justification by faith only, and the assertion of a God whose authority extends to establishing salvation and reprobation from always and before all time—each in its own way seeks to be a way of enabling people to live hopefully and with assurance.

At a deep level, therefore, a fundamental aspect of religion is its role of bringing together that which has been separated. One possible origin for the word "religion" is the Latin *religare* meaning "to retie," to reconnect, to put back together what has been broken. I find it always appropriate to ask of any religious phenomenon how it functions to meet the very human need to restore what is lost, to perform a work of reconnection and reconciliation, to overcome brokenness and disconnectedness. At times, this function of religion can be used to the benefit of some and the detriment of others; it can mean the support of an unjust political or social structure for fear of greater loss if that system were destroyed; it can also mean asking religion to do cultural and psychological work which a society might otherwise perform if it were willing to risk change. Those who see religion as in some form what Marx called the "opiate of the masses" limit religion to this version of this first role, but in so doing they ignore the creativeness and openness to possibilities for change that such a stance toward experience can bring with it.

They also ignore a second role that is essential at least in the Judeo-Christian religious tradition, the role of religion as transformer of human culture. Religion may also be from the Latin *relegere,* meaning "to reread," to change and renew understandings, to question old readings and make them new. Here again there are rich texts from the beginning—"I make all things new . . . I have come not to bring peace but a sword . . . the first shall be last, and the last first . . . when you have fed or clothed or comforted or visited the least of these, you have done it to me"—which make clear that the church to be true to itself must promote change in selves and society, even though that may bring disruption and threaten the assurance that it also must provide. Thus, the major traditions emerging from the Reformation had to come to terms with their need to promote change. The Roman Catholic emphasis on human cooperation with grace conveyed sacramentally, the Lutheran (although not Luther's) emphasis on good works as thanskgiving for saving faith, and the Calvinist emphasis on good works as signs of God's election all represent attempts to address that need.

I hope to be able to distinguish the Church of England from both its medieval predecessor church and its contemporary churches both Protestant and Roman Catholic. Simply put, the Church of England at least from the time of Edward VI grounded its effort to meet both of these needs in different places, by different means, and according to different senses of importance. The Church of England under the direction of Archbishop Cranmer joined other emerging Protestant traditions in rejecting papal authority and with it a view of the Bible and the Sacraments which made them the preserve of the professionally religious. It joined other Protestant churches in providing worship and Scripture in the language of the people rather than in medieval Latin. Yet it chose to locate the source of assurance not in a doctrine or an experience of conversion or election but in its life of worship made possible by the Book of Common Prayer, the Bible in English, and preaching as represented by the Book of Homilies. Cranmer wrote that by *"these holy mysteries . . . we be very members incorporate in [Christ's] mystical body . . . and be also heirs through hope of thy everlasting kingdom"* (emphasis added). Assurance thus resided in a series of occasions observed and in the lives articulated and revealed through those occasions, not in a body of doctrine to which assent was demanded.

Second, Cranmer made transformation and change, especially on a societal (rather than on an exclusively individual) level, far more important than did other Protestant traditions. When pressed, no Lutheran or Calvinist would deny the need for Christians to behave themselves, but good works were secondary in importance to both traditions. After all, to Luther the essential point is that we are justified by grace through faith and not works; to Calvin, salvation is conceivable precisely because it is an eternal decree of God from before creation and all time which cannot be affected by the actions of us miserable sinners. Yet Cranmer claimed, combining Paul and James, that the faith that saved is "a true and lively faith," and that in the life of the community gathered at the Lord's table we are given grace to "do all such good works as thou hast prepared for us to walk in," works which reveal the presence of that "true and lively faith." Following the lead of its true midwife Erasmus, the Church of England placed following Christ by loving one's neighbor and behaving charitably toward all, seeking to build up the Christian commonwealth through corporate worship, at the center rather than at the periphery of its theological and social agenda.

Thus the Church of England as it will be described here is concerned with developing a corporate life of worship as its place of assurance and furthering a societal transformation through the pursuit of active charity rather than private devotion as its overriding goal. This emphasis is marked in the use of the Book of Common Prayer instead of either the medieval missal or a service of preaching and extemporaneous prayer; it is also marked by the abolition of the medieval monastic and devotional system in favor of a definition of the Christian life as one of good works of love and charity that show forth a "true and lively faith." This way of thinking about the Church of England helps us understand why English religious controversies in the sixteenth and seventeenth centuries swirl around the Book of Common Prayer rather than around matters of doctrine. Supporters and advocates of the Church of England found their sense of identity through use of that book; their opponents found their Christian identity elsewhere. As a result, the established church could accept diversity in interpretation of the faith so long as the public worship of the Prayer Book continued, while those who found their identity in one or another doctrinal position demanded that the worship of the nation be brought into line with that doctrinal position, an untenable position for those in whose lives the use of the Prayer Book held the place that doctrine held in the lives of others.

This all has to do with poetry because my thesis in this study is that Spenser, Herbert, and Vaughan set out to promote the social agenda of the Church of England, both its assurance-giving worship and its transformation-promoting goal of realizing the true Christian commonwealth in England. At the same time, each worked under very different circumstances and thus understood the terms of that agenda quite differently. Spenser, for example, was concerned with the church as the source of a social agenda and of the ability to achieve it; he thus moves from a specific concern for the life of the Church of England in Book I of *The Faerie Queene* to a concern in the remaining books for the life of active charity it enables. Herbert is concerned with the nation-as-church, with building up the Christian commonwealth through building up the Body of Christ as a living temple. Vaughan, writing when the actual life of the church was absent, seeks poetic experience that enables his readers to experience Christian identity in its terms even in its absence.

Working as though it is of more importance to these writers what biblical texts the Prayer Book calls to be read on certain feast days than whether Spenser's, Herbert's, or Vaughan's understanding of predestination is that of Paul, Augustine, or Calvin requires a shift in our presuppositions about how poetry is to be read and understood. We must seek a social function for poetry, one in which its goals are understood not in terms of imagining doctrines poetically or in reproducing understandings already arrived at in other words, but in changing things. As in so many things in the Renaissance, Sidney will serve as a guide, for we will seek an understanding of poetry in terms of its "end and working," its ability "to teach, to delight, and to move."

We will encounter methodological difficulties, however, for as I have said I am concerned with change. A poet who seeks to write poems in the Sidneyan mode may acknowledge the need readers have to be reassured, but his poems must also seek to change the reader. This is especially true if they are put to the use of a church which seeks social transformation, the reign of charity, the Christian commonwealth. Thus, we will find that the writers examined here often provide the illusion of the familiar in generic or imagistic or narrative terms, only to reveal its illusory quality, providing no final rest in the text or its fictional world. These religious poets knew that the work of the church was in the world; reading was an instigation and, like worship, a source for understanding what needed to be done. Yet the aspect of a text that promotes transformation in the reader and the reader's world is not the subject of much study. We often posit a meaning in or behind a text rather than an intention for a text; I plan to find that the meaning of a text resides in what the writer intends to result from use of his text and not in the text apart from the reader's response to it beyond the actual act of reading.

For these purposes, I find that recent literary theory and poststructuralist practice provide at least the beginnings of a vocabulary of the issues that need to be attended to in articulating change. Jonathan Goldberg suggests of his project that it reveals how the "value of texts lies in their contingency, not in some security or consolation they may offer."[7] I would hope to show the same for the texts examined here precisely because the promotion of change is fundamental to the Church of England's agenda, and one of the things which a fully Christian literature struggles against is all the humanly created sources of security and consolation. The success of a truly persuasive Christian poetic is here found to lie in its acknowledgment of its contingency and its dependence on participation in the divine action for its efficacy.

Because the articulation of texts as agencies of change is not the customary manner of doing Renaissance scholarship, I hope to approach the central agenda of this study by surveying received expectations about the appropriate verbal contexts for construing religious poetry of this age; here, there is much to admire. The virtue of recent studies lies in the fact that they have dealt with this writing as religious literature and not merely as literature which happens to have a religious subject. They demonstrate that the specifically religious context and content of such writing provide not just the occasion or subject of writing, but also an array of distinctive sources, purposes, modes, and themes which must be taken into account if we are to understand the full significance of this work.

One way to describe the diversity and richness of such readings is to think of them as naming various occasions in religious history and in associated verbal contexts to inform the works they consider. Thus, Douglas Waters, in his *Duessa as Theological Satire,* asserts that the scene for Book I of Spenser's *Faerie Queene* is the verbal duel between English Protestants and their Catholic adversaries, especially concerning the theology of the Mass.[8] In this light,

Spenser's poem becomes an attack on the Mass as a symbol of corruption in the Roman Catholic church and a defense of reformed eucharistic doctrine. For Waters, therefore, the Renaissance in England manifests a break with the medieval tradition at least at the level of theological or polemical discourse. Rosemond Tuve's classic *A Reading of George Herbert* posits, however, a continuity of popular devotional language in England between the late Middle Ages and the Renaissance. From her perspective, George Herbert's poetry is intelligible in terms of its use of traditional imagery which had "ceased to be ingenious conceits and had become the natural language of deep feeling."[9] Louis Martz, on the other hand, locates the context for early seventeenth-century religious poetry in the practice of meditation, specifically that guided by Counter-Reformation techniques for using language to arouse profound emotional states of devotion.[10] Barbara K. Lewalski also offers a meditative context for religious literature, although her models are framed by a Calvinist formulation of the progress of the individual Christian life.[11] For Stanley Fish, religious writing is an essentially dialectic undertaking, modeled on the Platonic dialogue's process aimed at "changing, or exchanging minds."[12] Thus, in his view, the appropriate context for reading Herbert's poetry is provided by Herbert's writing on catechetical procedure, in light of which Herbert's poetic strategies may be seen to have direction and purpose.[13]

In each of these interpretive schemes, the common element is the positing of a tradition of using religious language which is presented as the contemporary verbal context in which the works of writers like Spenser, Herbert, and Vaughan can be understood. Implicit in all these studies is a response to the burden of prejudice toward religious literature which has been a part of the history of literary study at least since Samuel Johnson.[14] By the time of his "Life of Waller," the low estimation of poetry addressed in Sidney's *Defence* had been overcome, but in regard to religious poetry the net result was the same: serious writing was still "scourged out of the Church of God." Even in the midst of the metaphysical revival earlier in this century, T. S. Eliot could proclaim that "since the time of Chaucer, Christian poetry . . . has been limited in England almost exclusively to minor poetry."[15]

Recently, however, the proliferation of studies in Spenser, Herbert, Vaughan, Crashaw, and Traherne, to some extent at the expense of interest in the younger Donne,[16] reveals the occurrence of a profound change in our ability to concern ourselves seriously with the treatment of religious issues in poetry. My work is of course dependent on that of my predecessors, and I offer in this study what is, from one perspective, yet another tradition of religious discourse to serve as a context for understanding the poetry of Spenser, Herbert, and Vaughan. It is, as I have already indicated, the fundamental identifying mark of the Church of England—the ongoing worship of Englishfolk as enabled by the use of the Book of Common Prayer—which I would submit forms the indispensable frame for non-Catholic and non-Puritan religious discourse in Renaissance England and provides the definition of that "practical piety, and devotion"[17] espoused by all the writers whose works I will consider.

Within that context I wish to take seriously the overt claims to didactic purpose espoused by all these writers and to approach their works as primarily intended to further involvement in the practice and purposes of public worship in the Church of England. Although John N. King has recently argued that the origins of English Renaissance religious literature lie in the polemical writings of the reign of Edward VI,[18] I suspect that the official documents of the Church of England produced during that reign were of greater significance for the reigns of Elizabeth, James, and Charles than the works of Bale, Baldwin, Crowley, and the other writers of whom King reminds us. After all, the broad consensus for religious change on which Cranmer relied to support his work did not endure, as the post–Marian exile career of Crowley demonstrates. The energies of this "hot gospeler" quickly became marginal; the slow work of reform through use of the Prayer Book continued.

From another perspective, therefore, my concerns are quite different from those manifested in the works of earlier scholars. To establish some fundamental distinctions, I want to note that although the studies cited here, and many others like them, refute explicitly Johnson's denigration of religious poetry, they continue to apply to the sixteenth and seventeenth centuries what amount to distinctively eighteenth-century categories of thought about the role of religion in English cultural life. Such categories carry with them specific views of the role of language and of literary expression in the religious enterprise that I find anachronistic for the English Renaissance.

Let us recall Johnson's specific charges against religious poetry and the definitions of religion and religious discourse that inform them. In his *Life of Waller*, Johnson defines religious writing as having two subjects which differ in their appropriateness for poetic treatment. The subjects are "doctrine" and "devotion . . . [or] Contemplative piety."[19] The former is appropriate for treatment in a specific kind of poem ("The doctrines of religion may indeed be defended in a didactic poem"), but the latter is not, for "Contemplative piety, or the intercourse between God and the human soul cannot be poetical." Since "the essence of poetry is invention; such invention as, by producing something unexpected, surprises and delights," and the "topics of devotion . . . can receive no grace from novelty of sentiment, and very little from novelty of expression," Johnson argues that "poetical devotion cannot often please."

Embedded in Johnson's discussion is a set of distinctions which articulate an interpretation of the nature of religion and its relationship to society.[20] In the first place, Johnson's definitions create separate agendas for religious poetry and secular poetry. In terms of their subject matter, both doctrine and devotion refer to that which is "already known"; only the former is appropriate for poetry and only if it is what Johnson would define as didactic poetry. For Johnson, secular subject matter alone contains that which yields to the discovery, through invention, of "something unexpected" and is thus appropriately treated in a poetry which he would not call didactic. Such a division is patently false for sixteenth- and seventeenth-century England, in which the collapse of sacred discourse into secular language and the concern of the English Reformers for the conduct of daily life produced a constant interaction between the realms which was a consistent source of surprise. Johnson's use of the word "delight" in this context allies his tradition of critical thought with that of Sidney, who says the defining marks of poetry are its ability "to teach, to delight, and to move." For Sidney, however, it is precisely "the end and working" of poetry that render it worthy "not to be scourged out of the Church of God."

More serious, however, is the division created by Johnson's formulation between two kinds of religious discourse, that which defends doctrine and that which expresses devotion. What concerns me is the definition of religion which makes such a division possible. Implicit in Johnson's view of doctrine is a relationship between religion and theology in which what is believed is equated with a verbal formulation of belief produced by organized reflection about the faith. Johnson's evocation of God as "Omnipotence . . . , Infinity . . . , [and] Perfection"[21] suggests that for him "the Supreme Being" is understood primarily in terms of a philosophical concept or category or idea. In this light, Johnson's definition of the didactic in religious literature as that which defends doctrine may be understood to mean that Christianity is something already defined and expressed in verbal formulations which can then be defended in whatever terms, presumably those of rational argument, the audience for such a work would find convincing. For Johnson, a didactic poem is one which appeals to the intellect or the rational faculty, leaving all the rest of whatever makes up the category "religious" to the realm of "Contemplative piety."

I believe that when critics use a body of theological formulation to provide the context that explains religious poetry of the English Renaissance, they implicitly accept a Johnsonian definition of Christian belief as that verbal formulation to which one gives assent. Since neither Elizabethan nor Stuart England produced a theologian who achieved the international stature of a Luther or a Calvin or a statement of belief as detailed and comprehensive as the pronouncements of the Council of Trent, such approaches usually wind up taking their sightings on the Church of England and its literature from the perspective of Wittenberg or Zurich or Geneva, or even the Catholic colleges in Douai and Reims or the school for Jesuit novitiates at Tournai, instead of from Canterbury or London.[22] Such an imposition of foreign theological categories, however, forces writing at the service of the Church of England into categories of thought that are alien to the actual scene of religious literature in this period, in fact leading some scholars to conclude that the overt claims for didacticism in such writing, when it does not appear to defend doctrine, actually address life outside the realm of Christian concerns.[23]

This approach falsifies the scene for religious writing in the Renaissance in two ways. First, the English Reformation did not involve merely the substitution of one verbal code of doctrine for another. Instead, it denied that the medieval church subsumed all that Christianity could mean and sought to open up the possibilities for Christian meaning to Erasmus' insight that Christianity was a religion "on the way," furthered by diversity of thought united in reference to Christ as the action of God in the world.[24] Archbishop Cranmer sought the transformation of England into a Christian commonwealth through participation in Christ by active love of neighbor as the means to citizenship in the Kingdom of God. He was under no illusion that forcing a nation to subscribe to a single code of belief would accomplish that transformation. Instead, he placed, through the Prayer Book, basic Christian texts and events at the center of religious discourse. So long as the enactment of the Prayer Book rites was maintained, interpretive diversity could be not only tolerated but encouraged as providing glimpses into a mystery that transcended any single religious discourse.[25]

As a result, theological statements by the writers of the English church in this period are occasional and provisional, drawing on a wide range of theological resources from the Bible, the Fathers, and contemporary continental divines, often drawn from commonplace books rather than from systematic reflection and codification of belief. If there is a consistency to be found here, it is not to be sought through attempted construction of theological systems from occasional writings but through awareness of a faithfulness to basic texts and the desire to make those texts speak to particular situations and audiences. The theology of the Church of England is more concerned with how the received tradition is interpreted in the present than it is with the product of interpretation apart from the context in which it occurs.

My second point is actually another way of restating the first. At the heart of the Church of England is not intellectual assent to a specific doctrinal position but the entering in to something *done*. Thomas Cranmer, when he defined his beliefs about the church, made this point explicit:

But if thou wilt needs know where the true church of Christ is, and where the false, and not be deceived, herein take this for a plain and full answer, and wheresoever the word of God is truly preached, without addition of man's doctrines and traditions, and the sacraments duly administered according to Christ's institution, there is the true church, the very spouse of God, Christ being the head thereof.[26]

In this light, the significance of Cranmer's basic texts for reformation—the Bible in English, the Book of Common Prayer, the Book of Homilies, Erasmus' Paraphrases, and the Primers—becomes clearer. When he was free "to issue a theological declaration precisely as he desired it . . . for the first time in his life"[27] during the reign of Edward VI, he produced the texts which make possible the realization of "the true church of Christ" through the use of those texts, rather than by adoption of a formal statement of doctrine to take the place of medieval statements. Cranmer surely glimpsed what Dom Gregory Dix has more recently demonstrated,[28] that the eucharistic theology of the Fathers was particularly oriented toward the action of God in Christ and that medieval theologians had distorted that theology by substituting spatial metaphors for their temporal ones. To the Fathers, the church participated in the one redemptive act of Christ through its actions together with bread and wine, becoming the church and receiving Christ at work among them. Over this theology of eucharistic action medieval theologians laid a theology of objective presence, arguing that Christ was present at a static place there as opposed to an equally static here. To Cranmer, this theology obscured the real significance of the church as the *laos,* or people of God, doing the work in the world he called it to, enabled by the reception of Christ in the Eucharist.

Harvey Guthrie has formulated this orientation aptly:

The method of theology [for the Church of England] is not abstract reasoning. Its method is participation in and observation of the course of events which is the history in which the Church, the eucharistic community, lives and moves and has its being. . . . Its method is not primarily thinking about and lecturing on tradition and liturgy and cult. Its method is participation in liturgy and cult which puts a person and a congregation right into the tradition.[29]

Essential to Cranmer's reformed church is thus not assent to a statement of belief but participation in worship enabled by the Book of Common Prayer, which brings the biblical text and the sacramental enactment of the central event of Christian history into relationship with the present moment of celebration. As a result, when I refer to worship in this study I do not mean a general posture or stance or subjective attitude, but actual participation in corporate public activity using the Book of Common Prayer. Such activity, performed at least twice daily in English parishes and cathedrals, provided the context for reading the Bible, preaching, prayer, and performance of the Sacraments.

The writing I consider here needs to be understood in relationship to that worship activity. Prayer Book worship is an enactment of a conversation among basic texts by and for a congregation which interacts with those texts at a specific time of enactment and, it believes, is thus enabled to do God's work in the world. This interaction generates sermons and extraliturgical texts, including poems, which seek to further conversation between the central texts and the present moment rather than to conform to past doctrinal statements abstracted from either the Bible or Christian tradition. Texts of the established church in this period are appropriately read in terms of the aspirations of the English Reformers and the specific attacks on their reform program with its liturgical center. The poems examined here must be seen as taking their shape and articulation from those controversies, their writers drawing from available theological and literary resources what they believed would be found convincing by those they sought to persuade.[30] These texts are *rhetorical* and *apologetic,* seeking to encourage participation in the central act of the faith—active involvement in the life of the Christian community identified by use of the Book of Common Prayer—by using the language that would hold persuasive power for their audiences. To speak of any of these writers, therefore, as adhering to this or that philosophical tradition or theological -*ism* is to invert the actual relationship and confuse means for ends; it is to imply that the phenomenon so discussed has been reduced from its complexity in the experience of the corporate worship of the English church community to the categories of thought at work in an abstracted system. To make such claims is to affirm for human language an ability to be descriptive and truth speaking, and for Christianity a level of human comprehension that Cranmer and his followers would have found difficult to accept. Perhaps more serious, such claims make of the Church of England something static and fixed, something profoundly "other" than the lived activity of the faithful, an "otherness" to which intellectual assent is required rather than involvement in a community's practice.

On one level, therefore, critics who impose a theological system on the English church and its literature repeat the Johnsonian description of religion as doctrine. Other critics accept his complementary understanding of religion as "Contemplative piety." In this view, religious poetry and devotional writing are basically descriptive of the poet's own private religious experience. Inevitably, this approach plays down Renaissance writers' own didactic claims in favor of a view which isolates writers and texts in a one-to-one relationship with God, a scene for writing that Johnson called "the intercourse between God and the human soul." It espouses the view that Herbert's remark, reported by Izaak Walton, that *The Temple* is "a picture of the many spiritual Conflicts that have past betwixt God and my Soul"[31] should be interpreted to mean that such conflicts may be discussed without mention of their context in the corporate worship of the Church of England to which Herbert in *The Temple* constantly alludes[32] or without mention of the rest of Herbert's request: "if . . . it may turn to the advantage of any dejected poor Soul, let it be made publick."

The corporate and communal nature of English worship and its concomitant sense of a Christian identity which subsumes individual religious experience within the essential action of becoming "very members incorporate in thy mystical body, which is the blessed company of all faithful people" (BCP, p. 265) reorient our understanding of individuality in Christian identity and give to the speakers of Anglican poems what Heather Asals has called a "greater-than-individual personality as a member of the Body of Christ."[33] In Johnson's terms, the primary Christian relationship is between God and the individual; presumably, if he had been asked about the subject, he would have held that the public worship of the church functions to enhance that essentially private relationship. Again, in terms of the English Reformation, this relationship is reversed, the individual experience becoming that which enriches participation in the corporate, Christian identity-giving liturgical life made possible by the Prayer Book. In this view, the didactic role of writing comes to the fore, the writer seeking to encourage participation in Prayer Book worship and a fuller sense of its implications. Thus Henry Vaughan, in the midst of the Church of England's greatest crisis, would choose to praise about Herbert not his personal piety but "the end and working" of his "*holy life* and *verse*" because it "gained many pious *Converts,* (of whom I am the least)."[34]

Adoption of the Johnsonian view of religion as "Contemplative piety," however, affects some critics' views of the religious poetry of the English Renaissance. As biblical scholars have pointed out, the various texts of the Bible became part of the canon of Scripture because they were held to be the essential texts of the faith by the communities of the Old and the New Israel.[35] In England, at the Reformation, use of the Bible in Prayer Book worship became the chief means by which the English experienced the Bible, a practice reinforcing the ancient sense of the Bible as a community text. Barbara K. Lewalski, however, sees some biblical genres as analogous to private lyrics, and thus a "biblical poetics" or a "Protestant poetics" modeled on those texts, as manifest by Donne, Herbert, and Vaughan, must also be essentially "a private mode, concerned to discover and express the various and vacillating spiritual conditions and emotions the soul experiences in meditation, prayer, and praise."[36] Although his meditative and devotional models come from abroad rather than from England, Louis Martz would seem to agree about the essentially private and interior landscape for such texts.[37]

Through use of the Prayer Book, however, the Bible becomes the Word of God and therefore a source of models for Christian discourse in the context of its being read in public worship. As John Donne put it, "We must hear *Evangelium in sermone,* the Gospel in the Word, in the Word so as we may hear it, that is the Word preached; for howsoever it be Gospel in itself, it is not Gospel to us if it be not preached in the Congregation."[38] Thus, in Donne's terms, the Psalms of David, Lewalski's chief model for her "private mode," are the works of a "Prophet of every particular Christian; he foretells what I, what any Christian, shall doe and suffer and say."[39] Yet when Donne made that statement, he was delivering a sermon from within the Prayer Book's liturgical context, in which the Psalms were read through monthly (daily in cathedrals), thus literally becoming among the words of divine address for the English church community. Donne's point is to encourage his congregation to join in that cycle of reading, so that through such corporate activity David's words could become the prayers "of every particular Christian" through his joining in the prayers of the church.

To support this emphasis, Renaissance courtesy books and handbooks for using language from the time of the reign of Edward VI, including Elyot's *Boke of the Governor* and Wilson's *Arte of Rhetorique,* define the good as the active pursuit of the *public* good through living out one's assigned public roles.[40] They define evil in terms of the pursuit of self-interest. Cranmer's Prayer Book, as an exponent of that moral understanding, makes clear that engagement in worship involves an involvement of self in the corporate body, beginning with individual confession and profession of faith and moving toward corporate offering of "ourselves, our souls and bodies, to be a reasonable, holy, and lively sacrifice unto thee," so that through the liturgical action the individual may find his Christian identity through being "incorporate in thy mystical body." Cranmer's goal is not self-annihilation but self-realization through corporate membership in that body, leading to the doing of "all such good works as thou has prepared for *us* to walk in" (emphasis added).

Poetry framed by participation in such formative liturgical activity seeks to promote the purpose of that activity. Instead of imposing Johnson's categories, therefore, I propose to examine the religious literature of this age in terms of the context provided by the ongoing use of the Book of Common Prayer and to take seriously these writers' claims to be writing didactic literature to further that use. I believe we need to look in this literature not for either defense of abstract doctrines or descriptions of personal experience, but for the ways in which these writers marshaled the poetic and linguistic resources at hand to persuade their readers to engage in Prayer Book worship and respond to its working upon them. I am thus exploring more fully a suggestion made by Joseph Summers that in "the poet's and the preacher's experiments, the chief consideration was not how to convey personal experience honestly but how to use language most effectively for the subject, the aim, and the intended audience of specific compositions."[41] My thesis is that what one encounters in these texts is not a reference to what stands behind them, but an attempt to become for the reader a way of seeing the specific historical situation in which the reader encounters the text. What the text provides is tools for understanding, for seeing, for "reading" the audience for a text and the world in which the text is encountered, which are presented in a way that "teaches, delights, and moves" the reader toward the kinds of behavior the writer seeks to persuade him to adopt.

My concern is thus with what would be known by the seventeenth century as the Anglican tradition, the tradition of Cranmer and Hooker and Andrewes and Laud, and, I would argue, of Spenser, Herbert, and Vaughan. I use the term "Anglican" here in full awareness that it, like "Roman Catholic," is of seventeenth-century origin, even though the official name of the Church of England from the beginning was *Ecclesia Anglicana.* Thus the term has value for us, who know that the sixteenth-century struggle to claim words like "church" and "Christian" for one's own group while denying them to others ended in the uneasy truce reflected in different names for different traditions. The distinctive marks of Renaissance Anglicanism included its recovery of the Bible in the vernacular as a living text addressed to English-folk and its creation of a vernacular discipline of *common* prayer as the appropriate context for the reading of that Bible. They also included emphasis on a renewed sense of divine activity in English history in life, manifesting a divine claim on England and its people and calling for a renewed emphasis on moral and ethical behavior in public and private realms as the appropriate response to God's saving actions; abolition of the medieval system of individualized devotional practices in favor of corporate, outward-turning love of one's neighbor; and images of the Christian life as a life-long process of corporate growth in the Spirit subsuming individual growth. These distinctive concerns—emphasizing the public enactment of Word and Sacrament as vehicles of divine grace to those who participated in the Prayer Book rites, enabling charity and building community—all influenced Spenser, Herbert, and Vaughan in ways both obvious and subtle.

In the first place, they provide an agenda for literary activity—the emphasis on didactic proclamation aimed at provoking response to the text that will result in *praxis,* in love of neighbor aimed at transformation of society as the means of participation in the divine redemptive activity. Second, they perform a relationship between the Word and human words which informs these writers' attitudes toward models both biblical and classical and provides them with techniques for the use of language aimed at process and instigation, transformation rather than static depiction. Third, they provide a model for self-understanding and presentation in terms of process and emergence rather than stasis and fixity, a development that has a future fulfillment yet is always already begun, and that involves cancellation and disruption as well as renewal and transformation, dying as well as living. Fourth, they provide a historical place, a temporal locus for extraliturgical religious writing, a normative and authentic use of language which can function as a point of reference for poetic activity. Anglicans, as has often been said, are a people of the book, but what matters is not the book as object but the book made speech, the book in enabling use, enacted in specific moments of historical and communal and personal time.

For Cranmer and his followers, as for Erasmus, "Transformation . . . is the goal of theological discourse";[42] so, too for the poets considered in this study. Their point of reference for the use of language—the public worship of the Church of England—makes its claims for its texts as they are used in public worship, to further the divine activity. The Bible is the Word of God not in and of itself but through its use in public worship; thus it is what it is claimed to be only when it becomes a proclamation performed and thus a proclamation-as-event in and to the present moment of its use, predicated on a faith in divine use. The Bible and the sacramental rites which provide the historical context for the proclamation of the Bible become what they are claimed to be as God uses them to further his redemptive activity, reassuring the faithful, transforming the present, moving them toward future fulfillment. Even as the sense of self operating here is of self known in a relationship that transforms self, so the sense of language at work involves a relationship between extraliturgical texts and the texts which enable the performance of Prayer Book liturgy in specific moments of time—proclaiming, reorienting, demanding, redeeming, transforming, turning, "Speaking, and Doing."[43] As the Word-in-use interacts with human words-in-use, words both of the poets themselves and of those biblical and extrabiblical writers on whom they draw to make their poems, so this interaction models for their readers the interaction between the Word-as-doing and human action which is the subject of Christian proclamation.

In contrast to interpretive theories that imagine a text fixed in time to be acted on by the reader,[44] I would stress instead the text as furthering the becoming that is always already becoming, the text as homiletic in that it proclaims what is going on in a way that brings the pressure of the divine initiative to bear on the moment of enactment to further the working-out of that initiative. Religious poetry of the English Renaissance, at least from the tradition of the Church of England, is interpretive of the Word, bringing news of its doing to the present, in the sense that it functions in a way that furthers the Word's becoming now what it is claimed to be becoming, carrying out the divine injunction to go into all the world, preaching and teaching and baptizing, making all things new. I have, however, found useful the hermeneutic principle that a text is a historical event, interpretive of history in dialogue with the Word-in-use. I have thus paid attention to the specific historical circumstances of the writers whose poems I wish to examine, in terms of the ongoing historical worship of Anglicanism and also in terms of the historical situation faced by Anglicans at various points in the years between 1580 and 1660 by means of which the Church of England's sense of mission and purpose changed in time.

The texts on which I focus are a number of religious poems written in England between the establishment of the Church of England through the Elizabethan Settlement of Religion in 1559 and its restoration as the state church in 1660. I consider chiefly works by Spenser, Herbert, and Vaughan, with a concluding postscript on the ways in which the issues central to these writers fared in the post-Restoration writings of Traherne and Dryden. I have chosen these writers because they reveal three moments of understanding the social agenda of the Church of England and three attempts to promote it. Through the full integration of Anglicanism into English life in the early years of Elizabeth's reign, Thomas Cranmer's one "use" for the whole nation achieved the broad familiarity among Englishfolk that was necessary to provide a functional context for poetic allusion.[45] Spenser, Herbert, and Vaughan thus grew up in worlds in which process through time from cradle to grave was observed, informed, and articulated in the public realm by use of the Prayer Book. Essentially public, corporate, and transformational, that worship subsumed within itself reading of the Bible, preaching, prayer, and sacramental enactment, pursued as the means of transforming England into the true Christian commonwealth.[46] Yet each of these writers understood that social agenda in light of different historical circumstances and thus adopted different categories for understanding it and different methods for pursuing it.

Spenser and Herbert wrote within the ongoing performance of Anglican worship and could assume familiarity with that on the part of their readers. Spenser is the poet of societal transformation, Cranmer's original purpose, in which the activities of the church form the necessary frame and impetus for change, which must be carried out by "gentlemen or noble persons" in the arena of court and country. For Herbert, on the other hand, the church itself had become the body which must be built up into true Christian community. The difference here is one of emphasis only, since English society and the Church of England were the same people, at least legally and intentionally. But this difference, a product both of the development of Anglican identity and of the failure of Elizabeth's age to achieve the goals the church set for it, accounts for Spenser's use of specifically ecclesiastical concerns in Book I of *The Faerie Queene,* followed by more clearly moral and ethical concerns in subsequent books, and for Herbert's creation of a temple of words to teach involvement in the life of the church as the purpose of Christian living.

The victory of Cromwell brought public use of the Prayer Book to an end. If the works of Spenser and Herbert examined here are best understood in the context of the Church of England's ongoing efforts at transforming society, then the writing of Vaughan is best seen in terms of the *absence* of the ongoing life of that community which gave meaning to the language of earlier Anglican writers. Yet the Restoration did not return the religious situation in England to its pre–Civil War condition. By then, Anglicanism's role in English society had been significantly diminished, so that it no longer carried with it the kind of authority needed to play a determining role in the shaping and directing of poetic intention. The works of Traherne and Dryden manifest sharply differing views of the relationship between Anglican worship and the society in which that activity took place. In Traherne, the old communal emphasis on growth in the Christian life is reemphasized and celebrated, but with more limited scope and significance. In Dryden, the Anglican Church as *established,* as a static norm from which to judge and evaluate contrasting and conflicting religious and doctrinal positions, and with them the quality of one's Englishness, comes fully to the fore. Each in his own way, Dryden and Traherne reveal the roles the Church of England found itself playing in a society on which it was now dependent for its existence. Having, in effect, played out its opportunity to function as a major force for societal reform, the Anglican church then became primarily a force for the preservation of existing society and thus became much more the static institution, characterized by already-formulated doctrine and private devotion, that informs Samuel Johnson's views on religious poetry. Not until the beginnings of the religious movements of the nineteenth century was Anglicanism again to play a role aimed at changing the society in which it found itself.

Because of my sense that a rhetorical and homiletic model is the appropriate one for thinking about religious literature in England in the later sixteenth and seventeenth centuries, I begin with a consideration of the nature of language as it is used in Anglican worship, looking at the English Litany of 1544 because it is the first of Thomas Cranmer's efforts at creating worship in the vernacular and because it anticipates and clarifies the ways in which language is used in the Prayer Book itself. I then go on to examine theories of didactic writing in the age, especially as they apply to poetry. Finally, I examine the constellation of modes and genres that the writers of the Renaissance had available to make their poems and to make them function didactically. Such modes of discourse carry with them assumptions about the nature of reality and the place of humanity within it; as distinctively Christian writers, the authors I will examine in this study could not use the classical resources of genre, language, and form without taking a stand toward their conflicting claims in light of Christian proclamation. Indeed, these writers were able to use intertextual rivalries to amplify their claims for Christian perspectives.[47] I will use this discussion to raise questions about what happens to language when it seeks to mediate between the Bible as a text becoming what it claims to be only when used in a liturgical context which is also the context for writing that mediates biblical claims. These questions will then serve as openings into the body of literature by Spenser, Herbert, and Vaughan, writing which seeks to extend the homiletic voice of Anglicanism to, in Herbert's words, "finde him, who a sermon flies."[48]

I also examine the resources for writing in the Renaissance because I believe the writers examined here are understood appropriately within the constellation of beliefs about language revealed in the using of Bible reading, sermons, and liturgical texts. The promulgation of the Bible in English, within the liturgical context Archbishop Cranmer prepared for its use, manifests and promotes certain ways of thinking about and using language for didactic purposes. In this view, human use of language becomes primarily a vehicle for conveyance of the divine into the particulars of everyday life, into the events of history, and into the arena of social and communal relationships. It is no longer merely representational but becomes, in imitation of biblical speech, prophetic and transformational. It no longer seeks to preserve sacred and secular spheres, to distinguish the transcendent from the ordinary, but to facilitate the functioning of the divine in human history. It is thus profoundly incarnational; it at once performs the claims of God over the world, including the world of human discourse, and also offers itself for divine use in furthering God's purposes of redeeming a fallen humanity, including the fallenness of its language. The recovery of the Bible as prophetic and typological utterance in the context of Prayer Book worship is thus central to the English Reformation's sense of itself and the Anglican community's understanding of its relationship to the Word of God.

On occasion, my mode of presentation may seem slow or repetitious; in my defense I can only note that to abandon as historically untenable a view of discourse as static in favor of one that values movement and change is to sacrifice a degree of economy in articulation. A static scheme can be displayed once, in full, and later evoked by brief allusion. I have found, on the other hand, that concern for interchanges in discourse-in-process necessitates some review each time a new development is introduced. Among interactions, the introduction of a new element modifies existing relationships, requiring that the whole be surveyed to see where new connections have been formed, old ones changed, and relative positions modified.

My concern for change-producing interactions in relationships instead of the structure of static definitions of things also requires me to address the form of narrative known as myth and account for its relationship to Christian storytelling. Recently, from the comparative religions approach, the concept of myth has come into wide usage to describe nonscientific language that points to the human experience of transcendence. Especially in the work of Rudolph Otto and Mircea Eliade, "myth" has come to mean a special kind of language intended to engage the hearer in realities not accessible to other kinds of discourse. Some critics have begun to apply this terminology to the religious literature of the Renaissance.[49] Yet I have trouble with the term in reference to Christian writing because I find that it obscures what is central to the Judeo-Christian enterprise. Myth is the language of a religion which seeks to accomplish only the first function of religion I described earlier—to alleviate anxiety about change by reassuring its practitioners of the dependability of things. Even those who, like Northrop Frye, regard the Bible as myth acknowledge that it does not fit conventional manifestations of myth.[50] Its stress on an immanent or incarnate God manifest in specific moments of encounter with humanity, its aggressively linear time-scheme, its attacks on the mythic cultures of the ancient Near East, its future orientation are all exceptions to the characteristics of myth systems. The Christian "scandal of particularity," claiming the historicity of the saving acts of God as the central motif of biblical and Christian writing, is decidedly unmythic. In fact, I agree with Herbert Schneidau that the Bible is a *demythologizing* document, best seen over against the cyclical, anxiety-removing schemes of mythic cultures.[51] It is precisely this element of the Bible—its prophetic perspective on human life—that was reinforced in the early Christian community and in England at the time of the Reformation.

In this context, I find it intriguing that Jacques Derrida says that our current language situation derives from a loss of a sense of transcendent Logos.[52] Perhaps so, but the Judeo-Christian tradition has never simply made a proclamation about a *transcendent* Logos; that is the sphere of classical thought and of Christian apologetic aimed at mediating the claims of its God to a classical world. The *kerygma* of Christian proclamation is, in Old Testament terms, of an *immanent* Logos, and, in Christian terms, of an *Incarnate* Logos, the Word-made-Flesh to "pitch his tent" among us. Judeo-Christian proclamation is of a God unknowable except as he himself reveals himself in concrete, particular saving moments of human history.[53] Judeo-Christian apologetic may use all the terms of classical thought, as Judeo-Christian literature may use all the forms of classical literature, but there always comes a point at which such language and such conceptual frames stand under judgment and are found wanting in the face of narratives of divine behavior which enlarge rather than restrict human possibilities. What remains is the reality that the God proclaimed by this tradition is ultimately known more through telling stories about his past saving actions—"He brought us up out of Egypt"; "he was born of the Virgin Mary, suffered under Pontius Pilate, was crucified, dead, and buried"—than in abstract affirmations such as "eternal, omnipotent, transcendent." Basic Christian documents embody a theology of God who works in human history, which is always in conflict with theologies positing a God static and outside history; the English Reformation promoted the recovery of God as incarnate and renewed this conflict in its attacks on scholasticism. Renaissance English poetry which seeks to mediate that God uses language in light of biblical modes and puts itself to the service of that Word mediated through the Bible and the liturgical life of the community which is the context for biblical reading. It is this formative as well as informing context which I hope to recover and use as the perspective from which to understand the poetry of Spenser, Herbert, and Vaughan.

· 1 ·

Toward a Poetics of Persuasion

Liturgical Change for Social Reform

. . . scriptural laws postulate, not a beyond of representation, but a
transfusing and renewal of it. To the extent that they are inscribed
through and across the enunciations emanating from the multiple and
unnamable places of meaning occupied by the book-free subject, and to
the extent that they combine these enunciations together with their
agencies, they liberate new representations elaborated by the subject of
these enunciations. Such new representations of a world "in progress"
translate the suppression of the topos of *One Subject* of understanding
. . . as well as a violent *criticism* of ideologies, habits, and *social* rules (a
new world through and across the negation of the present world that
writing denies according to its immanent logic).—Julia Kristeva[1]

Against our often-practiced desire to still the object of inquiry so that we may
reduce it to one articulation we must contrast the actual historical and theological manifestations of the Church of England in a series of times observed
by means of a liturgy, itself always the same and yet always changing, which
was intended to change the behavior of its participants. Occasionally, we will
find it helpful to display things in a way that aspires to endurance when we
wish to take stock of where we are in a process, but we must be prepared to
regard claims to permanence with scepticism, or as part of some larger strategy. Moments of repose have their value not as ends in themselves but as
recreative moments anticipating and facilitating a resumption of the work.
Each time "Mr. *Herberts Saints-Bel* rung to prayers"[2] it defined a literal and
historical aural space (since English parish boundaries were drawn in terms of
parishioners' ability to hear the church bell ring) which was then occupied by

the enactment of the Prayer Book rites, creating and defining relationships among the congregation that gathered in response.

As Lawrence Stone and others have demonstrated,[3] the congregation that gathered was a cranky and contentious lot, quick to take offense, quick to feel encroached upon, eager to respond violently to real or imagined slights to personal and familial honor, in large measure because they found it difficult to feel emotionally and physically safe in the world. Old tribal and regional divisions still lingered, marked by the accents with which people spoke and preserved in the still largely agrarian and familial base of wealth and political power handed on from generation to generation through patterns of inheritance. Divisions of rank and class were inscribed across the congregation in forms and materials of dress and in arrangements of seating and behavior.[4] In the royal court, the language was that of power and authority, but the sheer fact of poor communication and the necessary survival of the old regional system of government meant that royal power was often more imaginary than real and was maintained through the manipulation of symbols in public and favors or rewards in private. Elizabeth did both well, dazzling her people with a display of splendor and majesty and charming them with a semblance of humility ("I count the glory of my crown," she said on one occasion from the splendor of her place of honor while delivering a state speech, "that I have reigned with your loves").[5] In private, she made her courtiers dependent on her often whimsical changes of mood and mind and kept them off-balance by making sure they were always uncertain of her deepest beliefs and commitments and of her future moves.

James and Charles, by claiming the private reality of their public image (king in spite of the consent of the governed, king in terms of the ability to compel obedience), were unable to inspire and evoke much more among their people than a grudging respect and fear or a sense that one must go on with things as they are only because alternatives are unimaginable or probably worse or not worth the cost.[6] Without the affection of ordinary Englishfolk for these necessary yet always alien men, the Stuart monarchs sought adulation from smaller and smaller coteries of favorites who pleased them by giving them what they wanted but always inevitably failed them at the last.

In any case, their people had reason to feel vulnerable, frightened, insecure, and uncertain of the future, and to accommodate themselves by making do, sacrificing dreams or ambitions (or pursuing them at any cost, to self or others), settling for the available comfort, small though it might be, and acting self-protectively at the expense of others. Life was usually short, with mortality rates especially high among infants and women in childbirth. Women faced with the prospect of each pregnancy the chance of debilitating or fatal infection or disabling bodily injury.[7] Men and women who survived into adulthood and beyond the child-bearing years were likely to marry repeatedly as they outlived their spouses. Their relationships were often forged more on the basis of perceived personal advantage (dowries or the promise of inheritance) or need (for a co-laborer or protector or caretaker or socially sanctioned bedmate) than on what the church defined as "mutual society, help, and comfort" (BCP, p. 291).[8] Much of the population went malnourished most of the year, making them more vulnerable to diseases for which the available cures were often more dangerous than the diseases themselves. The plague, if not as severe as in previous centuries, was still an all-too-frequent visitor. There was perhaps some security to be found in wealth and power, but that depended on the luck of birth-order and good growing seasons or one's skill at learning a marketable craft in the midst of unpredictable economic forces. One could aspire to move adroitly and successfully within the world of the court, but there one had constantly to prove oneself in the crafting of splendid appearances while guarding against a viciously duplicitous competition and an unpredictable source of reward.

To make matters worse from the point of view of those to whom a hedge against disaster was more important than theological niceties, the new religion had dispensed with many of the accommodations to the old securities of animistic religion that the medieval church had worked out to make its way among the unlettered (and the lettered, too, for that matter). Gone were the rituals of private devotion as well as the ceremonial trappings of a magical priesthood. As Keith Thomas has suggested, the medieval church understood the language of power in the popular vocabulary; it was magic, and the medieval church posed (in popular terms) as a practitioner of white magic against the forces of darkness and the uncontrollable and the unknown.[9] The reformed church saw all magic as evil and so risked appearing vulnerable and powerless against all the nameless things that seemed "out there" in strangers or in unforeseen ill tidings or the darkness of nighttime that filled too readily with projections of the darkness within. This is a time of witchcraft persecutions and the revival of folk magic. It is a time of an increase in marginal figures—vagabonds and thieves and homeless poor—and also a time of great public and official violence against the marginal. It is a time of bear-baiting and cock-fighting for sport, and of laughing at the victims of mental illness and physical disability. It is a time of making executions into public spectacle and of posting the heads of criminals at the gates to London. It is a time of torturing and mutilating the bodies of various kinds of criminals, according to prescribed rituals, as the society took vengeance for all its sense of vulnerability at the expense of those who rightly or wrongly for the moment embodied the figure of the transgressor or the violator or the victim of one's own fears for oneself.

This was a time in which one might appropriately expect people to be concerned above all with security, both emotional and social, choosing to hold on to what is, having little left over for risk or change or acceptance of differences. When the church bell "rung to prayers," it called forth (for they were legally required to go) from such a population trying to survive in a difficult time a congregation of the proud and defensive, the quick-tempered and the emotionally numbed, the frightened and the grief-stricken, the sick and the angry and vengeful and the confused and those eager to take advantage of every vulnerability. Many were literally unlettered, unlearned except in the oral wisdom that a subsistence economy depends on,[10] and those who were learned had been trained in a style of knowledge based on disputation and effective contentiousness, not on promoting consensus or negotiation of agreement. It was not a promising lot, perhaps, for a priest to call upon to "turn to the Lord, your God: because he is gentle and merciful, he is patient and of much mercy,"[11] urging them to respond "with an humble, lowly, penitent, and obedient heart," to acknowledge their limitations, to define themselves in terms of repentance, humility, and dependence on God for their daily bread. Nor, for that matter, was it a group likely to find immediately helpful a priest's response of a proclamation of forgiveness, of pardon, with "comfortable words" and talk of peace and concord, of freedom and hope. Or, to take seriously his offer of bread and wine, the feast of a merciful father, conveying "remission of our sins, and all other benefits of his passion."

Yet the language of the Prayer Book is of reassurance, seeking to enable those gathered to believe in enough continuity and predictability in their lives that they can give up their clinging to the safest and most familiar of ways and the narrowest circle of acquaintances. It seeks to enable them to discover what it is like to set aside differences and embrace the stranger in their midst, to be "very members incorporate in thy mystical body, which is the blessed company of all faithful people"; to listen perhaps to other words ("God is not unrighteous that he will forget your works and labor that proceedeth of love: which love ye have showed for his name's sake . . . You that do truly and earnestly repent you of your sins, and be in love and charity with your neighbors . . . O heavenly Father, so assist us with thy grace, that we may . . . do all such good works as thou hast prepared for us to walk in"), words that call for personal and corporate transformation, "a new life . . . walking from hence forth in his holy ways." In such terms the instinctive and habitual responses—fearful, wrathful, self-protective—are judged and found wanting. In their place is evoked a new language of behavior, a language of generosity and graciousness, of forgiving and sharing of "love and charity . . . to walk in." Such words might prove helpful to a fearful people, but they would need to be persuaded to enter wholeheartedly into the space of those words.

The poems of Spenser, Herbert, and Vaughan reside in that space as well, their agenda being to further the church's agenda as they each understood it, to encourage Englishfolk to participate fully in Prayer Book worship. What will be helpful to know about the liturgical context for Anglican poems does not, however, consist in schematic displays of material arrayed in a continuously available synchronicity, but instead is found in moments of interaction and interchange between texts and those who read them, or between texts and those who heard them, or between texts and actions performed to make texts available. Aggressively linear, Prayer Book worship links past and present in terms of the promise that they share a common future; it enables ancient texts to become what makes possible the saying of something vital to the present and to glimpse an as yet unsayable future while it also enables modern texts to become facilitators of such interchanges.

The burden of this part of my study is to move from the Prayer Book to poetry informed by the Prayer Book. As such it carries a multiple demand. One is that we note points of interaction in the Prayer Book rites, beginning at the most basic level of the formation of a group of people into a procession to read a text, when the text makes it possible for the group to come together in the first place and understand itself in a new way. We will thus begin with the Great Litany, Cranmer's first attempt at a vernacular liturgical rite and the first component of his Prayer Book.

Another demand is that we see the Prayer Book itself as the product of a number of intersections between changes in understanding of time and language as it becomes the site of their inscription into Renaissance culture. Finally, we must find a way of talking about poetry and its occupation of intersections between rhetorical culture and moral and ethical aims, on the one hand, and inherited traditions of articulation and accommodation used by humanity to insulate itself from change on the other. We must find how poetry could take its place in the "Church of God" when that church took the form of a process oriented by the Book of Common Prayer. Addressing such issues will require a glance at the resources of language and theory available to sixteenth- and seventeenth-century poets. Following the lead of Cranmer and his fellow Reformers, Spenser, Herbert, and Vaughan each sought to promote transformational participation in the new-making activity of God which they believed was available to them in the interchange of Prayer Book enactment, bringing both reassurance and the facilitation of change. Because of that we need to approach the poems of these Anglican writers first by understanding how language works in Prayer Book worship and second by exploring what Wayne Meeks calls "the whole matrix of social patterns within which it is uttered," including "conventions of language but . . . not limited to them." [12]

Let us begin, therefore, in 1544, on a morning in June, perhaps a Wednesday or a Friday, with an event which was not a beginning in the sense of ultimate origins, surely, but a moment in which something happened which makes possible other things. [13] It was a moment of national crisis, in which

Henry VIII had asked that "general processions in all cities, towns, churches, and parishes of this realm, [be] said and sung."[14] In response to this call, clergy and layfolk gathered to begin a procession. They were a people who had known only the Vulgate and the Sarum Mass, for whom all their lives God had been invoked *In nomine Patris, et Filii, et Spiritus Sancti.* Yet, that day they had before them an unfamiliar text. They formed a procession, as they had many times before, but this procession, enabled by the new text, would not lead them into the familiar confines of a religious world defined and circumscribed by Latin rites. It would, instead, lead them through a transformation of all that had become familiar and comfortable about their religion. It would change the basis for their understandings of the relationship between God and his people and between clergy and layfolk.

And so they began the procession, with the priest proclaiming the versicle, "O God the father of heaven," and the people responding, "Have mercy upon us miserable sinners."[15] Here, suddenly, *English* "understanded of the people" had become an authorized language for public divine address. No longer was God accessible only to the learned and the ordained; now the language of everyday speech among all sorts and conditions was also the language of divine address. One purpose of this new Litany was to make and to act out that proclamation. Since Cranmer envisioned from the 1530s a full English service, this rite also sought to prepare the people for that change. Historically, the Book of Common Prayer gives to Anglicanism its distinctive character as a branch of Christendom; as its first component, the Litany anticipates the larger book in ways that give us unique access to Cranmer's understanding of the role of language in Christian behavior. The English translation of the Bible, authorized in 1542, was an act welcomed by all English Reformers; the Geneva Bible looks back to it,[16] as do the Bishops' and the Authorized (King James) Bibles. But the Prayer Book would divide Englishfolk who sought religious reform, even while it sought to unite them in common prayer. With the Litany, we are already at several points of division—between the advocates of the vernacular and the espousers of Latin, as well as between the eventual Anglican mainstream and its Puritan dissenters.[17]

In this light, the first point to be made is that the English Litany is a rite to be used in procession; more, it creates the procession by giving an occasion for procession and a text for use to define and inform that procession. The Litany Cranmer devised stresses versicle and response, the stating of a petition by the leader of the procession and response to it by the congregation. By casting a role for the congregation, the Litany insists on participation by those in attendance because it creates a conversationlike interaction in which the prayer of the priest is completed only in and by the prayer of the people. In taking part, the attendants at this vernacular rite found that they became participants rather than passive observers or followers and that their participation was enabled by its language and form. The rite thus proclaims the nature of prayer as Cranmer understood it and invites corporate participation as one of the essential elements defining the term "prayer" itself.

Moreover, the English Litany is a prayer of a wayfaring people headed in procession from somewhere familiar to somewhere as yet undiscovered. Later, Cranmer made the corporate journey of the Litany more explicit by having the priest pause in procession to lead the Litany in the aisle in the midst of the congregation, so that the distance between priest and people was further overcome, the priest taking his place in the congregation for the performance of this rite. When the Litany was incorporated into the Book of Common Prayer, it was placed for use between Morning Prayer and Holy Communion as a way of moving literally as well as metaphorically from the Word proclaimed verbally to the Word enacted sacramentally, from passive hearing to active offering and receiving.[18] On the level of language this rite is the processional means of moving from the Latin, medieval church to the English, reformed church; on the level of liturgical action, it is a preparatory rite, a rite of claiming that participating in verbal proclamation is not an end, but the way to sacramental participation.

It is also a way toward societal transformation. We must be under no illusion that Cranmer envisioned the true Christian commonwealth in egalitarian terms, but that does not mean that he merely supported things-as-they-are. In fact, the close relationship between church and state created by the manner of the Reformation—mandated from above, taking advantage of the opportunity provided by Henry VIII's dissatisfaction with Rome over the matter of his divorce—made it inevitable that the polity of the new church would reinforce and promote certain forms of royal authority. But we also need to remember the impact of liturgical centralization on late medieval English society. The incorporation of English worship into a single rite in one dialect of the vernacular furthered the development of national identity and the decline of regional distinctions; it also undercut the influence of those members of the nobility whose power rested on regional land holdings and was reinforced by the existence of regional distinctions. Along with this came the decline of papal authority in England as well as the change in status of the clergy as a caste of special persons set apart to perform sacred mysteries. From Cranmer's position, a strong central authority supporting the church seemed a recourse against the arbitrary and inequitable power of the nobility to enclose their land and deprive the peasantry of their homes and source of livelihood. In our culture, wearied by long years of familiarity with bureaucratic inefficiencies and corruption in high places, we need to remember the gains in equity and uniformity of justice that centralized government brought to a feudal society controlled, if at all, by arbitrary local authority and the weight of tradition. Cranmer's vision of society involved divisions of status and power but also a compensating sense of mutual responsibility; in any case, the implications of his Litany would involve a good deal of societal sorting-out, the end result of which could not be specified except to offer images to guide the inevitable transformations.

On this level, therefore, the English Litany is a rite of beginnings and also movement from beginnings toward an as-yet-unclear future, but one that will surely be different from the past that it enables its participants to leave behind. It is a rite of in-betweenness, defining the Middle Ages and the Renaissance in terms of the contrast between one language of divine address and another, between the old sense of Christianity as a life separate from ordinary life and the new, as yet still forming community created in the midst of ordinary life by use of secular language. But it is also a rite of movement through in-betweenness, and so what is important about it is what it does, including what it signals, enables, and moves its participants toward—participation in a journey toward the new that it invites its hearers to join.

Here content allies with form, because what the Litany says reinforces its processional functions. The tone set at the opening is penitential; the point, its participants' situation: their sinfulness and their need for mercy. At the same time, it is, as an act of speech, both an expression of confidence that the one so addressed will have mercy and an act of faith, done as though it were true that God is characterized by being merciful.

In light of the situation in which the Litany was first enacted, its opening prayer is worthy of examination:

> Remember not lorde, our offences, nor the offences of our forefathers, neither take thou vengeance of our sinnes: spare us good lord, spare thy people, whom thou hast redeemed with thy most precious bloude, and be not angry with us for ever.
> *Spare us, good Lorde.*

Sinfulness—"our offences [and] the offences of our forefathers"—visited, according to Numbers 14:18, on children to the third and fourth generation, is of course always to be lamented, and God's favor sought to remove the burden of this ancestral guilt. However, these words now take on special importance. Reformation rhetoric identified the liturgical and theological practice of the medieval church as a departure from the right way of doing things; a later petition describes the medieval church as exhibiting "the tyrannye of the bishoppe of Rome, and all his detestable enormitie, . . . false doctrine and heresye, . . . hardnes of hearte, and contempt of thy worde and commaundemente." The use of Latin in the Mass and other public rites, as well as in the Bible, thus becomes a sign of "the offences of our forefathers." This petition, now offered in English, serves as both an appeal to the source of all authority that the sins represented by the use of Latin not stand in the way of English success in battle—Henry was about to leave for France to fight supporters of the old religion when this Litany was put into use—and a claim that the age of Latin and all it represented was now past, and inscribed as past under the sign of sinfulness. With this Litany, a new day of the vernacular was begun; those who joined in the way of this procession were now on a new path, enacted and enabled by Cranmer's rupture in what he saw as the seamless web of medieval religious discourse. Thus identified as "thy people" but in a new vocabulary, they were to find their identity as an Exodus people still. Now, however, the land of Egypt was reinterpreted as the immediate past, the *medium aevum,* the world of Latin texts, and the Red Sea passage a crossing into English, into a rebirth of the language of worship, and into a wandering in language in the hope of arrival at the last at a new promised land, one found through and recognized by the use of the vernacular.

The contemporary texts explanatory of this liturgical innovation stress its use as a corporate action, for they justify departure from former practice on the grounds of the need to promote corporate action. Henry's instructions to Cranmer[19] call for the use of the new Litany because "the people, partly for lack of good instruction and calling, partly for that they understood no part of such prayers or suffrages, . . . have used to come very slackly to the procession." Education and language are linked—the note attached to the new Litany explaining its use says it is for the increase of devotion that "the *common* prayer of procession is set forth in English." Careful instruction as to how laypersons are to take part is included.

The whole Litany ends on just this note of common prayer as a point of interchange between education, identity, and language. Cranmer departed most strikingly from his Latin originals to borrow from the Eastern church a prayer attributed to John Chrysostom. In Cranmer's translation from the Greek, the prayer takes a form now familiar from its later use in the Daily Offices of Morning and Evening Prayer:

> Almightie God whiche haste geven us grace at thys time with one accorde to make our commune supplications unto thee, and doeste promyse, that whan two or three bee gathered in thy name thou wilte graunte theyr requestes: fulfyll nowe, O Lorde, the desyres and peticions of thy servauntes, as may bee moste expedyente for them, graunting us in thys worlde knowledge of thy trueth, and in the worlde to come lyfe everlasting. Amen.

This prayer serves as a summary of what has happened in the Litany and an affirmation of its major themes. Stressing the interchanges performed in this common action (when two or three are gathered, God has promised to "graunte theyr requestes") and the status of that action (God has given "grace

at thys time with one accorde to make our commune supplications"), the
assembly created by the Litany is proclaimed possible by grace (his gathered
people depend on God's grace for their coming together) for the fulfilling of
their requests, not necessarily as they have been stated, but "as may bee moste
expedyente." At the same time, what is clear is that the validity of this
assertion is dependent on the enactment of the rite which contains it, made
possible by its use of a common language. Whatever truth for the community
the words of the Litany have, it arises from the context of their enactment and
depends on the specific moment of that enactment—"God . . . haste geven
us grace *at thys time.*" And what enables and empowers these words is not an
affirmation of doctrine but a recitation of the narrative of the central moment
in the history of Christian salvation, by which the moment of recitation is
linked to those defining moments:

> By the misterie of thy holy incarnation, by thy holy Nativitie and Cir-
> cumcision, by thy Baptisme, fastyng, and temptacion:
> *Good Lorde deliver us.*
> By thyne agonye and bloudye sweate, by thy crosse and passion, by thy
> precious death and buriall, by thy glorious resurreccion and ascension,
> by the commyng of the holy gost:
> *Good Lorde deliver us.*

To use the Litany is to engage in an act of self-discovery, for to use it is to
define oneself as someone estranged from God and yet living a contingent life,
dependent on the God from whom one is estranged both for life itself and for
the overcoming of estrangement. Yet the individual element in the Litany
moves toward the corporate—it is when "two or three bee gathered" that
"thou wilte graunte theyr requestes"—so that the divine response to the individual comes through that individual's participation in the rite that creates
and defines a community of faith. Cranmer's Litany does not efface individual
concerns but locates their resolution through corporate action enabled by the
use of this liturgical text. Thus, the Litany also becomes an act of faithful
expectation that God will respond in grace to the faithful supplication of his
people when they address him in common prayer.

On one level, therefore, the Litany is an appeal for God to work in England
as he has worked in times past:

> O God, we have hearde with our eares, and our fathers have declared
> unto us, the noble workes that thou dyddest in theyr dayes, and in the
> olde time before them.
> *O Lorde, aryse, helpe us, and deliver us, for thy honour.*

Cranmer in this Litany sought to put England once more in touch with the
God of biblical narrative, appealing to the God he believed was active in the

saving events recited in the Bible to act again in his day by making events like the forming of a procession saving events analogous to those depicted in biblical narrative. The people now gathered into community through procession become like the Israelites gathered to hear God's Word from the judges and the prophets and like the early church gathered to experience their risen Lord, present to them through Word and Eucharist. The translation of the Bible into English and the transformation of diverse Latin rites into a life of common prayer in the vernacular through a single use for all Englishfolk became the vehicles for realizing that new sense of God's actions in the present life of the nation.

Cranmer's Litany, therefore, claims English as a means of enacting a process of formation understood in terms of contingency and dependency on God and the creation through such informing of a wayfaring people, a community in which such speech is intelligible as an act of faith that there is a God who has acted in grace, who makes his grace available, and who thus empowers statements of faith such as this one. Faith in this instance is the act of recital—telling the salvation history and calling upon the God of that history. The Litany is an act of education precisely because it uses the vernacular to demonstrate and create an act of faith and an act of calling; its purpose is informing and facilitating procession to create a people on the way toward a somewhere that is as yet unclear but which will share a common future with the past acts of God with which the Litany associates the present moment of its enactment. Nevertheless, it would be defined when it was achieved in terms of the vernacular and through use of the vernacular; it would be a new place, as unfamiliar and different from the Latin past as the vernacular itself was in Christian worship in 1544, and yet recognizable as connected to what was new about the rite of 1544.

At the same time, the use of language in this act which creates a new set of relationships in the present and points to the future of those relationships is also done in the midst of denying the sufficiency of its participants' understanding of the words spoken by its users and framers. The community formed by this procession prays that God "fulfyll nowe, O Lorde, the desyres and peticions of thy servauntes, as may bee moste expedyente for them." If the speech of this community is acceptable, it is through the grace of the one to whom the litanist leaves the decision about what is really expedient, in spite of how the litanist or his community sees the issues. The Litany thus creates the kind of community which acknowledges its dependence on God not only for meeting its needs but also for knowing what they are, and for proceeding on the basis of that knowledge rather than on the basis of what the community's intercessory prayer actually asks for. The act of doing the Litany thus becomes contingent on grace as interchange, even as the act of participating in it through response is an interchange between the uses of the text and the response it enables them to articulate, because all proceeds in recognition that God must be relied on to interpret for himself categories like expediency and not be limited by the understanding of the community. The effectiveness of the doing of the Litany thus does not reside in the cognitive perceptiveness of the community but in its performance by that community. The Litany thus seeks response through participation in its text by repetition of its phrases, assent to its proclamations, and assent to its affirmation of faith that its words will be found acceptable, enabling the people to respond in faith to its petitions. It thus poses choices for those invited to participate in it, for to participate is to discover oneself among that company which is defined as putting its "whole truste and confidence in thy mercy" and who believes such trust is warranted because its requests are heard. On that company is placed the task of understanding itself in the terms put forth in the Litany. To choose not to participate is, in the terms of the Litany, to define oneself as being outside that company. In other words, as part of the nature of the Litany as a proclamation of faith there is an act of persuasion. In its use of language as enabling of the action it performs, it encourages those who hear it to join in its work of forming a procession into the new linguistic and liturgical and communal world to which it points and leads.

Thus, by 1544 the fundamental images of the Christian life as sought by the reformed Church of England were in place, embodied in a liturgical rite in the vernacular intended for use by clergy and layfolk. When Cranmer continued his liturgical project in the late 1540s and 1550s he both incorporated the Litany into the Prayer Book and expanded its model in his versions of the Offices, the Sacraments, and the pastoral rites. Building on its method of bringing all together and leading them to self-understanding and community participation, Cranmer prepared a Prayer Book transforming worship into a discovery of Christian life as procession and facilitating the journey toward Christian community which the Litany commenced. His Eucharist provided "all benefits of [Christ's] passion" so that those who participate in it can move on to do "all such good works as thou hast prepared for us to walk in" (BCP, p. 265). Cranmer's liturgical texts in use thus created a world of language "in process," the furthering of which was the task of the persuasive poets whose works will be the subject of this study.

The Scene of Religious Writing in the English Renaissance

Faith then being the root of all, and God having vouchsafed to plant this root, this faith, *here* in his terrestriall paradise, and not in heaven; *in the manifest ministery of the Gospell,* and not in a secret and unrevealed purpose, (for, faith comes by hearing, and hearing by preaching, which are things executed and transacted *here* in the Church) be thou content

with those meanes which God hath ordained, and take thy faith in
those meanes. . . . —John Donne[20]

The Prayer Book as the enabler of an expression of Christianity that places
importance not in beliefs held but in occasions articulated by texts performed
was itself made possible by interchanges in early Renaissance culture between
received modes of discourse and challenges to them arising from within the
scholarly and religious community. What characterizes the work of Erasmus,
for example, is not so much the substitution of a new interpretation of the
Bible for an old one, but the juxtaposition of interpretations that lead not to
resolution but to a community of discourse. Erasmus' methods became paradigmatic for Cranmer, even as his Paraphrases on the Gospels and Acts joined
the Prayer Book, the Book of Homilies, and the Great Bible in English parish
churches to provide a standard approach to the New Testament. His belief in
the importance of moral and ethical education centered on the imitation of
Christ and on growth in the Christian life; his marvelous and loving ironies
that comprise Folly's sense of a Christianity truly engaged in the Eucharist,
his concern for biblical study for all, his rejection of dogmatism in favor of
Christ-focused conversation offer the best available insights into the understanding of Christianity that Cranmer mediated through the Prayer Book. I
have examined this background elsewhere[21] and will return to it with special
regard for links between Erasmus' colloquy *The Godly Feast* and the experiential structure of Cranmer's Eucharist; now we must examine some of the
cultural interchanges that formed the context for Erasmus and for Cranmer as
well.

In his monumental study of Renaissance political discourse, J. G. A.
Pocock has defined the late Middle Ages and the early Renaissance as a period
of crisis in the use of language.[22] In Pocock's terms, what Ricardo J.
Quinones has defined as the "Renaissance discovery of time,"[23] a renewed
sense of the importance and potential of the particular event and the unique
moment, caused great difficulty for those who sought to give voice to it, for
this emphasis was not allowed in the received conceptual frame and its verbal
manifestations. For Pocock, the medieval view of reality "found the particular
less intelligible and less rational than the universal."[24] Because medieval verbal codes stressed the value of a conclusion to a process of reasoning, the
integrity of the particular was lost because it was subsumed within a rhythm
of order or recurrence believed to manifest the nature of God in the temporal
world.

Yet it is precisely in recovering the importance of the particular, the specific, the unique moment in time, and with it the sense of the present as the
arena of God's ongoing actions in history that Cranmer's reformed Church of
England distinguished itself from the medieval church in England. This re-

covery is implicated in a renewed emphasis on the importance of the Bible in a sacramental context, and with it a recovery of the biblical and early Christian sense of the significance of specific moments in time in which God encounters his people, moments related in biblical narrative and participated in sacramentally so as to realize in such moments the consequences of those past acts of God. It is also linked to the revival of rhetoric, with its emphasis on addressing a particular audience so as to "teach, delight, and move" them to change their behavior. [25] The English Reformers combined these two concerns in a single effort to use language so as to respond to what they perceived as the renewal of God's actions in English history by furthering the reign of charity and building up the Christian commonwealth. [26] Erasmus' claim that "in Christ everything is born anew, and the names of things utterly transformed" is thus descriptive of Cranmer's purpose for verbal change at the beginning of the great period of religious reform during the reign of Edward VI, when God became "Father, Son, and Holy Spirit" and was no longer "Pater, Filius, et Spiritus Sanctus."

To the English Reformers the rupture of the medieval view of reality and its distinctive modes for articulating that view created the opportunity to use language not for shoring up the claims of a lost world but for realizing and promoting change. To apply Julia Kristeva's terms, the recovery of "scriptural laws" for language in the vernacular Bible as used in Prayer Book worship produced a transfusing and renewal of representation, the creation through representation of "a world 'in progress'" rather than stasis, seeking "a new world through and across the negation of the present world," especially the received world of Latin worship and religious thought which the Reformation criticizes. The motives of such writing are not to copy, reproduce, or offer a static description of the "beyond of representation," but to transform by impinging on "things as they are" in ways that shape and direct the vectors of change. [27] Fundamental to this is discovering in and through received modes of language ways of articulating the new-found importance of specific present moments, even though those modes were not inherently well suited to the purpose and needed radical transformation if they were to achieve it.

The Book of Common Prayer was first used in England on the Feast of Pentecost, June 9, 1549, part of Cranmer's way of announcing the new church as the old at once recovered and made new. Pentecost is traditionally regarded as the birthday of the church, the specific historical occasion— "when the fifty days [after Easter] were come to an end, they were all with one accord together in one place," reads the account in Acts 2 which is the Epistle for Pentecost in Cranmer's eucharistic lectionary—when through the gift of the Spirit God enables the church to carry out its mission throughout the world by empowering it to speak all languages, so that according to Acts, "the multitude were astonied, because that every man heard [the disciples] speak with his own language" (BCP, p. 169). Pentecost is also traditionally called Whitsunday because it has for centuries been a day appointed for baptisms and for dressing in white as part of the preparation for baptism, the sacrament of admission into the "holy congregation" (BCP, p. 275). Thus to transform fully the worship of the Church of England from Latin to English on Pentecost, to further a reformation to be conducted through language on the day in which the church remembers its creative experience of the divine gift of language speaking, is to make significant claims indeed for what one is doing. Here, the baptismal action of moving from outside to inside the church is mirrored in the change from Latin to English, constituting the identity of the new church.

In Cranmer's lectionary for this day the Epistle from Acts is paired with the account from John's Gospel of Jesus' promise of a Comforter to come and his promise to love those who keep his commandments. Cranmer also provided lessons for the Epistle and Gospel for Monday and Tuesday of that week which continue the connection between the gift of language, tongues, and speaking and the fundamental Christian message. On Monday, the Epistle is the account of Peter's sermon from Acts 10 in which he recounts the narrative of Jesus' life and is heard with astonishment because of his gift of speaking. The Gospel reading for Tuesday is Jesus' parable from John 10 of the shepherd and the sheepfold; the sheep follow the shepherd because they know his voice, but they do not follow strangers because "they know not the voice of strangers" (BCP, p. 173). The act of reformation through putting the language of the Bible and the language of worship in the language "understanded of the people" now is claimed to have enormous significance in and of itself, becoming an extension and a redoing of the foundational act of Pentecost, making possible the astonishment of the English because they can now hear "comfortable words" in their own tongue. In addition, Cranmer emphasizes in this choice of lessons the ethical overtone of his Book of Homilies, issued two years earlier. The Gospel for the Monday after Whitsunday is from John 3, in which the writer claims that "he that doth the truth, cometh to the light, that his deeds may be known, how that they are wrought in God" (BCP, p. 172). The Gospel for the day itself stresses keeping of Jesus' commandments as the way to have the love of Christ and of the Father.

We need to remember that one element of Pentecost is the sending of a Comforter, echoed in the Collect for the Day with its petition that we "rejoice in his holy comfort," now underscored by the fact that the Book of Common Prayer makes it possible for the congregation to hear "comfortable words" in their own language. But another aspect of this is its transformational quality. The event is one of dramatic and utter un- and re-doing, a new event like that of Mount Sinai and its unconsumed burning bush that marks holy ground. Wind and fire "filled all the house"; those who are filled, although they were "these which speak of Galilee," now they "speak in our own tongues the great works of God." And the one of whom they speak, according to the Gospel for the Tuesday after Whitsunday, is the one who has "come that they might have life, and that they might have it more abundantly" (BCP, p. 173). Cranmer's goal, with his reformation by Prayer Book, was the communication of comfort, of reassurance, enabling the community that used his book to let go of some of their need for control so that a Spirit that transforms and changes and that also evokes reminders of prophetic ecstasy and divine foolishness might conduct its new-making work as well.

The transforming work of Cranmer's text also works through performative language. "This day," said John Donne of Easter Day in 1628, "this whole Scripture is fulfilled in your eares."[28] Taking his text from 1 Corinthians 13:12 ("For now we see through a glasse darkly, but then face to face; now I know in parte, but then I shall know, even as also I am knowne"), Donne claims that "these two secular termes ['Now and Then'] of which, one designes the whole Age of this world from the Creation, to the dissolution thereof . . . And the other designes the everlastingnesse of the next world . . . are now met in one Day; in this Day." Having stressed the importance of that specific Easter Day, he explores the terms in which he seeks to articulate it:

> For the first Term Now . . . is intended most especially of that very act, which we do now at this present, that is, of the Ministery of the Gospell, of declaring God in his Ordinance, of Preaching his word . . . And then the Then, . . . is intended of that time, which we celebrate this day, the day of the actuall possession of the next life. (Sermons, VIII, 219–220)

In another sermon, Donne made clear that for him "the Ministery of the Gospell" involves, as it did on that Easter Sunday in 1628, the unity of preaching and Sacrament, seen as "the outward means of salvation":

> They are a powerful thunder, and lightning, that go together: Preaching is the thunder, that clears the air, disperses all clouds of ignorance; and then the Sacrament is the lightning, the glorious light, and presence of Christ Jesus himself. . . . God hath joyn'd them, separate them not. (Sermons, IV, 105)

Thus Donne's point in his Easter sermon is that the fulfillment of his text is dependent on the context for his sermon, the whole action of Prayer Book worship as performed on that particular day.[29] Indeed, Donne's movement in this sermon, to its conclusion—"to know God himself, in himself, and by himself, as he is all in all; Contemplatively, by knowing as he is known, and Practically, by loving as he is loved"—replicates the movement of Cranmer's communion service. Beginning with the reading of the appointed Epistle and

Gospel, the Prayer Book rite moves to the Communion and then points beyond itself to demand a response in "loving": "We now most humbly beseech thee, O heavenly Father, so to assist us with thy grace, that we may continue in that holy fellowship, and do all such good works as thou hast prepared for us to walk in" (BCP, p. 265). Each specific celebration of the Prayer Book Eucharist performs and conveys "remission of our sins, and all other benefits of his passion" (BCP, p. 264) and then seeks its completion in the behavioral changes it claims to make possible. In another sermon, Donne made this connection explicitly:

> he preaches poorley that makes an end of his Sermon upon Sunday; He preaches on all the weeke, if he live well, to the edifying of others; If we say well, and doe ill, . . . if we doe build with one hand, in our preaching, we pull down with the other in our example . . . for the ill life of particular men reflects upon the function and ministery in generall . . . And as it is with us, if we divorce our words and our works, so it is with you, if you doe divorce your faith and your workes. (*Sermons,* V, 263)

In these terms, the Bible becomes God's Word when it is used in particular enactments of the Prayer Book rites ("this *calling* . . . is by the Word; but not by the Word read at home . . . nor by the Word submitted to private interpretation, but *by the Word preached*" [*Sermons,* VII, 3]), but the words of the preacher are incomplete without the action of the Sacraments and the behavior of preacher and congregation in response to participation in the Prayer Book rites.

Such use of language enacts a sacrifice which replicates the one asked of Christians as the role cast for them in Cranmer's Prayer Book: "here we offer and present unto thee, O Lord, ourselves, our souls and bodies, to be a reasonable, holy, and lively sacrifice unto thee" (BCP, p. 264). Cranmer recovered in this language the terms Saint Augustine used in *The City of God* to describe sacrifice:

> the true sacrifice is offered in every act which is designed to unite us to God in a holy fellowship. . . . the true sacrifices are acts of compassion, whether towards ourselves or towards our neighbors, when they are directed towards God . . . This is the sacrifice of Christians, who are "many, making up one body in Christ." This is the sacrifice which the Church continually celebrates in the sacrament of the altar, a sacrament well-known to the faithful where it is shown to the Church that she herself is offered in the offering which she presents to God. [30]

Augustine's terms here open the possibility of orienting all behavior, including the act of writing, "towards God" by having it function "to unite us to God in a holy fellowship" in relationship to "the sacrament of the altar" by furthering "acts of compassion . . . towards ourselves or towards our neighbors." The defining element of Christian writing thus becomes not employment of a specific vocabulary but the promotion of specific sorts of behavior in relationship to the defining rites of the church. For Cranmer, the use of language as an offering rather than as a pointer to a static view of reality is made possible by the rupture in language that defines the Renaissance; it does not seek to erase the historic rupture in religious language, but exploits it as one means of opening the world to the transforming activity of God.

Anglican use of language, viewed as an action analogous to the relationship between word and deed in liturgical use, is thus an enabling part of a larger action intended to produce change, an increase of "loving as he is loved," articulated as "all such good works as thou hast prepared for us to walk in." Anglican texts, created in the rupture of medieval thought and its modes of language described by Pocock, replicate that rupture to open the world to possibilities of transformation. They take their meaning not from an external reality to which they point, but from the specific occasions in which they are used and from the specific changes in behavior which result. From the use of the Prayer Book rites on that first Pentecost in 1549 the Church of England identified itself as a church because in that action the Word of God was preached and the Sacraments administered "according to Christ's ordinance." Yet the purpose of that church was not to be an end in itself; instead, it was to be "the means of grace" so that its participants can "lead a new life, following the commandments of God, and walking from henceforth in his holy ways."

Donne describes the behavior of Scripture read in Anglican worship and homilies preached to interpret that Scripture in terms of the disruption of received understandings and inherited verbal constructs. For Donne, the biblical text "de-signes" the world. The preacher "pierces us," he says; "Solomon (in Ecclesiastes) shakes the world to peeces, he dissects it, and cuts it up before thee" (*Sermons*, III, 48). What heals the world so disturbed is not another verbal code offered to replace the one swept away, but the action of worship ("he in us and we in him") and charitable behavior enabled by the complex of word and action that characterizes Prayer Book worship. Enacting Cranmer's Eucharist conveys "all . . . benefits of [Christ's] passion"; the proclamation of Christ's sacrifice enables the church to reside in a world which it wounds by its verbal acts because it inscribes suffering as the way to health. Christ as physician, says Donne, enjoins his followers to "Preach these sermons . . . cure thy Country . . . Live so, that thy example may be a precedent to others; live so, that for thy sake, God may spare others; and then, and not till then, thou hast done thy duty" (*Sermons*, III, 149).

As we have already noted, the dynamics of Cranmer's methods for reforming England are anticipated in the writings of Erasmus, who stressed in his work the regenerating, transforming, new-making qualities of Christian language, thus facilitating the relationship between language and religion as it was experienced and promoted by the English Reformers.[31] Cranmer titled his first eucharistic rite "The Supper of the Lorde and The Holy Communion, Commonly Called the Masse," a transformation into the vernacular inscribed by renaming the central act of Christianity in a way that recapitulates, in changing the words for things, the Reformation as a "making new."[32] Erasmus' desire for the Bible in the vernacular, coupled with his turn from medieval allegorizing to concern for the historic narrative of Scripture as the basis for interpretation,[33] reminded the Reformers that the Bible itself chronicles a sequence of divine acts in time each of which transforms and recreates those to whom God speaks and on whom he acts. To the Reformers, the events in English history in which they were participating and helping to create were analogous events through which God's purposes for England were being realized. While the authority of Scripture was the basis for attack on the traditions of the medieval church, Common Prayer and Holy Communion became the process through which English society was to be made new.

Erasmus also provided the English Reformers with models for the use of language to participate in God's new acts in English history. In his colloquy *The Godly Feast,* religious discourse leads not to verbal formulations of abstract doctrine but to charity. Erasmus' conversants take turns interpreting biblical texts in Latin, Greek, and Hebrew; each one's skill in languages enriches the understanding of the others. Their progress leads them to an altar where Christ presides and beyond it to tending the sick and seeking to bring peace where there is contention, thus acting out Christ's commandment to love God through love of one's neighbor. Eusebius draws the point: "Let us pray that since we can avail nothing of ourselves, he in his infinite goodness may never permit us to stray from the path of salvation, but . . . may guide us through gospel truth to life eternal—that is, draw us *to* himself *by* himself."[34] The literal and temporal path through Erasmus' garden of conversation thus leads from door to altar, from Word conveyed in words to Word made Sacrament, from Word as proclamation to Word-made-Flesh, incarnate in its working verbally, participated in through the transforming activity of generous conversation and charitable behavior.

In this view, Erasmus in no way denigrates the activity of speech but shifts attention away from the conclusions of discourse toward process itself as a way of drawing the reader into a larger ongoing conversation and teaching him how to participate in it. The charitableness and tolerance exhibited by Erasmus' discussants toward each other and their response in charitable behavior become models for his readers to emulate; in this way, they act out Erasmus' Christian humanism even as they are bound together by their Christ-focused and Christ-imitating dialogue.[35] Erasmus' goal, therefore, is more initiatory than conclusive; his texts subvert the aims of scholastic discourse while they involve their readers in the process they perform. In this way, Erasmus seeks to overcome the separation between Christ, art, and life; in the words of Marjorie Boyle, he proclaims

> . . . the godly feast, a conversation of Christian life and letters, [which] terminates where scholastic disputation seldom does: in a charity which goes forth amiably into other villages. It imitates perfectly the apostolic activity recorded in the New Testament where the *agape* was an incitement to such evangelization. . . . And so the colloquy copies that movement from text to life which Erasmus thought the dynamic of true theology. From philology to praxis, from the study to the village, is the plot of renaissance for that humanist theologian who affirmed language as the stuff of life.36

Erasmus thus deals with the received models for writing by putting them to uses that undercut the finality of specific statements in favor of emphasizing the overall referent of an ongoing conversation. What becomes important, finally, is not the truth or falsehood of a specific doctrinal or dogmatic statement but participation in Christ-focused conversation, generously and charitably engaged in, as a participatory model for human interaction. Theologically, the emphasis here is heavily incarnational; that is, Christ as God's action through speaking, the meaning of "God's Word," is referent, example, enabler, and goal. It is this model that Erasmus enacts in his colloquies, which become not only models for conversation aimed at reformation of the commonwealth, but instruments and instigators of that reformation because they invite the reader to join in their conversations.

When Thomas Cranmer created his Prayer Book, he made possible the joining of all Englishfolk into an Erasmian conversation with the biblical texts leading to the altar and beyond it to works of charity. In the words of Harvey Guthrie, "The ascetical *genre* of the Book of Common Prayer is that of the *Regulum* which makes it possible for the basis of the spiritual life of a community of Christian people to be the corporate, liturgical, sacramental, and domestic life of that community itself." The Church of England is "a pragmatic church which . . . defines both 'Church' and 'Christian' in terms of a series of times observed, a set of liturgical actions performed, a sacramental and corporate life together."37 Izaak Walton described George Herbert's understanding of this when he noted that "Mr. *Herberts* own practice [was] to appear . . . twice every day at the Church-prayers, in the Chappel . . . strictly at the Canonical hours of 10 and 4; and then and there, he lifted up pure and charitable hands to God in the midst of the Congregation." Walton goes on to claim that Herbert's parishioners who could not join him in church "would let their Plow rest when Mr. *Herberts Saints-Bel* rung to prayers, that they might also offer their devotions to God with him." Thus, says Walton, "powerful was his reason, and example, to perswade others to a practical piety, and devotion."[38]

Thus it was that in the reigns of Edward, Elizabeth, James, and Charles the Church of England came to understand itself and to understand Christianity less in terms of assent to doctrine than in terms of behavior. The Book of Common Prayer is not the worship of Reformation England, but is instead the text that *enables* worship through its enactment in specific moments of time. It is a text for, in Cranmer's word, *use*.[39] The combination of fixed texts and variable Psalms, lessons, and prayers, together with the variables of sermon, congregation, and clergy, as well as the changing historical context, meant that each discrete use of the Prayer Book called attention to itself both as an action in continuity with past and future enactments and as a unique, particular use unrepeatable because even when the same texts were called for again by the lectionary the participants and their situation would have changed.

The routine of Prayer Book use called for the reading of Morning and Evening Prayer daily. According to the Prayer Book of 1559 (the revision of Cranmer's 1552 Prayer Book made part of the Elizabethan Settlement of Religion), the two services, conflations of the seven-office monastic day, are quite similar. Each begins with the recitation by a priest of short biblical texts chosen for seasonal or daily appropriateness from a list printed in the book; this is followed by a call to confession, a general confession, and the pronouncing of absolution. The Lord's Prayer (without what Donne called in the *Satyres* Luther's "power and glory clause") followed, with an exchange of versicles and responses between the priest and the congregation. Next came, in Morning Prayer, the recitation of Psalm 95 (better known as the Venite), then the recitation of the Psalms appointed for the Office and the reading of one lesson from the Old Testament and one from the New Testament. Each lesson was followed by a canticle of praise chosen from listed alternatives. After the lessons came the Apostles' Creed, the Lord's Prayer again, another set of versicles and responses, and three collects or prayers—a Collect for the Day, the Collect for Peace, and the Collect for Grace. Evening Prayer followed essentially the same pattern, except that the canticles to be said or sung after the appointed lessons were different and included the Magnificat and the Nunc Dimittis; also, the second collect was a different version of a Collect for Peace and the third collect was for Aid against Peril.

On Sundays, Wednesdays, and Fridays, and at other times as appointed by the "ordinary," or bishop, Morning Prayer was followed by the Great Litany. On Sundays and Holy Days, after the Great Litany came the Eucharist or Holy Communion and a sermon. Again, according to the Prayer Book of 1559, the Eucharist began with the Lord's Prayer, the Collect for Purity, and the Ten Commandments, which were followed by the Collect for the Day and a Collect for the Monarch. The reading of the Epistle and Gospel and the Nicene Creed followed, together with a sermon or the reading of one of the homilies from the Book of Homilies of 1547 or that of 1558. The priest then read an offertory sentence from a list provided and the money contributions were collected. Following that the priest read a long prayer called the Prayer for the Whole State of Christ's Church Militant Here in Earth and exhorted the congregation to receive the Holy Communion. After the Exhortation came preparation in the form of a call to confession by the priest, the general confession by the congregation, and the pronouncement of absolution by the priest, together with the reading of "comfortable words." He then began the eucharistic prayer, or Prayer of Consecration, with its versicles and responses, its Proper Preface (or variable seasonal passage), the Sanctus ("Holy, holy, holy"), the Prayer of Humble Access, and the Words of Institution (or repetition of the narrative of the Last Supper). This was followed by the reception of bread and wine, the Prayer of Thanksgiving, the Gloria ("Glory be to God on High"), and the final blessing of the people.

Much has been written about Cranmer's interpretations of eucharistic theology; what is more significant here is to describe the experience of worship his Prayer Book made possible. The Prayer Book is not as some have said a Catholic book to go along with a Protestant theology. A Catholic book in the sixteenth century could not be in English; it of necessity had to be in Latin. Although vernacular worship had been part of Erasmus' goal, it was realized before the twentieth century only in the Protestant traditions. So the fact of the use of English in the Prayer Book makes it of necessity a "Protestant" book, but that does not mean that we can necessarily import into it the eucharistic theologies of any other reformed tradition. We need to allow the Church of England to be the kind of reformed tradition created by and informed by that Prayer Book and then inquire what sort of tradition that could be, rather than to begin with the assumption that it must be like this or that continental tradition and then force its formularies to fit that tradition's articulation of the faith.

We may approach the theology of the Prayer Book if we examine what it made possible in England. First, use of the Prayer Book established the irreplaceable context for reading of the Bible. John Donne made this point repeatedly in his sermons:

> . . . no Scripture is of private interpretation. I see not this mystery by
> the eye of Nature, of Learning, of State, of mine own private sence; but
> I see it by the eye of the Church, by the light of Faith, that's true; but
> yet organically, instrumentally, by the eye of the Church. And this
> Church is that which proposes to me all that is necessary to my salva-

tion, in the Word, and seals all to me in the Sacraments. (*Sermons*, III, 210)

The revised Prayer Book Lectionary (1561) provided for reading the Old Testament in the Offices of Morning and Evening Prayer once yearly, the New Testament four times yearly, and the Psalter monthly. The celebrations of Holy Communion on Sundays and Holy Days were also provided with their readings from the Epistles and the Gospels. In the process, especially through the constant repetition of the Psalter, coupled with the many echoes of biblical language in the Prayer Book rites themselves, the Bible became not just a work read but a living text which provided the actual language of worship and divine address.[40]

As a corollary of this, we need to note that Cranmer's emphasis in the Prayer Book is on the action of the corporate body, not the action of individuals. This emphasis is reinforced by the Primers, which make it possible for individuals and families to participate in corporate Anglican worship even when separated from it.[41] Donne also makes clear that the corporate worship of the community is the context in which God's Word becomes effectual to the people. The Word is manifest through the human actions of reading the Bible, preaching, and sacramental enaction; the relationship between God and the individual is effectual to the extent to which the individual becomes part of the congregation:

> [Salvation] is by the Word; but not by the Word read at home, though that is a pious exercise; nor by the word submitted to private interpretation; but *by the Word preached*, according to his Ordinance, and under the great Seal, of his blessing upon his Ordinance [the Sacrament]. So that *preaching* is this calling; and therefore, as if Christ do appear to any man, in a private inspiration, yet he appears but in weakness, and in an infancy, till he speak, till he bring a man to the hearing of his voice, in a setled Church, and in the Ordinance of preaching. (*Sermons*, VII, 157)

It is only in the use of the Bible in the context of Prayer Book worship that the Bible becomes for Anglican hearers the Word of God. Reading the Bible in private takes its significance from the understanding of public reading, not the other way around, since what occurs in private reading comes to be understandable only when it leads to or is guided by public reading and hearing. In this context, the texts of Scripture, the texts of the Prayer Book rites, and the texts of sermons delivered in the context of those rites become inseparable and interdependent components of the public action through which, to the faithful, God is conveyed to his people and they become the church. Or so Thomas Cranmer believed:

I say (according to God's word and the doctrine of the old writers) that Christ is present in his sacraments, as they teach also that he is present in his word, when he worketh mightly by the same in the hearts of the hearers. By which manner of speech it is not meant that Christ is corporally present in the voice or sound of the speaker (which sound perisheth as soon as the words be spoken), but this speech meaneth that he worketh with his word, using the voice of the speaker, as his instrument to work by; as he useth also his sacraments, whereby he worketh, and therefore is said to be present in them.[42]

Cranmer's theology of the close relationship between the Word in use and the Sacraments as vehicles of divine action in time had consequences for language when seen in light of the Prayer Book rites that embody Cranmer's theology. The set texts of the Prayer Book, in conjunction with the regular rotation of biblical readings, enabled the church to articulate its worship of God in the context of corporate use of the Prayer Book by supplying words for that purpose. At the same time, such language became also the vehicle of divine response to those words through their use in worship as they became vehicles of grace. In either case, the efficacy of language is dependent on the action of the divine Word, both in its supplying of the language in the first place and in its choosing those words as agents of its activity in the world. Through the public use of the Bible and the Prayer Book, Cranmer believed that God's Word became active in the world through its "work[ing] mightly . . . in the hearts of the hearers."

In this context, the importance of human words resides in the moment when they yield their authority in and of themselves and offer themselves for use as vehicles of the divine Word. This perspective on language stresses its functional dimension; words become meaningful not in any descriptive sense but in their effect on their hearers. That effect, in Prayer Book terms, is revealed not simply by the hearers' learning new knowledge but by their being moved to action. At the end of the Prayer Book communion rite, the congregation prays for grace to "continue in that holy fellowship, and do all such good works as thou hast prepared for us to walk in." In this light, Christian language has meaning only to the extent that its use motivates continuation of "fellowship and . . . good works."

Prayer Book rites thus need to be seen in terms of the enabling of process. Services other than the Offices and the Eucharist, notably baptism, confirmation, ordination, marriage, and burial, enabled individuals to articulate before God and the community significant moments in their lives in such a way that those moments became part of the life of that community and not just of the individuals involved. The language associated with these rites is always a language of becoming, not of finishing. At baptism, the priest prays that

God grant that "all things belonging to the Spirit may live and grow in them." At confirmation, the bishop prays that God "defend . . . this child . . . that he may continue thine forever, and daily increase in thy Holy Spirit more and more, until he come unto thy everlasting kingdom." From an Anglican perspective, therefore, the Christian life is never over, short of death, but is one of growth in the life of the Spirit as it works to transform the community of the faithful, orienting it toward the future of God's "everlasting kingdom," a transforming process effected in the world through the agency of the church, God's "holy congregation."

As part of the Prayer Book liturgy which is most open to variation, the Anglican sermon in its liturgical context was intended as part of a larger verbal enactment, mediating the Word effectively to the world. As an action that incorporates the Bible, and, in St. Paul's words, "proclaims the Lord's death till he come," the Prayer Book liturgy bridged the gulf between the "then" of past saving acts of God and the "now" of those who in Renaissance England heard the Word read, preached, and enacted sacramentally. In its variety the sermon is one special means of bringing the Word to bear directly on the present "now" of hearing and seeing and receiving, spelling out the full implications of the past events narrated in the Bible for the congregation in the present moment of worship. Thus, the role of the sermon for Cranmer was to bring the transforming pressure of the divine Word to bear on the present, to force an opening in the received, verbally structured understanding of reality to make room for the activity of that Word. But the sermon never stands alone as sufficient unto itself; it at best participates in the larger action, whose goal is "fellowship" and "good works," interdependent activities contributing to the realization of the Christian commonwealth seen as the human response to God's saving actions that bridges the gulf between the "now" of acting and the "then" of the future fulfillment of God's promises made in his past actions.

The liturgy of the Church of England always moves from past through present to the future, or, perhaps better, it informs the present in light of God's past actions and future promises while it directs and enables human present action to link past and future. As a result, we need to see Cranmer's view of the Christian life against the individuating tendencies of late medieval piety. In Cranmer's church the emphasis on corporate participation in Bible reading and sacramental reception had a future orientation. The Christian life became no longer a private pursuit of passive devotion but an active concern with other-directed charity, with the public living-out of Christ's summary of the Law leading to transformation of society as the goal of all Christian discourse. In this way, even as private devotion was subsumed within corporate worship, so private reformation was subsumed within public transformation.

Within this complex of emphases, Anglican language is didactic, concerned with impinging on the world of its hearers, bringing pressure on them to participate in the ongoing work of the Word mediated through corporate worship. We distort the texts of Anglicanism if we approach them as static descriptions of the faith or as theological statements descriptive of reality. Instead, we need to read them as enablers and facilitators of self-offering. In a fundamental sense, meaning of the texts is developed and clarified through the rite in use, but that is subordinated to the results of the rite in the behavior of its participants after the performance of the rite, and that, too, is subordinated to the future expectation of the fullness of meaning and knowledge. As in the case of Erasmus' conversants in *The Godly Feast,* the movement of the conversation is outward toward acts of charity and toward the fulfillment of meaning and the rite itself as a result of the congregation's "doing all such good works as thou hast prepared for us to walk in."

Cranmer's recreation of Christian worship in the vernacular meant, on one level, the intrusion of the sacred realm into the realm of the secular. In pre-Reformation modes, the artificial distinction between the sacred, centered in the Latin Mass, and the secular, centered in vernacular discourse, was made more pronounced by distinction in language. This compounded the division between clergy and layfolk exemplified by the performance of the Mass in the Latin *by* the priest *for* the congregation, which was reduced to the role of passive observer.[43] This was furthered by the proliferation of private devotional practices for layfolk which stress contemplative, inner-oriented behavior. But the recreation of English worship in the vernacular is in fact a claim that English is as "sacred" a language as Latin because it is also appropriate as a language for divine address. Some of those who objected to Cranmer's Prayer Book when it first appeared accused it of being a "Christmas game," a kind of secular, festive parody of the sacred text.[44] Just so—the transformation of worship into the vernacular effaced the concept of sacredness as a realm independent of the secular.

At the same time, it effaced the medieval sense of the secular as the world of ordinary human affairs conducted and facilitated through the use of the vernacular which has little to do with the sacred. Cranmer's attack on all the aspects of human devotional life that set apart certain human activity as sacred—all the private devotional practices of religious and devout laypersons—furthered this intrusion of the sacred into the secular.[45] Cranmer claimed, instead, that the realm of human relationships in social and everyday settings is the true arena of sacred action. His renewed emphasis on moral behavior, on active charity toward one's neighbor as the sign of "a true and lively faith" in God's redemptive act in Christ, infolded the medieval sacred realm into the secular world of English Renaissance culture. It also made available for Reformation worship the distinctive concerns of the patristic age, another reflection of the humanists' desire to transform the present by recovering the emphasis of the past, to return, as Erasmus desired, *ad fontes,* to the source.[46]

Renaissance use of late medieval and classical verbal codes is thus characterized by usurpation. While Cranmer sought to have his congregations unlearn their verbal habits, he also sought in the process to take over the authority of those codes and habits for his own verbal texts. Echoes of past forms and works reminded audiences that what was being offered was both similar and different—similar enough to be recognized as a certain kind of verbal artifact, but different enough to demand that the differences be taken into account. The Prayer Book's echoes of the medieval Mass in both form and verbal parallels served notice that its Eucharist is identifiable as a liturgical version of the Last Supper, but the differences make clear that Cranmer wanted it to be seen as the *true* liturgical version, the authentic version that takes to itself the authority claimed for past versions. This is yet another way of stressing the significance of the particularities of Cranmer's version and the particular liturgical events it made possible as they sought to make new the world in which they were performed.

Cranmer's sense of "presence" in relationship to the Eucharist, therefore, turns on the sense of the whole rite of Holy Communion as an opportunity to participate in the divine action in human history. In Cranmer's view, the medieval doctrines of the real presence of Christ in the Mass emphasized a static view of presence; Christ is present under the accidents of bread and wine spatially separated from the congregation, a reasonable view when only priests received the bread and wine regularly and Adoration of the Blessed Sacrament from afar was a common liturgical practice. But Cranmer rejected that view in favor of a participatory understanding; "the Bread which we break is a partaking of the Body of Christ; and likewise the Cup of Blessing is a partaking of the Blood of Christ" (Articles of Religion, Article XXVIII). To engage in the full eucharistic rite of hearing the Bible read and preached, of offering prayer for the church and the world, and of participating in the offering and reception of bread and wine is to participate in God's actions for the redemption of the world and to be enabled to participate in God's reconciling work; it is to participate in Christ as he is always present, at work in the world furthering the work of redemption. Cranmer's goal is to orient the life of a community in relationship to the altar and to God through the action at the altar and in the world. So Christ is present in the action of the communion rite, actively enabling the charitable work of his people, which Cranmer understood to be the point of a doctrine of Christ's presence for a people whose action together with bread and wine identifies them as "very members incorporate" in the Body of Christ.

Thus, Cranmer was not a "mere memorialist," as some have claimed. The

Christ he believed was present in the Eucharist was an active, transforming Christ, a Christ active in and through and for his people. He was not the static Christ Cranmer believed was defined by medieval doctrines of eucharistic presence, a Christ present in consecrated bread and wine available to be "reserved, carried about, lifted up, or worshipped" (Articles of Religion, Article XXVIII) but not to be received frequently, in both the bread and wine, by the people. This Christ, separated from the people and from the eucharistic action itself, was not Cranmer's Christ, who through the Prayer Book rites, Cranmer believed, was fully at work in the world enabling his people to gather, to confess, to be forgiven, to offer effectual prayer, to receive him, and to be enabled to further his redemptive work. That is how it was important to Cranmer for Christ to be present and that is how Cranmer believed him present, as the host of a banquet at the parish community table in anticipation of his hosting the blessed wedding feast of the Lamb, uniting Christ to the church as his bride, enabling the participants at the communion feast to become guests at the banquet to come.

Resources for a Homiletics of Poetic Discourse

. . . far from producing a weakened image of preexisting things, *mimesis* brings about an augmentation of meaning in the field of action, which is its privileged field. It does not equate itself with something already given. Rather it produces what it imitates, if we continue to translate *mimesis* by "imitation." Therefore the idea of a creative imitation will be what is at stake in our discussion.—Paul Ricoeur[47]

My concern in the rest of this study is with poems written by men who shared the Anglican emphasis on the transforming corporate experience of worship and the importance of moral and ethical behavior as the appropriate human response to the reconciling work of God. As English Christians, they wrote to promote participation in Prayer Book worship and the reforming goals of their church. As poets, they used language in ways they learned from their religious tradition and found in the process of Anglican worship a vocabulary of allusion enabling them to locate their works in relationship to the life of their church. It is thus the Church of England's stress on the importance of using language in relationship to communal sacramental action for preaching, prayer, and praise[48] and its use of language to bring about change in human behavior that make possible my discussion of these writers in terms of a common didactic purpose and homiletic technique. In this context, the inherited resources of imaginative literature also become available for the work of furthering cultural reform and the creation of Christian community. Central, of course, is the special sense for Anglicans in which the Bible is the

Word of God, not in its letters or its physicality but in the sense in which it comes to function as an instrument of the Word of God in the context of liturgical enactment of that Word. The Bible serves as divine instrumentality in a unique and irreplaceable sense, of course; but it does so only when it is read in the context of that liturgical action carried out by the very people who discover their identity as Christian people in the present through participation in that action. Thus, human language, extrabiblical language like that of the Prayer Book, and other forms of human language like prose and poetry, when they assume the ongoing life of the church as community formed by use of the Prayer Book as a context and also assume a relationship of interaction and creative proclamation with the Bible, can come to function in analogous ways.

To get at this sense in which the use of human language creates the occasion for divine action, which in turn uses it as a vehicle for acting in the world, let Richard Hooker get us moving closer to the functioning of language in specifically religious literature of the English Renaissance:

> For as much helpe whereof as may be in this case, I have endevoured throughout the bodie of this whole discourse, that every former part might give strength unto all that followe, and every later bring some light unto all before. So that if the judgements of men doe but holde themselves in suspense as touching these first more generall meditations, till in order they have perused the rest that ensue: what may seeme darke at the first will afterwardes be founde more plaine, even as the later particular decisions will appeare.[49]

These remarks appear early in Book I of Hooker's *Lawes of Ecclesiasticall Polity;* on one level they represent a plea for the reader to suspend his judgment about the more theoretical discussions of law and reason that appear early on in the *Lawes* until he reaches, in the later books, the discussions of particular aspects of church government and Anglican forms of worship. These remarks are therefore part of Hooker's rhetorical method, a method of eliciting a certain kind of reading response to his discourse.[50] On the one hand, he seeks to appear helpful to the reader, sympathetic to whatever difficulties the reader may encounter, but, on the other, his pose of helpfulness also advances the author's goal of getting the reader to read further, in hope of clarification, than he otherwise might have read. Hooker thus opens up for us the description of those rhetorical strategies a Renaissance religious writer might use to engage his reader in a particular kind of reading experience, one characterized by thoughtful, active, attentive searching for meaning. The reading experience here becomes a kind of quest for light, a search on the reader's part for that "plainness" which Hooker promises him.

On another level Hooker promises a reading experience quite extraordinary.

He defines what the reader will encounter early in the *Lawes* in terms of "more generall meditations"; what will follow he describes as "particular decisions."[51] It is the movement "in order" from generalities to particulars that interests me. In one sense, the particulars of the later sections of the text are "weak," however plain; they need the preceding generalities to "give strength" to them. In another sense, the particulars of the later text bring "light" to the darkness of the preceding generalities. Hooker thus describes the reader's experience of his text in terms of the reader's progressive ability to understand the words and sentences he reads. What Hooker claims is that the particulars presented later in his work will render "more plaine," more meaningful, the presentation of generalities he offers early in the work.

At once Hooker is urging his reader not to skip around if he wants to understand this work; the movement from generalities to particulars is so constructed that the reader must go through a structured process, must read them "in order" if he is to understand what Hooker has written.[52] At the same time, however, Hooker is making claims for the process of reading, or interpreting, what he has written. Hooker's central point is his attempt to persuade Anglicans attracted to Cartwright's Presbyterian movement to change Anglican worship and church structure that the Anglican way of doing things is just and appropriate. To do so, he begins with a point which he hopes will be universally agreeable, universally appealing, which is that the order of things manifests in some way the nature of God and his wishes for how his people conduct themselves. But Hooker's claim here is that this discussion is "dark" without the particulars of Anglican worship and church structure which follow it.

Hooker thus makes central to his argument the issue of the relationship between generalities and particulars which will also be of concern throughout this study. But, more than that, Hooker is claiming that while generalities may strengthen the presentation of particulars, the meaning of general statements is intelligible only in the context of particulars, in terms of particulars. To put this another way, Hooker is insisting that the meaning of the words and sentences he uses to present his general discussion of law early in the *Lawes* is unintelligible without the "light" cast on them in the mind of the reader by the particulars which follow.

My point here concerns the question of how words come to have meaning; Hooker says quite plainly that statements of general significance have meaning not in themselves but only in the context of particulars. Specifically, Hooker claims that the meaning of words resides in their conversation in and with the particular manifestations of Anglican worship and church polity. The particular things under consideration which will shed light on the generalities of words about the order of things are descriptions of Anglican worship and Anglican church government. The movement toward light and meaning

Hooker sets up in the *Lawes* is a movement from general discussions of law and nature toward particular discussions and descriptions of the ongoing worship of Anglicanism. What I want to make clear is that the meaning of the words Hooker uses early in the *Lawes* comes into being only in the context of his words about that particular institution and its life.

Hooker thus effectively sunders, at least for the purposes of reading his book, any immediate relationship between signifier and signified; words about generalities do not mean what he wants them to mean in reference to the natural world they might be thought to reflect, but only in reference to and in conversation with words about a specific and particular activity going on daily in the world Hooker shared with his original audience. Even here, however, Hooker does not promise total clarity of meaning; the presentation of particulars will only bring "some light," make "more plaine" the meaning of his generalities. Behind Hooker's language is an allusion to St. Paul's remark to the Church at Corinth which Donne would later use as the text for his Easter Day sermon in 1628.

> For we know in part, and we prophesy in part. But when that which is perfect is come, then that which is in part shall be done away. . . . For now we see through a glass darkly; but then face to face: now I know in part; but then shall I know even as also I am known. (VIII, 220)

In Hooker's terms, the glass of language about generalities "may seeme darke" but afterward may "be founde more plaine" as "the later particular decisions . . . bring some light unto all before." Yet short of the coming of that particular "which is Perfect" all he can promise is a greater degree of clarity, not full, face-to-face knowing.

There is thus a fundamental sense in which the signified of Hooker's discourse is intelligible only in terms of an expectation of future fulfillment of meaning. In Hooker's terms, what we can do is to set in motion, if "the judgements of men doe but holde themselves in suspense as touching these first more generall meditations," a process, in time, of reading sequentially, moving from "generall meditations" to "particular decisions . . . in order" toward a greater degree of clarity in the belief that such a process, if extended in time, will ultimately lead to signification, to knowing even as Hooker believes he is known. If one presumably joins that process of temporal movement toward full signification, then that process will not only lead one to Hooker's discussion of Anglican worship and polity, but to participation in that worship. For, after all, Hooker's *Lawes* is an apologia for use of the Prayer Book and its way of behaving with Christian language, aimed at putting to rest objections to that process of Christian worship.

The most that Hooker can claim is that he knows what words will be fulfilled in their meaning and which will pass away. Hooker's work sets the terms of the discussion in time and initiates the movement of discussion in time, but that is as far as it can go. If Hooker is fully attentive to Paul's remarks he alludes to, he knows that they are bracketed with Paul's proclamation that "Charity never faileth: but whether there be prophecies, they shall fail; whether there be tongues, they shall cease; whether there be knowledge, it shall vanish away" and his insistence that language use in church be intelligible to the congregation if it is to be for "edification, and exhortation, and comfort," a tenet of the English Reformation. There is a fundamental sense here in which language use is both necessary and inadequate; it is necessary because without it the movement is not begun that leads to full signification, but it is inadequate because the glass of language is always dark, always yielding up its claims to the act of charity, which will endure.

Thus Hooker offers in the *Lawes* a verbal text that moves from generalities to particulars as the initiating of a conversational process toward full signification which will not be complete at the end of Hooker's work but which at least his work can initiate. He does this in the context of a work intended to justify the use of a particular interpretation of Christianity which is just that particular toward which the whole work moves. His initiation of a temporal movement of reading is part of a larger rhetorical scheme to persuade his readers that they should be participating in that particular version of Christianity if they want to move, through the use of words that in use become vehicles of the divine Word, toward that perfection which is at once the goal of Anglican worship and the fulfillment of the meaning of Hooker's verbal text. I will argue in this book that the paradigm of language use Hooker defines here underlies the poetic and literary achievements of the writers I will survey.

In this light, the paradigm for language use that I find operating in Anglican religious works like Hooker's *Lawes* is one that reveals its authority in the world and over the world, including the world of human discourse, by bringing the biblical Word to bear on specific moments of human time through the enactment of that Word in the context of liturgical enactment of the central New Testament event. At the same time, if such verbal enactments are to be effective they must reveal their own inadequacy as utterance and their dependency on God's use of such human speaking if they are to have the effectiveness they claim for themselves. They cannot claim any independence of the human condition if they are to function for the redemption of that condition. Instead, they must at once counter the anxiety-reducing and stasis-inducing tendencies of ordinary human discourse; they must participate in the human experience of brokenness and death if they are to point toward resurrection. Such utterance is achieved through the refusal to use language in a conventional, referential, and designating fashion. Language appropriately used thus becomes a facilitator of process, an agent of change, an act of persuasion, rather than a means of reassurance or a depictor of reality. The desired functioning of language is also achieved through the refusal to use language as though it were a pointer toward another reality that does not participate in the conditions of temporal existence, that instead drains temporal existence of its significance as the arena of God's redemptive activity by denying the significance of human temporal experience. Such a reality may be posited as part of a rhetorical scheme that seeks persuasiveness, but it must be undercut if the full pressure of the Word is to be brought to bear on the specific historical moment, both of depiction in the work and of the reader's experience of the work. To put this another way, the meaning words come to have in such religious discourse must always be in terms of future fulfillment, not in terms of their pointing toward a previously existing or external reality that informs them and explains them.

To understand how this process of language use works in the religious poetry of this period, we must examine more closely the dynamics of Anglican speech acts themselves as well as the relationship between such instances of language use and other, non-Christian modes of discourse current in the English Renaissance which provide religious poets with many of the forms and vocabularies of expression they used in their work. I am arguing that religious poetry, especially in its didactic emphasis, provides the link between Renaissance and Reformation and shows religious writers taking over the new resources of language use provided by the Renaissance, not to achieve a sense of harmony or synthesis, but precisely to make the Christian claim about the relationship between God and his people. This they achieve, or at least seek to achieve, by undercutting the (potentially) rival claims implicit in the various literatures and language systems made available by the Renaissance interest in and recovery of the texts of classical antiquity in favor of the claims of the biblical God manifest in liturgical uses of the Bible, preaching, and sacramental enactment.

My concern in later chapters of this study is with the specific ways in which Spenser, Herbert, and Vaughan write poetry out of this tradition of language use for didactic enactment to further the goals of the English Reformation within the context of the historical situations in which Anglicanism found itself in the years from 1580 to 1660. I am always concerned to begin to think of religious texts diachronically rather than synchronically, as always changing in use from specific occasion to specific occasion, even as the Prayer Book is both always the same in each use and yet always different, both through the inclusion of differing biblical texts which shift emphases from one word or word pattern in the fixed text to others, and through the difference between historical situations in which each use occurs, again causing certain parts of the texts to stand out on one occasion and others on other occasions. Such a diachronic process of use is what enables the Prayer Book to have the same community-identifying, community-creating, and community-empowering function in each occurrence of its use.

Since meaning in this context is so occasion-specific it is difficult to pin down from the distance of so many years. What we can identify are those aspects of a literary work which contribute to the discovery of meaning whatever the historic situation might be. We can also identify those elements of a text which contribute to the creation of meaning. In a liturgical event, the texts of the Bible and the Prayer Book provide the words which must be interpreted;[53] the purpose of the sermon is the interpretation of those words to the specific historic situation into which they are spoken. At the same time, however, there is a continuity among events in Christian time so that the words of the biblical and liturgical texts also contribute to the interpretation of the sermon itself. Together, sermon, biblical readings, and liturgical texts interpret the present in light of the promise of future fulfillment of meaning that the past events read about in the Bible and the present events enacted through Prayer Book use come to share through liturgical use in the present. Finally, there is always a profound sense in which the interpretation of biblical, liturgical, and homiletic texts is not complete without the hearers' response, empowered by participation in the liturgical enactment of those texts and leading toward future fulfillment.

From this perspective, meaning becomes truly realized only in response, so that the use of language becomes meaningful as it furthers response. In a fundamental way, the meaning of language thus used is to be found not in relation to external referents but in terms of the action that results from such uses of language. For this reason, I am concerned with the ways in which nonliturgical religious texts contribute to participation in liturgical enactment and to the response it seeks to engender and with the kinds of responses the writers of such texts seek to further. In this way, I see religious poetry and prose of this period that was intended to be read outside a liturgical context as seeking to participate in the process of reformation, of provoking and directing response, which occurs centrally in liturgical action.

To use George Herbert's words, "A verse may finde him, who a sermon flies, / And turn delight into a sacrifice."[54] Such a stance takes the human delight in verse as a given; the religious poet would turn such response into "a reasonable, holy, and lively sacrifice," which the Book of Common Prayer claims to enable because it makes possible an offering of self to participate in God's redemptive work. Poems by Anglican writers were intended not to be contemplated and enjoyed only for themselves, but to result in what Ricoeur calls "an augmentation of meaning in the field of action," a change in the behavior of their readers resulting from their encounter with the text and enabled by that encounter. After all, as Sidney claims, it is "the end and working" of poetry that, when "rightly applied," justifies it "not [being] scourged out of the Church of God."[55]

In a fundamental sense, the subject of this study is "the end and working" of religious poetry, how it can be "rightly applied." Both are important for, as the attacks on imaginative literature in the age make clear, poetry was a more controversial verbal resource than classical rhetoric for Christian proclamation. I will explore this issue in more detail, but let it suffice to claim now that rhetoric's antecedents in Roman culture—in the context of its civil life and political and social relationships—made it more akin to the functions of Christian discourse in Renaissance England and thus more readily transferable to the new homiletic agenda. Poetry, on the other hand, came too closely associated with what Sidney called "a full wrong divinity" (*Defence,* p. 80) and what Herbert called "*Venus* Livery" to lend itself to Christian proclamation without transformation. Yet the struggle to achieve that transformation became one of the ways Christian poets in this age made the very claims that rendered their use of classical resources problematic.

The issues confronting poets turn on the matter of social utility, a point made by Stephen Gosson in his *Schoole of Abuse:*

> AS in every perfect common wealth there ought to be good laws established, right mainteined, wrong repressed, vertue rewarded, vice punished, and all manner of abuses thoroughly purged: So ought there such schooles for the furtherance of the same to be advaunced, that young men maye bee taught that in greene yeeres, that becomes them to practise in gray hayres.[56]

In creating this society, didactic writing obviously has an important role, but poets cannot share in it. In Gosson's view, poets are socially corrosive because poetry "drawes the mind from vertue, and confoundeth wit." Poets, therefore, detract from the building up of the "perfect common wealth" and ought to be banished. Gosson's use of the term "common wealth" deserves notice, because the establishment of the "true Christian common wealth" was the goal of the Reformers' use of language and the task of their attempts to reform English society through the introduction of the English Bible, the reemphasis on preaching, and the use of a vernacular Prayer Book.

The matter of the "common wealth" thus becomes the context in which we need to examine the arguments for the efficacy of language in poetry in regard to its ability to move or persuade its readers to change their behavior. The writer most closely associated with such a stance in the sixteenth century is, of course, Sir Philip Sidney. In his *Defence of Poetry,* Sidney counters arguments against the value of poetry precisely in terms of a claim for its usefulness in teaching, delighting, and moving.[57] Sidney's argument for poetry echoes the theology of language developed by the English Reformers, for it claims for poetry a special place within the universe of discourse because of its ability to further the reformation of those impaired by "that first accursed fall of Adam" (*Defence,* p. 79) and locates the specific powers of poetry in the rupturing of received images of the world exploited by Anglican texts.[58] After noting that David's Psalms "are a divine poem," that poetry "deserveth not to be scourged out of the Church of God," and that the moving or persuasive power of poetry is a reason to "give right honor to the heavenly Maker of that maker," Sidney makes the statement that links all that has gone before to his assertion of literary didacticism and persuasiveness: "Poetry therefore is an art of imitation, for so Aristotle termeth it in the word *mimesis*—that is to say, a representing, counterfeiting, or figuring forth—to speak metaphorically, a speaking picture—with this end, to teach and delight." As Sidney makes clear, mimesis here does not mean description of something already in existence, but is precisely that action of the poet which produces a change in behavior by the reader of the poem. It is, of course, Sidney's definition of "the end and working of" poetry that is to convince us that it "deserveth not to be scourged out of the Church of God." Such works therefore do not seek to be mimetic in the sense of reproducing or recreating or describing preexistent reality by translating the world outside the text into verbal constructs. Instead, according to Sidney, they "imitate . . . what may be and should be" with all the moral force of that qualifying "should." They seek to impinge on the worlds of their readers, making use of the residual powers of language artfully employed to provoke response, to judge the world as it is in terms of what it is not, or is not yet, and to invite the reader's participation in a process which, by taking "that goodness in hand," can move the world closer to what it yet "may be." Since to understand how these writers seek to persuade is the goal of this study, Sidney's argument here bears further examination.

At the heart of this issue is the word *mimesis* and its residual associations with reproduction or copying. The source of difficulty is the use of mimesis in Plato, especially in the *Republic,* where in his flight from the mutable and the particular he proposes that art is mimetic in that it copies experiential reality. It is banished from the ideal republic because it can be no more than a copy and inherently is doubly removed from reality. Art lies; the ethical opprobrium inherent in such a view colored attitudes toward art throughout the Renaissance. What Russell Fraser has called the "war against poetry" in this period surfaces in many places, trailing with it clouds of Platonic reference.[59] In *The Schoole of Abuse,* for example, Plato is heralded as one who "saw the doctrine of these teachers neither for profit necessary, nor to bee wished for pleasure" and thus "gave them all Drummes entertainment, not suffering them once to shew their faces in a reformed common wealth."[60]

If, as A. C. Hamilton has claimed, "Sidney's view of poetry remains stubbornly anti-mystical and severely practical, . . . rooted in man's life in this world,"[61] and, as S. K. Heninger has argued, Sidney's goal was "achieving a program of Protestant renewal among his countrymen,"[62] and if the thrust of the English Reformation and its transformation of classical rhetorical theory

and practice is toward the "reformed common wealth," then Gosson's argument seeks to sunder the relationship between poetry and "the Church of
God" precisely at the point that Sidney would affirm continuity. Whatever
the actual relationship between Gosson's *Abuse* and Sidney's *Defence,* Sidney's
justification for continuity between the Church of England's reform activities
and poetry as a human enterprise seems clearly to respond to this charge. His
concern is to affirm throughout that "the ends and working" of poetry will
enable it to withstand such a charge, thus securing poetry as an instrument
for the use of the church. While Gosson had claimed that "if people will bee
instructed . . . wee have divines enought to discharge that,"[63] Sidney would
also affirm the value of lay as well as clerical instruction through poetry.
Sidney's language for justifying poetry's role in the church is thus borrowed
from rhetoric, especially that concept of rhetoric advocated by Erasmus as his
method for religious reform.

The whole issue of mimesis must now be confronted; to the extent to
which Gosson claims poetry is a poor medium for didactic writing, some of
the burden of refuting him must address the terms of poetry's relationship to
that which is to be taught. I find Paul Ricoeur's interpretation of Aristotle
suggestive, for it is in anticipation of the terms of that interpretation that
Sidney presents his argument. Ricoeur contrasts the Platonic notion of mimesis, involving the concept of "redoubled presence," in which the imitating
works and imitated objects "borrow whatever tenor of meaning they have
from their intelligible models," with the Aristotelian concept of mimesis as
one in which the term denotes an *operation* within "the region of human
action, or production." Thus, mimetic works do not refer to "something
already given" but in fact are mimetic to the extent to which they bring about
"an augmentation of meaning in the field of action." The function of art as a
mimetic operation is to open possibilities of action through a redescription of
reality, reshaping the reader's perceptions of the world by creating new relationships through bringing together newly connected semantic fields, even
as, on one level, Sidney opens up new possibilities for poetry by bringing
together the semantic fields of poet as *vates,* maker, and *areytos.* In Ricoeur's
terms, "Word artisans . . . do not produce things but just quasi-things.
They invent the 'as if' "[64] which comes to be meaningful in terms of *praxis,* in
terms of what augmentation in action is produced. For Ricoeur, a mimetic
work "does not equate itself with something already given [but] produces
what it imitates."[65]

Sidney says, of course, that "it is not *gnosis* but *praxis* [that] must be the
fruit. And how *praxis* can be, without being moved to practise, it is no hard
matter to consider." In Sidney's argument the word *imitation* does not refer to
a relationship between the poem and a preexistent referent but to the poem
and *praxis.* Indeed, his summary statement ("Poesy . . . is an art of imita-

tion . . . a representing, counterfeiting, or figuring forth—to speak meta-phorically, a speaking picture—with this end, to teach and delight") re-capitulates Aristotle precisely along the lines sketched by Ricoeur, for, to Sidney, poetry is "an art of imitation" to the extent to which it teaches and delights, not to the extent to which it copies something preexistent. In this section of the Defence, Sidney has been careful, in fact, to create a rupture between preexistent "nature" and poetry as imitation. "There is," of course, "no art . . . that hath not the works of nature for his principal object, with-out which they could not consist" (Defence, p. 78), including, presumably, poetry, since, as Ricoeur points out, "fiction would never be understandable if it did not configurate what is already figured in human action."[66] The rela-tionship between poetry and preexistent reality is one of functioning for the sake of effectiveness in changing reality, not one of subservience to that reality.

But, Sidney goes on, "Only the poet, disdaining to be tied to any such subjection, lifted up with the vigour of his own invention, doth grow in effect another nature, in making things either better than nature bringeth forth, or, quite anew" (Defence, p. 78). It is in this rupture, again for the sake of produc-ing praxis, that the words Sidney uses for the poetic process must be located. Poetry is "a representing, counterfeiting, or figuring forth," terms presented as synonyms to indicate that the process of "figuring forth," like the others, is one of distinguishing the poem from whatever is preexistent for the sake of praxis. Indeed, the poet "doth grow in effect another nature," not in, but as a result of, the poem, using images of nature for the sake of intelligibility in the poem, yet re-presenting, counterfeiting, figuring it forth to produce a change in the behavior of the reader. Presumably the activities of all the other arts—the works of the astronomer, the geometrician, the musician, the phi-losopher, the lawyer, and the metaphysician, to name but a few on Sidney's list[67]—do not result in praxis because their works are informed by their relationship to what is prior to their actions, to which they are subservient. The ability of the poet, through his freedom from limitation by external referents, is to do that which produces action.

To make this point even clearer, Sidney then divides poetry that is a "speaking picture—with this end, to teach and delight" into three kinds. The first in his list, the "chief, both in antiquity and excellency," is the work of biblical poets "that did imitate the unconceivable excellencies of God": "Such were David in his Psalms; Solomon in his Song of Songs, in his Eccle-siastes, and Proverbs; Moses and Deborah in their Hymns; and the writer of Job" (Defence, p. 80). Part of Sidney's intent here is to counter Gosson, who used classical examples exclusively in his attack on poetry. Sidney's cloaking his argument in the authority of Scripture seeks at least a grudging admission from his adversaries that some poetry must not be dismissed lest one attack the value of the Bible: "Against these none will speak that hath the Holy Ghost in due holy reverence." Another part of his case is to ally the use of poetry with the ongoing task of the church in proclaiming the God of that Bible. He goes on to undercut the authority of non-Christian poets: "In this kind, though in a *full wrong divinity,* were Orpheus, Amphion, Homer in his Hymns, and many other, both Greeks and Romans" (emphasis mine). This is a point to which he returns, in rereading Plato's attack on poets in terms of an attack on "those wrong opinions of the Deity . . . nourished by the then esteemed poets . . . since they had not the light of Christ." Sidney argues that we no longer face that problem, since "now . . . Christianity hath taken away all the hurtful belief" (*Defence,* p. 108). He again affirms the value of biblical poets in terms of their function: "And this poesy must be used by whosoever will follow St. James's counsel in singing psalms when they are merry, and I know is used with the fruit of comfort by some, when, in sorrowful pangs of their death-bringing sins, they find the consolation of the never-leaving goodness" (*Defence,* p. 80). The value of biblical poetry resides in its ability to establish a transforming conversation; by enabling the articulation of "merry" and "sorrowful" feelings, it also enables the experience of "consolation." Again, the defining note of poetry is in terms of result, not in terms of a relationship to a preexistent reality. Biblical poets do indeed "imitate the unconceivable excellences of God," but, as we have seen, the terms in which God was recovered in the Renaissance involved the renewed sense of divine involvement in history and the affirmation of present participation, through liturgical action, in "thy mystical body." The God of Anglicans is defined as one who is "making all things new," not an abstract Idea. To "imitate" his "unconceivable excellences" is not to try to "conceive" them in the language of a poem, but to participate in "consolation," in the excellences of his redemptive acts through proclaiming them to the world effectively by creating texts that "teach, delight, and move."

Sidney's other link between the poet and God, his famous reference to God as the Maker of that maker, also emphasizes this point. If we can avoid the classical definitions of God as static and thus definable in terms of abstract categories of thought, then what becomes clear is that it is in the *transforming* (in Erasmus' terms, the name-changing and new-making aspects of divine action) and *recreative* aspects of divine action that the poet approximates "the heavenly Maker of that maker." In biblical terms and in contrast to the gods of myth, God made the world *ex nihilo.* His actions in remaking the world into the promised "new heaven and new earth" operate through words in use, as we have seen Cranmer claim. Thus, the poet is like God in that "with the force of a divine breath he bringeth things forth surpassing her doings." The "things surpassing her doings" are not his poems, but what is achieved through his poems by "the force of a divine breath" acting through them. It is through poetry, Sidney claims, that God works to correct "that first accursed fall of Adam" by enabling the poet to move people to "take that goodness in hand," to bring the "infected will" into action in accord with "our erected wit" (pp. 78, 81).

Sidney's second kind of poet includes those ancient poets who treat philosophical matters (in the Renaissance sense of philosophy, including moral, natural, astronomical, and historical subjects), but they are given short discussion since they do not invent their subjects and are thus limited to narratives already acted out which they are not free to vary. Sidney then moves quickly to the "third, indeed right poets." Some readers of Sidney have seen this transition as setting up a contrast between the first sort and the third,[68] but Sidney's definition of "right poets" does no such thing. The point here is whether the use of poetic forms is enough to make a writer a poet, or whether what is required is a fiction—whether a depicting of things as they are is enough, or whether the poet is the one who, "having no law but wit, bestows that in colours upon you which is fittest for the eye to see." The contrast is between the second and third types, not the first and the third. The third sort are in fact writers other than the biblical group who "most properly do imitate to teach and delight, and to imitate borrow nothing of what is, hath been, or shall be; but range, only reined with learned discretion, into the divine consideration of what may be and should be." Both biblical poets and this third sort teach, delight, and move; the role of the third group is to serve as intermediary between biblical proclamation and the present time of hearing, between the "divine consideration of what may be and should be" and the arena in which, as a result of "that first accursed fall of Adam" things are not as they may be or should be.[69]

Sidney returns to this point later in his discussion of the various classical genres of poetry. On the subject of lyric he notes, "Other sort of poetry almost have we none, but that lyrical kind of songs and sonnets: which, Lord, if He gave us so good minds, how well it might be employed, and with how heavenly fruit, both private and public, in singing the praises of the immortal beauty: the immortal goodness of that God who giveth us hands to write and wits to conceive; of which we might well want words, but never matter; of which we could turn our eyes to nothing, but we should ever have new-budding occasions" (*Defence*, p. 116). Not limited to old narratives, poets can tell new stories and thus open the world to new possibilities. Here Sidney is operating out of a vocabulary familiar from English church documents. In his "Homily of Fayth," Cranmer writes:

> THIS true faith wil shew furth it self, and can not long be ydle. For as it is written: The juste man doth lyve by his faith. He neither sleapeth, nor is ydle, when he should wake and be wel occupied. And God by his

prophet Hieremi sayeth: that he is a happy and blessed man, whiche hath faith and confidence in God. For he is like a tree, set by the water syde, that spreadeth his rotes abrode toward the moysture, and feareth not heate whan it cometh, his leafe wil be grene, and will not cease, to bring furth his fruit: Even so faithful men, (putting away al feare of adversitie) wil shewe furthe the fruite of their good workes, as occasion is offered to do them.[70]

Cranmer's imagery of works as fruit and of "new-budding" occasions through which the tree nourished by the water of faith produces its fruit becomes Sidney's image of poetry, functioning rightly, as being at the service of "the Church of God," functioning in the interchanges between the Word and the present time of encountering, empowered through the grace/faith relationship to persuade the faithful reader to produce, through faith empowered by grace, "heavenly fruit, both private and public." Sidney reemphasizes this point when he uses the biblical examples of Abraham and David to illustrate the difference between "eikastic" and "phantastic" imitation, the one "figuring forth good things," the other "infect[ing] the fancy with unworthy objects." With consequences ("good things" and "unworthy objects") again defining the characteristic act of poetry, Sidney here deploys biblical examples to support his claim that "the abuse of a thing [should not] make the right use odious" (Defence, p. 104). When Gosson would exclude poetry from the repertory of Christian proclamation, he echoes the Puritan bias toward limiting the effectiveness of Christ's Passion to the elect and the verbal means of reaching them to the sermon. Sidney, on the other hand, reaches out to include poetry in the Christian repertory, even as the Anglican tradition reaches out to use "all possible art," including public Bible reading, preaching, and sacramental enactment, to reach all, relying on God to provide what is needed to make human actions with language effectual. Sidney's theology of poetry therefore gives us a clue we need to locate the activity of various poems within the ongoing use of the Book of Common Prayer, creating and defining the "Church of God."

Persuasive Poetics and the Interchanges of Renaissance Writing

> Thou, whose sweet youth and early hopes inhance
> Thy rate and price, and mark thee for a treasure;
> Hearken unto a Verser, who may chance
>   Ryme thee to good, and make a bait of pleasure.
>   A verse may finde him, who a sermon flies,
>   And turn delight into a sacrifice.
>   —Herbert, "Perirrhanterium," ll. 1–6

Writers who in the sixteenth and seventeenth centuries sought to further the reforming goals of the Church of England had available to them a wide range of verbal resources to make their claims and to bring pressure on their readers to choose among those claims. George Herbert's address to the reader at the beginning of the first major poem in *The Temple* illustrates the confluence of verbal resources for the sake of Christian proclamation in poetry because it provides an intense cluster of images for the functioning of language in didactic Anglican poems. The first of these—"A verse may finde him"—points to the assertiveness of this literature, its concern to intrude into the world of its readers and command their attention. The second image—the comparison and contrast between "verse" and "sermon"—asserts a fundamental analogy between poetry and homily as modes of discourse; however they may differ in their uses of language they are worthy of comparison in terms of their intentions in regard to the audience they seek to "finde." The basis of contrast between them is put in terms of relative effectiveness in reaching that objective; verse "may" achieve their common purpose more effectively because of its ability to "finde" that part of their common audience "who a sermon flies." Poetry and homily as modes of discourse may differ in many ways, but these differences are here conceived as secondary to, although instrumental in the effectiveness of, their common function.

The third image—"turn delight into a sacrifice"—echoes Sidney's vocabulary while it defines the common objective of verse like Herbert's and of sermons like those Herbert (presumably) preached. As S. K. Heninger has pointed out, the sense that metaphor is transforming is at the heart of Sidney's theory of poetry.[71] According to Herbert, the homilist/poet will not settle for providing an audience with what Roland Barthes has called "the pleasure of the text"; the result of the homiletic poem's assertiveness must not be merely delight but the turning of delight "into a sacrifice." Since Herbert links poetry with preaching, it is appropriate to gloss "sacrifice" by the words of the Prayer Book with its description of the congregational role in the eucharistic action as "our sacrifice of praise and thanksgiving" and the offering of the people as an oblation of "ourselves, our souls and bodies, to be a reasonable, holy, and lively sacrifice unto thee" (BCP, p. 264). As we will see in more detail later, Herbert's goal is to bring the "sermon-flyer" to active participation in the worship of the church.

In addition, we might note that Herbert's opening for *The Temple* also makes use of a shared verbal methodology for effectiveness in both homilies and didactic poetry; that is, rhetoric.[72] An opening *laudatio,* or praise, of Herbert's imagined reader as one "whose sweet youth and early hopes inhance / Thy rate and price, and mark thee for a treasure" seeks to prepare the reader to respond positively to what is to follow, even as the use of *benevolentia* in the promise to "Ryme thee to good" coupled with the conditional "may chance" seeks to disarm any negative reaction the reader might have to the concluding assertion that what will be required of him is "a sacrifice." This approach reminds us that the language of biblical promise is a language of love and not of coercion, of persuasion, not condemnation.[73] The goal is enabling a process in which judgment is but the preliminary to forgiveness and reproach but the way to reconciliation. Indeed, the constellation of terms Herbert uses to describe the aims of his poetry—"good," "delight," "turn," "pleasure"—link poetry and homiletics to rhetoric, the three modes of discourse joined in Renaissance theory under the classic definition of the aims of didactic writing "to teach, to delight, to move" (or "to perswade").

In effect, what Herbert does in this stanza is to draw together techniques and vocabularies from a variety of verbal modes to begin as well as to explain the process of writing which, he hopes, will "turn delight into a sacrifice." Thus, his statement of purpose has become part of the means toward achieving that purpose and needs to be read in that context. His interchange of modes is also a crossing of the concerns necessary to this study. Linking the poem to the sermon with its assumed liturgical context and to the task of the sermon in teaching/moving, turning "delight into a sacrifice," Herbert also displays qualities of poetic functioning—assertiveness, overt didacticism, transformational aims achieved through delight—which are central to what I have chosen to call a poetics of persuasion, borrowing my key term from Sir Thomas Wilson's version of the traditional tripartite definition of and justification for using language didactically.[74]

To achieve the ends sought by the Anglican Reformers, language must take advantage of its persuasive resources; as a result, my concern must now be with the didactic dimension of this poetry, within the historical context of Reformation concerns, goals, and theories of persuasive writing. For if, as Sidney argues, the value of poetry for the church lies in its ability to produce *praxis*, not *gnosis*, in its "setting forth and moving to well doing," we must explore how the various aspects of a religious poem work together to achieve its forcibleness, or *energia*, which enables it to achieve this end persuasively.[75] Certainly, the writers I will consider in this study agreed with Sidney that poets "do merely make to imitate, and imitate both to delight and teach; and delight, to move men to take that goodness in hand, which without delight they would fly as from a stranger; and teach, to make them know that goodness whereunto they are moved" (*Defence*, p. 81). For Edmund Spenser, "the general end" of *The Faerie Queene* is "to fashion a gentleman or noble person in vertuous and gentle discipline."[76] As we have already seen, George Herbert, at the beginning of *The Temple*, states the purpose of the poetry to follow in terms which echo Sidney, since he promises "delight" as part of a poetic strategy to "Ryme . . . to good, and make a bait of pleasure" for those who would "fly" a sermon. And Henry Vaughan, in his "Preface to the Reader" for his volume of "solitary Devotions" entitled *The Mount of Olives,* declares that *"the ordinary Instructions for a regular life"* are *"as briefly delivered as possibly I could, in my* Sacred Poems."[77]

As poets and teachers, these writers unite in their affirmation that the purpose of poetry is didactic; its goal, moving the reader to action. These writers therefore seek to persuade; their art is an art of persuasion. The word derives, the *Oxford English Dictionary* tells us, from the Latin *persuadere,* "to bring over by talking," a usage just coming into currency in the sixteenth century. The dictionary's account of this word is rich in sixteenth- and seventeenth-century examples, all of which make clear the link between intention—"to bring over"—and the verbal methodology—"by talking." Some of these examples seemingly limit the change intended to one of mind or belief or attitude; others make clear that a change of mind is only preliminary to a change of behavior. Sidney, at least, understood the art of poetry in this latter sense: "This purifying of wit—this enriching of memory, enabling of judgment; and enlarging of conceit—which commonly we call learning . . . the final end is to lead and draw us to as high a perfection as our degenerate souls, made worse by their clayey lodgings, can be capable of" (*Defence,* p. 82).

In light of these claims, we need to pay attention in the works of these writers to the ways in which they seek to exercise such "forcibleness," such shaping and transforming power over their readers. The understanding of such texts involves letting go of our interest in using them as reproductions of past worlds, or as texts that take their meaning from preexistent or idealized frames of reference.[78] If Donne is correct when he claims for his sermon on Easter 1628 that "this day, this whole Scripture is fulfilled in your eares" through the agency of his preaching that Scripture, then the meaning of the words of his sermon derive not merely from their relationship to the Bible or to creedal formularies, although such relationships do provide the terms for understanding what Donne is claiming about this day. The meaning of those words comes to be in the response his words evoke in those who hear them in the context of Anglican worship. Or, to put it in words more akin to Donne's own argument, his sermon is meaningful to the extent to which it becomes a vehicle of the Word transforming the arena into which it is spoken through the instrumentality of the action with words and bread and wine that Donne and his fellow canons of St. Paul's and their congregation enacted on that day, which included—as a necessary but no less instrumental part—Donne's sermon.

My emphasis on the didactic, on the functioning of poetry to teach, to delight, and to move, inevitably aligns the poetics of these writers with other modes of discourse receiving renewed attention in the English Renaissance. The tripartite definition of the goals of persuasive writing is historically associated with the oration and sermon as well as with poetry. As historians of education and religion have taught us, educational reforms in England in the early sixteenth century stressed the importance of training in rhetoric as preparation for participation in public life.[79] At the same time, the English Reformers' emphasis on proclamation of the Word of God stressed verbal delivery as the medium of choice for instruction in the living of the devout life. And, as Sidney argues, it is because of the "end and working" of poetry that it "deserveth not to be scourged out of the Church of God" (*Defence*, p. 77).

What unites these modes in, for example, Herbert's use of them is a common motive, the desire to change the behavior of readers and hearers by impinging on their personal worlds to transform their behavior in the common social world. Oratory and homiletic are by definition public modes of discourse; the experience of poetry is private, unless, of course, it is read aloud, but Herbert makes clear in "Perirrhanterium" that the goal of his verse is to move the reader out of his personal world into the public arena:

> Through private prayer be a brave designe,
> Yet publick hath more promises, more love:
> And love's a weight to hearts, to eies a signe.
> We are all but cold suitours; let us move
> > Where it is warmest. Leave thy six and seven;
> > Pray with the most: for where most pray, is heaven.
>
> (ll. 397–402)

The constellation of verbs, "to teach, to delight, and to move," a description not only of the method of verbal persuasion but also of the justification for practicing these verbal arts, is an ancient association in each case and one that is repeated in Renaissance poetic, homiletic, and rhetorical treatises. These modes share fundamental aims and methods; verbal art for the Renaissance was understood chiefly as technique for rendering pleasurable and attractive what "otherwise they would fly as from a stranger."

In this light, Herbert's use of verse is yet another manifestation of his desire to "use all possible art" to reach his audience. The justification for using poetry to "turn delight into a sacrifice" lies in the most pragmatic intentions; Herbert's speaker expresses the faith that verse can achieve the goal of the sermon and do it better, at least for that audience who would "fly" a sermon. The image of the homilist that Herbert offers us in *The Country Parson* is similarly one constantly searching for ways of suiting a presentation to an audience in such a way that the proclamation of the sermon is heard powerfully, heard inescapably, heard as applicable forcefully to that specific audience.

If we may be concerned that such a line of thought seems to subordinate the act of poetry to nonpoetic ends, at least poetry shares with oratory and sermons the same kind of subordination in the critical theories of the age.

Outside the schoolroom in which students were allowed to sharpen their persuasive skills by taking indifferently either side of an issue,[80] oratory was viewed as having a God-given power to transform society for the common good. Indeed, Thomas Wilson defines the goals of rhetoric in explicitly religious terms; the power of organized persuasive language is God's gift to his people for the overcoming of sin-produced error because it can move them to do what is right. God's human agents, Wilson argues, should use rhetoric for the purposes of education, "that they mighte with ease win folke at their will and frame them by reason to al good order."[81] The ends of persuasive discourse or rhetoric are thus both religious and political, or, to put it in Wilson's terms, the will of God is that people be persuaded to live in community: "Neither can I see that men could have been brought by any other meanes to live together in fellowship of lyfe, to maintaine Cities, to deale truly, and willingly obeye one another, if men at the first had not by art and eloquence perswaded that which they full oft found out by reason."[82] Rhetoric, therefore, is an art of persuasion, the goal of whose use is social, moving its auditors to change their behavior so as to achieve "fellowship of lyfe."

The need for persuasive discourse stems, for both Wilson and Sidney, from the postlapsarian human condition. "[O]ur erected wit," Sidney says, "maketh us know what perfection is, and yet our infected will keepeth us from reaching unto it" (*Defence*, p. 79). The persuasive use of language is God's gift to correct this situation. Such an assertion is an act of faith; it reveals the profoundly theological implications of this theory of didacticism in writing, a theology of language that lies at the heart of the English Reformation.

Thomas Cranmer, in his sermon on faith in the first Book of Homilies, makes clear that the goal of the Reformers was a life of active charity, the expression and proof of that "true and lively faith." In his series of sermons on salvation, faith, and works, themselves examples of the Christian use of persuasive oratory,[83] he spells out the relationships among the basic elements of the Christian life:

> Let us therfore, good christen people, trye and examine our fayth, what it is, lette us . . . loke upon our workes, and so judge of our faith, what it is: Christ hymselfe speaketh of this matter, and saieth: The tree is knowen by the fruite. Therfore let us do good workes, and therby declare our fayth, to be the lively christen faith. Let us by such vertues as ought to spring out of faith, shew our election to be sure and stable, as S. Peter teacheth. Endevour your selves to make your calling and election certain by good workes. And also he sayeth: Minister or declare in youre fayth vertue, in vertue knowledge, in knowledge temperance, in temperance pacience, agayne in pacience godlynes, in godlynes

brotherly charitie, in brotherly charitie, love. . . . Therefore, let no suche phantasie and ymaginacion of faith at any tyme begile you, but be sure of youre fayth, trye it by youre livyng, loke upon the fruites that commeth of it, marke the encrease of love and charitie by it, toward God and your neyghbour, and so shall you perceyve it to be a true livelye faythe.[84]

Cranmer's point here is crucial; the word *faith* comes to have meaning, comes to be distinguishable from a "phantasie and ymaginacion of faith," precisely through examination of what results from it, defined in terms of actions rather than words. Only if one "trye it by your livyng" and "shewe in dede" can he "perceyve it to be a true livelye faythe." Such a fundamental connection between doing, using, behaving, and the meaning of words runs through all of Cranmer's reform program.

The various documents of the English Reformation, verbal acts all, were thus intended not primarily to be the defining marks of a new institution, but to be agents of change, verbal actions to transform through persuasion the society of Tudor England into the true Christian commonwealth. Rhetoric put to use, itself a God-given faculty to "win" and to "frame" its audience, is here sacramentalized, brought over "from a common to a holy purpose" by means of the ends to which it is put. Such ends, as Cranmer makes clear in his move from "fayth" to "love" through "brotherly charitie," come to be realized in a social context.

What I wish to note is the way in which the meaning of Cranmer's words becomes a matter of relationships; the efficacy of using language, a question of context and result. Cranmer's aim is the perception of history as the arena for the actions of God and the congregation's participation in those actions. "The tree is knowen by the fruite"; language takes its meaning from what results from its use. Cranmer's reforming documents were intended for public use, the rites of the Prayer Book becoming, through their use, the context for reading from the Great Bible and from the Book of Homilies. Later in this homily, Cranmer goes on to quote James: "Shewe me thy fayth by thy deedes." Thus, the key Reformation term "faith" comes to mean what results if the persuasive act of Christian language is successful.

If the meaning of faith thus resides not in the word itself but in the relationship between the public use of the word and the results of that use enabled by God, so, too, for the faithful the efficacy of didactic writing derives from the relationship between the use of language, the result of that use, and the One who empowers it. To these writers, God makes possible such a relationship through his use of the Word in Christ. Through the relationship between God and the historic Christ, and between the speaker and the spoken to, bringing the present into relationship with God's redeeming action in

Christ, "all . . . benefits of his passion" are made available to participants in Anglican worship in the present time of their participation. God thus promises and enables the successful completion of speech; what Cranmer proclaims is needed now is faith, a "true and lively faithe, in the merites of Jesus Christ whiche yet is not oures, but by Goddes workyng in us." According to this relational paradigm for meaning, God chooses his people by grace; he empowers them to respond and participate in his actions by faith. What gives meaning to the word "faith" are good works, defined as works of active charity toward one's neighbor. In terms of language and meaning as in terms of action, behavior both in speaking and in responding is radically contingent, unable to achieve of itself either successful meaning or successful action without the empowering action of God. What Cranmer and his fellow Reformers believed, however, was that through grace, by faith, mediated through the use of words and water, bread and wine, God enables his fallen creatures to do what the Prayer Book calls "all such good works as thou has prepared for us to walk in" (BCP, p. 265).

In terms of using language, therefore, the successful completion of persuasive speech is also contingent upon God's empowering grace and his enabling faith; in the words of Cranmer, "NOWE by Gods grace shalbe declared." This view of language is functional and sacramental; it is the use of language to facilitate sacramental enactment that best exemplifies the Reformers' theology of discourse, revealed in the use of language to create a text for liturgy in the Book of Common Prayer.[85] In such a view of language, the printed text of a poem, like the printed text of the Bible or the Prayer Book, does not become what it really is until text is realized through action when a text is read. It thus becomes an enactment in which one participates and finds oneself and is enabled to give voice to one's identity through a relationship with text so enacted and with the God who, according to Cranmer's theology of language in use, is revealed as involved in national and communal and personal life through such textual enactment, empowering and enabling texts and textual users to become what they are claimed to be by such use.

Yet such texts present problems as well. If a hearer is free to "fly" a sermon, so a reader is free to close the book or to manipulate his interpretation of such texts in ways that reduce the pressure they exert. Like Herbert's country parson, the Christian poet must constantly search for ways of suiting a presentation to an audience so that his proclamation is heard effectively as applicable to that audience specifically.[86] One of the strategies underlying the repetitiveness of Vaughan in his poems, or Herbert in the large number and variety of poems and poetic forms and moods in *The Temple,* or Spenser in the richness of his faerie world is just this sense of the need to "finde" the reader, to pursue a copiousness of effect so as to suit the text to the situation.[87]

It should come as no surprise, then, that Herbert and the other writers examined here drew on the languages and genres and modes of thought and presentation which carry power for their audiences.[88] The traditions of honoring classical and medieval literature as valued documents, the understanding of rhetoric as the study of powerful discourse, the claims to truth saying of classical philosophy, the life-giving authority of the homiletic voice all stood available to the Renaissance writer who would "finde" his reader, impinge on his world, and change his behavior in it. Use of such borrowed aids to effective writing must not be seen as implying the author's assent to the truthfulness of the works from which he borrows, but instead should be viewed as expressing the writer's sense of what kinds of language hold power for his readers because they command attention and shape understanding and behavioral response.

Humanist interest in the literatures of antiquity provided Renaissance speakers and writers who wished to make the divine claim in the world with three modes of discourse different from that reasoning mode Pocock has in mind as normative for the late Middle Ages—the Hellenic, reinvigorated through renewed interest in Plato and Neoplatonic thought; the Roman, emphasized by the renewed interest in Cicero, Quintilian, and classical oratory; and the prophetic, which uses as its model biblical speakers newly valued because of the recovery of the Bible in its original languages and in the vernacular.[89] In light of recent discussions, we can sort out these options in terms of their implicit methods of making their claims on their audiences and their implicit assumptions about the nature of things and the relationship each enacts between language and meaning.[90]

Hellenic discourse is the verbal mode of Platonic philosophy and its interpreters in their desire to discover among the changes of life a stable perspective from which to view the world. Hellenic thought posits a fundamental dualism between the material and spiritual realms, the former apprehended by the senses, the latter by the mind. In this dualistic cosmology, the material world always seeks to overcome the spiritual, to reduce its order and harmony to material chaos. Thus, the mental or spiritual faculties must always struggle to preserve their sense of cosmic harmony and participation in the spiritual order and their distance from the transitory world of the senses. In this light, Hellenic thought is revealed as a highly sophisticated version of mythic consciousness, the inherently human desire to escape temporal existence, to reduce the anxiety of experiencing our finitude.[91] Hellenic thought deprives the particular and unique event or person of meaning or value by denying its reality; from Plato forward, the truly "real" is found only in the changeless realm of Ideas. Late Hellenic thought merged philosophy and religion by stressing the ethical life of stoic discipline as a means to overcoming the material's claims on the individual and the cultivation of mystical experience as the means to salvation through anticipating an ultimate release of soul from body and union with the one reality as the ground of all existence. Ironically, this particular-denying mode of thought was highly individualistic because it stressed the individual's ascent to the divine through cultivation of the inner faculties rather than any societal or corporate movement. Only the enlightened few might escape the corrupting effects of the material world or the earthly city.

In its appeal to the human desire for release from the conditions of human existence, Hellenic writing resorts to claims for manifestations of the divine reality behind the temporal, absorbing the temporal into cyclical patterns which seem to deny or reverse the progress of time. At another level, it seeks to lead initiates into the mysteries of the individual soul's relationship to the divine. Indeed, the hiddenness of the divine and the promise of the initiate's access to it become part of the power of Hellenic speech. Stanley Fish has defined Hellenic discourse against Roman, or rhetorical, discourse by describing it as dialectical.[92] The form of the Socratic dialogue forces its audience away from concern for itself toward an increasing orientation upward, away from discourse, by forcing the audience into a process stressing purification of the soul. Language becomes a means toward somewhere, not a repository of truth; it aims toward the humiliation of its audience and their progress toward participation in the unsayable truth. Hellenic modes of language exploit the contradictions inherent in language to promote an inner experience that is independent of language, a "breaking-through" of language-bound perceptual frames; the result is assent to the profoundly individual experience of unity between knower and knowledge.

Hellenic modes of language permeated Renaissance England through the revival of interest in Greek and Greek texts, especially those of Plato, but also through the spread of interest in the hermetic tradition documented by Frances Yates and others.[93] As modes of interpreting, Hellenic models seek to put the audience into a relationship with text replicating that sought in their experience of the world. The reader of Hellenic allegories is led to distance himself from experience of the world and of the text toward increasingly abstract visions of reality experienced mystically. This mode is inherently divisive, creating an elite company of initiates who share the vision of truth as much hidden as revealed through the agency of the verbal text.[94]

The goal of Hellenic language is thus *gnosis,* Truth as hidden and known only to initiates; in theological terms, its concern is with God as concept or category or idea. Behavior is subordinate to knowing, an adjunct to enable the deepening of knowing; *praxis* is never the goal of Hellenic discourse. Language exercises power through its ability to conceal truth as well as its ability to move the initiate toward truth. Interpreting allegory becomes a process of perceiving truth hidden behind and pointed to by language's images and signs of abstractions. The goal of reading for the informed is transcendence of the text to achieve contact with the hidden power of the universe, enabling detachment from the conditions of temporality.[95] The speaker of a Hellenic text exercises power through his claim to possess *gnosis* and to be able to reveal that truth to those willing to subject themselves to the rigors of his text. The pose of the initiate, with its concomitant power to claim those who wish to set themselves off from the mass of humanity through the possession of arcane cabalistic secrets, contributes to the power of the Hellenic stance.

If the ideal reader of Hellenic discourse is thus someone who seeks transcendence from the temporal, the ideal audience for Roman discourse is a citizen of the state, for whom use of language as an exercise of power functions in relationship to the whole of society rather than to an elite of initiates. The great age of classical rhetoric was the age of Augustan cultural reform, during which orators linked forwarding the interests of Rome to the fulfilling of individual destiny and the achievement of meaningful existence. To this end, Roman orators borrowed from the Greeks ethical material and modes of persuasion to argue that individuals should abandon their own private interests to work for the welfare of Rome rather than to advocate the overcoming of passion in the interest of the intellectual development of the soul. This effort to reduce the empire to a unified whole dedicated to forwarding the interests of the principate is manifest in the art of the period as well as in its oratory; Virgil's *Aeneid*, "overgoing" Homer by combining two epics into one, proclaims that the meaning of history is to be found in the emergence of Rome as the agent of peace in the world.

As Jane Tompkins and Stanley Fish have pointed out, the Roman orator is able to exercise power because he forcefully reminds his audience of what they already know and assent to.[96] The proper concerns of classical rhetoric are the bonds of society and culture which already bind a people together into an organized state. Unlike Hellenic language modes, Roman rhetoric works to reassure its audience of the fundamental rightness and appropriateness of existing structures toward the end of eliciting their aid in the maintenance of that established social order. Its orientation is thus public and social, not private and individual. If Hellenic writing is disorienting, Roman rhetoric is reassuring; if Hellenic language exploits contradictions and difficulties in signifier-signified relationships, Roman rhetoric avoids or papers over such problems. The rhetor becomes a model of the good citizen; his discourse, the repository and vehicle for communicating commonly held values.[97]

If Hellenic discourse addresses the problem of temporality by denying its reality and gives value to the individual only through the effacement of his uniqueness, Roman rhetoric effaces the individual by seeking to involve him in a temporal process which ultimately has no place for him yet to the fulfillment of which he is called to contribute. The pursuit of Roman civic glory involved the yoking of Roman religion to civic goals; thus, the resources of myth were employed to create a myth of Roman destiny and, on occasion, the deification of a caesar.

The power of Roman rhetoric lies in its ability to persuade the mass of citizens to relinquish personal concerns in the name of a larger concern—the perpetuation of a social order. Its emphasis is on the value of that order, a sense of value derived from the ability of such a vision of order to give meaning and direction to the lives of individuals and thus to efface the anxiety of temporal existence. In such a mode, the significance of the present is lost as it becomes subservient to the past act creating that order. In this view, religion becomes significant only to the extent to which it can further the subservience of the society to abiding political structures. Religion thus functions as a means of preserving order, providing a myth of divine sanction for the past act that determines the present and preserves the existing order while prescribing punishment from the gods for those who would upset the already-given order of things.

The most important mode for the purposes of this study is, however, the prophetic mode, which received renewed attention in the Reformation period through the Reformers' recovery of the Bible and their offering of that text to Englishfolk in a language "understanded of the people." Prophetic speech shares some concerns with both the Hellenic and the Roman modes, but it is in fundamental conflict with them in other regards. In fact, one of the major techniques employed by Anglican writers in the Renaissance was to force Hellenic and Roman models for speech to function like prophetic speech. In the process, however, such classical modes had to be made to give up their distinctive claims and yield to the claims of biblical discourse.

Like the Hellenic mode, prophetic utterance raises questions about the ability of human words to point simply to external referents; unlike the Hellenic mode, however, the prophetic mode is addressed to people in their temporal situations and takes an affirmative stance toward the historical dimension of human life. That it shares with the Roman mode, but unlike the Roman mode it refuses to affirm unquestioningly the kinds of societal norms classic rhetoric implicitly affirms. Instead, it functions re-creatively, making all things new through judgment, renewed call to relationship, and promise of future fulfillment. Indeed, in the great Old Testament prophets the new speaking of God affirms that the breaking open of the present social and verbal situation is necessary to the new act of God. Thus, Isaiah and Jeremiah attack those who would assert the inviolability of Jerusalem, but they also attack those who would claim that the fall of Jerusalem represents an invalidation of God's promises to his people.

The prophetic mode is also a manifestation of a social role, in that the prophet, although called by and functioning as a spokesman for God, must use language and genres of speech—conventions, in fact—which are recognizable to a people as those appropriate for a prophet if his prophetic utterance is to be accepted. Thus, prophetic speech which proclaims judgment on the present and demands radical change must make use, transforming use, of inherited tradition.

The source for examples of the prophetic mode is, of course, the Bible, which conveys what it holds to be God's Word, which always comes, through prophetic discourse, to make its claim on humanity.[98] The prophetic speaker delivers to his audience a Word which always comes to God's people in specific, concrete, particular events; his proclamation creates the people of God anew, gives them their identity as his people, and calls them to a renewed relationship with him. Prophetic speech was thus understood, primarily, as proclamation, as the vehicle conveying God's Word to the present moment of its speaking. In this view, the Bible is not primarily a compendium of history or a work of theology but a proclamation of God's Word to "this present time," to the historical and temporal moment of the reader's experience. Literature which seeks to enter "into the service of [that] text"[99] must also be proclamation of that Word to the same "present time." This Word always reminds God's people of their past experience with him, calls them anew out of their cultural expectations into a new creation, and carries with it a promise of future fulfillment of the relationship now being created. This Word always comes to a community which it creates through its speaking in the world; it comes to individuals as they respond to that Word by identifying themselves with the promise given to the community and to them as individuals through their membership in that community.[100] For this reason, the sequence of such moments of creation through divine speaking becomes a history of salvation, a sequence of stories which through its recounting in the cultic life of the people of God restores that people to historical continuity with the saving events of the past and reaffirms the validity of God's promises about the future.

The Bible as a text enables the retelling of the defining events of the salvation history in a way that continues its recreative work. The Bible is a repository of these stories and of human response to the events recounted in these stories. These stories are told in such a way that the claims of God upon his people are expressed in the moment of biblical reading about past expressions of those claims. The Bible becomes a vehicle for making God's claims and for demanding the response God called for in past saving events in the history of his people. Response to those stories invests the moment of reading with the significance of the relationship with God described in those stories. Thus, the historical moment of reading can become a saving moment, a moment of exodus, a moment of being called into participation in the salvation history of God's relationship with his people.

The Bible also exists in intimate and conversational relationship with the cultic life of the people it tells stories about. It is the community that establishes *canon*, that recognizes and affirms for the specific stories in the Bible the authority they have within that community. At the same time, it is the Bible that tells that community who it is and who the God is who creates that community. Through the cultic recounting of the biblical stories, the community is restored to historical continuity with the people of God in times past and experiences now the call of God to relationship with him and incorporation into his future promises for his people.[101]

The cultic life in its reenactment of past saving events, such as Cranmer recreated through the Prayer Book, enables the people of God to enter into the full reality of past saving events and experience the full benefits of God's reconciling work in human history. Though these events are historically past and remain past, the community experiences an incorporation into them as eternal acts of God and experiences through them participation in God's present activity and call to a future relationship with him. What happens in the Hebrew celebration of Passover or the Christian celebration of the Eucharist must be seen in terms of "re-presentation," or "actualizing in the present" an event which always remains past, concrete, historical, never timeless or mythic, to effect the relationship now, in the moment of celebration, that God made with his people in that past historic event. At the same time, such rites anticipate the future fulfillment of God's promises made in that past event, again in the now of celebration.

If biblically modeled speech subverts the claims of mythic discourse, it also undercuts the intent of classical rhetoric since its aims are not preservation but transformation. The status of the present is never subservient to the past creative act; the conveyance of the Word to the present invests the present with the full creative significance of all such divine intrusions into human history. As in Cranmer's Book of Homilies, all members of society, from monarch to laborer, stand under judgment, the call to relationship, and the future promise. Biblical speech affirms the experience of the temporal as transforming; hope is found through change, not in its avoidance or denial.

What biblical language provides in its description of God's saving acts are the terms in which to understand the present moment as a moment like the past saving moments, as a moment of God's saving action now. It also provides the terms which make this recognition possible in the present. In a conversational relationship between description of the present and analogous description of the past, actions in the present come to be seen in terms of the actions of the past and thus are perceived as entering into and taking on the saving significance of the past moment of God's acting in human history. I find it helpful, therefore, to use A. C. Charity's term "applied typology" for this use of language to distinguish it from the looser and more general term "typology."[102] The discovery that the present can be described in terms of past saving actions carries with it renewing, recreating power as well as a radical insistence on God's claims over the present, and thus impinges on the world of present experience, demanding response, demanding choice as to how the expression of God's claim will be responded to. Thus, when Thomas Cranmer described the young King Edward as a "new Josias," he was claiming that God was again at work in the events of Edward's day in the same way he had been at work in the Deuteronomic reformation, and, as a result, the same claims God exercised over Israel during the reign of Josiah were again applicable to England in the mid-sixteenth century, as well as the same call to relationship and the same promise of divine presence and future fulfillment.

The biblical text and with it all human discourse which seeks to convey the Word to the particular and concrete situation into which it is addressed are thus proclamation of God's Word, are evangelical in that they proclaim to the now of the present audience the creative word of God, with all its transforming, time-defining, and community-creating force. The Greek origin of our word *evangelical* means proclamation of the good news, of the God who is present in his Word making all things new. Anglican sermons and poetry which sought to make this proclamation aspired to confront their readers with God's Word in their concrete moment of reading, or hearing, to inform them of the significance of their time, and to persuade them to choose how to respond. Because such utterances were spoken by someone who believed that the biblical Word is good news, they ought to persuade their readers to respond to this encounter with the Word by choosing to enter into the relationship with God that the Word calls them to, as enabled by use of the Prayer Book.

Because their method of discovering God's actions in the present was through discovering actions and situations in the present analogous to actions in the past saving events of God, the language and forms of biblical conversation with God provided Anglican writers with paradigms for their work in the present. In all the writers we will survey, we will find their works grounded in specific biblical genres (especially the narrative, the cultic proclamation, the psalm in all its modes, the prophetic utterance, the gospel, the epistle), not merely as models for copying but as the vehicle of the Word which is to be brought into a conversational relationship with the present. These exercise controlling authority over all the other genres and forms incorporated into the work from other available modes of human discourse, especially from the classical age.

Unlike mythic speech, which seeks to accommodate the randomness of human existence into some overarching order or scheme, or classical rhetoric, which seeks preservation of "things-as-they-are," biblical language comes as judgment on human modes of understanding in discourse. The biblical Word

thus comes into the world unexpectedly, and, instead of restoring some pri-
mal order or affirming the rightness of an existing order, makes a new situation, a new community, a new creation. Biblical language, as Herbert
Schneidau points out, demythologizes the forms and constructs of human
language and refutes their claims to authority, so as to make the divine claim
of human dependence on God.[103] It calls humanity out of its verbally constructed world, whether that be the world of myth or logic, of Hellenic or
classical rhetorical discourse, and into a new world of faithful response to the
divine Word that transforms the situation into which it is spoken. It claims
that the biblical narrative mediating God's Word to the world is the defining
act of verbal discourse and rejects the implicit or explicit claims of all other
verbal structures.

Into a world newly aware of the riches of classical literature, philosophy,
and other manifestations of mythic consciousness, Anglicans thus addressed
once more the biblical claim that ultimate significance lay in the specific,
temporal, and particular actions of a God otherwise mysterious. In mediating
between the Word and the world, Anglican writers used all the resources of
language available to them to make what Eric Auerbach has defined as the
essential thrust of Judeo-Christian writing, that of "the claim to absolute
authority."[104] In biblical terms, truth lies not in abstract statements about
experience but in the consequences of the very telling of the stories of God's
encounters with humanity.[105] It is through retelling of such stories, literally
for Anglicans in the reading of the Bible which contains those stories in a
liturgical context, that God's claims over his creatures are made present,
made to apply to the historic particular of the moment of reading.

Such a view of the biblical text underlies Richard Hooker's assertion that
true preaching is the reading of Scripture in church.[106] The sermon as prophetic discourse is a clarifying of the relationships between God's past actions
and his action in the present moment of reading, a bringing-to-bear on the
present of God's claims made in the past. In this assertion, Hooker affirmed
the Anglican association of its worship with biblical examples, in which the
Word of God, manifest in the recitation of the narrative of past saving acts, is
spoken in the context of the assembly of God's people. The use of such stories
in the Anglican liturgy in connection with the enactment of the Holy Communion identifies that rite as a successor in the present to the ancient assem-
blies of the Hebrews and of the early Christian community, as Cranmer argued. In this context, biblical texts become the lived language of divine
address. That is to say, such usage identifies the using community and places
it into a living relationship to the past events retold through biblical reading.
The Bible thus ceases to be a text from the past searchable for wisdom about
how to live in the present and becomes a work that provides the means to

understand present-day events, informing them and placing them into a living relationship with the common future to which past divine acts point.[107]

In light of the views held by Cranmer and his fellow Reformers, the mythic consciousness which biblical discourse subverts has a twofold component in the Renaissance. In the first place, it is the mythic interpretation of Christianity inherited from the Middle Ages. Controversies about biblical interpretation in the English Reformation turn on whether the Bible points allegorically to a realm of eternal reality external to the temporal world, draining the temporal of meaning and significance, or whether the Bible points to the significance of human life as it is really lived in light of biblical proclamation. One strategy of carrying out this controversy is to claim the infolding of allegorical meaning into the literal text, so that the significance humans attribute to abstractions is claimed for the biblical narratives and their present-day analogues. Another is to undercut the transcendent emphasis of much late medieval piety and to insist that the Christian life is lived in active charity to one's neighbors rather than in passive contemplation of abstract ideas of divine mystery or cyclical repetition of rosaries. In the English Reformers' view, the Christian future is achieved through living out Christ's Summary of the Law through the temporal succession of events rather than through retirement and transcendent meditation aimed at release from the world seen as a vale of tears.

The other focus of the Reformers' subversion is toward the classical tradition as the bearer of mythic consciousness; this reveals itself in literature that borrows from the classical tradition to make Christian proclamation. The Reformers' strategies, as old as Augustine or Prudentius, are to undercut the claims of the classical tradition by juxtaposing them with Christian claims even while adopting the forms and linguistic strategies of the classical writers. In the same way as John's Gospel seeks to usurp the claims of Hellenic philosophy for the *logos* by rewriting the beginning of Genesis to proclaim that "the Word became flesh," so Augustine railed rhetorically against rhetoric and Prudentius epically refuted Virgil. To write a Christian epic or pastoral is to claim for Christian narrative authority over classical discourse and is thus to enact biblical claims for God's authority over his creatures. It is to claim to be doing the classical task but doing it correctly. Such a claim becomes an intrinsic part of the Christian writer's method of proclaiming the world's relationship to the divine Word.

A poetry that "deserveth not to be scourged out of the Church of God" is thus a poetry that can be used to further the pragmatic and functional ends of Anglican writing by persuading its readers to "take that goodness in hand" as well as "to make them know that goodness whereunto they are moved." In other words, the end sought by Anglican didactic discourse, including sermons and homiletic poems, is participation in the sacrifice that is the offering of self through the offering of the community in the Prayer Book Eucharist, resulting in the incorporation of self into "that holy fellowship" and the doing of "all good works." In considering religious poems by Anglican poets in the English Renaissance, we need to keep in mind always their homiletic model in its role as part of the liturgical action which functions as conveyance of the Word and enabler of response through participation in the ongoing actions of that Word. Poem and sermon sacrifice their authority as independent verbal acts to the source of their authority, the Word they seek to convey. They also sacrifice their integrity to that verbal context to which they allude, the liturgy which embodies them, informs their purpose, and enables it to proceed. But the whole verbal enterprise itself sacrifices its claims for self-sufficiency to the societal context in which it occurs and toward which it addresses itself. The role of words in the human response to God's actions in Christ is understood in terms of God's purpose for conveying his Word, this Christ-made-Flesh—the creation of "that holy fellowship" defined in terms of participation in the actions of the Word through good works.

The Prayer Book liturgy in use is thus the meeting place between the Word and the arena of its present enactment; an enactment of the central event in Christian history, it conveys the consequences of that event ("all . . . benefits of his passion"). So, too, the independence of liturgy is undercut; its efficacy is dependent on response, on the extent to which it enables its participants to participate in what the Prayer Book calls "all such good works as thou hast prepared for us to walk in." In this light, Anglican poetry is never complete nor ever intended to be complete in itself, but instead replicates the place in the worship service held by the sermon, as a part, drawing its authority from the biblical and liturgical context of its use and dependent for its efficacy on the sacramental action that follows it in the Prayer Book service as well as on the response of the people both during and after the enactment of the rite.

What we should be alert to by now is the need to understand this poetry in terms of its functioning, more specifically its functioning at the margins of discourse in the relationships between homily and congregation, always yielding its claims over its readers to a larger realm of discourse, always pointing its readers beyond the reading moment to the ordinary context for such a moment as well as to the ordinary ends of such a moment. And yet marginality brings the freedom to be audacious, to function with self-conscious risk in the seam between the customary and the disaffected, between the ongoing worship of the nation and those who "would fly" a sermon. Poems of this sort, although they are finally caught up in a larger process of discourse, are free to reveal the world as a construct of human language, and to refute the claims to authority of such constructs, so as to make the divine claim of human dependence on God. Such poems call humanity out of its verbally constructed world and into a new world of faithful response to God as transforming Word. They claim that the use of biblical narratives mediating God's Word to the world defines the proper use of verbal discourse and reject the claims of all other verbal structures. In these ways, through the transformation, the "making new," of models and predecessors, the Anglican poets of the English Renaissance expressed the divine claim over humanity, proclaimed the presence of God to his people in the events of their day, and demanded response. Through the use of biblical models for speech and constant echoing of biblical language, they proclaimed that the God who exercises his claim now is the God of whom the Bible speaks and who speaks through use of the Bible. Through the use of all human verbal techniques for evoking meaning and moving people, such as rhetoric, imagery, and all the rest, they sought to impinge on the world of their readers while at the same time undercutting the claims of all human verbal structures, even their own. In this way, they directed to the Bible and the Christian community their reader who discovers through their works who he is and what kind of world he lives in. They used their own works as instigators of change and then expressed the divine judgment on themselves so that their readers would never confuse the biblical Word with the words of the poets. Thus, they reminded their readers of the biblical proclamation that God is only in his Word and never in human words about him and alerted their readers to God himself in his specific actions in human history.

Finally, they mediated the claims of One whose actions contain not only judgment and call to relationship but also promise of future fulfillment. As texts whose meaning resides in *praxis,* in what results from the reader's experience of them, these poems call their readers to a relationship whose history is intelligible ultimately in terms of promises whose fulfillment is still to come in a future of peace and rest with One who promises to meet human need, One who comes primarily not to be served but to serve. This sense of divine initiative in the history of the people whose works we will consider gives to their works a particular urgency, a desire to transform their readers, either by catching them up in the sense of God's actions in history or by bringing them to points of choice in terms of how they will respond to the claims mediated through these poems.

For all these reasons, the writers we will consider employed a poetics of persuasion, a use of language aimed at expressing the claims of the Word they mediate and at evoking specific responses to those claims. As such, they become enablers of process, writers of language for use. I am thus concerned with the ways in which this Anglican tradition of discourse informs the writings of Spenser, Herbert, and Vaughan. As all these writers were fond of saying, their works are didactic. That is to say, they are confessional, autobiographical, epic, lyric, meditative, allegorical, or even self-consuming only to the extent that such verbal strategies enable them to be didactic, to fulfill an essentially rhetorical and homiletic function of seeking to change the behavior of their readers. And not change for the sake of change only, but change in behavior shaped and informed and directed by the Anglican agenda for the reformation of society into the true Christian commonwealth, as that agenda came to be understood in the various historical situations in which Anglicanism defined itself and its purpose in the years between 1580 and 1660.

· 2 ·

Edmund Spenser

Spenser's Celebration of the Word

Spenser, to whom we often turn for images of Elizabeth's court and of Elizabethan culture, was actually a rigorous critic of her court and the society that supported it. What we now read as idealized portraits and effusive encomiums were originally strategies of reform in a culture where criticism had to be voiced in the language of compliment if it were to be heard at all. Cranmer's vision of the Christian commonwealth to be built through the enabling of charity found in Spenser its most articulate spokesman and effective proponent. The sweeping inclusiveness of Cranmer's vision of a society living out his reign of charity at every level is realized in Spenser's plan to promote through the narratives of knightly quest and discovery ethical behavior at every level of social interaction. *The Faerie Queene* is thus a religious poem, as are most of Spenser's poems, for they bring all of English society within the perspective of the divine activity in history and reveal what possibilities for transformation may be released within it through the enabling use of the Prayer Book.

Categorizing Spenser as a religious poet is a controversial act,[1] yet in a fundamental sense Spenser remains, at least for me, the quintessential poet of the Church of England. As a poet who places in the penultimate canto of Book IV of *The Faerie Queene* a wedding between the Thames and the Medway, the "salt Medway," the "middle way" of Anglican apologetic,[2] the church as salt and leaven as it merges with the great water highway of English history and flows out to command all the ways of talking about natural forces in divine terms, Spenser deserves attention in terms of the goals and aims of the English Reformation. Indeed, I will argue here that Spenser sought through his major poems the achievement of a Christian commonwealth to result from

Prayer Book worship leading to charitable behavior. This was, as we have seen, Cranmer's aim in his reformation by use of the Prayer Book; Spenser took up this quest at a time in which controversy over use of Cranmer's books threatened to divert attention from his goals.

Spenser composed the early books of *The Faerie Queene* during the 1580s, a period of renewed controversy over use of the Prayer Book. The tenure of Archbishop Grindal (1576–1583) had seen a lessening of tensions, but at the cost of laxity in enforcing conformity to Prayer Book use. His successor, Archbishop Whitgift, attempted in 1584 to reverse this drift through issuing a number of articles which demanded that the Prayer Book be used "in public prayer, and none other."[3] The result was a strong reaction by the Puritan party, beginning in 1585, which took the form of public complaints and a series of publications, the most famous of which are the Marprelate tracts of 1588 and 1589.

These developments posed serious dangers for the program put forward by the English Reformers. Already, under Archbishop Grindal, Cranmer's plans for improving the educational level of Anglican clergy ran afoul of political controversy. In the form of "prophesyings," gatherings of clergy for instruction in Scripture called for as early as Cranmer's *Injunctions* of 1547 appeared to Elizabeth to be opportunities for fomenting social unrest; she suppressed them. One result was that the Puritan party championed the prophesyings, claimed to be on the side of an educated, preaching clergy, and labeled the Church of England as a defender of the situation inherited from the Middle Ages.[4] Because the queen on whom the Church of England depended reacted to political pressure by trying to use her church for social control rather than reform, she, too, represented an obstacle to the fulfillment of Cranmer's program, albeit one whose involvement called for cultivation rather than suppression.

We know of Spenser's support for Archbishop Grindal in his struggle with the queen over the prophesying controversy.[5] In the 1580s and early 1590s Spenser set out to move both queen and country on toward the English Reformers' goal of societal transformation aimed at creation of the true Christian commonwealth. Reasserting Cranmer's view of religion as functional for change, Spenser employed allusions to Prayer Book modes of language to assert the need to participate in God's actions in English history through Word and Sacrament. Seeking to avoid Puritan confessionalism and the destruction of English worship, he sought to involve the queen once more in supporting the aims of the church created in her father's and brother's reigns.

Such an agenda was rich and complex; to deal with it here I will emphasize two aspects of it. As we have seen, the central vehicle of change for Cranmer was the transformation of the liturgical life of England from the Mass celebrated by the priest distanced from the congregation through language, theology, and manner of life to the Holy Communion shared by the congregation through the facilitation of a priest joined to the congregation by language, theology, and mode of life. The celibate performer of seemingly magical rites in Latin was to become the married enabler of the work of God in the world through the use of English. Spenser thus begins his epic of the English Reformation with an assertion of the transforming efficacy of the vernacular Eucharist, with Red Crosse Knight's quest becoming the enabler of transformations and pointing toward marriage as one way of articulating its goals. No longer an aristocratic or noble warrior achieving a dynastic union, Red Crosse as "meer English" finds his adventures leading to betrothal to Una more significant than any offered by Virgil or Ariosto. Spenser's, and Red Crosse's, work here is thus inscribed through the transformation of epic genres, wrenching old texts into new purposes, "overgoing" past models.

Another of Spenser's agendas flowing from this one—as do all the agendas of *The Faerie Queene*—is the redefinition of the Christian life as one based not on the monastic model of private devotion, celibate living in same-sexed communities, and individual devotion on a heroic scale but on the ancient and now-recovered familial model in which the communion table is the focus of parish life as a family meal, cutting across divisions of English society, making the nation one family and everyone capable of significant devotion. Central to this would be what I will call the domestication of *eros,* or the sacralization of *eros,* the reinscription of Christian love to include the sexual, even as English conflates the three Greek words (*agape, eros,* and *philia*) and the two Latin words (*amor* and *caritas*) for love into one. The official translations flinched at this, even as Queen Elizabeth and others found difficulty with a married clergy, substituting "charity" for *caritas* in such texts as Paul's injunction that there are three great gifts of the Spirit, but "the greatest of these is charity" (1 Corinthians 13:13). But Spenser did not: "So let us love, deare love, lyke as we ought, / love is the lesson which the Lord us taught" (*Amoretti* 68, ll. 13–14).

Such a transformation of eroticism is inscribed in *The Faerie Queene,* and especially in the *Amoretti* and *Epithalamion* in terms of a reinvention of the Petrarchan conventions for articulating human feeling. Romeo is "for the numbers that Petrarch flow'd in," says Mercutio (II.iv.38–39), and Juliet says of him, "You kiss by the book" (I.v.110), yet the continued articulation of erotic feeling in Elizabethan writing and culture by means of Petrarchan conventions must not obscure the fact that the plot of Petrarch's *Rime sparse* is the plot of medieval courtly love with its goal of the diversion of erotic energy into ascent of a spiritual ladder, ending with prayer to God made possible by devotion to the Blessed Virgin Mary. Dante and Petrarch make clear the cultural problem posed by the energies of eroticism; love's disruptiveness of domestic and civil order continues as a major theme in Renaissance England, as the plots of so many of Shakespeare's comedies and tragedies suggest.

Yet the reformed Christianity of the Prayer Book took away the hierarchy of ascent through the Blessed Virgin; it dared at once to channel the directions of the Christian life through the domestic and social arrangements of English society and to insist that those same structures accommodate the sexual energies so widely perceived as disruptive to them. Red Crosse will seek to turn from "the world, whose joyes so fruitlesse are," but is told, "that may not be," since in his world the "*vergine umana . . . chiara . . . santa*" of Petrarch[6] has become "that royall maide," and the Seven Sorrows of the Blessed Virgin Mary and medieval devotion have become "that virgins cause disconsolate" (*FQ,* I.x.63–65), to be relieved in Faerie Land or England, not in private prayer or pilgrimage to the shrine of a saint. From the beginning, Cranmer's Prayer Book makes marriage a major social feast, to take place on Sunday or Holy Day mornings at the Eucharist, for "the procreation of children," for the active exercise of sexuality among those "as have not the gift of continency," and for "mutual society, help, and comfort," thus "signifying unto us the mystical union, that is betwixt Christ and his Church" (BCP, pp. 290–291). In the absence of a celibate ideal, of the monastic social structures, of contemplative devotion to the Virgin Mary, marriage moves strongly into the center of societal life. Cranmer reinforced this by having the official Primers be books of family prayer, not individual devotion, which orient religious life outside of church in relationship to the worship of the community, not in devotion to saints or other private exercises.

Although Spenser's role in encouraging the domestication of *eros* will concern me here, I want to introduce the subject by examining how Sidney's major work appears in this light. The *Arcadia* displays all the disruptive potential of *eros;* the many twists and turns of the plot are motivated by desire and its effects. At least in the version Sidney completed, however, the case made by the work as a whole is that *eros* can be dealt with only in the context of ongoing domestic relationships; otherwise it leads to death or to the destruction of the fabric of trust in society. For love, Pyrocles and Musidorus abandon their appropriate roles as heroic youths and violate the standards of conduct that accompany those roles. For love, and for fear of love, King Basilius abandons his social and familial responsibilities, as does his queen. These narrative consequences of *eros* are displayed against a background of subplots in which rampant evil and cruelty are perpetuated repeatedly in the name of love or as an enraged response to the frustration of desire. In a society in which personal, familial, and national safety were thought to reside in the continuity of family ties and in the acceptance of social roles, these are serious problems indeed.

In spite of this, however, Sidney clearly values human feeling, especially sexual desire, as the basis for significant relationships and social interaction. Our sympathies in the work are clearly with those struggling to work out the consequences of desire; we never wish someone would resort to forced relationships and arranged marriages. Although the actual resolution of the many plots requires a miracle (patterned not unlike Christ's paradigmatic resurrection), we leave the work convinced that Sidney believes such miracles are possible and worth waiting for. There is no structure here either for avoiding the realities of human desire or for channeling it outside the social structures of marriage, family, and family-ruled society.

Astrophil and Stella, in this light, reveals the limitations of Petrarchan structures for dealing with *eros* or of social structures not based on the domestication of *eros*. Astrophil, for example, can get through thirteen lines of pure Petrarchan rationalization in Sonnet 71 about how Stella's beauty "drawes the heart to love" while "As fast thy Vertue bends that love to good," yet "ah, Desire still cries, give me some food."[7] We have no sense that Astrophil's desire is evil; only the exercise of it outside existing social structures would create problems, for "Rich she is." What stands criticized here is the rest of the Petrarchan plot, as a by now unworkable solution to the urgency of desire and the social convention of making marriages on bases other than mutuality of affection. Sidney's treatment of Astrophil articulates a critique both of fantasies of unbridled eroticism and of the Petrarchan mode of repression and denial through redirection. Neither offers a solution to the realities of erotic desire; the former threatens legitimate individual and social needs for predictability and growth of relationships in time while the latter makes of erotic desire a personal inner battle that succeeds only at the cost of denial and retreat from the interpersonal. What is called for is a transformation of social structures which allows for an affirmation of erotic desire and the achievement of its fulfillment as well as for amelioration of its destructive potential.

In Cranmer's view, espoused in the claims made in the Prayer Book marriage rite, the goals of the English Reformation involved developing a community built up through the domestication of *eros* and the forming of a commonwealth around the one table of the Christian family. Spenser sought to promote those goals. To achieve this end in Book I as well as in the rest of *The Faerie Queene* and, especially, in the *Amoretti* and *Epithalamion,* works that stand, in effect, at the beginning and the end of *The Faerie Queene,* Spenser brought biblical, classical, liturgical, and homiletic/rhetorical modes together to make the Reformers' proclamation about God's renewed activity in the events of English history. In examining these works, I reject the approach to Spenser which sees his work as being fundamentally about abstractions, claiming that his allegory points beyond the work itself to a timeless realm of reality.[8] I suggest instead that, in Spenser's narrative, abstractions (including the words that name abstractions) take on meaning not apart from the narrative, but precisely because of the ways they are used in specific moments of a narrative which is always a vehicle for bringing the power of those abstractions to bear on the real historical situation in which Spenser's audience found itself. The abstract words displaying virtues and vices in the work come to have meaning only in the context of the specific moment of reading[9] and only in a prophetic act of reading which sees the narrative as fundamentally "about" Spenser's historical situation, describing it, bringing to bear the pressure of biblical imperatives upon it, and working to change it. What Spenser gives us is not a naive redoing of historical allegory in which figures in the poem point to actual figures in English history so as to replicate in the poem their past behavior in the world.[10] Spenser is not giving us an allegorized description of how things were in the England of his day; rather, his method is one of presenting his readers with an instrument by which to interpret that world, which points out, in Sidney's terms, not "what is, hath been, or shall be," but "what may be and should be." Putting a grid of possibility over "what is," Spenser opened before his contemporary reader directions for behavior, emphasized the significance of certain of those options, and thus enabled his poems to function (at least potentially) in a didactic way. He therefore made of his work not an object of knowledge but an instrument for knowing, transforming the contemporary social and political landscape into a place of new opportunities for change, moving it through ethical behavior toward the English Reformers' goal of community and commonwealth.

The Poetics of Christian Commonwealth in The Faerie Queene

Toward the end of Book I of *The Faerie Queene,* a "godly aged Sire" leads the Red Crosse Knight, the central figure of that book, to "the highest Mount" of the faerie landscape and shows him "a litle path" which directs Red Crosse's "vew" to "a goodly Citie."[11] This episode bears careful examination because it comes at a critical point in Red Crosse's journey from the Court of Gloriana to the land where Una's parents are held prisoner by the dragon which Red Crosse has set out to slay. Prior to the episode in which this ascent to the "highest Mount" takes place, Red Crosse has wandered aimlessly through Faeryland, meeting with one disaster after another, until he is finally rescued from the giant Orgoglio by Prince Arthur and reunited with Una. Taken by her to the House of Holiness, he is instructed, as the headnote to Canto x tells us, about "repentance, and the way to heavenly blesse." His guides in the House of Holiness are Fidelia, Speranza, and Charissa, evocative of association with faith, hope, and charity, Saint Paul's three cardinal virtues. It is Charissa who leads Red Crosse finally to the Hermitage on the "steepe and hy" hill where they meet the "godly aged Sire" who directs Red Crosse's attention to the path that leads his view to the City of God. The sight of that city thus comes as the culmination of the process of instruction undergone by Red Crosse in the House of Holiness.

In addition, the pace of events in Book I quickens markedly after Red Crosse descends the "highest Mount." After his sight of the city, Red Crosse rejoins Una, who, understandably, considering her past experience with him, awaits him "still with pensive mind." The events which follow suggest that Red Crosse is now ready for his battle with the dragon, for he journeys swiftly with Una to her "native soyle" and encounters the dragon within the first four stanzas of Canto xi. This is blinding movement indeed for anyone accustomed to the leisurely pace of the earlier cantos; clearly something of major importance has just transpired to facilitate such haste.

In light of its place in the plot, therefore, we are encouraged to find that the sight of that "goodly Citie" marks a crucial stage in Red Crosse's preparation for victory in the battle he has been pointing toward since before the beginning of Book I. Since I want to discover just how Spenser's poem functions as a didactic work, "to fashion a gentleman or noble person in vertuous and gentle discipline,"[12] this central passage in a process of instruction from within the poem is an appropriate place to begin. The relevant stanza reads, in full:

> From thence, far off he unto him did shew
>   A litle path, that was both steepe and long,
>   Which to a goodly Citie led his vew;
>   Whose wals and towres were builded high and strong
>   Of perle and precious stone, that earthly tong
>   Cannot describe, nor wit of man can tell;
>   Too high a ditty for my simple song;
>   The Citie of the great king hight it well,
> Wherein eternall peace and happinesse doth dwell.
>
> (I.x.55)

Because Spenser sets up Red Crosse's experience of the New Jerusalem as both an act of seeing and an act of reading (the presentation of a visual image as a text in words intended to teach its audience, including both Red Crosse and the reader), this episode can help us understand how Spenser used words to teach his readers. As such, this passage is instructive as to Spenser's method because it stresses both the uses and the limitations of language. The "godly aged Sire" leads Red Crosse to a place where he can see a path that at once links Red Crosse to the "goodly Citie," since it leads his sight to it, and at the same time separates him from that city, since it is still "both steepe and long." Spenser's poem also leads us as readers to the city by telling us that it is there in the world of Red Crosse's experience and by giving us a few details of its appearance. At the same time, however, what in the poem presents us with the city also distances us from it by confessing the limitations of the poet's language to present it to us. Although we know the city has walls and towers "builded high and strong / Of perle and precious stone," they are such "that earthly tong / Cannot describe, nor wit of man can tell."

Spenser's language here takes nothing away from the city; it is really there, at least in the terms of "reality" operative in the faerie world, since Red Crosse can see it clearly. The problem lies with using language—with the powers of "earthly tong" or "wit of man" to "describe," to "tell"—and with interpreting language—the ability to "read" the "way to heaven." The image of the city is here evoked, but its depiction can only be approached, never encompassed, by the conceptualizing and verbalizing skills of even so adept a poet as Edmund Spenser. There is a fundamental sense in which this "goodly Citie" can only be brought into the verbal world of *The Faerie Queene* by the poet's denying his ability to get it in, by confessing his limitations rather than displaying his descriptive skills. Presumably, in the conceptual frame operative here, we are to imagine the existence of a "ditty" of the city (and, later, we will consider what it might be), but for now it is "too high" for this speaker's "simple song."

What we have here is, of course, not so much an actual admission of failure on Spenser's part as it is a deliberate rhetorical strategy to locate any possible "ditty" of the city in relationship to Spenser's poem as verbal construct. Whatever image of the city Spenser might have created would represent a distraction because it would provide for his text a false sense of completion or achievement which would detract from Spenser's larger objectives. Red Crosse experiences the city as competitive with his quest as well as its culmination; Spenser refuses to give us an image of the city to compete with its more customary depiction, a point to which we will return. We may note, however, that one consequence of Spenser's strategy is that at this point in the poem there develops a split between Red Crosse's experience of Faeryland and ours. In terms of the plot, Red Crosse must see this city if he is to complete his quest, and so he does. Although it is still at the end of a path "both steepe and long," he sees it clearly enough to notice at least that "The blessed Angels to and fro descend" and to compare it favorably with Cleopolis, "For this great Citie [Cleopolis] does far surpas, / And this bright Angels towre quite dims that towre of glas" (I.x.58). If we are to learn from Red Crosse's experience, presumably we, too, must be shown this city for ourselves, but this is precisely what Spenser refuses to do for us. We proceed, from this moment in the poem, aware that the poet has not given us, and claims that he is unable to give us, something he claims we need.

This reverses situations earlier in the poem in which Spenser is careful to point out to us the things Red Crosse sees and to help us establish their significance. This is especially true of the episode in Canto i, which anticipates in many of its details Red Crosse's sight of the eternal city in Canto x.

The occasion is of course Red Crosse's sight of Archimago's false Una, a verbal seeing again associated with an "aged Sire" (I.i.29). Archimago is at once the "arch-magus," the first of magicians, and thus "arch-imager," the great maker of images. His image created for Red Crosse, who is prepared for this sight of the false Una with the aid of erotic dreams fetched from the realm of Morpheus, is "made . . . of that other Spright, / And fram'd of liquid ayre her tender partes / So lively, and so like in all mens sight, / That weaker sence it could have ravished quight" (I.i.45). As maker and framer, Archimago is a kind of Renaissance artist, here literally giving "to aery nothing / A local habitation and a name." What Spenser wants us to be aware of throughout is the quality of artifice as falsehood in Archimago's work as well as its power to affect the senses. Archimago is "Simple in shew"; "Sober he seemde . . . And well could file his tongue as smooth as glas."[13] As Spenser notes, through his repeated use of the word "seems" and its various forms in describing Archimago and his actions, we, as readers of the words that present the false image of Una to Red Crosse and to us, are alert to her falsity and the duplicity of her maker. At this point we know more than Red Crosse; Spenser here lets us both share the maker's and the viewer's perspectives on this artistic creation, since we know both its falsity and its apparent appeal.

Red Crosse wakes from his dream of "wanton blis and wicked joy" to behold this image of Una, which for us is totally verbal and which for Red Crosse takes on a verbal quality. The image of a woman with "gentle blandishment and lovely looke, / Most like that virgin true, which for her knight him took," soon begins to speak "words, that could not chuse but please, / So slyding softly forth, she turnd as to her ease," providing a verbal enrichment or equivalent to her visual seductiveness. When Red Crosse, although profoundly disturbed, does not yield to this speaking picture of Una, Archimago takes another approach. Arranging his false Una in an amorous pose with "a young Squire" made of yet another sprite, he goes to rouse Red Crosse and urges him to "Come see, where your false Lady doth her honour staine." As later with the "godly aged Sire," Red Crosse goes to see the sight prepared for him, but, as a result of what he is taken to see by Archimago, coupled with Archimago's reading of that sight, Red Crosse sets off come morning, leaving Una behind.

Spenser parallels these two stories of Red Crosse's sights, using the principle of organization announced by Richard Hooker for his Lawes of Ecclesiasticall Politie, that "every former part might give strength unto all that followe, and every later bring some light unto all before."[14] On both occasions, Red Crosse is taken to see something by an "aged Sire"; on both occasions, as a result of what he has seen, coupled with the account of that sight provided by his guide, he sets off on a journey. There are, as well, sharp differences. In the case of Red Crosse's mountaintop sight of the eternal city, his guide is a "godly aged Sire," not the false Archimago, the merely "aged Sire" of Canto i. In this latter case, his journey is with Una, toward fulfilling his quest, not away from her. The sight of the city enables Red Crosse to proceed with Una; the sight of the false Una leads him away from her and provides room in the poem for Archimago to disguise himself as Red Crosse: "And when he [Archimago in disguise] sate upon his courser free, / *Saint George* himself ye would have deemed him to be" (I.ii.11). Spenser here subverts the received cultural expectation of what "Saint George" would be like, revealing the problems he saw inherent in a readership trained by medieval assumptions about the saints. On the basis of a traditional religious education, Elizabethan readers, Spenser thought, would have difficulty distinguishing Archimago from Saint George; only after seeing Red Crosse go through his education can we discern that he is the one worthy to inherit the cultural authority that the title "Saint George" evokes. At this point, however, Red Crosse has not yet learned who he is, and appearances here can deceive even so well-informed readers as we. It is only, Spenser seems to imply, the "reading" ability he models for us in the role of his narrator that keeps us from making the confusion of the false and true knights that others in the poem, including Una, fall prey to.

Since the way Spenser will inscribe the fulfillment of Red Crosse's quest is as a betrothal to Una, however, there is more here that needs paying attention to. The sight of the false Una is an occasion for exploring the potential destructiveness of *eros;* it is depicted as placing Red Crosse in a double bind. He winds up "going astray" and abandoning Una not by yielding to the desires aroused by his dream of "loves and lustfull play," or the opportunities presented by his sight of the false Una as "a loose Leman to vile service bound" (I.i.47–48) or his equally false sight of her joined with another apparition "in wanton lust and lewd embracement" (I.ii.5). Instead, his flight is an escape from conflicts he experiences between desire, opportunity, and expectation. The problem is not the presence of erotic feeling between Red Crosse and Una, or of the bodily manifestation of human life. After all, the tempting false Una is not real body at all, but the fantasy of a body that Archimago thought Red Crosse would find desirable. Una as the embodiment of truth is not the issue, for we will eventually find the true Una as an embodied creature later in the poem, as Red Crosse looks desirously on her in a different way:

> Thrise happy man the knight himselfe did hold,
> Possessed of his Ladies hart and hand,
> And ever, when his eye did her behold,
> His heart did seeme to melt in pleasures manifold.

> Her joyous presence and sweet company
>   In full content he there did long enjoy,
>   . . . swimming in that sea of blisfull joy.
>
> (I.xii.40–41)

And, of course, underlying this and linking it with the city of Canto x is the traditional biblical imagery of the church as the bride of Christ and the new Jerusalem coming down out of heaven as a bride prepared for her bridegroom.

The issue is what will move *eros* from the arena of fantasy to the arena of fulfillment; that, Spenser claims, involves its incorporation into a socially acceptable and socially supported context, moving it from the realm of the private to the realm of the public with all its attendant risks. Indeed, the language which Spenser uses to describe Red Crosse's emotional state as he sees the false Una in Book I is that used by the Prayer Book to describe the alternative to the married expression of human sexuality. According to the marriage rite, this is "not to be enterprised nor taken in hand unadvisedly, lightly, or wantonly, to satisfy men's carnal lusts and appetites" (BCP, p. 290). In Una as truth or the true church, Spenser creates an image through Red Crosse's relationships, both with the false and true Unas, that embody, or give movement and form to, the language of the Prayer Book. Also part of Spenser's agenda here is to make clear that it is through the life of the body, involved in a social and public context, that the kingdom or the holy city or the body of the bride of Christ is built up. Thus, Red Crosse sees the body of the false Una and the City of God and the body of the true Una, and there is a rich sense in which his experience of the former helps him recognize the latter two and recognize them, finally, as one body. There are also suggestions here about how to read the Prayer Book as a text that takes its meaning from its use in a context in which meaning functions as a result of what one sees, how one sees it, and what action that "seeing" leads to. Reading is thus for now both an active and a passive behavior, both something one does and a recognition of what situation one is in.

Errour, we may remember from earlier in Canto i, combines in depiction features of a dragon with features of "womans shape," but distorted so that in this case Errour is "most lothsom, filthie, foule, and full of vile distaine" (I.i.14). "She" pours out from her "hellish sinke . . . a fruitfull cursed spawne" which she feeds with "poisonous dugs" (I.i.15, 20–22). In her dragon aspect she vomits "bookes and papers" accompanied by "frogs and toades, which eyes did lacke." This linking of blind regard for erroneous books with a perversion of female anatomy and generativity prepares for Archimago's false Una and for the depiction of the stripped Duessa, who shares many of Errour's physical characteristics, including especially her distasteful "dugs," her shameful "neather parts," and her "taile, with dong all fowly dight" (I.viii.47–48). When Red Crosse delights in regarding Una's body, her physical presence in the poem, he has moved beyond the whole complex of associations Spenser sets up here between a distorted femaleness, an inability to "read aright," and a perversion of eroticism.

Two things need to be made clear. The first is that there is a close relationship in *The Faerie Queene* between the kinds of experiences depicted for us as readers and that presented to the central character within the poem's fictional world. We experience the world of Faeryland as language; the world that Red Crosse sees takes its nature from the nature of language. There is a real sense in which Red Crosse, like us, needs a skillful reader, indeed needs to become a skillful reader, if he is to distinguish between verbal fantasies and verbal allusions to reality. He lacks this when he is in the company of the false maker and duplicitous reader Archimago but has this sort of companion when he is on the mountain in the company of the figure Contemplation. Archimago is first seen by Red Crosse in the guise of a contemplative, and his confusion of appearance and reality in Canto i is the result of Archimago's tongue, filed "as smooth as glas"; in Canto x, he can distinguish between the "angels towre" and "that towre of glas." The nature of Faeryland is shaped by the possibilities of the language that depicts Spenser's fictional world; the experience of Faeryland demands response, initially, in the form of reading, a reading that actively seeks contact with what is being depicted. [15]

Second, when Red Crosse finally sees his sight of the New Jerusalem, the city John describes as "a bride come down out of heaven adorned for her bridegroom," we are reminded of the limits of language. Spenser indicates either directly or indirectly no difficulty in presenting us with the image of the false Una in the language of his poem. The profound tension we have noted in his account of the city is nowhere present in his account of Archimago's making, framing, and reading activity. The city as bride is juxtaposed with the false Una and later with Duessa as aggressively unfaithful yet potential brides; just before Red Crosse wakes to see Archimago's false image of Una, he seems to hear in his dream the Roman wedding song, "*Hymen io Hymen*" (I.i.48). Spenser's own language is capable of showing us that false bride as well as how to read her aright, but for the heavenly bride he must admit it is "too high a ditty for my simple song." Similarly, his monstrous Errour of Canto i is articulated vividly as a perversion of female generativity, anticipating Duessa's own deformed appearance, while Una's own generativity is depicted by its absence, brought into the poem only under the unspokenness of future possibility for the betrothed who delights in the physical presence of the other.

Reading or choices among readings here also affect participation in narrative. Spenser uses the plot conventions of medieval romance (knight errant with damsel in distress on quest) to structure events in *The Faerie Queene*, but the mispairing of Red Crosse with Duessa and Archimago with Una cannot advance beyond a certain point in this story. Elimination of this doubling at the point of Red Crosse's vision of the city restores Spenser's borrowed (albeit highly distorted) plot structure to its traditional pattern. Although Spenser will later reject the ideal of one true story to shape all experience, here he uses the arresting of a story as a way of linking his characters' problems in understanding how to stay in the plot that inscribes them with their difficulty in interpreting the words that furnish their world. Spenser's depiction of his faerie world constitutes a profound reinterpretation of his medieval inheritance that is as much judgment of it as acceptance. Shorn of the trappings of medieval religion (the grail quest) as well as of medieval culture heroes (the knights of Arthur's round table), Spenser's version can point to a new potential ending for Arthurian writing, substituting the building of a Christian commonwealth in Tudor England for the societal failure represented by the collapse of the round table fellowship. Since in at least some versions the disruption of the round table society is the result of *eros'* disruptiveness—the adulterous relationship between Guenevere and Lancelot, an example of courtly lovers stepping outside, or misreading from inside, the bounds of their genre as it defines acceptable channels for passion in a world of arranged marriages—it is appropriate that Spenser's attempt to write a version of Arthurian epic with a happy ending would begin with, enact repeatedly, and move toward a multiplicity of marriages that are based on mutually felt erotic feelings. To domesticate *eros* is not to deny its disruptive potential but to risk disruption while learning how to accommodate the recreative play of *eros* in channels that contribute to the life of society rather than annihilate it. Spenser's great experiment is to attempt a new reading of married love as *eros* and passion disruptive of society as lust, a transformation of truth and falsehood in societal understanding through a transformation in its terms of understanding.

While language is thus good at depicting false images, it is less adequate in presenting sights that promote desirable results. Adept at articulating private erotic fantasies, it is less helpful at depicting interpersonal and social displays of erotic feeling. Faced with the task of depicting the city, Spenser must admit that his language is under judgment, that it falls short because it inevitably falsifies, and, before an image so important, had best resort to admission of its own inadequacy. Spenser's method enacts a judgment on human powers of conception; to be under judgment means to face the limitations of language and with it the limitations of human powers of thought and articulation. Red Crosse's problem in the episode with the false Una lies in deciding that the sign, or text, of the false Una points to, is, the text of the real Una; Spenser solves that problem in depicting Red Crosse on the mountain by pointing out the distance between the sign and that to which it points, by in fact not giving us a sign of the city at all, but only of the path to it and of others' reactions to it. The other side of the paradigm also holds. Spenser can teach us how to read false images because he informs us of the nature of language's falsity; when faced with the city, we know of its presence because it forces us once again to acknowledge the limitations of the very medium that would teach us by presenting images of "what should be." The city is "true" because it remains outside the "falsification" of language, even Spenser's language.

This candid admission of the nature of language brings us to recognize the importance of reading when undertaken in full knowledge of the nature of what is being read. In the first episode, Spenser's narrator himself serves as our guide to reading "aright," while Red Crosse has a false guide, one who would hide the falsifying nature of language. In the second, the "godly aged Sire" acts as a "right reader" for Red Crosse, but, since Spenser's language fails, by his own admission, to present us with what Red Crosse sees, we are left on our own. Red Crosse accepts the validity of the reading offered by Contemplation ("thou hast my name and nation *red* aright, / And taught the way that does to heaven bound" [emphasis mine]), but we are left to judge whether that reading is right and provided with inadequate knowledge from within the poem to make that judgment. As a result, we must seek it elsewhere. At this point, Red Crosse catches up with us as readers and moves beyond us in terms of how clearly he sees and reads the world of Faeryland.

There is a very real sense in which Spenser himself is a kind of Archimago, since both are arch image makers, the one for his self-created reality, the other for the fiction of Faeryland. Both are aware that there is a real distinction between the images they create and the reality they would depict. The difference is that Archimago offers his images *for* reality and urges his observers to act as though they *were* reality, while Spenser candidly admits that his images of the eternal city both point to it and separate us from it. Archimago's world is the world of myth, a human-shaped world accommodated through language and the mental processes that create language to the needs of humanity for possession, for order, for control. And so, inevitably, is Spenser's, with the small but vital difference that he does not ask us to accept his fiction for truth, but forces us into a position of seeking other contexts, referents, or interpretations than "earthly tong" can "describe" or "wit of man can tell." A confirmation of Archimago's method occurs in Canto ii, where, true to the mythic pattern of medieval romances, Red Crosse rescues a damsel in distress and takes up her quest. At least part of the explanation of what is going on here has to do with the satisfaction of expectations. To one steeped in the genre of the romance, this course of events is appropriate to expectations created by that genre; this is what happens to get narratives under way in works like *The Faerie Queene*. In this case, as we know, however, the lady is not Fidessa as she claims to be, but Duessa in disguise. Spenser is able, like

Archimago, to tell "all" about characters who fit conventional patterns, even their duplicity, yet he cannot bring the true "bride," the New Jerusalem, into his poem except by negation or by, as we will see, pointing out the direction for finding it and the terms for knowing it when we do.

Spenser's point here is that the process of learning from a Renaissance poem is more than observing patterns of behavior and copying them, as in medieval texts, but is a task that must come to terms with the medium of communication being employed and use the character of that medium to understand the nature of what that medium presents. Archimago the magician is one who communicates by hiding the nature of text, demanding that the observer/ reader accept as given the conceptual world Archimago's images figure forth. Much of Book I of *The Faerie Queene,* before Red Crosse's sight of the eternal city, is devoted to tearing down Archimago's world, exposing it for the falsity it really represents; the high point of this is the stripping of Duessa at the end of Canto viii, in which the "reality" of her body is in sharp contrast to expectations of it she created earlier, or even of Red Crosse's experience of it at the beginning of Canto vii before he had learned of his need for an informed reader of bodies, including bodies of text. The rest of Book I is devoted to telling a story which points constantly, not to a world of self-generated and self-enclosed fictions, which are the generalities and abstractions our minds develop to structure our experience, but to a world of narrative which intrudes upon and informs not only the world of Red Crosse's adventures but the everyday world of concrete particulars that made up life in Elizabethan England.

Before examining that more fully, however, we need to return once again to Red Crosse on his mountaintop to see exactly what Red Crosse is taught there, how that teaching process takes place, and how it is mediated to us as readers. Whatever happens there, it is explicitly bound up in an act of reading.[16] Una was able to "read" Errour easily (I.i.13), but Red Crosse did not heed her advice to "beware." Now the "aged holy man" who leads Red Crosse to his sight of the city tells Charissa that she "better can the way to heaven *aread"* but takes on the task at Charissa's insistence. In this scene, Red Crosse will learn Contemplation's point—doing charity is true "reading" of the world, not exchanging one set of words for another. At the end of this scene, Red Crosse can thus assert that this "holy Sire . . . hast my name and nation *red* aright, / And taught the way that does to heaven bound."

At the same time, if our experience of the city Red Crosse sees from this mountaintop is in any way parallel to Red Crosse's experience of that city, then the words of the poem mediate to us the way to that city through our reading of it. In the poem, Red Crosse is taught something, but what he is taught is not easily expressible in abstract terms. It is *praxis* instead of *gnosis,* a way necessarily associated with charity and faith by the reading action of

Contemplation. What Red Crosse is taught is also bound up in discovery—of the city, of the path to the city, of Red Crosse's identity (his past and his name), and of his future, a promise of future citizenship in that city with the name of Saint George and the role of "thine owne nations frend / And Patrone." All this—self-discovery in terms of past origin and future promise—is brought to bear on the present moment of Red Crosse's instruction by Contemplation, based on his "reading" of the "text" that is the sight of the city.

What language can do, therefore, for Red Crosse in the poem is what Contemplation does with it—present a sight of the city and point the way toward that city—through reading "aright." The way which is read aright is not a general notion of living faithfully and charitably, however, but is very specific in terms of the narrative of Red Crosse, resumed after and as a result of this episode. It is "that royall maides bequeathed care," the quest given Red Crosse by Gloriana to free Una's parents from the clutches of the dragon that holds them captive. The resumption of this specific quest is what Contemplation's reading directs Red Crosse to, and for the knight it is a persuasive reading: "Then shall I soone, (quoth he) so God me grace, / Abet that virgins cause disconsolate." And after hearing Contemplation's reading of his situation, Red Crosse does indeed quickly resume his quest. Thus, when Contemplation says of Charissa that she "better can the way to heaven aread," he is being literally correct, since Charissa *is* "all such good works as thou hast prepared for us to walk in." To *do* Charissa is *to read* the way to heaven; what Contemplation does is direct Red Crosse on that way, which he then perceives as a "reading aright" of Red Crosse himself, since true reading is not an act of imaging or an act of abstracting but a doing.

Since Spenser says, however, that he cannot show us the city Red Crosse sees, at least not in the terms in which Red Crosse sees it, we must ask how we as readers benefit from the reading act of Contemplation. We learn the importance of the sight of the city for what happens to Red Crosse from what he does in the poem. Before he sees the city, he is in some way not yet ready to continue his quest, but after he sees it and hears Contemplation's reading of it he renews his quest with single-minded resolve. Spenser goes to great lengths to reveal the significance of the city to us so that, even if he cannot show it to us, he at least can let us know what kind of place it is. Red Crosse sees the heavenly city, Spenser tells us, from a place like the one from which God gave Moses the Ten Commandments and like the one where "that deare Lord . . . oft thereon was fownd, / For ever with a flowring girlond crownd"; it is also "that pleasaunt Mount, that is for ay / Through famous Poets verse each where renownd." And, because it is a mountain from which Red Crosse sees the new Jerusalem, it is like that mountain from which Saint John the Divine also tells us he saw the City of God. Leaving aside for a moment the analogy with Mount Parnassus and its traditional associations, as Spenser reminds us, with "the thrise three learned Ladies," the Muses who inspire poets and others to verbal pronouncements, and also leaving aside the allusion to Christ as Poet contained in the image of a "flowring girlond" with which Spenser says "that deare Lorde" was "for ever . . . crownd" when he was "oft . . . fownd" on the Mount of Olives, let us consider briefly the other mountains with which the mountain of Red Crosse's sight of the city is compared. The result may take us closer to understanding what Spenser is doing with the city that is not there in the poem.

The conventional reading of Spenser's comparison of Red Crosse's mountain with Mount Sinai, the Mount of Olives, and the mountain of Saint John the Divine is that the four mountains are places where, as James Phillips puts it, "after similarly arduous spiritual trials, men have been given a revelation of ultimate truth."[17] The problem with this reading is that, according to Spenser's narrative, Red Crosse does not see "ultimate truth" on his mountain. Nor does Moses on Mount Sinai; he receives the Ten Commandments from God, a text outlining the terms of the relationship in time between God and his people. Nor does Christ on the Mount of Olives; there he is betrayed by Judas into the hands of the Roman authorities for trial and crucifixion. Nor does John the Divine receive "ultimate truth"; he gets a message to deliver to the seven churches in Asia Minor and he, like Red Crosse, sees a city. These are not trivial distinctions. Indeed, they raise the central issue for any attempt to come to grips with the interplay between the vehicle of presentation in Spenser's poem (narrative, character, setting conveyed in words) and what that vehicle conveys (the "meaning" of Spenser's poem). If our understanding of what we are reading about in this poem is informed by our sense of the nature of the language which presents us with its fictional world, then how we deal with that information will shape radically our sense of what the poem is about and how it works. Phillips' remark about what the various figures experience on their respective mountaintops suggests that the standard approach to *The Faerie Queene* seeks the "meaning" of the poem at the expense of rather than in terms of the immediate, particular details of the poem through which that "meaning" is presented. Yet Spenser's concern for "reading aright" calls for us to pay particular attention to just these details.

I have put the word "meaning" in quotation marks in the preceding paragraph because I see what Phillips and others are seeking is to make sense of *The Faerie Queene* in certain specialized ways. This approach to meaning posits the presence behind the poem of an ordered, changeless, universally true, atemporal vision of reality which Spenser is seen to be dramatizing through the vehicle of his poem.[18] Imitating or pointing to this is supposedly the purpose of Spenserian allegory, the sense in which, conventionally, Spenser's poem is understood as an allegorical poem. In Angus Fletcher's theory of

Spenserian allegory, for instance, the narrative of the poem proceeds through a wilderness to certain garden spots of tranquility and meaning, our reading of which gives us the clues we need to make sense of the poem as a whole.[19] In Michael Murrin's view of allegory, the "truth" of the poem is deliberately hidden behind the veil of allegory to protect it from the prying eyes of the uninitiated.[20] In each case, significance is seen to reside in categories of truth, in ideas or abstractions, and thus in our thoughts about events rather than in the events themselves. In the case of Spenser's poem, the focus of such interpretation lies on teasing out the abstraction seen as "figured forth" in the text and regarding that abstraction or pattern as the "meaning" of the text.

In fact, what such approaches to Spenser do is make of his poem a myth; such readings are expressions of mythic consciousness, which always seeks to distance specific experience from the experiencer, to lose it in the general, reliable, manageable, universal truths which the mythic consciousness posits as lying behind the shifting, particular, unique occurrences of experience.[21] This approach is already enacted in the poem and rejected, for it is the world of Archimago, who seeks to organize Red Crosse's relationship with Una into a perception of reality that answers Red Crosse's needs for understanding, for meeting his physical appetites, for resolving his uncertainties over his quest. Throughout the poem, Red Crosse's experiences are unexpected, confusing, open-ended; to accept Archimago's interpretations is to have all resolved, closed, made static. To Red Crosse's credit, he does not give himself over fully to Archimago's image; to Spenser's credit, he is careful to expose the essentially human, language-based, need-fulfilling, and therefore appealing nature of what Archimago has to offer.

Such a view of things also differs from the claims of biblical proclamation which Spenser would have us remember when he brings Red Crosse to his sight of God's city and locates that seeing on a mountain he associates with biblical mountains on which God acted in human history. As we have noted, mythic consciousness has little regard for history, for individual experience, or for the new, unique, or particular. In contrast, the biblical view is that the God of its tradition speaks and acts and reveals himself only in specific encounters with humanity which in turn invest those specific moments with the significance which myth would locate in abstract, timeless, or cyclical rhythms. The sequence of such events in the Bible creates a sense of history with a past narrative and a future expectation; each event in the sequence always "makes all things new," always has the qualities of newness, surprise, and recreation of community, identity, and promise.

If, as Kornelis Miskotte argues, the mythic mode is the distinctive mode of human consciousness,[22] then the process of reading through allegorizing is the interpretive manifestation of that mode. Allegorizing transforms narrative into a static array of relationships; it deprives narrative of its sense of process and takes away the value of its particulars.[23] Spenser uses allegorical elements in his poem because they constitute the mode of depiction which carried authority and power for his audience and thus represent the language to which they would respond most immediately. His letter to Raleigh discusses both the advantages and drawbacks of this choice. On the one hand, he knows "how doubtfully all Allegories may be construed," but on the other they are what "the most part of men delight to read." His choice of Arthur derives from his position as a personage "made famous by many mens former workes," an authority he wants for his own purposes. But Spenser uses allegory in a way that undercuts its claims and reveals its inadequacy for dealing with the reality to which he would point; to put it another way, he *infolds* the meaning of abstractions into the specific events of his narrative, arguing that words which evoke abstractions have power and significance only in the context of specific narrative events. In Canto i, for instance, Red Crosse functions in an allegorical landscape when he invades the Wandering Wood and does battle with the dragon identified as Errour by Una. Red Crosse slays this dragon; he immediately thereafter makes an error in his response to Archimago's image of Una. In allegorical terms, Errour can be slain in combat; when Red Crosse, having slain Errour, still makes mistakes, our whole sense of the ability of allegory to tell the truth about reality is opened to question. For Spenser, the reading technique of allegorizing will only lead to more error while giving a false sense of confidence in our ability as readers. Allegory is, after all, a product of human wit and tongue of man, whose products are misleading unless they take on meaning in specific moments of narrative time informed by divine activity.

In this light, we may again visit Red Crosse on his mountaintop, now seen as one to be understood not in allegorical terms but in terms of analogy with biblical mountaintops. The biblical parallels which Spenser draws for Red Crosse's mountain are among those events which the Bible proclaims and recalls as moments of God's encounter with his people and which the Prayer Book enacts as antitypes of its own experience of hearing the divine Word. Moses on Mount Sinai, Jesus on the Mount of Olives, John on his mountain—in each case these are not mythic spaces, not points of a mythic geography where in some general sense the gods are present to mankind and thus organize humanly experienced space, but are presented in the Bible as specific places significant only because, on one particular occasion, something happened which is best accounted for by saying that God encountered a man and acted in history. The God who had acted to lead Israel out of Egypt and bring it into being as a people then led it to Mount Sinai, where in a specific moment of time he laid out the terms of their new relationship. That same God, revealing himself to humanity in a specific historical life, acted again to complete the work of redemption by being betrayed and handed over to

Roman authorities to be crucified. Then, at a time when the promises made by God to his people seemed in doubt because of Roman persecution, God spoke once more to a man on a mountaintop with a message that even in these events God was at work, using them to bring about the full deliverance of his promises.

This is the kind of mountaintop on which Red Crosse sees his city and the kind of experience he has of that city. What Red Crosse sees from that mountaintop does not reassure his human categories of expectation but confounds them. To Red Crosse, "Till now, . . . I weened well, / That great *Cleopolis,* where I have beene, / . . . The fairest Citie was, that might be seene." Now, however, "this great Citie that does far surpas, / And this bright Angels towre quite dims that towre of glas." From Red Crosse's perspective, the New Jerusalem is the unexpected sight, the new city which confounds his expectations about cities.

Some critics have seen in all this a conventional treatment of the Augustinian doctrine of the two cities (the one of humanity, the other of God), but to stop with such an appraisal is to overlook major elements of the scene. 24 Red Crosse of course chooses the correct "reading" of his vision in such dualistic terms: "O let me not (quoth he) then turne againe / Backe to the world, whose joyes so fruitlesse are; / But let me here for aye in peace remaine, / Or streight way on the last long voyage fare." But his choice is rejected by his guide in favor of his returning to earthly service to the Faerie Queene in the continuation of his quest to free Una's parents from the clutches of the dragon. Red Crosse acts here in a manner parallel to the behavior of Peter, who, having seen on yet another mountain Jesus transfigured and joined by Moses and Elijah, tells Jesus that he wants "to make three tabernacles" (Luke 9:28–33), but, as the King James Version continues, he says this "not knowing what he said."

In Red Crosse's view, after his sight of the New Jerusalem, worldly joys "so fruitlesse are" that he would escape the realities of his temporal existence in favor of the contemplation of things divine. His guide, who is, after all, named Contemplation, might be expected to embrace this view. Again, expectations are not met, however, for the guide insists, "That may not be." Instead, he instructs Red Crosse to return to his initial quest: "ne maist thou yit / Forgo that royall maides bequeathed care, / Who did her cause into thy hand commit." Only then can he "bend . . . [his] painefull pilgrimage / To yonder same *Hierusalem.*" This pattern of proceeding is finally affirmed by Red Crosse, who praises his guide: "O holy Sire . . . how shall I quight / The many favours I with thee have found?" There is no answer to this question provided in the text except Red Crosse's own resumption of his quest; here, again, interpretive answers come in the form of *praxis,* of engaging in charitable action, and not in the form of verbal formulas or *gnosis.*

Spenser in this passage is clearly not concerned with a conventional dichotomy between the City of Man and the City of God; in fact, that reading is firmly rejected by Red Crosse's guide in favor of a sequential pattern.[25] For Red Crosse, service to the Faerie Queene and thus to her city of Cleopolis is a necessary prerequisite for beginning the journey to the New Jerusalem, or, to put it another way, the exercise of citizenship in the earthly city is a requirement for eventual citizenship in the City of God. This point is made on a visual level as well; although the poet claims that "earthly tong / Cannot describe" Red Crosse's vision of God's City, what images we are given closely parallel those used to present Cleopolis. Both cities have towers, both have jewellike or glasslike qualities, and both are filled with communities, the one of angels, the other of elves and humans. In other words, what we *do* see of the New Jerusalem comes to us through the terms used to present Cleopolis, the prior city in Red Crosse's experience providing the vocabulary and imagery to depict the latter, superior city, although this latter sight in effect redefines the words used to describe it and to react to it.

Red Crosse thus experiences a transformation, or "making new," of what the category "city" means for him, including the loss of orientation and of interpretive ability characteristic of moments when old definitions become unstuck and new ones break in. Yet such moments of linguistic crisis can also be moments of growth; Red Crosse enacts here a giving up of the insistence on interpreting things for himself and a turn to reliance on a voice from outside his limited interpretive frame. As a result, he can begin to glimpse a new way of thinking about meaning. For him, now, "city" comes to involve a promised future fulfillment and his own behavior in anticipation of and leading to that fulfillment rather than any comfortable equation between the category and Cleopolis. Although if he ever returned to Cleopolis he might still refer to it by the word "city," he would do so while being aware that the word now also functioned as a way of articulating the goal of a journey which arrival at Cleopolis would not satisfy.

He also knows that the direction of this journey is in and through various bodies and through making the kinds of distinctions that characterize a "false" and a "true" Una, or a Duessa and a Una. The journey he now makes is one of building up the body of a human society through marriage which "signif[ies] the mystical union, that is betwixt Christ and his Church" and through action in relationship to an altar where a body is received ("the Body of Christ which was given for thee") and a body is made ("thou dost vouchsafe to feed us . . . and dost assure us thereby . . . that we be very members incorporate in thy mystical body"), both at marriages ("The new married persons [the same day of their marriage] must receive the Holy Communion") and regularly on other occasions. The eucharistic language of bodies thus creates interdependent interactions, or defines the arena of human interactions as also the arena of divine action in Spenser's, and Cranmer's, sense of the Christian life as a wayfaring life, building and journeying, in which the meaning of things is realized in action, in active charity, not in the realm of passive *gnosis*.

What Red Crosse receives on his mountaintop is thus not a vision of "ultimate truth" but a renewed call to his vocation. What he sees is not abstract *gnosis*, a concealed vision of ultimate, atemporal reality, but a renewed invitation to *praxis*, to a way or a journey. This is another pervasive biblical motif; God in his creative, saving actions calls into being a new or renewed relationship between himself and his people, calls on Israel to respond by embarking on a path leading from the present moment of encounter to the fulfillment of God's promises made in that moment of encounter. Moses departs Mount Sinai with the terms of a way of life for God's people embodied in the Ten Commandments. Jesus departs from the Mount of Olives to follow the way of the cross, the way taken by the one who proclaims, "I am the Way," the way his followers must take if they "take up their crosses and follow him." John writes of his vision to encourage the churches of Asia Minor to persist in the way even in the face of persecution. It is a way characterized by faithfulness to the relationship God calls his people to have with him, to his promise, and to anticipation of their future fulfillment.

It is also a way that leads the called from their reliance on mythic constructions of reality, even as Abram was called to turn away from Babel and its significance as a mythic point of reference, into a land unstructured by mythic schemes, equipped only with an occasion-specific but not location-specific relationship with God. Myths organize landscape by locating sacred points within it so that surroundings can be located and attended to, a point noted by Fletcher in his study of *The Faerie Queene.* Yet landscape at this point in the poem actually disappears; the spatial arrangement of places displayed through the first ten cantos of Book I vanishes in the space between Stanzas 1 and 2 of Canto xi, between Una's reference to "the tedious toyle, ye for me take" and her announcement, "Now are we come unto my native soyle." Replicating the technique of biblical narration, which ignores setting almost entirely to emphasize the importance of God-human and interpersonal relationships, Spenser here makes clear that the developing relationship between Red Crosse and Una, with all its larger implications, is now (un)creative of space, making possible the dispatch with which this journey occurs. Thus, the achievement of narrative movement in Spenser's poem is enabled through its achieving an informing relationship with biblical modes of depiction.

Such is the world Red Crosse enters on his mountaintop. It is no accident, in this light, that after he accepts the renewal of his call to the way that leads to the dragon—"Then shall I soone, (quoth he) so God me grace, / Abet that virgins cause"—he receives his name. The guide sets this up as a kind of test:

"Then seeke this path, that I to thee presage, / Which after all to heaven shall thee send . . . / For thou emongst those Saints . . . / Shalt be a Saint . . . / thou Saint *George* shalt called be." Then, when Red Crosse has tried and failed to reject his calling and has accepted anew the way he is directed to go, the guide explains fully the derivation of Red Crosse's name. Born an English-man, Red Crosse was brought to Faeryland where he was found in a furrow by a Ploughman, who gave him the name Georgos. Like Abram/Abraham, Jacob/Israel, Saul/Paul, and other biblical figures who discover their real identity in their faithful response to God's call, Red Crosse too finds his new name as a consequence of accepting his vocation.

It is also an important moment for us as well. We were told earlier that we would have thought on the basis of appearance that Archimago in disguise "when he sate upon his courser free, / *Saint George* himself ye would have deemed him to be" (I.ii.11). We now, with Red Crosse, have been told who the real Saint George is; on the basis of this discovery, we ought now to be able to "read his name aright" on the basis of behavior (*praxis*) rather than appearance, which is so easily confused with true *gnosis*. Here, the transforma-tion of names inscribes the meaning of a journey—leaving the old and antic-ipating the new, a process of transformation. Red Crosse himself makes this connection in expressing his thanks to his guide: "O holy Sire (quoth he) how shall I quight / The many favours I with thee have found, / That hast my name and nation red aright, / And taught the way that does to heaven bound?" In such a narrative situation, "reading" ceases to be arriving at a conclusion or a translation of one set of words into another set of words, but the marking out of a way through participation in that way. We may talk about what has happened here by saying that meaning has been deferred indefinitely, if we think of "meaning" in terms of categories of thought, but another way to describe it is to say that the meaning of meaning has changed categories, has effaced conventional categories, so that meaning now comes to reside in doing, not in intellectual conclusions. Or, perhaps better, doing on the way has come to absorb and subsume "reading" as a process of intellection through undercutting it as an end but rescuing it as a means. Thus another way for Red Crosse to understand the difference between "wanton lust" and the domesticated eroticism envisioned by Cranmer in the Prayer Book is by living in and through the life oriented toward the altar made possible by the Prayer Book. Or, to put it another way, bodies become part of the Body of Christ by becoming embodied in and by bodying forth the life of charity that builds up the body that is the city that is a bride. Red Crosse is thankful for a "reading" that points out a way that has arisen in a conversation that tests interpretations and results not in a conclusion but in a new beginning, an opening out of possibilities.

At this point, having described the parallels between Red Crosse's mountaintop sight of the New Jerusalem and biblical mountaintop encounters with God, we have to note the most glaring difference, one that will be increasingly crucial. Spenser's *The Faerie Queene* is not a part of the Bible; on the most obvious level, the moments similar to Red Crosse's mountaintop experience we have described are claimed by the Bible to be actual, particular historical experiences had by people at least as "real" as Spenser himself to the readers of his poem. In fact, they are the kinds of moments which constitute history itself, or at least the biblical sense of it. Spenser makes no such claim for *The Faerie Queene*. Its world is not historical; it is not even a copy of the Elizabethan world. It is a fiction, and its role in Spenser's didactic efforts is not to supplement or supplant the Bible but to enable interchange to occur between Spenser's world and the biblical world as it is encountered in Prayer Book worship.

To grasp the dynamics at work here, we need to look at the mountain associated with Red Crosse's mountain in Canto x that we have hitherto ignored. Along with Mount Sinai and the Mount of Olives, Spenser also says this mountain is like Mount Parnassus, "That pleasaunt Mount, that is for ay / Through famous Poets verse each where renownd." In short, we need to consider the role of poetry itself as one dimension of the didactic method at work in Spenser's poem. The reference to Mount Parnassus and its resident Muses is prepared for by the image of Christ as poet in the preceding lines, as he sits on the Mount of Olives "for ever with a flowring girlond crownd." The Muses sing "a lovely lay" in juxtaposition with the "bloudy letters" of the Ten Commandments in the depiction of Mount Sinai with which Moses receives "the bitter doome of death and balefull mone." Spenser thus evokes the image of Christ as poet, as the new David, singing a song of love to God's creation, functioning as the lover in the Song of Songs, wooing Israel back to its relationship with God, here evoked in the juxtaposition of Old with New Law, the Law of Judgment versus the Law of Love or Grace. Christ's passion fulfills the old law and institutes a new law, as God acts again in history to sing a new song, to call Israel anew, creating a new Israel, the church, which is the earthly body of the Risen Christ. God's incarnate Word here becomes both song and singer, poet and poem, "he in us, and we in him."

The alternative to Archimago as poet and language user in *The Faerie Queene* is thus not Spenser but Christ. The biblical Word in *The Faerie Queene* is the Word whose activity in the world is paramount, providing us with a perspective from which to view Spenser's words as well as the words of Archimago. The role Spenser's words play is that of proclamation, of establishing a conversation between the reader and the Word, of freeing the reader from his bondage to human words so that he can respond in faith to the Word that empowers and informs the language of *The Faerie Queene*. Yet that Word is not another version of the static, atemporal, abstract world of mythic consciousness, but a Word that is by definition transformational, that in Erasmus' words "utterly transforms . . . the names of things" (and of people). The world of the Word is not another world at all, and certainly not a denial of this world, but this world in the process of being wooed by a "new song," a new speaking and thus creative acting of God that makes all things new, including the words we use to name things. Spenser can thus openly risk confusion with Archimago and use this comparison to illuminate the limitations of his skill and also teach us how to use his didactic method because of his reliance on the Word enacted in use of the Prayer Book.

Also worth examination is the relationship Spenser sets up in *The Faerie Queene* between his poem and the classical tradition of poetry more closely connected with the Muses than is the biblical tradition. Spenser, in the letter to Raleigh, claims that his poem is patterned after classical epics and notes the works of Homer and Virgil as classical predecessors. In the episode of Red Crosse's vision, he borrows a narrative motif of classical epic exemplified most readily by Aeneas' vision of the future in Book VI of *The Aeneid*.[26] There, Anchises describes for his son events to come in the history of the city Aeneas will found on the fields of Latinum. Like Red Crosse's, Aeneas' vision is of the future of a city; unlike Aeneas', however, Red Crosse's future is stated in terms of personal participation. Contemplation describes Red Crosse's role in the eternal City of God as one with both individual and social consequences; because of his deeds to come in defeating the dragon, Red Crosse "Shalt be a Saint, and thine owne nations frend / And Patrone." On the other hand, Aeneas' future glory derives only from the glorious deeds of his progeny, culminating in the deification of Julius Caesar; while Red Crosse will marry Una, their marriage itself will teach how to build—and to recognize and reach—the kingdom.

Spenser's treatment of this epic motif, therefore, must be seen as a transformation of the shape and content of the classical model. Transferring the place of vision from Hades to the mountaintop of biblical encounter with God and changing the terms of the vision's future promise, Spenser "over-goes" Virgil in terms of the way he handles this epic motif. Such a transformation is made possible because of the material Spenser borrows from the two other literary models incorporated into this passage. The first is the Saint's legend, specifically the Legend of Saint George, which Spenser uses to give Red Crosse the basic plot motif of his victory over the dragon and his identity as England's patron saint.[27] The second is the sight of the New Jerusalem contained in the Book of Revelation, which provides Red Crosse with the substance of his own sight of the city. Red Crosse thus owes his identity to one sort of literary work, this event in his history to another, and the substance of his experience to yet another. As a result, Spenser is able to create an epic narrative of future vision which is not limited to one person or one city; Red Crosse participates in a story and becomes the patron saint of a whole nation on its way toward the eternal city, which is the common destiny of all God's people. Yet this is not to be read allegorically; Spenser does not claim insight into a universal process. He instead gives us tools for interpreting future events through which they can claim to be part of the salvation history.

Spenser's running commentary on the epic tradition functions in more subtle ways as well. When Red Crosse, after seeing the false image of Una created for him by Archimago, rushes away from her in the early morning, the world he enters is that of classical epic:

> Now when the rosy-fingred Morning faire,
>   Weary of aged *Tithones* saffron bed,
>   Had spred her purple robe through deawy aire,
>   And the high hils *Titan* discovered,
>   The royall virgin shooke off drowsy-hed,
>   And rising forth out of her baser bowre,
>   Lookt for her knight, who far away was fled,
>   And for her Dwarfe, that wont to wait each houre;
> Then gan she waile and weepe, to see that woefull stowre.
>
> (I.ii.7)

The language here echoes many classical sources, including Homer, Virgil, and Ovid. The closest analogue is probably Dido's moment of discovery that Aeneas had fled her in pursuit of his divine destiny, but of that tragic example of the cost of divine/human encounter Spenser has made a remarkable transformation. Red Crosse enters this classical epic world and opens it for Una through his inability to interpret his own feelings and Archimago's false images correctly. Yet, by the end of the poem, Spenser finds a way, through his redaction of epic plotting, to reunite his Aeneas with his Dido. The classical roles thus do not become prisons of narrative; Spenser can use generic motifs to get his poem written yet can transform them at will. What makes this possible is Spenser's location of his text in recreative proximity to the transforming energies of the Bible. Spenser claims, in effect, that the world of classical epic functions in terms of and as a result of the kinds of false images Archimago has conjured up for Red Crosse, who enters the world of classical discourse here as a result of misreading. On the other hand, after Red Crosse has reaffirmed his quest by "reading aright" the action at the beginning of Canto xi moves with the radical economy and dispatch that characterizes biblical narrative.[28]

Again, Spenser effaces Virgil's vision of Aeneas' future in Canto v of Book I. After Red Crosse has defeated Sansfoy in battle, his companion Dwarf reports on explorations in the basement of Lucifera's House of Pride. There, he reports to Red Crosse, he has found "strowne" in a "corner":

> The antique ruines of the *Romaines* fall:
> Great *Romulus* the Grandsyre of them all,
> Proud *Tarquin,* and too lordly *Lentulus,*
> Stout *Scipio,* and stubborne *Hanniball,*
> Ambitious *Sylla,* and sterne *Marius,*
> High *Caesar,* great *Pompey,* and fierce *Antonius.*
>
> (I.v.49)

The proud story Aeneas hears in Virgil's Hades, leading forward through time to the deification of Julius Caesar, here is collapsed into a pile of words, the "ruines" of a "fall," a fitting metaphor for Spenser's designs on the claims to cultural authority held by Virgil's *Aeneid.* Red Crosse's flight from Lucifera's house, after hearing the Dwarf's report, is again in the early morning, but in this case it is not out into the landscape of Virgilian epic. Instead, it is past a "donghill of dead carcases," another fitting metaphor for what Spenser has sought to make of the promise inherent in Virgil's view of history.

Spenser's treatment of classical precedent for his poem thus functions in a variety of ways. At once it enables him to borrow generic form and episodic and scenic detail from classical models to provide material for his poem. At the same time, however, it undercuts the authority of classical form by exposing the limitations inherent in classical narratives of human possibilities. Finally, it demands that we transfer our sense of textual authority from classical literature to Spenser's poem. Spenser claims that the story of Red Crosse is the true epic, the story that ought to carry with it the weight of classic, epic authority for his culture. In yet another way, therefore, Spenser insists on the importance of the story he is telling in this poem by asserting its superiority to its classical antecedents, even as it uses those antecedents to achieve literary form for that narrative. At the same time, however, Spenser yields the authority of his own narrative to that of the Bible; Spenser's poem functions in a usurping relationship to classical antecedents precisely because it can claim for itself a biblically based authority over them. Replicating in its relationships to the Bible the stance Spenser urges for his readers, *The Faerie Queene* thus functions to assert the claims of biblical narrative over classical forms of discourse. The evidence for the validity of that claim Spenser presents through the narrative transformations it makes possible.

So far, however, our account of Red Crosse's experience has limited its attention to this one character in Spenser's fictional world, although he has been identified with a character familiar to all of Spenser's contemporary audience as a part of England's cultural inheritance. If this episode is to become didactic, it must bring pressure to bear on its audience to discover the possibility that the story of Red Crosse is, or can be, the reader's story which informs and thus directs his own actions in the real world of his experience.

To understand how Spenser achieves this, we need to examine how Spenser gets Red Crosse out of the ancient legend of Saint George and into the fictional world of *The Faerie Queene*. The "father grave" is of great help; to explain to Red Crosse why he must continue in his quest of the dragon, he must tell Red Crosse his story, "Sith to thee is unknowne the cradle of thy brood":

> For well I wote, thou springst from ancient race
> Of *Saxon* kings, that have with mightie hand
> And many bloudie battailes fought in place
> High reard their royall throne in *Britane* land,
> And vanquisht them, unable to withstand.
>
> (I.x.65)

So far, Spenser's "godly sire" has provided Red Crosse with English parentage, domesticating a figure whose origin was traditionally in Asia Minor. He also gives Red Crosse a family heritage like that of Aeneas, who was also of "ancient race" through his Trojan ancestry and who fought to raise his throne in Italy. Now, however, Spenser changes the legendary account still further; the figure of English religious tradition is suddenly translated yet again, this time into the arena of Spenser's fictional world by an agent of that world:

> From thence a Faerie thee unweeting reft,
> There as thou slepst in tender swadling band,
> And her base Elfin brood there for thee left.
>
> (I.x.65)

Red Crosse's role shifting, his "change by Faeries theft," opens the closed world of possibilities defined by classical epic as appropriate for those of "ancient race." Red Crosse is brought into the world of "Faerie lond," where he is deposited in "an heaped furrow" and found by "a Ploughman . . . / As he his toylesome teme that way did guyde" who "brought thee up in ploughmans state to byde, / Whereof *Georgos* he thee gave to name" (I.x.66). Literally, Red Crosse has entered the world of the georgic, which Spenser now brings into the world of the epic, crossing classical genres in a way Virgil would never have done. His model of course is the biblical one, of the one who "didst not abhor the Virgin's womb" (Te Deum, BCP, p. 54), who "hath regarded the lowliness of his handmaden" (Magnificat, BCP, p. 61), and who, like Red Crosse, "slepst" in "swadling band." Red Crosse is not Christ, but the New Testament narrative of Christ gives Spenser the possibility of enriching the narrative of epic to include "the humble and meek" (BCP, p. 62) so that a figure out of georgic can seek fame in "Faerie court" and "prove thy puissaunt armes" in a battle so fundamentally important for the English. One consequence of God's actions in Christ, Spenser argues, is the transformation of stylistic and narrative possibilities in epic and perhaps in human lives as well.

The consequences of kidnapping and transfer into the realm of Faeryland are twofold: first, the conditions of his arrival in Gloriana's realm provide Red Crosse with his name. Second, the faerie context of his new life provides the opportunity for him to achieve the heroic deeds which are the reason for his reputation in his native England. At the same time, however, it is Red Crosse's connection with England which enables him to discover a goal for his actions other than his search for "fame," the only goal possible to achieve if one remains totally within the faerie realm. Spenser's transformation of the legend of Saint George claims for his faerie world a defining and naming function; the relationship that world has to the real world of England provides for Faeryland an expansion of its fictional significance. In Gloriana's realm, Red Crosse will attain fame for his deeds; in England, he will use his faerie name but will find himself the patron saint of his nation.

Spenser's transformation of the legend of Saint George is an act of daring. Against the Puritans, who wanted abandonment of the liturgical calendar with its observations of seasons and saints' days, Spenser aggressively asserts the importance of this medieval figure, one of the very few post–New Testament saints retained on the Anglican calendar, not in any sense as intercessor but as one whose example can teach his audience. Yet Spenser's recreation of George into a figure with English origins as well as an English scene for his life articulates his claim to the special power of his fiction to remake the meaning of things. Through this transformation of narrative, Spenser aspires to authority among the narratives of his culture not just to enliven old tales but to remake narratives of past authority so they become transforming for the present moment of retelling. Historically a figure associated with the Crusades, where he served as the patron of the Christian warriors who sought to free the Holy Land, George in Spenser's version can become a way of talking about what it means to find the central conflicts of Christian living in the events of Spenser's own day rather than in the remoteness of the past or distant lands. Bringing George into the realm of Faeryland thus becomes a way of bringing pressure to bear on Spenser's readers to discover all that the medieval cult of the saints could now mean in the experience of the church that found its identity in relationship to involvement in the history of England and which was fundamentally changing so central an aspect of medieval folk religion.

One feature of the reforming English church was Cranmer's plan to jettison the medieval cult of saints, with all its trappings of private devotions and pilgrimages and the magical aura of its pantheistic overtones. In setting the tone for the new direction for piety, in which only God, as Father, Son, and Spirit, would be addressed in prayer and yet the most ancient of the saints—those mentioned in the New Testament and a few later ones—would be retained, Cranmer must have taken great care with the texts and prayers on the saints' feast days. Chief among them is All Saints' Day, November 1, for which Cranmer composed this Collect for the first Prayer Book of 1549:

> Almighty God, which hast knit together thy elect in one communion and fellowship, in the mystical body of thy Son Christ our Lord: grant us grace so to follow thy holy saints in all virtues and godly living, that we may come to those unspeakable joys, which thou hast prepared for them that unfainedly love thee; through Jesus Christ our Lord.

Here all the themes we have seen as significant are raised (the emphasis on "communion and fellowship" in the "mystical body" of Christ moving toward "unspeakable joys" through "godly living" [BCP, p. 244]), but what is significant, of course, is that the saints serve as ways of articulating "virtues" and "godly living" as actions, transforming human experience and opening "unspeakable" possibilities for the future. There is no *ora pro nobis* here; the saints are significant as figures who inform our experience and give us a way to "follow," to "walk in." The saints are part of the "one communion and fellowship"; they make possible joining that company in the present not by intercession but by making pathways to "follow."

What finally links the world of Red Crosse with the world of the reader, therefore, is just that sight of the eternal city that Red Crosse sees and that Spenser says he cannot depict for the reader of *The Faerie Queene*. Although Spenser says he cannot show it to us, since the "ditty" of the city is "too high . . . for my simple song," Spenser's Elizabethan reader knew that he had many occasions to identify and anticipate the sight of that city. He had Saint John's account of it read to him in church on the feasts of All Saints, Saint John, Saint Michael and All Angels, Holy Innocents, and Trinity Sunday. He heard that the lives of the saints defined a way to the heavenly city, creating a path for him to follow. He heard preachers tell him that the city was the Church Triumphant anticipated now in the reality of the Church Militant, so that in a real sense he saw that city in the process of becoming every time he gathered to use the Prayer Book with his fellow churchgoers. He also heard preachers tell him that the Supper of Holy Communion was itself an anticipation of the blessed wedding feast of the Lamb, at which he would become part of that city as the Bride of Christ. He was told that every marriage was a sign of that city, as the act of marriage signifies the relationship between Christ and his church. At Morning Prayer in singing Te Deum and in the Eucharist in singing the Sanctus, he joined in the song of that city as John reports it (Revelation 4:8). Finally, he was told that the promises of that city come to those "which die in the Lord," in the Burial Office (BCP, p. 310).

Indeed, Spenser prepares us for this transfer of attention from the faerie landscape to the scene of ongoing life of the Church of England through his depiction of the process through which Red Crosse prepares to make the discovery of "reading aright" which results in his resumption of his quest to free Una's parents from the power of the dragon. Reading aright is *praxis,* not *gnosis,* is in performing the fruits of faith, not in contemplation of abstract truth. Thus what Spenser gives us in his depiction of the House of Holiness and his narrative of what Red Crosse does there is a performing, a doing, a "right reading" of the functioning of Cranmer's church, both physically and liturgically. "Governd" and "guided" by the female figure of heavenly wisdom from the Old Testament's Wisdom literature, this building is entered through the "streight and narrow" path to the Kingdom, echoing the tradition of church architecture in which the small door in the church portal was positioned under a "last judgment" sculpture, so that one in a way entered the Kingdom when entering the church building. The "spacious court" leading to the Hall reminded the reader of the narthex and nave. The experiences and characters Red Crosse encounters here echo the pattern of movement from faith to hope to charity basic to Cranmer's interpretation of Christianity; the linking of the eucharistic "cup of gold / With wine and water fild up to the hight" and the "booke, that was both signd and seald with blood" echo his affirmation, articulated in the Prayer Book, of the essential connection between hearing the Bible read and taking part in baptism and Eucharist as preliminary to and enabling of acts of charity in the world.

Caelia's house is described in the terms Anglican apologists used to articulate their claims for their church; it is at once "auntient" (I.x.3) and also reformed, characterized by adherence to "sacred lore / And pure unspotted life" achieved through the way it "governd was, and guided evermore" by Elizabeth, the "Supreme Governor" of the Church of England. This house is indeed a "schoolehouse"; here, appropriately for so education-oriented an institution as the reformed Church of England, Red Crosse undergoes a cleansing and regenerating experience so that "His mind was full of spirituall repast" (I.x.48) when he approached the Mount for his sight of the "Citie." Red Crosse's experience here thus becomes a "reading aright" of Anglican worship, the experience of Christ as "spiritual food and sustenance" (BCP, p. 256).

The terms used to describe Red Crosse echo those used by the Prayer Book to describe the posture and understanding of the faithful participant. Red Crosse experiences "remembrance of his wicked wayes" and is "prickt with anguish of his sinnes so sore" (I.x.21); the English were exhorted to "acknowledge and confess our manifold sins and wickedness" (BCP, p. 50) to proclaim "there is no health in us," for "the remembrance of [our sins] is grievous unto us, the burden of them is intolerable" (BCP, p. 259). He despairs, but Speranza provides "comfort sweet" (I.x.22), reminding him that Fidelia promised hope, and Caelia offers Una "comfort" and "counsel and advisement right," echoing the Prayer Book's promise of "counsel, advice, and comfort" so that he can continue "in weeping, fasting, and praying" (BCP, p. 323; Red Crosse fasts [I.x.26], cries [I.x.28], and prays [I.x.26]) until his "body [has been] made clean" and his "soul washed" (BCP, p. 263). Then he is brought by "wise Patience, / And trew *Repentance*" to Una, now with "cured conscience" (I.x.29). He literally "comes . . . with faithful repentance" (BCP, p. 320); he has experienced being "called to earnest and true repentance," a "hearty repentance and true faith" in a God "whose property is always to have mercy" (BCP, pp. 316, 263). He is now ready to meet Charissa, to be taught about "all such good works as thou has prepared for us to walk in."

Cranmer created a life of worship in which a process of moving from a sense of illness, bondage, unworthiness, uncleanness, or limitation to a sense of health, freedom, blessedness, cleanness, and opportunity is reenacted over and over in various ways and on many different occasions. Spenser infolds references to a wide range of these in his account of Red Crosse's preparation to take on the life of Christian charity. In a number of fundamental ways, for example, Spenser's description of what happens to Red Crosse in the House of Holiness is patterned after the baptismal rite of the Prayer Book. The knocking at the door, the reference by Caelia to the "narrow path," the "multitude of babes" that hang around Charissa, the imagery of Red Crosse's burial ("he laid him privily / Downe in a darksome lowly place farre in"), and his washing in "salt water" to purge him of "the filthy blots of sinne" all have their references to the prayers, biblical texts, and actions of Prayer Book baptism. The fertility of love here finally encompasses Red Crosse himself, who comes to Charissa in place of her newly born child and is treated by Mercy "As carefull Nourse her child" (I.x.35). Cranmer believed that the Church of England would become truly what it claimed to be through the doing of Charity; here Red Crosse becomes a kind of child of Charity, "born again" to the meaning of Christian living. When this is linked with the instruction in the seven charitable acts of mercy ("Grant that whosoever is here dedicated to thee by our office . . . may also be endued with heavenly virtues"), what becomes clear is that Red Crosse in the House of Holiness is entering into the significance of baptism and the Christian life as acted out in Prayer Book worship in the Church of England. English congregations heard these words constantly; indeed, Cranmer urged that baptisms occur on Sundays so that the whole congregation would be present to welcome the newly baptized into "the congregation of Christ's flock" and to experience renewal of their baptismal vows as they were spoken in the name of the child being baptized.

Further, all of Book I, from the entry of Red Crosse into the House of Holiness to the end of the poem, is in fact an extended seeing of what England is being called to do through the perspective provided by the Prayer Book's celebration of All Saints' Day, a traditional day for baptisms.[29] Red

Crosse's discovery that he is to become "a Saint . . . emongst those Saints, whom thou doest see" alludes to the Collect for that day, with its references to the granting of grace "so to follow thy saints in all virtues and godly living." The lines spoken by Contemplation about "The new *Hierusalem,* that God has built / For those to dwell in, that are chosen his" are supplemented by the Epistle for All Saints (Revelation 7) with its description of the gathering of "a great multitude . . . of all nations and kindreds and people." The description of "blessed Angels to and fro descend[ing]" expands the reference in this Epistle to John's sight of "another angel ascending from the rising of the sun" by way of reference to Jacob's dream in Genesis 28. The description of Red Crosse's mountain as one like "that sacred hill . . . / Of our dear Lord" derives from the Gospel, which is Matthew's account of Christ going "up into the mountain" and proclaiming the Beatitudes, with their promise that "great is your reward in heaven" for perseverance in the face of verbal adversity, the speaking of "all manner of evil sayings . . . falsely . . . against you."

Also, the treatment accorded Red Crosse in the House of Holiness parallels the pattern of Anglican morning worship, beginning as it did with Morning Prayer. The general confession describes Red Crosse's condition:

we have erred and strayed from thy ways, like lost sheep. We have followed too much the devices and desires of our own hearts. We have offended against thy holy laws. We have left undone those things which we ought to have done, and we have done those things which we ought not to have done, and there is no health in us. (BCP, p. 50)

And Fidelia gives him "heavenly learning" in her "schoolehouse," echoing the fact that the readings at Morning and Evening Prayer are called "Lessons." Indeed, the readings at Morning Prayer on All Saints' also provide the language for describing what Red Crosse experiences here. At Morning Prayer, the First Lesson is from the Wisdom of Solomon, chapter 3, which claims that "They that trust in him, shall understand the truth, and the faithful shall remaine with him in love: for grace and mercy is among his Saints, and he regardeth his elect" (3:9). The Second Lesson is from Hebrews 11 and 12; it lists the faithful from Abel to the prophets to support the proposition that "faith is the ground of things, which are hoped for, and the evidence of things which are not seen." Hebrews 12 claims that "we are compassed with so great a cloud of witnesses" so that we can "run with patience the race that is set before us," and also alludes to the battle with "a beast" to be "thrust through with a dart" so that "ye are come unto the mount Sion and to the city of the living God, the celestial Jerusalem, and to the company of innumerable Angels," encapsulating the whole of Red Crosse's narrative while linking feast, text, rite, and poem.

If the initial instruction received by Red Crosse invokes the process of

Morning Prayer, his treatment at the hands of Caelia invokes the images of the Collect for Purity with which Holy Communion begins. Her attention to his "wounded hart" is response to the petition of that prayer, that God "Cleanse the thoughts of our hearts by the inspiration of thy Holy Spirit, that we may perfectly love thee, and worthily magnify thy holy name." The rite then continues with the recitation of the Ten Commandments, which on that day, like Red Crosse's mountain, are juxtaposed with the Beatitudes in the Gospel and with them Moses' and Jesus' mountains. As we will soon see, Red Crosse's story continues with evocations of the Sacrament of the Eucharist in his battle with the dragon, drawn from the language of Revelation 19, the Second Lesson for All Saints' Day at Evening Prayer, with its reference to a warrior on a white horse named "the Word of God" and his battle with "the beast" juxtaposed against "the marriage of the Lamb" to "his wife . . . arrayed with pure fine linen and shining, for the fine linen is the righteousness of Saints." Even the ship journey with which Book I ends finds its source in the passage from Wisdom 5 that serves as the First Lesson for Evening Prayer on All Saints', in which life is compared to a journey by ship and the just are promised armor from God so that they may withstand evil.

Spenser, through these structuring allusions to the biblical texts and rites for All Saints' Day, infolds Book I inside another process of discourse while also infolding those allusions into their enactment in Book I. By using these allusions to the books of the Apocrypha and to Revelation in an eschatological but not an apocalyptic way, Spenser takes his place with the established Church of England against its Puritan detractors who rejected the authority of the Apocrypha and who often read Revelation apocalyptically. Such allusions are also not to the Bible as a static text or to the Prayer Book as a model, but to a realized enactment of discourse that defines a specific moment of historical time in England (November 1) as being part of the sequence of moments that lead to the promised future fulfillment in a city. Such moments become both defining and enabling moments as well as anticipations, in the communion banquet, of the blessed wedding banquet of the Lamb that is both now and to come. In such moments, the city is seen not by being described but by being participated in.

In fact, the sight of the city that Red Crosse has inside the poem is the only aspect of the faerie landscape that is directly visible to the readers of the poem outside the world of that poem and that is presented to them in the same terms in which a figure in the poem sees it and not in the fictional language of Spenser's faerie world. Instead, that "sight of the city" was available to them, just as Red Crosse had seen it, in the complex of texts enacted in Prayer Book worship. The importance of this cannot be overstressed. As a result of reading the poem, members of Spenser's audience would have realized that the sight of the city which is so crucial to the narrative of Red Crosse inside the poem was available to them as well, in the real world of Prayer Book worship addressing the particulars of their everyday lives, and not inside the poem with Red Crosse. Having read the poem, however, they could now approach the next time they were reminded of the city and see it in their future which is also in their midst, by bringing with them what they have read Contemplation say of that city to Red Crosse and find that it applies to them as well.

With this vital link between the world of faerie and the world of Tudor England in place, we may go on to another, for Spenser's readers were aware of one element of Red Crosse's vision that Spenser's hero seemingly does not know. The characters and landscapes in *The Faerie Queene* repeatedly evoke specific people and places in the real world of Spenser's England. In his letter to Raleigh, Spenser makes clear that Gloriana herself and her faerie kingdom are fictional particularizations of various qualities possessed by "the most excellent and glorious person of our sovereign the Queen, and her kingdom." In commenting upon Red Crosse's vision, critics through the years have posited a number of buildings as candidates for Spenser's model in his depiction of Cleopolis and its "towre of glas."[30] The fact that they have not been able to agree on a single satisfactory original does not detract from their consensus that Spenser did have a specific building in mind, one that existed in the real world of Spenser's England. In the episode of Red Crosse's vision, as throughout the whole of *The Faerie Queene,* the world of the poem is in fact a fictional transformation or metaphoric re-presentation enabling a new perspective on Spenser's own world, a point that his original readers surely would have recognized.[31] Spenser's treatment of England first deprives his readers of a familiar landscape but then gives it back as a place where important things are happening and new things are opening through the instrumentality of Spenser's poem. Thus, what *The Faerie Queene* gave an Elizabethan reader was a new perspective on himself and on his age, one from which he could see himself and his age in a startlingly new way, full of hitherto unrealized possibilities for new and as yet uninscribed narrative directions and outcomes.

At this point, let us consider that reader's experience of Red Crosse's vision. What he discovers in Spenser's poem is a character who, like himself, has been brought from England into the fictional world of Spenser's poem. In that world, this reader sees Red Crosse discover his identity and find that in this landscape he is enabled to perform the heroic deeds that will ensure his role in the building up of Gloriana's Cleopolis and gain him access to that country's "immortall booke of fame." At the same time, he sees Red Crosse finding that his heroic deeds in Faeryland are the beginning of a journey toward citizenship in God's eternal city and a role and identity as England's patron saint. Yet this reader also knows that what Red Crosse discovers as Faeryland is a fictional version of his own country, a country in which the eternal city can also be glimpsed, suggesting the realization that the heroic deeds enacted by Red Crosse in Faeryland are at least possible in his own native England. As a result, Spenser expects his reader to discover that to follow the way defined by Red Crosse in the real world of England is to join in Red Crosse's journey toward the New Jerusalem. In short, Spenser makes possible in this episode his reader's realization that to participate in the creation of a true Christian commonwealth by working to transform the world of his day-to-day existence into a realized version of Cleopolis is to be involved in God's salvation history, to be working toward eventual citizenship in God's eschatological city which he knows from Revelation will be God's gift to his chosen people at the end of time, realized through participation in Prayer Book worship.

As William C. Johnson has pointed out,[32] Spenser everywhere in *The Faerie Queene* moves from the individual to the communal, as in the acts of Anglican baptism and Communion. Each of the knights in the poem pursues not merely the end of his personal quest but returns to Cleopolis, presumably to celebrate the wedding feast of Prince Arthur and Gloriana. Other prospective weddings—that of Red Crosse with Una, of Britomart with Artegall—await the fulfillment of that relationship before they can take place. Marriage as the communal recognition of individual relationships and the necessary societal prerequisite to private fulfillment of those relationships is a constant motif in *The Faerie Queene*. At the same time, if Red Crosse's quest in service to Gloriana and her city points ultimately to and prepares for citizenship in the New Jerusalem, so the communal act of marriage also anticipates the revelation of God's City to God's people. It is "as a bride prepared for her bridegroom" that the writer of Revelation sees the holy city descending to inaugurate the new age of God's dwelling with his human creatures. Humans enter society in a fundamental way by becoming brides and grooms; through the actions of their bodies, people become "one flesh" and "one body" in and through Christ. Christian community on earth created by the generative marital unit founded on a domesticated *eros* and lived in anticipation of eternal communion with God is therefore the goal of all actions in Spenser's poem.

In this light, Spenser's didactic method in *The Faerie Queene* becomes clearer. The reader of Spenser's poem may discover through it the possibilities inherent in his native country and the means to realize those possibilities. The world of *The Faerie Queene* can thus become a map to lay over his perception of the real world, an exhortative and evaluative perspective from which to sense both the shortcomings and the opportunities inherent in the godly kingdom of England. At the same time, he is taught the urgency of action, the pressing need to follow in his own world the paths toward knowing and doing exemplified by Spenser's male and female heroes. In light of what Spenser proclaims in *The Faerie Queene,* involvement in the real world of England aimed at making it over into the true Christian commonwealth is also the means by which to gain entrance into the New Jerusalem. With Red Crosse, Spenser's reader may join in praise of that "holy Sire": "how shall I quight / The many favours I with thee have found, / That hast my name and nation red aright, / And taught the way that does to heaven bound?" He may also answer this question the same way, by getting on with the quest for a life of active charity.

Like the narratives in the Bible enacted in Prayer Book worship from which Spenser works and the worship to which he alludes, his story of Red Crosse has the quality of open-endedness. It is incomplete without the response of the reader and becomes intelligible in terms of that response. The biblical indicative always carries with it either explicitly or implicitly an imperative, a claim exerted on the reader demanding his response. To have the Bible read in English and in church was for sixteenth-century worshippers to find the moment of reading a moment of encounter with God, a moment of calling, a moment of self-discovery which takes away human claims to self-sufficiency either in knowledge or in action in the midst of that re-presentation of past saving acts of God which sees the present moment of enactment as being in continuity with those past events and thus a source of grace to "do all such good works as thou hast prepared for us to walk in." It rendered them incapable of understanding their world on their own, incapable of self-salvation, by reminding them of God's claim upon them and their dependency on him for their sense of self and their sense of purpose in life, and also of the divine gift of grace to enable human participation in the working out of his future. It also made their lives of charity pilgrimages and quests and struggles as noble, significant, and "epic" as any they might read about.

Spenser's poem functions by never claiming to be history but to be a fiction which constantly gives way to the claims of the Bible from which it takes didactic strategies and its authority to recreate classical forms. That fiction is written in such a way as to bring the Church of England's claims to the attention of the reader so that he perceives God at work in the specificities and particularities of his world as surely as the Bible proclaims God's presence in the events of Israel's history so that the reader will be persuaded to respond. What Spenser sought in Book I of *The Faerie Queene* was to force his reader to confront the nature of language as customarily used, to find language inherently false, inherently duplicitous, and thus the version of reality it conveys equally false, and to compare that with the functioning of language in Prayer Book worship, where it confesses its limitations but offers itself for divine use. He therefore offers us a new way of dealing with experience, for which he promises the sight of the eternal city, or, better, points his reader to sights of the city in the world of his own experience. Spenser's reading of that city points toward not an abstract view of truth but a way of life, the consequences of which can be called eventual citizenship in that city as a member of the communion of saints. Thus, Spenser seeks to proclaim the biblical Word about that city and with it the biblical Word about the world of his readers in such a way that they will be drawn to become citizens of that city.

This description of Spenser's didactic method and intention in the episode of Red Crosse's vision of the heavenly city aligns his work decisively with the intentions of the English Reformers. At this point, it is appropriate to quote John Hales, writing to Protector Somerset while engaged in a journey to ensure compliance with the reform program instituted by Archbishop Cranmer during the reign of Edward VI:

> yet am I fully persuaded, and certainly do believe in your Grace's sayings, that, maugre the Devil, private profit, self-love, money, and such-like the Devil's instruments, it shall go forward, and set such a stay in the body of the commonwealth, that all members shall live in a due temperature and harmony.[33]

As I have argued earlier, the English Reformers sought through education of the people in active charity empowered through sacramental participation a transformation of English society into the true Christian commonwealth. The various official documents of the Church of England present the promise of what English society could become that Spenser evokes imaginatively in *The Faerie Queene* and incorporate the theology of language Spenser uses fictionally in his didactic poem.

That Spenser knew intimately the defining documents of mid-Tudor Anglicanism is without question; required for use in all English churches as part of the Elizabethan Settlement of Religion in 1559, they had by the 1580s become integral parts of English daily life. From his participation in their use Spenser learned his emphasis on the communal as the primary dimension of religious life, his belief that transforming English society is the appropriate goal of Christian living, and his strategy for using language to bring about the reality of his communal societal vision.[34]

The individualism we often associate with the Renaissance was actually an inheritance from late medieval Christianity which the Puritans, ironically, perpetuated, albeit with a new theological justification.[35] A developing Calvinistic emphasis on election and reprobation, coupled with the search for inner signs of the individual's eternal destiny, could not long coexist with the Church of England's insistence on the inclusive national scope of Prayer Book worship and its offer of the way of salvation to all.[36] Archbishop Cranmer's rejection of late medieval individualistic devotional practices and the eucharistic theology which separated the priest from the people and made of the Mass a private devotion of the priest signaled in England a new effort to create a communal sense of the Christian life. Cranmer, in his Homily of Good Works, attacks "papistical supersticions, and abuses" such as "beades, . . . lady psalters and

rosaries, . . . xv. Oos, . . . S. Barnardes verses . . . with suche like marchan-
dise"[37] (perhaps anticipating Spenser's depiction of Archimago) and proposes
instead texts intended to "move the people to honor and worshippe almightie
GOD, and diligently to serve hym . . . to serve their Kynge . . . and godly
and honestly, to behave themselves towardes all men."[38] This statement of
purpose embodies an interpretation of Christ's summary of the law which gives
to loving God and one's neighbor dramatic communal and societal
consequences.

It is, therefore, no accident that Red Crosse's deeds in Book I lead him to
the celebration of his victory over the dragon in the community of Una's
parents. As a result of his victory, the gates of their city are thrown open to
him and he is welcomed among them; further, his victory makes their celebration possible. The dancing, the singing, the banqueting are all communal
acts for which the betrothal of Red Crosse and Una is both the occasion and
the culmination. For Spenser, the point of Red Crosse's victory is not, finally,
the individual triumph over the forces of evil, but the building up of community which that victory makes possible.

Nor, if the pattern set forth for the Christian life in the Prayer Book or
Book of Homilies is paradigmatic for *The Faerie Queene,* is it surprising that
the virtues Spenser celebrates are not overtly religious ones. Part of what the
English Reformers reacted against was the understanding of religion as
pertaining to an arena separate from the world of everyday interactions. Rejecting the medieval practices of monasticism, mystical contemplation, and
private devotion that separated Christian living from ordinary personal interactions, the English Reformers promoted an understanding of the Christian
life in which the two worlds of religious and day-to-day living coincide.[39]
The ethical life of active charity in the everyday world was, to them, the
appropriate response to God's saving actions and, indeed, the life of "virtues
and godly living" which reveals the presence of that essential, saving, "true
and lively faith."[40]

At the same time, for Cranmer and his followers, the community which
their efforts at religious reform sought to build up was coextensive with the
nation of England itself. The vision of English society evoked by the language
used in the official documents of the English Reformation to discuss the dual
role of the monarch as governor of the church and king of the nation is one of
a hierarchic people whose prelapsarian state of harmonious interrelatedness
can be recovered through participation in the community life of active charity. In the Book of Homilies, this point is made in both positive and negative
ways. In the famous homily "Of Good Ordre and Obedyence," the homilist
glowingly celebrates the hierarchies of nature and then moves in a parallel
kind of hierarchy upward from the natural world to the "little world" of the
human body and, finally, to the hierarchy of human society:

ALMIGHTY God hath created and appoynted all thinges, in heaven, earth, and waters, in a moste excellent and perfecte order. . . . The water above is kepte, and rayneth downe in dewe tyme and season. The Sonne, Mone, Sterres, Raynebowe, Thundre, Lyghtnynge, cloudys, and al byrdes of the ayer, do kepe their ordre. . . . And man himselfe also, hath all his partes, bothe within and without . . . in a profitable, necessary and pleasaunt order. Every degree of people, in their vocation, calling, and office, hath appointed to them their duetie and order . . . and every one have nede of other, so that in al things, is to be lauded and praysed, the goodly order of God, without the which no house, no citie, no common wealth, can contynue and endure.[41]

The building up of this reciprocal hierarchic vision ("every one have nede of other") in the midst of a world characterized by Hales in terms of "private profit, self-love, money, and such-like" is the goal of the English Reformation; all the values taught in its official documents tend toward the realization of this vision. In the same way, vices are described in terms of their detrimental effect on this hierarchy of national life. In his homily "Agaynst Whoredome, and Adultery," Thomas Becon proclaims that "the outragious seas of adultry, fornication, and unclennes, have not onely braste in, but also overflowed, almoste the whole worlde, unto the great dishonoure of God, the exceding infamie of the name of Christ, the notable decaye of true religion, and the utter destruccion of the publique wealth."[42] This vision of the potential disruptiveness of *eros* underlies the terms Spenser uses to create Errour, Duessa, and the false Una. In the dynastic structures of Tudor society, in which the family bore much of the responsibility for the preservation of a degree of predictability and economy of effort in living that we now assign to a sense of individual responsibility or to a complex system of legal enforcement, this perception of the rupturing power of *eros* is perhaps not inexplicable. In any case, for Elizabethans undomesticated *eros* promoted contentiousness, about which Hugh Latimer argued that "this vice is so muche hurtful to the society of a common wealth" that "they [who practice it] be unworthy to live in a common wealth."[43]

People and king, church and state, one national body living harmoniously in interactive and mutually responsive charity and obedience: this was the goal of the English Reformers. The thrust of the English Reformation was, therefore, not just toward ecclesiastical reform as an end in itself but toward the reformation of society through the agency of the church. John Booty, in his eloquent description of the Elizabethan Prayer Book, strikes just the right note: "In the parish churches and in the cathedrals the nation was at prayer, the commonwealth was being realized, and God, in whose hand the destinies of all were lodged, was worshipped in spirit and in truth."[44]

Such is the context in which we need to see Spenser's ongoing allusions to England and her monarch in *The Faerie Queene*. In his tantalizing proem to Book II, Spenser notes that some will regard "all this famous antique history" as "th'aboundance of an idle braine / . . . and painted forgery." On the other hand, the world constantly reveals things "Which to late age were never mentioned": "Why then should witlesse man so much misweene / That nothing is, but that which he hath seene?" The poem is thus a challenge to human discovery: "Of Faerie lond yet if he more inquire, / By certaine signes here set in sundry place / He may it find."

> And thou, O fairest Princesse under sky,
> In this faire mirrhour maist behold thy face,
> And thine owne realmes in lond of Faery,
> And in this antique Image thy great auncestry.
>
> (II.proem.4)

Spenser's landscape is an instrument for seeing England as a realm where possibilities exist which "to late age were never mentioned"—the learning of Holiness, of Temperance, of Chastity, of Justice, and all the rest. And if such possibilities can come to be understood in such a way that his readers could learn them, then they might also come to exist in the realm of Elizabeth I. In *The Faerie Queene*, Spenser sought to educate his nation into the same virtues, the same community, the same Christian commonwealth sought by the English Reformers two generations earlier in the reform program of Edward VI.

In this light, "praise" of Elizabeth, either directly in the prefaces or indirectly through praise of the figures of Una, Belphoebe, and Britomart, functions not to describe Elizabeth but to encourage her to take her own part in this transformation of English society by spelling out for her the kind of behavior that would further that end in terms of a rhetorical scheme that would allow her to shape her behavior according to those models without having to admit that she had not already been doing so. Spenser thus uses the strategy for addressing princes outlined by Erasmus and embodied in his *Enchiridion militis christiani*, in which images of desirable behavior are offered in terms which serve to encourage princes to emulate them. According to Erasmus in a letter of 1504, the use of *encomia* "consists in presenting princes with a pattern of goodness, in such a way as to reform bad rulers, improve the good, educate the boorish, reprove the erring, arouse the indolent, and cause even the hopelessly vicious to feel some inward stirrings of shame."[45] As I have argued elsewhere, Erasmus' educational program in the *Enchiridion* provided Thomas Cranmer with the basic images of Christian living and the methods for teaching them he used in his Book of Homilies.[46] The English Reformers believed that through education and corporate experience of word and sacrament the reforming aims of Erasmus could be extended from a small elite to incorporate an entire nation. Spenser, in *The Faerie Queene,* picks up Erasmus' strategies, applies them to Elizabeth, and extends them, after Cranmer, to include all Englishfolk. The rhetorical use of praise—the descriptions of things and behavior that "should be" as though they were already—thus functions in Spenser's poem to encourage his readers to realize the images he offers so as to merit the praise he attaches to such images, a strategy especially appropriate in a cultural situation in which negative remarks about those in authority were extremely risky undertakings.

Spenser's discourse in *The Faerie Queene* operates within this framework. As we have already pointed out, the episode of Red Crosse's vision of the New Jerusalem in Book I transforms a classical epic device while claiming for itself the authority granted Spenser's classical generic prototype. The truly epic vision of the future, Spenser claims, is the vision of God's City, not that of Augustan Rome. He achieves this claim by juxtaposing Virgil's *Aeneid* with John's Revelation; here, through Spenser's poem, the biblical vision exercises its claim of authority over the classical. Spenser's poem thus claims authority for itself over classical epic because it derives its authority from its constant allusion to its biblical sources as mediated through their use in Prayer Book rites.

If, after his "sight of the city," Red Crosse can proceed with dispatch to his fight with the dragon, we must also explore the ongoing relationships between Bible and Prayer Book worship that are evoked in the development of Spenser's narrative. Red Crosse's sight of the New Jerusalem is an allusion to the biblical text (Revelation 19) used in the Eucharist for All Saints', and to Revelation 20–22, which amplifies that story. His actual victory over the dragon in Canto xii occurs through the agency of the sacramental life of the church, the acts of baptism in "the well of life" and Eucharist in "the tree of life," images of the fulfillment of the church's Sacraments drawn from Revelation 22. By accepting his quest through the world rather than by abandoning his quest to attempt to go directly to the heavenly city, Red Crosse finds that the city has come to him, as the church's Sacraments are defined and described in terms Saint John uses to describe features of the heavenly city. This battle takes three days; so it was that three days separate Crucifixion and Resurrection in the climactic events of Jesus' earthly career. It is important to note that Red Crosse's victory is wholly fortuitous; he is actually defeated by the dragon twice, and only because "it fortuned" him to fall into the "well of life" and near the "tree of life" is he able to "freshly up arise" to renew the fight. Or, at least in the terms of human narrative, these "falls" are "fortuned"; no one in Spenser's audience, I suspect, could have missed the references to the worship of his or her own parish, here displayed in its full eschatological significance. Some scholars have undervalued the importance of this allusion to the Sacraments, seeing instead a reference to a more general bestowal of grace.[47]

While the Church of England did acknowledge that God's grace was not limited to the Sacraments (nor does any Christian tradition limit the power of God in such a way), it taught and practiced participation in the Sacraments as the ordinary "means of grace and hope of glory." Only in the Calvinist traditions did an emphasis on divine omnipotence lead to a vestigial role for the Sacraments in parish life, which was not the case in the Church of England. In Spenser's church the Eucharist was celebrated weekly and on holy days in cathedrals. This set the standard for parishes, where the Eucharist was celebrated as frequently as layfolk appeared to take part.

What Spenser is getting at here involves at once the gratuitousness and inexplicability of divine action on behalf of God's creatures, at least in human terms. All one can say is that the way to avail oneself of divine aid is to render oneself available, to undertake the earthly pilgrimage guided and enabled by participation in the worship of the Church of England, with its "sight" of a future promise realized through the path of charity. In this light, Book I of *The Faerie Queene* becomes a "reading" of the cross, a narrative enacting the "re(a)d cross," the "bloudie Crosse" marking Red Crosse as a "deare remembrance of his dying Lord" (I.i.2), entering into what it means to follow in the way of the Christ, who promises, at least to Anglicans, to provide in the complex of Prayer Book worship "all . . . benefits of his passion."

We need also to note here the differences between Spenser's intertextual relationships with the Bible and his classical antecedents. If classical modes had to be transformed to serve as models for episodes in *The Faerie Queene*, if entering into a classical world of language is a result of a crafted misreading, then here the poem's relationship to the Bible is an enabling relationship. Red Crosse at the end of Book I is in effect "reading" through chapters 19 to 22 of Revelation; as a result, he resumes his quest and achieves victory over the dragon. He thus models "right reading" of the biblical text, a reading that is not an act of mind only, but a behavioral process. His "reading" is in fact a "doing," an engagement in the struggles of his quest "that thou hast prepared for us to walk in," undertaken in an openness to the Word conveyed by reading, proclamation, and participation in the Sacraments. Taking Red Crosse as a model reader, we find that the appropriate reading of Spenser's poem is not an act of mind achieving *gnosis,* but an act of becoming through *praxis,* of taking up one's own cross, performed as a "reading" of the cross itself. To read *The Faerie Queene* aright, therefore, is to "do" Red Crosse by entering into the narrative he opens before us.

Instructed in the virtues as it observed the various knights discover them, Spenser's Elizabethan audience had in *The Faerie Queene* patterns of life as pilgrimage, as quest, following the saints in a process of growth in knowledge and action in the world of the poem. These quests lead to the building up of the fictional community of Gloriana's Cleopolis. At the same time,

Spenser's constant allusions to the real world of England in the poem make clear that Faeryland is not what is but a way of furthering "what may be, and should be" in England itself. Spenser's poem raises the tantalizing possibility that his readers can convert their world into a true Christian commonwealth if they act out in the world quests for it inspired by those presented in the poem. Spenser's constant reminders of the "make-believe" nature of his fictional world make clear that it is never an end in itself but a means to an end which can only be found in the world of human interactions for which the fictional world always offers inciting and enticing ranges of possibilities.

The final measure of incentive for Spenser's readers to "take that goodness in hand" comes from the consequences of Spenser's ongoing biblical and liturgical allusions. Even as the goal of Red Crosse's pilgrimage is that heavenly city which is the goal of all Christian living, whether in Faeryland or in England, and even as Red Crosse's victory comes through his participation in the familiar Sacraments of the Prayer Book, so Spenser's readers are to see through this poem the meaning of their historical moment. In the events of Spenser's England, he would have his audience see, God was at work once more, building up his city, calling his people into community by reconciling them to himself and thus giving them their identity and their purpose. To participate in the creation of God's salvation history by realizing the Christian commonwealth and thus to become a citizen of the city which represents the end of that history is seen as the overriding issue of Elizabethan life. To point this out and to equip his readers for that activity are Spenser's tasks in *The Faerie Queene*.

Spenser's fictional world is thus never an end in itself but always a means to a larger end. In the same way, it derives its meaning from Cranmer's process of reformation—both of church and of society—to which it constantly alludes. While the Book of Homilies presents images of the Christian commonwealth directly and overtly instructs its audience in the life of active charity intended to build up that national community, it does so in the context of the living liturgical action through which people are empowered to live that life. Spenser's poem presents its images fictionally, but always in cooperation with and in reference to that same ongoing liturgical action and its process of societal reform started in England by Cranmer in the reign of Edward VI and continued in the reign of Elizabeth through the established church. As we have seen, the documents of the Edwardian Reformation were not intended as the defining marks of a religious institution but as agents of change designed to effect a transformation of English society. In the same way, Spenser's *Faerie Queene* is not a static depiction of a fictional world but a didactic poem intended to move its readers toward active participation in that process of transformation. It thus represents the first stage in the story of the way in which writers involved in the life of the Church of England put "all possible art" to the work of her reforming agenda at a time in which years of use had made the Prayer Book so familiar that it was available as informing context for enabling allusion.

The Homiletics of Marriage in Spenser's Epithalamion

What we have of *The Faerie Queene* ends with language that anticipates in striking fashion the language Spenser uses to end his wedding song, his *Epithalamion*. The linking term is the motif of time as "short"; a comparison of Spenser's image of time and his use of it in each poem allows us to view the *Epithalamion* not only as an appropriate continuation of his sonnet cycle *Amoretti* but also as a complex redoing and reemphasizing of themes and methods basic to the didactic undertaking of *The Faerie Queene* itself. Time for Cranmer is the arena of human work and God's work; he sought to have people participate in God's work and contribute to its fulfillment. The shortness of time for Paul (1 Corinthians 7:29; read at Evening Prayer on May 24, 1594) was an argument for remaining single, or so it was in the Middle Ages; in Cranmer's terms, marriage is part of the work that people do to further God's work, even when time is experienced as near its end. Thus, for him, marriage functions as an act in time that teaches and enables something basic about the relationship between human and divine endeavor that can lead to participation in God's promised future for his people. Cranmer married; his reform program abolished institutionalized celibacy and his Prayer Book made marriage a rite as significant as any except baptism and Eucharist.

The kingdom of God, the eternal city of fulfilled promises, is thus to be reached, and built, through the moment-to-moment and day-to-day interactions of men and women in marriage and family and local and national community created, defined, and nurtured in their relationships by the ongoing worship of the Prayer Book. The work is through specific occasions, not of a timeless ideal in light of which human actions must always be counted loss and failure, but of occasions whose future promises the redemption of failure. Nor is it a return to a mythic state of blissful release from responsibility and adulthood, but instead works through acceptance of adult responsibility in relationships. Thus it moves beyond "the devices and desires of our own hearts" toward the restoration of "holy fellowship."

In Spenser's work, the task of continuing the activity of Book I is to expose the duplicity and falsehood of received images and myths, of projected wish fulfillments and manipulative understandings, in this case, in the realm of human sexuality. Or, to put it another way, *eros* must now participate in the furthering of the work of the kingdom, but to do so it must be inscribed in English culture in a new way, its old myths exposed, its texts rewritten, and its possibilities evaluated. Spenser's work is much about the exposure of the ways in which human fears and fantasies about sexuality are traditionally dealt with in ways that frustrate more than they make possible fulfillment. It is about those fears and fantasies as the continuing activity of Archimago against which the realities of human sexuality are both disappointingly unglamorous and also truly life giving. It is about finding a place for *eros* in a culture just now stable enough to incorporate within itself what had earlier been by definition outside, in the realm of the marginal and the exploitative.

Spenser's concern is also with the significance of human endeavor and the desire for release. The ending of Book I of *The Faerie Queene*, in fact, enacts a double deferral of meaning. In terms of "meaning" as an end of an act of reading, a quest is relinquished in favor of a shift to an affirmation that true reading is now to be understood as doing in response to verbal experience, *praxis* not *gnosis* becoming the fruit of poetic encounter. Such a deferral results from the sense that such action is not a conclusion but a beginning, in the initiation of which the poetic experience has a role to play. But this role results as much from the discovery of the duplicity of language itself and thus the relinquishment of a quest for final "meaning" in the work as it does from the assignment of meaning to language.

The other deferral involves the narrative level of the poem. The future promise of fulfillment in marriage for Red Crosse and Una comes to be a way to hold open the narrative of Book I; only when that marriage is consummated in the narrative of the poem can we say that we know when the work of Book I either as a poem to be finished or a didactic enterprise to be engaged in is at an end. But the two are related; if the deferral of meaning is implicated in the future promise of the blessed wedding supper of the Lamb, so too the narrative of Book I, as it infolds references to that eschatological banquet, points to the same future as a sign of closure. In other words, if the reader discovers that to engage in *praxis* to build the city is the only way to "read aright" Book I (and the rest) of *The Faerie Queene,* then such action also furthers the completion of Book I's narrative. Thus, to know what Book I means, one has to further its work through participation in the community defined and created by the Prayer Book and become thereby a guest at that wedding feast, seeing the city "face to face" instead of in the "dark glass" either of Spenser's text or of human experience apart from the orienting and informing work of participating in use of the Prayer Book.

The role a deferral of closure might play in *The Faerie Queene* has been the subject of much recent and fruitful speculation, the most helpful vehicle of which has been Jonathan Goldberg's *Endlesse Worke: Spenser and the Structures of Discourse.*[48] Goldberg's work gives us ways of talking about the narrative of Spenser's poem that avoid fruitless inquiry about whether the poem is incomplete, complete but unfinished, or actually finished. I would distinguish my own argument about *The Faerie Queene* by noting that I reject Goldberg's seemingly arbitrary distinction between the "readerly" and the "writerly" texts; Goldberg lumps traditional approaches to Spenser's poem under the "readerly" category and privileges the attributes of the "writerly," which he finds to include playfulness and resistance to closure. Yet Spenser's refusal to provide closure is surely but another part of his strategy to change behavior in the world to which the poem is addressed; if his text is to change things, it must undercut through playfulness and other means the received structures of texts and worlds which people use to eliminate change in their experience. Readings of Spenser which find closure and stasis answer similar needs we have for texts to yield to our control. Goldberg's view finds reading *The Faerie Queene* an "endlesse worke"; in my view, the endless work of the poem is in transforming the world of the reader, and all the open and opening characteristics of the poem work toward that end.

So, too, the *Epithalamion* "ends" the *Amoretti* in its first great movement to the altar, but such movement leads not to closure but to the making of "endlesse matrimony."[49] This extends, surely, the work of the marriage of the couple at that altar because it leads through transformations of meaning to the wedding feast of the Lamb, the endless marriage of Christ and his church built through liturgical enactment and its aftermath in which the couple at the *Epithalamion*'s altar have a role as they move to the nuptial chamber, their rest coming "in hope" that their actions there will result in "blessed Saints for to increase the count."[50] Here, too, the ending of the narrative and the completion of its "meaning" are deferred, the last lines of the poem opening out toward future promise and action to reach that promise. Thus, the *Epithalamion,* far from circling back on itself, becomes literally an "endlesse moniment," a monument whose work is without end in "short time" until time itself ends in the fulfillment of the promises proclaimed in biblical texts and enacted in the Prayer Book rites.

The *Epithalamion* also, for Spenser, inscribes a continued rethinking of the central language of human sexuality. Goldberg draws our attention to the unending of Book III of *The Faerie Queene* in the 1596 edition, continuing an approach to the poem helpfully articulated earlier by Leigh De Neef. In De Neef's reading, one of the major issues for Books III and IV of *The Faerie Queene* becomes the rereading of what it means for women to engage actively in realizing their sexuality.[51] Amoret's heart-wound, her flight, and her imprisonment in the House of Busirane are, at least in part, self-inflicted as expressions of a fear of adult female sexuality, for "who can love the worker of her smart?" (III.xii.31). In the 1590 version, of course, Britomart frees Amoret from the debilitating consequences of such fear ("As she were never hurt") and facilitates her union with Scudamour. The language Spenser uses to describe their embrace promotes an image of sexual union as total and effacing of self and of language ("No word they spake . . . / So seemd those two, as growne together quite") a condition to which Britomart aspires ("to her selfe oft wisht like happinesse") in 1590. By 1595 and the *Epithalamion,* however, Juno "still dost patronize . . . wedlock" and "for comfort often called art / Of women in their smart" (ll. 390–395) and the couple joined in that poem expect to enjoy "the sweet pleasures of theyr loves delight" (l. 401); in 1596, the self-obliterating image of Amoret and Scudamour embracing is gone from *The Faerie Queene* to be replaced by a deferral of closure for their narrative into another book of the poem. What may be happening here is Spenser's own realization that in the image of Amoret and Scudamour at the end of Book III (1590) he had made his own myth of sexual union that was in its own way as debilitating to actual human interactions as the fears Amoret herself creates and must relinquish. In the *Epithalamion,* his images are more plural, human sexuality becoming an interactive behavior of selves in actual occasions rather than a merger into a myth of obliteration. Such a textual inscription of sexuality may be less inspiring to the young who lack clear boundaries to their selves anyway and would just as soon relinquish identity to another, but is probably less than helpful to adults who know that reality is missed if it is discounted in a fruitless pursuit of another version of childhood.

By the years 1594 and 1595, when Spenser wrote *Epithalamion* and resumed his work on *The Faerie Queene,* the Puritan challenge to the Church of England had for the time been effectively countered.[52] In these poems, then, it is possible to observe the courage of a fuller acceptance of time and a different strategy for proclaiming Anglican concerns. The deferral of marriages in *The Faerie Queene* here yields to the celebration of a marriage, albeit one in a different fictional world. If *The Faerie Queene* enables us to see what the narrative of English time *could* be, *Epithalamion* explores the full significance of what has happened and *is* happening in England through use of the Prayer Book. In addition, if Book I of *The Faerie Queene* draws its controlling language from a specific and particular moment of time and human activity enabled and defined by the Prayer Book, the *Epithalamion* incorporates Cranmer's marriage rite in a way that infolds the proclamation of that rite into the poem's specific moment because it announces that moment as a saving divine encounter and proclaims it to be so through the process of poem making and Christian prophetic proclamation. It does this in a way that also opens the moment of reading to a similar interpretation. Time continues here to be the arena of divine action that is significant for all potential audiences of this poem; central to Spenser's task is the way his poem takes up the questions of human-divine relationships in time so as to define the moment of narrative as well as the moment of reading as linked to the future promise of endings and beginnings that will enact the closure of time. Generative human interaction here constitutes the ongoing life of the body that links present enactment to future fulfillment through its actions in time.

In the two stanzas known as "The Eighth Canto, Unpertite," of the fragmentary Book VII of *The Faerie Queene,* the speaker presents an image of Mutability's "greatest sway" in this world, so that "flowring pride / Short *Time* shall soon cut down with his consuming sickle." The *Epithalamion* of course also ends with an image involving "short time"; in the poem's final line, the speaker calls on his poem to be "for short time an endlesse moniment." In both cases, time, so often depicted by Spenser as the enemy of humankind, a sign of sinful estrangement from God because it is the agent of death, takes on more positive connotations. In the broken ending to what we have of *The Faerie Queene,* it becomes an agent of human redemption as its destructive aspect is turned on pride, "cut down with his consuming sickle," thus freeing us from the traditional source of all our woe. Time precisely in its shortness now becomes an agent of human deliverance, the pathway to "that same time when no more *Change* shall be, / But stedfast rest of all things." At the end of the *Epithalamion,* the poem itself, "cutting off through hasty accidents" that in "dew time" would have produced "many ornaments" for "my love," functions like time at the end of *The Faerie Queene* to hasten the sought-for day of fulfillment and thus must stand as "unto her a goodly ornament, / And for short time an endlesse moniment."

In both cases, time functions eschatologically, as both the arena and the agent of the process of redemption and fulfillment and not merely as the ally of judgment, suffering, and death. *The Faerie Queene* casts the present into a new light through seeing it in terms of future promise; the *Epithalamion* proclaims and looks toward a fulfillment in/of time, even through the action of "cutting off through hasty accidents," which, as we have seen, points to a fulfillment intelligible only in terms of a future promise, of the possibility of "heavenly tabernacles," to be approached through the actions in time celebrated in the poem.

We may get closer to a linking term for these texts if we consider the source to which Spenser is alluding at the end of *The Faerie Queene,* for we are in fact back into the intertextual relationship with Revelation 19–22 so central to the ending of Book I. The speaker's memory of Nature's speech, her claim that a time will come when "no more *Change* shall be, / But stedfast rest of all things . . . / With Him that is the God of Sabbaoth hight," echoes Revelation 21:3–4:

Behold, the Tabernacle of God is with men, and he will dwell with them: & they shall be his people, and God himself shall be their God with them. And God shall wipe away all tears from their eyes: & there shall be no more death, neither sorrow, neither shall there be any more pain: for the first things are passed.

Depicting a powerful image of the end of Mutability and all its effects subsumed into "stedfast rest," this passage follows the beginning of Revelation 21 with its picture of the New Jerusalem coming down out of heaven as a bride prepared for her bridegroom. In fact, Book VII.iii of *The Faerie Queene* ends at the point at which the whole book of Revelation ends, in prayer for the coming of the time evoked by the preceding images, Spenser's "O that great Sabbaoth God, graunt me that Sabaoths sight" functioning in the same way as John's concluding "Amen. Come Lord Jesus." In both cases, what is to come is becoming already because it is promised of the one who can fulfill such promises; thus, the events described in Revelation are narrated as though they were past although they are yet to come, while the tone of Spenser's poem evokes something of the "rest" that is to come. In both cases as well, the existence of such texts is implicated in the coming of that which they ask to come, for the act of prayer is implicated in the answering of prayer, yet at the same time the one to whom prayer is addressed is one "to whom our needs are known before we ask." Thus prayer is not a magic act creating outcomes, but the text of interaction between faithful partners in a relationship through which the future is reached and negotiated.

John's images for the future fulfillment of biblical promise, as we have seen before, are here bound up in the language of human marriage. The status of Revelation as a canonical text was open to question during the Reformation, with Luther and other Reformers questioning its inclusion in the biblical text and radical Protestants making it their central text. Cranmer's lectionary omits large portions of it from regular reading and locates its use in the larger context of the whole cycle of biblical readings. For present purposes we need to note that Revelation contains apocalyptic material—the graphically violent visions of a semignostic battle between cosmic forces of good and evil—and eschatological material—the proclamation of the full revealing of divine love. Spenser draws on the first part of this material most heavily in Book I of *The Faerie Queene* and on the second part most heavily in *Epithalamion*. He saves himself from falling into a gnostic position in the story of Red Crosse because he refuses to use the Revelation material to predict a cosmic battle to come on a fixed timetable for which we are passive observers; instead, he uses the language of Revelation to clarify the significance of what was going on in the emergence of the Church of England from what Spenser saw as its Roman captivity, a process in which both his poem and his audience had a definite role to play. In *Epithalamion,* he uses the specific occasion of a wedding to proclaim how divine love works through such seemingly insignificant events by which the kingdom is being built and the promises of divine love move toward their fulfillment.

The eschatological moment is inscribed in Spenser's poem in terms of its relationship to the wedding of heaven and earth and of Christ and his Bride, the church becoming the New Jerusalem "prepared as a bride adorned for her husband," whose speech—"the Spirit and the bride say, Come"—becomes the prayer of John at the end of Revelation. In the context of the biblical episode, John is taken to see "the bride, the Lamb's wife," and thus has the "sight of the city" also given Red Crosse in Book I of *The Faerie Queene*. We will have occasion shortly to review the other biblical texts John draws on to develop his "sight of the city," which is also a "sight of the bride." What I am now about is building up the context for Spenser's poem which is a "moniment" to "short time" and which is a poem that builds into the specifics of a particular wedding the full significance of that wedding in terms of Christian proclamation about its future promise, as demonstrated by liturgical enactment. Spenser here links his poem to the language pattern that recurs throughout the Bible, from Genesis through the Song of Solomon and Isaiah, Jesus' miracle at the wedding in Cana, and the passages from Revelation cited here. The result is a powerful set of associations which clarify the role of marriage as an effective sign of the workings of divine love in time and which Spenser exploits fully in his poem.

For this reason I wish to claim that *Epithalamion* actually represents Spenser's "ditty of the city," the poem in which he finally risks giving us, to the extent to which "earthly tong" or "wit of man can tell" (*FQ,* I.x.55), a description of the City of God. A wedding which is full of song and color and life, a banquet characterized by copious feasting and drinking, an action which encompasses the world and calls it forth to altar and banquet table— here Spenser at once describes the subject of *Epithalamion* by borrowing from biblical depictions of the City of God and also makes clear his claim that this wedding connects its time to the time of the fulfillment of the City of God. By so doing he brings the City into our time by showing how human weddings tell us about the blessed wedding feast of the Lamb and also by claiming that human weddings open the way to the City to come. *Epithalamion* thus becomes an outpost of the City of God in time because it is a temporal gate to the City.

In these terms I want to enrich the implications and complexities that time may hold for the *Epithalamion*. In so doing, I will expand on but also correct the implications of Kent Hieatt's argument for the role of time in structuring this poem. Hieatt has claimed for this poem an elaborate numerological structure which manifests images of eternity in the poem's temporal world. Spenser's wedding hymn, Hieatt argues, is filled with circles, with rings, with the great arc of the sun in its circular progress through the sky.[53] In Hieatt's reading, the poem itself is a circle, beginning in darkness and ending in darkness twenty-four hours and stanzas later. In this sense, at least, the poem becomes "endlesse" in that, in Hieatt's terms, it turns back upon itself to end where it began.

Yet this does not answer fully the question posed by the poem's ending request, that it be an "endlesse moniment" for "short time." Nor, for that matter, does it clarify in what sense the poem is, or can be, "unto her [whose wedding with the speaker the poem celebrates} a goodly ornament." Although the numerical patterns Hieatt notes do create a kind of circle, they just as forcefully create a sense of the day's uniqueness, for only the summer solstice has just the number of hours of light and darkness from which the poem takes its construction, and only on one unique Feast of "St. Barnaby the Bright" was Spenser himself married. Nor does the poem ask that we accept the day it defines as in any way "typical" or normal; in fact, the uniqueness and unrepeatability of this day are constant claims of the poem.

Yet we may be closer to an answer to these issues if we think of the poem, to the extent to which it inscribes a circularity, as a ring, a verbal version of the wedding ring central to weddings in the Church of England, one of the chief points of controversy between the English church and Puritans, who objected to its use as a remnant of papistical departure from the biblical ceremonial of the primitive church. The wedding actually takes place in Stanza 13, or the "middest" of the poem, where the giving of a ring is not mentioned. Through making of the ring a poem, and of the poem a ring, Spenser can make the poem into an "ornament" to the beloved and for "short time an endlesse moniment." In the Prayer Book rite itself, the ring plays a central and defining role: "With this ring I thee wed." But the giving of the ring is not an end in itself, not a completion of an action, but a beginning, for the priest goes on in the rite to pray that "these persons may surely perform and keep the vow and covenant betwixt them made, whereof this ring given and received is a token and pledge." Thus, the giving of the ring, like the giving of the poem, is an action in anticipation of future action which will give meaning to the former action, since the giving of the ring is a "token and pledge" that the "vow and covenant" it initiates will be performed and kept, so that only through such ongoing action does the giving and receiving of the ring come to have meaning.

Thus the ring missing from the poem is rediscovered as the poem itself, yet not in any static way. Here words form a ring independently of their "meaning," yet the meaning of the ring given is for us pointed to by the poem even as the "meaning" of the poem is directed by the form of the ring given. The acts of giving a ring and/or a poem-as-ring enter into a mutually enlivening conversation, opening up new possibilities in relationships, including that created by words and deeds at the altar (they both "pledged their troth" and performed a "giving and receiving of a ring") that are otherwise closed without this interchange and without it specifically. The groom gives the bride a ring and Spenser gives us a poem-as-ring; here displacement of action into language opens a space that is in conversation so that other actions can result. "Meaning" here is in those resulting actions.

The use of the ring in relationship to the language of the poem and of the Prayer Book wedding rite thus defines another of those situations in which the language of a printed text comes to effect things only in enactment in particular situations. The script provided by the Prayer Book for the groom instructs him to say, "With this ring I thee wed," the modifier "this" making clear that the meaning of this text comes only as a description of a specific ring given by the groom to the bride in the context of a specific moment in the life of the couple and in the life of the community; indeed, both parties to the wedding *and* the community must consent to the wedding. The giving of the ring becomes an action that can be spoken of as "final" only in the sense that it brings to an end the ability to speak of the couple as not married; otherwise it is the initiation of an action, a beginning of that which the giving of the ring effects, the proclamation of which is given to the priest and deferred for several lines until he summarizes what has taken place. In spite of popular belief that the wedding ring is symbolic of the unity and indissolubility of marriage, the Prayer Book rite makes no mention of such an interpretation. Instead, the ring is "a token and pledge" of "the vow and convenant betwixt them made," that they "live faithfully together," a far cry from the fusion and self-obliteration implied by a static and changeless image of marital harmony.

The priest prays in the rite for God's "blessing upon these thy servants . . . so these persons may surely perform and keep the vow and covenant betwixt them made . . . and may ever remain in perfect love and peace together, and live according unto thy laws." Only in terms of actions joined with words that mark the initiation of action to come—"Forasmuch as N. and N. have consented together in holy wedlock, and have witnessed the same before God and this company, and thereto have given and pledged their troth either to other, and have declared the same by giving and receiving of a ring, and by joining of hands"—can he pronounce them married.

Although marriage had no official status as a Sacrament in the Tudor Anglican church, the rite follows the models of baptism and Eucharist in joining the enacting of a verbal text with things and actions—the giving and receiving of the ring and the joining of hands—to create through its enactment a relationship. Like the use of biblical and liturgical language in such situations, the giving of the ring participates in that which it signs, becoming a tangible "declaring" of what is begun in this action and a contributor to the discovery of what that means by contributing to the keeping of the "troth" which over time will reveal what is meant by these actions. Once more, "doing" subsumes "meaning," as action following the enactment of the marriage rite informs the meaning of that rite.

Also, as we have seen before, the achieving of such meaning is again not dependent on the words used or the action performed, in a constitutive sense, but on the God who promises to act through such words and actions. As the opening language of the rite makes clear, we are once again in the realm of Cranmer's argument that language, when enacted, facilitates and reveals divine action in the world which is joined in by human beings through participation in the enactment of the rite. The priest greets the congregation and proclaims the significance of what is taking place:

> Dearly beloved friends, we are gathered together here in the sight of God, and in the face of his congregation, to join together this man and this woman in holy matrimony, which is an honorable estate, instituted of God in paradise in the time of man's innocency, signifying unto us the mystical union, that is betwixt Christ and his Church.

In other words, one function of marriage is to tell all "beloved friends" assembled on this particular occasion something about God and his relationship with his people. It is also for the enabling of the responsibilities of the Christian life, again defined in societal terms, for the priest's opening remarks define "the causes for which matrimony was ordained":

> One was, the procreation of children to be brought up in the fear and nurture of the Lord, and praise of God. Secondly, it was ordained for a remedy against sin, and to avoid fornication, that such persons as have not the gift of continency might marry, and keep themselves undefiled members of Christ's body. Thirdly, for the mutual society, help, and comfort, that the one ought to have of the other, both in prosperity and adversity. (BCP, pp. 290–291)

All of these reasons affirm the health of the Body—the continuity of the nation-church, the preservation of Christ's body, the establishment of the "society" of the marital relationship, the well-being of the bodies of those being married—as the reasons for marriage. The rite here stresses the special particularity of the action it makes possible. The "afterlife" of God's establishment of marriage in Eden, his using the image of marriage in the Song of Songs as the image for the relationship between Christ and his Church (at least according to traditional interpretations), God's promise in Isaiah that he will wed himself to Israel in an indissoluble union, and Christ's "adorning and beautifying" marriage "with his presence and first miracle that he wrought in Cana of Galilee"—all such consequences for humanity of those specific historical acts of God are revealed and made significant through the specificity of the historical marriage which the Prayer Book rite enables through its enactment.

There is thus at the center of the *Epithalamion* a situating of the poem in relationship to another ongoing process of discourse; as in the case of Book I of *The Faerie Queene,* consequences for action and meaning are brought to bear on the poem and are acted out within it. I have belabored this point because some readings of the *Epithalamion,* including Hieatt's, move not from the general through the specific but from the specific to the general. Hieatt's reading of the poem moves progressively further and further away from the literal world of the poem into the realm of abstraction about the poem. In the terms we have come to understand, Hieatt uses his discovery of the poem's numerical structure as a way of constructing a myth about the poem, as Christian proclamation is rewritten in terms of a "dissolving surface" that leads us to contemplate, not specifics, but "cyclical return."[54] In other words, Hieatt constructs from the poem a myth that draws back from the details of the poem's verbal world into another humanly constructed world of abstraction and atemporality.[55]

Such a reading overlooks the relationship that exists in the poem between the poem itself and the marriage rite it expounds, as well as the tensions that exist between the poem and its classical antecedents, and, within the poem, between the lover/speaker and his beloved, the world of the poem, and the world of the reader. What Spenser has done in this poem is to use this numerical structuring to stress the concrete specificity of June 11, 1594 (Saint Barnabas' Day), the day on which the wedding depicted in the poem took place, and the significance of that event in all its specificity. To the extent to which images of the eternal become present through being infolded into the temporal world of the poem, they show us the importance of that day in terms of its relationship to past saving acts and to the future they have in common. By drawing our attention to that day in the very structure of the poem as well as in its language, Spenser underscores radically the importance of the specific event of that day—the wedding, which he depicts in the poem. Spenser would remind us that the God of his faith, the God who joins together the couple in the Prayer Book's wedding rite, invests the specific events of life with far more significance than we wish them to have. Our response to temporality is mythic escape; God's is specific action to redeem temporality, not to obliterate it. By the end of the poem, this argument will come to have serious consequences for readers of the poem.

We might begin by noting how radical is Spenser's handling of the genre of his wedding song. Paul Miller describes Spenser's poem as the beginning of an epithalamic tradition in Renaissance England which draws on classical models.[56] In many ways, Spenser echoes the conventions of the classical genre—the invocation of the Muses, the use of the traditional wedding chant "Hymen io Hymen, Hymen they do shout" (l. 140 and elsewhere), the gathering of the wedding guests, the celebration of the bedding of bride and groom. In terms of the classical tradition, however, there are marked differences.[57] In the wedding songs of Catullus and others, the singer is a guest at the wedding; here, he is both guest and host, both singer and bridegroom. Thus Spenser brings his speaker within the events depicted in his poem; he is both observer/celebrator and participant. In addition, of course, Spenser teases us with the possibility that he is the speaker, that the wedding celebrated is his own, fusing bridegroom/speaker/poet into a single role.

Spenser has also given his poem several settings linked in narrative sequence, a fundamental restructuring of his classical examples. If we may use Catullus' *Carmen LXI* as representative—and the most recent editor of Spenser's poem finds clear echoes of this Latin text in Spenser's work[58]—then we may note the single movement of narrative in Catullus' epithalamion: the procession of the couple, culminating in their being put to bed for their wedding night. Spenser incorporates this narrative but places before it the procession to the altar, the wedding service itself, the wedding celebration, and only then, with the shift in mood from the celebratory tone of all of Catullus' poem to the ceasing of sound and the dismissing of the wedding party, does he pick up the narrative of *Carmen LXI*. Whereas the bedding *is* the wedding in Catullus' poem and becomes a public and celebratory moment that includes lots of bawdy banter, Spenser shifts all that to the earlier parts of his poem and makes of the public world of Catullus' narrative an interpersonal and, above all, a quiet moment. In banishing Catullus and his audience from the nuptial bedchamber, Spenser also banishes Catullus himself as the definer of the epithalamic genre and the subsumer of marriage's meaning for poets and poems and their audiences. As the public recedes into the private in Spenser's *Epithalamion,* so the static and already-written and impersonal and fixed narrative of the Roman wedding gives way to the open-ended and problematic and yet faithfully and hopefully contracted narrative of Spenser's lovers. Their future is not yet over; it stretches before them.

The community at the end of Spenser's poem is, as we have seen already, a community being created but as yet not complete, not just the community that joined the couple at the altar earlier in the poem, although part of the point is the poem's role in creating and linking these communities. Thus, in the *Epithalamion,* which Spenser by his title claims to be the true epithalamion, the wedding ceremony comes to share equal place with the bedding ceremony. The altar rites create what the act of sexual union demonstrates; sexual union becomes the action that in *praxis* defines the meaning of the wedding ceremony. Although the wedding ceremony requires its bedding sequence, since in Christian terms a marriage is not a marriage until it is consummated, the public ceremony is required first to distinguish the acts of the marital bed from acts of "carnal lust." This displacement of emphasis, created through the rewritten narrative of an epithalamion, coupled with the changed role of the speaker, marks Spenser's most striking appropriation and radical transformation of classical models for poems about weddings.

Spenser also performs other transformations of the classical tradition of epithalamia, for his poem extends the redoing of his classical models to other matters of language and convention. In the first place, Spenser invokes "the learned sisters," not Hymen, as the Muse of this poem, and it is the lady of the poem, not Hymen, who gets the flowered garland. Although Catullus gives Hymen, "good love's conjugator," authority over the results of marriage (he is the guarantor of "opinion" in regard to "heirs" and "lineage" and is thus the "protector of boundaries") and as a result can proclaim Hymen the god "whom in the heavens ought men . . . to worship,"[59] Spenser decisively displaces Hymen from center stage. He can say that "Hymen is awake, / And long since ready forth his maske to move" and boys can shout Hymen's name, but clearly this reflects the employment of language as conventional usage in a way that undercuts the significance and the ontological status of that to which it alludes, even as it draws on the traditional associations of such language to give the poem's world the right sort of traditional atmosphere. Hymen is the god of epithalamic poetry, after all, or so Catullus would demonstrate. To operate in this genre, Spenser suggests, involves the use of such language; the way he uses it argues that we need not take it seriously.

There are, however, important echoes of the end of Book I of *The Faerie Queene* imbedded in Spenser's wedding song. We may well remember that Red Crosse hears *"Hymen io Hymen"* only when he departs from the false Una, whom he has seen displayed as "a loose Leman to vile service bound" (I.i.48). The modest beloved of *Epithalamion* reduces the allusion to a conventional aside—"Bid her awake; for Hymen is awake" (l. 25). At Red Crosse's betrothal to Una, "sweete Musicke" of earthly musicians is joined by "an heavenly noise / Heard sound through all the Pallace" (I.xii.38–39), replicating the Sanctus in the Prayer Book Eucharist when "with angels and archangels, and with all the company of heaven" the congregation joins in the "Holy, holy, holy, Lord God of hosts" (BCP, p. 262). This song is also sung "continually" (BCP, p. 53) by the angels; it is the angelic song of the angels who "continually / About the sacred Altare doe remaine" in *Epithalamion* (ll. 229–230). Other details, including the "two hands" of the officiant (see *FQ* I.xii.37 for Una's father's "own two hands [which] the holy knots did knit"), the humility of the bride, the abundance of the wine (Una's house "did sweat with great aray"), and the feasting, make clear that Book I is evoked in *Epithalamion,* inviting us to see the significance of the former now invested in the latter, while the latter wedding clarifies how the events of Book I come to have meaning for real inhabitants of Elizabeth's England. It is through specific weddings like this one that the betrothal of Red Crosse and Una both yields significance and reveals new understandings.

In addition, Spenser's use of biblical language is so pervasive and so central to the articulation of the poem that it evokes a radically different response from the array of classical allusions. The allusions to Catullus are here to provide generic window dressing and to be deprived of their cultural significance; the biblical allusions are here to tell us what Spenser claims is the significance of this wedding. These references to the Bible's resources of language run the spectrum from echoes of details (the Song of Solomon's "daughters of Jerusalem" now include in their number the "merchants daughters" of stanza 10; the generosity of the Song of Solomon's male speaker in calling for "drink abundantly" provides a model for *Epithalamion*'s speaker's generosity) to the language of major moments of the poem (the Song of Solomon's passages provide language for the calling of the bride, for her description, and for the proclamation of her significance; Psalm 45's description of the king's daughter also provides details of description and episodes of movement) to major thematic references (the tradition of interpreting a link between the bride of the Song of Solomon and the church as bride in Revelation 21 forms a frame of reference for Spenser's claims for his bride and for the wedding), the Pauline image of the "bed . . . / Without blemish or staine" (ll. 399–400) leading to the "high heavens" and the "count" of "blessed Saints" (ll. 409, 423). So central to the Bible's developing language for talking about the relationship between God and humanity in time is the imagery of marriage, and so fully does Spenser display here echoes and quotations and allusions to that biblical language that such a list of biblical references could be extended indefinitely.

The point of so thorough an incorporation of biblical material into *Epithalamion* is not just to provide words to get a poem written. It is to draw a contrast between a classical understanding of the significance of human relationships and Spenser's understanding of the biblical one. The language of classical epithalamia provides decorative touches for Spenser's poem, while the language of biblical allusion so permeates the poem that it may be said to provide the vocabulary which enables Spenser to get the poem written. While his adaptations of classical language are without precedent and thus reveal Spenser's sense of freedom in using that language, his use of biblical language has biblical authority and the authority of the church's own usage behind it, thus locating Spenser's text within the scope of that authority. A comparison of two transformations of inherited language use in the poem will illustrate my point.

In Stanza 6, the speaker calls on "ye three handmayds of the Cyprian Queene," the three Graces traditionally attendants of Venus, to "Helpe to addorne my beautifullest bride," and while doing so, "as ye use to Venus, to her sing." To ask that the Graces substitute the beloved of the poem for Venus is thus to pay the bride a high compliment. Such use of language is at once a form of praise of the woman and an undercutting of any claim to authority this language might have apart from such specific occasions as this. It is, in effect, a renaturalizing of classical nature-personification, a reversal of the process through which the figure of Venus got its identity in the first place. The beloved thus becomes the true Venus, "Venus" given meaning in a way that the classical figure of the love-goddess could no longer have. The figure of Venus thus takes its meaning from the specific particularity of the woman so named and compared at the expense of the classical image of Venus. Yet in the process Spenser has revitalized classical imagery, giving Venus a currency and immediacy through the association she now has with an Elizabethan woman. Here Venus is no longer a timeless repository of ideals but a term for inscribing beauty now informed by her relationship with Spenser's beloved; the realization of beauty now becomes its characteristic source of significance, not the distance between the real and the transcendent.

Another image of diversion occurs in Stanza 13. Here, the lady "stands / Hearing the holy priest that to her speakes." She responds to the wedding— "How the red roses flush up in her cheekes, / And the pure snow with goodly vermill stayne," he says, "Like crimsin dyde in grayne." As a consequence, "even th'Angels which continually / About the sacred Altare doe remaine, / Forget their service and about her fly." If there is an allusion to Cupid here,[60] it is Cupid incorporated and thus transformed into the "angels and arch-angels, . . . and all the company of heaven" with whom the priest invites the congregation to praise God by saying, "Holy, Holy, Holy"—the Sanctus from the rite of Holy Communion. The word "continually" echoes the depiction of the same scene from Te Deum, a canticle from the rite of Morning Prayer:

> To thee all angels cry aloud: the heavens and all the powers therein. To thee Cherubin and Seraphin, continually do cry. Holy, Holy, Holy, Lord God of Sabbaoth.

This, too, echoes the depiction of the heavenly assembly in Isaiah 6, the source of the angels' song, and the image of the heavenly altar from Revelation:

> in the midst of the throne, and round about the throne, were four beasts full of eyes before and behind. . . . And [the beasts] rest not day and night, saying, Holy, holy, holy, Lord God Almighty, which was and is, and is to come. (Revelation 4:6–8)

Without biblical and churchly precedent for the cluster of associations Spenser pulls together here, we might well conclude that Spenser is making claims for his subject that it cannot sustain. In fact, we can complicate the picture even further. The language Spenser uses to depict the bride also has traditional associations:

> How the red roses flush up in her cheekes,
> And the pure snow with goodly vermill stayne,
> Like crimsin dyde in grayne.

On one level, we are in the midst of language like that of Isaiah 1:18: "Come now, and let us reason together, saith the Lord: though your sins be as scarlet, they shall be as white as snow; though they be red like crimson, they shall be as wool," central to the Prayer Book's penitential rite for Ash Wednesday (BCP, p. 319). In the tradition of biblical imagery about sin, the bride's blush is a sign of her sinfulness; the woman on a "scarlet-colored beast . . . arrayed in purple and scarlet" in Revelation is the Whore of Babylon. All of these associations Spenser implicates in his depiction of the woman whom the angels leave their tasks at the heavenly altar to "about her fly."

Yet the imagery Spenser evokes has even broader ramifications. It is through the "precious blood of Christ" that we are redeemed, shed in his passion and shared in the Eucharist, the union of bread and wine, of "crimsin dyde in grayne." The first Epistle of Peter makes the connection: "ye know that ye were . . . redeemed . . . with the precious blood of Christ as of a lamb without blemish and without spot." In Hosea, God proclaims Israel a whore, yet he promises to woo her back: "Therefore, behold, I will allure her, and bring her into the wilderness, and speak comfortably unto her. . . . And I will betroth thee unto me for ever; yea, I will betroth thee unto me in righteousness, and in judgment, and in loving kindness, and in mercies. I will even betroth thee unto me in faithfulness; and thou shalt know the Lord" (Hosea 2:14, 19–20). 1 Peter and Hosea are part of the readings assigned on the Daily Office calendar of the Prayer Book in late August; on the day that the Hosea text is read at Evening Prayer (August 27) the second lesson is chapter 4 of the first Epistle of John, which also functions as the Epistle reading for the First Sunday after Trinity, which in 1594 fell on June 2, just over a week before Spenser's wedding to Elizabeth Boyle. That reading develops the argument of *Amoretti* 68, that the love of the speaker and his beloved is an appropriate reaction to God's love revealed in the Resurrection of Christ. John's Epistle claims that "God is love, and he that dwelleth in love dwelleth in God, and God is in him." John goes on to find in love the way to link present and future: "Herein is the love perfect in us, that we should trust in the day of judgment."

This tradition of imagery also lies behind the conventional reading of the Song of Solomon as the love song of Christ to his church which culminates in the imagery of Revelation: "And I John saw the holy city, a new Jerusalem, coming down from God out of heaven, prepared as a bride adorned for her husband." This is also the tradition of imagery that the Prayer Book marriage rite evokes at its beginning, when the priest proclaims that the joining of "this man and this woman in holy matrimony" signifies "unto us the mystical union, that is betwixt Christ and his Church." The imagery which Spenser uses to present the bride at the altar combines the juxtaposition of red and white as a sign of sinfulness ("though your sins be as scarlet") and as a sign of redemption ("our souls washed through his most precious blood"), a fitting image for one who is at the moment of description standing before the altar engaged in one of the actions through which she joins with the speaker to participate in God's actions for their redemption and for the redemption of the society which they help to build through this action together. Here, the sinfulness of human bodies is redeemed, not by denial of the body but through the offering of the body in its sinfulness to be transformed by God through his use to further the divine redemptive work in the world. It is as she finds herself as she is, even in her sinfulness, to be beloved by God and wooed by God as well as by the speaker that she stands forth as one engaged in a process which moves through history toward the end of history, which is described as the transformation from red to white. As the female speaker of the Song of Solomon announces in light of her beloved's call to her, "I am [through this calling both] the rose of Sharon and the lily of the valleys."

Spenser's claim to use such language for a description of his bride and his claim that the Angels "forget their service and about her fly" are examples of hyperbolic overreaching, unless we see that, in light of what the Prayer Book marriage rite says about specific marriages, what is taking place here facilitates, or demarcates, a particular involvement in God's action for human redemption, surely a worthy object for angelic interest. Such use of language underlies Spenser's poetic enterprise at this point; not only is he indebted to the Bible for the very words which enable him to make his poem, but he is also engaged in making, through the application of those words to the specific event being depicted, the Church of England's claim about the redemptive significance of such events as enacted in the Prayer Book rites. In other words, Spenser has put his poem at the service of the biblical Word mediated liturgically to enact through it the biblical claim about God's actions for the redemption of humanity.

This enables Spenser to use the classical tradition of epithalamia with such ease, all the while demystifying its authority. Further, in claiming his role as singer of the poem in the first stanza, Spenser's speaker compares himself to Orpheus: "Helpe me mine owne loves prayses to resound, / . . . So Orpheus did for his owne bride" (ll. 14–16). On the one hand, the speaker evokes for himself the Orphic role of poet, a classical tradition demonstrating the authority and power of poetry to be so great that it could charm Pluto and bring him to release Eurydice from Hades.[61] The speaker replicates that role; he calls his bride to "Wake . . . forth to come." In that regard, Spenser's singer must appear as the lesser poet, since he does not call her forth from Hades, only from her "bowre." Yet Spenser *does* "overgoe" Orpheus, for although Orpheus did convince Pluto to release Eurydice, he violated the conditions of the agreement by looking back at her on their way out of Hades, only to see her receding into the underworld. Spenser's speaker, however, not only looks back at her but describes her fully, both outwardly (Stanza 10) and inwardly (Stanza 11), and urges "ye merchants daughters" to see her as well. Yet the beloved is not lost; she moves steadfastly forward to give her lover her hand.

In a real sense, therefore, Spenser in this poem evokes the Orphic role and the Orphic story not to fail, as Orpheus, but precisely to succeed, something Orpheus himself could not do, thus proving Spenser the more powerful poet.

To reinforce this point, Spenser alludes to another part of the Orphic story. Orpheus sang alone, as this speaker does, but his song, heard, as here, by the woods, resulted in Orpheus' dismemberment. Orpheus' song while alone in the woods was one of despair at his loss, precisely the kind of song Spenser's speaker asks the Muses not to sing:

> And when ye list your owne mishaps to mourne,
> Which death, or love, or fortunes wreck did rayse,
> Your string could soone to sadder tenor turne,
> And teach the woods and waters to lament
> Your dolefull dreriment.
> Now lay those sorrowfull complaints aside.
>
> (Ll. 7–12)

In making this appeal he succeeds in controlling their response while avoiding Orpheus' fate. The speaker in this poem thus enacts a new role for the poet, one that completes the task at which Orpheus failed. The role created here is thus a usurpation of the classic role of poet as enacted by Orpheus; this song, Spenser claims, is the true act of poetry at the service of love. Classical models of the true poet are dismembered, as Orpheus was dismembered, to be replaced by this singer with his song. The unconsummated love of Orpheus, like that of Petrarch, no longer is part of the plot of love in poetry. The roles of poet and lover merge to sing a new song, at once using the forms and language of the classical precedents and usurping their authority. Thus Spenser also enacts a claim to the domestication of *eros,* literally changing the plot of the Orphic role so as to deprive *eros* of its destructive potential. Spenser thus seeks to open the plot of marriage, at least for poets, rewriting the narrative of Orpheus' marriage so as to make it less destructive to brides, to poet/spouses, and to poetry itself. For the classic narrative of poetry is of its achievement at the expense of the practice of *eros,* even as the traditional plot of Christian sexuality values celibacy and is suspicious of *eros.* Spenser here conflates several plots and aspires to give them a new ending all at once.

Indeed, Spenser's words at this point in Stanza 1 pose the issues presented by this poem precisely in terms of the efficacy of poetry. As Enid Welsford has pointed out, Spenser here is alluding to his earlier poem "The Teares of the Muses," in which each of the Muses in turn expresses her lament that poetry no longer achieves the ends intended for it.[62] Spenser's "Teares" is a poetic version of Sidney's negative evaluation of English poetry in his *Apology;* in the poem, each Muse weeps that humanity has lost the educative benefit of the arts. The cost is "Blind Error, scornefull Follie, and base Spight," says Terpsichore, and her sisters echo her charge. The benefit of revival, on the other hand, would be "my heavenlie discipline," according to Urania, "th'heavenlie light of knowledge . . . And th'ornaments of wisdome."

By asking in the opening stanza that the Muses "Now lay those sorrowful complaints aside" and by using once more the variable refrain in the *Epithalamion,* Spenser invites comparison of the two poems. Implicitly, the *Epithalamion* is a positive response *as a poem* to the Muses' complaints about the state of English poetry. It achieves this because it proclaims what wisdom is and finds it in acknowledgment of the human situation as well as the opportunity for redemption from that situation available through placing oneself in the same transforming relationship to the Word as the poem does to the biblical and liturgical texts to which it humbly and yet joyously alludes. It is just this image that is evoked at the end of Stanza 13:

> But her sad eyes still fastened on the ground,
> Are governed with goodly modesty,
> That suffers not one looke to glaunce awry,
> Which may let in a little thought unsownd,
> Why blush ye love to give to me your hand,
> The pledge of all our band?
> Sing ye sweet Angels, Alleluya sing,
> That all the woods may answere and your eccho ring.

The "blush" here evokes *eros* at the moment of angelic song. The bride is "governed with goodly modesty"; her "blush to give to me your hand" anticipates the physical giving and receiving of the ring and of the consummation of the wedding night. In this light, the angelic song is as much in appreciation of the beloved's relinquishing of a self apart, separated by myths of *eros* as "awry" from adult sexuality, and of the erotic joy made possible by her decision to let that go as well as by the altar rites as it is in celebration of the arrival of the bride in all her beauty. Only by isolating herself from the speaker ("her sad eyes still fastened on the ground") does the lady preserve a world in which a "glaunce awry" might admit what she fears will be "a little thought unsownd." When she extends her "hand" for the beloved's hand and for his ring, however, she admits a lover-to-be and begins to enter into an adult sexuality (like Amoret overcoming her fear of the "worker of her smart") from which will emerge "Saints for to increase the count."

The redemptive work Spenser celebrates here is thus one that affirms and incorporates human physicality and sexuality, transforming it in the process. In a sense on the way toward Adam's affirmation of a "fortunate fall" in *Paradise Lost,* Spenser here proclaims that the way to human salvation is through the exercise of human sexuality in the context of marriage, not through a denial of it. For the angels to sing "Alleluya," Spenser's speaker claims, the beloved must acknowledge her physicality and her sexuality, even if that means also to acknowledge the fallenness of that bodily existence. To do so is to make oneself available for transformation, available for use in the redemptive work of God in the world and thus part of the "blessed company" who are "very members incorporate" in the Body of Christ. The mood here replicates that surrounding the reception of the Holy Communion in Cranmer's Prayer Book. The priest approaches the altar in humble prayer: "We do not presume to come to this thy table (O merciful Lord) trusting in our own righteousness. . . . We be not worthy so much as to gather up the crumbs under thy table." Yet, after the priest's reciting the narrative of Institution, the priest and people receive the bread and wine and move to sing "Glory be to God on high. . . . We praise thee, we bless thee, we worship thee, we glorify thee, we give thanks to thee for thy great glory." In the same way, the lady's humility is appropriate and yet incomplete; she must take him by the hand, complete the action, for the angels to sing "Alleluya."

In the context of the biblical and liturgically enacted Word, therefore, Spenser's poem can complete and surpass the Orphic parallel. Although Orpheus called his bride from Hades, while the speaker of *Epithalamion* calls his only from her "bowre," in terms of the biblical proclamation about God's actions in history, the success this speaker has in his "calling forth" is itself an assertion that the Word that speaks through *Epithalamion* acts in such ordinary and specific moments to call God's people from death into life, from darkness into light, from a fear of *eros* and its destructive potential into a sexually charged marital relationship blessed in its (potential) fecundity by the church. It is, therefore, appropriate that Spenser ends this poem in prayer to "ye high heavens":

> Poure out your blessing on us plentiously,
> And happy influence upon us raine,
> That we may raise a large posterity,
> Which from the earth, which they may long possesse,
> With lasting happinesse,
> Up to your haughty pallaces may mount,
> And for the guerdon of theyr glorious merit
> May heavenly tabernacles there inherit,
> Of blessed Saints for to increase the count.
> So let us rest, sweet love, in hope of this.

The ultimate implications of the action described in this poem lie in their future consequences, which are not within the power of the speaker to effect. Instead, he and his bride must live in hope of them, in hope of the "blessing" that translates the present act in all its specificity into an act with an afterlife, fully intelligible only in terms of a future dependent on Word and Sacrament working through those who open themselves to that divine work by offering themselves, their "souls and bodies," through participation in Word and Sacrament through use of the Prayer Book rites. Although one can only live in hope of such an outcome, this is the sort of hope that transfigures human relationships. So, Spenser ends his *Epithalamion* on a note of honor for "the Maker of that maker" and an expression of his dependency on that Maker both for finishing his poem and fulfilling his speaker's desires. Our sense of the last lines of the poem as an ending for the poem is dependent on "hope" that the God who provided the language for the poem will also provide the fulfillment of its desires.

Exploring the implications of this affirmation of contingency will lead us further into the workings of Spenser's language in his wedding song. For Spenser has sundered one vital relationship in his redoing of the Orpheus myth. Orpheus' rescue of Eurydice was enabled precisely because of the power Orpheus' poetry had to affect the real world, including the powers of death. His failure to rescue Eurydice was not one of poetry but of personal faithlessness to the bargain he struck with Pluto. In the *Epithalamion,* on the other hand, this relationship between poetry and action in the world is more problematic. The speaker bids his bride "Wake now my love, awake; for it is time" (l. 74), yet a few lines later she is still asleep: "Ah my deere love why doe ye sleepe thus long, / When meeter were that ye should now awake." Events in this poem are commanded by the speaker, and they happen, but the connection between their being asked for by the poem and their happening are at best unclear. The lady, at the altar, has "her sad eyes still fastened on the ground"; the act of marriage requires the joining of hands, yet the lady resists doing her part: "Why blush ye love to give to me your hand, / The pledge of all our band?" But the beginning of the next stanza, "al is done."

The direct connection between events in the world depicted in the poem and the words of the poem is thus at best problematic. Things happen, and the speaker asks that they happen, but the causal link between the two is not clear. For the completion of the action which is both the occasion and subject of the poem, what is required is outside action in conjunction with and in completion of the speaker's requests, rather than mere response in obedience to the speaker's commands. The beloved is the one who, finally, freely, gives her hand, not because she is told to, but because she joins with the speaker in the completion of their joint action, overcoming her own resistance to make possible the joining of their stories into a single, unfinished narrative. Unlike the conventional love-sonnet plot, in which the speaker seeks, and fails, to enable the beloved to become part of his own story, here Spenser succeeds in creating a single narrative of two because he yields control of his speaker's future to a larger action incorporating both his and his beloved's stories and giving them a future together. The poem thus evokes a context where so many established narratives can find they are not limited to their stock of traditional endings. What Spenser relinquishes, of course, is the security that the familiar or the separate gives; in relationship with an open future there is the possibility of disappointment as well as of fulfillment.

The articulation of this poem, therefore, is itself an act of faith, a problematic act fraught with the possibility of failure, which leaves lots of room for changes in direction—for either a rejection or an acceptance of the poem's implicit invitation. It is not a reflection of or a pointer to a static reality but a text that achieves its ends by facilitating interchanges between its antecedent texts, its narrative, and its readers. It is therefore a profoundly contingent utterance, a leap of faith into an action, both of poetry and of marriage, of art and of living. The *Epithalamion* is art as proclamation about the events it describes, performed through the language it uses to present those events. It is the sort of discourse that brings the beloved to a point of affirmation or rejection of the event through which the poem moves. In the language of the rite of wedding Spenser must have in mind, the "holy priest . . . shall say to the woman":

> Wilt thou have this man to thy wedded husband, to live together after God's ordinance in the holy estate of matrimony? Wilt thou obey him and serve him, love, honor, and keep him, in sickness, and in health? And forsaking all other, keep thee only unto him, so long as you both shall live? (BCP, p. 292)

And "The woman shall answer. I will." The nature of this action is that the woman must answer if the action is to proceed, but there is always that moment between the asking and the reply in which everything is radically problematic, for there is no way to insure that such response will follow.

In the same way, the poem presents its readers with a similar choice. For us, it is a question of whether or not we affirm "I will" to the proclamation the speaker makes, not about marriage as a generalized notion or an abiding reality, but to the specific claims the poem makes about this particular marriage. The marriage "rings" the beloved; the poem seeks to "ring" us with its claims, but in the same way that the wedding is dependent on the woman's response, from the man's perspective, the "ringing" action of the poem depends on our response. Our challenge is to relinquish the secure and familiar for a call to relationship in an open future.

The complementary acts of "ringing" that make up the expression of this poem thus function on several levels. In Spenser's day, parish boundaries in England were created by the literal extent to which a given church's bell could be heard when ringing. Spenser's speaker here acts like a church bell, even as he links ringing of bells and writing of this day (ll. 261–264), calling all to the creation of a community at the altar. This is community which is able to form to celebrate a wedding as an appropriate continuation of the narrative of the *Amoretti-Epithalamion* sequence because Spenser has in that sequence transformed the erotic by a process inscribed through his treatment of Petrarchan expressions of love, reinterpreting them in the context of Christian love.[63] The central moment in this transformation is of course Sonnet 68, which is built on Christ's summary of the law and which invites the beloved to "love . . . lyke as we ought, / Love is the lesson which the Lord us taught." Cranmer in his Book of Homilies had urged charity as the appropriate response to God's love, to what Spenser calls God's act to "bring away / Captivity thence captive us to win." Spenser links the love between a man and a woman as one of the ways we can respond "for thy sake . . . / With love may one another entertyane." After this affirmation has been achieved in *Amoretti, Epithalamion* comes as a great celebration of the speaker's claims, a poem which "completes" the process of the sonnet cycle by presenting the marriage which is Spenser's revolutionary solution to the central issue of courtly love in a way that completes nothing but only transforms *eros* from a divisive into a community-building activity and leaves much more to be done before its vision of possibilities can be achieved.

The *Amoretti-Epithalamion* sequence thus stands in close relationship to Spenser's didactic intentions in *The Faerie Queene,* for it represents a redoing and furthering of *The Faerie Queene*'s central motifs. Although we can never know for sure, it is probable that Spenser was at work on the *Epithalamion* at about the same time he was drafting the Mutability Cantos. In the *Amoretti,* Sonnet 80 refers to his "race . . . / Through Faery land / . . . halfe fordonne." If we accept the validity of Spenser's plan of twelve projected books for the completed *Faerie Queene* which he outlined in his "Letter to Sir Walter Raleigh," this means that with six books completed—the six books of *The Faerie Queene* as we know it—he now had resting space to "gather" himself so that he might "breake anew: / And stoutly will that second worke assoyle, / With strong endevour and attention dew." When he began his "second work" we do not know, but the stress on "eternitie in mutability," on the specificity of time which is the arena of divine action in the mutable, in both the Mutability Cantos and the *Epithalamion,* makes it possible to argue that what we have finally in *Epithalamion* is none other than Spenser's vision of "Sabaoths sight," his perception of the implications for short time of the signs of God's actions within it. Spenser's wedding song is more than a celebration of a particular marriage; it is in fact an image in "short time" of the promised marriage of heaven and earth, the sight of God's Sabbaoth toward which actions like the wedding evoked here finally move. *Epithalamion* is a poem of process; against the background of eternity's circular lines the speaker's process is linear, a movement in time from the temporal to the eternal which time, in the final assessment, makes possible. In addition, this progress is not the speaker's only; if we understand persuasive poetics aright, reading the poem makes its readers potential guests at the poem's wedding feast, participants in the speaker's song, and thus participants in a transformation which opens the possibility of incorporation into the temporal event which is, ultimately, none other than the sight of Sabbaoth, the effective sign in time of the promised wedding supper of the Lamb.

The *Epithalamion* thus becomes a facilitator of the interpretation of human relationships which have a future, which promote the building of Christian community, and which further the work of the kingdom. Spenser charts here the creation of a new relationship based on a mutuality of desire yet which is structured in a way that it can achieve recognition in a public act of a community. What Spenser gives us is a fully domesticated *eros,* an *eros* transformed from disrupter of society to builder of society, especially of a society that anticipates and contributes to a kingdom anticipated and recognizable in words like love and charity and nurture. One way of tracing Spenser's work in *The Faerie Queene,* therefore, is to notice the quests of the knights in terms of their exploration of falsity and illusion and their relationship to success or failure in human interactions. Spenser is not naive about the deep-rootedness of *eros* as a problem for individual and community, nor about the difficulty of making it functional rather than disfunctional in human relationships over time. Neither is he pessimistic, for the finding of a sight of Sabbaoth in the real and particular marriage celebrated in the *Epithalamion* argues for an enduring confidence in human ability, nourished by the community-building rites of the Prayer Book, to participate in the divine redemptive work to overcome human limitations and effect reconciliation, not of myths like "male" and "female" but of real men and women.

In this light, it is worth remembering that at the start of Book II, immediately after the betrothal of Una to Red Crosse at the end of Book I of *The Faerie Queene,* we find Archimago back at his old tricks with Duessa, creating false images, weaving a "web of wicked guile," in ways that explore an undomesticated *eros.* Duessa here, as one Archimago uses to "draw [good knights] from pursuit of praise and fame, / To slug in slouth and sensuall delights" (II.i.23), of course anticipates the figure of Acrasia and her Bower of Bliss, one subject of Guyon's quest in Book II of *The Faerie Queene.* Acrasia as she appears to Guyon is a creation of Archimago ("Her nathelesse / Th'enchaunter finding fit for his intents, / Did thus revest, and deckt with due habilliments" [II.i.22]); one way of describing the issues of Book II is in terms of undomesticated *eros* and male wish fulfillment. We have already suggested that the "cruel steele" that penetrates the heart of Amoret in Book III (xii.38) and must be removed by the actions of Britomart *as a woman* in some sense is a self-inflicted wound based on a distinctively female fear of undomesticated *eros.* Much the same language and situation appear to Guyon in the person and situation of Amavia, whom he meets after being told by Red Crosse who Duessa really is. Amavia, too, has a "deadly smart" in the form of a "bleeding hart" pierced by "cruell steele" (II.i.40–43); again, the wound is self-inflicted, but Guyon cannot cure it. Amavia dies, and Guyon sets out on his quest, which is to respond to Amavia's story of her "smart," the result of her grief at her husband's betrayal of her and death at the hands of Acrasia. Amavia, in "Palmers weeds" (a version of Guyon and his Palmer, without Guyon), has tried and failed to free her husband from Acrasia's powers.

Anticipating the need for Britomart, a woman, to free Amoret, this episode suggests the need for Guyon as male to deal with Acrasia and casts the issues of Book II in terms of male difficulty with undomesticated *eros*. Mortdant, Amavia's husband, lacks the male excuse of an unwilling spouse to rationalize his wandering; Amavia's feelings for him are strongly positive, as revealed by the child (which may be one of Spenser's many versions of Cupid) they conceive together, by her willingness to forgive and forget if he will leave Acrasia behind, by her disappointment at her failure to free him, and by her sorrow at his death. The issue in Book II is not the female as temptress—after all, Duessa here (and her successor Acrasia) is the creation of male image making ("Her . . . / Th'enchaunter . . . deckt"), not some innate female seductiveness. What is of concern to Spenser are the ways in which male fantasy turns women into temptresses, objects of desire, who can be yielded to and then blamed for the yielding, denying abandonment of adult male responsibility. As I have suggested elsewhere, the Bower of Bliss, situated on an island, may well be Spenser's parody of the terms in which early explorers described Roanoke Island, as a new Eden where food grew without human effort and the natives wore no clothing—an image promoted in England which proved disastrous for Raleigh's colonizing efforts because it attracted as colonists those who sought a place promising release from labor and sexual restraint.[64] In any case, the Bower is populated with those who, in the language of the Prayer Book marriage rite, have become "brute beasts that have no understanding" and who "lightly" and "wantonly" seek to "satisfy men's carnal lusts and apetites" (BCP, p. 290), the details of Homer's Circe episode from the *Odyssey* giving Spenser the means to articulate in narrative this language. The Bower, as the terms of description for Roanoke Island make clear, is an Eden of the mind, a place of male wish fulfillment, its full terms delineated in the image of Acrasia and Verdant sleeping after enjoying the delights of "bed and bowre." She holds his head in her lap beneath her "snowy brest" which bears "through languour of her late sweet toyle, / Few drops . . . / That like pure Orient perles adowne it trild, / And her faire eyes sweet smyling in delight" look down on Verdant, who is characterized as a "young man . . . [who] on his tender lips the downy heare / Did now but freshly spring" (II.xii.75–79). This evokes, of course, Mars, Antony, or any number of other mythic figures who put aside their arms to enjoy undomesticated *eros*, but it is also mother and child. So long as the experience of being mothered remains as the dominating object of male desire, that desire will be manifest in fantasy as Bowers of Bliss whose inhabitants are all-knowing, all-satiating, and all-caretaking females who are never found, and *eros* for men is a regression to infancy. Or, perhaps better put, for men to be adult in their sexuality they must understand and put into perspective their relationship with their mothers as at once the source of much that was good but also over, not an available experience in the present. Giving up the illusion of Verdant's desire fulfillment as an available possibility is part of what is required if men are to love real women in real relationships.

In Book III, as we have already noted, Spenser's concern is with myths blocking female participation in full adult sexuality, concentrating finally on Amoret's fear of sexuality which she imagines in terms of wounding, of a painful "smart." Here, also, in the episode of the Garden of Adonis, Spenser gives a positive image of female sexuality and of human sexual generativity to contrast with and expose the duplicity of the Bower of Bliss. Human sexuality (and anatomy) makes possible in the Garden of Adonis a depiction of a grounded and reassuring ongoingness of things, linked to and thus authorized by the divine initiative: "of their owne accord / All things, as they created were, doe grow, / And yet remember well the mightie word, / Which first was spoken by the Almightie Lord, / That bad them to increase and multiply" (III.vi.34). Spenser's task here is to create a mood of reassurance to contrast with Amoret's fear of her own role in human generativity and thus to enable a transformation of that fearful attitude. Of course, in one sense Spenser's ongoing treatment of this issue is to transform the *Amoretta* of Book III.vi.28 into his own *Amoretti* in which the problem of female wariness of love is transformed through bringing it into the story of Easter, in which God's redemptive love of humanity is a call to humans to "love, deare love, lyke as we ought," which will lead to the celebration of adult sexual union in *Epithalamion*. Here, however, Spenser's task is a simpler one, that of linking engagement in adult sexuality with the ongoing life-creating work of God.

One of Spenser's goals, therefore, is to explore how conventional role expectations for women could be enriched to allow for a full and active partnership in an adult relationship characterized by mutual acknowledgement of sexual desire. With women no longer as simply their fathers' possessions to dispose of for the enrichment of the family estate, no longer required merely to endure their procreative roles to ensure the orderly transfer of property from generation to generation, the whole social structure imaging a role for women and an accompanying set of attitudes toward self and other to support that role needed transforming. That is part of Spenser's agenda in Books III and IV of *The Faerie Queene;* it requires an examination of the received images of women and their roles. I have already noted the ways in which Sidney criticizes the Petrarchan imagery and narrative of male sexuality and love in his *Astrophil and Stella;* note now the creation of the "false Florimell" in Book III of *The Faerie Queene.* Made by a witch, she is "in shape and looke / So lively and so like [the real Florimell], that many it mistooke" (III.viii.5). Yet the false Florimell is a literalization of Petrarchan conventions for describing the object of male desire:

> The substance, whereof she the bodie made,
>   Was purest snow in massie mould congeald . . .
>   . . . .
> In stead of eyes two burning lampes she set
>   In silver sockets, shyning like the skyes,
>   And a quicke moving Spirit did arret
>   To stirre and roll them, like a womans eyes;
>   In stead of yellow lockes she did devise
>   With golden wyre to weave her curled head.
>
>   (III.viii.6–7)

Spenser's narrator claims that "many mistooke" the False Florimell for the real one; if so, it must be because they have learned or are to be characterized as having learned to expect women to appear describable in terms of Petrarchan conventions of description rather than as they actually appeared. There is an implicit undercutting of such conventions at work here; I do not believe that Elizabethan readers really needed to wait for Shakespeare to write Sonnet 130 to know that "My mistress' eyes are nothing like the sun." Yet clearly the images inherited from the Petrarchan tradition need to be examined and revised if a new domesticated *eros* is to have its desired effects. The "false Florimell" figure offers Spenser the chance to encapsulate received images of female appearance and behavior, ground them in human fantasy, both male and female, and reject them. He is thus able, in the rest of the poem, to move beyond Petrarchan models of human expectation, to expose the falseness of fantasy images, and to revise and transform the Petrarchan narrative of male/female interaction.

The ending of the 1590 version of *The Faerie Queene,* with Scudamour and Amoret merged so that the reader, "Had ye them seene," is told that he would have thought them one double-gendered creature, seems to arrive at closure more than its predecessor books, yet it leaves open the resolution of Britomart's quest for Artegall and thus provides many possibilities for resumption of the poem and getting closer to Spenser's goal of a twelve-book work. It therefore in the end repeats the deferral of closure we have noted at the end of Books I and II; yet even the apparent "closure" of Amoret and Scudamour must have seemed too much in hindsight, for Spenser unclosed them and deferred resolution of that plot strain in his 1596 version, making the issue of closure even more central, and thus even more problematic, in the books added to the poem in the version of 1596. Since my main concern here is with the *Epithalamion,* I want to leave full examination of that for another place, but I do want to note that movement through Books IV through VI reveals increasingly a sense that public and private are interactive and interdependent so that the domestication of *eros* and the furthering of God's redemptive work cannot be described as happening on any one level alone. Part of Spenser's achievement in *The Faerie Queene* must lie in his bringing us to sense the full arena of human actions, and yet the significance of individual and particular actions within that arena, an awareness that structures the *Epithalamion* in its reaching out to depict and include the human, the natural, and the divine societies in the world that comes to center on the altar and the bed and on the movement of people in relationship to them.

At least some of the direction of Spenser's movement of his text, and of his readers, can be traced in the *Amoretti,* which begins with the Petrarchan roles intact. The speaker is the idealizing creator of images that distance as much as bring into language the beloved's appearance: she is a "soverayne beauty" of whom he claims to be "now with her brightness dazed, / . . . looking still on her I stand amazed, / At wondrous sight of so celestial hew" (*Amoretti* 3, ll. 1, 5–8). His beloved is at once his "Angel," attracting his "hot desyre" (30, l. 3), but in proper Petrarchan fashion also coming "to lead fraile mindes to rest / In chast desires on heavenly beauty bound" (8, ll. 7–8). Yet she is also his "Faire proud (27, l. 1), whose resistance to this desire arises from "so hard a hart" (31, l. 1) and who can be described as "cruell and unkind" (56, l. 1).

The "Lord of love" in the early poems (here Sonnet 10) is an "Unrighteous Lord" (10, l. 1); the first reference to the Anglican calendar in Sonnet 22 (a reference to Ash Wednesday, called the First Day of Lent in Spenser's Prayer Book) involves borrowings from the lessons and Collect to create an image of the self-sacrificial lover of the Petrarchan narrative. The Epistle is from Joel 2, with its promise that God is "gracious and merciful, long suffering, and of great compassion" and its request that "the priests serve the Lord between the porch and the altar, weeping and saying, 'Be favorable, O Lord, be favorable unto thy people.'" The Gospel is from Matthew 6, with its assertion that "where your treasure is, there will your hearts be also." In the Collect for the day, the priest prays that God "Create and make in us new and contrite hearts" (BCP, pp. 108–109). Of this, Spenser's lover makes of his beloved a "sweet Saynt" who deserves "service fit," and so, behaving like "sacred priests," he will "builde an altar to appease her yre: / And on the same my hart will sacrifise" in the hope that she will accept it as a relic "to be kept" (22, ll. 4, 8–14). In these lines Spenser's speaker makes of his love a kind of counter-religion, contradicting directly the instructions of the Ash Wednesday commination rite, which says that "the man that maketh any . . . molten image . . . and putteth it in a secret place to worship it" is "cursed," for God (using Psalm 51 to make this claim) "delightest not in burnt offering . . . [but in] a broken and contrite heart" (BCP, pp. 316, 321). Whatever meaning Lent has for the speaker at this point is to be found in personal and private terms, without regard for the larger perspective sought by the biblical texts.

Yet by Sonnet 57 the beloved has become a "Sweet warriour" who can change her role in the narrative of such relationships. By Sonnet 59 her self-assurance can be articulated by the speaker as a source of happiness, for the one who is loved by a woman so assured is loved indeed. Sonnet 62, a sonnet for the New Year of Annunciation Day, with its emphasis on the blessedness of Mary because of her role in the salvation history, brings an appeal to the beloved that they *both* change their roles in the traditional plot of *eros:* "So let us, which this chaunge of weather vew, / Chaunge eeke our mynds and former lives amend, / The old yeares sinnes forepast let us eschew, / And fly the faults with which we did offend" (62, ll. 5–8). The roles and their attendant behavior characteristic of the Petrarchan tradition on the part both of the lover and his beloved are now brought under judgment ("the old yeares sinnes"), so that since neither emerges a victor, neither need consider himself or herself a loser. Thus the way is clear for Sonnet 63, in which the speaker can see "the happy shore"; for Sonnet 64, in which the lovers kiss and he finds her a garden; for Sonnets 65 and 66, in which the speaker explains why the beloved has gained rather than lost in loving him; and for Sonnet 67, in which the speaker says that it was when both the lover and beloved in this narrative of *eros* were weary of their roles in the traditional version ("When I all weary had the chace forsooke, / The gentle deare returnd the selfe-same way" and "sought not to fly") and accepted new ones ("I in hand her yet halfe trembling tooke, / And with her owne goodwill hir fyrmely tyde. / Strange thing me seemd to see a beast so wyld, / So goodly wonne with her owne will beguyld") that they were able to break with the traditional outcome of the Petrarchan narrative of *eros* and write a new version. As a result, her love of him can now be seen as participating in the resurrecting love of God (it is she "by whom my spirit out of dust was raysed" [74, l. 10]), so that this account of love will bring renewal to later readers and thus become a narrative with an afterlife ("my verse your vertues rare shall eternize . . . [so] / Our love shall live, and later life renew" [75, ll. 1, 11–14]).

The transformation which Spenser inscribes here is revealed in other shifts in language and situation. The two have a real conversation, recorded in Sonnet 75, a contrast to their performer/observer roles of Sonnet 54. He is still drawn to her physical appearance, finding "her paps like early fruit in May" (76, l. 9), but this image is restrained, even realistic, its tone less hyperbolic and contrived than the extended comparisons of her features to the "treasures . . . of the Indias" in Sonnet 15. Her qualities of character, of "gentle wit, / And vertuous mind" (79, ll. 3–4), are still her "trew fayre," but missing is the sense that such virtue is either angelic or perverse. Her hair has become merely "fayre golden heares" (81, l. 1), not the "golden wyre" of the false Florimell or the hair so like gold wire that "which is gold or heare, may scarse be told" of Sonnet 37.

What Spenser is of course performing here is a new language of love, in which the extremities of the Petrarchan roles and their languages are given up in exchange for new ones. These appear on the one hand to be quieter versions of the old ones—he still describes their relationship as one in which she is a superior who accepts him, an inferior—and thus preserve recognizable connections to the old roles and modes of articulation. But they are fundamentally different in what they make possible; namely, a relationship that can continue and take its place in the salvation history, becoming finally an arena of the ongoing divine reconciling activity leading to the kingdom. This is a narrative of *eros* that can lead to *Epithalamion,* not to Petrarchan redirection or to Sidneyan defeat. It is one that allows the woman a role other than passive resistance onto which the speaker projects his own drama; it is one that allows the man to emerge from his own fantasies of *eros* into interactive conversation with one who responds. No wonder that the central image here is not the radical hermaphroditic merger of the first version of the end of *The Faerie Queene* but a taking of hands, in weariness and thirstiness, now dissatisfied with the sterilities that the old modes had come to be, but also in "trembling" at the newness and radicalness of this step (67, l. 12).

Spenser thus realizes in the sonnet form what he had sought on a larger scale in *The Faerie Queene*—the possibility of a domesticated *eros,* integrated into the old marriage forms and transforming them from a place of combat and forced male dominance into a space where new narratives of relationships can be written and rewritten as the way to link present to future. The couple, wed according to the marriage rite in the Prayer Book, give and pledge their "troth" and declare "the same by giving and receiving of a ring, and by joining of hands" (BCP, p. 293). The lover and beloved in the *Amoretti* have already anticipated this by joining hands in a mutuality of "troth," of trust, faithfulness, and confidence on which they will base their futures. It is no accident that in the *Amoretti* sequence Spenser follows the sonnet of joining hands with Sonnet 68, in which the grounds for this rewriting of the Petrarchan narrative of *eros* are declared to be the "Lord of lyfe, that on this day, / Didst make thy triumph over death and sin," not the "unrighteous Lord of love" who appeared in Sonnet 10 and whose demystification is achieved in the *Amoretti* sequence.

Since the action of God which overcomes the separation between heaven and earth, between life and death, between the temporal and the eternal, is an act of love, Spenser argues in Sonnet 68 that his speaker's love, merging *eros* with *caritas* in his feeling for his beloved, is an appropriate response to that divine act. Indeed, this sonnet makes clear that the overcoming of the courtly love dichotomy, which Spenser effects in *Amoretti,* is entirely dependent on the Easter-act of God's love for humanity. In light of this, the biblical readings appropriate for a nuptial Eucharist on June 11, 1594, the one day of that year which fits all the numerical symbolism of *Epithalamion,* are worthy of our attention. William C. Johnson has recently shed light on the *Amoretti* sequence by pointing out in it echoes of the eucharistic lectionary readings for the Sundays of spring 1594.[65] If we extend this approach to *Epithalamion,* some interesting conjunctions appear to help us see how this poem functions as the ring which complements the "joining of hands" effected in the *Amoretti.* "The Form of Solemnization of Matrimony" from the Prayer Book of 1559 begins as the priest greets the assembled throng: "Dearly beloved friends, we are gathered together here in the sight of God, and in the face of this company to join together this man and this woman in holy matrimony." He then declares the importance of the action about to take place by listing a series of biblical images of marriage drawn from both the Old and New Testaments:

> [Marriage] is an honorable estate, instituted of God in paradise, in the time of man's innocency: signifying unto us the mystical union, that is betwixt Christ and his church: which holy estate Christ adorned and beautified with his presence and first miracle that he wrought in Cana of Galilee, and is commended of Saint Paul to be honorable among all men.

The focus of this declaration is on human marriage in time; its purpose is to stress the importance of marriage both in the creation as God made it and also as a sign in time of God's promised relationship with a redeemed creation. Those in the *Epithalamion* who enter into "endlesse matrimony" through "hearing the holy priest" read these words are reminded of the context of their actions in the course of events that constitute salvation history; they find that they participate, through marriage, in the actions of God beginning in the first creation and continuing in the new creation of heaven and earth in Jesus Christ and that they share a common future with those events.

But June 11, 1594, was not just an ordinary day on the Church of England's liturgical calendar; it was also Saint Barnabas' Day, the feast of "Barnaby the bright." Because of that, when the wedding had taken place and the priest obeyed the rubric to begin the communion service, the assembled congregation would have heard read in the Collect for the Day a petition that God "Let us not be destitute of thy manifold gifts, nor yet of grace to use them alway to thy honor and glory." The priest would have also read for the Gospel a familiar passage from John:

This is my commandment, That ye love one another, as I have loved you. Greater love hath no man than this, that a man lay down his life for his friends. Ye are my friends, if ye do whatsoever I command you. Henceforth I call you not servants; for the servant knoweth not what his lord doeth: but I have called you friends; for all things that I have heard of my Father I have made known unto you. Ye have not chosen me, but I have chosen you, and ordained you, that ye should go and bring forth fruit, and that your fruit should remain: that whatsoever ye shall ask of the Father in my name, he may give it you. (John 15:12–16)

The language here reminds us of Christ's own sacrifice and its associations with human love of other humans, as Christ has demonstrated it. Other connections with marriage come in the Gospel's concluding lines: "Ye have not chosen me, but I have chosen you, and ordained you, that ye should go and bring forth fruit, and that your fruit should remain." In light of this reading, the speaker's request, in Stanzas 22 and 23 of *Epithalamion,* for prayers that the wedded and bedded couple "bring forth the fruitfull progeny, / . . . the timely fruit of this same night / . . . a large posterity" which "May heavenly tabernacles inherit" (ll. 403–404, 417, 422) takes on more than conventional significance. Marriage, with its opportunity for bringing forth of marital fruit, becomes a vocation to which people are called, affirming the value of a domesticated *eros* which is then implicated in the appeal for gifts and the grace to use them as a loving response in time to Christ's own love expressed in his sacrifice.

The language which begins the wedding service and the language of the prayers and readings for Saint Barnabas' Day place the love celebrated in *Epithalamion* squarely into the context of Christian love evoked first in Sonnet 68 of the *Amoretti* sequence. A further dimension to this love feast is provided by the wedding rite's exhortation, which quotes extensively from Saint Paul's Epistle to the Ephesians:

Husbands, love your wives, even as Christ also loved the church, and gave himself for it; that he might sanctify and cleanse it with the washing of water by the word, that he might present it to himself a glorious church, not having spot, or wrinkle, or any such thing; but that it should be holy and without blemish. So ought men to love their wives as their own bodies. . . . For this cause shall a man leave his father and mother, and shall be joined unto his wife, and they two shall be one flesh. This is a great mystery: but I speak concerning Christ and the church. . . . And he is also the Savior of the whole body. (5: 25–33)

We have noted Spenser's borrowing from the language of the Song of Solomon in *Epithalamion;* this exhortation links the traditional reading of the Song of Solomon as the love song of Christ for his church to the community enacted by the performance of such rites. Since the setting for the Elizabethan marriage service was the Eucharist (the rubrics instruct the newly wedded couple to receive the Sacrament), the marriage celebrated in *Epithalamion* inevitably occurs in the context of liturgical participation in Christ's redemptive action uniting himself with his people.

If the love celebrated in *Epithalamion* is a response to God's love for humanity, then the wedding itself becomes the action of God uniting that love, even, or even especially, in its erotic dimensions, to his own love of humanity and his furthering the redemptive activity in the world. Even as the rings and circles of *Epithalamion* are signs of the action of the eternal in the temporal, so the wedding which is at the center of the poem is to be seen as a sign of the promised wedding of heaven and earth as well as a means of linking the present to that future. For, of course, in biblical terms what the whole process of human time is moving toward is the transformation of the earthly church into guest and participant at yet another wedding, the wedding feast of heaven and earth at the end of time, depicted so vividly in the Revelation to Saint John:

> And I saw a new heaven, and a new earth; for the first heaven, and the first earth were passed away, and there was no more sea. And I John saw the holy city, new Jerusalem, come down from God out of heaven, prepared as a bride trimmed for her husband. . . . And I heard like a voice of a great multitude, and as the voice of many waters, and as the voice of strong thunderings, saying, Halleluiah: for our Lord God almighty hath reigned. Let us be glad and rejoice, and give glory to him: for the marriage of the Lamb is come, and his wife hath made herself ready. And to her was granted, that she should be arrayed with pure fine linen and shining, for the fine linen is the righteousness of Saints. Then he said unto me, Write, Blessed are they which are called unto the Lamb's supper. (Revelation 21:1–2; 19:6–9)

Such is the context in which Spenser calls us to set the unique wedding celebrated in his *Epithalamion*. The bride of the Lamb approaches the heavenly altar to a hymn sung by "a voice of a great multitude," the "voice of many waters. . . . the strong thunderings"; the bride in Spenser's poem comes to her earthly altar as the woods answer the song "As if it were one voyce" of "the roring Organ" and of "all the Nymphes that you can heare / Both of the rivers . . . / And of the sea." The heavenly bride, the church, is "arrayed with pure fine linen and shining"; the bride of *Epithalamion* with her "sunshyny face" is "Clad all in white, that seemes a virgin best. / So well it her beseemes that ye should weene / Some angell she had beene." The bride of Revelation is a city; the bride of *Epithalamion* is a "pallace fayre" (l. 178). As the angelic choruses of both weddings join in singing "Alleluya," the wedding in Spenser's poem, on June 11, 1594, in all its particularity, is claimed to participate in God's love for his creatures and thus becomes a sign of the divine redemptive activity, a human action of love in response to God's love which is a sacrament of that love, an effective sign of its presence and its ultimate promise for humanity which makes that promise effective for those who participate in it. In this way, it furthers the fulfillment of God's prophecies in Isaiah that he would create a new heaven and a new earth, linked to the "city" as bride in Revelation.

But it is not a static sign. The Collect for Saint Barnabas' Day calls for God to bestow his gifts and the grace "to use them alway to thy honor and glory," and so *Epithalamion* becomes a celebration of gifting. Itself a gift to the woman it calls forth and a "moniment" to the time of its giving, it calls forth the gift of the beloved's hand and enables the woods to bestow their gift, along with the rest of nature and humanity. It also asks of the divine "all thy blessings unto us impart" so that the couple created in this action can give of themselves to "the count" of "blessed Saints."

As an evocation and example of the abundance of giving, the poem extends its range of those on whom gifts are bestowed to include its audience. Sidney's images of persuasive poetics involve giving of instruction and delight that create community because it overcomes the distance between poet and audience characterized in terms of flight "as from a stranger." Spenser's persuasive strategy in *Epithalamion* is to place a wedding before us characterized by a joyous wastefulness—"Poure out the wine without restraint or stay, / Poure not by cups, but by the belly full, / . . . That . . . all the postes and wals with wine, / . . . may sweat, and drunken be withall"—that seeks to overcome separation and thus becomes the metaphor of a copiousness of divine giving and of speech and action in imitation of divine giving. For, after all, the priest prays in the wedding rite that God "Pour upon you the riches of his grace" (BCP, p. 297).

Certainly, Cranmer believed that a copiousness of language transformed those who received it; for him, congregations receiving the Word obtained "that thinge, whiche . . . depely prynted, and graven in the harte, at length turneth [it] almost into nature." Spenser's *Epithalamion* is a poem of process copiously engaged in; that is to say, it delightfully enacts the creation of relationships and the overcoming of separation with such abundance of giving and absence of restraint that its readers, too, are gifted, drawn to think of themselves in its terms as part of its community who can participate in its expression by themselves behaving with copious generosity toward one another.

Spenser thus finds in celebrating a specific wedding a way of replicating the copiousness of God's gift of love in Christ and exploring its significance in terms of time and the formation of community. In the poem, the speaker describes a linear movement in time, a movement through which the lovers, separated at the beginning of the poem, advance toward each other to meet at the altar for the marriage itself. They then move together from the altar to the nuptial bed, and, through anticipating the fruits of that bed, move beyond it to contemplate union among the "high heavens . . . / In which a thousand torches flaming bright / Doe burne" with the "blessed Saints," echoing the language of Te Deum in Morning Prayer. This linear movement in time is set against the circles of eternity expressed in the form of the poem, finally to merge with them in the poem's concluding images of sainthood and endless rest. As the poem ends, we realize that the speaker has in a way come full circle, through twenty-four stanzas and twenty-four hours, to where he began. And yet, of course, he is not where he began at all, but a day later, to be lived in the aftermath of the events celebrated in the day of the poem. That kind of day is one in which we are now taught to expect and embrace not stasis and sameness but recreative rebeginning and the opening-up of the predictable to a copious bestowal of new possibilities. With this merging of the temporal and the eternal, the specific day, June 11, 1594, can promise an end to days, as the specific marriage celebrated in the poem points to the final marriage, now signs in time of the eternal wedding of heaven and earth to come, made possible through the divine activity bestowing his love abundantly on his people.

Because the poem is a process designed to delight us and to move us, we are invited to join the speaker in his linear movement and merge with him toward that kingdom, not into an endless day but through a succession of days. As the speaker moves through the poem in time and with time, he calls on all creation to join him in his song of praise to his beloved; because we are part of creation as readers of his poem we may join in his song and thus join in the procession to the altar and to the bed. The poem's litanylike catalog addresses, in turn, every level of creation in the cosmos, from woods and waters through animals and humanity to saints and angels; at some point in the ascendancy of the human hierarchy of "bachelors" and "fresh boyes," of "damzels" and "virgins," of "servants" and "people / standing all about," of "gazers" and "merchants daughters," of "Choristers" and "young men of the town," all in the poem's audience will find themselves called to a place in the poem's procession. Spenser argues that the occasion he both celebrates and creates in *Epithalamion* is that sort of occasion which makes possible the formation of Christian community Cranmer sought through the documents of the English Reformation, precisely because it is in dialogue with their use that the narrative of *Epithalamion* takes place and replicates their promise of God's copious grace.

Spenser creates in this poem a "reading" in terms of *praxis* of the invitation to the wedding in one of Jesus' parables of the Kingdom of God:

Then Jesus answered, and spake unto them again in parables, saying,
The kingdom of heaven is like unto a certain King which married his

son, and sent forth his servants, to call them that were bid to the wedding, but they would not come. Again he sent forth other servants, saying, Tell them which are bidden, Behold, I have prepared my dinner: mine oxen and my fatlings are killed, and all things are ready: come unto the marriage. But they made light of it, and went their ways, one of his farm, and another about his merchandise. . . . Then said he unto his servants, Truely the wedding is prepared: but they which were bidden, were not worthy. Go ye therefore out into the high ways, and as many as ye find, bid them to the marriage. So those servants went out into the high ways and gathered together all that ever they found, both good and bad: so the wedding was furnished with guests. (Matthew 22:1–10)

The divine generosity, defining love as obliterating human categories like "good" and "evil," thus opens the possibility that acting in accordance with such copious openness is what makes possible the constitution of human community, the opening of closed narratives of human possibility to opportunities as yet unimagined, and the effacing of the category of "stranger" that separates one person from another. In similar fashion, Spenser makes of his wedding poem an invitation, bidding to the wedding everyone whom the poem finds, in the faith that, as the writer of Revelation declares, "Blessed are they which are called unto the marriage supper of the Lamb." Spenser's *Epithalamion* presents us with an image of a marriage, a particular marriage in time whose temporality is stressed by the poem's intimate connections with the particular day, June 11, 1594. But because the poem also conveys signs of divine action, the marriage it celebrates, in all its particularity, becomes a sight of Sabbaoth, a sign of the wedding feast of the Lamb, the constitutive song of the City of God celebrating the union of heaven and earth, in which all time finds its rest and community becomes all-inclusive. And because the poem is intended not only to present an image of the good but to delight us and move us to imitate the good, its intent is also to be a vehicle through which we as readers become members of the wedding party at that particular marriage and thus discover we are blessed guests at the eschatological wedding feast of heaven and earth.

The process of deferring meaning also has its role to play. For if the giving of the ring and the giving of the poem are not conclusive in the sense of producing a final meaning for these actions but instead open up and initiate a process of action which will progressively give the words and actions of the poem their meaning, to be fulfilled only in the final marriage of heaven and earth, of Christ and his church, which will give words like "marriage" their "face-to-face" meaning, so the process of discovering meaning initiated by the poem contributes to our coming to that place and that event. If the poem defers the meaning of the wedding rite until the bedding, and if the bedding itself takes its meaning from the event to come of the final wedding to come, in which the "blessed Saints" inherit "heavenly tabernacles" by becoming members of the "bride prepared for her bridegroom," then the process of reading the poem becomes that process of human loving through which we move toward that final wedding. Such process is engaged in not out of a fullness of meaning, but in faith and hope that such fullness of meaning is to come. Thus, the thrust of Spenser's discourse is toward the opening of possibilities in the closed world of classical images of marriage and poetry, the closed world of human myths about sexuality and about marriage, to make of specific and particular marriages, as they are really lived, moments in the divine salvation history.

The theology of the Church of England, lacking either Catholic purgatory or Calvinist certainty of election, made even more important human relationships with God in time, as the arena in which humanity's ultimate destiny must be settled. Coupled with this, poetry written in accord with the rhetorical theory of persuasive poetry sought to be a vehicle in time for the working out of that relationship. In the Renaissance, therefore, time became of crucial importance. Spenser's *Epithalamion* is not merely "an endlesse moniment" *in* short time, as Hieatt suggests, but "an endlesse moniment" *for* short time, a tribute to time itself, as the arena in which human relationships to God are established. It does so because it is an effective indicator of process, through which those of us who live in short time are made over into residents of eternity. We read Spenser's poem incorrectly if we overlook this element of the role we as readers in time have in the poem, to join in its process which takes us from our own isolation in time to its altar, and from that altar to the bed, to the always-being-completed union of man and woman in marriage which is the effective sign in time of God's Sabbaoth, his eternal resting place, achieved through the wedding of heaven and earth in the risen body of Christ.

Spenser's use of his own marriage in the *Epithalamion* thus serves, like Red Crosse's "sight of the city" in Book I of *The Faerie Queene,* to ground the poem's proclamation in the specifics of time and history in late Tudor England and the aims of the English Reformers. Marriage, the sign of fulfillment and completion in *The Faerie Queene,* here becomes a sign of divine involvement in human history as well as the means to participate in that course of divine action. Even as Red Crosse is, in a real sense, during his fight with the dragon, in the landscape of Faeryland, the landscape of Tudor England, and the landscape of Revelation 22's depiction of the landscape of the new Jerusalem all at once, so, too, the wedding celebrated in the *Epithalamion* becomes, at the end, the "sight of Sabaoth" prayed for at the end of *The Faerie Queene.* To "read" the *Epithalamion* fully is to engage in the life of that nation-church aimed at building up the Christian community. Specific acts of marriage become both proclamations of divine love of humanity and processes through which people move toward citizenship in the future eschatological community of divine promise.

The *Epithalamion* thus becomes a "sight of Sabaoth" and a "ditty of the City of God" because it engages its readers in the biblical/homiletic/liturgical enactment of language that points to the future fulfillment of God's promises. It is precisely the biblical proclamation about God's investing specific moments of time with ultimate significance, realized liturgically in Tudor England, that enables Spenser to make such claims about a marriage on June 11, 1594. To an audience familiar with the rites themselves, Spenser's poem would come as a homiletic proclamation of the significance of those rites, encouraging and enabling them to take on their full meaning. Even as the marriage described in the *Epithalamion* creates around it a society of "virgins," "fresh boyes," "Minstrels," "merchants daughters," "holy priest," and "Angels," and even as it proclaims marriage as one of the foundations of Tudor community achieved through replication of the divine generosity, so Spenser seeks to further the English Reformers' goal of "true Christian commonwealth."

In this, Spenser sought to further the goals of the Church of England during the reign of Elizabeth. By espousing the furtherance of Cranmer's program of religious reform that sought cooperation in God's saving actions aimed at the building up of community and commonwealth, he contributed to the development of the English church as a Christian community in process defined by its worship which was concerned with the future of a culture bound together by a language and a history. As a result, he helped the Church of England avoid the pitfalls of confessionalism and personalistic piety. By creating what is in effect a fictional and imaginative version of Hooker's *Lawes*, he helped place decisively the emphasis in Anglicanism on the experience of a people together interpreted in light of promises recovered from the past and the expectation of their future fulfillment.

It is precisely because Spenser was a layman that he manifests this situation. Later, as we will see in considering the poems of George Herbert, the direction of Anglican concern turned from community as English society, empowered and enabled by the actions of the church within it, to community as church itself with a destiny separate from England as a nation. In that self-understanding, it was appropriate that the role of the priest as the one who calls the community together for prayer and praise would come more to the fore in the articulation of a Christian poetry. What Spenser manifests, however, is a situation in which the poetic voice of religious proclamation could be turned outward toward society at large in a celebratory way, emphasizing the role of the whole *laos* (people) of God in his work. Spenser's lack of

Holy Orders becomes a sign that at least for a brief time in Renaissance England it was possible to proclaim the religious life as the undertaking of all the people of God and not just the professionally religious. As we will see, Henry Vaughan sought the same role for his age, but only when the nation for which Anglicanism was the church prohibited its priests from calling the people together.

· 3 ·

George Herbert

Herbert, Spenser, and the Poetics of Church and Commonwealth

One of the difficulties we face as a result of the way we conceptualize the past is that we imagine normative examples and then define variance from those norms in terms of difference in kind rather than degree. Edmund Spenser and George Herbert are not frequently discussed together; each occupies a different conceptual space, the one "Elizabethan" and "pastoral" or "epic" or "allegorical," the other "Jacobean" and "lyric" or "metaphysical" or "meditative." Some also locate them in spaces marked "secular" and "sacred." In bringing them together in terms of their relationship to a common tradition of understanding Christianity, I intend to locate each as exhibiting different ways of reaching the same didactic goals, drawing on the same liturgical and theological and experental resources, rather than as functioning in different categories or worlds of writing. The experiences of reading *The Faerie Queene* or *The Temple* are different; both, however, have similar intentions—to promote the social agenda of the Church of England, to encourage participation in its worship as the enabling means to further God's reconciling work in the world, promote the reign of charity, and realize the Christian commonwealth.

Herbert's and Spenser's works, I find, are most helpfully conceived as examples of the varieties of didactic writing made possible by the manner and intent of Anglican worship. Certainly Herbert had occasion to be aware of Spenser as a distinguished predecessor. Born in 1593, Herbert moved to London in 1601, where he attended the Westminster School and thus had occasion to see where Spenser had been buried in the Abbey only two years before. He was there, and at Cambridge, Spenser's old university, when the first folio edition of *The Faerie Queene* was published in 1609, to be followed by the first edition of Spenser's collected *Works* in 1611 and a second edition in 1617. He was still at Cambridge when a memorial to Spenser was installed in Westminster Abbey in 1620. Such a chronology reminds us of these poets' proximity in time and of Spenser's growing posthumous reputation when Herbert was forming his own images of what a religious poet might do.

Yet by the time Herbert began to write the poetry that makes him of interest to us, the religious climate in England was quite different from the one that had nurtured and also challenged the didactic skills of Spenser in his desire to "fashion a gentleman or noble person, in vertuous and gentle discipline." One way of marking that change is to note that during the early years of the seventeenth century terms such as "Roman Catholic" and "Anglican" became current for denoting competing religious traditions. Opposition to the episcopate and the Prayer Book in the late sixteenth century had made the term "Puritan" useful to describe those who took such positions; otherwise, the struggle over religion in England was in terms of which group could claim for itself the word "church" among Englishfolk. As Richard Hooker makes clear, the Church of England aspired to become in fact as well as in legal definition the church of, in, and for England. The abusive vocabulary of that time seeks to efface alternatives, to undercut their claims to legitimate existence, thus the blanket use of terms like "Antichrist," "papistical," "so-called Romanish" church. The Church of England, in its reflection on itself, believed it had reformed the abuses of the Middle Ages and recovered the apostolic and thus ancient character and agenda of the church. From this position it attempted to eradicate other alternatives, at least within its own rhetoric. Thus, the Church of England was, to itself at least, the church; rival groups were to be denied the use of the word "church" as a term for themselves.

Yet the emergence of the more neutral and accommodating and parallel terms "Roman Catholic" and "Anglican" suggests that by the 1620s there had evolved for English churchfolk a new sense of self-identity which was at least better defined if more limited and modest in claim than the one implicit in the aspirations of the earlier Reformers. The former term, more polite than "whore of Babylon," emerged during the reign of James I during the negotiations for Prince Charles' proposed marriage with the daughter of the King of Spain; the latter term, an Anglicizing of *Anglicana ecclesia,* the Latin name of the Church of England from the 1530s, also came into wide use at about the same time. With these terms the Church of England now seemed at least grudgingly to accept the existence of alternatives to itself, abroad if not at home, and concede that however distasteful they might appear to an Anglican they were not likely to disappear. In exchange, it got back a sharper sense of its own identity, with clearer boundaries. Herbert's church, unlike Spenser's, could now think of itself as having a life of its own separate from the nation or from other Christian groups. This identity—as in Herbert's terms, "Christians" first and then "Commonwealth's men"—could now be developed and cultivated and celebrated for its work in the world. With the rupture here of the close link between church and nation characteristic of Spenser, Anglicans could now think of themselves as having a future separate from the national future, and thus a role in national life distinct from and within the national life rather than equal to or bound to the national life.

One sign of this, inscribed in Herbert's work, is again in the arena of love and poetry. Spenser transformed the received modes of depicting significant human concerns in poetry, including love and human relationships, often by appearing to set out on the conventional path but radically transforming the terms of proceeding while on the way. Herbert starts his poetic enterprise in opposition: "Cannot thy *Dove* / Outstrip their *Cupid* easily in flight?"[1] And so his poems take on the work of transforming human lives into the life of charity with a more overt acknowledgment of the central place of the church as agency in that transformation. In the process, love comes to be love only in relationship to the church and its Christ and its work.

Thus we may say that for Petrarch love as *eros* exists as a force disruptive of society and of Christian devotion—a sign of a baser aspect of human nature which therefore must be renounced or transfigured into love as *agape* or *caritas*. For Spenser, love as *eros* is real and may be domesticated through being brought within the Christian community by the transforming work of divine love by which *eros* can become part of the work of building the Christian commonwealth. For Herbert, however, love is recognizable as love, whether *eros, philia,* or *agape,* only in terms of the relationship between God and his people as mediated through Word and Sacrament through use of the Prayer Book. The church recognizes itself in terms of participation in that use leading to its realization of itself as a charitable community; in relationship to that process, the word "love" comes to have meaning, whatever its form or manifestation. Otherwise, the language of love is "fiction only, and false hair" ("Jordan [I]," l. 1). In Herbert's perspective, the language of human love, at least as received through the Petrarchan tradition, is "only" convention, like gold wires for blond hair, having no referent unless it comes to have meaning in relationship to the divine love for humankind.

The erotic is not evil; the country parson's decision to marry is a matter of "temper," not a failure to overcome a baser or corrupt nature. Instead, male-female relationships become matters of community concern. The country parson marries (and Herbert married in 1630, before becoming a priest and rector of Bemerton) if his work for the reign of charity is furthered thereby, either because of "the temper of his body" *or* "the temper of his Parish."[2] The wife he chooses (by "ear" rather than by "eye," as in the Petrarchan tradition) is a woman who will conduct herself, rear the children, and discipline the household so as to "make Christians, and then Commonwealth's men." *Eros* is thus an aspect of human living, potentially disruptive perhaps, but able to be channeled appropriately if placed in the right relationship to the future of church and nation.

Thus, the word "love" has meaning for Herbert as human actions promote the loving and reconciling work of God in the world; otherwise, human behavior, of whatever sort, is "false" and language about it "untrue," rather than "evil" or "secular." One of Herbert's goals in his poems is to explore how the varieties of love are to be found in the relationship between God and his people. By transforming the received modes of openly didactic utterance, lyric sequence, and prophetic exhortation, Herbert is able in his own way to recreate the Petrarchan narrative of love as well as to perform a startling and dazzling display of poetic and verbal forms. He seeks to "overgoe" Petrarch by finding in the divine-human relationship, as it is experienced in the Anglican life of worship, depths of variety in love and its forms of articulation undreamed of by the writers of Venus and Cupid.

One of the chief modes of transformation Herbert employs is the speaker's move from the role of lover to that of beloved; many of the characteristics of the speaker in *The Temple* are drawn from the conventions of the Petrarchan lady—hardness of heart, pride, resistance to the lover's advances—who is wooed by God in Christ, thus enacting in poetry the roles envisioned for Christ and his church in the traditional interpretation of the Song of Solomon and other biblical texts. "Love is the lesson the Lord us taught," claimed Spenser, opening the possibility that a man and a woman could abandon conventional roles and write, or live, new ones in Christian community. To discover that we are loved and therefore can love becomes Herbert's text of surprise and transformation in human relationships. For him this is the stuff of daily interactions, informed by the Offices and rites of the Prayer Book and through them in the give-and-take of community life enabled by the love "the Lord us taught." Herbert's is therefore a very "practical piety, and devotion," as Walton called it, getting something, at least, right about George Herbert.

The Practical Piety of The Temple

Herbert's poems come to us as a collection—*The Temple*—with the subtitle *Sacred Poems and Private Ejaculations* and with an epigrammatic quote from Psalm 29 ("In his Temple doth every man speak of his honour"). The temple alluded to in the Psalm is the temple in Jerusalem, and the Psalm praises God for his generosity to his people: he "shall give strength unto his people; the Lord shall give his people the blessing of peace" (vv. 9–10). The Psalms were used in Herbert's Prayer Book in a regular rotation at Morning and Evening Prayer on a thirty-day cycle (Psalm 29 was read at Evening Prayer on day five of the cycle). The Psalter Herbert knew contained 149 Psalms, plus Psalm 119, which is so long that for convenience it was divided into 22 sections, read over a period of three days. The 149 Psalms plus the 22 sections of Psalm 119 add up to a total of 171 songs, or poems, as Sidney reminded us.[3] The numbering of short poems in "The Church" section of *The Temple* varies from editor to editor; Hutchinson's edition has 166, while my edition has 172.[4] Clearly, however one counts, Herbert here calls our attention to the fact that his poems in their conception *as a collection* owe much to the Psalms and their use in the Prayer Book as part of the corporate prayers of the Church of England. Like the Psalms, these poems present themselves as both "sacred poems" and "private ejaculations" (or short prayers uttered in emergencies); in the context of Prayer Book worship, the Psalms become texts that honor God as the source of strength and blessing, that enable corporate and individual concerns to be articulated in the temple, in the presence of the assembly of God's people, since that is where prayer is especially effective in Anglican terms. As Herbert puts it in "Perirrhanterium":

> Though private prayer be a brave designe,
> Yet publick hath more promises, more love:
> . . . .
> Pray with the most: for where most pray, is heaven.
>
> (Ll. 397–398, 402)

The Temple as a title for a collection of long and short poems is an allusion to that activity with words where the temple as the people of God become themselves and recognize what they become, through their speaking in God's honor, as enabled by the Prayer Book. What follows in the book of Herbert's poems is a complex interplay of word, text, and action to further the building of the community of love and promise into the Body of Christ.

The Prayer Book Herbert used in his adult life was the edition of 1604, a lesser-known (compared to the Bible it also produced) by-product of King James' conference with the leaders of the various parties within the Church of England at Hampton Court in 1603. The 1604 Book of Common Prayer is essentially the same as the Book of 1559, with slight revisions in language and rubrics, such as instructions that only priests perform baptisms to meet authoritarian Puritan complaints about midwives performing this function. As a follower of his ordination vow to participate in the daily use of the Prayer Book and its calendars and lectionary, George Herbert read every December 21 from 1625 to 1632 the lessons appointed for the Feast of Saint Thomas the Apostle, including the following verses from the second chapter of Paul's Epistle to the Church at Ephesus:

> Now therefore ye are no more strangers and foreigners, but fellow citizens with the saints, and of the household of God; And are built upon

the foundation of the apostles and prophets, Jesus Christ himself being the chief cornerstone; In whom all the building fitly framed together groweth unto an holy temple in the Lord; In whom ye also are builded together for an habitation of God through the Spirit.

Paul's vocabulary of citizenship is distinctively secular, yet he applies it to the community of the faithful at Ephesus. As a citizen of the Roman Empire, Paul was aware of the special nature of that claim, for it distinguished the status of a free person from those in the empire who were merely captive peoples. He was also aware of the Hebrew heritage of identity as the people of God. Now he uses the term to apply to a new body; in Christ, all distinctions ("strangers" or "foreigners") based on the Ephesians' former relationship to Rome or Israel are effaced in favor of "fellowship with the saints." Paul here echoes a pervasive Old Testament notion; one of the shocking things Israel's God called it to was to overcome innate fear and suspicion of the stranger and foreigner, who was to be treated under the law as one familiar, a neighbor or relative. It is Christ, for Paul, who enables this distinctively Hebrew notion to be adopted by Gentiles.

This also makes possible the claim that what "temple" meant in either the Hebrew or the Roman world has also been transformed; the sacred places of Roman religion where their caste of priests appeased the gods and the temple in Jerusalem, the survival of which was a sign for many Israelites of God's continuing favor and presence, have been displaced into the living temple of Christian fellowship, composed of the faithful themselves, who must welcome the stranger. Paul is, of course, writing to encourage the Ephesians to discover their identity in this new definition which seeks to efface both Jewish and Roman concepts of belonging; his is a didactic text.

The Gospel for Saint Thomas' Day, from John 20, also points to itself as a text for didactic use: "Jesus saith unto him, Thomas, because thou hast seen me, thou hast believed: blessed are they that have not seen, and yet have believed. And many other signs truly did Jesus in the presence of his disciples, which are not written in this book: But these are written, that ye might believe." The Collect for the Day emphasizes the themes of these texts: "Almighty and everliving God, which for the more confirmation of the faith didst suffer . . . Thomas to be doubtful in thy Son's resurrection: Grant us . . . to believe in thy Son Jesus Christ, that our faith in thy sight never be reproved" (BCP, p. 217).

To explore the juxtaposition of these texts as they stood revealed in the context of an act of worship by which Herbert and his congregation at Bemerton could proclaim themselves members of a "holy fellowship . . . he in us and we in him," we might note that Thomas' doubt was for "the more confirmation of the faith"; John's Gospel "writes" of it "that ye might believe," and Paul's Epistle suggests that such writing is of the sort that defines readers as being "of the household of God," enabling the growth of "an holy temple of the Lord." Thomas believed because he touched the body of Christ after Christ offered his body for proof; the Christ of this text offers blessing on those who believe yet who "have not seen." Yet the text itself, as a text for a Eucharist, becomes involved in a "touching of the Body," since it is written that those who see/read it "might believe." So Paul argues that in believing one ceases to be a stranger and becomes part of the Body which is, and is still becoming, "an holy temple in the Lord." The Anglican Eucharist on Saint Thomas' Day enacts a double offering of the Body, in text and Sacrament, to make of one body/temple its receivers, who overcome their estrangement by offering it for reconciliation in the forming of Christ. So there is here beneath the word "building" a constant giving way from noun to verb, so that the "framing" offered in the text is at once a description of what is and an instigation of what is to come. Paul thus evokes an image of a double framing, of the church into a temple "in the Lord," which thus becomes "an habitation of God through the Spirit," God without and within, a double enclosure which is not a freezing of motion into static description but an orientation of motion through the use of words that at once frame the congregation and also unframe and reframe them to incite growth whose end is God and yet whose origins and process are God.

Paul's importance for the English Reformation is never so clear as in such texts in which the significance of Christian community formed by baptism and developed through eucharistic participation stands forth in terms of the image of the Body of Christ. The act of baptism in Cranmer's Prayer Book is an action with words and water through which the child and/or the stranger becomes "regenerate, and grafted into the body of Christ's Church." The act of Eucharist is undertaken that "we may evermore dwell in him, and he in us" as "very members incorporate in thy mystical body." Such references make clear that Cranmer followed Paul, in the many occasions in which he writes to the various churches about their being "temples," in understanding such references as to the corporate body of church, and not to individuals in their private and interior spiritual lives except insofar as individuals are related sacramentally to that body.[5] George Herbert in his *Country Parson* stresses the corporate goal of his endeavors; his goal is "to feed my Flocke," "to raise up their mindes to apprehend Gods good blessing to our Church, and State," to grow "with the growth of his Parish."[6] In terms of this imagery, the "spiritual Temple" is the goal of the ongoing life of the corporate body, life enabled by the Holy Spirit, not spiritual as opposed to physical. In this light, the experience of the individual is not excluded but becomes important as it encompasses the move from stranger to member and, in the recounting, enables participation in and building up of the corporate community of Christians. In the Prayer Book Eucharist, the play of pronouns is suggestive: "I believe" in the Creed but, at the climax of the rite, "we . . . thank thee, for that thou . . . dost assure us . . . that we be very members incorporate in thy mystical body."

At his ordination to the diaconate, Herbert vowed "to serve God, for the promoting of hys glorie, and the edifying of hys people."[7] Taking literally the root meaning of "to edify"[8] as "to raise an edifice," what Herbert offers us in *The Temple* is an extended exercise in "building" in all senses of that word. On the one hand, he creates something written that builds into a *Temple* of words and texts; at the same time, his work constantly reminds us of the church as building through its allusions to the architectural features of a church building and to the activities that take place inside it. Its purpose, however, is to be the kind of writing that will bring its readers to "believe that Jesus is the Christ . . . and that believing ye might have life through his name" by participating even more fully in the "building" of "an holy temple in the Lord, . . . an habitation of God through the Spirit." To participate in the life of the community that takes place in a building (the church) is to give up one's fear of the stranger to participate in the "building" of the Body of Christ (the church).[9] Basic to Herbert's strategies in *The Temple* is this multiple play with "building" as both noun and verb form, in its references to *The Temple* itself as a church built of words and to the process of writing and reading as a process of building, for to read Herbert as he would be read is to engage in the worship of that church as a people on the way, constantly overcoming estrangement, adding to the building, and thus growing into "an holy temple in the Lord," always now a Church Militant on the way toward "time and place, where judgement shal appeare" and with it, but only then, becoming the Church Triumphant.[10] Yet such acts of reading and writing take place in a context in which even doubts or misreadings, like that of Thomas, become part of the way toward "confirmation of faith," in which engagement in process becomes more important than conclusions or "correct" readings of texts or situations.

The thirty-nine years that separate Spenser's proclamation about his wedding on June 11, 1594, and the publication of Herbert's *Temple* in 1633 reveal a profound shift in the relationship between the Anglican church and English society, albeit one that still resides within the dynamics of Anglicanism as a church which understands itself in terms of its common life together made possible by use of the Prayer Book. That shift is manifest in the contrast between Spenser's vision of Christian proclamation addressing directly the whole of English society, claiming it has a role in the divine history of salvation, and Herbert's vision of the church as the primary arena of and context for Christian living. In Spenser's view, the church is leaven, the source of empowering grace to effect the transformation of England into the true Christian commonwealth. In Herbert's view, the church continues to have implications for life in society, but he thinks of them as occupying distinguishable categories and his intention is the incorporation of strangers in a move toward the building up of the church. Especially in "The Church Militant," although history continues to be the context of Christian living, that history becomes defined as the history of the church itself, rather than the broader history of peoples and nations. Indeed, Herbert's work would run afoul of government censors because of his claim that Christianity might be leaving the old world behind: "Religion [shall] to *America* flee: / They have their times of Gospel, ev'n as we" (ll. 247–248). In beginning to separate church from nation by distinguishing them in terms of separate futures, Herbert contributes to an establishing of Anglican identity but at the cost of a sense of estrangement from that nation. Herbert risks becoming a stranger, of setting the church against the nation. This anticipation of the experience of becoming a sect suggests why many English dissenters felt in Herbert a kindred voice in spite of his obvious devotion to the Church of England.

Later, as we will see at the conclusion of this study, Anglicanism would undergo an even more profound change in achieving its post-Restoration manifestation, becoming once again implicated in the broader political and social order, but by means of a much narrower and more negative and defensive self-understanding. Anglicanism, by the time of Dryden's *Religio laici,* would be well on its way to becoming what Samuel Johnson thought of it as being—a minimum set of doctrinal statements requiring intellectual assent and a worship primarily intended to further personal and private devotion. Since this is our inherited frame for locating and interpreting Herbert, we need to be careful to remember that it was still in the future when Herbert wrote his *Temple.*

Nevertheless, events were already well under way which would at least promote such developments. The persistence of the Puritan movement suggests that even among opponents of the old religion adherence to and full participation in the Anglican program for reform of society would not be achieved. Indeed, it can be argued that the Puritan movement was able in the years leading up to the Civil War to take over much of the hopeful thrust of Anglican concern for creating the true Christian commonwealth.[11] At the other extreme, as the events of November 5, 1605, and its aftermath made clear, neither persuasion nor coercion would eliminate all English adherents to the old religion. The persistence of both Catholics and Puritans in making their claims resulted in a heightened awareness among Anglicans of their church as one church among many and not as the sole expression of Christianity in England. Donne's request "Show me deare Christ thy spouse" in Holy Sonnet XVII thus becomes no idle question, as it would have been had Anglicanism's aspirations been realized. This would lead both to Herbert's concern for its well-being and Laud's use of coercion to achieve a minimum level of compliance with his understanding of how its Prayer Book should be used. At the end of the century, having once experienced defeat at Puritan hands, Anglicans would settle for preservation of their legal status rather than again risk survival for a more aggressive stance in regard to changing things as they are.

It must be also conceded that the Anglican movement failed to achieve its goal of creating the true Christian commonwealth. The optimism we noted in quoting John Hales' letter to Protector Somerset—"I [am] fully persuaded . . . that . . . it shall go forward, and set such a stay in the body of the commonwealth, that all the members shall live in a due temperature and harmony"—and in Spenser's exultant vision of the building up of Cleopolis as the way to the eternal city had its later manifestation in the masques performed at the courts of James and Charles, but these works were performed for a small audience of the already converted and only reveal the extent to which those at the top of the social hierarchy were by then out of touch with broader societal developments. Cranmer's vision of a weekly Eucharist uniting all England at the table of Christ's enabling feast was achieved only in cathedrals and some parishes; increasingly prescriptive legislation was required to achieve even quarterly communions in the whole of the church. The grip of the late medieval emphasis on individuality in religious matters was in the end too powerful to break; its revival in a Puritan emphasis on sermons rather than Sacraments as the means of grace and on rigorous self-discipline rather than other-oriented charity proved, finally, the more enduring and effective means of social mobilization.

In any case, Spenser and Herbert represent two emphases in Renaissance Anglicanism, the one of the vision of God's engagement in human history and poetic effort to promote human involvement in that divine activity, and the other of the church as the body through which God proclaims his actions to the world and a poetic effort to promote participation in its transforming work. The biblical voices closest to Spenser's own are the narrative and prophetic voices of the Old Testament with their aim of revealing the actions of God in the history of a people. The biblical voices closest to that of Herbert are the Psalmic voice and, especially, the Pauline voice, which, as we have seen, defines the church as the new people of God by transforming the meaning of words like "citizen" and encourages the life of the church as the historic enterprise through which God acts for the reconciliation of all estranged people to himself.

Herbert's offering of words in *The Temple* in fact represents a complex expansion of the didactic principle enunciated in the Gospel reading for Saint Thomas' Day—"these are written that ye might believe . . . and that believing ye might have life"—through giving examples of the discovery of belief, as in the case of Thomas and as also in the case of Saint Paul, who goes on in chapter 3 of Ephesians to emphasize that the story of his own reception of "the dispensation of the Grace of God" is written "Whereby, when ye read, ye may understand my knowledge in the mystery of Christ . . . to make all men see what is the fellowship of the mystery." To "read" Herbert as he would be read is not merely to experience his poems but to respond by taking part in the "building" which is both an active response of the reader and a description of what God is doing in the world in which the reader can participate by grace through faith, through "the power that worketh in us," in the use of the Prayer Book rites.

Nothing is more difficult about Herbert, or more central to his work, than discussing how in his poems this play between grace and faith is manifest, because in a fundamental sense Herbert must depend on an interchange which is by definition outside or inadequately pointed to by the words of the poems. One of his most explicit references to this amplifies the point. In "The Windows," the preacher of "thy eternall word" is "a brittle crazie glasse," whose words are "watrish, bleak, & thin," since "speech alone / Doth vanish like a flaring thing, / And in the eare, not conscience ring." The act of preaching becomes, in this presentation, at best in itself an opportunity "To be a window" through the offering of language by definition inadequate to the task in the faith that God by grace will "restore the image." In the context of the poem's subject, "The Windows" therefore becomes a prayer that God provide "thy grace . . . [to] anneal in glasse thy storie, / Making thy life to shine within / The holy Preachers; then the light and glorie / More rev'rend grows, & more doth win" (ll. 5–9). This bears on both the subject to which the poem points—the act of sermon delivery in church—and the act of writing and reading the poem in the context of *The Temple* as a building of words. The phrase "Doctrine and life, colors and light" (l. 11) provides clues, for if as a result of this poem one listens to and observes the combination of "doctrine," that text which reflects on what one believes, and "life," the behavior that reveals and informs belief, then the poem has itself become a "window," for it has led to a "reading" which manifests itself in action in the context of the life of the church as a people acting together in preaching and listening and behaving, thus "building" up the "building" both of the "holy temple" of the community and *The Temple* of poems. Yet the function of language here, both in the poem and in "doctrine" as a verbal statement of belief, is to provide the "window" or occasion for divine action and the "colors" for life and light, not to take their place. Opening the world to divine action, giving to life and light color to make them visible, the poem as an act of language becomes an offering of its speaker lending itself to interchanges with the divine. Owing much to the form of the lament Psalm and to intercessory prayer, this utterance emphasizes language's inadequacy on its own and its speaker's inadequacy on his own, yet claims for human speech its appointed role as the vehicle and revealer of divine action. And, of course, it is the relationship between the preacher's words and God's "storie," not abstract "doctrine" about God, that gives the poem's words and the words of the preacher their power. The narrative of God's saving actions, continued through the "windows" of sermons in their liturgical context, enables the claim that it "more doth win." The poem thus becomes a prayer for its own efficacy as well as a proclamation about the efficacy of preaching because God has chosen to use it, both in church and in poems. The poem answers its opening question by becoming a text that makes possible a response that will reveal the presence of divine action furthering the "fellowship of the mystery." Like the relationship between objects like church windows that depict aspects of God's "storie" and preachers who tell those stories in their sermons, act them out in the Sacraments, and use them to understand their lives, the links between "Doctrine and life, colours and light," between texts and readers are found in relationships and interactions ("when they combine and mingle"), not in any part "alone."

Herbert's poems thus become homiletic because they insist that the meaning of "reading" resides in such interactions that require the involvement of the reader. At once skillful creations by Herbert and gifts of God to Herbert ("my first fruits . . . / Yet not mine neither: for from thee they came"), they provoke explorations of issues like "mine" and "thine"—causality, responsiblity, the need to embrace the stranger in oneself and in others—which resolve only in the reader's behavior in response to them. The difficulty in distinguishing between "mine" and "thine" and between God as ultimate and immediate, as hidden yet direct source of all goodness, is part of Herbert's point. The poet/preacher's skill denied becomes part of his offering to the God he proclaims even as his poems become "windows" in human experience with language for a fundamentally transforming encounter, an occasion for the revealing of the divine activity in the world making all things new. Such activity is made known in the reader's response to Herbert's poems; their "meaning" comes to be in that response, through the action they enable and advance. Such texts become extensions of Herbert's priestly functioning in his congregation, because God works through his people, regarding their acts as self-oblations to further his recreating activity.

Building a speaking voice on Psalmic, Pauline, and liturgical models of speech, defining the self in terms of possibilities in relationship with God as revealing of the divine action in human history, Herbert completes the transition we have noted between Spenser's use of the biblical voice of the narrator of events in the sacred history and a voice dramatizing human and divine interaction around or in consequence of those events, between Christian proclamation about human society at large and Christian proclamation about the human society of the church. On the other hand, however, we must be clear that in this shift the audience has not changed; seeking to be coterminous with English society, the Anglican church not only ministered to the spiritual needs of the entire nation but also defined, through universal baptism, the meaning of citizenship in that body politic. What Herbert reflects in his stress on the church is a change in the terms in which that audience is defined as well as a concomitant change in didactic strategy. The same group of people is on the way to citizenship in the New Jerusalem; what has changed is the question of whether or not the life of the nation or the life of the nation-as-church is the center of attention and the arena of growth and transformation. Spenser is of the former orientation, while Herbert is decisively of the latter.

The *Didactic Priesthood of* The Country Parson

Herbert's images of the country parson, and thus ultimately of the speaker in *The Temple,* derive from the rite for the ordering of priests, in the charge given by the bishop to those seeking ordination. In this address, the bishop exhorted the ordinands "to have in remembrance how high a dignity, and how chargeable an office ye be called":

> to be the messengers, the watchmen, the Pastors, and the stewards of the Lord: to teach, to premonish, to feed, and provide for the Lord's family: to seek for Christ's sheep that be dispersed abroad, and for his children which be in the midst of this naughty world, to be saved through Christ for ever. . . . they be the sheep of Christ, which he bought with his death and for whom he shed his blood.

In the midst of such richly biblical and traditional imagery, drawn from Jesus' examples as well as from his parables and from Paul's instructions about appropriate behavior of church leaders, several themes emerge. There is a sense in which the priest here is called to take on a Christlike role; there is also a sense in which the images are drawn from expectations for the behavior of parents toward children. The priest is to teach and protect, like an Elizabethan father, or feed and care for, like an Elizabethan mother:

> The church and congregation, whom you must serve, is his spouse and his body. . . . Wherefore consider with yourselves the end of your ministry, towards the children of God, toward the spouse and body of Christ, and see that you never cease your labour, your care and diligence, until you have done all that lieth in you . . . to bring all such as are, or shall be committed to your charge, unto that agreement in faith, and knowledge of God, and to that ripeness and perfectness of age in

Christ, that there be no place left among them, either for error in religion, or for viciousness in life.[12]

After having defined the priest's role in terms of nurturing and disciplining action to build up the Body of Christ, the bishop then described the contingent nature of the office: "ye cannot have a mind and a will thereto of yourselves, for that power and ability is given of God alone. Therefore ye see how ye ought and have need earnestly to pray for his Holy Spirit. . . . ye perceive how studious ye ought to be in reading and in learning the Scriptures, and in framing the manner, both of your selves, and of them that specially pertain unto you, according to the role of the same Scriptures." Inadequate in and of himself, the priest must always offer himself as one prepared for use by God in his reconciling work.

Herbert's images of the parson, given in his address to the reader at the opening of *The Country Parson,* echo the language of this exhortation, noting that "the way to please [God as a priest], is to feed my Flocke" (p. 224). His definition of the priestly office quotes Paul, but the citation is to a passage that also lies behind the language of the ordination rite: "[the priest] fils up that which is behinde of the afflictions of Christ in his flesh, for his Bodie's sake, which is the Church" (p. 225). Further, his images of the parson's diligence in reading and studying Scripture and his care to make sure that his family and household are proper examples to his parishioners also follow from the bishop's exhortation. Herbert's images thus stress the corporate orientation of the priestly office and the didactic emphasis inherent in the Anglican concern for its role in the building up of the visible earthly Christian community with its dual role as body and bride, as a flock tended by the priest in the place of Christ as the great shepherd, both protector and nurturer, to prepare it for his coming again.

The bishop's exhortation, as well as Herbert's desire to have "a Mark to aim at," makes clear that what Herbert offers us in *The Country Parson* is not so much a description of Herbert's own conduct of his ministry at Bemerton as it is a work written to facilitate the learning of such an image both by the writer and the reader. In this sense, Herbert actually "wrote" *The Country Parson* only as he discovered the meaning of those images in the actual conduct of his ministry and thus became more like his images, even as the reader truly "reads" *The Country Parson* to the extent to which the work instigates changes in the conduct of the reader's behavior. In his discussion of "The Parson Catechizing," Herbert reiterates this and generalizes it to include catechizing and preaching:

in Catechizing there is an humblenesse very suitable to Christian regeneration, which exceedingly delights him as by way of exercise upon himself, and by way of preaching to himself, for the advancing of his own mortification; for in preaching to others, he forgets not himself, but is first a Sermon to himself, and then to others; growing with the growth of his Parish. (P. 255)

By making himself part of the congregation for his own didactic efforts, Herbert thus undermines any claim the parson might have to be a repository of truth to be conveyed to his parishioners. Instead, Herbert interprets the Prayer Book's images of priesthood in terms of growth "with the growth of his Parish," making the process of living the Christian life one of mutual enrichment for priest and congregation alike. The priest's role is one of facilitator of that growth.

The "ordinary Church-Catechism" Herbert refers to as the one the parson "useth, and preferreth" is found in the Prayer Book as a part of the service of confirmation; learning it is thus linked to the process of growth in the Christian life as defined by the progress of official church services from baptism through confirmation to participation in the Eucharist. Providing a textual way station which centers around learning to recite and interpret at least minimally the three basic documents of the faith (the Apostles' Creed, the Ten Commandments, and the Lord's Prayer), confirmation is the occasion at which young people assumed for themselves the vows taken for them at baptism by their parents and godparents, a step for which catechetical instruction was the prescribed preparation. In Cranmer's stucturing of the Christian life in the Prayer Book, confirmation was intended to guarantee a minimum level of knowledge about the Christian faith and to underscore the importance of growth in knowledge for the development of a life-long process of living in relationship to the altar and to the doing of charity. To instruct one's congregation in the catechism is to repeat fundamental texts and to have one's congregation repeat such texts; it enacts a bringing of that congregation into an ongoing interpretive relationship with these texts as well as with the baptismal life itself. By the time one did this very often, one surely knew the words of these texts firmly by heart, as well as the interpretations of them which make up the text of the catechism. Approaching these texts as Herbert does, by defining the relationship of the person to them in terms of growth, suggests that fundamental Christian texts constantly incite change which in turn causes us to read the texts as new texts.

Herbert's discussion of ways of altering the language of the set catechism has been justly noted by Stanley Fish as a model for at least some of the poetic strategies employed in The Temple.[13] I hope now to clarify and expand this point. Herbert's "socratic technique" of putting the catechism's questions in terms of things more familiar to the audience is itself a process of interpretation, but one aimed at creating a situation in which the answers to the catechism's questions come as answers to other questions as well. The catechetical process becomes one of placing the catechized in a relationship to ancient biblical and liturgical texts in a way in which growth in understanding and engagement is more important than the specific interpretation arrived at on any given occasion. In Herbert's view, interpretation is conditioned by things like age and experience, so there is no one interpretation that is "correct" in that it is a final goal to be striven for by everyone. The process of interpreting is thus to enable growth in the Christian life, not to be an end in itself.

We also need to realize that the model of catechizing Herbert has in mind is not exclusively or primarily one-on-one questioning but took place in a group setting in which a given question was the occasion for a variety of answers. Catechizing took place according to the Prayer Book during Evening Prayer on Sundays and Holy Days. The parson, says Herbert, requires that "all" be present for different reasons:

> First, for the authority of the work; Secondly, that Parents, and Masters, as they hear the answers prove, may when they come home, either commend or reprove, either reward or punish. Thirdly, that those of the elder sort, who are not well grounded, may then by an honourable way take occasion to be better instructed. Fourthly, that those who are well grown in the knowledg of Religion, may examine their grounds, renew their vowes, and by occasion of both, inlarge their meditations. (P. 255)

Catechizing thus takes on a role in the parish community larger than its ostensible one of preparing young people for confirmation by bringing them to know and to some extent understand the essential texts of the Christian faith. As the center of community instruction, it appeals to people of different ages in different ways. That is, the same words will be interpreted by various people differently and serve different functions for them according to their various ages, levels of understanding, and depths of faith. What holds this process of instructive interpretation together is not a unanimity of understanding which all have to reach but the liturgical and community context and, related to that, its function as a builder of Christian community.

Although the need for individuals to have a sense of success in interpretation that does arise in a specific moment of interrogation is obviously important to the sustaining of the process, as is their need to be allowed to grow "in an honourable way," the catechizer at least is clear that such senses of resolution are, and are of necessity, only provisional and open to later deepening, expansion, or revision even by the "well grown." In this light, let us look at "Love-joy," one of Herbert's poems from *The Temple* in which questions and answers play a central role:

> As on a window late I cast mine eye,
> I saw a vine drop grapes with *J* and *C*

> Anneal'd on every bunch. One standing by
> Ask'd what it meant. I, who am never loth
> To spend my judgement, said, It seem'd to me
> To be the bodie and the letters both
> Of *Joy* and *Charitie*. Sir, you have not miss'd,
> The man reply'd; It figures *JESUS CHRIST.*

The object referred to here is, presumably (or at least it so becomes in the context of the poem), a window by which God has acted to "anneal in glasse thy storie"; we need to ask how such has happened. The poem turns on an interactive process of dialogue in which two people announce different readings of the same ambiguous sign, but one of them asserts that because the other speaker is right, he is also right. The first speaker, one "never loth / To spend my judgement," interprets the "*J* and *C* . . . / Anneal'd on every bunch" of the grapes as "*Joy* and *Charitie,*" and so the other speaker in the poem interprets them to be Jesus Christ and also tells the speaker that he has interpreted them correctly.

Here is, at once, the juxtaposition of one sort of reading with another sort, the realization that in a profound sense "*Joy* and *Charitie*" is an appropriate and helpful interpretation of "*J* and *C*" if one also accepts that "*J* and *C* . . . figures *JESUS CHRIST.*" In this sense, the anonymous "other voice" acts like Herbert's example of the catechist who "will draw out of ignorant and silly souls, even the dark and deep points of Religion." The poem thus enacts a narrative of interpretation that seems to move from ignorance to knowledge, from letters to words, from image to understanding. One might, from this narrative, assume an intention on the part of the maker of the window to create an opportunity for discovery and its resulting satisfaction on the part of the viewer, except for the fact that the second speaker says the first speaker is both right and wrong. He is right that "J" and "C" may be said to mean, or stand for, "Joy" and "Charitie"; if they stand instead for "Jesus Christ," then he is wrong, at least on one level. He is of course right, but on another level, the level of Christ as encompassing a multiplicity of interpretations, of figurings, of letters making one body.

At the same time, however, the poem suggests that interpretation itself operates in a complex way, for nothing is to prevent the reader from offering his own reading of "*J* and *C,*" as, for example, justice and compassion.[14] To such a reading the other speaker could still respond, "you have not miss'd." In either case, the point is the "building" of the body of Christ through engaging in a process of interpretation in relationship to texts and images and buildings that have windows like the ones mentioned in the poem. Interpretations like that offered by the speaker "figure" Jesus Christ because they promote engagement in the interactive life of the community which is and is becoming Jesus Christ. The second speaker's response is also figuring or acting out *"Joy* and *Charitie,"* delighting in and rewarding the first speaker's interpretation rather than calling it a prideful misreading, so that the first speaker might be encouraged to go on with his process, to see links between joy, charity, and Christ. To realize that the reader's interpretations, although perhaps different from the first speaker's, can also be treated with joy and charity is also an incentive to continue interpretation by making letters into "bodie," engaging more deeply in the life of the institution which gives interpretation its context and orientation. Interpretation here enters the arena in which the point is not the reading itself but the charitable engagement in a communal act of interpretation and the resolution in the proclamation that *any* reading "figures *JESUS CHRIST"* when it operates as both these readings do in the context of biblical imagery of vines and grapes and the eucharistic language of sacramental usage.

As we have seen, the use of "letters" and actions with bread and wine constitutes the "bodie," which realizes itself in such actions as they lead to "charitie." In this light, the role Herbert takes as both writer and reader of his own texts teaches that the process of writing and reading is one of interpreting in such a way that we are oriented not toward coming up with "correct" readings but toward furthering the discovery of Jesus Christ by becoming "the bodie and the letters both." Every particular engagement in this process is at least potentially one of discovery of new ways in which to interpret, so that all "read" Jesus Christ, all interpretations leading to and furthering the life of the "bodie and letters both," the earthly Body of Christ, built through the use of "letters" (the Prayer Book text) which, when used, makes grapes read Jesus Christ. Herbert's point, following Erasmus, is that a copiousness of reading is enriching of the community when all are brought into a charitable relationship with the eucharistic process of the corporate Christian life. The second speaker's role in this is important because it affirms the interpretation of the first speaker and provides the terms in which that affirmation is possible, not only of the first speaker's interpretation but of potential ones by the reader as well, since it is when two or three are gathered in his name that Christ is with his people.

In Herbert's view, as expressed in *The Country Parson,* this process was not over at confirmation, but could be engaged in with profit by people of all ages. Learning to interpret so that in whatever new particular situation of life the old and familiar words could take on the reinvigoration of being found to figure *"JESUS CHRIST"* is thus central to the parson's calling, both for himself and for his parishioners. Herbert's didactic efforts mirror the whole Prayer Book enterprise in which the play of texts from the lectionaries, the variable Psalms and prayers, and the set texts of the rites and Offices enact discrete and particular interpretations in light of their historical context in the corporate life that subsumes the individual lives of the participants. The "individual" in Herbert's poems is realized in terms of a specific interpretive stance; the many times in which such a stance is undercut, although without uncharitable delight in proving someone wrong, reflect Herbert's emphasis on mutually enriching conversation about interpretation rather than on the importance of reaching a "correct" conclusion. It is the process of charitable conversation that leads to the building up of the Body of Christ, not an exclusionary desire for someone to arrive at truth. One reaches the goal of discourse for Herbert when one is engaged in the actions that lead to the corporate goal—that is, the worship of the church—and it is to that which Herbert's poems always point us as readers.

Herbert's images of the country parson are consistently didactic, of which the two most significant manifestations are personal example and homiletic discourse, under which I would group catechizing, preaching, and personal reproof or commendation. "The Countrey Parson's Library is a holy Life," says Herbert, for "even it selfe is a Sermon" (p. 278); so all aspects of his life and that of his household are organized to serve as growth-producing examples of the faith. Further, "the Forme and Character of a true Pastour," Herbert claims, is shaped in terms of his teaching function:

> there being three points of his duty, the one, to infuse a competent knowledge of salvation in every one of his Flock; the other, to multiply, and build up this knowledge to a spirituall Temple; the third, to inflame this knowledge, to presse, and drive it to practice, turning it reformation of life. (P. 255)

"Inflaming" is the task of the sermon, for the sake of which the preacher is to use "all possible art." On the other hand, "to infuse a competent knowledge of slavation" is the task of catechizing. Herbert judges catechizing especially effective because it involves direct address to individuals to alert them to the necessity of interaction by which identity is realized: "at Sermons, and Prayers, men may sleep or wander; but when one is asked a question, he must discover what he is" (p. 257). Note here that both for the parson and the parishioner the "self" or "what he is," the significant sense in which these people have a self to discover and know, is found in interactions and not apart from the community which forms the context for those interactions.

We will have occasion to return to this method of promoting self-discovery at a later point; now, however, I want to note how Herbert is concerned here, as with preaching, for "particularizing of his speech," for finding through a copiousness of approach the method that will make contact with the different particular situations of his parishioners. Of the act of preaching, he says,

> When he preacheth, he procures attention by all possible art, both by earnestnesse of speech . . . and by a diligent, and busy cast of his eye

on his auditors. . . . He often tels them, that Sermons are dangerous things, that none goes out of Church as he came in, but either better or worse. (Pp. 232–233)

"Particulars ever touch, and awake more then generals": the preacher, according to Herbert, combines "stories and sayings they will well remember" with "hart-deep" cloaking of "words and sentences in our hearts, before they come into our mouths" and with direct addresses or "Apostrophes to God." What makes the sermon memorable and effective as an act of speech are both the content and the manner of delivery ("earnestnesse of speech" and "a diligent, and busy cast of his eye on his auditors"), all within the context of Prayer Book worship. Here, narrative ("stories they will well remember"), including the narrative of interpretation, has a central role to play.

In the case of personal reproof or commendation, Herbert is also concerned to make the speech fit the situation in which the hearer finds himself and his own position in life. "Blessing," says Herbert, "begets a reverence, and makes him esteemed according to his Profession" (*CP*, p. 286); part of the parson's calling is to comfort the sick, to commend acts of charity, to praise learning, and to encourage such behavior among his parishioners. Another part of his calling involves correction; here again he seeks to present his observations in ways that suit them to their intended hearers:

Those that the Parson findes idle, or ill imployed, he chides not at first, for that were neither civill, nor profitable; but always in the close, before he departs from them: yet in this he distinguisheth; for if he be a plaine countryman, he reproves him plainly; for they are not sensible of finenesse: if they be of higher quality, they commonly are quick, and sensible, and very tender of reproof: and therefore he lays his discourse so, that he comes to the point very leasurely, and oftentimes . . . in the person of another, making them to reprove themselves. (P. 248)

Even as in the case of catechizing and preaching, Herbert's emphasis here is on suiting the didactic methodology to the situation and to the person; in each case, the goal is to find that approach which will produce the response Herbert seeks. At the same time, Herbert is aware that the same discourse may be effective with different persons in different ways, all of which are acceptable so long as they incorporate the taught into the ongoing activity of interpreting rather than shut any out.

Herbert's verbal strategies thus work to create moments of interpretation for people at different conceptual levels; for Herbert, any word is far more than just "this or that" but in fact is the occasion for an inexhaustible list of interpretations the process of engaging in he desires to set in motion. As in the case of "charity," the process of reading Herbert is to participate in interpretation so that what results is action which provides the real definition:

To Charity is given the covering of sins, *1 Pet. 4.* 8. and the for-givenesse of sins, *Matthew 6.* 14. *Luke 7.* 47. The fulfilling of the Law, *Romans 13.* 10. The life of faith, *James 2.* 26. The blessings of this life, *Proverbs 22.* 9. *Psalm 41.* 2. And the reward of the next, *Matth. 25.* 35. In brief, it is the body of Religion, *John 13.* 35. And the top of Christian vertues, *I Corin.* 13. Wherefore all his works rellish of Charity. (P. 244)

Herbert's interpretive scheme here weaves biblical references into allusions to creedal formulas ("I believe in . . . the Forgivenesse of sins: the Resurrection of the body: and the Life everlasting") and to the eucharistic body, placing his definition in the context of Cranmer's own claims for charity as the fruit of a true and lively faith and the consequence of eucharistic participation. Thus, all the didactic activities of Herbert's country parson are framed by Prayer Book worship, notably on Sunday:

having read divine Service twice fully, and preached in the morning, and catechized in the afternoone, he thinkes he hath in some measure, according to poor, and fraile man, discharged the publick duties of the Congregation. The rest of the day he spends either in reconciling neigh-bours that are at variance, or in visiting the sick, or in exhortations to some of his flock by themselves, whom his Sermons cannot, or doe not reach. And every one is more awaked, when we come, and say, *Thou art the man.* (P. 236)

Since *The Temple* begins at this point—"Thou . . . / Hearken unto a Verser . . . / A verse may finde him, who a sermon flies"—it is appropriate to ask what we might expect of Herbert's didactic strategies in his poems. In the first place, the poems themselves reflect Herbert's anticipation of a variety of situations and personal locations in the common journey toward building up the earthly Body of Christ, the church. In this light, we may define the audience of "The Church Porch" in Herbert's terms as those who might "fly a sermon," who need encouragement in terms of readily understandable moral and ethical choices to begin to orient their lives toward fuller participation in the body which positions them to hear what the speaker has to say, including Herbert as part of the audience for his own texts. The most significant move-ment in the long poem "Perirrhanterium" is from the opening address to one "who a sermon flies" to the conclusion, which gives intruction for listening to a sermon, suggesting the direction Herbert would have his reader take in response.

Again, the audience for the poems in "The Church" consists of all those who are "holy, pure, and cleare, / Or that which groneth to be so"; Herbert enacts a copiousness of strategies, a veritable multitude of different ways of teaching along the lines Herbert gave in *The Country Parson* for preaching, catechizing, and blessing or reproving. In "The Church Militant," we find a text aimed at an audience "groning" to be "holy, pure, and cleare" but needing encouragement to prevail in its efforts. In each case, however, the focus is on the church, on the ongoing life of that community which Herbert says the priest is to care for, to inform and inflame, and to "drive . . . to practice, turning it to reformation of life." In "The Church Porch," the movement of "Perirrhanterium" is from isolated and individual existence in the world to gathering "Where it is warmest . . . / Pray with the most." In "The Church," we are never more than a few poems from those which remind us of the church itself, either as the building which houses worship or as the ongoing liturgical life which creates and enables worship and thus the discovery and furtherance of Christian identity. In "The Church Militant," the focus is on the history of that institution, from its beginnings through the present of Herbert's address to that future "where judgement shall appear."

What follows is a description of some of these strategies in more detail. Herbert makes clear in *The Country Parson* that the task of the priest is to find his congregation where it is and address himself to it in ways that will evoke responses from everyone. At the same time, as he demonstrates in his discussion of catechizing, people in different places will respond in different ways, all potentially helpful, to the same process of instruction. Rather than postulate a single, overarching structures for *The Temple,* other than the broader task of building, I find it more helpful to notice the various structures *The Temple* incorporates within itself in terms of Herbert's rhetorical, didactic conversation with his readers and to see all those structures subsumed in the single continuing reference to the ongoing life of the church, which includes a wide variety of instruction, prayer, preaching, and sacramental worship in their individual and corporate dimensions.

With this in mind, we may now move through *The Temple,* noting as we go the various stances and strategies of the speaker as he seeks to encounter his readers and to incorporate them in a movement that he is himself a part of. Although I do wish to group a number of the poems together as examples of various strategies, I do not pretend to exhaust the possibilities; instead, I only hope to illuminate a few of those strategies. These are strategies that turn on *opening* rather than closing interpretation, on the discovery of possibilities of meaning in regard to the reader that renders reading these poems "dangerous," both to the human striving for processes of intellection that bring order and stasis out of experience and to concepts of language that reinforce such images. To "build" the temple of the church is to "let go," to use Stanley Fish's term,[15] but it is also to discover that a full reading of Herbert is found not merely in interior processes of intellection, even self-defeating ones, but in an offering of the self, an opening of the self to participation in knowledge which in Herbert's terms is a participation in the ongoing work of the Spirit for the building up of the church and the redemption of the world. For Herbert, like Sidney, *praxis* is the fruit; his parson seeks above all to "inflame knowledge, to presse, and drive it to practice, turning it to reformation of life" (*Country Parson,* p. 255).

The Dialectics of Choice in "The Church Porch"

Herbert begins *The Temple* with a clearly preparatory or transitional section, "The Church Porch," which starts with a rhetorical invitation to the reader aimed at enlisting his involvement in a text that "may chance / Ryme thee to good." Herbert's stance and mode of address in "Perirrhanterium" begin by assertively seeking to move the reader toward changes in his behavior. The tone of this poem is best characterized as an example of "earnestnesse of speech," valued by Herbert because, he believed, "it being naturall to men to think, that where is much earnestness, there is somewhat worth hearing" (*Country Parson,* p. 232). By proposing choices of actions and by judging them, he asks the reader to locate himself within such categories, to decide where he is, and to move toward amendment. The movement here is strongly linear, through what begins with a reaching out for the sermon-flier, then broadens its scope to encompass a variety of readers and situations and moves those so "found" toward enclosure within the church itself and within the life now enclosed in this process of examination, definition, and interpretation that the poem sets in motion.

The intent and occasion of "The Church Porch" are illuminated by realizing the close links between the Prayer Book catechism and the rite of confirmation.[16] In Herbert's day, according to the Prayer Book, "there shall none be admitted to the Holy Communion, until such time as he can say the catechism, and be confirmed" (BCP, p. 289). Confirmation is a rite in which the "youth" make for themselves the promises made in their names by their parents and godparents at baptism and receive through the bishop's laying on of hands a "strengthening" with the Holy Spirit so that they may have "increase . . . [of] thy manifold gifts of grace" to "continue thine forever" and "in the end . . . obtain the everlasting life." Confirmation thus is a rite of growth, of living-on-the-way, which admits the confirmed to full eucharistic fellowship in the church. It is a rite that marks the achievement of a certain age and level of understanding among those who are ready to move onward. Those who receive it are already baptized and therefore "have all things necessary for their salvation, and be undoubtedly saved" (BCP, p. 283), so that what is marked by confirmation is an entry into the full process of adult growth and nurture in the Christian life.

In this light, the catechetical tone of "Perirrhanterium" becomes appropriate as a transition between a situation of "flying a sermon" (avoiding the rites of the church) and "approaching" to "taste / The churches mysticall repast" ("Superliminare," ll. 3–4), entering into that eucharistically centered life which is explored in "The Church" section of *The Temple*. The self-acceptance of baptismal vows by the confirmand is prepared for by learning from the catechism that his life is implicated in that of active charity; as a renewal of baptismal vows, the teachings of the catechism and of "Perirrhanterium" are thus appropriately referred to as a "sprinkling" ("Superliminare," l. 2), because they take their meaning from the rite of baptism in relationship to the process of growth in age and in the Christian life through time and thus signal a continuation and development of the effects of baptism by water and the Holy Spirit.

The argument and content of "Perirrhanterium" represent an expansion in hortatory fashion of the response to the question "What dost thou chiefly learn by these commandments?" in the Prayer Book catechism. As in the catechism, the answers (or, in this case, the exhortations) come in terms of traditional lists of vices and virtues. In fact, Herbert evokes the traditional list of the seven deadly sins:

> Beware of lust (l. 7)
> Boast not (l. 50)
> Lie not (l. 73)
> Flie idlenesse . . . / O England! full of sinne, but most of sloth
>   (ll. 79, 91)
> Look on meat, think it dirt, then eat a bit (l. 131)
> Be thriftie, but not covetous (l. 151)
> Envie not greatnesse (l. 259)
> Be calm in arguing: for fiercenesse makes / Errour a fault (l. 307)

He also evokes the traditional virtues:

> Abstain wholly, or wed (l. 13)
> Drink not the third glasse (l. 25)
> Take not his name, who made thy mouth, in vain (l. 55)
> Dare to be true (l. 77)
> Do all things like a man (l. 121)
> Be thriftie (l. 151)
> Be sweet to all (l. 211)
> Towards great persons use respective boldnesse (l. 253)
> Thy friend put in thy bosome (l. 271)
> Entice all neatly to what they know best (l. 295)
> Be usefull where thou livest (l. 325)
> Scorn no mans love (l. 348)
> In Almes regard thy means, and others merit (l. 373)

If we note the Prayer Book text which lies behind these lists, we can see in "Perirrhanterium" an expansion and specific applicative interpretation of Christ's community-oriented summary of the law:

Question: What is thy duty towards thy neighbor?
Answer: My duty towards my neighbor is, to love him as myself. And to do to all men as I would they should do unto me. To love, honor, and succor my father and mother. To honor and obey the king and his ministers. To submit myself to all my governors, teachers, spiritual pastors, and masters. To order myself lowly and reverently to all my betters. To hurt nobody by word nor deed. To be true and just in all my dealing. To bear no malice nor hatred in my heart. To keep my hands from picking and stealing, and my tongue from evil speaking, lying, and slandering. To keep my body in temperance, soberness, and chastity. Not to covet nor desire other men's goods. But learn and labor truly to get mine own living, and to do my duty in that state of life, unto which it shall please God to call me. (BCP, p. 286)

Here, the traditional virtues have been given a strongly social interpretation; they are not behavioral practices which can be understood in isolation as the actions of one alone or before God, but describe possible behaviors among persons in a community which goes corporately before God to confess its shortcomings and to be forgiven and made once more "very members incorporate in the mystical body of thy son."

The rhetorical frame for Herbert's expansions on the catechetical model is one that actively "seeks" different persons in different situations and thus aspires to reach an ever-wider audience. Starting with the one "whose sweet youth and early hopes inhance / Thy rate and price, and mark thee for a treasure," Herbert's homiletic voice moves outward as he first considers those who might "sinne in wine or wantonnesse," instructing them not to overindulge and then addressing those who do: "Yet, if thou sinne . . . / Boast not thereof." His course through the sins also expands to include more and more groups: "Art thou a Magistrate? then be severe: / If studious, copie fair, what time hath blurr'd" (ll. 85–86). He also addresses those with "sonnes," those who need direction in spending money, those who "play," those who need advice in conduct toward "great persons," those who are "single," who are guests, and many others; the effect is to catch up more and more "sorts and conditions" of humanity in the sweep of his discourse. Like Spenser listing the guests invited to the wedding in *Epithalamion,* his scope is sufficiently wide to include at least once, and probably more than once, all of those he imagines making up the audience for this poem.

The end of the poem brings this diverse gathering to church: "Though private prayer be a brave designe, / Yet publick hath more promises, more love . . . / Pray with the most: for where most pray, is heaven" (ll. 396–402). Herbert continues to give instructions for behavior in church that apply to all: "Bring not thy plough, thy plots, thy pleasures thither." In the end, the rhythm of the examined life takes its paradigm from the two Daily Offices of Morning and Evening Prayer: "Summe up at night, what thou hast done by day; / And in the morning, what thou hast to do" (ll. 451–452). These lines allude to the motifs of these two Offices as defined in their Collects. In the evening, Anglicans asked, "Give unto thy servants that peace which the world cannot give, that both our hearts may be set to obey thy commandments, and also that by thee, we being defended from the fear of our enemies, may pass our time in rest and quietness" (BCP, p. 64). In the morning, they requested, "Defend us . . . with thy mighty power; and grant that this day we fall into no sin, neither into any kind of danger, but that all our doings may be ordered by thy governance, to do always that is righteous in thy sight" (BCP, p. 60).

On one level, we are in this poem at the simplest function of language in didactic discourse—the giving of instruction and reproof—and the poem is aimed at an audience which would respond at such a level. That is, implicit here is a view of language in which the words of the text will have meaning in the sense that warnings to avoid certain kinds of behavior and follow others can be easily translated from the specific moment of reading into specific expression in behavior. In this context, the interpretation of language poses no major problem. But there are also those readers who will raise questions about what such general terms as lust, envy, and sloth or love, alms, and thrift really mean. In part, Herbert has anticipated that response by the copiousness of examples he gives; on another level, however, he offers a more subtle answer. The response to the poem by a reader is put into the context of procession to church; as in the Great Litany, to begin to act as Herbert directs is to locate oneself in the context of such a procession. When Herbert gets his readers into church, the question of interpretation comes once more to the fore:

> Judge not the preacher; for he is thy Judge:
> If thou mislike him, thou conceiv'st him not.
> God calleth preaching folly. Do not grudge
> To pick out treasures from an earthen pot.
> > The worst speak something good: if all want sense,
> > God takes a text, and preacheth patience.

Presenting a case which he will articulate more subtly in "The Church," Herbert here puts the burden of dealing with inadequate preaching (a major charge of the Puritan party against mainstream Anglicans) on the shoulders of the hearer who objects. The act of objection is a self-judgment, requiring reinterpretation of the situation, the content of the sermon, and the roles of preacher and hearer. If what the hearer desires is not found, then the problem lies with the hearer, not the preacher. Indeed, Herbert goes on, patient endurance of bad preaching and the blessing even a bad preacher gives with full efficacy (the sacramental dimension of priesthood here again pointing up Herbert's difference from the Puritan understanding of the nonsacramental minister who functions effectively only in a good sermon) makes church attendance worthwhile:

> He that gets patience, and the blessing which
> Preachers conclude with, hath not lost his pains.
> He that by being at church escapes the ditch,
> Which he might fall in by companions, gains.
> He that loves Gods abode, and to combine
> With saints on earth, shall one day with them shine.

Herbert's point here is that engaging in a common action with the company—"saints on earth"—of gathered people is what is most important about church, not the efficacy of the sermon. It is the priest's role in that community, not the skill with which an individual might or might not fill that role, that is of importance:

> Jest not at preachers language, or expression:
> How know'st thou, but thy sinnes made him miscarrie?
> Then turn thy faults and his into confession:
> God sent him, whatsoe're he be: O tarry,
> And love him for his Master: his condition,
> Though it be ill, makes him no ill Physician.
>
> (Ll. 427–444)

In one way, this is an injunction to make the best of church, including the quality (or lack thereof) of the preacher and his sermon. It functions as a response to the Puritan charge that Anglican preachers were dull and unlearned and the use of set prayers was repetitious and distancing. In another, however, it is an invitation to the kind of "misreading" we noted earlier that makes all signs in the context of Prayer Book worship "figure *JESUS CHRIST*," or makes of the act of preaching an opportunity for God to be seen as the real preacher, because it makes the full act of discourse dependent on the response of the reader or hearer to God's use of the speaker and not to the speaker himself. In this context, preaching becomes divine "folly," human speech in full knowledge of all its difficulties and complexities which makes sense only in that God has chosen it as the means of furthering his activities, which may in fact necessitate the freeing of language from its conventional usage if it is to reveal the divine activity. Thus, even bad preaching has its utility, and even if we must question the universal effectiveness of the kind of language Herbert has engaged in heretofore in "Perirrhanterium," we can rest in the assurance that whatever words like abstract terms for sins and virtues will be found to mean, they take on their effective meaning in the context of corporate Anglican worship.

At one level, therefore, "Perirrhanterium" employs a very straightforward didactic strategy, appropriate for the relatively untutored, which instructs in personal conduct and directs all such efforts toward right conduct in church. At the same time, however, Herbert begins a more complicated rhetorical strategy which will ultimately have a major role to play in the poems of "The Church." He is, after all, building a church with poetry in both senses—in the book and in the world—and to read "Perirrhanterium" is to be sprinkled with holy water preparatory to entering "The Church" section of *The Temple* as well as the church itself as a body of Christians. The purifying use of holy water characteristic of the medieval church has become, in accord with Cranmer's transformation, a metaphor for a reorientation of behavior.

The one who truly would "flie a sermon" is not to be won back with a mere list of precepts; if Herbert's intention in *The Temple* is to "Ryme [us] to good . . . / And turn delight into a sacrifice," we need to notice the ways in which he seeks to engage and involve such a reader, through the experience of reading, so as to persuade him to change his behavior. The short poem "Superliminare," which ends "The Church Porch" and provides a "doorway" to "The Church," provides us with some clues as to how Herbert seeks the kind of persuasive engagement with the reader that is essential to the achievement of his task in *The Temple:*

> Thou, whom the former precepts have
> Sprinkled and taught, how to behave
> Thy self in church; approach, and taste
> The churches mysticall repast.
>
> Avoid Profanenesse; come not here:
> Nothing but holy, pure, and cleare,
> Or that which groneth to be so,
> May at his perill further go.

The two quatrains which make up this short poem form a bridge between "Perirrhanterium" and what follows in "The Church." Like all bridges, this one at once makes connections between two separated points and reminds us of the gulf that separates them, making the bridge itself necessary. The heavy ruled line that divides, or joins, these stanzas in some early editions of *The Temple* reemphasizes the point. This poem marks a kind of line to cross, or a threshold distinguishing one space from another. One knows, upon reading this poem, that a moment of decision or of significant transition, or of the making of distinctions, has occurred. The first quatrain centers on the word "approach"; it offers the reader of the work who has responded to the "precepts" of "Perirrhanterium" an invitation to the rest of the volume: "approach, and taste / The churches mysticall repast." But although we know that the next section of the work is entitled "The Church," the use of the possessive form and the phrase "mysticall repast," with its eucharistic overtones, reminds us that "church" is both the next section of *The Temple* and the literal Church of England of which Herbert was a priest. In a way not yet clearly defined although clearly evoked, learning from "the former precepts" is preparing us both for reading the next section of *The Temple* and for participation in the actual eucharistic community of the church as a visible institution.

On the other hand, if the first quatrain of this poem centers on invitation, the second quatrain emphasizes exclusion. The key word is "avoid," made more emphatic by its placement as the first word in the stanza. The tone of the second quatrain reminds us that the invitation issued in the first carries with it a qualifying clause: "Thou, *whom the former precepts have / Sprinkled and taught, how to behave / Thy self in church;* approach" (emphasis mine). The reader is now brought to a position of having to evaluate whether he has in fact been "Sprinkled and taught, how to behave" by reading "Perirrhanterium." The second quatrain reinforces this sense of the need for choosing between two possible self-definitions: "Nothing but holy, pure, and cleare, / Or that which groneth to be so, / May at his perill further go."

These quatrains thus provide a set of categories which apply to the reader as reader of *The Temple* and also as (potential) participant in the full eucharistic life of the church. Indeed, the parallels Herbert creates between the structure of his poem collection and the architecture of a church building suggest that what applies to the informed reader of Herbert's poems also applies to him as a member of the visible worshipping community. Since the words Herbert uses to define the sections of his poem collection apply literally to the church building and only metaphorically to the poems, what we learn about reading *The Temple* and from reading *The Temple* is employed completely and realized fully only through participation in the activities within the church (building), not through reading within "The Church" (poems).

But Herbert is also using the relationship between the two "churches" to bring pressure to bear on the reader of his poems. Let us consider briefly the position in which the reader of *The Temple* finds himself at this point in his reading. Herbert, in *The Country Parson,* notes the confrontational nature of Christian proclamation. The parson, he says, "often tels them, that Sermons are dangerous things, that none goes out of Church as he came in, but either better, or worse" (p. 233). What Herbert is in effect asking of his reader in

"Superliminare" is to decide whether, after reading "Perirrhanterium," he is better or worse. The two quatrains of this poem urge the reader, for the sake of reading as well as attending church, to evaluate himself in terms of the set of categories provided in the poem. Has the reader learned "how to be-have / Thy self in church"? Is he "holy, pure, and cleare"? If not (and who is?), is he at least one "which groneth to be so"? If none of these categories applies, Herbert insists, the reader had best turn away.

What Herbert offers here is thus a complex interplay of incentives and disincentives, both in terms of reading and church going. To be permitted to read on is itself an incentive to conform to the categories Herbert offers, another linking of the reading and the reforming processes. In any case, the reader, brought to a point of self-analysis by a confrontation with categories of evaluation in terms of which he will find himself "either better or worse" than he thought he was as he (more or less) innocently began to read through "Perirrhanterium," is thus led to discover "what he is" (*CP*, p. 257), but such self-definition is created in terms of the reader's relationship to "The Church" as text and the church as worshipping body, not as he is apart from them.

If we can see in these quatrains a connection being made between how one reads and how one behaves, we must say that the stress in "Perirrhanterium" is on the behavioral, personal-conduct-of-life side of this relationship. In this long poem a single pattern is repeated. To a series of issues involving personal and social conduct, Herbert offers a prescription for behavior, then defines both sides of the reader's alternatives. Stanza 3 provides a paradigm:

> Abstain wholly, or wed. Thy bounteous Lord
> Allows thee choise of paths: take no by-wayes;
> But gladly welcome what he doth afford;
> Not grudging, that thy lust hath bounds and staies.
>> Continence hath his joy: weigh both; and so
>> If rottennesse have more, let Heaven go.

The reader is provided a choice within a choice. The intitial decision—"Ab-stain wholly, or wed"—is actually one side of a choice, that between "conti-nence" and "rottennesse." What is at work here is, again, a play of incentives and disincentives: the positive side, in Herbert's terms, is made more attrac-tive by its apparent variety and openness, while the negative side is preju-diced by the term in which it is defined—"rottennesse"—and the definition of its consequences—"let Heaven go."

Herbert in "Perirrhanterium" thus establishes a procedure of confronting the reader with choices in which the alternatives are defined in such a way as to suggest their implications. There is also a buried allusion to the Christian motif of "the way"—the "choise of paths: take no by-wayes." To make the choices Herbert proposes is to participate in "the way"—the "way of righteousness," the path of the One who said "I am the Way" even as this poem itself leads the reader from the personal and social conduct of his life to, by Stanza 65, the conduct of his behavior in the earthly Body of Christ, the church. Yet even as Herbert makes clear that catechetical questioning will provoke different interpretations in different "sorts and conditions" of parishioners, he does not propose a myth or normative pattern for the life of that community. "Perirrhanterium" is at best a beginning, seeking out the one who is not responsive to religious discourse at all. It tries to get him back in the context of normative religious language use; that is, in the worship of the church. There is yet much, much more to do and a long way to go. The copiousness of didactic strategies in "The Church" is best met with a copiousness of interpretive response, again making clear that for Anglicans what unites is what is done together and not uniform allegiance to a single definition of the faith.

"Perirrhanterium," informed by and informing the rite of confirmation as a preparation by the already baptized for full eucharistic participation in the life of the church and as a reminder to those already confirmed of what that action meant in terms of taking on for oneself an orientation of life, is thus a poem for youth that serves as a reminder that, although one is free to make choices, the arena of Christian life becomes the context for meaningful choice and the source of divine aid in making ones that provide useful self-understanding. In this light, the making of private choices takes its meaning in the context of divine activity from the public catechetical preparation for confirmation (the Prayer Book prescribes that such instruction take place "openly in the church") and the public rite of confirmation itself (the Prayer Book requires that "every child . . . have a witness of his Confirmation") and as preparation for public participation in the Eucharist.

Since Herbert continues this pattern of confronting the reader with choices in "Superliminare" and there makes the connection between choice of conduct and ability to read, it is no accident that the end of "Perirrhanterium" places the reader in church, deciding how he will respond to the words he hears. It is a time of self-examination: "In time of service, seal up both thine eies. / And send them to thine heart." What Herbert seeks in church is an active listener: "Judge not the preacher; for he is thy Judge: / . . . Do not grudge / To pick out treasures from an earthen pot. / The worst speak something good: if all want sense, / God takes a text, and preacheth patience." The goal of the hearer or reader throughout is active engagement in language, not as an end in itself, but as a means chosen by the One whom the words convey: "Jest not at preachers language, or expression: / How know'st thou, but thy sinnes made him miscarrie? / Then turn thy faults and his into confession: / God sent him, whatsoe're he be: O tarry, / And love him for his Master: his condition, / Though it be ill, makes him no ill Physician." In such a situation, the preacher's words have lost their easy referentiality. Rhetorical or homiletic language can now be seen as the vehicle of divine action. The "condition" of the preacher, his authorized role in a liturgical rite and in the community identified and created by that rite, comes to be more important than his homiletic skill. Indeed, the true "text" and sermon may have little or no relationship to the actual words of the preacher. The role of the reader here is once again an interpretive role, an ability to hear what Donne called the "Sermon of the Sermon" instead of, or in spite of, the actual words or their delivery.

"Perirrhanterium" thus charts a move toward community as well as a move away from easy referentiality in language. By the end of the poem, the kind of behavior shaping sought by the speaker early in the poem is transformed into a questing for meaning in the context of community action, a meaning that may come to be understood apart from the actual language used in the context of that community's defining action. The reaching of an interpretation or the failure to do so now involves the reader—"How know'st thou, but thy sinnes made him miscarrie?"—as the one who "flies" at the beginning of the poem is asked to "tarry, / And love him for his Master." What Herbert provides here is a means for turning the quest for meaning into a part of the growth-producing process—"turn thy faults and his into confession"—as the public acts of the Prayer Book come to enfold all aspects of the handling of language and the understanding of self in growth.

What such a prescription of a reader does is to create again a choice and the incentive to adopt a stance toward language as at once necessary and dispensable, involving an attentiveness to self, to what about oneself that language conveys, and to the One with the Word about oneself that the preacher's words seek to convey. One must decide to become that sort of reader if one is to be the kind of reader Herbert seeks. To make that decision is to locate oneself in a set of relationships enabled through language, a conversation between God and the world, between Christ and his church, which creates a typological triangulation of the present, the world past, and the world to come. Herbert's poetics set up this conversation, if the reader will decide to join, because Herbert brings the reader to a moment of self-definition, in light of the terms he sets forth, which has immediate bearing both on the reader's personal conduct in the larger world and on his skill and abilities as a reader of Herbert's poetry. Or, to put it the other way around, Herbert makes it clear that one's abilities as a reader of his poetry have implications for how one conducts oneself in the process of living.

One of the ways in which Herbert achieves persuasiveness in his Temple poems is thus through engaging the reader in a process of reading that involves the making of choices, which include the making of decisions about reading, that will have implications about the reader's own situation in life. If the reader of "The Church Porch" has persevered to its end, he has chosen to give up being a flier of sermons and is listening to one. Perhaps it is a bad one (perhaps it is "Perirrhanterium" itself, which is not one of Herbert's most highly regarded poems), like the one he might earlier have flown, but he has also learned a way of listening and interpreting that evokes the larger context of that sermon. He is less concerned with the actual words of the sermon than with its existence as a performative activity of the kind God chooses to make a "window" in time through which to work his redemptive activity. Having reached that point, both in learning to respond to words and to participate fully in the Prayer Book service being enacted, he is ready to move with the rite to its next stage, which is the performance of the eucharistic action, combining biblical text and sacramental participation. In relationship to that Herbert finds and hopes to persuade his readers to find the life that leads from Christ to Christ, from life to life abundantly.

The Eucharistic Work of "The Church" in the Dissemination of Christ

Herbert frames "The Church" section of *The Temple* with eucharistic references. The poem that confronts us first when looking into "The Church" through the door of "The Church Porch" is "The Altar," one of Herbert's most arresting poems because of its visual appearance. This is a highly appropriate place for Herbert to locate this poem in a collection of poems built on analogy with the church as building and as community in Anglican terms. The sight lines of Anglican churches are such that, upon entering, one's eyes are drawn to the altar, a visual manifestation of the liturgical reality that the altar and its communion rites are the focus of Prayer Book worship around which all else revolves and, in terms of the events it enacts, the community is built.

Herbert's final eucharistic allusion in "The Church" is not "Love (III)," although that is a profoundly eucharistic poem to which we will return; it is instead the lines that Herbert places after "Love (III)" and the finis of the text: "*Glory be to God on high / And on earth peace / Good will towards men.*" If Herbert were as well informed about medieval liturgies as Rosemond Tuve finds him to be,[17] then he would have known that Cranmer's major reorganization of the medieval Mass was the removal of the *Gloria in excelsis* from its traditional position early in the rite and its relocation at the end of the Eucharist, where it becomes the triumphal song of praise to God that the rite just completed has achieved its claims to incorporating its participants into the ongoing divine activity in the world and empowering them to do "all such good works as thou hast prepared for us to walk in." By quoting its opening line in Cranmer's translation at the end of "The Church," Herbert concludes his exploration of the eucharistic life with a reminder that activity with his text is and must be enclosed in the actual eucharistic activity of the Anglican church. What Herbert can supply in "The Church" as text is the dissemination of Christ as the way to read his text; he cannot supply a substitute for Christ as the feast itself. That only the church as community formed by eucharistic action at the altar can supply, if the reader chooses the way of reading Herbert charts, making his reading an offering in faith that God will work through that oblation where the Gloria, which is the song of the community at the altar, can be sung in its entirety by the reader.

Heather Asals has explored brilliantly the functioning of Herbert's language in its play on the role of the priest in breaking the bread and the poet in breaking the word so that Christ is distributed. [18] I want to show that Herbert's ongoing references to the life of Anglicanism as a community gathered at the altar also manifest themselves on a larger scale than the interplay of individual words. As Asals makes clear, one of the ways in which Herbert seeks to orient the reader to the eucharistic action of the church is by linking the act of writing to the act of distributing the communion elements; by extension, our reading is a kind of reception. Yet there is no doing without the Eucharist itself. To read such writing is to glimpse the difference between reading words and the reception which completes and informs the sermon (or poem) it follows.

In *The Country Parson*, Herbert describes the Eucharist as a "feast of Charity" in which the priest comes "not only to receive God, but to break, and administer him." He finds himself "in a great confusion": "Neither findes he any issue in this, but to throw himself down at the throne of grace, saying, Lord, thou knowest what thou didst, when thou appointedst it to be done thus; therefore doe thou fulfill what thou didst appoint; for thou art not only the feast, but the way to it" (*CP*, p. 257). Yet it is also a time of increased didactic activity on the way: "hee . . . applies himselfe with Catechizings, and lively exhortations," and encourages participation so that his congregation will have "many excitings of grace" (*CP*, pp. 258–259). Thus, to "Throw [oneself] down at the throne of grace" is not to abandon effort but to suspend simplistic causal expectations about the link between effort and outcome.

As a paradigm for what Herbert is about in *The Temple*, the image he gives us here is enormously helpful. It enables us to modify the image of Herbert's strategies presented by Stanley Fish, that in his poems lies a contradiction, in that the poems' "conscious aesthetic strategy (to drive the reader to a deep and dark point of religion)" is also "one for which [the poet] finally cannot claim responsibility." Fish goes on to find that the effacing of responsibility comes in terms of a "realization [that] the work has already been done." [19] I would suggest that what is actually going on in Herbert is a different kind of displacement of responsibility; the agency of success in Herbert's didactic efforts resides, of course, in God and not in the poet, but it resides in the ongoing divine activity of the Eucharist rather than in the "already done" of God as abstract Idea or category of thought. As Donne says in the *Devotions upon Emergent Occasions,* God may be "considered in thy selfe . . . a Circle . . . but considered in thy working upon us, art a *direct line*"; the Anglican emphasis on incarnation stresses the constantly renewed sense of the opening of possibility, both in language and in behavior, that makes of human time and history the arena of salvation which is acted out and engaged in through the Eucharist. If there is an "always" to be retrieved, it is in terms of an "always already going on" that concerns Herbert and his readers here and now, because the Eucharist opens the possibility of involvement in that "going on" which leads to future fulfillment.

In this light, the "feast" includes both "feast" and "way"; what matters in Herbert is "discoverie," that Christ mediated temporally in the Eucharist is both "way" and "feast," means and ends. Herbert's didactic activity thus has purpose; enabled by grace, it leads to grace. Reading, too, has purpose; the discovery of an opening in the seamless web of words constructed in language as projections of human need for stasis raises possibilities for the orientation of life in time by grace toward grace. The discovery of unconditional love frees speaker and reader from the need for self-imposed language structures as defenses against change and nothingness. To find that salvation is not dependent on human effort, even as meaning is not, is to find the freedom to engage in the Christian journey. That is of course the great insight of Paul about the Christian proclamation against which the medieval system for earning merit and buying indulgences seemed a "works righteousness." Without the redactions of either Luther or Calvin, but in the context of the Anglican concern for creation of a community in which such an understanding could have meaning in an ongoing life of a community together, Herbert repeatedly lets the power of Paul's insight transform the world afresh. Christ as "full, perfect, and sufficient sacrifice," the Word broken so that all can be transformed and made new, frees texts and readers from their bondage to old patterns and expectations. It enables them to take up their cross, offer their brokenness up for healing, and love their neighbors, in a round of feeding and being fed that builds the City of God. That is Paul's claim, a claim never far from the breaking of bread to "proclaim the Lord's death until he come again."

It is thus important to approach "The Altar" as well as the altar from the perspective of "The Church Porch" as few do these days. To have become the kind of reader Herbert describes for us at the end of "Perirrhanterium" and then to "groan to be holy, pure, and cleare" is to be available for the actions of Herbert's speakers as well as for the work of the God he hopes will make windows of his poems, preaching patience at least, if not confession and blessing. The self-oblation implicit in such an attitude of participation acts out a self-offering that makes one available for the redemptive work of God. Herbert's Eucharist acts that out; his poems would bring his readers to engagement in that nurturing and growth-producing behavior. Christ distributed through the poems of "The Church" is thus the way to Christ distributed in the Eucharist of the church.

Spenser moves us past the Eucharist proper to send us out into the world; Herbert seeks to extend the ongoing doing of the Eucharist to incorporate into the fullness of its meaning all human action, including the before, the during, and the aftermath. In Spenser, the Eucharist is that which enables "all such good works" which inform the Eucharist of its meaning; in Herbert, it is life in relationship to the Eucharist as an ongoing human activity on which the emphasis is placed and in which meaning is found. Paul enjoins that we "do this," and in doing this we "proclaim the Lord's death until he come" to every new and unique moment of human experience. Herbert is always aware that "until he come" the Eucharist will always be offered, sending people out surely, but always to come again to the altar at which "all benefits of his passion" are received to incorporate more of time into the salvation history. I do not mean to suggest that Herbert "centers" life on or in the Eucharist any more than he affirms a static eucharistic doctrine, but that the doing of "this" becomes what is done over and over along the way, inexhaustibly making things new even as it renews the divine action and the proclamation of divine promise of future fulfillment.

"The Church" begins and ends with eucharistic references; what "frames" "The Church" here is not an eternal return but an action that yields to such radically different experiences and interpretations in different times and places the means of grace and the hope of glory. The poems framed by Herbert's eucharistic allusions come to take their meanings in relationship to the ongoingness of that action, not to an interpretation of it. Herbert's strategies in "The Church" are to bring all of human life in relationship to that action as the "means of grace and the hope of glory" as those words come to have meaning, however provisional, in the strategies for choice and interpretation he offers to further participation in it.

To begin "The Church" after reading "The Church Porch" and to think of the Prayer Book Eucharist at "The Altar" is to realize that Herbert has already transformed the terms in which we have come to think of "The Church Porch." Confirmation, prepared for by catechetical instruction, was an unrepeatable rite, but in "making new" the medieval Mass Cranmer transformed the preparatory rite of the priest, which was essentially a private rite before the altar, into a public preparatory rite that is a kind of redoing, or remembering and updating, of confirmation. The priest prays that "Almighty God, unto whom all hearts be open, all desires known, and from whom no secrets are hid: Cleanse the thoughts of our hearts by the inspiration of thy Holy Spirit, that we may perfectly love thee, and worthily magnify thy holy name; through Christ our Lord. Amen" (BCP, p. 248). He then recites the Ten Commandments and the congregation responds, "Lord have mercy upon us, and incline our hearts to keep this law." And it is of course the action of the Eucharist that follows that informs and enables what is sought here and thus answers this preparatory prayer. In this light, the elements of "The Church Porch" that evoke images of the catechism and confirmation are absorbed into the eucharistic emphasis of "The Church"; what we are promised is that what follows will transform our understanding of what was taught in "The Church Porch" in ways that will enable the accomplishment of its teaching. Whatever resolution in interpretation we thought we might have reached in "The Church Porch" is now reopened, bringing us to a place in which all the issues it raised must be examined again in a new context in relationship to the altar and the action that gives it meaning. Yet such redoing keeps the conduct of the Christian life an open and thus potentially growth-producing arena of behavior, a way of perceiving necessary to the future attainment of the divine promises, one that requires continued making of choices in interpretations, revising old ones and discovering new ones.

As Dom Gregory Dix has taught us, the action of the Eucharist is one involving offering, giving thanks, breaking, and receiving, each of which is distinct and yet but a version of the others.[20] "The Altar" meditates on the parts of the eucharistic action as it involves the "heart" of the Collect for Purity ("cleanse the thoughts of our hearts") and the recitation of the Law ("incline our hearts to keep this law") mediated by texts like Jeremiah 31:33 ("I will . . . write [my law] in their hearts . . . and they shall be my people"). It is thus a poem of preparation for approach to the altar itself as well as an encounter with the "making new" action of the eucharistic life.

"Meaning" in "The Altar" is found in the conversation between "feast" and "way," between offerer and receiver in the enactment of the altar rite. The conventional thing to say about this poem is that it is emblematic; that is, the appearance of the poem gives visual form to its subject. In the poem, the speaker tells God that he is building an altar out of the pieces of his heart and the cement of his tears. At the end, the speaker prays that God "let thy blessed SACRIFICE be mine, / And sanctifie this ALTAR to be thine." We might conclude, following the readiest argument,[21] that the poem is about building an altar within, and that the visual image of the poem shows us that altar, so that even when the speaker is silent—"if I chance to hold my peace"—the visual shape of the poem "to praise thee may not cease."

In other words, the shape of the poem is the altar the speaker refers to in the first line of the poem. In these terms, the poem evokes some of the parts of the eucharistic action described by Dix. We have offering, surely, of the heart/altar and at least a request for blessing ("sanctifie this ALTAR to be thine"). We also have a breaking, so that the shape of the heart can become the shape of the altar: "each part / Of my hard heart / Meets in this frame, / To praise thy Name." In this sense, the poem, in relationship to the eucharistic action, is incomplete; poised in offering, seeking "thy blessed SAC-RIFICE" as "mine," it lacks distributing, reception, or response.[22] We may attempt to explore this incompleteness by seeing the speaker's lines as a leap into offering and brokenness, as a prayer in search of response, and the poem's shape as a finding.

Moving there requires noting the disjuncture between the words of the text and the shape they form. The altar we see before us in the text is built of words; the altar the speaker is talking about is not made of words but of the pieces of his broken heart. At no point in the poem does the speaker show any awareness that his words about his heart happen to go together to make up the visual image of an altar. Indeed, the speaker says he is raising a "broken ALTAR," while the visual image we see is not broken at all. We know that, and Herbert knew that, but the speaker does not. Thus, the shape of the poem represents not a reflection of the speaker's remarks but a comment upon them by the poet.[23]

If that be the case, then we must ask what that comment is; to answer that question, we need to remember the biblical and liturgical allusions in this poem. The primary allusion is to Psalm 51, in the context of passages from Deuteronomy, Jeremiah, and II Corinthians. In Deuteronomy 27:5–6 God instructs the people of Israel to build an altar out of stones and offer burnt offerings upon it. In Psalm 51 the speaker proclaims that God no longer wants burnt offerings but "the sacrifice of . . . a broken and a contrite heart." In Jeremiah 24:7 God promises to "give [Israel] an heart to know me." In II Corinthians 3:2–3 Paul tells the church at Corinth that "Ye are our epistle written in our hearts, known and read of all men . . . the epistle of Christ . . . written not with ink, but with the Spirit of the living God; not in tables of stone, but in fleshly tables of the heart." Paul's words also pick up other Old Testament images from Ezekiel 36 about God giving Israel a new heart, one of flesh and not of stone.

Psalm 51 is also a central text in the Prayer Book's penitential rite for Ash Wednesday, "A Commination against Sinners," done between Morning Prayer and Holy Communion on that day. In that rite, the minister reminds his congregation that those who violate the Ten Commandments are "notorious sinners" and calls upon his congregation to "return unto our Lord God, with all contrition and meekness of heart, bewailing and lamenting our sinful life, knowledging and confessing our offenses, and seeking to bring forth worthy fruits of penance." Citing II Corinthians, Jeremiah, Isaiah, and other prophetic texts, the minister goes on to urge his congregation to "cast away from you all your ungodliness that ye have done, make you new hearts and a new spirit." Psalm 51 follows, and the people join the minister in praying that God "be favorable to thy people, which turn to thee in weeping, fasting, and praying" (BCP, pp. 316–323).

In this context, Herbert's "The Altar," especially in light of its proximity to "The Sacrifice," stands as a poem related to the liturgical cycle as a preparation for the contemplation of the events of Good Friday and Easter. It is an Ash Wednesday and Lenten poem, a response to the injunctions of the minister in the commination service to engage in confession, contrition, and reorientation of behavior, coupled with an appeal to God to act as he has promised as a God whose "property is to have mercy" (BCP, p. 322). It acts out the role of confession in relationship to the life of a community of prayer and not just as an individual action. The speaker locates himself in relationship to a community, is indeed creative of a community which includes God as actor in relationship to his heart, the speaker as actor and acted upon ("Turn thou us, O good Lord, and so shall we be turned," prays the community in the commination rite), and others who will hear the speaker praise God and see his praise in the form of the poem when he falls silent. Thus one informing action for "The Altar" is liturgical prayer, which creates a community through its enactment.

If we put all this together what becomes clear is that the poem evokes a development that has already begun and is continuing, and that the new act of God which makes offerings of hearts better than burnt offerings on the altar is the offering of God in Christ's sacrifice, which writes, in the life of the Spirit, God's law on the hearts of his people rather than on Moses' tablets of stone. The church, like the church in Corinth, is a living testimony, or epistle, to God's saving actions. There are thus profound links here to language and its use. The psalmist, just before talking about a broken and contrite heart, asks God to "Create in me a clean heart, . . . and renew a right spirit within me."

Such language, in the context of the commination rite, has specific references to the cleansing action of the Spirit in baptism as well as to the beginning of the Prayer Book Eucharist. And, immediately after making this prayer, the speaker says, "O Lord, open thou our lips; and my mouth shall show forth thy praise," lines borrowed for use daily in both Morning and Evening Prayer. Herbert would thus remind us of the public context in which the speaker's words of self-offering come to have their meaning and are able to become part of the story of God, altars, and hearts. He would also remind us of the liturgical calendar, with its annual retelling of the story of Christ's earthly ministry and its anticipation of Christ's return in power and great glory. Ash Wednesday comes at a pivotal moment in that story, shifting the emphasis from the joy of the infancy narratives to a more somber tone in anticipation of Good Friday. To behave as the speaker of "The Altar" behaves is to open oneself to an act of God including the speaker in the narrative of salvation, an open-ended narrative written and told through divine-human interactions like the one enacted here.

One theme that runs through all this is the contingency of human language as a manifestation of the contingency of human action. The cleansing of the heart, the writing of God's law as an epistle in our hearts, is an action of God, so that human response in praise and action is contingent on God's prior action. And, if Paul is right, it is the corporate body of the church at Corinth that manifests the epistle written in the heart, not the individual Christians at Corinth. The renewal in the heart made possible by Christ's sacrifice is manifest in the corporate speaking action of the church in Morning and Evening Prayer and the Eucharist. The Anglican altar is the altar of God and his people, not the altar of individuals apart from that corporate body.

In this light, the speaker's statement turns on several metaphors, both explicit and effaced. The first is between the speaker's heart and the stones of the altar of Deuteronomy. The second is between the speaker's literal heart and human resistance to divine action. These metaphors function in a variety of ways. The speaker's (literal) heart is God's creation, "Whose parts are as thy hand did frame"; the speaker thus acknowledges that he is God's creature. Even as the heart itself, however, is God's creation, so the brokenness of the heart as a sign of willfulness or hardness of heart is also God's action: "A HEART alone / Is such a stone, / As nothing but / thy pow'r doth cut." The heart as metaphor for human existence as well as for human redemption is as it is because of divine action. The speaker's words thus presuppose divine action on both fronts; his reponse is in terms of "tears" and "rears," his offering in contrition for his broken heart. But such offering is also contingent on God's actions; the joining of the two metaphors of the heart makes clear that the speaker's framing of his broken heart—"each part, / Of my hard heart / Meets in this frame"—is a manifestation of the action of the one whose "hand did frame . . . [the] parts . . . of [my] heart."

The speaker's own role in the building of the heart/altar is thus undercut, not to drain it of volition, but to make clear its contingency and thus to manifest the claim that the speaker's action as well as his situation is dependent on and revelatory of the divine initiative. Indeed, as the speaker's act of address in its biblical context makes clear, the very fact of the speaker's speaking is a sign that his prayer has been answered; his God has opened his lips, has made him part of the divine activity in the world. And, since the table becomes an altar through corporate liturgical usage, the altar as sign and response makes the connection between the speaker's own act of offering and the liturgical offering of "our selves, our souls and bodies, to be a reasonable, lively, and sufficient sacrifice unto thee" that we may be "members incorporate in thy mystical body," the link between individual offering and corporate reception which the Prayer Book communion makes possible.

This is also one claim of the poem's shape. Even as the speaker asks that the altar of his heart become God's altar, his words complete an altar of words which will remind the reader of the importance of altars even when the reader only looks at the poem. Thus, the speaker's prayer literally becomes the answer to that prayer. And if that be the case, then we enter into a process of unfolding—if the prayer for God's actions becomes a sign of God's actions, then the poem becomes a sign of God's working in those whom he enables to pray. Thus, by a process of reading, we are drawn to the altar of the One who makes reading possible, for it is his sacrifice, made known at that altar, which we learn makes possible the whole series of reading acts we have performed.

As Robert B. Shaw has recently noted, the shape of "The Altar" strongly resembles the capital letter *I* as well as an altar.[24] Just so; the process of interpretation enacted by this poem engages the reader in an interchange in relationship to the altar that results in the offering of self-apart-from-God and the reception of the self-in-Christ, which is the end of the eucharistic action. In "The Church," this *I* will soon become the *I* of "Iesu," both the monogram of Christ and the action of Christ ("*I ease you*") who is "in us and we in him" through eucharistic participation giving speakers like the speaker of "The Altar" their new identity in Christ. Herbert's final turn on this motif will come in "Love (III)," in which the speaker will object to his worthiness to "look on thee" and Love will respond, "Who made the eyes but I?" As in this poem, God refuses to accept our self-readings and insists on reading us as we are in Christ, not as we are apart from the eucharistic body. Here, however, the *I*/altar becomes Herbert's way of urging us to see in the self-oblation enacted by this speaker the way toward the kind of answer that heals and transforms, making new the speaker who responds to God by joining in the church's offering of itself.

As a result, we can see in the poem the full shape of the eucharistic action as the literal shape of the poem becomes the healing response of God to the speaker's prayer, making the broken heart into a "healed" altar of words, a visual metaphor of the poet's claims about how God works with human offerings of self through words to make all things new. What Herbert gives us in this poem is a weaving of biblical and liturgical language and imagery in which the speaker's bringing into language of his situation (description) and his request for response (intercession) (re)present the situation of Christians before the altar of the church who use biblical language to bring the brokenness of the world before God and to engage in an action with words and bread and wine at an altar in expectation of divine response that makes all things new. If the words of the poem present the speaker's leap into faith that there is some One there to respond, the fullness of the poem, including its shape, acts out Herbert's faith that response comes in a way that relates "mine" and "thine" in a common enterprise in human time through the agency of discourse modeled by the speaker of the poem.

One result of this "framing" of the speaker's request in the shape of the eucharistic action is the breaking down of expectations about asking and getting answers. We customarily use the transaction between a request and its response as a way of defining outsides and insides, so that to make a request is to define oneself as outside that in which one wishes to be included, and to receive an answer is to receive that incorporation into the inside one seeks by asking. Herbert's play of language back and forth between inside and outside suggests, however, that to be able to ask the question in these terms is already to find oneself inside. Or, so the shaping of the question into its answer would raise as a possibility for the reader, as an occasion of his choice to take part fully in the conversation which makes "he in us and we in him."

Herbert's style thus works to open itself and its reader to such creative and redemptive activity in texts and lives. It keeps us off balance by confusing our normal expectations of reading experiences and keeps suggesting that conventional expectations of referential discourse are inadequate to express what Herbert seeks to convey. In the enigmatic

$$Ana \begin{cases} \text{Mary} \\ \text{Army} \end{cases} gram,$$

Herbert's claim "How well her name an *Army* doth present" is more puzzling than clarifying, even when we know the accidental anagram hidden in the word "Mary," until we also know the play Herbert is making with the beginning of John's Gospel, which, translated literally, says "the Word became flesh and pitched his tent among us." Even then, what the poem does is set up a play between the words "Mary" and "Army" which evokes a whole world of interaction far removed from their usual functions in the world of English discourse. Mary gave her humanity to the Word so that it could spell God's victory in the world. And when we notice the way "Mary" becomes an anagram of another word, we might well notice that "anagram" itself is a complex word, for, after all, Mary's mother was Saint Anne, even as Jesus is the Word from God. From Anna to Mary to Christ is the genealogy of a grammar of the Word as well as the recitation of a narrative in time which gives life to language through its employment in the name of Christ.

In such terms we find that even so short and epigrammatic a poem opens up possibilities of language in a liturgical context. The Gospel text alluded to here from John is the traditional reading for the Gospel at the Eucharist on Christmas Day, when in liturgical terms the coming of God's Word in Christ is replicated in his coming in bread and wine—the use of the elements of communion entering into the use of human language to manifest the Christ among us. Even as the elements must be "misread" in the experience of faithful reception to become the body and blood of Christ, so the use of language to proclaim the Christ also involves a "misreading," so that all words, all signs, may contribute to the process by which they may someday be made to "figure *JESUS CHRIST.*" Dissociation of referential language becomes unsettling in such a context, but a necessary preliminary to hearing its full import, that since things are not what they seem to be, as mediated through language, there is hope that the final word about human existence is not ours but God's, or so it is the reader's choice to affirm.

Herbert's poems thus become interpretations which seek fuller interpretations, all pointing to the ongoing life of that community created by the eucharistic action which incorporates and reorients interpretive behavior. The poems in "The Church" instigate participation in this process in the church where the knowledge gained from reading can be performed and identified. Barbara Harmon has described well the situation of Herbert's speakers at the end of many of his poems and, I might add, the situation of his readers as well:

> Ultimately, . . . the idea that it is possible to represent the self in ways either coherent or safe is reduced to the status of a cherished fiction and is, at last, relinquished. What replaces it is a view of the world almost violently open, made vulnerable by interpretation, sensitive to the free play of meaning, unbounded, unsafe, and, I would add, inhospitable to the representation of the self.[25]

In this description of the speaker of "The Collar" at the end of the poem, she puts him in precisely the situation of those in biblical narrative who are encountered by the God of that narrative. Abram, confronted by God and led away from the world of the ancient Near East represented by Babel with all its mythopoetic constructs of the world, finds himself not in the terms of that world but in terms of the call given him by God. The new name for him— Abraham—is a divine gift, a result of his new identity achieved not through his own interpretive efforts but through his participation in the relationship he is called to.

Herbert of course seeks, and seeks for us, a new identity, one defined not in terms of "representations of the self" but in terms of the opportunity to offer oneself in Christ presented by the Eucharist. Harmon contrasts "The Collar" to other poems in "The Church" in which the speaker is able to articulate his identity in terms of biblical narratives rather than personal ones. I find Harmon's argument persuasive as far as it goes, but would note that "The Collar" is as indebted to biblical narratives as any other poem in "The Church." In the biblical tradition, the experience of separation is as much a part of the ongoing relationship with God as any other. In effect, Herbert enables the articulation of such an experience in ways that bring it into proximity with the Eucharist. This "wounding" of self-presentation is a way to discovering Christ in the abyss of collapsed self-articulation; wounds are here revealed as places of darkness where the crucified One makes his dwelling.

Conventional readings of "The Collar" argue for its ending as a resolution of the problems the body of the poem acts out, an example of a successful way of bringing poems to a close,[26] because the dramatic shifts in tone that reflect the verbal conflicts in the first thirty-two lines of the poem are resolved in the calm achieved in the closing lines:

> But as I rav'd and grew more fierce and wilde
> At every word,
> Me thoughts I heard one calling, *Child!*
> And I reply'd, *My Lord.*

Herbert's presentation of this ending appears to overcome the problems posed in the opening lines, problems Harmon describes in terms of human efforts to deal with the world through conceptualization in language. Herbert does this by affirming human contingency, human dependency, on another kind of word, a word from without naming the speaker "*Child.*" The speaker's response, now undivided in accepting this new name and the relationship of dependency it implies, takes the form of naming the external speaker—"*My Lord.*"

Resolution for this speaker, therefore, must come in the terms of this ending, yet for all its efficacy it too is problematic. The best the speaker can do is affirm "Me *thoughts* I heard one calling" (emphasis mine); his response is an act of faith, one which Herbert affirms by his control of the poem's tonal shifts, but nevertheless an action *as if* there were such an external speaker. More cannot be said, except to note that if the speaker is mistaken in what he heard then whatever resolution the poem achieves certainly falls apart. Our experience of the poem therefore argues for the efficacy of faithful response; it at least raises the possibility of such response and affirms its utility for getting poems finished as well as for furthering the relationship with God that leads to salvation. But Herbert does not want to make claims that go beyond possibilities to assertions of certainty. The language of parent and child here, as we will note later in more detail, functions to emphasize the depths of these issues. The God who would break into the stasis and paralysis of human conflict, to get us moving by providing effective orientation for our energies, must be a God who can address us at the deepest level of human origins. Thus, the language of parent and child is appropriate here for that task.

Let us now note another aspect of this poem's language. As Harmon points out, critics have argued that the way to interpret the poem's images of "board," "wine," "corn," and "fruit" for which the speaker "hast hands" is in eucharistic terms. The "board" becomes an altar; the "wine" and "corn" the wine and bread of Holy Communion; the "fruit" of the "rode" as rood, through which the Anglican communicant receives "all. . . benefits of his passion." But, as Harmon also points out, nothing in the poem necessitates such a reading: "The assignment of sacramental and eucharistic meaning is an interpretive act performed by the poem's speaker." If *we* do it, however, as readers of this poem, then the narrative of the early part of the poem takes on greater import. The speaker's divided state of rebellion struggling with submission to "good cable, to enforce and draw, / And be thy law" enables interpretation in relationship to biblical narratives of human rebellion from God, and the poem's ending replicates human actions through a "child," the God-man Jesus. Through choosing to accept a new self-in-relationship as a child of God, the speaker is now welcome at God's board, free to take the "fruit" in his hands that will make new his "sigh-blown age."

Such a reading also "restores" cognitive force to the various images and words of the poem by reinstating a sense of relationship to what is otherwise a disparate set of images. In other words, this perspective on the images of the poem replicates for us as readers the same experience the speaker has when he acknowledges the perspective on himself provided by accepting himself as Child, yet this setting of the poem's images in an eucharistic context is just as tentative and just as requiring of our assent to an assumption as is the speaker's own assent at the end of the poem. In other words, Herbert suggests to us how to achieve an interpretation of his poem by showing us how his speaker achieves a sense of release from the earlier self-defeating attempts to express experience in terms of myth making; both require an act of faith. The speaker achieves release through accepting on faith that the voice he thinks he hears is that of God; the reader achieves a helpful reading of the poem through accepting on faith that the board struck at the beginning of the poem is an altar.

The poet thus presents us not only with a problem but a solution, yet one that requires our involvement in the world of eucharistic action the poem alludes to if it is to be adequate to resolve the problem the poem presents to us. Herbert has played with our sense of need to resolve in an intelligible way the scene the poem offers us; he suggests that the way to resolve the problem of the poem is implicated in what is required for living a life of faith, for becoming guests at God's table. Thus, not only does the poem argue that a relationship with God, and its concomitant view of the world, is a solution to the speaker's sense of being divided against himself, it also insists that a solution to the problem of poetic meaning, to the problem of words that make us even more fierce and wild, comes only when we respond to the Word that causes them to fall into coherent relationships. The poem thus becomes an offering of the brokenness of the world it enacts. It makes an offering of the failure to achieve identity through language by means of the breaking of habitual forms of discourse and a reception of blessing through the distribution of a new kind of identity in relationship to the One who in such actions in human history comes to deserve the name "Lord." It is, as Harmon suggests, a poem that argues "that in the world of the New Covenant needs are met through . . . a displacement of the personal by the collective solution," achieved by "reading the interior story in the contexts—both sacramental and biblical—to which it truly belongs."[27]

What the poem is "about" in any conventional sense, therefore, is not our experience of it or interpretation of it alone, but another experience which it makes possible, perhaps even necessitates for the faithful reader, so that "true" reading of the poem comes to be in participation in the activity to which it points. Yet nothing forces us to make that leap of faith and cognition. Shown the benefits of such a leap through the way it resolves the speaker's problems, we are left to decide whether we want to have a poem that is fierce and wild, confused and self-defeating, or whether we want an affirmation of faith. We are encouraged to take that leap for ourselves, yet we are left to do it on our own. What Herbert seeks here is not a myth of understanding but a sense of who one is in terms of relationship and purpose; we find here our freedom to make that choice.

At the end of "The Collar," therefore, Herbert leaves us to decide whether we will choose the path that will render the poem meaningful and also find ourselves drawn with the speaker of that poem to an act of faith at God's board, or whether we will renounce meaning and leave the board; the poem suggests to us the cost of the latter choice, yet it, and its speaker, cannot decide for us. "The Collar" thus exemplifies Herbert's poetics of persuasion, a dialectics of choice which uses the resources and the limitations of language to confront readers with processes of reading that raise options and force examination of the nature of language itself and the ways we use it to frame and shape our world. In this way, Herbert seeks to catch us who might fly a sermon, to turn our delight in reading into a sacrifice of ourselves, or in the words of the Prayer Book, into an offering of "our souls and bodies, to be a reasonable, holy, and lively sacrifice unto thee."

Such self-oblation includes, of course, the offering of prior self-definitions for the sake of receiving the new "self" of participation in Christ. Herbert's bringing of the whole of the world as it is conceived in human terms within an ongoing relationship to the ever-unfolding eucharistic action can only be spoken of, only brought into language, at the point at which old words pass away, for the new is not yet spoken nor can it yet be spoken. The choice he confronts us with, ultimately, is to hold onto the old or to follow his speaker into the as yet unspoken and unspeakable, except in relation to prior acts and as yet unfulfilled promises of God as they are mediated through enactment in the Prayer Book rites.

In light of this, all human efforts to talk about God are at once necessary and yet provisional and flawed; when they seek to substitute human abstractions for the radical particularity of his self-revelation, they lose touch with the very experience they seek to understand. Words about God come to have this meaning only in the performance of the knowledge God reveals in the Eucharist. On the other hand, without the use of language there is no communication at all; successful discourse must lead to, or be fulfilled in, performance rather than abstract systems of thought, although it may use a failure of interpretation as a way of revealing the failure of human construction in discourse.

In "The Sacrifice," Herbert departs from his otherwise universal practice of creating a speaker contemporary with the time of composition to act out this situation; here the speaker is Christ himself in the act of performing human salvation, and his lament from the cross reflects the paradoxes of human interpretation. The speaker calls *"all ye, who passe by"* (ll. 1–3) to contemplate his Passion. The grief felt by the speaker derives from his reading of texts and situations which exclude the significance of this particular act. The Jewish leaders, "Princes of my people," desire his death because they are unable to interpret the narratives of their past relationship with God to include this particular new manifestation of divine action—"Without me each one, who doth now me brave, / Had to this day been an Egyptian slave" (ll. 9–10)— and because his interpretations of himself conflict with theirs—"they accuse me of great blasphemie, / That I did thrust into the Deitie" (ll. 61–62). Herod and Pilate are also called to interpret the meaning not just of his sayings but of his actions and presence. The culmination of all this is the Crucifixion itself, becoming an interpretation manifest in the ironic reading *"Hail king."* Yet what validates Christ's own interpretation is not a vindication in the realm of interpretations but the action of the Passion itself as he juxtaposes to all interpretations the lament, "Was ever grief like mine?" In this light the Passion is defined as a divine action which changes interpretations into performance that achieves the meaning of the events—"I, who am Truth, turn into truth their deeds" (l. 179)—even when the course of this leads to Christ's sense of abandonment by God himself in the broken line that is a quotation from Psalm 22:1: *"My God, my God"* (l. 215). At that point the mystery that confounds interpretation comes fully into play, the words of the biblical text, even in (or because of) their absence, becoming the only words that "interpret" this action in all its awful particularity.

At this point of the text, the Crucifixion functions as a particular divine event that results from and thus judges human inadequacy in understanding and yet transforms human interpretive processes, new wine bursting old wineskins, making from them effective ways of entering into the mystery of divine particularity. How Christ, who must be God as well as human according to Christian proclamation, can be abandoned by his divinity defies all interpretive skill, and yet the openness of that event in the Prayer Book Eucharist, where "all benefits of his passion" are made available, is the central

Christian claim. Herbert's response to the Passion in "The Thanksgiving" thus comes in terms of interpretive difficulty and failure:

> 'Tis but to tell the tale is told.
> *My God, my God, why dost thou part from me?*
> Was such a grief as cannot be.
>
> (Ll. 8–10)

The speaker's efforts to find an appropriate response to God's actions are frustrated; they also stand revealed as at once presumptuous (that a human speaker could devise an appropriate response) and negotiatory (that he could offer an appropriate exchange). The point is not that the description of the Christian life given here is inappropriate, but that any human act of giving, or interpretation of the gift of God in human terms, is bound to fail before exploration of the divine gift. In response to such a situation, Herbert can think of interpretations in terms of action for many of God's gifts, but before something that "is told" only "to tell the tale," or that is fulfilled only in the telling, interpretation fails: "Then for thy passion—I will do for that— / Alas, my God, I know not what" (ll. 49–50). Only in telling the tale is "the tale told"; in Pauline terms, only by "telling" the tale by recounting the narrative, doing the meal that "proclaims the Lord's death until he come," and living out its consequences can the event be "interpreted." Yet such a "reading" of the Passion has meaning again in terms of a future fulfillment of that event which will render human language about it finally meaningful in any "full" sense, while at the same time make it no longer useful; we proclaim the Lord's death only until he comes. In "The Reprisal," therefore, the full light of the eucharistic claim of the church is brought into words: "by confession will I come / Into thy conquest . . . in thee I will overcome / The man, who once against thee fought" (ll. 13–16). For in the Prayer Book Eucharist, confession is made possible only "for thy Son our Lord Jesus Christ's sake" and is followed by discovering in reception of the elements that we "obtain remission of our sins" because "we be very members incorporate in thy mystical body."

Herbert's point here is the necessity of seeing words as actions or actions as the only way really to interpret or "read" such words. Again, following Erasmus' paradigm, events such as the Passion of Christ are explicable only as charitable actions that proceed from them; there is no "dealing with thy passion" in the sense of responding to it or interpreting it in another set of words. There is only loving response, or response through loving. Words about these events are meaningful only if they lead to opening out interpretation rather than leading to a "true" conclusion; that interpretation itself is meaningful only if it leads to actions of love. If it becomes an end it is no longer in any sense "true." There is much to dismantle here—in the arena of defining "truth" as arriving at a final text—and also to promote—in the arena of becoming readers through loving neighbors—and both involve words. Yet words as ends are part of the problem; only words as means promote the reign of charity.

In "Assurance" Herbert performs this model; writing, thoughts, and language combine to raise questions, to introduce "cold despairs, and gnawing pensivenesse" into the speaker's sense of what pertains "Betwixt my God and me." In imitation of the lament Psalms, the speaker demands a response from the One from whom relief must come in such a situation. Part of the strategy here is, of course, to acknowledge that the speaker is dependent on God:

> But I will to my Father,
> Who heard thee say it. O most gracious Lord,
> If all the hope and comfort that I gather,
> Were from my self, I had not half a word,
> Not half a letter to oppose
> What is objected by my foes.
>
> (Ll. 19–24)

In opposing God as Word with human "words" here, the speaker brings to the fore the dialectic between human words and the divine Word. Without divine aid, there are no human words, "not half a word," to oppose humanly constructed articulations of doubt originating both from within and without the speaker. Against this, the speaker juxtaposes his claims for the divine activity through language:

> But thou art my desert:
> And in this league, which now my foes invade,
> Thou art not onely to perform thy part,
> But also mine; as when the league was made
> Thou didst at once thy self indite,
> And hold my hand, while I did write.
>
> (Ll. 25–30)

Yet Herbert is after more than just a juxtaposition of languages, divine and human, but a sense of the function of human language in relationship to what is desired of the divine. If God is really his "desert," he is there both in the sense of the speaker's deserving and in the sense of "desert" as wasteland, the verbal space where in Stanza 1 language brings into being a "bitter thought," "rank poyson," and "torture." The abyss of text like the wounding of text thus becomes yet another context for the beauty of God in "discourse." The next stanza affirms the "ruine" or abyss in relationship to God:

> Wherefore if thou canst fail,
> Then can thy truth and I . . .
>
> . . . .
>
> Yea, when both rocks and all things shall disband,
> Then shalt thou be my rock and tower,
> And make their ruine praise thy power.
>
> (Ll. 31–36)

Because of the centrality of the wounded Christ in Christian imagery, sites of wounding become the place of Christ in the world, making suffering the way of the cross, the way to be with Christ. In these allusions to Psalm 31:4 ("thou art my strong rock") and Psalm 61:3 ("thou hast been my hope, and a strong tower for me against the enemy"), Herbert in effect answers the question posed earlier; by using God's text, he is able to articulate to God his claim for protection, although on his own he has "not half a word." Taught by the use of the Psalter in the Prayer Book, Herbert can find help from God in asking for help from God. Because of this, the speaker can pray that the "ruine" of his "desert thought" refute itself as a claim against the God-human relationship and come to be a source of praise rather than detraction. If that happens, then the speaker is free to let even the language of "deserts" go on playing itself out:

> Now foolish thought go on,
> Spin out thy thread, and make thereof a coat
> To hide thy shame: for thou hast cast a bone
> Which bounds on thee, and will not down thy throat.
>
> (Ll. 36–40)

Human use of language here stands revealed as a defense, a "coat" to hide "thy shame"; time, which it seeks to obscure and hide from, will refute it. There is no refuge in hiding from temporality in human language constructs; the body within the "coat" of language will reveal the effects of temporality, the "bone" it cannot swallow. Running through this poem is therefore an undercurrent of Ash Wednesday imagery—"Remember, O man, that dust thou art and to dust thou shalt return"—and its reversal in the divine promise of Resurrection (Ezekiel's "valley of dry bones") acted out and made effectual through baptism and the Eucharist, healing the divided self Herbert articulates here. And so Herbert concludes, "What for itself love once began, / Now love and truth will end in man." Time, as that from which human discourse would hide, is also the arena of divine activity, mediated through the Bible put to use, to transform death and deserts of dust into life, making all things new.

But, of course, the poem is a lament, an asking in the hope of answer. It is no accident that the poem which follows "Assurance" in "The Church" is "The Call," a prayer built on the end of Revelation and its prayer, "Come Lord Jesus," the one who said, "I am the way, the truth, and the life." This poem is an extended process of definition, in which the transforming function of the Word is revealed in its ability to make words mean what they need to mean to make the Christian proclamation. The interlacing of language here reminds us at some point that every attribute the speaker asks for here is Christ, "figures *JESUS CHRIST*," who reconciles words to each other and the world to himself through a process of divine action in time that Herbert enacts here as a demonstration of the fluidity of language. When Christ is the referent, Herbert argues, these desires can be expected to come to pass:

> Come, my Way, my Truth, my Life:
> Such a Way, as gives us breath:
> Such a Truth, as ends all strife:
> Such a Life, as killeth death.
>
> Come, my Light, my Feast, my Strength:
> Such a Light, as shows a feast:
> Such a Feast, as mends in Length:
> Such a Strength, as makes his guest.
>
> Come, my Joy, my Love, my Heart:
> Such a Joy, as none can move:
> Such a Love, as none can part:
> Such a Heart, as joyes in love.

The eucharistic experience is one of being made new "in him"; it is "a Feast, as mends in Length."[28] Yet the life of the church is also one lived in hope, an at once now and yet to come. What Herbert creates in these poems is a pressure toward orientation of life by means of the Eucharist in and through time, a raising of the possibility of being made new which is itself part of the way to being made new, which seeks the reader's assent, depends on that assent, yet attributes the moving of the reader to the ongoing work of the Word through human language. It is by raising of possibilities that go beyond human expectation, faithful asking for the fulfillment of those possibilities, and claiming that the one who is able to fulfill them is enabling their fulfillment that Herbert's didactic strategy operates.

Assurance is therefore always an "as if," a word whose meaning is sought for, and thus a process which becomes part of Herbert's didactic strategy because it constantly refers us to the Eucharist as the action in which "thou . . . dost *assure* us thereby of thy favor and goodness toward us, and that we be very members incorporate in thy mystical body" (emphasis added),

where action ruptures language and its self-contained world with the proclamation of measureless love. In "The Agonie," a poem that combines the
Passion text with eucharistic allusions and thus situates itself in relation to
the Prayer Book's eucharistic readings for the Thursday before Easter (the feast
in commemoration of the establishment of the Eucharist), Herbert rejects the
claims of philosophers to encompass the world in their writings. A better
task, he says, is "to measure . . . two vast, spacious things . . . / Sinne and
Love." The first is "measured" by reference to the "man so wrung with pains";
the second by what proceeds from one of his wounds: "Love is that liquor
sweet and most divine, / Which my God feels as bloud; but I, as wine" (ll.
17–18). The fulfillment of God's promises is thus independent of human
interpretive skill or its separation from divine "reading," and dependent on
God's experience of humanness. Functioning through love, which is still love
although God "reads" it as "bloud; but I, as wine," God's actions overcome all
that separates one from another. The connection between Sin-as-event and the
speaker is the ongoing action of Eucharist, which defines love in relationship
to the reception of wine and also links the speaker temporally to the Passion
which confines the "measure" of Sin to that moment and opens the "measure"
of Love to the as yet unmeasurable because still ongoing and not yet ended
succession of Eucharists which brings "all . . . benefits of his passion" to
those who partake in it. Herbert does not deny the real presence of Christ's
blood in the Eucharist when he says that God feels love as "bloud; but I, as
wine." The wine of the Holy Communion or of the Mass still tastes like wine
after consecration no matter what theology of presence the priest holds. Herbert's point is that our salvation is not dependent on our sensory or interpretive skills but on God's skills; we are loved and known in Christ as part
of his mystical body because God chooses to regard us in that way because of
his love of us. Love as eucharistic tasting thus defies "measure" because it
becomes Love through God's dissemination of it in time and the world, a
process as yet unfinished and therefore unavailable to human measurement.

In the lines that end "Good Friday,"[29] blood is proclaimed "fittest . . . to
write / Thy sorrows" in the speaker's heart, which contains "both ink and
sinne." As a result of such writing, "sinne may say, / *No room for me,* and flie
away." Yet such divine writing cannot banish sin finally:

> Sinne being gone, oh fill the place,
> And keep possession with thy grace;
> Lest sinne take courage and return,
> And all the writings blot or burn.
>
> (Ll. 29–32)

Like "The Agonie," this poem links the divine saving action in the events of
Good Friday with the Eucharist, the ordinary means of being "fulfilled with

thy grace," so that "we may evermore dwell in him and he in us," and with writing and reading. Participation in the Eucharist is thus what Herbert seeks as that which will prevent the effacing of divine writing, "blotting or blur-ring" what is mediated to us through the text of the biblical account of the Passion. What Herbert is doing in this poem is exploring the Epistle for Good Friday in the Prayer Book, making it into a statement in the present of Herbert's time. The Epistle, from Hebrews 10, reads in part:

> After those days (saith the Lord) I will put my laws in their hearts, and in their minds will I write them, and their sins and iniquities will I remember no more . . . Seeing therefore brethren, that by the means of the blood of Jesu, we have liberty to enter into the holy place by the new and living way which he hath prepared for us . . . let us draw nigh with a true heart and a sure faith, sprinkled in our hearts from an evil conscience, and washed in our bodies with pure water. Let us keep the profession of our hope, without wavering (for he is faithful that prom-ised) and let us consider one another, to the intent that we may provoke unto love, and to good works, not forsaking the fellowship that we have among ourselves.

God's promise to reinterpret our behavior ("their sins . . . will I remember no more") enables us to hope and to enter the life of active charity. The echoes here of the language I have had occasion to cite so frequently—"that we may continue in that holy fellowship and do all such good works as thou has prepared for us to walk in"—from the end of the Prayer Book Eucharist, locate Herbert's poem squarely in the context of that moment in the rite. As in "The Altar," the action of God makes possible participation in a restorative "living way." What Herbert seeks in the poem is "possession of our hope" defined in terms of what the Eucharist provides.

In "Obedience" Herbert conceptualizes the writing of poetry in a way that replicates the divine act of writing in blood/ink as one of offering:

> On [this poor paper] my heart doth bleed
> As many lines, as there doth need
> To passe it self and all it hath to thee.

Yet writing takes divine aid—"Let me not think an action mine own way, / But as thy love shall sway"—and the reading of such a text will multiply the consequences, even as the doing of the Eucharist defines love in a way that defies "measure":

> He that will passe his land,
> As I have mine, may set his hand
> And heart unto this Deed, when he hath read;

> And make the purchase spread
> To both our goods, if he to it will stand.

Herbert thus sees in writing and reading a "breaking" of the words, so that there is a multiplication of readings and responses beyond "measure," instigating an action in language which replicates the eucharistic action and is fulfilled in it. What is required is not a limiting of meaning but an opening out of response, a dissemination of the Word through the actions of the Word in the Eucharist, "if he to it will stand." Herbert's method is always to offer a glimpse of the possibilities when the prison house of language as "measure" is broken open by the recreating Word, yet he always reminds us that the reader must choose to read with an openness to interpretive possibilities, even as he must choose not to "fly" a sermon.

As Heather Asals has pointed out,[30] Herbert here plays with the image of ink as blood and poetry as the outpouring of the broken heart, redeemed by the eucharistic blood of Christ in his sacrifice. In these terms, the "breaking" of language in Herbert, the breaking of ordinary interpretive schemes into paradoxes and contradictions, replicates the fraction of Christ on the cross and in the Eucharist as a healing fraction that proceeds in terms of its own brokenness and self-offering. If that occurs, the poem can have its intended didactic effect, making of the reading and interpreting process the beginning of another act of writing, that by God in "heav'ns Court of Rolls":

> How happie were my part,
> If some kinde man would thrust his heart
> Into these lines; till in Heav'ns Court of Rolls
> They were by winged souls
> Entred for both, farre above their desert!

Only the grace conveyed to participants in the Eucharist has the copiousness to "spread . . . into every part, / Meeting sinnes force and art." Defining grace in verbal terms as "Dispatches from their friend," Herbert here in "The H. Communion" juxtaposes the actions of the Word with that of human speech. The divine text as action ("Making thy way my rest") heals the ruptures in humanity at its depths ("the souls most subtle rooms"); the copiousness of Herbert's own art enables the articulation of particular human situations in ways that orient them toward the Eucharist as the source of both the text that defines people in terms of wounding and inadequacy and the text that finds Christ present in wounding to heal it ("Thou hast restor'd us to this ease"). Unlike the Host of the Roman Catholic Mass, which is sometimes displayed for adoration in a monstrance of jewel-encrusted gold ("rich furniture") covered with a rich fabric veil ("fine aray"), Herbert's eucharistic bread and wine are described in terms of a nurturing meal that transforms categories like "way" and "rest" ("Making thy way my rest") because "thy grace, which with these elements comes," is able to meet the speaker's needs at the most fundamental depths and recesses of his being, "Op'ning the souls most subtle rooms." Herbert here reminds us of the prayer that begins Cranmer's Eucharist and describes God as one "unto whom all hearts be open, all desires known, and from whom no secrets are hid" (BCP, p. 248).

Interpretation which proceeds to find hope in misreadings and broken interpretations is that which Herbert urges upon us, as in "Iesu":

> JESU is in my heart, his sacred name
> Is deeply carved there: but th'other week
> A great affliction broke the little frame,
> Ev'n all to pieces: which I went to seek:
> And first I found the corner, where was *I*,
> After, where *ES*, and next where *U* was graved.
> When I had got these parcels, instantly
> I sat me down to spell them, and perceived
> That to my broken heart he was *I ease you*,
>   And to my whole is *IESU*.

Again, it is through the breaking of the text that the way to a healing through an interpretive process can occur. What appears to ordinary acts of interpretation as a dissolution actually results in a manifestation, or showing forth, of meaning in greater copiousness. In such poems, Herbert raises the possibility of restoration from limitations, brokenness, and death precisely through the agency of those elements which appear to ordinary human interpretive methods as things which must be avoided or denied reality or papered over. In "The Pearl," for example, the interpretive acts of "Learning," "Honour," and "Pleasure" create worlds apart from the process through which the speaker claims the divine-human relationship proceeds; he must reject each in favor of passage through "these labyrinths," led not by "my groveling wit" but by "thy silk twist" which is "let down from heav'n to me."

In "Divinitie" we find a similar situation; "men, for fear the starres should sleep and nod," have created "spheres" and "Epicycles" which stand in stark contrast to biblical injunctions about human conduct, which Herbert summarizes as "*Love God, and love your neighbor. Watch and pray. / Do as ye would be done unto.*" His speaker notes, ironically, that these are "dark instructions," but they are as "dark as day" in contrast to human wisdom based on the triumph of "Reason" to account for the predictability of the stars in the night. What matters in human affairs, therefore, is not the product of human imagining that seeks to insure that things will always remain the same, that the stars will stay in their courses, but an orientation of living—"such good works as thou has prepared for us to walk in"—in relationship to the Eu-

charist. The speaker addresses one of the central matters of Reformation controversy—whether and in what way Christ is present in the bread and wine of
Holy Communion—and asserts that human speculation, again, is a diversion
rather than a furthering of the way:

> But he doth bid us take his bloud for wine.
> Bid what he please; yet I am sure,
> To take and taste what he doth there designe,
> Is all that saves, and not obscure.
>
> ("Divinitie," ll. 20–24)

Thus, "Faith needs no staffe of flesh"; that is, belief in the real presence of
Christ as an enabling meal on the way—"Thou dost assure us in these holy
mysteries"—is not dependent on human explanations, but itself "stoutly
can / To heav'n alone both go, and lead." Herbert here again makes clear that
the life of participation in the action that forms the eucharistic community
("To take and taste what he doth there designe") is the defining action of
Christians ("all that saves") so that life apart from it is not a life on the way
that is the way of the cross that leads to the fulfillment of God's promises.
God's actions with bread and wine are a "designing," a part of a divine activity which intends the salvation of the participants and is therefore a kind of
design, but which also depends for its understanding on our "de-signing" the
signs of bread and wine so they "figure *JESUS CHRIST*." Again, Herbert
shifts issues of "divine" and "human," "knowledge" and "faith" into a new set
of categories. What is at issue is not a static understanding of the world as
"this or that," but knowledge as what is discovered in experience of the
Christian life as life on the way; human desire for fixity of things that leads to
the imagining of "Epicycles" to guarantee the courses of the stars stands
revealed as human pretension, "As if a starre were duller then a clod," that
must be given up for a life of faith, of charitable action, of eucharistic reception as interdependent manifestations of an orientation of living. For that
orientation Herbert's speaker claims ultimate significance, not for the products of human reason.

Experience in "The Church" as text is thus shaped by one who would be
hearkened to, who would "finde him, / Who a sermon flies," would "infuse"
and "build up" knowledge of salvation and "inflame" it, "drive it to practice."
Such a poetic homilist seeks for a congregation only those who are "holy,
pure, and cleare, / Or that which groneth to be so" who are appropriate
readers of "The Church" section of *The Temple*. The ongoing life of the Christian community, which leads to "all such good works as thou hast prepared
for us to walk in," here becomes the way of sustaining and furthering that
community's sense of being "heirs through hope of thy everlasting kingdom"
because it provides the context of writing and reading in "The Church."

Herbert's poems thus become interpretations that themselves evoke and demand interpretations, all subordinated to the ongoing life of that institution created by the eucharistic action which gives shape and direction to his play of writing and reading. Herbert underlines the life of the church enabled through Prayer Book worship, which facilitates "confession" and becoming "in thee," and the performance of interpretation that at once wounds discourse and also redeems it through the wounds of Christ as Word. The life in Christ proclaimed as the life of the church as his earthly body becomes a life of transformation and growth, of a new song that is coming to be sung, making the old into the new. In this process, the poems in "The Church" instigate participation as the way to read or interpret them fully.

Herbert builds "The Church" as a body of texts that ends where the Prayer Book text ends, with the singing of "Glory be to God on high / And on earth peace / Good will towards men." As Herbert makes clear in "The Agonie," the measuring of "Sinne and Love" is a task of more consequence than the customary interpretive tasks of "Philosophers," yet "few there are that sound them," because the way to do so is by entering into "all benefits of his passion" through participating in the Eucharist, "that liquour sweet and most divine, / Which my God feels as bloud; but I, as wine." Between these two poles, "The Church" performs the proclamation of Christ as the interpretation of all texts, including the human failure in interpretation or the human insistence on interpretation that would deny or cover over human woundedness, human immersion in temporality, and the divine action in time and history.

Herbert is careful in *The Temple* never to allow us to lose sight of the worshipping body defined by the use of the Prayer Book. On the one hand, he offers poems specifically on the Prayer Book rites. The poems "Mattens" and "Even-song" are filled with echoes from the canticles and prayers of the Daily Offices. The lines "[man] did not heav'n and earth create" and "Teach me . . . / That this new light . . . / May both the work and workman show" echo themes of the Venite and the Benedicite in "Mattens," while the lines "Blest be God above, / Who gave me sight . . . his sonne" echoes the Song of Simeon in "Even-song." Other poems remember baptism and Holy Communion with imagery drawn from their prayers and interchanges.

Further, Herbert builds in "The Church" section of *The Temple* references to the ongoing cycle of the church year. The poems "Good Friday" and "Easter (I)" and "(II)" occur early in "The Church"; they are surrounded by poems on the Passion and the Resurrection. Two poems on baptism are also situated here, since to Anglicans Easter was a traditional occasion for baptisms to take place. Somewhat later, Herbert inserts his "Whitsunday" poem and follows it a few poems later with one for "Trinitie Sunday," as well as the poems "Christmas" and "Lent" later in the collection. Poems between "Easter" and

"Whitsunday," or Pentecost include two poems on "The Holy Scriptures," two poems on "H. Baptism," and one on "The H. Communion" which stress the participation of humanity in Christ's Resurrection through Word and Sacrament. Other poems in this section focus on basic aspects of human life— on "Nature," on "Sinne," on "Affliction"— and on defining characteristics of the Christian life—on "Repentance," on "Faith," on "Prayer," and on "Love." Between "Whitsunday," traditionally the birthday of the church, and "Trin-itie Sunday" come poems on the activities that take place within the church—"Praise I," "Mattens," and "Even-song"—as well as the poems that reflect the physical features of the church—"Church-monuments," "Church-musick," "Church-lock and key," "The Church-floore," and "The Windows." Poems between "Trinitie Sunday" and "Christmas" explore various aspects of the Christian life, notably "Humilitie," "Frailtie," "Constancie," and "Afflic-tion III." "Sunday" treats any of the many Sundays numbered in the Anglican liturgical calendar after Trinity Sunday as a "day most calm, most bright, / The fruit of this, the next world's bud," the "day my Savior rose," since every Sunday is a little Easter. "To all Angels and Saints" alludes to All Saints' Day, while "Employment II" and "Denial" suggest the pentitential and preparatory tone of Advent. The poems from "Christmas" to "Lent" reflect human response to God in "Ungratefulnesse," the speaker's renewed sense of despair in "Sighs and Grones," and the entry of sin and death into "The World." The stress on human pretensions to knowledge in "Vanitie I" makes appropriate the opening line of "Lent": "Welcome deare feast of Lent: who loves not thee, / He loves not Temperance, or Authoritie." With "Lent," Herbert has in a sense started anew "The Church" as both text and as ongoing worship community, since the poems that begin "The Church" are those which would follow Lent—the Holy Week emphasis on the altar and the Passion and Resurrection of Christ. Herbert does not need to duplicate in text the full Anglican liturgical year; he in fact leaves out Epiphany and the saints' days, except perhaps by allusions too remote for us to note who do not live in a society which marked legal, educational, and agricultural terms and seasons by its progress. Nor need he do so to declare his hostility to the Puritans, who objected to all special seasons and days. Instead, his combination of similarity and difference reminds us of the difference be-tween texts of poems and that to which they would direct us, the space in time that must be overcome by the reader's decision to take up Herbert's invitation to join him at the altar. *The Temple* is not a replica of the Church of England but a text in conversation with it; Herbert's intent is to enable richer participation in Anglican worship. Thus he constantly reminds us that we are reading text which realizes its meaning in our behavior in response to it, not in what we might think about it.

After Herbert establishes his ongoing allusion to the life of the visible church he is free to expand upon it, using it as a more remote reference to develop and guide more fully the experience of those who participate in that life. After noticing his allusion, we need only the slightest promptings to remember that the church's liturgical life was always going on in cathedrals and parish churches, in the royal chapels and those of the great country houses, in the universities, in places like Little Gidding, and in the grandest and humblest of rectories, creating and informing that body which encloses, instigates, and informs Christian living; structuring the poems in this way, Herbert constantly orients our attention toward this ongoing conduct of Anglican worship while it leads to deeper involvement in that life.

Of course, the Prayer Book does not end the eucharistic observance with the Gloria; it ties the meaning of the rite into the doing of good works. In the same way, Herbert at the end of "The Church" as much as at the end of "The Church Militant" not only has "relinquish[ed] any claim to have finished his work, in the sense either that it *is* finished or that *he* has finished it,"[31] but also refuses to let his reader feel a sense of closure. If "The Church" works as a didactic text, then the reader knows that before the realization of the divine promises, God's work is to go on loving, and his people's work is to go on in the way that is both feast on the way and way to the feast. Herbert's dialectic with the ongoing worship of Anglicanism is itself revealed in the extensive additions and reworkings which separate the Williams manuscript from the manuscript and printed versions of "The Church" of 1633; his reader is also called to the constant reopening of time and self and language to the Christ that through time makes all things new, conveyed to the community that gathers to do what it is called to do so that it can sing "Glory be to God on high."

Herbert, Sidney, and the Petrarchan Tradition of Love

Love is, for Herbert, the eucharistic host and host/feast, making the eucharistic guest into love as well. Love for his audience, Herbert knows, is understood as existing chiefly in another realm of language and reference, that of *eros* and the Petrarchan tradition. In sonnets (appropriately) sent to his mother in 1610, Herbert described this tradition for articulating love in terms with which we have by now become familiar. He attacks the traditional imagery—"Why should I *Womens eyes* for Chrystal take"—but also adds another dimension to the critique we have found in Sidney and Spenser. "*Roses* and *Lillies* speak thee," he says, addressing God, "and to make / A pair of Cheeks of them, is thy abuse." He wonders, "Why are not *Sonnets* made of thee? . . . / Cannot thy love / Heighten a spirit to sound out thy praise / As well as any she?" Spenser could put "*Roses* and *Lillies*" in the beloved's cheeks in *Epithalamion* and have them function religiously because he described them there as the beloved presents herself at the altar to join the speaker in marriage. For Herbert, however, there is the risk of separating love from the defining source of love when it is incarnate in any human form other than God in Christ. Herbert's point, finally, is that love is the name and the action of God; it is in relationships with God as love and lover and beloved that human love for God and for other humans comes to have meaning as part of the category "love."

Poems of love are thus appropriately addressed to God and to human beloveds in the context of their joint relationship to God, not in the language of Venus.[32] Herbert thus extends Spenser's critique. We may "love . . . lyke as we ought" because the "Lord of lyfe" taught us what love means in a way that, now, for Herbert, comes to exclude or pass judgment on our ability to label erotic feelings apart from their Christian context as belonging to the category "love." One dimension, therefore, of "The Church" section of *The Temple* is a running dialogue with and overgoing of English adaptations of the Petrarchan tradition of addressing poems of love to women, with their concomitant inscription of love as Venus and Cupid and their role as "*Venus'* livery." Love for Herbert does not exclude the erotic dimension or version; he is not a gnostic who rejects the bodily as evil or corrupt. Instead, the point of contention is the ability to speak of feelings or behavior as within the category of love. For Herbert, the criterion for use of that term is the divine-human relationship; in that context, the word "love" can be used meaningfully but not outside of it.

In this light we may examine Herbert's relationship to the most famous, surely by 1610, of Elizabethan Petrarchan sonnet sequences, Sidney's *Astrophil and Stella,* published in 1598.[33] Herbert may or may not have understood Sidney's dispraise of the Petrarchan tradition; he surely recognized that many of Petrarch's, and Sidney's, imitators were like Romeo early in Shakespeare's play in their use of the conventions and thus more in love with loving and playing the role of lover than in taking seriously the larger function and meaning of love in a Christian context. My claim, therefore, is that Herbert's use of the *Astrophil and Stella* sequence as a scene for poetic transformation is more a critique of Astrophil than it is of Sidney. It is, after all, Astrophil whom Sidney has say that "Who will in fairest booke of Nature know, / How Vertue may best lodg'd in beautie be, / Let him but learne of *Love* to reade in thee / Stella, those faire lines, which true goodnesse show" (Sonnet 71, ll. 1–4), and thus it is Astrophil to whom Herbert has his speaker respond, "Starres are poore books, & oftentimes do misse: / This book of starres [the Bible in the immediate context, but perhaps also *Astrophil and Stella* as a book of stars which shows the limitations of *eros* without an informing relationship to God] lights to eternall blisse" ("The H. Scriptures II," ll. 13–14).

Astrophil and Herbert's speaker begin at the same place in their explorations of love and its language; that is, with the heart. After considering the resources of "others leaves," Astrophil finds that his Muse insists he "looke in thy heart and write."[34] Later, Astrophil's heart will be the source of the experience of love's pains, for it is where he is wounded, since love's "dart . . . pierc'd my heart" (Sonnet 20, ll. 13–14); it is also the place that is "burthned" by love (Sonnet 34) and the place that can be called a "temple" for adoring Stella and the image of Cupid's dart (Sonnet 5, ll. 5–7) until "Church and Churchman starve."

In contrast, or in transformation, Herbert begins with the heart, but a heart broken by divine power ("A HEART alone / Is such a stone, / As nothing but / Thy pow'r doth cut"), not the attractiveness of a human woman or the irresistibility of Cupid's darts. Immediately, in contrast to Astrophil's view, Herbert points out that only God, not Cupid, can injure the heart with love. Divine action pierces the speaker's heart and also reassembles it "To praise thy Name" so that "if I chance to hold my peace, / These stones to praise thee may not cease" ("The Altar," ll. 6–8, 12–14). Astrophil, in Sonnet 2, describes how Cupid effected his "wound," his "conquest"; Herbert moves from "The Altar" of his wounded heart to "The Sacrifice," described in "The Reprisall" as "thy conquest" (l. 14). What of course transfigures Herbert's version of a Petrarchan sequence is the fact that his speaker is the loving beloved who must respond to a wounding ("A broken ALTAR, . . . / Made of a heart"), yet finds it in contrast to the wounding of the beloved lover. Astrophil would present Stella with his "paine" in verse to move her to "pitie" and "grace"; Christ offers his Passion to those "whose eyes and minde / To worldly things are sharp, but to me blinde" ("The Sacrifice," ll. 1–2), those who "denie themselves all pitie" (l. 143). In this version of the conventions of Petrarchan love language, Herbert condenses the movement Petrarch followed (from beloved female to beloved God through a beloved Virgin Mary) and which Sidney rejected. In Herbert's *Temple,* the lover-beloved relationship is between the speaker and God throughout, although Herbert finds ways of switching the roles from time to time in interesting ways. One might call this a parodic relationship, except that Herbert claims his version to be the authentic one and not merely a pastiche of the original.

For Herbert, the *blazon* of the beloved is therefore the broken body of Christ; in these terms, love has meaning only in relationship to that broken body as eucharistic gift: "Love is that liquor sweet and most divine, / Which my God feels as bloud; but I, as wine" ("The Agonie," ll. 17–18). For Astrophil, here defined as among those "eyes . . . to worldly things are sharp," Stella's body inspires Astrophil to love, and in spite of "sweetest soveraignite / Of reason / . . . Desire still cries, give me some food" (Sonnet 71, ll. 6–7, 14). The feast of love for Astrophil is Stella; for Herbert, it is the eucharistic feast: "God is here prepar'd and drest, / And the feast, / God, in whom all dainties are" ("The Invitation," ll. 4–6). For Herbert, our relationship to the offering of Christ's body is what enables the relationship of human bodies to have significance: "I will not marry; or, if she be mine, / She and her children shall be thine" ("The Thanksgiving," ll. 23–24).

Astrophil can claim that "in *Stellas* face I reed, / What Love and Beautie be, then all my deed / But Copying is, what in her Nature writes" (Sonnet 3, ll. 12–14). Herbert can agree—"*There is in love a sweetnesse readie penn'd: / Copie out only that, and save expense*" ("Jordan [II]," ll. 17–18)—but the love to be copied here is not from Stella's body—"how then shall I imitate thee, and / Copie thy fair, though bloodie hand?" ("The Thanksgiving," ll. 15–16). Astrophil claims that his art does not reside in "allegories," in "Philosophie," or in "eloquence"; he says instead, "I in pure simplicitie, / Breathe out the flames which burne within my heart, / *Love* onely reading unto me this art" (Sonnet 28, ll. 1, 9–10, 12–14). Herbert also claims the importance of simplicity in terms quite as complex as Astrophil's; he has his speaker ask, "Nor let them punish me with losse of rime, / Who plainly say, *My God, My King,*" after eloquently using philosophical categories allegorically ("Jordan [I]," ll. 14–15).

What, of course, happens in these two lyric sequences is that categories of love, simplicity, and art, even though couched in much the same terms and drawing on the same traditional forms of lyric narration, have fundamentally different meanings and functions. We will note other, notably liturgical and biblical, sources for the vocabulary and forms of the poems in "The Church" section of *The Temple,* but what we are observing here is the way in which Herbert takes one strand of language, form, and narrative and transforms it in very daring ways to make a different but related claim about fundamental human concerns. Allusions to *Astrophil and Stella* make the earlier sequence into a site where Herbert performs his eucharistic work as priest/poet, breaking, and breaking through, received conventions so that love can come to be that which is distributed rather than closed up in a relationship between two people. We get the private spaces of *eros* back, of course, but only after the language and roles of the Petrarchan sequence have been exploited for what they can do to articulate and further the divine-human relationship and the erotic dimensions of human interaction have been brought into socially creative spaces of community life.

Much of the persuasiveness of "The Church" as poetry turns on its ability to transform the scene for understanding courtly love and erotic feeling for poems of love as well as for lovers. Unlike Spenser, who achieves his effects by pointing to new options in human behavior in *Amoretti* and *Epithalamion* by starting out with two lovers in their traditional Petrarchan roles and then charting their way toward new positions through bringing their relationship into the terms of Christian love, Herbert starts with the divine-human relationship but evokes association with the Petrarchan tradition both by direct reference and by deliberately echoing the language of *Astrophil and Stella.* The closure of the narrative of *Astrophil and Stella* is deliberately contrasted to the openness—a contrast also echoed in the limited variety of Sidney's forms and the enormous variety of Herbert's—of narrative in "The Church" portion of *The Temple*. Or, to put it another way, *Astrophil and Stella* and all its possible imitations will always end in the frustration of love and desire and the ending of the lovers' relationship. This must be, given the closure of options Sidney might otherwise have employed, as well as the number of "ways out" Astrophil tests and finds wanting, even though "sweetest soveraigntie / Of reason" indicates otherwise—"Desire still cries, give me some food." Yet Herbert's version of a love relationship "ends" in continuation, in the ongoingness of a banquet in which the beloved persists in finding a way to facilitate the satisfaction of desire—"So I did sit and eat" ("Love [III]," l. 18).

The Petrarchan narrative, as it stands exposed to Herbert's critique, reveals the radical limitations of its assumptions. As we have seen, Herbert deliberately juxtaposes art as falsity in the Petrarchan tradition—"The wanton lover in a curious strain / Can praise his fairest fair; / And with quaint metaphors her curled hair / Curl o're again"("Dulnesse," ll. 5–8)—with the (apparently) simple truthfulness of true Christian art which "plainly" says, "*My God, My King.*" Given the resources in language and traditional narrative available to an Astrophil as poet, there can be no other outcome of his story; what must result is repetition ("her curled hair / Curl o're again"), including the repetition of frustration. As Herbert himself admits, the access to the Blessed Virgin Mary which made it possible for Petrarch to go beyond the limitations of his original situation is no longer available; although he "would addresse / My vows to thee most gladly, Blessed Maid, / And Mother of my God, in my distresse . . . / alas, I dare not," because for the Church of England God demands that we approach him directly and without an inferior intermediary ("To All Angels and Saints," ll. 8–16). In such a situation, from Herbert's perspective, Astrophil is limited by his role to be the desirous one and Stella to be the desired. In this plot of *eros,* only desire and its frustrations can come to speech, never its fulfillments.

Because of the all-inclusiveness of Herbert's claims for his elaboration on the biblical language of God as love, the Petrarchan tradition of bringing *eros* into language stands revealed as being merely about language, with no actual referent in the world either as it is or as it could be. According to the conventions, the vocabulary of Petrarchan love and the speaker's skill in using it derive from the Muses; if the characteristic act that defines the "wanton lover" is that he "curl o'er again" the already curled hair of the beloved, making "fictions onely and false hair" the subject as well as the text of Petrarchan love, then "purling streams" refresh a lover's loves." Herbert's reference is to the "purling spring" which "from the ribs of old Parnassus flowes" in Sonnet 15 of *Astrophil and Stella;* Astrophil, like Herbert, aspires to claim immediate experience as the true source of "love and skill." But for Astrophil it is the experience of Stella, rather than water, or inspiration from the Muses, that evokes "love and skill." Herbert's logic is that Stella is available to the reader only in Astrophil's language and thus can only enable repetition ("curl o're again") of a pattern of feeling, relationships, and narrative outcomes that Astrophil has already followed to an inevitable absence of an ending satisfactory for the fulfilling of desire. Thus, the "purling streams" have become only Astrophil's own words which cannot "refresh" any other lover's loves. For Herbert, therefore, the problem with Astrophil's understanding or definition of love is that it is limited to a narrow range of narrative possibilities and is always devolving toward a myth of love's failure.

In contrast, what appears so shocking about "The Church" section of *The Temple* is the variety of roles its affirmations about love enable its characters to play. Herbert's speaker can, like Astrophil, praise his beloved as "infinite sweetnesse" ("The H. Scriptures," l. 1); remember that Stella's kiss "even of sweetnesse sweetest sweetner art" (Sonnet 79, l. 2). The last stanza of "Longing" uses without modification the language Astrophil uses in wooing Stella. Herbert writes:

> My love, my sweetnesse, heare!
> By these thy feet, at which my heart
>   Lies all the yeare,
>   Pluck out thy dart,
> And heal my troubled breast which cryes,
>   Which dyes.
>   (Ll. 79–84)

Astrophil of course calls Stella his love and his sweetness; in Sonnet 36, his "soule . . . at thy foot did fall" (l. 12) and in Sonnet 50 his "panting breast" seeks healing from his wound, defined in Sonnet 20 as a "dart" that "pierc'd my heart." And, of course, "dying" had significance as a concealing metaphor in Herbert's day, allowing direct reference to active sexuality to be articulated in public texts.

Like Astrophil, Herbert's speaker is willing to give up the worldly rewards of "Learning," "Honour," and "Pleasure" ("The Pearl," ll. 1, 11, 21) in exchange for his beloved. Herbert's speaker can protest that his beloved does not pay attention to his "devotions," and thus he feels his "heart broken" ("Deniall," ll. 1–5); Astrophil experiences "inward smart" because although his words "do well set forth my mind," in Stella "no pitie I find" (Sonnet 44, ll. 1–5). Herbert's speaker can insist that his Lord come, for "my head doth burn, my heart is sick" ("Home," ll. 1–2), while Astrophil can describe his response to Stella's inaccessibility in similar terms: "My mouth doth water, and my breast doth swell, / My tongue doth itch, my thoughts in labour be"

230 · GEORGE HERBERT

(Sonnet 37, ll. 1–2). Herbert's speaker is "tenant long to a rich Lord" ("Redemption," l. 1), while of course it is Lord Rich whose claim on Stella prohibits the full expression of Astrophil's suit for her love.

Like Astrophil, Herbert's speaker can respond to other speakers within the sequence, although while Herbert usually finds commentators to be helpful and informative, Astrophil usually rejects as unwanted advice the remarks of his friends; see among others Sonnets 14, 21, and 28 and compare them to "Love-joy," "Love Unknown," and other of "The Church" poems. Both also find consolation in the complexities of language. For Herbert, "We say amisse, / This or that is: / Thy word is all, if we could spell" ("The Flower," ll. 19–21), while Astrophil is able, because of "grammer rules," to make "this" mean "that," or, to turn Stella's "No, No" into a "yes" (Sonnet 63, ll. 1, 8, 14).

One of the effects of this kind of comparison between the language conventional for Petrarchan lovers and Herbert's speaker's addresses to God is to reveal the level of intimacy or desire for intimacy characteristic of Herbert's speaker. Herbert's justification, of course, is the intimacy of address to the divine so often a characteristic of psalmic speech. Yet there is on occasion both a sense of appropriateness and a sense of shock over the effects Herbert achieves by using this language taken from a male-female dialogue to articulate his relationship with God. On the one hand, Herbert's use of such language performs a commentary on the appropriateness of Astrophil's claims for Stella, his willingness to place her above him, and his eagerness to attribute ideal characteristics to her, either of virtue or of hard-heartedness. Praise in such ideal terms seems appropriate when addressed to God in Herbert's poems; after them, we return to *Astrophil and Stella* to find Astrophil less playful, less sincere, in fact using the appropriate language of love but using it to address the wrong beloved. Shakespeare has Rosalind say in *As You Like It,* "men have died from time to time, and worms have eaten them, but not for love" (IV.i.106–108), words that another Petrarchan lover needs to hear at that point in the play if anything is to come of his relationship with Rosalind. Herbert would provide the same service for *Astrophil and Stella,* revealing Astrophil's hyperbole and also his high expectations in claiming to look for and find in Stella such things as "grace" (Sonnet 27, l. 14), "Vertue" (as an ideal characteristic), "Love," ultimate "power" over the conduct of his life, and of course "faith." From the perspective of Herbert's use of such terms, Astrophil's seems strikingly inappropriate and misguided, the outcome of his wooing less tragic than comic and grounded in his lack of understanding about where and about whom and in what conversation such language is appropriately used.

At the same time, however, Herbert's use of such language has its consequences for his art. To the extent to which Herbert's speaker assumes the traditionally masculine role of lover in the Petrarchan tradition, to that same extent God or Christ becomes the female beloved. Like Stella, this God is sought often in vain—"Whither, O, whither art thou fled, / My Lord, my Love?" ("The Search," ll. 1–2). The same resources of sensual imagery, such as the appearance of flowers, the smells of spices and woods, flavors such as sweetness, characteristics such as light and brilliance, appetites like hunger and desire, feelings like pain and joy that are available to the Petrarchan love poet are also available to Herbert to create this speaker in his wooing of God. Christ in "The Sacrifice" invites this by taking the passive role of the one looked upon; thus, at least some of the power of this poem—strong enough to leave Herbert's speaker speechless at the end of "The Thanksgiving" ("Then for thy passion—I will do for that— / Alas, my God, I know not what")—derives from the juxtaposition of the convention of Petrarchan description of the beloved, including her form, her appearance, her clothes, her behavior, with the experience of having the speaker do his own description and have it be of a crucifixion. We are invited to "see" (ll. 1–3, 29, 30, 35, 37, 45, 50–51, 57–58, 109, 119, 134–135, 149–151, 158, 183, and 201 all refer to eyes, seeing, seeking, watching, and the like) even as Astrophil is concerned with seeing Stella, her eyes, and the effect her eyes have on him.

Moments of bodily description in Petrarchan sequences are moments of readerly voyeurism; there is much at stake here, including how much of the beloved's body the speaker will reveal, how the conventions of description will be manipulated, and how the play between an implied intimacy and the distancing result of verbalization will be teased out. Astrophil wants Stella's body; the closest he will ever get to it is in the accounts of it he makes public in his own verbal descriptions, so that what he wants in private he gets but also loses by making it public. There is thus loss at every turn. The male voyeur, offered the female form in the conventions of Petrarchan language, is invited to feast on form; he is allowed to make an object of that form, ignoring the person of that body, responding in fantasies and wish fulfillments, not in interaction or engagement with that body. Men know that male sharing in the observation of women is a mode of togetherness that expresses hopes and desires at the expense of sharing fears or anxieties about personal adequacy, or feelings about each other. The observed female body can be viewed socially because the looking reinforces male aspirations to control and mastery by making the woman an object of imagined desire who asks nothing in response. Men can thus believe in their own omnipotence in such situations because they are asked to do nothing to demonstrate it; what one might do remains safely within the realm of fantasy.

Herbert's depiction of Christ, on the other hand, begins with body, continually offers more and more body, alludes to the eucharistic reception of the body as well as the building up of the body of Christ through eucharistic reception, making us "incorporate in thy mystical body . . . we . . . in him, and he in us" (BCP, pp. 264–265), and ends with the making of the body—"Who made the eyes but I?" ("Love [III]," l. 12). At least part of the power Herbert finds in "The Sacrifice" derives from the shock of having the beloved function as the agency of self-revealing, insistently demanding a response and challenging readerly distance and passivity. We are asked to see, through the medium of poems, and yet challenged on the grounds of the privileged position such "seeing" grants us. The readerly position thus becomes one of complicity with those onlookers who saw Christ's agony and did nothing or who actively engaged in his tormenting. The challenge of "The Sacrifice," in light of its associations through Herbert's depiction with the Petrarchan *blazon,* is to break through the passive comfort and illusion of powerfulness conveyed by so privilged a position as the traditional readerly role and instead to "come / Into thy conquest," to join through the opportunities offered by the church in the building of the body of Christ, proclaiming the triumph of the body in his Resurrection and participating in the life of his reconciling work. The conventions of reading as well as writing Petrarchan sequences thus provide Herbert with a vocabulary for his work because through using those conventions he is able to articulate his texts, but by breaking those conventions he is able to generate the discomfort and energy to change required of the effective didactic poet.

At the same time, of course, Herbert's speaker frequently has occasion to give voice to situations outside the received role of the Petrarchan lover. In fact, he has the chance to articulate the role of Stella or other Petrarchan beloveds, none of whom ever gets to speak much if at all in the actual Petrarchan sequences. Astrophil would of course be delighted to find his feelings for Stella called by her a "mighty passion" and her unyielding response termed sinful, deserving his "condemnation" ("The Reprisall," ll. 2, 4). Astrophil with "my horse, my hand, my launce" wins the prize and hopes to move Stella to grant her favor to him; he would be thrilled if she responded by confessing her passion for him:

> Yet by confession will I come
> Into thy conquest: though I can do nought
> Against thee, in thee I will overcome
> The [one], who once against thee fought.
> ("The Reprisall," ll. 13–16)

Poems like "Affliction," "The H. Communion," "The Temper (I)" and "(II)," "Mattens," "Church-musick," "Constancie," "The Starre," "Sighs and Grones," and "Unkindnesse," among others, exhibit a speaker who responds to God as active lover by exhibiting the resistance, the doubts, the pride, the fear of intimacy, and the desire for concealment which are all among the attributes of the Petrarchan beloved. Unlike her, however, Herbert's speaker is also able to respond with gratitude for the lover's expressions of feeling—"When first thou didst entice to thee my heart, / I thought the service brave" ("Affliction [I]," l. 1)—to encourage persistence, to ask for understanding and gentleness in overcoming the beloved's resistance, and to find in the lover strength to change in the beloved what stands between the two:

> . . . by the way of nourishment and strength
> Thou creep'st into my breast;
> Making thy way my rest,
> And thy small quantities my length;
> Which spread their forces into every part,
> Meeting sinnes force and art.
> ("The H. Communion," ll. 7–12)

Herbert's speaker/beloved can acknowledge the energy and devotion of the lover and ask for more of his loving work. He can lament the suffering his resistance provokes in his lover ("Sinnes Round") and ask "pardon," finding in Christ's Passion the making "good / My want of tears" ("Ephes. 4:30," ll. 35–36).

While Astrophil would use his poems to teach Stella of his love and fills them with his experiences of love night and day, Herbert's speaker also finds God as lover ever attentive and also working to convey that love; unlike Stella, however, he can be unequivocal in asking for more:

> I cannot ope mine eyes,
> But thou art ready there to catch
> My morning-soul and sacrifice:
> Then we must needs for that day make a match.
>
> . . . .
>
> Teach me thy love to know;
> That this new light, which now I see,
> May both the work and workman show:
> Then by a sunne-beam I will climbe to thee.
> ("Mattens," ll. 1–4, 17–20)

One of Herbert's great achievements, therefore, in his lyrics in "The Church" is the ability to write a side of the lover-beloved dialogue available in the Petrarchan tradition only by inference and limited to very restricted patterns, chiefly along the lines of persistence in rejection or a teasing but half-hearted and easily revoked acceptance. Herbert's interchange of conversation between lover and beloved goes beyond even that achieved in his own variations on the Petrarchan tradition by Spenser, who could bring into text his beloved's joining of hands with him, again through the transforming effects of divine love, but the beloved of the *Amoretti/Epithalamion* remains mute except for her implied responses at the *Epithalamion*'s marriage rite. Herbert, on the other hand, develops the beloved role at length, allowing for a very wide range of feeling, negotiation, interaction, give-and-take of relationship. The speaker, in the role of beloved, can bring into speech dimensions of love not allowed Astrophil because they are part of Stella's role which she never gets to say.

Part of Herbert's persuasiveness in "The Church" section of *The Temple* therefore resides in the power for articulating human love that he finds in making God into the One about whom love language should be used, not "any she." This extends to the understanding of divinity, for Astrophil criticizes Cupid, manifesting "Love in boyish kind," since he made Stella his beloved and "seekst not to get into her hart" to make her love him in return. In contrast, God as lover/beloved is fully adult, is fully and by definition love, and thus "all heart." Taking the biblical language of lover/beloved found especially in the Song of Solomon, the Psalms, the prophets, and Revelation and using it as a means to transform the limitations of the received Petrarchan tradition, Herbert thus argues that God as lover/beloved makes poems possible that extend the powers of speech in articulating human experience. This opening of possibilities through the rupture of received patterns of speech and writing is characteristic of Christian language use and enables Herbert to achieve much of his distinctive power and persuasiveness.

In addition, Herbert is able to extend the vocabulary of love beyond the roles of lover/beloved in "The Church" to include other members of the human community. Unlike Astrophil, Herbert's speaker finds the intrusions of comments and observations by other figures in the community that gathers in relationship to the altar of *The Temple* to be helpful and supportive. This sets up a categorization of love; to Astrophil, love as Venus and Cupid is an essentially private experience which he cannot get his beloved to share with him in spite of his poetic work. Even when she does give him a kiss, the result is a massive misunderstanding between them that leads him to ask for more and her to deny all, destroying the relationship. That kind of love, with its resulting isolation of the speaker and privatization of his experience, is characterized by a withdrawal from community and from the world. Even Astrophil's instructions from his Muse to look into his heart, rather than in traditional sources, for a language of love reinforce his isolation. This is reflected in Astrophil's reaction to the comments of a "friend" in Sonnet 14; his remarks become "Rubarb words . . . / To grieve me worse" (ll. 5–6); the friend who speaks in Sonnet 21 is granted the praise of speaking "healthful caustics" (l. 1), but Astrophil compares all the world to Stella's fairness and refuses to listen. Love sets Astrophil against other people, against himself, and against all that might be subsumed under categories of discourse like "virtue," "reason," and the like. Love, Stella, and their articulation in verse deprive Astrophil of those resources, an isolation reinforced because there can be no socially acceptable arena for fulfilling his desire. Lord Rich may be a "rich foole" (Sonnet 24, l. 8), but he effectively stands in the way of any possibility of resolution. Astrophil does not exist in this sequence as anything but Stella's lover; even after the relationship is over, he is still, and only, a speaker of the "joyes" and "woes" she brings him (Sonnet 108). Who he is, therefore, is so totally dependent on this one manifestation of love that without it he is nothing and with it he is alone.

Herbert's speaker, on the other hand, lives in a much larger and fuller community of love. Other speakers can criticize his interpretations of love and he can accept their remarks and incorporate them into his own sense of love. Others, like the "other" speaker in "Love-joy," can join in an interpretive dialogue. In "Love Unknown" the outside speaker can take over the poem. This is a fictive world in which others may have joys and sorrows, not just the speaker. There is thus established a sense of commonality which widens and enriches the range of human experience which it is possible to bring into speech. Such inclusiveness derives, of course, from the fact that the lover/beloved relationship here is with Love as creator of all things and the source of human redemption who actively woos his creatures. The relationship between God and his person here does not have a problem with exclusiveness; its richness is so abundant, and grace so ever-flowing, the feast so bountiful, that no one is an impediment to another in the enjoyment of it. The eucharistic meal that is the central source of language and imagery here is a community meal, and thus the arena of love is a community arena. Spenser shows the way here; his lover and beloved find that their love, as God's lesson, leads out of the isolation of Petrarchan narrative into the community of a wedding feast. Herbert assumes that context for his explorations of love; as a result, his explorations of love break through the limits imposed on them by their original tradition. *Eros* now has a definite place, but it is a place where *eros* is part of a larger definition of love and can enable the articulation of all aspects of divine/human and male/female relationships as well as find in the Prayer Book rites a socially acceptable arena for its own full expression. The speaker here is fully a part of a loving community, enabled by the feast of love which orients him toward community and the kingdom.

Herbert's freedom to enact so many variations on the Petrarchan conventions and roles and narratives derives of course from the relationship he creates for his texts with biblical models as they are experienced within a lived community in the world. In contrast, love as Venus and Cupid remains an illusion, existing only in the realm of language and of imagined but never realized desire. Any approach to fulfillment thus requires giving up the fantasy-world of text, risking the chance that experience will not measure up to expectation, thus experiencing love as loss rather than fulfillment. Or so appears Astrophil's world from the perspective of Herbert's critique. On the other side, Herbert's text can posit love as discovery of new possibilities, as encountering persons at the depths of their being and aspirations, as revealing possibilities in human relationships in love beyond the stereotypes of the Petrarchan tradition (since the Bible already provides models for both male and female roles in describing God and his people in their relationship), as pointing toward a radically open future. Herbert's love is interactive, not projected, in which both parties in the relationship have voices, not the univocal text of a single speaker who desires control, but the multivocal text of lived relationships. Thus Herbert enlarges Spenser's understanding of the role of love, including *eros,* in the experience of the divine and of the human.

I must also note that among the roles played in the drama of love that Herbert creates to build the temple are parental ones. The God who speaks the word "Child" and is responded to as "My Lord" at the end of "The Collar" and who uses "darts" and deprivations to teach the speaker ("Affliction [I]"), who is "Almightie Judge" ("Judgement," l. 1), and who has "wrath" and a "rod" ("Discipline") is the paternal figure of traditional western culture. We need to see these images of God in terms of the Prayer Book's rites for ministry to the sick and dying, in which the presence of God in human suffering and fear is found through an act which it calls love. God here is One "which dost correct those whom thou dost love, and chastisest every one whom thou dost receive" (BCP, p. 307); illness and suffering thus achieve articulation as signs of divine favor, not disfavor or absence, again, for Herbert, a redefining and a reorganization of the world through a loving reorientation of things in relationship to love. Astrophil's sufferings were a sign to him of Stella's disfavor; for Herbert's speaker, they become a way of relating oneself to God as love since God "chastisest every one whom [he] dost receive."

Yet Herbert's God is maternal as well. The figure of Love that speaks "sweetly" and takes his hand "smiling" and insists that he eat meets human needs for nurture and irresistible and unquestioning acceptance that are associated with the maternal role in our cultural tradition. Such language is characteristic of the role assigned God in other eucharistic poems in "The Church" such as "The Invitation" and "The Banquet"; God as maternal figure reaches out to "All" rather than forcing divisions between sheep and goats or passing judgment. God is also "Home" where one can go when "my head doth burn, my heart is sick," where God "dost ever, ever stay." On other occasions, such as in "The British Church" and "Church-rents and Schismes," the maternal role is explicitly assigned to the Church of England, but that is the passive dimension of the maternal, that which needs "protection," needs to be "double-moated" with grace. The active maternal role, the establishment of a sense of orientation from having a sense of "home," the caretaking and feeding and giving of long-suffering and unqualified acceptance—these also are roles that Herbert's speaker assigns to God.

My point is that part of Herbert's persuasiveness in encouraging and enabling the life of his church comes from his ability to incorporate so many
understandings of and definitions of and open-ended plots for the narrative of
love into his dramatization of the divine-human relationship. Herbert's
claim, of course, is that through orienting the language of love around God
rather than around other humans we are free to live lives of love that incorporate and support and enable the Christian community to participate in the
divine reconciling work and thus connect the present to the future fulfillment
of desire in the kingdom. Such narratives of love incorporate rather than
isolate, offer the chance for fulfillment rather than promise inevitable frustration and separation, and thus have open futures rather than pasts that can only
be repeated. Herbert has thus shifted the grounds and the methods, but his
aims are still those of Spenser: to incorporate all humanity into the process of
building up the Christian commonwealth, a community of love, enabled by
love, and going toward love—"the lesson which the Lord us taught."

Love is thus the eucharistic work of the Church of England; against the
background of its ongoing worship, Herbert's *Temple* breaks the culture of
Petrarchan love language so that the biblical understandings of love can come
into speech in Herbert's world, mediating in charitable action the ancient
texts that at once judge human texts of love and then give back the ability to
love openly rather than in accord with human scripts. Because of Anglican
worship, the Bible becomes a living text in the world; in Herbert's "The
Church" it builds anew, with the verbal materials of the Petrarchan tradition,
enacting in the verbal *Temple* the transformation of language that is a sign for
the world of what its Lord is doing in his own redemptive work, promising in
life the openness and the inclusiveness and the fulfillment it achieves in text.
Rather than excluding *eros* from *The Temple,* Herbert finds a way to make the
Christian proclamation of recreation in its terms as well; the places in society
named for the play of *eros* by the Prayer Book and created in society by its use
provide Herbert with the terms to describe and enact a uniquely complex
articulation and exploration of the divine-human relationship in which all
that is human is redeemed.

Herbert's Uses of the Bible in The Temple

In the context of the Prayer Book Eucharist, the central act for Herbert other
than reception of the consecrated bread and wine was reading of the Bible.
His congregation heard the Bible read and then interpreted in sermons and
responded to it in prayer and praise and entered into the enactment of its
central episode in the Eucharist itself. Yet to be involved in the round of
reciting the Daily Offices of the Prayer Book and observing the eucharistic
lectionary is to be engaged in an experience of the Bible fundamentally different from simply reading through it the way one would any other book.[35] As I

have noted earlier in this study, the Bible for Anglicans did not become what it was claimed to be until and unless it was read in church in the context of Prayer Book worship. Then, however, it became the Word of God, again not in any simple sense of its words equaling the Word of God, but in the sense that through its use God as recreative possibility was conveyed to those by and for whom it was read, preached, and enacted in the Eucharist.

What happens in such usage is that the biblical texts appointed for any given day set up a conversation among themselves and with the present moment of reading. They become, in a very real sense, addresses to the present moment of reading, texts which connect the time of reading to the events recounted in the reading, in fact, as in "The Agonie," "measuring" the present in terms of such "past" events. The Daily Offices of Morning and Evening Prayer in Cranmer's Prayer Book call for the reading of three texts at each service—a portion of the Psalter, an Old Testament lesson, and a New Testament lesson—while the eucharistic lectionary appoints two lessons—an Epistle and a Gospel. Many of the invariable texts of the Prayer Book are also quotations from the Bible. Since Christians claim that the Bible tells one story of many saving acts of God in human history, each of the appointed lessons becomes a piece of that story which takes on a special coloring from its being brought to stand in relation to the other pieces of the story appointed for that day and to the historical situation into which they are addressed. The Prayer Book brings about the public reading of the whole Bible annually, with the Psalter repeated once a month, the New Testament once every four months, and the Old Testament once a year. Although one could, of course, read the Bible privately, for Anglicans the primary experience of the Bible was in terms of the shape given it by the way in which the Prayer Book separated it into individual episodes and brought those episodes into relationship with each other, with the prayers and sacraments of the Prayer Book, and with the ongoing conduct of people's lives. This experience gave to each day, for those like Herbert who were faithful to their ordination vows by reading the Offices, or those like Herbert's parishioners who had the chance to hear them read publicly, the special emphases of whatever texts were appointed for that day as those texts were brought into juxtaposition with the day's events. Herbert notes in "Charms and Knots" that "Who reads a chapter when they rise, / Shall ne're be troubled with ill eyes" (ll. 1–2), since the lessons for Morning Prayer called for the reading of whole chapters of the Bible's books each day. The regular, daily routine of reading the Offices, in conjunction with regular celebration of the Eucharist, thus forms the essential biblical experience for faithful Anglicans, shaping the way in which the world is perceived in biblical terms.

In "The H. Scriptures II," Herbert refers to the "configurations" of biblical texts and his desire to see "not onely how each verse doth shine, / But all the constellations of the storie" (ll. 3–4). Alluding to the interactions among the three texts appointed for the Offices and their conversation with the day of their reading, he notes that "This verse marks that, and both do make a motion / Unto a third, that ten leaves off doth lie . . . / These three make up some Christians destinie" (ll. 5–8). He then describes how the experience of the texts in light of what is going on in the reader's life is what gives these texts their meaning, while the texts themselves inform the reader's own present experience:

> Such are thy secrets, which my life makes good,
> And comments on thee: for in ev'ry thing
> Thy words do finde me out, & parallels bring,
> And in another make me understood.
>
> (Ll. 9–12)

He concludes by seeing the process of the interpretive conversation among texts and present experience as part of the process of Anglican worship aimed at realizing meaning in the future fulfillment of God's promises: "Starres are poore books, & oftentimes do misse: / This book of starres lights to eternall blisse."

Interpretation of Scripture is thus an opening of the present to meaning in biblical terms, not a closing or a subordinating of the present to something past or over. It enables the articulation of present experience in ways that bring it within the context of God's always new-making salvation history. Herbert's poems constantly affirm the achievement of meaning as contingent on God's acts and their biblical record, asserting the inadequacy of human language apart from that record to achieve the goals of writing. In "Faith," Herbert notes that "thou [dost] make proud knowledge bend & crouch / While grace fills up uneven nature." Faithful reading of the Bible together with its use to bring present experience into speech are God's gifts:

> Faith makes me any thing, or all
> That I beleeve is in the sacred storie:
> And where sin placeth me in Adams fall,
> Faith sets me higher in his glorie.

For Herbert, one's experience in the present makes biblical episodes intelligible ("thy secrets, which my life makes good") when through a reciprocal relationship the language of biblical passages makes possible the articulation of present experience ("parallels bring / And in another make me understood"). Thus his speaker finds that through musing over biblical analogues to describe his own experience and situation he becomes "understood . . . in another," presumably by himself, by others, and by God:

> If I go lower in the book,
> What can be lower then the common manger?
> Faith puts me there with him, who sweetly took
> Our flesh and frailtie, death and danger.

Part of the point here is that if one aspect of the biblical narrative enables the speaker to understand and articulate his situation ("sin placeth me in Adams fall") then the rest of the story told in biblical narrative is also available as a possibility or even promised as a future hope for him ("Faith sets me higher in his glory . . . / puts me there with him, who sweetly took / Our flesh and frailtie, death and danger"). Through faith, past becomes open to the present to incorporate present experience and enable the speaker to give voice to it; the future also becomes open as the past of biblical events comes to inform the speaker about the significance of present events and to link past and present in a common promise for the future. In this light, the Bible, in a way a radically closed book, a complete book, becomes in the context of Christian worship a book to open the world,[36] including the world of meaning, to the operations of a God who works by transformation, to make all things new, to make all signs "figure *JESUS CHRIST.*"

To understand the use of the Bible in "The Church," we need to keep firmly in mind both the process and the significance of the way in which use of the Prayer Book makes the Bible available. Herbert's method is that of Spenser; to bring into language a present moment through use of biblical "parallels"—modes and forms of speech, language, moments of narrative—is to locate the present moment of speaking within the history of salvation because to do so is to replicate in extraliturgical writing the role taken by the Bible in Anglican worship, as well as to locate that moment of speaking in relation to the normative use of the Bible in Anglican worship. For, as we have already noted, the Bible provides the Prayer Book not only with texts with which to address the congregation but also texts which enable the congregation assembled on any particular day to articulate itself to God. The regular use of the Psalter, as well as the invariable use of biblical texts such as the Lord's Prayer, the Venite, the Magnificat, and the Nunc Dimittis in various of the Prayer Book rites, makes for a weaving of Prayer Book and Bible together in use. To draw on this resource is, once more, to identify the occasions of Prayer Book use as the appropriate arena for coming to understand both the Bible and the world into which the Bible is spoken, as well as the future they both may be said to hold in common.

We have already noted how the replication at the end of "The Collar" of the biblical situation in which Abram is called away from all that Babel represents enables Herbert not only to give up human ways of creating selves through personal narratives but also to locate the speaker's "performance of knowledge" at the end of the poem in the context of the eucharistic enactment of God's salvation history. In light of Herbert's remarks in "The H. Scriptures II" about a "constellation" of three texts, we might also note that the account of Abram's call, from Genesis 12, was read annually at Evening Prayer on January 7 and that the Psalm appointed for that day was Psalm 37, which contains these lines:

> Leave off from wrath, and let go displeasure:
> Fret not thyself, else shalt thou be moved to do evil.
> Wicked doers shall be rooted out: and they that patiently abide the
> Lord, those shall inherit the land.
>
> (vv. 8–9)

On that day as well the second reading is Romans 5, which begins, "Therefore being justified by faith, we have peace with God through our Lord Jesus Christ: By whom we have access by faith into this grace wherein we stand, and rejoice in hope of the glory of God" (vv. 1–2). In this light, "The Collar" emerges as a way through the enclosure of humanly devised narratives into the appropriation of the instructions and promises held in these texts by means of recreating in the present the calling-forth of Abram, again in terms of the speaker's relationship to the "board" or altar of the eucharistic action.

A more complex example of the way in which appointed texts "do finde me out" is displayed in "Affliction (I)." This poem has been read as a quasiautobiographical text; certainly it seems to describe events in the life of the speaker that sound like events in Herbert's own life. The speaker remembers an initial experience of delight in God and an early inclination to divine service; we know that Herbert went to Cambridge University in 1609 with the intention of seeking holy orders. The speaker also mentions illness and "Academick praise"; we also know that Herbert did have bouts with sickness and that he did achieve notable academic success as university orator.

Yet the thrust of the poem describes a speaker who has increasing difficulty in understanding the narrative of his life in terms of God's actions. At the same time as he approaches a presentation of his present situation, our ability to locate that situation in the narrative of Herbert's life is diminished. While early pleasure in God and his creation leads to sickness and loss motivated by God, so too the speaker's ability to define himself in relation to a biographical narrative also becomes problematic. The one who initially gave joy soon "tok'st away my life," "didst betray me to a lingring book," "throwest me / Into more sicknesses" (ll. 31, 39, 52). God's good gifts in the early part of the poem soon turn to ashes, so that the speaker can say "thy power [doth] crossebias me, not making / Thine own gift good, yet me from my wayes taking" (ll. 53–54). At the end, the speaker must admit that "what thou wilt do with me / None of my books will show," and the poem will end in paradox: "Let me not love thee, if I love thee not."

Part of the point here is the claim that "books," the repositories of received language used to explain and account for things, fail to inform the speaker of what is going on in his relationship with God. Books only lead him to long for a functional role in creation, the way a tree is useful by providing a home for birds (ll. 57–60), rather than the more human sense of separation from the easy resolution of purpose exhibited by nature. The speaker's depiction of his situation and his struggle through language in the poem to account for that situation retreat into mystery, into puzzlement, into confusion, even as our ability to read the poem as autobiographical also becomes increasingly difficult.[37]

A further complicating factor comes from the fact that the lines that end the poem allude to 1 John 4:8—"He that loveth not knoweth not God: for God is love." If we locate the use of this reading at Evening Prayer on April 28, we find that the Old Testament reading for that day describes the gifts God gave to Solomon:

> Judah and Israel were many, as the sand which is by the sea in multitude, eating and drinking, and making merry. . . . And God gave Solomon wisdom and understanding, exceeding much, and largeness of heart, even as the sand that is on the sea shore. (1 Kings 4:20, 29)

The description of God's blessings to Solomon—the fulfillment of the ancient promise that God would lead Israel to a land flowing with milk and honey and fill it with a people more numerous than the stars in the sky or the sand on the seashore—becomes in "Affliction (I)" a way of describing what the speaker experienced early in his relationship with God: "Such starres I counted mine . . . At first thou gav'st me milk and sweetnesses" (ll. 11, 19). More of this description comes from Psalm 136, also among the texts appointed for that day:

> O give thanks unto the Lord, for he is gracious: and his mercy endureth for ever . . . Who by his excellent wisdom made the heavens . . . Who laid out the earth . . . Who hath made great lights . . . The sun to rule the day . . . The moon and stars to govern the night . . . Who giveth food to all flesh. (Vv. 1, 6, 9)

Herbert's speaker had experienced "starres" and "heav'n and earth" as "gracious benefits"; now, "Turning my purge to food, thou throwest me / Into more sicknesses." The world of wisdom in Herbert's day ("a lingering book . . . Academick praise"), first seen as a divine gift to "Melt and dissolve my rage," now becomes "books" which will not explain God's ways. In other words, praise of divine goodness and bounty that makes up these lessons appears as a memory or trace in the poem; in its place in the present of the poem come loss, suffering, and perplexity, a sense that he is "clean forgot."

What Herbert has done in this poem is to bring the speaker's situation into language in terms of a reversal of the Old Testament promises. Yet that strategy too is a using of an Old Testament model, the lament Psalm, of which Herbert had been reading several examples before April 28. The following seem to have contributed images to the speaker's articulation of his "Affliction":

> Have mercy upon me, O Lord, for I am weak . . . my bones are vexed . . . My soul also is sore troubled . . . I am weary of my groaning. (Psalm 6:2–6)

> O let my prayer enter into thy presence . . . For my soul is full of trouble . . . Thine indignation lieth hard upon me: and thou hast vexed me with all thy storms. . . . My lovers and friends hast thou put away from me and hid mine acquaintances out of my sight. (Psalm 88: 1–2, 6, 18)

> My heart is smitten down, and withered like grass: so that I forget to eat my bread. For the voice of my groaning: my bones will scarce cleave to my flesh. (Psalm 102:4–5)

The stance of the lamenter is to hold God accountable for both present ills and relief from those ills; Herbert's speaker here "entangles" the articulation of his situation in biblical lament language even as he finds God's ways with him a "crossing," an "entanglement," a being "where I could not go away, nor persevere" (ll. 46–47). The final bringing-into-language of this situation occupies the last stanza, in which the speaker remembers other biblical injunctions like that in Psalm 22, in which the psalmist can go from demanding of God, "Why hast thou forsaken me?" to asserting, "The meek shall eat and be satisfied." He also invokes the Pauline reminder in Hebrews 11:34 of those who "out of weakness were made strong." He then recoils in rejection of the demands such references appear to make on him: "Well, I will change the service, and go seek / Some other master out." But, crossed again by the echo of Christ's injunction in Matthew 6:24 ("no man can serve two masters"), he ends with yet another crossing: "Ah my deare God! though I am clean forgot, / Let me not love thee, if I love thee not" (ll. 65–66). On one level, this poem articulates the struggle to bring the meaning of divine action into human conceptual frames, into articulation in thought and writing. The speaker remembers his response to the early display of divine favor in such terms:

> I thought the service brave:
> So many joyes I writ down for my part . . .
> I looked on thy furniture so fine,
> And made it fine to me.

> . . . .

Thus argu'd into hopes, my thoughts reserved
No place for grief or fear.

. . . .

I had my wish and way.
(Ll. 2–3, 7–8, 15–16, 20)

Issues like causality, the ability to control things, and the ability to articulate experience are here defined in terms of personal responsibility for success, which the rest of the poem proves to be illusory. The turn in fortunes effaces such considerations and shifts the level at which things are known, achieved, and articulated from "thoughts" and personal volition to feelings and experience, from "my thoughts reserved / No place for grief" to "I scarce beleeved, / Till grief did tell me roundly, that I lived." The speaker who remembers his sense of an active role early in the poem finds himself now passively "blown through with ev'ry storm and winde" (l. 36).

The articulation of divine action changes as well, from "entice" and "entwine" to "betray" and "cross-bias"; the speaker's resulting sense of motion forward toward self-created and self-oriented identity shifts to a sense of being caught between: "I could not go away, nor persevere" (l. 48). God, too, is seen as behaving in perplexing ways: "Thus doth thy power . . . not making / Thine own gift good, yet me from my wayes taking." The contrast between the celebration of God's gifts in the readings from the Psalms and 1 Kings and the speaker's lament for gifts lost functions to heighten the sense of his frustration at his entrapment in God's "cross-bias." The situation at the end of the poem is one which lacks even the relief from "raving" provided by the ending of "The Collar"; the inability of humanly devised self-narratives to reach understanding combines with the failure of resources like human initiative—"I threatened oft the siege to raise"—and human learning; perhaps even the Bible itself—"what thou wilt do with me / *None* of my books will show" (emphasis added)—reaches only the stasis of the final "crossing."

At the end of "Affliction (I)" the speaker has not found that the "constellations of the storie . . . make up some Christians destinie"; instead, "what thou wilt do with me" remains unclear. Yet the very ability to articulate this situation in terms of a Psalmic or Jobean lament places it within the context of the ways in which Anglican use of the Bible comes to inform present moments. Shakespeare has Edgar say, as he confronts his blinded father, "the worst is not / So long as we can say, 'This is the worst' " (*Lear,* IV.i.27–28). When the Bible, as used in Anglican worship, can provide the resources to bring situations like this one into language, then the situation can come to be understood in terms of the speaker's ongoing relationship to the God mediated through that worship. We can still note that the speaker has relinquished his own efforts at understanding in favor of letting God be the actor, even if

that, for the moment, must be in negative terms: "Ah my deare God . . . /
Let me not." What the speaker performs at the end of this poem is letting
God be God. If this is a poem articulating the human struggle to bring the
meaning of divine action into human conceptual frames, then "thy power
[doth] cross-bias" those frames, rendering inadequate the ones achieved so far
and described early in the poem. Yet part of the point of this poem is to teach
the difficulty of conceptualizing God and his ways and to locate that difficulty
in the relationship with God himself as part of the process of taking part in
the way that is Christ and is in Christ, and is the way of the cross.

In this context, the speaker may soon come to be able to hear more of 1
John 4, especially verse 10 ("Herein is love, not that we loved God, but that
he loved us, and sent his Son to be the propitiation for our sins"), in light of
the kind of language interpreting that sense of love found in the Prayer Book
rite for the Visitation of the Sick: "whom the Lord loveth, he chastiseth"
(BCP, p. 302). But that time is not yet at the end of "Affliction (II)" as a
bringing into language of a situation which seems to deny the efficacy of
divine promises ends still seeking a way for its articulation to become part of
the process that leads to the fulfillment of those promises.

A poem like "Affliction (I)" points to the locating of the articulation of the
God-human relationship in moments with language that do not end so much
as they open possibilities before us. Words, cut loose from the possibility or
even the necessity of constructing a closed narrative of beginnings, middles,
and ends, can play against each other to set up resonances and associations
within the enactment of Anglican worship as a verbal field of interplay between action, text, and world, seen as the vehicle of God's action in human
time and history, which can open the closure of discourse to the playful renewal of the world by the Word. The speaker's story at the end of "Affliction
(I)" is not yet over; meaning is deferred, yet it is deferred to another story,
that of God's dealings with his creatures, which itself is not yet over, so that
the meaning of the poem comes to reside in yet another deferral of meaning.
As long as biblical language can be used to bring texts like this into being,
however, the events related in this way can teach and persuade to deeper
engagement in a life that enables the articulation of both human joy and
human suffering and thus finds both as episodes in the way of Christ.

This poem thus makes sense in terms of what A. C. Charity has called
"applied typology";[38] the biblical text is a living language with which to talk
about a present reality because the events described in typological language in
the Bible are still open to the speaker's participation. As a result, the events
described in this poem and others in *The Temple* are informed by interchanges
with biblical events and come to function didactically in relationship to those
events. In this way, Cranmer's theology of participation in the afterlife of
God's actions in Christ through community use of bread and wine finds its

signifier and enabler in the interchanges of behavior among the Word, biblical words, and contemporary words.

In such poems, Herbert creates a speaker who performs texts in the psalmic mode, using stances, vocabulary, and themes drawn from biblical example ("parallels bring"), thus reinforcing the argument that through using such models to dramatize moments in the divine-human relationship one becomes part of that relationship even when the theme of the poem is estrangement or distance from God. By finding biblical situations as analogues to present moments and therefore providing the appropriate means to make poems out of such moments, Herbert is able to bring present experience into persuasive language. In this, the use of "applied typology"—the language of the Bible itself for indicating the significance of the events it describes—is extremely significant. We are familiar with some uses of typology, expecially in the New Testament, in which for example the Israelites' passage through the Red Sea becomes an antitype, an anticipation, of Christ's baptism. But the Bible's use of past events to describe later events has deeper implications. On the one hand, it is an admission that human language fails before the acts of God in time. The only language appropriate to talk about a new act of God is the language of past divine acts. Thus, Jesus is a new Moses or a new Elijah; his resurrection a new Exodus or a new act of creation.

More than that, however, the use of typological language says something about the nature of the new act; it puts that act into continuity with past saving events. Thus, when during the eucharistic prayer the celebrant recounts the history of divine acts, he locates the present moment of celebration in the sequence of those acts and thus provides the present moment with a future, sharing in the future promise inherent in the past acts. God called Abraham and promised a land of plenty for his descendants; he called Moses and promised deliverance from Egypt. In the same manner also he calls his people together in the present and makes the same promises anew to them. Thus, when Herbert uses this language to articulate present experience, he is making the claim that the Bible is not a closed narrative but an account of a story that is still going on. In fact, he is making the claim that the events he relates are part of that narrative precisely because it is possible to articulate them in the language that narrative uses.

Herbert is thus able to populate his poems with biblical figures and recapitulations of biblical events. In "Aaron," for example, the speaker finds his ability to claim a priesthood like Aaron's because of his incorporation into the Body of Christ through his role in the celebration of the Sacraments. He thus can describe his present situation in terms of the past biblical figure because of his participation in that community which is created by its use of the text from which such descriptions come. In "Christmas" Herbert finds "My dearest Lord" at "the next inne"; in "Redemption" he finds his "rich Lord" among "theeves and murderers: there I him espied, / Who straight, *Your suit is granted*, said & died." The point is that for the speaker of these poems, as (potentially) for us as readers, the past event of the Crucifixion is not "past" in our sense of time but part of the present moment of our experience. If it were not, our "suit" could not be granted; we would be excluded from incorporation into God's salvation history. But because Herbert, through using the language of "applied typology," claims that the saving events of God's history are present to us and demonstrates that claim by finding in biblical language the resources to articulate present experience, we gain the sense of the openness of that salvation history to us.

Such a way of applying biblical language to present moments of experience makes two claims. First, it stresses the urgency of the present moment and heightens the importance of the reader's response. Second, it points out that the reader is in a position of choice. Herbert first uses the rhetoric of presenting choice in the "Perirrhanterium" section of "The Church Porch," where clear options are offered for living out the Christian life and the implications of making choices are clarified. Our need to make choices is heightened in importance; to accept the claim that God's salvation history is open to readers in the present and to find ourselves within it is one of our options; the other is to reject the claim those events have over us and to find ourselves excluded, the events merely "past." In this way especially Herbert acts out in his poems the didactic function he outlines for the priest in *The Country Parson*. The possibilities that open before the reader in Herbert's poems, achieved through his distinctive incorporation of biblical modes of presentation, are part of his persuasive strategy. To adopt the perspective made available through biblical claims is to experience the breaking-through of human narrative frames, an experience Herbert hopes will move his readers to share that perspective with him.

Herbert is able to use biblical language in *The Temple* to create a sense of the ongoingness of God's actions because of the way in which he locates that usage in the context of the church's corporate life, where the Bible provides the language used to bring pressure to bear on the present and to articulate that present before God. Since in the Anglican tradition the important thing is participation in the life of the community gathered at the altar rather than adherence to a particular verbal code of belief, the role of the Bible in Anglican worship is to bring the community into contact with the ancient stories in the context of that community's life together formed by the sacramental enactment of those stories, so that those stories can come to have meaning for the present moment of hearing and enactment. Herbert enacts and contributes to the conversation between the gathered community and the biblical texts that speak a transforming word to that community. The constant invitation of this conversation is to find that the biblical narrative is not closed but open to continuation in the present by means of continued use of biblical language to articulate the present to that community.

What Herbert achieves in *The Temple* is a relationship between speakers and biblical texts that replicates the use of the Bible in Anglican worship. By enclosing his poems within the texts of the Bible and the Prayer Book or within the biblical narrative as enacted in the use of the Prayer Book, a "double-moating" of his text ("The British Church," l. 29), Herbert mirrors the theme of enclosure that functions throughout *The Temple*[39] and teaches his readers how to use these resources to bring the present moment of their own experience inside God's narrative of salvation. Human life, enclosed by death, thus also becomes enclosed by God's saving actions. The "intombing" of flesh ("Church-monuments," l. 2), the "locking" and "binding" effects of sin ("Church-lock and Key," ll. 1–2) that destroy the "stately house" ("The World," l. 1) of love and the "house" of human endeavor are all transformed, or set free from their conventional referents through God's "double-moating," so that "all these dyings may be life in death" ("Mortification," l. 36). What is formed is a new enclosure, built by "Love and Grace . . . a braver Palace then before" ("The World," ll. 19–20) that is not binding but freeing. Yet Herbert also combines the image of the church as building with the church as journey, as in the process of building, in which "death is fair, / And but a chair" ("The Pilgrimage," ll. 35–36), moving toward images of climbing and building and singing: what builds is the new song which is already being sung but between the words of the old songs, in the struggle to use them, in the process of effacing them, of acting out language's complex situation in the midst of all the texts that convey the Word:

> Wherefore I sing. Yet since my heart,
> > Though press'd, runnes thin;
> O that I might some other hearts convert,
> > And so take up at use good store:
> That to thy chest there might be coming in
> > Both all my praise, and more!
> > > ("Praise [III]," ll. 37–42)

Herbert's "building" of "The Church" is thus a prayerful enactment of language in offering that it be an agency of the divine action, enabling the building up of the body that is journey and song, the enclosure of Christ and the enclosing of Christ, "that we may evermore dwell in him, and he in us." In this light, all the pain and struggle and dying become part of the journey, part of the seeking, part of the building (as seeking becomes part of the process of building), to sing the new song:

> Let the wonder of his pitie
> > Be my dittie,

And take up my lines and life:
Hearken under pain of death,
                Hands and breath;
Strive in this, and love the strife.
                ("The Banquet," ll. 49–54)

Spenser's "dittie" was (and was not) of the city to come, an appropriate emphasis for a poet seeking to orient the conduct of public life toward the building up of the Christian commonwealth. Herbert's "dittie" is of the "wonder of his pittie," an emphasis on the divine concern for and response to human suffering appropriate for a poet who actively seeks to nurture and heal human brokenness as the way of incorporating the private and personal of human life into the building up of the Body of Christ as the community on the way to the city of God's promises. Against the conventional portrait of Herbert as the "sweet singer of Bemerton" we need to notice here the importance of conflict ("love the strife") in Herbert's depiction of the relationship with God we are called to have. He is honest about conflict as part of the divine-human relationship and in fact claims that conflict does not define one as being outside this relationship. One does not, and does not have to, please God all the time; conflict here is essential to the relationship since through struggling with God one moves to deeper awareness of divine love and forgiveness. In enacting such moments of discovery, Herbert makes his poems didactic in that they seek to persuade his readers to articulate their experience in such terms and thus to understand the moment of reading as productive of a confrontation between them and God's acts and thus transformational of the reader. And that response is defined in Herbert in terms of the reorientation of the reader toward the ongoing life of the church:

For as thy absence doth excell
                All distance known:
So doth thy nearenesse bear the bell,
                Making two one.
                ("The Search," ll. 57–60)

It is the scene of the church, realized through use of the Prayer Book, to which Herbert called his parishioners by the ringing of his "*Saints-bell*"[40] and where he proclaimed "God is more there, then thou" ("Perirrhanterium," l. 404), in which we may make two one "in him, and he in us" (BCP, p. 263).

In regard to its uses of language, "The H. Scriptures I" takes a similar approach. This poem, a hymn of praise to the Bible, presents a series of images for a "book," providing terms which enable the Bible to be seen as a different kind of collection of words than the books of "Affliction (I)" which could not tell the speaker what to expect from God. To achieve this, Herbert describes the Bible in heavily sacramental language. In quatrain 1 it is a kind of feast, as the speaker asks his heart to suck honey from every letter, an image of Eucharist as well as of nursing, or Eucharist as nursing. In quatrains 2 and 3 it is a glass that "mends the lookers eyes," but it is also "the well / That washes what it shows" (ll. 9–10), a combination of baptismal imagery, restorative in its creation of a new life to mirror as well as to "wash" the old life apart from the eucharistic community, with the reflective properties of water that form the vehicle of divine action in the sacrament of baptism. But again, Herbert's discourse is paradoxical; rather than filling the breast of the one who sucks in quatrain 1, the Bible works "To cleare the breast" in quatrains 2 and 3, the distorting effect of the mirror or well-bottom image becoming a correcting rather than a confusing one. At the end, the paradox is caught up in a final turn: "heav'n lies flat in thee, / Subject to ev'ry mounters bended knee." How heaven can lie flat is unclear, as is how a mounter is also a kneeler, except in the sense that kneeling to receive the Eucharist is the way to hope of "thy everlasting kingdom." What Herbert is asking here is that we experience the Bible as text, seen in the context of a sacramental life, which opens up the world to possibilities the human mind, or human language, is unable to grasp or enable language to mean, thus opening a "window" in the world for divine activity. The copiousness of divine self-disclosure ("heav'n lies flat in thee") through the Bible and through the invitation to participate in Christ through eucharistic reception is what Herbert would delight us with.

In this way, Herbert seeks to open his readers to receive that which the human tendency to distance and isolate would close off. He would remind us of the profound sense of sinfulness that attaches to the ways language is used to distance through distinctions and generalities the very God on whom all are dependent for everything. Certainly, Herbert himself seeks to make his own art open to the divine action in the Spirit; as he says in "Easter," "Consort both heart and lute, and twist a song / . . . Or, since all musick is but three parts vied / And multiplied, / O let thy blessed Spirit bear a part, / And make up our defects with his sweet art" (ll. 13–18). A similar motif enables the ending of "Denial" to tease us into the possibility of divine art, as God acts to "mend my ryme" (l. 30), or, as in "Josephs Coat," when "his power . . . once did bring / My *joyes* to *weep,* and now my *griefs* to *sing*" (ll. 13–14). As Herbert claims in "A True Hymn":

> if th'heart be moved,
> Although the verse be somewhat scant,
>   God doth supply the want.
> As when th'heart sayes (sighing to be approved)
> *Oh, could I love!* and stops: God writeth, *Loved.*
>
> (Ll. 16–20)

Part of the point here, of course, is that what enables the writing of poetry in a eucharistic context is not what the speaker can do but what God is doing for the speaker, and for the reader. Thus the image of God as poet, supplying what the speaker-as-poet lacks, often in surprising and unexpected ways ("God writeth, *Loved*"), enables Herbert to act out in his poems what Cranmer presents as the enabling love of God through "grace . . . [to] continue in that holy fellowship, and do all such good works as thou hast prepared for us to walk in" (BCP, p. 265).

In "Divinitie," Herbert contrasts the "Epicycles," the "spheres," products of the "curious questions and divisions" which humanity has devised "for fear the starres should sleep and nod," with the "doctrine" of Christ, which appears to humans as "dark instructions . . . / Who can these Gordian knots undo?" (ll. 19–20). These "beams of truth" are the ones with which we are now familiar: *"Love God, and love your neighbour. Watch and pray. / Do as ye would be done unto"* (ll. 17–18). What clarifies doctrine, "undoes" the knot, is not thought like that which produces epicycles, but eucharistic participation leading to charitable action:

> But he doth bid us take his bloud for wine.
> Bid what he please; yet I am sure,
> To take and taste what he doth there designe,
> Is all that saves, and not obscure.
>
> (Ll. 21–24)

The simple doing of the Eucharist becomes what gives meaning to words, not "Reason." Thus we are enjoined, "burn thy Epicycles . . . / Break all thy spheres," for "Faith needs no staffe of flesh, but stoutly can / To heav'n alone both go, and leade" with Christ as way and enabler of the way, both goal for the journey and food and drink to nourish us on the way.

Faithful reliance on the Spirit is what Herbert claims enables him to use language in spite of its problematic nature, especially to force an opening, in effect to "wound" human confidence in and insistence on interpretive language, and yet to see such acts of wounding as ways of opening the universe of human discourse to the transforming powers of the Spirit and to weave yet another web of words, the "Fine nets and stratagems to catch us in," in which all things, all words, become new in figuring Christ.

We might also see a poem like "Prayer (I)" as a text that opens possibilities by effacing generic forms. Herbert asks in an early poem, "Why are not *Sonnets* made of thee?" In "Prayer (I)," he transforms the conventional expectations of the sonnet form in ways that raise questions about the genre that parallel the kinds of questions raised by the text itself about its subject. At every point, this poem resists conventional definition and thus generic "pinning down." Herbert's audience was accustomed to the varieties of the secular sonnet in both its Italian and English forms and some late Renaissance experiments with them, but "Prayer (I)" upsets any conventional anticipation of how it might proceed. Unlike the Italian sonnet, with its clearly defined octave and sestet, Herbert's poem varies the rhyme scheme of the first eight lines, making them into two quatrains as in the English form, but that pattern is not sustained. The rhyme scheme of the poem is *abab cdcd effe gg*, a form that reflects neither standard pattern. If one begins the poem expecting an English sonnet, one looks in vain for a clearly defined grouping into three image and idea units with concluding couplet. If there is a "concluding" image, it is found in the ending "something understood," but that occupies less than half of the final line, not the entire concluding couplet. If, on the other hand, one changes expectations in the middle and looks for the two-part division of the Italian form, one is again frustrated. There is no sense in which the first eight lines form a unit or octave responded to by the sestet. Herbert, by ending the first and second groups of four lines with a semicolon, reinforces our expectation of finding an English sonnet, but that only makes the absence of strong end-punctuation at the end of line 12 and the failure to offer the concluding couplet even more confusing. The complete absence of a verb in this poem only serves to heighten our sense of a deliberate effort to play the poem and its subject off against conventional expectations of both.

What Herbert does give us in "Prayer (I)" is an extended list of images for prayer, perhaps twenty-seven, more or less, depending on how one makes key interpretive decisions. These, too, evoke conflicting responses—each reader will find some of Herbert's definitions of prayer familiar and others unfamiliar, thus feeling at once affirmed in his understanding of prayer and also stretched and broadened to accept other ways of describing it. At the same time, such a conscious display of images raises questions about the adequacy of any such list; once the process of listing has begun, the reader may find himself drawn to extend the list and thus engaged in a process of thought about prayer. But if that is the case, prayer becomes something that extends beyond the capacities of any human listing process, a mystery that at once demands human discourse and reminds us of its limitations, including the failure of "Prayer (I)" to encompass prayer. One is left with the divine injunction to pray in spite of the limitations of human abilities to conceptualize and verbalize such activity, having as a result of this poem both learned something about prayer and unlearned something about language. Prayer's mystery exceeds our abilities to conceptualize it, yet the attempt to conceptualize coupled with the frustration of that activity is the necessary path to participation in that mystery. One answer to the question posed here is of course Cranmer's Prayer Book, but its copious variety only echoes Herbert's sense of abundance.

Such a technique is also manifest in "Easter-Wings," another of Herbert's "shaped" verses. Having taken language from Psalm 57, one of the Psalms appointed for Morning Prayer on Easter Day to write "Easter," he continues this practice in its companion poem. "Easter" expands on verses 8 and 9 of Psalm 57: "I will sing, and give praise. / Awake up, my glory; awake, lute and harp: I myself will awake quite early." "Easter-Wings" takes the imagery of wings from verse 1 of that Psalm—"under the shadow of thy wings shall be my refuge"—and other language from Psalm 113 appointed for Evening Prayer on Easter Day—"He taketh the simple out of the dust: and lifted the poor out of the mire" (v. 6). The Gospel for Easter in the Prayer Book is John's account of the discovery of the empty tomb, with its attendant reference to the issue of interpretation ("they knew not the Scripture that he should rise again from the dead"), which suggests once more the paradigm of using what Herbert in "The H. Scriptures II" calls "parallels" from the Bible to inform present events in a way that enables participation in those events.

With this in mind, "Easter-Wings" may be described in light of the way it uses an enactment of its biblical references to usurp the claims of classical literature in a way similar to that employed by Spenser in *Epithalamion.* "Easter-Wings" depends for its full impact on the reader's knowing Herbert's models for the poem's shape, the two poems from *The Greek Anthology* by Simias entitled "Wings" and "The Axe."[41] Herbert objects to secular love poetry in an early sonnet ("Doth Poetry / Wear *Venus* Livery? only serve her turn?"), a question in effect responded directly to here, because the form of "Easter-Wings" in the Williams manuscript is in the shape of Simias' "Wings," which are the wings of *eros.* In Herbert's poem, however, the conventional effects of love, made familiar in secular Renaissance love poetry, become not proofs of love but of "sicknesses and shame," the punishment of "sinne," that make the speaker "Most poore" and "Most thinne." In Herbert's final version of "Easter-Wings," however, the shape had become that of another poem by Simias, "The Axe," which is the axe of Epeus, who made the Trojan horse. While this may have appealed to Herbert because Simias refers to Epeus as one who was a servant and who brought water from "living springs," as Christ did, Herbert also works a more profound reinterpretation of Simias' work.

Simias' "Axe" is a very special kind of shaped poem, one intended to be read from the outside in, by reading the first and last lines, then the second and next-to-last lines, and so forth, working in to the middle; the narrow central lines thus contain the concluding words of the poem. By in effect turning the poem inside out, Herbert makes the progress of reading replicate the process of experiencing sin's punishment by having the lines as well as the speaker's statement become "Most poore" and "most thinne"; in reversing Simias' pattern, the speaker and the reader also achieve a move outward away from poverty and thinness into expansion of lines and "flight." By taking the lines of the earlier version of "Easter-Wings" and forming them into the shape of Simias' "Axe," Herbert also achieves the shape of the Greek *chi,* literally "x-ing" out *eros,* incorporating it into the name of Christ, effacing pagan love by Christian love using the change of shape to transform its meaning, thus making the instrument of Epeus' death-dealing treachery into a sign of God's life-giving love. What one now moves into at the center of these stanzas is not a line achieving the end of the poem but a space, an opening between words, even as the empty tomb is the event of Easter celebrated in the text of the poem,[42] which means the poem can continue. What was the conclusion of Simias' "Axe" now becomes the (apparent) conclusion to human life (death) which is reversed as the lines again lengthen when the speaker asks to "rise" with the one who leaves the tomb empty.

This opening in words, in time, in human conceptual and interpretive efforts becomes that which informs Herbert's use of language. It is, after all, "with thee" that the speaker prays to "rise" and "combine" to make true what the pattern of the words performs, the expansion of meaning and lines into the action as well as the shape of wings. As in the case of "The Altar," the speaker gives no sign that he knows his words take this shape; it is in the play of shapes for the reader that Herbert is able to efface the older forms of love in the name of a love that promises a resurrection, making what in the poem appears as the "empty tomb" of space between the *extremis* of the speaker's condition—"Most poore" and "Most thinne"—into the prayerful affirmation that "With thee" the speaker can "rise" and "combine" in a way that reverses interpretations and expectations, so that "Affliction shall advance the flight in me."

Poetic manifestations of language, when seen as human interpretation, thus become the tomb of interpretation, of meaning imposed on experience, and yet can also be the vehicle of grace, or at least the vehicle of instituting in the reader a move toward sources of grace in the church's liturgical life. In "H. Baptisme (I)," the speaker alludes to the renewal of baptismal vows, part of the purpose in the Prayer Book of having baptisms as part of regular Sunday services and not in private ("when I view my sinnes, mine eyes remove / More backward still, and to that water flie"), which enables an interpretation of present and "future sinnes" as discredited in the divine interpretation of the speaker:

> You taught the Book of Life my name, that so
> What ever future sinnes should me miscall,
> Your first acquaintance might discredit all.
>
> (Ll. 12–14)

God's book, as opposed to human books, can rewrite human narratives in ways that transform them into texts with different endings so that through God's Word "future sinnes" can only "miscall" the speaker's name. In Christ, human activity in time is rewritten; God as reader of his book makes his misreadings true and the truth of human behavior a "miscalling" which divine activity discredits so that the narrative of humanity can have an ending open to as yet unspoken possibilities.

Such a paradoxical conclusion points to locating the articulation of the God-human relationship not in the language of philosophical or even conventional poetic discourse but in those moments enacted through language in which articulation comes to reside in moments that do not end so much as they open possibilities before us, opening the closure of discourse to the playful renewal of the world by the Word. A similar pattern is acted out in "Love unknown," in which the speaker seeks to tell a "tale" that "is long and sad" (l. 1); it involves an effort to interpet the Christian life as it moves in relation to the Sacraments ("font" and "holy bloud") as well as experiences defined as *"AFFLICTION."* In each case, what results is not what the speaker expects, but what the second speaker he encounters terms as the action of One who would "renew," make "supple," and "mend." This poem raises for the speaker the possibility of finding in such terms the ability to bring the agonies of Christian living within the eucharistic process of making all things *"new, tender, quick."*

The second speaker's counter-interpretations literally "pierce" the body of the text in three places (ll. 18, 37, and 56), wounding the speaker's self-composed narrative; his remarks enact the elision the speaker notes at lines 51 and 52 ("some had stuff'd the bed with thoughts, / I would say *thorns*"). As thorns, the second speaker's remarks interrupt the narrative constructed by the first, who repeatedly incorporates the second speaker's interpretations favorably ("Indeed 'tis true"; "Indeed it's true"; "Indeed," respectively) yet persists in telling the tale as one "long and sad."[43] Finally, the second speaker takes over the telling of the tale to make it one of "more favour then you wot of" by giving a counter-ending that retells the speaker's tale but casts it in the light of words like "renew," "supple," and "mend." As readers, we do not get the chance to see what the speaker would do with such a reinterpretation; he disappears into silence, leaving us to evaluate this reading in light of actual experience of the sacramental life. It is thus as vehicle of the Spirit that human words, even the words of the Bible, function meaningfully, not as mirrors or pointers to meaning or truth expressed in abstract terms. The function of extraliturgical language, such as Herbert's poetry, is to take away from our reliance on the world structuring of conventional language use and thus open experience to the transforming power of the Spirit that is working to make all things new.

In such terms we may examine Herbert's repeated image of God as artist; poems that appeal to the divine creativity manifest their dependence in the insistence that God make a poem of the speaker, but in so doing themselves become proclamations of the divine activity on which their very existence is based. In "Deniall," the speaker describes a past experience of the absence of divine hearing, resulting in a broken heart and broken verse; the poem itself, because of its failure to rhyme its concluding lines, becomes the broken verse that resulted. Yet by the end of the poem, the speaker's prayer that "thy favours granting my request," a future expectation, becomes present in the poem's ending, "They and my minde may chime, / And mend my ryme." As in other poems in "The Church" based on the psalmic lament model, the act of requesting in "Deniall" becomes the vehicle of response, or at least the claim to response, that opens the possibility of divine activity in the world, available to the reader by means of his own search for it.

The theme of God as poet and the speaker as God's poem recurs frequently throughout *The Temple.* In "Love I" God is "authour of this great frame"; in "Nature" to tame the speaker's heart is God's "highest art," to be achieved when God "Engrave thy rev'rend Law and fear" in the speaker's "rugged heart." In "Perirrhanterium" the effects of sin are described in terms of impairing our ability to read God's text: "It blots thy lesson written in thy soul; / The holy lines cannot be understood." God's redemptive action restores humanity to an earlier state of obedience through teaching us to read correctly: "All knees shall bow to thee; all wits shall rise, / And praise him who did make and mend our eies" ("Love II," ll. 13–14). Thus,

> The grosser world stands to thy word and art;
>   But thy diviner world of grace
>   Thou suddenly dost raise and race,
> And ev'ry day a new Creatour art.
>   ("The Temper [II]," ll. 5–8)

In this light, the speaker's poetry is effective when it is joined with God's poetry, expressed in his divine actions, as in "Christmas":

> The shepherds sing; and shall I silent be?
>   My God, no hymne for thee?
> My soul's a shepherd too; a flock it feeds
>   Of thoughts, and words, and deeds.
> The pasture is thy word: the streams, thy grace
>   Enriching all the place.
> Shepherd and flock shall sing, and all my powers
>   Out-sing the day-light houres.

God's Word is thus not "word" but place where divine action ("Enriching all the place") performs its transfiguration of human experience, including human expectations about narrative outcomes, to "out-sing" the limitations of human ability apart from the divine activity. Together, however, "His beams shall cheer my breast, and both so twine, / Till ev'n his beams sing, and my musick shine" ("Christmas," ll. 15–22, 33–34).

Herbert's use of the metaphor of God as poet translates the activity of God in the church into the terms of "The Church" as a collection of poems. Herbert's speakers exist in poems; the "metaphorical God" of *The Temple* acts to overcome the limitations in articulation experienced by these speakers. Their words stand revealed as inefficient, distorting, counter-productive ("We say amisse, / This or that is: / Thy word is all, if we could spell" ["The Flower," ll. 19–21]), but at those points at which God acts to correct or rewrite them, they are also revealed as vehicles of divine action which God can choose to use in spite of their insufficiencies. When that happens, the speakers have to release their desire to write their lives and thus control them in favor of using language as an offering of "ourselves, our souls and bodies, to be a living sacrifice unto thee."

To do so, however, is to find oneself involved in a relationship and process of opening oneself to God's Word as it is heard in the context of Prayer Book worship. The song of the shepherds, which the speaker of "Christmas" would make his own, is, according to Luke 2:14–20, a song of "glorifying and praising God" taught them by the angels; it is the opening of *Gloria in excelsis,* found at the end of "The Church" and of the church's eucharistic rite. Reading Herbert, therefore, is a process of constantly being referred to another Word as the source of informing poetic power and meaning through allusion to the biblical text as used in Anglican worship. If we admire what we find in Herbert, he implies, we are thus directed to the original of what we like.

At the same time, if we are drawn from Herbert's poetic craftsmanship to wonder at God's framing and redeeming art, so we are drawn from delight at our own abilities as readers to see ourselves as God sees us. In "The Temper (I)," for example, the speaker sets out to find a stance from which to "praise thee, Lord"; he feels his rhymes "should . . . / Gladly engrave thy love in steel" if he could experience always what his soul feels sometimes. What the speaker is about is an attempt to strike a bargain with God, asking that God not "rack" him "to such a vast extent," sometimes taking him "above fourtie heav'ns, or more," sometimes "to hell." Instead, he wishes refuge in church ("thy roof") where "Then of a sinner thou art rid, / And I of hope and fear." As a result, he argues, this poetry will be better able to praise enduringly once he is rid of the changes and chances of this life. Yet by the end of the poem the speaker is reconciled to God's way with him ("Yet take thy way; for sure thy way is best") and thus can use God's way with him to produce poetry that God will find acceptable: "This is but tuning of my breast, / To make the musick better" (ll. 23–24). What makes the speaker's assent possible is a change in his understanding, away from the human tendency to divide, to categorize, to label:

> Whether I flie with angels, fall with dust,
> Thy hands made both, and I am there:

> Thy power and love, my love and trust
> Make one place ev'ry where.
>
> (Ll. 25–28)

Thus, because the speaker has changed his concept of where God is to be found, his ability to write "praise" is restored; because Herbert has taken us through the speaker's thought processes, our own perceptual constructs are also changed as we come to see the speaker, and ourselves, in a world in which God is always active in spite of evidence to the contrary. A similar pattern of change in perception is charted in "Even-song," in which the speaker begins with a sense of God's love in giving him the ability "Both to be busie, and to play" and God's judgment on how he spent his time. The speaker finally reconciles both his work and his worry:

> Not one poore minute scapes thy breast,
> But brings a favour from above;
> And in this love, more then in bed, I rest.
>
> (Ll. 30–32)

God's service is freedom; participation in his actions, rest.

Herbert's poems, therefore, are poems of process which function in a variety of ways to engage us as readers. We are challenged to behave in certain ways, to "grone" to be "holy, pure, and cleare." We are taught our inadequacies of thinking, of reading, of interpreting and thus see ourselves anew in light of the images and processes Herbert offers us and puts us through. At the same time, however, we are taught the source of hope, of light, of right reading; we are told whose Word not only judges us but also transforms us into a new creation through love. Herbert's poems always point us beyond and through themselves to the God whose Word is the standard for all Herbert's words, a Word which judges but which accepts in love a copious range of caring responses to that judgment. The most obvious source of that Word is the Bible, "joyes handsell; heav'n lies flat in thee." Yet for Herbert that is only one source. Herbert points us primarily to the Word made flesh, to God's act of love in Christ, and to the church, which is his earthly body, the context for Herbert of Bible reading, the living extension of God's Word, a continuation of his saving actions, as it is the continuing context for the Bible to be read and discovered as the story of God's actions.

In this light it is again the process of Christian poem making that matters, not the conclusion. In "Jordan (II)" the ending—"*how wide is all this long pretence! / There is in love a sweetnesse readie penn'd: / Copie out onely that and save expense*" (ll. 16–18)—would seem to undercut what has gone before, including Herbert's speaker's description of his "lines of heav'nly joyes . . . / Curling with metaphors a plain intention" (ll. 1–3). Yet in the poem it is the copiousness of the speaker's mind that leads not to poetry but to the speaker's "blott[ing] what I had begunne." Only in the process that moves between the depiction of the struggle with copiousness and the injunction to "Copie" the sweetness "readie penn'd" in love that results is to be found the intent of the poem Herbert gives us.

Herbert's "Church" thus enacts a leap of faith, an act of proclamation that if the poet's "heart be mov'd," then "Although the verse be somewhat scant, / God doth supplie the want" (ll. 16–18). In this poem "A true Hymne," as in other poems in "The Church," the Christian proclamation about divine love for God's creatures becomes that which not only enables poems to be written but also answers the speaker's and reader's human needs: "As when th'heart sayes (sighing to be approved) / *O, could I love!* and stops: God writeth *Loved*" (ll. 19–20). This play with the image of God as poet and his creatures as poems he is writing teaches a vocabulary for considering humanity as that which is being made into God's new song and models an engagement in that process in the writing of Christian poetry itself. In "Sepulchre," the speaker contemplating human culpability in Christ's Passion notes that "as of old the Law by heav'nly art / Was writ in stone; so thou, which also art / The letter of the word, find'st no fit heart / To hold thee" (ll. 17–20). Yet even as "heart" always holds "art," whether fit to do so or not, so "nothing can . . . / from loving man / Withhold thee" (ll. 22–24).

In "Love (III)" this persistence of divine loving action becomes the re-capitulative paradox in which Herbert develops "The Church." This poem is not another effort at "the reducing of Man to the Obedience of God," although it acts out a process of becoming obedient. It is not another praise of divine power expressed in temporal action, although it might lead to such praise. This poem that comes just before Herbert's allusion to the *Gloria in excelsis* is not another humbling of self before God, although that, too, might result. It is not another attempt to find a strategy in which God can be brought to speak "My servant," thus assuring enclosure in the divine salvation history. It is, instead, a dramatization of Herbert's final didactic play on the paradox that the divine promise is not dependent on human agency, even human interpretive skill or skill in discourse, since the One Christians proclaim was and is and is to come comes not to be served but to serve:

> Love bade me welcome: yet my soul drew back,
>> Guiltie of dust and sinne.
> But quick-ey'd Love, observing me grow slacke
>> From my first entrance in,
> Drew nearer to me, sweetly questioning,
>> If I lack'd any thing
>
> (Ll. 1–6)

Herbert in these lines takes the Anglican Eucharist and interprets it in terms of Jesus' parable in Luke 12:31–40: "Blessed are those servants whom the lord when he cometh shall find watching: verily I say unto you, that he shall gird himself, and make them to sit down to meat, and will come forth and serve them." The speaker's persistent response in "Love (III)" is in terms of a self-interpretation that sees only human unworthiness, a coming-to-understand self precisely as that which separates the speaker from God. This human sense of unworthiness comes to be seen as that which provokes interpretive activity that would deny human contingency and assert human rather than divine responsibility for meeting human needs: "A guest, I answer'd, worthy to be here: / Love said, You shall be he" (ll. 7–8). In response, Herbert casts Love/Christ/God as refusing to take the speaker's sense of unworthiness as a final and concluding answer, as constantly undercutting the sense of self that would create identity in separation, and as substituting a new self, one in relationship, that is as a result worthy to be at the table, since it acknowledges the creative role of God at every level:

> I the unkinde, ungrateful? Ah my deare,
>   I cannot look on thee.
> Love took my hand, and smiling did reply,
>   Who made the eyes but I?
>
>   (Ll. 9–12)

Playing on the tropes of Christ as recreative love, Herbert reminds us that the Eucharist is done in Christ; at his altar, God sees the church as Christ and makes the church into Christ. In this poem acts of touch, acts of greeting, acceptance, interposition of Love between the speaker and his isolate sense of self consume that sense of self and the words that display it. Abstract doctrines of self and of the Eucharist are effaced in favor of the speaker's entry into and discovery of a relationship that cannot be evaded.

> Truth Lord, but I have marr'd them: let my shame
>   Go where it doth deserve.
> And know you not, says Love, who bore the blame?
>   My deare, then I will serve.
> You must sit down, sayes Love, and taste my meat:
>   So I did sit and eat.
>
>   (Ll. 13–18)

Christ as both server and served is the final paradox of the Gospel. The church as gathered community at the altar becomes what God calls it to be through this action of language and performance and divine activity, both encloser and enclosed, offerer and receiver—"very members incorporate in thy mystical body, which is the blessed company of all faithful people." Herbert had observed in "The Invitation,"

> Lord I have invited all,
>> And I shall
> Still invite, still call to thee:
> For it seems but just and right
>> In my sight,
> Where is All, there All should be.
>>>> (Ll. 31–36)

Herbert here describes his role as priest in the Anglican Eucharist, where he bid his congregation, to "all that be here present, [I] beseech you for the Lord Jesus Christ's sake, that ye will not refuse to come thereto, being so lovingly called and bidden of God himself" (BCP, p. 254). Herbert's task in "The Church," as it is in "The Church Porch," is to move his congregation "to come thereto"; his final incentive is the promising of the discovery in that action of a gracious and loving God who comes more to serve than to be served. So it is appropriate that he concludes "The Church" with "Glory be to God on high," a quotation from the song of glory with which Cranmer chose to end the rite of that discovery.

Time, History, and "The Church Militant"

With a final incentive to choose "groning . . . to be holy, pure, and cleare," achieved through evoking involvement in that community whose life empowers its participants to "do all such good works as thou hast prepared for us to walk in," Herbert leaves off writing "The Church," not with a sense of closure as much as a perpetuation of strategies for bringing enclosure and an identification of that through which enclosure is to be achieved. But that is not where he ends *The Temple;* instead, he goes on to expand the process of enclosure beyond his didactic presentation of Anglican "building" by evoking an image of the process of the church in time:

> Thus do both lights, as well in Church as Sunne,
> Light one another and together runne.
>
> . . . .
>
> But as the Sunne still goes both west and east;
> So also did the Church by going west
> Still eastward go; because it drew more neare
> To time and place, where judgement shall appeare.
> *How deare to me, Oh God, thy counsels are!*
>> *Who may with thee compare?*
>>>> (Ll. 270–279)

The sun, conventional marker of time, moves west toward its reappearance in the east; the church, moving through time, also approaches the east by moving west. This time-bound journey is, however, the way toward the end of time, toward that "time and place, where judgement shall appear," and not toward an eternal return.

After this poem, which expands the enclosing activity of "The Church" to incorporate past, present, and future, "The Church Militant" moves to "L'Envoy," a prayer in which the speaker asks that the "King of Glorie, King of Peace" make "warre to cease" and also "blesse thy sheepe" by refuting the claims of sin that "thy death is also dead . . . / That thy flesh hath lost his food, / And thy Crosse is common wood" and by making sin's breath "sigh" at "thy conquests and his fall" and "bargain with the winde / To discharge what is behinde." "The Church Militant" then concludes with a proclamation about God: *"Blessed be God alone, / Thrice blessed Three in One."* This appeal to divine action, again modeled on biblical lament Psalms with their appeal to God to vindicate the faith and faithfulness of the lamenter, finds Herbert resting his claims for his persuasiveness again not on God as Idea but on God as actor in human history.

This section of *The Temple* has not met with much favor from critics, many of whom have tried to define it as separate from or at least problematic in relation to the rest of *The Temple.*[44] I am not so concerned to defend the quality of this section as poetry as much as I am to see what results from bringing it in relationship with what has gone before. The royal censors, who delayed publication of the entire book because of their concerns about this section and especially about Herbert's claim that "Religion [shall] to America flee: / They have their times of Gospel, ev'n as we," were in their own way acute readers of this poem.[45] For I would posit a double consequence of Herbert's proclamation in "The Church Militant." The first is the undercutting of any desire we might have to see the "building" of "The Church" to which "The Church Porch" leads us as in any way final or definitive. The engagement in life pointing toward the "new-making" of all things leads to death as part of that process of renewal; what Herbert is about in "The Church Militant" is to raise the possibility that such a death may not be merely individual but institutional as well. If the Anglican church, in this view, is to be faithful to its Christ, it must be prepared to die if that is what is required of it. The second is what might well have concerned the royal censors even more; Herbert seems prepared to raise the whole issue of the church-state relationship as potentially a detriment to the mission and function of the church itself, not in any merely oppositional way, as with the Puritans, but in a profound way by questioning what Christ as spouse of the church might require of his bride to remain faithful in assisting with his reconciling work in the world. The Puritans were clearly not interested in, nor valued highly, the existence of the Church of England; they wanted to make of it something quite different, a church to endure which would satisfy their sense of what the "true" church would be. Herbert's position is more radical; for him in "The Church Militant" the whole matter of the church's ability to continue to exist is open to question, so that being the church that is true to its Lord might mean ceasing to be a church at all.

As we have previously noted, the uniting of church and state in England under the supreme governorship of the crown was viewed by sixteenth-century Anglicans as an opportunity for national reform through the life of the church, leading to the creation of a true Christian commonwealth. By Herbert's day, however, the tensions implicit in such a relationship—posited in "The Church Militant" in terms of "power" *versus* "love"—were beginning to make themselves visible in increasingly striking terms. By the early 1630s, the English settlements in America, in Jamestown and Massachusetts Bay, the one a loyal Anglican colony and the other a refuge for Puritan dissenters, posed nicely the growing conflict over the nature of religion in England itself. The easy identification of the future of the church with national destiny so central to Spenser's interpretation of the Gospel is here seen as fraught with complexities that are as yet unresolvable. Herbert would seem pessimistic: "one may foretell, what sinnes next yeare / Shall both in *France* and *England* domineer" (ll. 245–246).

If this be the case, then we may see the central issue in "The Church Militant" as concerning whether or not such a fundamental conflict for the Church of England stood inside or outside the sequence of divine acts in human history. On the one hand, "The Church Militant" defines the "building" activity of "The Church" as toward that which will pass away. In no sense final, the incorporation of human life into the church is for the sake of future transformation into "The Church Triumphant" and is not an end in itself. According to the Prayer Book, Anglicans offered prayer for "the Church Militant here in earth." This is another way of saying that what is sought is that which only God can give in the fulfillment of his promises. Anything short of fulfillment points toward that end and is not an end in itself, although it may be part of the way toward fulfillment. Meaning, too, participates in this deferral, for words like "judgment" cannot be known in the fullness of their referents until the "time and place" when those referents come to be. Until then, the use of such language can only orient our attention toward that "time and place"; it cannot provide answers.

We need now to review Herbert's proclamation in "The Church Militant" about Christian time in its appropriate context in Anglican usage. The Christian view of time, manifested in the Bible in both content and literary form, sets itself firmly against mythical views of time. From a mythical perspective time is illusory, always dissolving into either an eternal cycle of beginnings and endings or an eternal present stretching infinitely before us. Christian time, however, is aggressively linear, with an already, a present, and a yet to come. Although God may be postulated as having eternal and immutable existence, all that can be known of him is from his self-revelations in linear temporality; in fact, it is precisely because of the uniqueness and unrepeatability of those divine intrusions into human time that the Hebrews developed their sense of linearity in time.

Anglican liturgics at the time of the Reformation contributed to the recovery of this biblical sense of time. The Prayer Book Eucharist stresses the uniqueness and unrepeatability of God's action in Christ: he "made there (by his one oblation of himself once offered) a full, perfect, and sufficient sacrifice, oblation, and satisfaction, for the sins of the whole world" (BCP, p. 263). This language is deliberate; it is intended to counter medieval doctrines of the Mass as including a repetition of Christ's sacrifice. In Anglican terms, the Eucharist is not a redoing of the Crucifixion but an effective sign of the Risen Christ's continuing redemptive activity, the operative means through which the people of God are enclosed and sustained in the life of the Spirit and empowered to charitable acts. In other words, the Eucharist is the action through which the effects of Christ's sacrifice—a past action—are made available to the present moment and to the present congregation, enabling them to achieve an expectation of future fulfillment.

The poetic experience that Herbert creates for us in *The Temple* is also linear. In "The Church Porch" the poem that begins with the speaker seeking "him, who a sermon flies" ends with instructions about how to listen to sermons; it moves from the individual in need of instruction about how to conduct his life to the corporate community gathered in prayer. In "The Church" the speaker moves from "The Altar" to "Love (III)," from altar as sign of repentance and sacrifice to altar as banquet table, from the contrite speaker to the speaker as guest. In "The Church Militant" the speaker moves from east to west, from past to present, and beyond the present to "time and place, where judgement shall appear."

The issue of time in *The Temple* turns on the relationship between Herbert's poetry and the Bible as a narrative proclamation in and to human experience in time about the meaning of human time. The claim of the New Testament is that in Jesus Christ God acted once for all to fulfill his promises made to the Old Israel and to open the path to salvation for all humanity. The New Testament in Revelation contains the end of the story started in Genesis; as the world was made by God, so it will end with the full revelation of his glory at the last. Yet that history is incomplete insofar as the present moment of any reader is concerned who comes to it after the close of events recorded in the historical sections of the New Testament. The problem facing Herbert or his intended audience is their need to be included in the history of God's saving actions recorded in that narrative if God's promises are to apply to them at the last.

At this point the importance of the church becomes clearer; as the context for reading the narrative of God's actions for humanity in history and as the occasion for the celebration of those events in the Sacraments, the church proclaims the openness of God's salvation history to those who participate in its defining acts of baptism and Eucharist. The church thus becomes the sign of God's continuing activity to incorporate his people into his kingdom and also the source of grace to make that inclusion possible.

Part of Herbert's point in *The Temple,* therefore, is to make the fundamental Christian assertion about linear time. But he does more than that. If in fact Herbert seeks to teach us, "inform and inflame" us, and if the focus of his address is the reader in the present moment of reading, then part of what he is about is to inform us about the significance of the present and inflame us in the present so that we too will choose to become a part of the linear narrative of God's salvation history. The most immediate example of this proclamation about time is "The Church Militant," with its "readings" of time and history as well as its readings of readings of time and history.

The repetition of the refrain *"How deare to me, O God, thy counsels are! / Who may with thee compare?"* divides "The Church Militant" into five sections, each one recounting one episode in the history of the church, from its origins to the present, through a movement geographical as well as temporal. Herbert's subject is the spread of the church in time and space: by the end of the second section it has reached England and "the higher victorie":

> *England . . .*
> Giving the Church a crown to keep her state,
> And not go lesse then she had done of late.
>
> . . . .
>
> Thus both the Church and Sunne together ran
> Unto the farthest old meridian.
>
> (Ll. 90–98)

Along the way, the progress of the church has subsumed the heritage of Israel and Egypt; classical philosophy has been undone and forced to spell a new language of assent to the new religion:

> *Plato* and *Aristotle* were at a losse,
> And Wheel'd about again to spell *Christ-Crosse.*
> Prayers chas'd syllogismes into their den,
> And *Ergo* was transform'd into *Amen.*
>
> (Ll. 53–56)

The crucifixion becomes an act that forces language into new forms, undercuts the claims of logic, and demands assent (*"Amen"*) rather than humanly devised proofs (*"Ergo"*). Thus, the second section of "The Church Militant" ends with the spread of the church to "the farthest old meridian," to the last geographic point of land moving westward from its origins in the Near East.

At this point, however, when one might expect Herbert to continue the story to the present day and include Anglican hopes of the transformation of the state, he instead goes back to the beginning of his story to pick up the parallel westward journey to "Sinne" as it dogs the heels of the church, becoming pagan gods in Egypt and Greece, the emperor in Rome, and also, in the Rome of a later day, the pope. Thus, a theme that was implicit at the beginning of "The Church Militant" comes to the fore. In the early lines of this narrative of the poem Herbert notes that

> Common-weals acknowledge thee,
> And wrap their policies in thy decree,
> Complying with thy counsels, doing nought
> Which doth not meet with an eternall thought.
> (Ll. 5–8).

In such lines Herbert suggests the images of state and church working in harmony we noted as being part of the rhetoric of the early Anglican Reformation. He goes on, however, to point out, "But above all, thy Church and Spouse doth prove / Not the decrees of power, but bands of love." In that "But" there occurs the articulation of a new situation, in which interpretations of God in terms of commonwealths, policies, and power no longer are "proven" by "thy Church and Spouse." The church, if it is to be true to its own interpretation of God, must therefore, at least potentially, be prepared to find love and power in conflict and thus to find itself in opposition to "Common-weals."

This theme is renewed in the fourth section, in which the effects of sin are seen in its work to "bewitch, and finely work each nation / Into a voluntarie transmigration. / All poste to *Rome:* Princes submit their necks / Either t' his publick foot or private tricks" (ll. 193–196). In terms of the rhetoric of the sixteenth century, this union was undone and reformed in England in the Anglican Reformation, but here Herbert asserts that "The latter Church is to the first a debter. / The second Temple could not reach the first: / And the late reformation never durst / Compare with ancient times and purer yeares" (ll. 224–227). In light of the Anglican claim to take the patristic church as its model, Herbert's language must be read as judgment on what it had (or had not) achieved. Thus it is that "sinnes next yeare / Shall both in *France* and *England* domineer" and "Then shall Religion to *America* flee."

Indeed, what could have appeared as a triumphal story of the church's progress in fact becomes a story of decline, of the spread of sin constantly plaguing the church in its journey: "Thus Sinne triumphs in Western *Babylon;* / Yet not as Sinne, but as Religion." The effects of sin are most pronounced in the church itself, almost as though the church were the bearer of sin rather than its foe. What should appear as the triumph of the church may signal its decline; the complicity of the church in the spread of sin profoundly complicates distinctions created by a vocabulary easily separating "sin" from "religion."

Herbert now begins to move into highly controversial ground. If we remember that at the beginning of "The Church Militant" Herbert sets up a dichotomy between "Common-weals" and "thy Church and Spouse" in terms of "power" and "love," we cannot escape noticing that the image he presents of the function of sin is in terms of its using the power of the state, cloaked in the guise of religion, to force its way:

> From *Greece* he went to *Rome:* and as before
> He was a God, now he's an Emperour.
> (Ll. 139–140)

> As Sinne in *Greece* a Prophet was before,
> And in old *Rome* a mightie Emperour;
> So now being Priest he plainly did professe
> To make a jest of Christs three offices.
> (Ll. 171–174)

> As new and old *Rome* did one Empire twist;
> So both together are one Antichrist.
> (Ll. 205–206)

> Thus Sinne triumphs in Western *Babylon;*
> Yet not as Sinne, but as Religion.
> (Ll. 211–212)

"Princes submit their necks / Either t' his publick foot or private tricks"; the nature of sin is to aggregate power to itself using the state to further its ends. In light of this, Herbert's opening reference to "Common-weals" wrapping "their policies in thy decree, / Complying with thy counsels, doing nought / Which doth not meet with an eternall thought" (ll. 5–7) becomes ironic; such behavior stands revealed as one of the ways sin advances itself—using divine authority as a tool for achieving the demonic ends of power.

Against this, from the beginning, Herbert posits "thy Church and Spouse" as proving "Not the decrees of power, but bands of love." At the heart of authentic Anglican proclamation, as we have seen, is the persuasion to active charity—"all such good works as thou hast prepared for us to walk in"—and to this emphasis Herbert returns to proclaim judgment on the use of state power in its relationship to America:

> Then shall Religion to *America* flee:
> They have their times of Gospel, ev'n as we.
> My God, thou dost prepare for them a way
> By carrying first their gold from them away:
> For gold and grace did never yet agree:
> Religion alwaies sides with povertie.
> We think we rob them, but we think amisse:
> We are more poore, and they more rich by this.
> Thou wilt revenge their quarrell, making grace
> To pay our debts, and leave her ancient place
> To go to them, while that which now their nation
> But lends to us, shall be our desolation.
>
> (Ll. 247–258)

In light of European foreign policy toward America, the Gospel here comes as a judgment on Europe and as grace to those it despoils of their gold. Clearly Herbert is not concerned with the English settlers either at Jamestown or in the Massachusetts Bay Colony; the "they" who "have their times of Gospel" are the ones whose gold has been "carried away," that is, the native Americans. We might note here Thomas Cain's recent argument that part of what is at stake in Book II of *The Faerie Queene* is how Raleigh will manage his foreign exploits; handled intemperately, "the gold of Guiana and fruitfulness of Virginia become destructively opposed goals."[46] In 1617–18, when Herbert was at Cambridge, Raleigh, having long abandoned his goal of colonizing Virginia, made a last desperate effort to gain Guianan gold; his failure cost him his life. War with Spain, in part over the control of New World gold, contributed to Herbert's abandonment of public life and his taking of orders in 1624.[47] At this time, Nicholas Ferrar, a friend of Herbert's and a member of the Virginia Company, also resigned his seat in Parliament and his association with the colonizing effort in the New World, in part over the government's efforts to take control, for reasons of power and wealth, over the administration of the Virginia Colony. Both Herbert and Ferrar took Holy Orders as a response to their experiences with governmental power, an action positing an oppostion between church and state. Herbert went on to become a priest, to write *The Temple,* and to become the rector of the parish at Bemerton; Ferrar retired to his family's estate at Little Gidding and established what the Puritans called his "Arminian Nunnery." In "The Church Militant," Herbert raises the vision of the Christian life at the heart of Anglicanism and contrasts it with the functioning of state power. The ongoing association of the two is here proclaimed prophetically to be to the detriment of the former; the church "shal ev'ry yeare decrease and fade; / Till such a darknesse do the world invade / At Christs last coming, as his first did finde" (ll. 229–231).

If the very institution which Herbert celebrated in "The British Church" as "thy praise and glorie" has encountered fundamental problems in its relationship with the society it sought to transform, we might wonder where the good news is in this poem. It comes in holding onto the role of the church in the history of salvation as Herbert defines it. As we approach the end of the poem, sin's power seems to increase: "Yet as the Church shall thither westward flie, / So Sinne shall trace and dog her instantly" (ll. 259–260). Sin, which started out one hundred lines behind, has caught up to cut the gap to an "instantly." In fact, the next line crosses the two: "The Church shall come, & Sinne the Church shall smother" (l. 266). We remain poised between sin and church, not able to distinguish which will "smother" the other. But in the next lines the image of the "Sunne" returns to light the church's way: "Thus do both lights, as well in Church as Sunne, / Light one another, and together runne." Herbert, in "The Sonne," had pointed out the English sun/son pun in just these terms:

> A sonne is light and fruit; a fruitfull flame
> Chasing the fathers dimnesse, carr'd farre
> From the first man in th'East, to fresh and new
> Western discov'ries of posteritie.
> So in one word our Lords humilitie
> We turn upon him in a sense most true:
>> For what Christ once in humblenesse began
>> We him in glorie call, *The Sonne of Man.*
>>> (Ll. 7–14)

As a result, with the church relocated in relationship to "the Sunne," although "Sinne and Darknesse follow still / The Church and Sunne with all their power and skill" (ll. 272–273), the "time and place" they are headed is still one "where judgement shall appeare." In spite of what sin can do to the church, all its efforts take it closer to the point at which the real source of power, through love, will reassert itself to the ultimate detriment of sin.

What Herbert would remind us here is of another dichotomy; "The Church Militant" is at best provisional, at best a passing thing. "The Church Triumphant," that church to come which subsumes and transforms and makes new what has gone before, is what the whole story is really all about. And that church to come is again dependent on God, again to be looked for, again a future promise. Our relationship with that church to come is complex and paradoxical. We are at once on the way to that church, yet also we are in the way of sin. Only God can make the necessary separation, the necessary distinctions.

Or so is Herbert's proclamation, one which he asks God to make into a meaningful statement in "*L'Envoy*": "make warre to cease; / . . . blesse thy sheep." Thus, the role cast for the church in "The Church Militant" is an enacting of the role of the Son with the same result; the future of the church takes with it the future of sin and leads once more to the ultimate revelation of divine power in the fulfillment of divine promises. And what comes again as good news to Anglicans in Herbert's prophetic claims is that what enables such a text to come into being is a use of biblical texts shaped after their use in Anglican worship. Beneath Herbert's presentation of the relationship between the church and sin as it functions through the nations in this poem is Christ's parable, from Matthew 25:31–46, of the division at the last of the nations into the sheep and the goats:

> When the Son of man shall come in his glory, and all the holy angels with him, then shall he sit upon the throne of his glory. And before him shall be gathered all nations: and he shall separate them one from another, as a shepherd divideth his sheep from the goats. And he shall set the sheep on his right hand, but the goats on the left. Then shall the King say unto them on his right hand, Come, ye blessed of my Father, inherit the Kingdom prepared for you from the foundation of the world.

Annually, according to the Daily Office calendar, this chapter from Matthew was read on January 28; on the following day, at Morning Prayer, one of the Psalms appointed is Psalm 139, from which Herbert got part of the refrain in "The Church Militant." Verse 17 reads, "How dear are thy counsels unto me, O God: O how great is the sum of them!"

If we note that the rest of that refrain answers the question posed by God in Isaiah 46:5 ("To whom will ye liken me, and make me equal, and compare me, that we may be like?"), we may come closer to grasping what Herbert is about in this poem. Part of what Isaiah had to do was to proclaim to Jerusalem that it was not inviolable, that it could not rely on God to preserve Israel as a nation or the temple worship of God at Jerusalem. But the good news in Isaiah is that even this destruction-to-come of what had historically given Israel its identity as God's people was not a denial of God's promises. Like Isaiah, Herbert is able to envision a situation in which even that eventuality in England in regard to the Anglican church as an agent of the state could be part of the divine action for human redemption. In this light even the destruction of the life of that institution Herbert worked so hard to build up could be seen as but one more manifestation of the death that is the way to life itself.

For Herbert to be able to make this claim by bringing it into speech in the present through employing biblical narratives mediated by use of the Prayer

Book is a way of affirming the value of the church and its function in the world, even if that functioning must lead to its own demise. In Christ's parable, the sheep are those who keep faith with the essential proclamation about the Christian life as one of active charity:

> Come . . . inherit the kingdom . . . For I was an hungered, and ye gave me meat: I was thirsty, and ye gave me drink: I was a stranger, and ye took me in: Naked, and ye clothed me: I was sick, and ye visited me: I was in prison, and ye came unto me . . . Inasmuch as ye have done it unto one of the least of these my brethren, ye have done it unto me. (Matthew 26: 34–40)

As Herbert says, "Religion alwaies sides with povertie." Thus, in the final analysis, the source of the church's true "praise and glorie" is its faithfulness to the role in his saving activity God calls it to, whatever that role might be. What is important is not what Anglicanism has achieved in terms of a "mean" between Rome and Geneva, but its use of God's "double-moat[ing]" of grace for his ends. The purpose of the Church of England is not, therefore, to achieve an ideal of purity, but to keep faith with its Lord in the reconciling work of love he calls it to.

Herbert's last words in *The Temple* are a prayer that the church's destiny as a crucified institution may be redeemed in these terms—"blesse thy sheep, / Thee to love, in thee to sleep" (*"L'Envoy,"* ll. 3–4)—and that the promises of God to conquer sin be fulfilled. The final task of his persuasive power thus lies in his desire to involve us in the life of an institution which itself may have to be let go of if its ultimate purposes in God's divine activity are to be fulfilled. Remembering Christ's last words from the cross, he ends *"FINIS,"* "it is finished"; a work is finished which ends only in its self-offering to the One on whom it depends for its efficacy. Use of text replicates the cross as paradigm of life and the way to life, as enactment of text opens the present to the fullness of future meaning. The text as body/embodied is offered up as lost and broken, in a way that becomes the way to life.

Herbert did not live to see the kinds of issues he anticipates in "The Church Militant" come to the crisis of the 1640s in which the Anglican church as institution did die. Through benefit of hindsight, we may see in these lines an anticipation of the issues which Henry Vaughan, Herbert's successor as Anglican poetic voice, would be forced to face and with which he would be forced to struggle. For Spenser and Herbert, the ongoing life of Anglicanism was the context for and the enabler of a reading of the cross that would move readers to take it up, whether to live in the new action of God transforming the commonwealth or in the new action of God calling the church to faithful watching even through its own crucifixion. For Vaughan, as we will see, the issue becomes moving the reader to take up that cross even when the defining and enabling institution, the normative setting for such reading, is absent. Herbert began his collection of religious poems with a quotation from Psalm 29—"In his Temple doth every man speak of his honour"— and created a verbal church which would function like the Primers to provide the means for its readers to articulate their concerns in the real church, which is the community as the Body of Christ. Vaughan, on the other hand, must begin with a quotation from Job 35 ("Where is God my Maker, who giveth Songs in the night?"), for the absence of that Body must confront the mid-century Anglican with a question no less fundamental than that of where God might yet be found when all customary signs of his presence are silenced.

· 4 ·

Henry Vaughan

Vaughan and the Poetics of Absence

In the preface to the second edition of his *Silex Scintillans,* Henry Vaughan announces that in publishing his poems he is communicating "this my poor *Talent* to the *Church,* under the *protection* and *conduct* of her *glorious Head:* who (if he will vouchsafe to *own* it, and *go along* with it) can make it as useful now in the *publick,* as it hath been to me in *private.*"[1] His concluding prayer defines "publick" usefulness in terms by now familiar, that "I may flourish not with *leafe* onely, but with some *fruit* also." We are, of course, again in the midst of a theology of poetic functioning that stresses the agency of Christ in the public effectiveness of didactic poetry, teaching by articulating what Izaak Walton was to describe in Herbert as "a practical piety, and devotion"[2] and Vaughan refers to in this preface as "a true, practick piety" so as to produce "publick fruit." Vaughan clearly puts himself in the tradition of Herbert, "whose holy *life* and *verse* gained many pious *Converts* (of whom I am the least)" (p. 390); indeed, his description of what is needed by those who wish to write effective religious poetry echoes Herbert's desire for readers who "grone" to be "holy, pure, and cleare," for he asserts that "he that desires to excel in this kinde of *Hagiography,* or holy writing, must strive (by all means) for *perfection* and true *holyness,* that a *door may be opened to him in heaven,* Rev. 4:1, and then he will be able to write (with *Hierotheus* and holy *Herbert*) A *true Hymn.*" Just so; Herbert's "A True Hymn" asserts that "if th'heart be moved . . ./ God doth supplie the want."

In Vaughan's image of "leafe" and "fruit" we are also back in the tradition, reflected in Cranmer's Book of Homilies, of the Christian life of active charity as the fruit of faith; the poet's production of printed "leaves" is offered in the faith that such efforts will produce in its readers what Vaughan called in his

"Preface To The Reader" in *The Mount of Olives* "a regular life," the "ordinary Instructions" for which he claims are "as briefly delivered as possibly I could, in my Sacred Poems" (p. 140). Vaughan thus locates his poetic efforts in that tradition of discourse we have been defining in Herbert and his predecessor Spenser in the Anglican tradition; this is reinforced when Vaughan says he seeks in these "leafes" "to communicate . . . to the *Church*" and ends his preface with echoes of language used in the Prayer Book's communion rite. Vaughan's "*hope* and earnest *desire*" is for "fruit"; "I humbly beseech him to perfect and fulfill for his dear *Sons* sake, unto *whom*, with *him* and the most holy and loving *Spirit*, be ascribed by *Angels*, by *Men*, and by all his *Works*, All Glory, and Wisdom, and Dominion, in this the *temporal* and in the *Eternal* Being. *Amen*" (p. 392). The Prayer Book Eucharist repeatedly uses the petition form "beseech" + infinitive and infinitive:

> We beseech thee . . . to save and defend
> we most humbly beseech thee . . . to comfort and succor.
> (BCP, p. 254)

And such prayer is asked "for Jesus Christ's sake" (p. 254), "for thy Son our Lord Jesus Christ's sake" (p. 259). Other prayers end "through Jesus Christ our Lord, to whom with thee and the Holy Ghost, be all honor and glory, world without end. Amen." Thus, allusions to Prayer Book rites and use of its structuring patterns and vocabulary are what enable Vaughan to bring to speech his own prayer for the efficacy of his own didactic poetry.

We must remember, however, that Vaughan wrote this in 1654 when the "Church" to which Vaughan offers his "poor *Talent*" was in a radically different situation from that of 1633, when Herbert's *Temple* was published. On January 3, 1645, Parliament declared the Prayer Book illegal, and a week later William Laud, archbishop of Canterbury, was executed on Tower Hill. Four years later, Charles I followed his archbishop to the scaffold. Anglican worship, from Vaughan's position in the early 1650s, was officially forbidden, conducted clandestinely if it occurred at all, and appeared unlikely ever to be restored. Such records as exist imply that Prayer Book worship did continue, but infrequently, on a drastically reduced scale, and in the secrecy of private homes. Penalties for noncompliance with the new order of worship and persistence in the old rite were progressively increased until, after December 15, 1655, "none of the Church of England should dare to preach or administer Sacraments, teache schoole, &c. on pains of imprisonment or exile."[3] Use of the Anglican Prayer Book in any form, including its liturgical calendars and accompanying ceremonial, was abolished as a public occurrence; the ongoing life of the Anglican church had come to an end, at least in the forms in which it had been known and experienced since 1559.

In considering Vaughan, therefore, we have to keep firmly in mind the situation of Anglicans after the Civil War. That community where Spenser and Herbert found their understanding of God through participation in the tradition of liturgical enactment enabled by the Book of Common Prayer was now absent. Vaughan is the poet of that absence; writing in the 1640s and 1650s, he is the chronicler of the experience of that community when its source of Christian identity was no longer available. What Vaughan engaged in during this period was an effort at keeping alive the implications of the Prayer Book church during a time when the church was a part of the past, or at best a surreptitious activity in which to participate was to put one into opposition to the very state whose destiny had once seemed informed, created, and enabled by the ongoing life of that church.

One of the things that resulted from the abolition of the Prayer Book church was that the artifacts that remained took on even greater importance through a sense of their loss as places where important activities go on all the time. What Anglicans were left with was a deep sense of their past importance and a present, poignant sense of what had been lost or was in danger of being lost by their abandonment. Amidst such feelings, as well as in anger and apprehension, Vaughan writes in *The Mount of Olives*:

> These reverend and sacred buildings (however now vilified and shut up) have ever been, and amongst true Christians still are the solemne and publike places of meeting for Divine Worship: There the *flocks feed at noon-day*, there the great *Shepherd* and *Bishop* of their souls is *in the midst of them*, and where he is, that *Ground is holy*; Put off thy shoes then, thy worldly and carnall affections, and when thou beginnest to enter in, say with *Jacob*, *How dreadful is this place! sure this is none other then the house of God, and this is the gate of heaven!* Such reverence and religious affection hath in all ages been shew'd towards these places, that the holy men of God detain'd either by Captivity, or other necessary occasions, when they could not remedy the distance, yet to testifie their *desire and longing for the Courts of the Lord*, Psal. 84. they would always worship towards them. (P. 147)

The devotion that Herbert would show toward the activities ongoing in such buildings in his time is applied by Vaughan to the buildings themselves, precisely because they are "now vilified and shut up." To describe the "holy men of God" as being "detain'd either by Captivity, or other necessary occasions" is to define from their perspective the situation Vaughan and his fellow Anglicans found themselves in after the 1640s. This passage describes Vaughan's stance in his poetry exactly—a "worship *towards* them" (emphasis added), toward the signs that remain of the lost community life, either in the physical manifestations of that life in buildings or in the memories of those who had worshipped in them according to the use of the Prayer Book. His effort is to act out a keeping of the faith, and his works seek to teach and enable such a keeping of the faith in the midst of what was for that faith the most fundamental and radical of crises.

Here, too, Vaughan is in a different place in regard to his concern for the social, the domestic, and the political. The rites of the Church of England no longer were the vehicles through which private and interpersonal events, behavior, or desire could become public and enter the larger fabric of social interactions, yet births, marriages, and deaths continued to be features of English life. Since Vaughan's concern was to maintain at least something of the Anglican experience as a part, although of necessity a private part, of English life in the 1640s and 1650s, the relationship between the language and modes of behavior characteristic of Anglican worship and the social and domestic world of personal interactions was forced to change. For many Englishfolk, the language and rites of personal passage were now different from what they had been before. Therefore, the religious life Vaughan articulates cannot—because it was now officially outside human endeavor—have the encompassing dimensions of a public, officially sanctioned religious life.

This had its consequences for the telling of human narratives in regard to the aspects of human experience that could or could not be included. For Petrarch, both *eros* and divine love could occupy the same narrative only by placing them in opposition so that the former is rejected to get to the latter. Spenser's revolution was to declare that all of human love was properly understood in relationship to a single narrative—the divine work in human history—with a domesticated *eros* functioning as a channel for the divine activity. Herbert's variation was to declare that love came to have meaning as a term for human experience, including erotic experience, when it took its place within and in relationship to the narrative of a divine-human relationship. All, through variations on the relationship between erotic and divine love, find ways to hold both within the same narrative. For Vaughan, however, the divine-human interactions created in and through his poems must proceed perhaps side by side with other human narratives but to a great degree independent of them. The consequence of social change for Vaughan, therefore, was to make what Vaughan thought of as the narrative of true religion take place parallel to the narratives of *eros,* but on separate paths. Their stories, their worlds, had been put asunder.

As a result, the plots and varieties of love that are an important part of both Spenser's and Herbert's agendas and resources in Vaughan retreat into the realm of the metaphoric or the lost. While official Anglicanism had once functioned as a public umbrella and enabler for human interaction through which the personal became related to the community, its loss as a creator of community now meant that the public energies of love would be articulated in other texts. What we regard from a modern perspective as Herbert's quaintness often merely reflects the daily vocabularies and structures of a society still moving out of a feudal ruralism; in Vaughan, there is a deliberately archaic quality to the terms in which interpersonal and social situations are described. This often derives from Vaughan's reliance on biblical terms and situations; it also suggests a struggling for a language in which to depict a totally new social situation for a church now rapidly becoming "past" and of an older time.

Vaughan defines this situation in terms of a persistence in the affirmation that in spite of the fact that the "reverend and sacred buildings [are] now vilified and shut up," they "*still are* the solemne and publike places of meeting" (emphasis added), so that worship can be directed "towards them . . . to testifie their *desire and longing for the Courts of the Lord.*" In the absence of that communal activity which gives Christian identity to individuals, a sustaining of faith in that activity as the source of identity becomes a way of linking past with future expectation, of manifesting desire that the divine promises still be fulfilled, even though the primary focus both for the proclamation of those promises and for the means of reaching "time and place" for their fulfillment (*"this is the gate of heaven"*) is no longer functioning.

Vaughan's focus must therefore be on the self, but on the self estranged both from that corporate sense of self we noted as one helpful way of conceiving the voice of Herbert's poems and from that community whose ongoing worship activity was where definitions and understandings of the self were to be found: "They are all gone into the world of light! / And I alone sit ling'ring here" (ll. 1–2).[4] This sense of isolation raises fundamental problems with the creation of a speaking self in poetry; Vaughan's speaker must seek to articulate the situation of the Anglican separated from his identifying community, but he must do so as one who, as a result of that separation, cannot readily find his voice as Anglican, since the resources for Christian utterance were by definition absent. There is no opportunity to find a self-identity as an individual here, for the character of Anglican identity was such that individual selves were identified in relationship with the developing community and not apart from it. Without that community, the speaking self will be articulated, at least at first, in terms of loss. Later it will find itself able to speak in terms of memory; still later it will realize itself in terms of expectation of future fulfillment.

In his images of the "reverend and sacred buildings" and of the feeding of the flock by the "great *Shepherd . . . in the midst of them*" in places now "shut up," Vaughan evokes painfully a profound sense of loss, both of the life of those places and of the sense of identity that came with them. The central issue with Vaughan is to find out how to talk about what has happened in a way that enables his reader to have a sense of still being part of that life now past, of still having an identity as Christian that is informed by that life and is also able to be sustained even in the midst of its absence, so that it is possible to go on saying that "the great *Shepherd*" is still "*in the midst of them.*"

Vaughan's concern in his religious poetry is thus to struggle toward a sense of identity in Anglican terms even when the source of that identity is lost, to understand events as, in Herbert's terms, "figuring *JESUS CHRIST*" even when the particular events to which one must look to find that identity argue not for its presence but its absence. To see how Vaughan achieved the teaching of that discovery is the task of this section of my study. Initially, however, I want to examine some aspects of Vaughan's prose writings contemporary with his poems because I find in them anticipations of the strategies of articulation in which he couches both this special new sense of Anglican identity and instruction in how his audience of faithful Anglicans could also achieve it. I also want to devote close attention to the uses of Herbert's *Temple* in Vaughan's poems, because reading *The Temple* comes to be for Vaughan the closest thing available in the late 1640s and 1650s to actual participation in Anglican worship as Herbert knew it and thus functions in Vaughan as a source of allusion in the way in which use of the Prayer Book itself functioned for Herbert.

One way to understand the events of Vaughan's day for faithful Anglicans is to affirm them as Vaughan does in his prose works, as in some sense "necessary occasions" of being "detain'd," and to look to those who do keep the faith in the midst of their detaining as exemplary. What one finds, at least among some Anglicans after the war, is a willingness to risk persecution to keep up the life of the church even if they had to do so in secret; indeed, some found this experience increased their enthusiasm for the old religion. John Evelyn in 1656 twice made the journey from his home in Depford to London to receive Holy Communion according to the Prayer Book from one Dr. Wild in a clandestine service in Dr. Wild's lodgings in Fleet Street, "the first time the Church of England was reduced to a chamber and conventicle," where he found "a greate meeting of zealous Christians, who were generally much more devout and religious than in our greatest prosperity."[5] In southern Wales, the parliamentary Act for the Better Propagation of the Gospel (1649–50) resulted in the deposing of nearly three hundred clergy from their cures, including among them Thomas Vaughan, Henry's brother.[6] Yet the efforts of Vaughan's friends Thomas Powell and Thomas Lewes to keep the doors of parish churches open, along with Vaughan's extensive publishing activities in both poetry and prose, suggest that although the Church of England was "crippled,"[7] there continued to exist a community of the faithful who, like their London counterparts, found the new situation an incentive to increased rather than diminished activity on its behalf.

In his dedication of *The Mount of Olives* to Sir Charles Egerton, Vaughan alludes to this community:

It must be counted for a great *blessing,* that there is yet any left which dares *look* upon, and *commiserate* distressed Religion. *Good men* in *bad times* are very scarce; they are like the *standing eares of Corne escaped out of the Reapers hands,* or the *Vine-dressers last gleanings after the first ripe fruits have been gathered.* Such a *precious generation are the Just* in the *day of trouble,* and their *names* are like to *afflicted truth,* like the *shadow of a great rock in a weary land,* or a *wayfairing mans lodge in the waste and howling Wildernesse.* The *Sonne* of *God* himselfe (when *he* was *here,*) had no place to put his head in; And his *Servants* must not think the *present measure* too hard, seeing their *Master* himself took up his *nights-lodging* in the cold *Mount* of *Olives.* (P. 138)

Vaughan's praise of those who "dare *look* upon, and *commiserate* distressed Religion" is a complex of biblical allusions and quotations; in these allusions, Israel faces and reacts to the fall of Jerusalem by coming to see the survivors as a saving remnant. The images of corn and grapes "escaped out of the Reapers hands" and the "Vine-dressers last gleanings" derive from Isaiah 17:5–7:

And it shall be as when the harvest man gathereth the corn, and reapeth the ears with his arm; and it shall be as he that gathereth ears in the valley of Rephaim.

Yet gleaning grapes shall be left in it, as the shaking of an olive tree, two or three berries in the top of the uppermost bough, four or five in the outmost fruitful branches thereof, saith the Lord God of Israel.

At that day shall a man look to his Maker, and his eyes shall have respect for the Holy One of Israel.

The image of the "shadow of the Great rock" is also from Isaiah: "And a man shall be as an hiding place from the wind, and a covert from the tempest; as rivers of water in a dry place, and the shadow of a great rock in a weary land"(32:2). The image of the "wayfaring lodge" is from Jeremiah:

Oh that my head were waters, and mine eyes a fountain of tears, that I might weep day and night for the slain of the daughters of my people!

Oh that I had in the wilderness a lodging place of wayfaring men; that I might leave my people, and go from them! for they be all adulterers, an assembly of treacherous men. (9:1–2)

Isaiah 27:5 links the image of the "day of trouble" with that of a "remnant" that will escape and "again take root . . . and bear fruit," a fulfillment Vaughan identifies with the events of the New Testament. The image of a "precious generation" combines numerous Old and New Testament references to emphasize the favor and blessing of God upon those who keep the faith in the face of difficulties. Vaughan is able to articulate the present situation of

Anglicans because he compares it to Jesus' own earthly suffering and to the situation of Israel during and after the fall of Jerusalem. Vaughan thus re-enacts the prophetic response to that past critical situation, in which the destruction of the historical enterprise that gave Israel its sense of identity was redeemed by faithful prophets who proclaimed that even in such calamitous circumstances God was not absent from his people but was in fact at work in human history once more to prepare for the full realization of his promises. The company of those who sustain their faith has a role to play here; by seeing these as "necessary occasions" and seeing themselves as a "saving remnant" they can find their faithfulness a link between the past of Anglican experience and future fulfillment of God's promises. This is made possible by linking present difficulties to the sufferings and loneliness of Christ in his death, typologically joined to the situation of Israel so that the victory over suffering, isolation, and apparent defeat, revealed in Christ's Resurrection, renews the promises of eventual deliverance by means of their suffering God made to the old Israel and reveals that God has the power to make good those promises. The kinds of typological links made here by Vaughan are anticipated in such biblical passages as the following one from the First Epistle of Peter:

> Ye also, as lively stones, are built up a spiritual house, an holy priesthood, to offer up spiritual sacrifices, acceptable to God by Jesus Christ.
> Wherefore also it is contained in the scripture, Behold, I lay in Sion a chief corner stone, elect, precious: and he that believeth on him shall not be confounded. . . .
> But ye are a chosen generation, a royal priesthood, an holy nation, a peculiar people; that ye should shew forth the praises of him who hath called you out of darkness into his marvellous light. (2:5–6, 9)

What Vaughan does here, using "applied typology," is to view the "saving remnant" of Anglicanism as a refuge in the wilderness, claiming that in their faithfulness is the "seed" of the promise of fulfillment. This situation is thus treated typologically, analogous only to the postexilic situation of Israel and the situation of Jesus' earthly ministry.

In this light, Vaughan's dedication "To the Peaceful, humble, and pious Reader" is of great interest. He begins by granting that *the world . . . triumphs over Manuals* such as the one he has written. His purpose is not to *envie . . . [the] frequent Extasies,*" of those victorious in the Civil War, or their *"raptures to the third heaven; I only wish them real, and that their actions did not tell the world, they are rapt into some other place*" (p. 140). True to a pragmatic Anglicanism, Vaughan makes clear that what is important is not devotion that takes someone elsewhere, *"into some other place,"* but the Christian life lived out here, in the *"real"* as opposed to the "other" place. Then, in an aside aimed at the Puritans, Vaughan claims, *"nor should they, who assume to themselves the glorious stile of Saints, be uncharitably moved, if we that are yet in the body, and carry our treasure in earthen vessels, have need of these helps."* Vaughan uses the phrase "the body" here in at least two senses. On the one hand, his claim is a self-effacing one. Given a vocabulary which discusses the true Christian life as "in the spirit," in the sense of making "extasies" and "raptures" the marks of religious experience, then, he says, we are still "in the body," are novices on such a journey and need devotional aids such as set prayers for devotions analogous to those of the Prayer Book that the Puritans attacked in their advocacy of extemporaneous prayer open to the speaking of the spirit. On the other hand, and this is actually an undercutting of the pretentions of Puritan religious concepts and experience, we who are still "in the body" are "very members incorporate in the mystical body of thy Son," as the enacted language of the Prayer Book proclaims at the end of the communion service, and are thus the ones who know the real meaning of religious language, not the newcomers who believe they have found something missing in the old religion. What Vaughan offers through the language he uses to describe his situation is an argument for and a way of keeping faith with that body created through Prayer Book worship which is the context in which religious language has its true meaning.

Vaughan intends, as well, an undercutting of Puritan claims that their interpretation of Scripture and the church is the true interpretation. The most charitable version of the Puritan claim about the old religion was that the Anglican church was incompletely reformed, that it needed additional reform in belief and practice to make valid its claims to authenticity as the church. Less charitable versions abounded, asserting that the Reformation had in fact never occurred and that the church in England between the Elizabethan Settlement of Religion and the victory of the Puritan forces was as corrupt as the medieval church, *"Antichristian,"* in fact (p. 186). In either case, the war created conflicting images of the church, each manifest in warring verbal exchanges, each seeking to command the field for establishing what a church in England might be. Vaughan's entry into this field of verbal combat comes in the form of an *apologia* for those who persist in their loyalty to the texts of the Church of England as they facilitate Christian living—"we . . . have need of these helps"—as well as a statement supportive of their loyalty in the face of increasingly harsh Puritan efforts to dissuade them from their persistence in supporting the forms of the old faith.

Vaughan also distinguishes his understanding of the Christian life as one "in the body," as one lived socially in the "blessed company of all faithful people," from a radically private, interior, and individualized faith based on inner experiences of "extasies" and "raptures to the third heaven" which can only be claimed or described but never shared. The relationship Vaughan wants his readers to have with his text is one of finding in it a common meeting ground in a shared experience of loss, joining in the use of "these helps" to preserve something of life "in the body" now lost. In this light, his final comments come as a plea to fellow Anglicans to persist in their faithfulness:

> Onely I shall adde this short Exhortation: That thou wouldest not be discouraged in this way, because very many are gone out of it. Think not that thou art alone upon this Hill, there is an innumerable company both before and behinde thee. Those with their Palms in their hands, and these expecting them. If therefore the dust of this world chance to prick thine eyes, suffer it not to blinde them: but running thy race with patience, look to JESUS the Authour and finisher of thy faith, who when he was reviled, reviled not againe. Presse thou towards the mark, and let the people and their Seducers rage; be faithful unto the death, and he will give thee a Crowne of life. Look not upon transitorie, visible things, but upon him that is eternal, and invisible.
> (P. 141)

This exhortation is, again, a complex of biblical and liturgical references. The original audience encouraged "in this way" were the people of Israel "discouraged because of the way" in Numbers 21:4. The "Hill" on which one can feel alone is the hill of Isaiah 30:17–18, where after "One thousand shall flee at the rebuke of one, ye be left as a beacon upon the top of a mountain, and as an ensign on an hill," on whom God will "wait, that he may be gracious unto you." "Those with their Palms in their hands" are the crowd at Jesus' entry into Jerusalem (Matthew 21, Mark 11, Luke 19, John 12). The "innumerable company both before and behind thee" is, echoing the Gospel narrative, the company of Revelation 7:9–10, the "great multitude, which no man could number, of all nations and kindreds, and peoples and tongues, [that] stood before the throne, and before the Lamb, clothed in white robes, and palms in their hands," who cry "with a loud voice, saying, Salvation to our God which sitteth upon the throne, and unto the Lamb." This passage is the Epistle for All Saints' Day in the Prayer Book, on which day the Collect asks God "which hast knit together thy elect in one communion and fellowship [to] grant us grace so to follow thy holy saints in all virtues and godly living, that we may come to those unspeakable joys, which thou hast prepared for them that unfainedly love thee" (BCP, p. 244). The Gospel for that day is the account of the Sermon on the Mount, itself a typological redoing of God's gift of the Ten Commandments on Mount Sinai, which raises the possibility that through keeping of the faith the "Hill" upon which Vaughan's audience found itself could be a situation of learning, a mountain like that one from which Moses looked into the Promised Land, or the Mount of Olives or Golgotha, in which suffering led to resurrection. Hebrews 12:22 ties these together, proclaiming that its audience is "come unto mount Sion, and unto the city of the living God, the heavenly Jerusalem, and to an innumerable company of angels, to the general assembly and church of the firstborn," the "blessed company of all faithful people," in the vocabulary of the Prayer Book.

Hebrews 12:1 also provides Vaughan with another image, that of the race:

> Wherefore seeing we also are compassed about with so great a cloud of witnesses, let us lay aside every weight, and the sin which doth so easily beset us, and let us run with patience the race that is set before us, looking to Jesus the author and finisher of our faith; who endured the cross . . . and is set down at the right hand of the throne of God. For consider him that endured such contradiction of sinners against himself, least ye be wearied and faint in your minds.

This Vaughan links with Philippians 3:14, in which Paul asserts, "I press toward the mark for the prize of the high calling of God in Christ Jesus." He also takes a line from Psalm 2—"Why do the heathen so furiously rage together, and why do the people imagine a vain thing?" (also quoted in Acts 4:25)—and makes it apply to "Seducers" of the people rather than heathens, a more appropriate category for the Puritans. Vaughan's injunction is that of Christ in Revelation 2:10: "be thou faithful unto death, and I will give thee a crown of life." Vaughan's "Look not" passage is a transformation of Paul's words to the Colossians: "seek those things which are above. . . . Set your affection on things above, not on things on the earth" (3:1–2).

Vaughan here locates his fellow Anglicans in the situation of the Old and New Testament peoples addressed in these passages. To people of the promise faced with a new situation, Vaughan counsels keeping of the faith in light of the future promise. His view of the time is again eschatological. The old injunctions hold; now, however, they are seen in a new light. The community is not here or at best it is scattered, each member "alone upon this Hill." But the true community, of which he and his audience are still members, is from the historical past or is yet to come, "both before and behinde thee." The aspect of Jesus' life to be lived out, imitated now, is that of reviling not even though we are reviled, of keeping to the old injunctions, remembering the old community, finding oneself still to be a member of that company through hope in the promises of God, living in expectation of the resumption of the life of that community to make possible those who will come "behinde thee," all pointing toward the fulfillment of the life of that whole company which is yet to come which will unite those who are not alone with their predecessors and their successors. Vaughan finds in such texts the verbal resources to claim that the present situation of Anglicans is a special one that creates the opportunity to live out roles and models for the Christian life which are available and appropriate only in circumstances of deprivation, isolation, and persecution, such as those then prevalent. He is thus able to recreate the present as a time of special opportunity to experience the fullness of traditional resources. Faithfulness to the old forms and images of the Christian life here takes on power and importance because to it apply unique assurances of salvation—"be faithful unto the death, and he will give thee a Crowne of life"—as well as special responsibility to be the continuity between those who are "before and behinde thee."

Vaughan also accomplishes in this passage the assertion that to use the special language of the fellowship of the saints that is so much a part of Prayer Book worship and to use the biblical texts that underlie and inform such usage are themselves ways of keeping the faith. Even though the normative use of Prayer Book texts has been lost, so long as its language remains the language that enables one to give voice to the experience of such a new situation, that use becomes one way of making the proclamation that even those events which deprive the writer and the reader of so much that is essential may in fact be God's actions to fulfill rather than to destroy what has been lost. This is linked to the task of faithfulness in adversity given to Vaughan's Anglican contemporaries; since part of the company of which one discovers one is still a member through the use of such language is "behinde thee," is still awaiting the palm branches of a Palm Sunday celebration, or of the triumph of Revelation, the keeping of the faith now becomes the path, the "way," toward a restoration of what has been lost so as to make possible the future expectation of those "behinde thee."

Vaughan's work that follows—*The Mount of Olives*—is in fact a companion volume to the Prayer Book, a set of private prayers to accompany Prayer Book worship, a kind of primer for the new historical situation. There are prayers for going into church, for marking parts of the day (getting up, going from home, returning home), for approaching the "Lord's Table," and for receiving Holy Communion, meditations for use when leaving the table, as well as prayers for use in time of persecution and adversity. Vaughan's model for this work is the official Primer of the Church of England as well as such works as Lancelot Andrewes' *Preces Privatae* (1615) and John Cosin's *Collection of Private Devotions* (1627). These books, written when the Prayer Book was still in use, were intended to orient the lives of their users more fully to the corporate life enabled by the Prayer Book. Vaughan's version, by alluding to the Daily Offices and Holy Communion as though they were available for use, serves at once as a constant reminder of what is absent and as a means of living as though they were available.

The prayers and meditations Vaughan published in this volume also remind their readers of what is lost because they are filled with verbal echoes of the Prayer Book. For example, the "Meditation before the receiving of the holy Communion" begins with the phrase "*Holy, holy, holy, is the Lord God of*

Hosts, the whole earth is full of his glory," which is a close paraphrase of the Sanctus of the Prayer Book communion rite: "Holy, holy, holy, Lord God of hosts; heaven and earth are full of thy glory." The confession which makes up part of this meditation echoes the language of the prayer which comes between the Sanctus and the prayer of consecration. Vaughan provides this text to enable the voicing of confession: "I confesse, dear God, I confesse with all my heart mine own extreme unworthyness, my most shameful and deplorable condition. But with thee, O Lord, there is mercy and plenteous redemption" (p. 161). The Prayer Book's text reads as follows: "We do not presume to come to this thy table (O merciful Lord) trusting in our own righteousness, but in thy manifold and great mercies. We be not worthy so much as to gather up the crumbs under thy table, but thou art the same Lord, whose property is always to have mercy" (BCP, p. 263). Later in the same meditation Vaughan quotes one of the "Comfortable words" (Matthew 11:28) that follows the absolution and also echoes the blessing of the priest after confession:

Vaughan: O Lord be merciful unto me, forgive all my sins, and heal all my infirmities. (P. 163)
BCP: Almighty God . . . Have mercy upon you, pardon and deliver you from all your sins, confirm and strengthen you in all goodness. (P. 260)

Words of comfort once spoken by the priest to the congregation during the ordinary use of the Prayer Book can now facilitate the writing of a prayer asking that mercy, forgiveness, and healing be available although their old sources are not. Such examples only suggest the copiousness of Vaughan's allusions to the Prayer Book in *The Mount of Olives*. What Vaughan offers in this work is a manual of devotion to a reader who is an Anglican "alone upon this Hill," one cut off from the ongoing community which once gave him his identity. The title makes this point. Vaughan's audacious claim is to align the disestablished Church of England, the Body of Christ now isolated from its community, with Christ on the Mount of Olives, isolated from his people who have turned against him and who will soon ask for his crucifixion. Because Vaughan can locate present experience in those terms, he can claim that to endure now is to look forward both to an execution and a resurrection; the times call for the living out of that dimension of the meaning of a desire to imitate Christ and give special understanding to the command to "take up thy cross and follow me."

This work thus serves as a reminder of what has been lost, a source of echoes and allusions to keep memories alive, and, as well, a guide to the conduct of life in this special sort of world: "And what else is the World but a Wildernesse? A darksome, intricate wood full of *Ambushes* and dangers; a Forrest where spiritual hunters, principalities and powers spread their nets, and compasse it about" (p. 146). It seeks to make the time of Anglican suffering a redemptive rather than merely a destructive time, hence its title. One who follows and lives out the image of the Christian life that Vaughan offers in *The Mount of Olives* conducts a life that extends the orienting function of the Prayer Book routine of services to the moment-to-moment conduct of living while constantly being reminded of what is missing—the very Prayer Book which Vaughan echoes over and over again. He also covertly argues for its recovery and importance. In his "Admonitions for Evening-Prayer," here envisioned as taking place in private, Vaughan reminds the reader familiar with the Prayer Book of the value of that Office:

> Remember that in the *Levitical* Law there is a frequent Commemora-
> tion and Charge given of the two daily Sacrifices, the one to be offer'd
> up in the morning and the other in the Evening, Exod. 30:7, 8. These
> offerings by *Incense,* our holie, harmlesse and undefiled High-Priest hath
> taken away, and instead of them every devout *Christian* is at the ap-
> pointed times to offer up a Spiritual Sacrifice, namely that of *Prayer.*
> (P. 150)

This argument for prayer at morning and evening, assigned to Christ, cannot help but remind the Anglican "alone upon this Hill" of the Prayer Book Offices now proscribed, so that he must "withdraw from all outward occupations to prepare for the inward and divine." How different the situation of Vaughan's readers from Herbert's parishioners, who could, instead of withdrawing, go out to attend Herbert's reading of the Daily Offices or stop their work in the fields to join with him when the church bell rang, signaling his reading of the Offices. To make his readers' memories more poignant, Vaughan alludes to the invariable Collect of Evening Prayer—"Lighten our darkness we beseech thee O Lord"—in his evening meditation—"As long as thou art present with me, I am in the light, but when thou art gone, I am in the shadows of death" (p. 151). He also alludes twice to the Magnificat, the song of the traditional Prayer Book canticle after the first lesson in his "Prayer for Evening."

> Vaughan: I know, O my God, it is not in man to establish his own
> ways, it is thy Almighty arm must do it . . . in the day time I will
> be speaking of thy wondrous works, thy must merciful and liberal
> arms. (P. 152)
> BCP: For he that is mighty, hath magnified me: and holy is his name.
> And his mercy is on them who fear him: throughout all generations.
> He hath showed strength with his arms: he hath scattered the
> proud in the imagination of their hearts. (Pp. 61–62)

The Puritan abolition of the Prayer Book deprived Englishfolk of God's word—the Magnificat—and substituted "man's ways"—extemporaneous prayer. Vaughan's web of allusions thus defines the new religious situation in terms of human pretension. It also acknowledges that the place for Christian experience, even the recovered experience of the public and communal, is now within, since it cannot be either public or corporate.

During this time when use of the Prayer Book was forbidden, a number of Anglican clergy devised alternative versions of Prayer Book services to circumvent the prohibition. Vaughan takes a more subtle approach by creating a work designed to remind its readers of the lost book through repeated echoes and allusions and to inculcate an ordering of daily living according to the routine of the Prayer Book, perpetuating its influence and informing purpose much as they were when its public use was not proscribed. In other words, Vaughan seeks to enable, in spite of the absence of public use of the Prayer Book, the continuation of a kind of Anglicanism, linking those who continued to use the Prayer Book in private and those who might have wished to through identification with each other in their common solitary circumstances. Vaughan's texts facilitate a working sense of Anglican community through the sharing of exile, connecting those who, although they probably were unknown to each other, had in common their sense of the absence of their normative, identity-giving community. He makes this clear in his preface "To the Reader" of his *Flores Solitudinis*, written in 1652 but published in 1654.

> In those sad Conflicts I dedicated the Remissions to thy use, Reader, & now I offer them to thy view. If the title shall offend thee, because it was found in the woods and the wildernesse, give mee leave to tell thee, that Deserts and Mountaines were the Schooles of the Prophets, and that Wild-hony was his diet, who by the testimony of the Sonne of God was the greatest amongst those that are borne of women. (P. 216)

Vaughan's works are for the use of his readers; his comparisons of himself to the prophets and to John the Baptist who cried out in the wilderness "prepare ye the way of the Lord" reinforce our sense that Vaughan finds in the events of his day analogies with the situation of the prophets as they experienced the fall of the historical enterprise that gave them their identity as people of God, and the later prophet, John, who, like the earlier prophets, saw in the apparently destructive events of the fall of Israel signs of God's actions renewing human history, enabling and promising a future divine activity fulfilling at the last the promises that apparently seemed to be abrogated by the fall of that enterprise. For Israel in exile, the presence of the prophet was itself that act of God that redeems the time and signifies God's faithfulness to his people even in the midst of circumstances which seem to assert the contrary. Vaughan's argument, in fact, turns on the question of interpretation. A negative understanding of current events is, to Vaughan, malicious:

> I protest seriously unto thee, and without Scepticisme, that there is no such thing in this world, as misfortune; the foolish testinesse of man arising out of his misconstruction and ignorance of the wise method of Providence, throwes him into many troubles. . . . what ever falls upon us from that Almighty hand, it is a diamond; It is celestiall treasure, and the matter of some new blessing, if we abuse it not. (P. 217)

The human effort to make a diamond out of what has now befallen Anglicans is a matter of struggling to undermine "misconstruction" and "ignorance" so as to see these events as evidence of "the wise method of Providence," and so Vaughan ends his entreaty:

> All that may bee objected is, that I write unto thee out of a land of darkenesse, out of that unfortunate region, where the Inhabitants sit in the shadow of death: where destruction passeth for propagation, and a thick black night for the glorious day-spring. If this discourage thee, be pleased to remember, that there are bright starrs under the most palpable clouds, and light is never so beautiful as in the presence of darknes. At least intreat God that the Sun may not goe down upon thy own dwelling, which is hartily desired and prayed for by Hen: Vaughan. (P. 217)

Rhetorically, this passage is a backing up from the prior claims, a moving from the audacity of the earlier assertion that "there is no such thing in this world as misfortune" to a request that "at least intreat God that the Sun may not goe down upon thy own dwelling." The end is, finally, in what one can be sure of—that Vaughan joins the reader in a prayer at least to raise the possibility that a community, no matter how small, exists in one act of speaking to God "out of a land of darkenesse," and to claim that in the keeping of faith in entreaty to God there is hope that Vaughan's other claims are true. At the least, such language puts Vaughan's interpretation of the present situation into a typological relationship with Job, whose description of his situation as "a land of darkness and the shadow of death" (Job 10:21) is part of the lament process, his persisting in which led to the revelation of God at the last, and then to the fulfillment of promises like that of Isaiah: "The people that walked in darkness have seen a great light: they that dwell in the land of the shadow of death, upon them hath the light shined." In such terms Vaughan would teach the means of keeping the faith in the face of such profound challenges, arguing that the very act of bringing the present before God in faithful lament is itself the way to promote the dispelling of darkness so that the stars that burn so brightly at the end of Spenser's *Epithalamion* might be glimpsed once more.

Vaughan's Uses of The Temple

To teach his readers how to understand membership in the church when that body is absent and thus keep faith with those who have gone before so that it will be possible for others to come after is Vaughan's didactic undertaking in *Silex Scintillans*.[8] To achieve that intention he tests the resources still available in the Anglican way of viewing the Bible as a text for use in articulating present circumstances and in the possibility that memories of Prayer Book rites still linger or that they are still available either through private observation of the Daily Offices or occasional clandestine sacramental use. At the same time he adds yet another allusive process, this to George Herbert's *Temple*.[9] In the experience of reading *Silex Scintillans*, the context of *The Temple* functions in lieu of the absent Anglican services. Using *The Temple* as a frame of reference cannot take the place of participation in Prayer Book rites; it can only add to the sense of loss by reminding us of their absence. But it can also serve as a way of evoking and defining that which cannot otherwise be known—the experience of ongoing public involvement in those rites—in a way that furthers Vaughan's desire to produce continued faithfulness to the community created by those rites.

The ending of *The Mount of Olives* provides us with a paradigm of Vaughan's combining the Bible, the Prayer Book, and Herbert's *Temple* to achieve both an ending for a devotional work and the didactic functioning of that ending. After providing texts for articulating a devotional stance toward the Daily Offices and Holy Communion, *The Mount of Olives* moves to a reflection on death which serves to facilitate the death, or ending, of the work as well as the experience of death itself from the perspective of the Prayer Book rites as though they were available for facilitating the Christian dying of its readers. The work ends thus:

> Lord *Jesus Christ* my most loving Redeemer, into thy saving and *everlasting Armes* I commend my *spirit*, I am ready my *dear Lord*, and earnestly expect and long for thy good pleasure; *Come quickly*, and receive the soul of thy *servant* which trusteth in thee.
>
> *Blessing, and honour, and glory and power be unto him that sitteth upon the throne, and unto the Lamb and to the holy Ghost for ever and ever Amen.*
>
> *Glory be to God on high, and on earth peace, good will towards men!*
> *Blessed be God alone!*
> *Thrice Blessed three in one!*

This articulation of a text that facilitates Christian dying is achieved, first of all, through biblical quotation. The speaker uses Christ's words—"Father, into thy hands I commend my spirit"—from Luke 23:46 at the end of Christ's life to evoke both that situation and a reminder of what would follow (Christ's Resurrection), which makes possible the quotation from Christ's words at the end of Revelation and the writer of Revelation's response: "Surely I come quickly. Amen. Even so, come, Lord Jesus." In "longing for thy good pleasure," Vaughan also echoes Psalm 71 from the Prayer Book's rite for the visitation of the sick. He then goes on to quote Revelation 5:13 ("Blessing, and honour, and glory") in praise of the Lamb who makes possible the speaker's confidence in God's deliverance as well as the promise that holds for the one who can use such language of divine appeal in regard to his own death. He then quotes the opening line of the *Gloria in excelsis,* which we have already noted in discussing the close of "The Church" section of *The Temple* is both the ending song of the Prayer Book communion rite and the ending line of Herbert's "The Church." Finally, he quotes the trinitarian blessing of God Herbert puts at the end of "The Church Militant."

This triple quotation of endings from biblical, liturgical, and literary sources is, of course, of endings that do not end anything but conclude in expectation, long for the same future that is not yet but is to come, and thus articulate themselves as (un)endings that reach toward and further the relationship between the speakers of these conclusions and the ending they all desire. By using them to articulate his own concluding, Vaughan points to them as three complementary resources for bringing into speech the kind of situation in which he finds himself in a way that informs and enables that situation to be more than merely desperate, but in fact a part of the salvation history. In this light, Vaughan's use of Herbert becomes yet another resource for articulating a text that will continue the Anglican poetic task, the use of language that will further the building of Christian community and the reign of charity in anticipation of its participation in the fulfillment of divine promises at the last.

One of the things a reader familiar with Herbert's *Temple* will notice immediately upon reading *Silex Scintillans* is the frequency and complexity with which Vaughan makes use of Herbert's poems. As Sharon Seelig has pointed out, Vaughan borrows twenty-six poem titles directly from Herbert and uses nine more with slight variation.[10] Other poems by Vaughan adapt their subject matter or their phrasing or imagery from Herbert's poems. For example, Vaughan's "Rules *and* Lessons" recasts the basic intention and content of Herbert's "Perirrhanterium," while "The Holy Communion," although its title is different, treats the same subject as Herbert's "The Banquet" and adopts a modified version of Herbert's first line; where Herbert declares, "Welcome sweet and sacred cheer, / Welcome deare" Vaughan gives us "Welcome sweet and sacred feast; welcome life." Vaughan's "Sun-dayes" borrows the method of stringing together images of its subject from Herbert's "Prayer (I)." Other poems by Vaughan make use of verbal echoes from Herbert in abundance. In "The Search," line 74 reads, "Me thought I heard one singing thus," while Herbert's "The Collar" reads "Me thoughts I heard one calling, *Child*" (l. 34). The opening lines of Vaughan's "The Passion" and Herbert's "Good Friday" both begin "O my chief good." Vaughan's "Christs Nativity" begins "Awake, glad heart!" which reverses the sense of the opening line—"Awake sad heart"—of Herbert's "The Dawning."

Other examples of Vaughan's extensive indebtedness to Herbert can be found in echoes and allusions as brief as a word or phrase or as extensive as a poem or group of poems. So thoroughly does Vaughan invoke Herbert's text and allow it to speak from within his own that there is hardly a poem, or even a moment within a poem, in either *Silex I* (1650) or *Silex II* (1655) which does not exhibit some relationship to Herbert's work. Indeed, this thorough evocation of the older poet's work begins with Vaughan at the dedication for the 1650 *Silex,* which echoes Herbert's dedication to *The Temple,* with Herbert's "first fruits" becoming Vaughan's "deaths fruits"—and continues these echoes in the expanded version of this verse printed in the 1655 edition, where Herbert's "present themselves to thee; / Yet not mine neither: for from thee they came, / And must return" becomes Vaughan's "he / That copied it, presents it thee. / 'Twas thine first, and to thee returns." In addition, Herbert's "Avoid, Profanenesse; come not here" from "Superliminare" becomes Vaughan's "Vain Wits and eyes / Leave, and be wise" in the poem that comes between the dedication and "Regeneration" in the 1655 *Silex.* Vaughan also follows Herbert in addressing poems to various feasts of the Anglican liturgical calendar; indeed, he goes beyond Herbert in the use of the calendar by using that calendar's list of saints to provide, as the subject of poems, the names of Saint Mary Magdalene and the Blessed Virgin Mary.

By using *The Temple* so extensively as a source for his poems, Vaughan set up an intricate interplay between his *Silex* poems and Herbert's poems, a deliberate strategy to provide for his work the rich and dense context Herbert had ready-made in the ongoing worship of the Church of England. Although the actual Anglican church buildings were "vilified and shut up," Vaughan found in Herbert's *Temple* a way to open the life of the Anglican worship community if only by allusion to what Herbert could assume as the context for reading his word/church. With *The Temple* open before him and his readers, Vaughan could treat it as a text for use, writing poems which function in relation to poems in *The Temple* as poems in *The Temple* function in relation to biblical and Prayer Book texts. If the Prayer Book cannot be used to enact the church, at least Vaughan's poems can be used to enact *The Temple,* to use the articulations of experience provided in Herbert's work as events with an afterlife to enable the bringing-into-discourse of Vaughan's fundamentally new situation, thus linking it with the church of Herbert's day in terms of the common future they share. Vaughan's *Silex Scintillans* thus becomes his "reading" of *The Temple,* his deed that reinterprets Herbert's texts, that becomes the proof that while Vaughan may be "the least" of Herbert's products he certainly is the one who gives *The Temple* whatever meaning it can have in the world of the 1650s.

There is also a sense in which Vaughan begins *Silex I* where Herbert left off in "The Church." Remembering that Herbert considers, toward the end of "The Church," the traditional "last things" in poems entitled "Death," "Dooms-day," and "Judgement," we must note that Vaughan has poems entitled "Death," "Resurrection and Immortality," and "Day of Judgement" as the second, third, and fourth poems in *Silex I.* Vaughan here enacts a reopening of *The Temple* and a resumption of Herbert's enterprise precisely at that point at which Herbert presumed it appropriate to stop and in the terms which allude to the end of human history and the beginning of God's eternity. Yet history had ended for the Church of England in one form; in searching for another form, Vaughan begins with the classic theological terms and occasions for ultimate endings and beginnings.

In addition, in his *Mount of Olives,* Vaughan describes Herbert as being "of blessed memory" and praises his "incomparable prophetick Poems," especially "Church-musick," "Church-rents and schisms," and "The Church Militant." It is not hard to see why Vaughan valued these texts.[11] "Church-musick" claims that its speaker and church music "say sometimes, *God help poore Kings*" (l. 8); "Church-rents and schismes" claims that "Mother" church, as a result of "debates and fretting jealousies," has had her "serv'rall parts . . . cast . . . in the dirt" (ll. 11, 16, 21, 23); and "The Church Militant" proclaims, as we have seen, the growing darkness in and about the church in England and religion's imminent departure for America. Walton notes that the vice-chancellor of Cambridge University had licensed *The Temple* for publication in the hope that Herbert would not be taken "to be an inspired Prophet"; clearly Vaughan views Herbert in just the terms the vice-chancellor hoped he would avoid.[12]

We may therefore see *Silex Scintillans* as resuming the work of *The Temple* in the context of a situation defined by Herbert's expectation of "the *British Church* . . . trodden under foot, and branded with the title of *Antichristian*" (*Works,* p. 186). Herbert's "last things" anticipated for all become for Vaughan events realized in the history of the Church of England; *Silex* becomes an attempt to find what life after institutional death might occasion. In this context, *The Temple* serves as a textual manifestation of a "blessed Pattern of a holy life in the *Brittish Church*" now absent and libeled by the Puritans as having been the reverse of what it claimed to be. *Silex Scintillans* comes to be a resumption in poetry of Herbert's undertaking in *The Temple* as poetry—the teaching of "holy life" as it is lived in "the *Brittish Church*" but now colored by the historical experience of that church in the midst of a rhetorical and verbal frame of assault.[13]

What now becomes important is to understand the terms in which Vaughan sees his relationship to Herbert, both as Christian exemplar and as Anglican poet. As we know, Vaughan praised Herbert as a "blessed man," one whose religious poetry alone among many who "dash *Scriptures* and the *sacred Relatives* of *God* with their impious conceits" was worthy of commendation. Indeed, Vaughan claims that Herbert's "holy *life* and *verse* gained many pious *Converts* (of whom I am the least)" (*Works*, p. 391). Vaughan's quotation of Paul—"I am the least of the apostles" (1 Corinthians 15:9)—identifies Vaughan as taking on a role as Christian and as poet in the succession of true apostles, who will hope to "labour more abundantly than they all" (1 Corinthians 15:10) because of his role as "one born out of due time" (1 Corinthians 15:8), the separation between Paul and the original apostles repeated in the situation that separates Vaughan from Herbert, both in terms of a temporal succession and a separation resulting from the fate of Anglicanism in the succeeding years.

This sense of "handing on" an apostolic function as Christian exemplar and poet underlies Vaughan's argument in "The Match," a poem which Jonathan Post has described as informed by its relationship to the Anglican rite of confirmation,[14] but which is more closely related to the rite of ordination for a priest. The poem opens with an address to Herbert as poet, in echo of the reference to Herbert from the preface to *Silex:*

> Dear friend! whose holy, ever-living lines
>   Have done much good
>   To many, and have checkt my blood,
> My fierce, wild blood that still heaves, and inclines,
>   But it is still tam'd
>   By those bright fires which thee inflam'd;
> Here I join hands, and thrust my stubborn heart
>   Into thy *Deed,*
>   There from no *Duties* to be freed,
> And if hereafter *youth,* or *folly* thwart
>   And claim their share,
>   Here I renounce the pois'nous ware.
>
> (Ll. 1–12)

It is "into thy *Deed*" as poet that the speaker thrusts "my stubborn heart"; Vaughan claims a performance of what Herbert sought in "Obedience," that "some kinde man would thrust his heart / Into these lines," in anticipation of which Herbert promised "How happie were my part." Herbert in this poem makes clear a play on "Deed" as an action with words as well as an action with consequences in the real world evoked through the idea of a deed as a gift of a possession:

> He that will passe his land,
> As I have mine, may set his hand
> And heart unto this Deed, when he hath read;
> And make the purchase spread
> To both our goods, if he to it will stand.
>
> ("Obedience," ll. 36–40)

Vaughan here defines his own poetic vocation as a "reading" of Herbert, a joining into Herbert's task of making "the purchase" of writing/proclaiming God's "death and bloud . . . spread / To both our goods." A "deed" is both act and text which records and makes binding a transfer of title, authority, and power. Such is Vaughan's "deed" from Herbert's poetic "deed"; he joins Herbert in a common prophetic and literary enterprise and accepts the role of, or creates himself as, the heir to Herbert's title and vocation. Here, too, the joining of hands and the evoking of images of pentecostal fire suggest both confirmation and ordination, for in both rites the bishop lays his hands on the person receiving the rite, prays for additional gifts of the Holy Spirit, and proclaims that in the laying on of hands those gifts are bestowed. But to join hands with Herbert in his priestly role as poet and to accept his "Duties" is to suggest the functioning of the latter rite, in which priests join with the bishop in laying hands on the ordinand.

The rite of ordination is further invoked in the second part of "The Match," in which the speaker performs the prayer which the bishop in his charge to the ordinand requests that "ye ought and have need earnestly to pray for [God's] Holy Spirit . . . by the mediation of our only mediator and Saviour Jesus Christ . . . that ye may so endeavour yourselves . . . to sanctify the lives of you and yours . . . that ye may be wholesome and Godly examples and patterns for the rest of the congregation to follow."[15] Vaughan's prayer to Christ is to "Afford me life, / And save me from all inward strife . . . / Settle my *house,* and shut out all distractions" (ll. 5–16), thus again echoing the bishop's charge "to forsake and set aside . . . all worldly cares and studies" evoked by Herbert in his "passing his land." Further, Vaughan's prayer is "Thy will in all be done, not mine," responding to the bishop's charge not to have "a mind and a will thereto your selves" but "according to the will of our Lord Jesus Christ." "To thee therefore my *Thoughts, Words, Actions* / I do resign" (ll. 14–15), says Vaughan's speaker, again reflecting the bishop's charge to pursue study of Scripture, prayers, and ministry of "the doctrine and Sacraments . . . as the Lord hath commanded."[16] His prayer concludes with a request that "this *grain* which here in tears I sow / Though *dead*, and *sick*, / Through thy *Increase* grow *new* and *quick*" (ll. 28–30). The word "increase" comes from the prayer over the ordinand offered by the bishop "that he may daily increase . . . in the knowledge and faith of thee, and thy son . . . that . . . thy holy name may be always glorified, and thy blessed kingdom enlarged."[17] The image of sowing grain comes from Jesus' parable of the sower (Matthew 13, Mark 4, Luke 8), a traditional ordination text: "other fell on good ground, and did yield fruit that sprang up and increased; and brought forth, some thirty, and some sixty, and some an hundred" (Mark 4:8). Vaughan's last words are also an echo of the last words of Herbert's "Love Unknown," in which the second speaker of the poem instructs the first speaker in the actions of God to "*have you be new, tender, quick*," although Vaughan turns them into a prayer for the results of his offering himself as a "poor Oblation" which "through thy Mercies may be more" in terms of being more productive of the fruits of his sowing.[18]

Vaughan here in effect asks that his "dread Lord" ordain him to a priesthood as poet, in a poem placed at the center of *Silex I*; he follows this with "Rules *and* Lessons," a sermonlike poem transforming Herbert's "Perirrhanterium," and adds poems later on the Holy Communion ("Dressing" and "The Holy Communion"), thus replicating the general structure of the Prayer Book Eucharist in which sermon precedes Sacrament.[19] I stress a priesthood *as poet*, for without the presence of a bishop no ordination to a real priesthood in the Anglican church would be possible, and no bishops were ordaining anyone in the late 1640s. Thus the "*grain* . . . I sow" will produce a poetic harvest, not eucharistic bread. To ask that his efforts take on Herbert's "Deed" in "ever-living lines" is to affirm, first of all, the contingency of even a truly ordained priest on the functioning through him of Christ and thus the dependency of a priestly office as poet on the functioning of God through the poet's language. Second, it is to seek the only kind of priesthood available in the Commonwealth period, a making available of "lines" to carry out the priestly office now closed to real priests. Only Herbert's role as priestly poet, not his other role as priest of the Anglican church, is open to Vaughan. His brother Thomas was a priest who was deprived of his living by the new government; Vaughan's prayer is that God use his poetry to continue the functioning of the priestly office as Vaughan had experienced it through reading *The Temple*, arguing that this is a time when there is no other way for that office to function.

Again, Vaughan's triple set of textual echoes at the end of "The Match"—from the Bible, from the Prayer Book, and from *The Temple*—defines the way in which such a poetic priestly office might come to be performed. Through the articulation of the speaker's stance by means of these three texts he is able to act out what a priesthood might mean in his historical situation, informing it through reference to the priest's biblical and sacramental resources and *The Temple* as a verbal manifestation of the ongoing life that the use of such resources by a priest would facilitate. *Silex Scintillans* takes *The Temple* into itself along with the Bible and the Prayer Book in the same way in which the doing of Prayer Book rites incorporates the Bible and the larger arena of Christian living, reflected in *The Temple,* includes both the Bible and the Prayer Book. In Vaughan's unique circumstances, the incorporation of these texts makes possible the articulation of Vaughan's situation, even as the Bible makes possible the effectiveness of the Prayer Book and the use of the Prayer Book makes possible the doing of "all such good works as thou hast prepared for us to walk in."[20] To be able to articulate that situation in these terms is to open the world so addressed to the possibility that the meaning of Christianity as Herbert understood it is still a possibility, that even in such a situation the present moment of address can come to be seen as a moment of potential incorporation into the divine history of salvation. It is also to seek persuasiveness about the validity of the understanding of Christianity which empowers such an articulation. That is what Vaughan would achieve in *Silex Scintillans,* and that is why he both draws on the allusive resources of *The Temple* and offers his poetic efforts to the God on whose activity they must depend for their persuasiveness and effectiveness.

Yet to see how Vaughan seeks persuasiveness in a situation different from the one in which Herbert wrote *The Temple* we also need to note the differences between Herbert and Vaughan in putting together a didactic collection of religious poetry. One of the most obvious is the fact that Vaughan does not continue Herbert's practice of alluding to the features of the church building, a feature of almost as many poems by Herbert (seven) as there are poems on feasts from the Prayer Book calendar (eight). Nor does Vaughan follow Herbert in poems that describe the actions of the clergy in the church building, a feature of several of the poems in *The Temple.* In his situation in the late 1640s and 1650s, as we know, Vaughan could not find in those images and activities the kinds of poetic resources available to Herbert; after all, those "sacred buildings" are now "vilified and shut up." Vaughan draws the contrast explicitly in his version of Herbert's "The British Church," in which Herbert's "fit aray" becomes Vaughan's "seamlesse coat" which "These dare divide, and stain." In other words, the ongoing life of that institution Herbert celebrates and works to build up is in Vaughan's experience "a little dust."

But if the larger context of allusion in Herbert's *Temple* is missing in Vaughan's experience, Herbert's own *Temple* is very much a part of Vaughan's experience. To Vaughan, Herbert's work serves not as a work to copy, merely, much less a work to refute and "overgoe," but a constant reminder of what has been lost which thus functions in relationship with the speaker of Vaughan's *Silex* analogous to the relationship in Herbert's poetry between the experience of Herbert's speaker and the ongoing life of the Anglican church. Even as the life of that institution informs the activities of Herbert's speaker, so the desire for the restoration of those activities or at least the desire for the fulfillment of the promises which those activities make possible informs Vaughan's speaker. Thus it is appropriate that while Herbert's *Temple* ends with an image of the sun as the guide to progress in time toward "time and place, where judgement shall appeare," so Vaughan ends *Silex II* with praise of "the worlds new, quickning Sun!" which promises to usher in "a state / For evermore immaculate"; until then, the speaker promises, "we shall gladly sit / Till all be ready" ("L'Envoy," ll. 1, 16, 26–27). While Herbert's speaker can claim to participate in a historical process through the agency of the church's life, Vaughan's, in the absence of that life, can keep the faith by expectantly waiting for that time when the images of Christian community central to Herbert are finally fulfilled in those divine actions which will recreate Christian community:

> Dear Lord, do this! . . .
> Incline each hard heart to do good
> And cement us with thy sons blood
> That like true sheep, all in one fold
> We may be fed, and one minde hold.
>   (Ll. 43–48)

Such images, given meaning in Herbert by the ongoing activities of the church, are still usable in Vaughan as a way of talking about what is to come rather than what is now. Here, Vaughan's echo of the Prayer Book's recital of the Ten Commandments ("incline our hearts to keep this law," BCP, pp. 248–249) is linked to an image of the church to come as having "one minde . . . all in one fold," lines Vaughan borrowed from John Cosin's *Collection of Private Devotions* he wrote in 1627 to accompany the burial of the dead, as a way of imagining the expectation and hope of the faithful. What was formerly for Anglicans the subject of daily prayer has now become future expectation. Vaughan's allusions to Herbert make clear the terms in which to understand what has been lost, as well as a way of giving meaning to such language so that Vaughan's projection of it into the future will have power and evocative effectiveness.

We have already noted Vaughan's use of Herbert in poems like "The Brittish Church" and "Rules *and* Lessons." We can see something more of Vaughan's use of Herbert if we compare his expansion of Herbert's "Decay" in his "Religion." Herbert's poem contrasts present experience of God with past experience as recorded in the Bible: "Sweet were the dayes, when thou didst lodge with Lot, / Struggle with Jacob, sit with Gideon, / Advise with Abraham . . . / Encounter Moses" (ll. 1–4). Now, however, "thou dost thy self immure and close / In some one corner of a feeble heart" (ll. 11–12).

God's presence now seems less, seems in "retreat, / Cold Sinne still forcing it" (ll. 18–19). Hope lies in the divine promise to "return / And calling *Justice, all things burn*" (ll. 19–20). Herbert's poem develops a paradox that the Incarnation, through which God becomes part of human experience, is, in human terms, weakness, although in Christian terms such "closing of God in a grave" is the source of human hope. In his sense of time here Herbert anticipates his treatment of time leading to judgment in "The Church Militant." Through his use of images of "Sinne and Satan, thy old foes" he alludes to the rite of baptism, with its heavy stress on "release of sins" and forsaking "the devil and all his works" (BCP, p. 273), thus remembering baptism is part of the process which leads to the final defeat of "Sin and Satan" when Christ "shall come again at the end of the world to judge the quick and the dead."

Herbert's poem, in the context of Anglican sacramental life, is thus a way of accounting for the present situation of Christians, of finding God's presence in their lives in a new way which points to a final fulfillment, which, because of the apparent power of "Sin and Satan," suggests that "the world grows old" and that the fulfillment of God's promise is near. Vaughan's poem also presents a contrast between God's relationship then and now; picking up Herbert's list of names—Lot, Jacob, Gideon, Abraham, and Moses—and his list of places—"fair oak, or bush, or cave or well"—he presents the same scene:

> Under a *Juniper,* some house,
> Or the coole *Myrtles* canopie,
> Others beneath an *Oakes* greene boughs,
> Or at some *fountaines* bubling Eye;
>
> Here *Jacob* dreams, and wrestles, there
> *Elias* by a Raven is fed,
> Another time by th'Angell, where
> He brings him water with his bread;
>
> In *Abr'hams* Tent the winged guests
> (O how familiar then was heaven!)
> Eate, drinke, discourse, sit down, and rest
> Untill the Coole, and shady *Even;*
>
> Nay thou thy selfe, my God, in *fire,*
> *Whirle-winds,* and *Clouds,* and the *soft voice*
> Speak'st there so much, that I admire
> We have no Conf'rence in these daies.
>
> (Ll. 5–20)

But Vaughan's stress is not, as is Herbert's, on a new way God is present; instead, lacking ability to allude to the rite of baptism, Vaughan must question the divine activity altogether. We will have occasion later to examine this poem in more detail; for the moment I want to note how Vaughan's recourse is to a redoing of Herbert's image of the church in time from "The Church Militant," claiming that religion is now a "tainted sink," if you will, a polluted baptismal font—"that *Samaritans* dead *Well*" (l. 46–47)—compared to the purity of Herbert's font. He ends his poem with a request that the purity of baptismal life return—"Heale then these waters Lord"—or that God act again in human history decisively—"turn once more our *Water* into Wine!" (l. 52). Vaughan's poem thus takes as its context Herbert's poem, allowing Herbert's work to inform its interpretive processes, casting Herbert's language and images into a new situation which makes them function as a prayerful petition that God resume the fundamental sacramental acts and relationships in which the Anglican church once found its identity and its role in the divine saving activity in the world. The interplay with Herbert's poem also allows *The Temple* to function as a way of defining what is lost and what must be resumed again.

A similar interplay takes place between Herbert's "Christmas" and Vaughan's two poems on "Christs Nativity." Vaughan's first nativity poem takes its opening motif from Herbert's "The Dawning," transposing its "Sad heart" into a "glad heart," but the deeper relationships are with Herbert's "Christmas." The "Consort" that natural sounds of woods, winds, and springs make in "Christs Nativity (I)" comes from the second section of Herbert's "Christmas" poem, a motif that recurs in Vaughan's "Christs Nativity (II)," where Herbert's "shall I silent be? / My God, no hymne for thee?" (l. 15) becomes Vaughan's "And shall we then no voices lift?" (l. 5). While Herbert's poem ends with song—"His beams shall cheer my breast, and both so twine, / Till ev'n his beams sing, and my musick shine" (ll. 33–34)—Vaughan's first poem laments that the speaker needs to be "some *Bird,* or Star . . . / Then either Star, or *Bird,* should be / Shining, or singing still to thee" (ll. 13–18), but no song comes. Thus, he ends his second nativity poem with an image of human ingratitude expressed by the lack of song or celebration of Christmas—"alas, my God! Thy birth now here / Must not be numbred in the year" (ll. 17–18).

The context for Vaughan's creative reworking of Herbert's poems on the nativity is of course the Puritan abolition of the Anglican liturgical calendar and with it the observation of Christmas itself. In light of Herbert's poem, Vaughan's poem, with its intercession for a renewed act of God—"let once more by mystick birth / The Lord of life be bourne in Earth" (ll. 29–30)—takes on added power and poignancy. Without the Anglican celebration of Christmas as a context, Vaughan's poem makes the fulfillment of the Collect for Christmas— "Grant that we being regenerate and made thy children by adoption and grace, may daily be renewed by thy Holy Spirit"—seem even more remote. With that celebration as context, Herbert can use in "Christmas" a paraphrase of that

Collect—"Furnish & deck my soul, that thou mayst have / A better lodging then a rack or grave" (ll. 13–14)—and then go on to proclaim a kind of fulfillment of that prayer in the second part of the poem, with its triumphant "His beams shall cheer my breast . . . / Till ev'n his beams sing, and my musick shine." In the context of the sacramental life of Anglicanism which enables words like "faith" to have meaning for Herbert, he can claim that "Faith puts me [in the common manger] with him, who sweetly took / Our flesh and frailtie, death and danger" ("Faith," ll. 22–23); lacking that life, Vaughan can only wish he "were some *Bird* or Star, / Flutt'ring in woods, or lifted far / Above this *Inne*" (ll. 14–16). There is now no room in the inn for Vaughan, either. He can only live in anticipation and hope—"I am all filth, and obscene, / Yet, if thou wilt, thou canst make clean" (ll. 23–24)—but his second "Nativity" poem moves not toward a realization of an answer in poetry and song but, lament-fashion, regrets that "Thy birth now here / Must not be numbred in the year," either in the numbers of the calendar or the numbers of song. Part of what is at stake here is the loss of the ability to celebrate Christmas, including the writing of poems about it. Vaughan's double poem replicates the form of Herbert's poem, which also has two distinct sections, but Herbert is able to use the second section to provide the "hymne" for Christmas, while Vaughan cannot do so. In his historical circumstances, the second section of a poem on the nativity can only lament that Christmas "Must not be numbred in the year," which only reinforces the speaker's plea in Part I that God act once more "by mystick birth" and recreate "the year" so that proper response to it can be made in poetry. In this light, Herbert's poem works to inform our sense of the issues in Vaughan's poem. Although the eager Puritan censor could have passed over the implications of Vaughan's poem because the speaker blames himself ("I am all filth, and obscene" [l. 23]), the reader informed by Herbert's poem would see such confession as an echo of the Prayer Book's petition that "our sinful bodies [may be] washed clean by his body" because "if thou wilt, thou canst make clean." Such allusion ties the speaker's stance to the act of public confession in the Prayer Book and identifies the source of difficulty in the poems as those who prevent the "numbring" of Christ "in the year."

What I am suggesting, therefore, is that for Vaughan's *Silex Scintillans* Herbert's *Temple* functions as a source of reference, one which joins with the Bible and the Prayer Book to enable Vaughan's speaker to give voice to his situation and thus, ultimately, to teach how to redeem the time by keeping faith with those who had gone before through orienting present experience in terms of the common future that Christian proclamation asserts they share. To use Herbert in this way is to claim for him a position in the line of priestly poets from David forward and to claim for Vaughan a place in that company as well, in terms of the didactic functioning of his Christian poetry. To use Herbert's work as a model, even when transforming it, is to understand the present in typological terms once more by being able to make the affirmation that even in duress, when the context Herbert assumed was absent, Vaughan and those who learned from him were able to keep faith with their Anglican predecessors and thus make endurable the time of Anglican exile. In Vaughan's day, the activity of writing *Silex Scintillans* becomes a "reading" of *The Temple,* not in a static sense as a copying but in a truly imitative sense, Vaughan's text revealing how *The Temple* had produced, in his case, an "augmentation in the field of action" in a way that could promote others to produce similar "fruit" through reading Vaughan's "leaves." Standing in relationship to *The Temple* as Vaughan would have his readers stand in relation to *Silex* itself, Vaughan's poem collection models the desired relationship between text and life both he and Herbert sought. Using the living text of the past to make communion with it, to keep faith with it, to understand the present in terms of it, Vaughan "reads" Herbert to orient the present through working toward the restoration of community in their common future. Vaughan's audience did not have the church with them as it was in Herbert's day, but it had *The Temple;* together with *Silex Scintillans* they taught how to interpret the present through endurance, devotion, and faithful charity so that it could be made a path toward recovery at the last. Vaughan, through his use of Herbert, thus orients the activity of priestly poetry once more toward the results of *"Deeds"* with "lines." He, too, would claim to be a poet whose meaning is in results, in promoting the transformation of what is *"dead,* and *sick"* into the *"new,* and *quick"* through "thy *Increase,"* the actions of God through the words made available by the writing of the poet/priest, creating an occasion for divine action in the reading moment. Thus it is with special urgency that Vaughan's speaker recounts the offering of his tears as "grain" for the divine "Increase"; if Vaughan's deed with Herbert produces "fruit" then the speaker will know that the expectation of the psalmist will have been fulfilled, that "they that sow in tears shall reap in joy" (Psalm 126:6), so that Vaughan would know that he had found a way to "sing the Lord's song in a strange land" (Psalm 137:3).

The Homiletics of Searching in Silex Scintillans (1650)

Silex Scintillans is much more about the possibility of searching than it is about finding. It is more about the possibility of living out Christian identity in an Anglican sense when the source of that identity is absent, except in the traces of the Bible, the Prayer Book, and *The Temple* Vaughan echoes. It is also more about anticipating God's new actions to come than it is about celebrating their present occurrence. The danger Vaughan faces is that the church Herbert knew will become merely text, will be reduced to a Prayer Book unused on a shelf, or a Bible read in private, or *The Temple* itself. If that happened, the Anglican moment would become fully past, known only as an occasion for sorrow or affectionate memories, serving as a perspective from which to criticize the various Puritan alternatives, but not something to be lived in and through. Vaughan could then no longer claim to be "in the body," for Christ himself would be absent. Vaughan's challenge in *Silex Scintillans* is to teach how someone, through continuing to use the Bible and Prayer Book to articulate present experience as though the Prayer Book were in public use and adding to that the reading of *The Temple* to evoke the vocabulary of public use, could experience the possibility of an opening in the present to the continuing activity of God leading to the fulfillment of God's promises, and thus to teach faithfulness to Anglicanism, making it still ongoing despite all appearances to the contrary.

Ultimately, in the portions of *Silex Scintillans* added in the edition of 1655, Vaughan would be able to celebrate rather than lament the experience of Anglicans in the Commonwealth period because he could proclaim that experience of loss as necessary to the fulfillment of God's promises at the last in the inbreaking of his kingdom. The isolated Anglican is called to keep faith with his tradition by seeing its times of trouble as part of what must be endured faithfully by God's people if they are to function as "saving remnant" and help to usher in as well as to achieve citizenship in that kingdom. In that hope, and in the resources he is able to provide for articulating and interpreting present experience, Vaughan ultimately finds cause for rejoicing. But the development of that eschatological perspective is gradual; although we will note its appearance toward the end of *Silex I* where it functions as a way of claiming usefulness for the strategies which lead up to it, we will not find its full development until *Silex II*. In the experience of reading, this perspective vindicates Vaughan's exploration of the consequences for living and writing of the loss of the Anglican church as a public institution and of the resources that remained within its tradition for understanding and responding to the events that had overwhelmed it. I want now to explore the ways Vaughan sought in the 1650 *Silex* to teach faithfulness to Anglicanism in light of its demise; the next section will examine his new strategies for understanding that demise as itself an act of God in continuity with his past acts.

Among the ways one might regard the edition of *Silex Scintillans* which Vaughan published in 1650, I want to describe two and use them to help us gain access to this remarkable body of poetry. Although most readers proceed as though the larger work of 1655 (*Silex II*) were the work itself, for which the earlier version is a preliminary with no claim to separate consideration, I first want to examine *Silex I* as a work unto itself. For a few pages at least I want to regard it as a work written and published by a poet who did not know that five years later he would publish it again, with significant changes in the context of presentation and with significant additions in length. I want to restore to it the opening Latin poem and emblem and dedicatory verse of the

1650 edition. Then, in the next section, I want to look at it as part of the larger work of 1655, tracing the consequences for the work of the fact that Vaughan then dropped the Latin poem and emblem, expanded the dedicatory verse and joined it to a prose preface, and added a large new body of poetry at the end of the 1650 collection. That section, emphasizing *Silex II,* will take into account the difference in our experience of *Silex I* created by the revised and augmented frame for the older poems created by the 1655 edition.

The title, *Silex Scintillans: or Sacred Poems and Private Ejaculations,* exists at once to distance Vaughan's work and his situation from Herbert's and to link them. Not merely acknowledging Vaughan's indebtedness to Herbert, his simultaneous echoing of Herbert's subtitle for *The Temple* (Sacred Poems and Private Ejaculations) and use of a very different title reminds us that Vaughan writes constantly in the absence of that to which Herbert's title alludes. Richard Crashaw could, of course, entitle his 1646 work *Steps to the Temple* because in 1645 he responded to the same events constraining Vaughan by changing what was for him the temple; by becoming a Roman Catholic, Crashaw could continue participation in a worshipping community but at the cost of flight from England and its church. Vaughan remained loyal to that English institution even in its absence by reminding us of what is now absent, or at best present only in a new kind of way in *The Temple* itself. Vaughan's goal for *Silex Scintillans* is to find ways of giving us the experience of Anglicanism apart from Anglicanism, or to make possible the continued experience of being a part of the Body of Christ in Anglican terms in the absence of the ways in which those terms had their meaning prior to the 1640s.

Silex I thus begins with material that replicates the disjuncture between what Herbert built in *The Temple* and the situation Vaughan faces; again, it serves for Vaughan as a way of articulating a new religious situation. The Latin poem *"Authoris (de se) Emblema"* that begins *Silex I* in the 1650 edition, together with its emblem, represent a reseparation of the emblematic and verbal elements in Herbert's "The Altar." While Herbert combined visual appearance with verbal construction, Vaughan puts the language of "The Altar" about God breaking the speaker's rocklike heart into the poem and depicts in the emblem a rocklike heart being struck so that it gives off fire and tears. In the poem, the speaker accounts for what follows in terms of a new act of God, a changing of the method of divine acting from the agency of love to that of anger. Linking this with the bringing-forth of water from the rock struck by Moses, the speaker finds, "I live again in dying, / And rich am I, now, amid ruins lying."[21]

This poem and emblem, when set against Herbert's treatment of the same themes, display the new Anglican situation. Herbert's "Church" from "The Altar" to "Love (III)" shifts in its reading of the Anglican Eucharist from a place where what God breaks is made whole to a place where God refuses, in love, to take the speaker's sense of inadequacy, or brokenness, for a final answer. In *Silex I,* the altar shape is absent, even as the Anglican altar was absent; amid the ruins of that altar, again divided into the pieces of the broken heart of the speaker of "The Altar," the speaker finds an act of God, changed from the love of "Love (III)" but an act of God nonetheless, which enables the speaker to find and affirm life even in brokenness, "amid ruins lying." In addition, Vaughan reaches back through Herbert's recreation of Sidney's *Astrophil and Stella* to the situation facing Astrophil in Sonnet 37 in which Stella "Hath no misfortune, but that Rich she is." Here Vaughan can find a way to have his speaker assert "rich am I" amid his misfortunes, restoring in the process the sexual overtones of Resurrection language—"I live again in dying"—to their function as articulations of experience informed by Christian paradigms. By placing his revision of the first poem in Herbert's "Church" at the beginning of *Silex I,* Vaughan asserts that we will find life amid the brokenness of Anglicanism when it can be brought into speech that at least raises the expectation that such life will come to be affirmed through brokenness itself, here through the brokenness of language and language-framed worlds as well as of the speaker's sense of self. So, Herbert's *Temple* is broken here, a metaphor for the brokenness of Anglicanism, but broken open to find life, not the death of that institution Puritans hoped to destroy by forbidding use of the Prayer Book.

The poem that forms the dedicatory verse of *Silex I* takes us back to the beginning of *The Temple,* as Herbert's offering of "first fruits . . . yet not mine neither" becomes Vaughan's of "thy deaths fruits" (l. 2). It is thus the Crucifixion of Christ that provides the typological moment used here to bring this situation into speech; as in *The Mount of Olives,* it is "drops of thy all-quickning blood" that made "my heart . . . bud" into the poems that follow. Vaughan is again in the midst of the traditional Anglican language about the "fruit" of human effort enabled by and dependent on divine action. He characterizes the Puritans as "some here to hire . . . / That ston'd thy servants," thus describing the Anglican situation as a replication of the martyrdom of Stephen; the stones of Herbert's "The Altar" become agents of destruction rather than components of building. The speaker can characterize historic events in terms of actions in and to the church, yet because of what he implies about what has occurred he reminds us that the English themselves have brought about the destruction of the Anglican church and furthered the effects of the fall; note that the "ground" on which the divine blood falls is "void of store," reversing the creation as Herbert defined it in "Easter-Wings" as "in wealth and store." But the "I" here has expelled those "here to hire" who "ston'd thy servants, and did move / To have thee murthred for thy love"; the speaker defines himself as one who is striving to be true to the old way of participating in the divine activity rather than to the new Puritan alternative, and so he "begs" God that he "wouldst take thy Tenants Rent" (l. 14). While Herbert in his dedicatory poem would ask God to "refrain" readers "who shall hurt themselves or me," Vaughan defines this act as one of "expelling" those who "ston'd thy servants," something his "I" has done to further the possibility of offering language to God for his use.

To make poems in this historical situation, articulating that situation in persuasive speech to argue that even in that situation is to be found the action of God so that his readers will be brought to keep faith with the Anglican community even in the absence of its defining activity, Vaughan thus takes into his own action with words the breaking up of Anglicanism, mirrored in the breaking up of Herbert's language and structure of persuasive experience in *The Temple*. It is obviously not enough merely to juxtapose what was with what now is; if the Anglican way with the Bible and community-creating worship were to remain valid, there needed to be a means of affirming and involving oneself in that being-on-the-way even when it is no longer going on. Otherwise, the Anglican enterprise is over and finished, and brokenness yields only "dust," not the possibility yet of water from rocks or life from ruins. Vaughan thus writes of brokenness in a way that makes his poems a sign that even in that brokenness there remains the possibility of finding and proclaiming divine activity and offering one's efforts with words to further it. In that light, Vaughan can reaffirm Herbert's claim that to ask is to take part in the finding by arguing that to be able to ask and to seek is to take part in the divine activity that will make the brokenness of Anglican community not the end of the story but an essential part of the story itself, in spite of all evidence to the contrary. If Vaughan can persuade us of that, then his work can become *"Silex Scintillans,"* "flashing flint," stone become fire, in a way that will make it a functional substitute for *The Temple,* both as title and as poetic text.

It is in this light that we need to approach "Regeneration," the first poem that we face after the prefatory material in the version of *Silex Scintillans* Vaughan published in 1650. This is not a poem in which regeneration occurs, nor does the speaker claim that it has occurred.[22] It is, instead, a poem which concerns itself with issues of how the world is to be perceived in Vaughan's new situation. In the world Vaughan addresses in this poem, regeneration, as defined by the Prayer Book (baptism by water and "thy Holy Spirit" so that "these children be regenerate and grafted into the body of Christ's congregation" [BCP, p. 275]), is no longer a possibility. Yet the faith of Anglicans was that "our Lord Jesus Christ hath promised in his gospel to grant all these things that ye have prayed for; which promise he for his part will most surely keep and perform" (BCP, p. 273). What is at issue here is how the world looks when the action with water and language which gives meaning to that prayer and words like "regeneration" is absent, so that words like "regeneration" are cut loose from their liturgical context and others stand ready to give them new definitions. The issue here for Vaughan is how under such circumstances Anglicans can continue to have faith in their claims about asking for divine "performance."

This poem, which is a redoing of Herbert's "The Collar" as well as his "The Pilgrimage,"[23] raises problems for us in terms of interpreting the situation which Vaughan is eager to create but less ready to resolve. At the beginning of "The Collar," Herbert's speaker proclaims that he struck the board and cried, "I will abroad"; later, he debates whether his "lines and life are free," or whether he has "rope of sands . . . / Good cable" (ll. 4, 22–24) to hold him back. Vaughan's speaker "stole abroad" even though he is "still in bonds" (ll. 1–2), thus suggesting that in this situation the speaker has a freedom from constraint Herbert's speaker lacked and thus can complete, for better or worse, the action Herbert's speaker contemplated but never acted out. Nevertheless, both poems end in an exchange of dialogue between the speaker and one he defines as "Lord." Vaughan may also be alluding to the journey taken by Herbert's speaker in "Affliction (I)," but that journey is from a place which the speaker understands to one where "I could not go away, nor persevere," while Vaughan's speaker, although he is always going away from one place to another, is never able to achieve the interpretive clarity Herbert's speaker has, at least at the beginning of his journey. Herbert's "The Pilgrimage" and Vaughan's "Regeneration" share other similarities. Both speakers describe a journey through a landscape that carries in its geographic details obvious allusions to issues and settings from other sources; in Herbert's poem, however, the speaker's destination is defined early in the poem as "the hill, where lay / My expectation" (ll. 1–2), while in Vaughan's poem this destination is never so clearly defined as part of the speaker's understood goal for his journey, so that the settings he finds himself in are more unexpected discoveries, mere features of a landscape, than goals for a journey.

In the poems from *The Temple* Vaughan alludes to in "Regeneration" there is a clarity about the nature of issues like direction and the terms of debate which underlie Herbert's work, even though problems arise for Herbert's speaker in the pursuit of those issues. The events that separate Vaughan from Herbert are inscribed in "Regeneration" in terms of a difficulty in interpreting that distances speaker from setting and action. If Vaughan indeed read Herbert's "board" in "The Collar" as the Anglican altar, then his separation from it and from the traditions of language it represents in "Regeneration" provides a kind of freedom to go "abroad" in spite of "bonds," yet that freedom does not lead to the kind of journey through a landscape Herbert presents in "The Pilgrimage." *That* landscape can be brought into the language of traditional allegorization, marked as it is by things like "The gloomy cave of Desperation" (l. 4), "The rock of Pride" (l. 6), "Fancies medow" (l. 7), "Cares cops" (l. 11), and "the wilde of Passion" (l. 14). Herbert's poem can lead through such a landscape to a place where the goal of journeys like this one can be seen to be deferred to where *"none goes that way / And lives"* and the speaker can affirm death itself as "but a chair" (ll. 33–34, 36).

In the case of "Regeneration," however, the freedom to steal abroad never leads to a landscape in which there is the appearance of clarity in direction and setting, but always to landscapes in which problems arise in terms of understanding where this speaker is and where he is going, problems so severe that they throw into doubt the whole notion of the religious life as a narrative of a journey with a goal. Herbert's speaker in "The Pilgrimage" is able to discern at least that "I was deceiv'd" (l. 30); Vaughan's, however, "wonder'd much, but tyr'd / At last with thought" (ll. 61–62), overcome by wonders he has encountered yet also wondering what they mean, moves without achieving the kind of clarity, even in negative terms, that is open to the speaker of Herbert's poem. This kind of difficulty in making distinctions is characteristic of the poem from the beginning. He starts, "A Ward, and still in bonds, one day / I stole abroad" (ll. 1–2); his journey is in some unspecified sense forbidden, a "stolen" voyage, "stolen" presumably from whatever creates his bondage, although the details about who or what does the binding remain unspecified. We do, however, gain a moment of clarity in the next line: "It was high spring." At least we know what time of the year it is in which he takes his "stolen" trip "abroad." Yet immediately there are problems, for he notes "and all the way / *Primros'd,* and hung with shade" (ll. 3–4). We have difficulties negotiating this line because of the syntactical ambivalence over whether *"Primros'd"* is a verb or an adjective. The next phrase seems to resolve the issue in terms of an adjectival usage, for we read "and hung with shade." Yet this line, which conjures up images of trees dark with foliage, casting their dark shadows on spring paths rich in primroses, before the end of the stanza becomes more sinister, for "sinne / Like Clouds ecclips'd my mind" (ll. 7–8). Between these two images of shade, we encounter a change of scene: "Yet, was it frost within, / And surly winds / Blasted my infant buds."

The conventional reading of these lines is in terms of a move from without to within the speaker, a juxtaposition between the delights of natural, earthly springtime and the inner turmoil of sinful humanity perhaps defining the "bondage" of line 1. That structuring of the experience described here is supported by the traditional Pauline image of being bound to sin set in juxtaposition to the freedom of new life the baptized have in Christ (Romans 8:15). Unfortunately for any faith we might put in such a reading, an equally traditional image of the baptismal life is to be a "ward," having received the "Spirit of adoption," and thus "bound on earth" (Matthew 18:18) to become "children of God" (Romans 8:16), whose "service is perfect freedom" (BCP, p.

59), a situation from which this speaker steals away. In any case, the poem does not demand either reading; it merely juxtaposes the "high-spring . . . abroad" and the "frost within," leaving the reader to wonder at the (lack of) connection and thus at the problems this situation creates for the ability to articulate such perceptions in conventional nature metaphors.

Vaughan may also be evoking here echoes of Donne's "The Primrose," a poem associated in the editions of Donne available to Vaughan with a hill near the Herbert family estate in Montgomeryshire. In Donne's poem, the hill and flowers are images of nurturing abundance, like God's gift of manna to the Israelites during their desert wanderings; Donne makes little of the primroses and manna in the poem, except that they encourage his speaker to think in terms of ideals of womanhood which no real woman can achieve, so he decides to take women as they are. For Vaughan, the significance of the Herbert estate is precisely now in what it cannot guarantee (that is, understanding and significance without struggle), but Vaughan decides to make what he can of the reality of his situation rather than abandon it, and to await divine manna, or renewal of divine generosity in the midst of a new situation experienced by Anglicans as a kind of wilderness wandering.

We do know, for example, that "sinne / Like Clouds ecclips'd my mind," which ought to make us suspicious of the quality of the perception stated in the beginning of the second stanza: "Storm'd thus; I straight perceiv'd my spring / Meere stage, and show." Yet it is that very perception that turns the outward journey into "My walke a monstrous, mountain'd thing / Roughcast with Rocks, and snow" (ll. 9–12). While in Herbert's "Collar" the speaker can say "I rav'd and grew more fierce and wilde / At every word," Vaughan's speaker can only say "Storm'd thus," raising and not resolving questions of agency and causality and thus also raising questions about the function of his perceptions and what they tell him, since it is unclear whether he is the subject or the object for "Storm'd." Vaughan's speaker thus enacts a situation in which the ability of words to articulate relationships is disrupted, so that doers and receivers of action are hard to distinguish, even as outer and inner scenes of experience are hard to separate. Vaughan can create expectations of clarity in perception—"I straight perceiv'd my spring"—and take them back in the next line—"Meere stage, and show." He poses situations that demand the sorting-out of relationships between subjects and objects, but then withholds the relation-creating words that permit that clarification. However we might regard the significance of Herbert's allegorical landscape in "The Pilgrimage," he at least has access to that sort of language in a way that enables the journey in that poem to be seen as a pilgrimage; Vaughan, however, lacks that verbal resource. One consequence is to make the speaker's account of his experience hard to define, even as he has trouble defining where he is or what he is doing. His movement is patterned after Herbert's speaker's ("as a Pil-grims Eye . . . / So sigh'd I upward"), echoing Herbert's lines:

> I fell, and cry'd Alas my King!
> Can both the way and end be tears?
> Yet taking heart I rose, and then perceiv'd
> I was decev'd.
>
> (Ll. 27–30)

But the clarity afforded Herbert's reader at this point is denied Vaughan's; from what he "takes heart" is not specified, leaving us only to conjecture. The process of perception is taken from Herbert's poem, not the result. One way of describing what Vaughan is presenting here is a sense of experiencing "the way and end" of journeying as "tears," including the "tears" of Herbert's "Altar" without their "cementing" function, since they here can only "rain for grief" (l. 16) but do not lead to a point of understanding the role of "decep-tion" that produces tears in the perception of things.

A further sign of this difficulty in perception comes in the speaker's sight of the "paire of scales" at the "pinacle" of his "monstrous, mountain'd" walk. He "took [the scales] up and layd / In th'one late paines / The other smoake, and pleasures weigh'd" (ll. 19–24). If the speaker had then said "And," he would have made clear which "prov'd the heavier graines," but he says instead "*But* prov'd the heavier graines," making it impossible to tell which is which. Nor does he say what difference it makes; conventionally, "smoake, and plea-sures" have been used to suggest the lightness of worldly pursuits in such comparisons and thus are usually less valuable than "late paines," but here they may (or may not) "prove the heavier graines."

In the next stanza this pattern recurs: the speaker hears "some cryed, *Away*," and the speaker leaves, but whether "I [was] led / Full East" or whether "I . . . led" is again unclear. In any case, the next scene raises the possibility of typological interpretation of the setting: "a faire, fresh field could spy / Some call'd it, *Jacobs Bed;* / A virgin-soile, which no / Rude feet ere trod, / Where (since he stept there,) only go / Prophets, and friends of God" (ll. 25–30). Let us for the moment ignore the question of who is doing the spying of the "faire, fresh field," whether "I," "some," the unknown leader, or even the "field" itself. This is an allusion to Genesis 28 where Jacob wrestles with God for a blessing and declares the place to be holy ground because of the encoun-ter with God in a specific moment of historical time. The problem, of course, is that it may or may not be "*Jacobs Bed*," since "*Some* call'd it," and of course some do not; nor does the speaker help us by giving us his perception.

There are good reasons for expecting a biblical allusion like this one to prove helpful. Genesis 28 was read annually at Evening Prayer on January 15, on the Daily Office calendar in use when the Prayer Book was outlawed, during the season of Epiphany, with its emphasis on the revealing of Christ to the Gentiles. In the late 1640s, January 15 fell between the first and second Sundays after Epiphany, with their concern that the people of God "perceive and know what things they ought to do" and have "peace all the days of [their] life." On that day, Genesis 28 is joined by Romans 13, with its emphasis on subjection to higher powers as agents of God and its belief that "our salvation is nearer than when we believed" (v. 11). Morning Prayer for that day calls for the reading of Matthew 13, with its several fields providing landscapes for Jesus' parables of the sower, the wheat and the tares, and the treasure hidden in the field. Such texts promise to orient the poem because they suggest a concern for Christ as the treasure which makes the field worthy and thus the appropriateness of desiring Christ as the way to salvation.

In Vaughan's handlings of these texts, although they provide elements of the landscape (changing the place of Jacob's encounter to the field of Jesus' parables, for example), they are not able to shed interpretive light on the experiences of Vaughan's speaker in this problematic landscape. "Regeneration" thus enacts the consequences for religious language when the context that gives it the possibility for rendering present experience meaningful is taken away. Under those circumstances, basic orienting metaphors like the journey or pilgrimage or details of the natural setting cease to function in an informing way but instead produce confusion, misdirection, hints of possible meaning that always prove distractions rather than clarifications. "Regeneration" thus ceases to have much to do with the consequences of baptism by water and the Spirit and takes on more of a concern with "re-generation," "having to do with generation," either the creation of multiple possibilities or the passing of time from one generation to the next. In that light, the youthful "Ward" ventures into an adult world and finds the territory of his elders a space of contradictory and fragmentary voices; even so strong a reference as this one to *"Jacobs Bed"* only divides the (potentially) orienting voices into "some" who call it Jacobs Bed and those who do not.

What happens here is symptomatic of the poem as a whole. The loss of Herbert's "board," the altar displaced from its position both in the Anglican church and in *The Temple* and with it the ongoing process of discourse around that altar, deprives Vaughan's speaker of a context in which typological language like *"Jacobs Bed"* can be meaningful in a way that would inform the speaker's use of langage to define what is at stake in his poem. Vaughan evokes the potency of such language; if the speaker could say that this *is* "Jacobs Bed," then those who "go" there could be identified as "Prophets, and friends of God," but such language retains its potency only in a controversial sense, because Anglicans and Puritans could not agree on how and when to use such language meaningfully. Even as "Regeneration" evokes rumors of the possibility of making distinctions about actor and agency, inner and outer, so too it reminds us of the residual power of biblical language but dramatizes the consequences of the controversy about when that language has such power in a situation in which the normal context for interpreting the Bible (Prayer Book worship) is no longer available.

In any case, Vaughan has transformed Herbert's "Cares cops," which his speaker "got through / With much ado," into "A grove . . . / Of stately height" where "all was chang'd, and a new spring / Did all my senses greet" (ll. 34–40). One way of reading these lines is to describe what has happened as an inner experience of regeneration, a transformation of the before-evoked wintry images "within," yet the speaker defines this as an outer, sensory experience ("a new spring / Did all my senses greet"), and Vaughan withholds any understanding of how the speaker got there. The change is a feature of the outer landscape, although it is unclear whether the speaker or the grove is "scarse well set" or who is doing the "descrying" that reveals it. Nevertheless, it is a place where "The unthrift Sunne shot vitall gold / A thousand peeces, / And heaven its azure did unfold / Checqur'd with snowie fleeces" (ll. 41–44). The splendor of such a place remains undeniable, although its relationship to the spring of the poem's first stanza is never specified.

Perhaps more significant is the claim that the scene "fed my Eyes / But all the Eare lay hush. / Only a little Fountain lent / Some use for Eares, / And on the dumbe shades spent / The Musick of her teares" (ll. 47–52). Herbert's discovery on "the gladsome hill, / Where lay my hope" of a "lake of brackish waters on the ground" which produces in him "many a sting / Of swarming fears" has become a fountain flowing with water, a "Cisterne full / Of divers stones," presumably suggesting that the water is clear and flowing, not still and salty like Herbert's. At least Vaughan urges us to "pray marke" how the "bright, and round stones . . . / Danc'd through the floud" while "others ill-shap'd, and dull . . . / more heavy then the night / Nail'd to the Center stood" (ll. 57–60). This is a place where it is still possible to discern centers, but not one where it is clear whether the speaker "drew her neere," or "drew neere her"; certain spatial relationships in the scene can be defined, but the speaker's relationship to them is again problematic. This scene produces in the speaker a response in terms of "wonder much," but it does not yield to this attempt at interpretation; instead, "tyr'd / At last with thought, / My restless Eye that still desir'd / As strange an object brought," again raising the question of whether the "restless Eye" "brought" or "was brought" the "banke of flowers" that next he "descried."

Although the scene of the cistern causes the speaker to "wonder much," we are not told the kinds of questions, the ways of defining that scene, that cause him to wonder. Yet we are given enough to cause us to wonder with him. This could be the cistern of Jeremiah 2:13, which has been "hewed out" by

Israel after forsaking "the fountain of living waters," a "broken cistern, that can hold no water," which is part of the problem God has with Israel. Or it could also be that of Isaiah, promised of the king of Assyria, that if "ye . . . come out with me, drink ye every one the waters of his own cistern" (Isaiah 36:16). Or, in New Testament terms, the rocky contents of the cistern suggest Christ nailed to the cross, the "stone which the builders rejected, the same is become the head of the corner" (Psalm 118:22). In this light, the "bright" stones can be seen as the components of the wall of the New Jerusalem, whose light "was like unto a stone most precious, even like a jasper stone, clear as crystal" (Revelation 21:11), so that the water of the fountain becomes "living fountains of waters," related to Jacob's Well, and Jesus' proclamation about the "well of water springing up into everlasting life" (John 4:14), and thus to images of Anglican baptism, which, as we have seen, traditionally underlie the whole discussion of "regeneration" itself. In the baptismal rite the priest proclaims that "None can enter into the kingdom of God, except he be regenerate and born anew of water and the Holy Ghost" (BCP, p. 270). Vaughan's speaker insists we "pray mark" the stones in the water, echoing the voice of the "other" in Herbert's "Love Unknown," who says, "*Mark the end. / The Font did onely, what was old, renew*" (ll. 63–64), again suggesting the baptismal images we are to recognize here.

Such possibilities might well come into the mind of Vaughan's reader, any of which would suggest ways in which the speaker's experience could be understood, but the speaker does not stop to decide which is applicable, or to help us reach such a decision. Since this takes place where meaningful distinctions cannot be made because the context in which they would appear meaningful and not tiring and strange is absent, only the sound of water, in all its possibilities, offers itself to the ear, not the language of Prayer Book usage which might have provided an arena for interpretation, because it would connect so problematic a sight/site to the speaker's interpretive understanding. The occasions for this which offered themselves to Herbert on a daily basis are absent; there is no situation in which God can "anneal in glass thy storie." Instead, the speaker's restless eye turns to another enigmatic scene, the "banke of flowers," where he sees "Some fast asleep, others broad-eyed" and hears "A rushing wind," which again presents an interpretive problem which yields to no answer: "whence it stirr'd / No where I could not find" (ll. 65–72). This wind is clearly linked to the "rushing mighty wind" of Pentecost in Acts 2:2, the manifestation of God in the Spirit, but without Anglican services of baptism, confirmation, ordination, and Eucharist to proclaim the particular acts of God in the Spirit, the speaker can only look for outward signs, "dispatch an eye, / To see if any leafe had made / Least motion," seeking "My mind to ease" (ll. 74–78). Then, finally, he does get a kind of an answer, the answer of Christ in John's Gospel: "The wind bloweth where it listeth, and thou hearest the sound thereof, but canst not tell whence it cometh, and whither it goeth: so is every one that is born of the Spirit" (John 3:8).

In this light, Vaughan's speaker is one who seeks knowledge of his moment in time, in a situation in which such knowledge is not available and the poem about the search can end only in indeterminacy, its involvement with the speaker still unclear in spite of Vaughan's ability to bring in direct biblical reference—"But while I listning sought / My mind to ease / By knowing, where 'twas, or where not, / It whisper'd; *Where I please.*" Thus, in spite of the Puritan claim that the Bible provided all answers to human questions without benefit of an interpretive tradition, such is not the experience of Vaughan's speaker. One way of describing what he encounters in this journey is to say that traditional language for situating and interpreting significant religious experiences fails in this poem. Without the ongoing worship of Anglicanism to inform and direct uses of such language, discourse can at best raise possibilities of significance but offer only "dumbe shades" on which to spend language, only a "restless Eye" to attract with "strange objects," only a speaker who "wonder'd" and "tyr'd." Vaughan's speaker is "Amaz'd" by his experience; it provides a maze for us as well. Even the One who provides significance to human experience through his actions, according to the traditional approach to understanding the divine initiative in human history, enters the poem through a text of whimsical arbitrariness, *"Where I please"*—not comfortable words. Some scholars claim Vaughan's acceptance here of a Calvinist celebration of the inscrutability of the divine will; it seems far more likely that to the extent to which this does echo emphases in Calvin's thought it underlines the cold, remote, unsatisfactory character of such a role for God, at least as far as the speaker is concerned. The divine address to the speaker here certainly does not achieve what the speaker seeks—"I . . . sought / My mind to ease"—but leaves him still beseeching at the very end of the poem. This poem thus does not end anything, as it would if it argued for a positive reading of one interpretation of God. Instead, it posits the mystery of God as an issue to be struggled with, and the speaker, again in the pose of the lament psalmist, is left, appropriately, wrestling with God for a blessing, demanding that God be held accountable for his behavior. What *is* asserted is the difficulty of the situation in which the speaker finds himself, yet the struggle to find understanding is the way through that situation. Vaughan does affirm that the God of Anglicans is clearly not who they had assumed him to be, at least on the basis of the events of the 1640s; there must be a taking-into-account of a degree of divine independence, even of his old promises and actions. The motif of the Christian journey here leads through landscapes characterized by the confusion of language rather than by its reorientation in terms of future fulfillment of meaning. Vaughan thus creates a powerful experience of the distance between his situation and the conduct of Anglican worship whose memories he can evoke but whose resources for interpreting language he cannot readily use.

What Vaughan thus achieves is a text which enacts a fundamental disorientation. What has become problematic is not Anglicanism as answer or conclusion, since that is not what the Church of England sought to provide. What is at issue is a process of language which had traditionally served to incite and orient change and process. Now such resources are no longer available; as a result, Vaughan's speaker, seeking in motifs of journey or biblical reference or liturgical practice that orientation, finds instead a lack of direction which raises fundamental questions about the enterprise he is engaged in.

Yet, by the end of the poem the speaker has also achieved a kind of clarity of expression and position in the midst of such a maze of words and suggestions of (un)meaning. That clarity of stance comes in the ability to call upon God for a renewal of divine action: "Lord, then said I, *On me one breath,* / *And let me dye before my death!*" (ll. 81–82). These lines come as an expansion of Herbert's speaker's reply to God's "*Child*" at the end of "The Collar" and reflect the speaker's sense of the need for clearer perception of God's behavior. The difference between the divine reply here and in Herbert's "The Collar" finds God much less active to overcome the distance between the speaker and himself; Herbert's "*Child*" becomes "*Where I please,*" suggesting the presence of the divine activity even in a world like the one the speaker has described, yet also suggesting the distance between the speaker's perceptions of where he is and where he encounters God as acting. Yet, even in terms of the allusion to John's Gospel—"so is every one that is born of the Spirit"—the speaker's depiction of his journey is still unclear about where he stands in relationship to the divine action.

Ironically, it may be precisely the speaker's inability to bring his world and his experience of it into the poem with any clear sense of relationships like coming and going that forms the strongest argument for even such a world as the arena for divine activity still. "Regeneration" raises the possibility of regeneration even in a world so opaque to knowing as the one the speaker offers us in this poem, since the poem can end with a biblical allusion. The poem's final line lends itself to exegesis in the terms with which we have become familiar, a prayer for inclusion that becomes effective in the offering of it: "Lord, then said I, *On me one breath,* / *And let me dye before my death!*" But if regeneration *is* still possible, then it is, as always, radically dependent on the speaker being found by God, not by his finding God. This is a world that remembers the possibility of religious language and imagery, in which images can suggest baptism or crucifixion, can evoke the language given power through liturgical enactment, but it is also a world in which the speaker can at best be said to have "wonder'd much, but [without coming to any conclusion] tyr'd / At last with thought." It is a world in which one must be aware of the absence of that community created by liturgical enactment which gives to religious language its meaning, but it is also a world which we can see, through this poem, as one in which God can still act "Where I please," and that is something to hold onto in such a world. A God who at least acts "Where I please" and can be appealed to bestow "on me one breath" is still better than no God at all.

Given the historical context of this poem, we can see the brokenness of its syntactical relationships and the interpretive difficulties it poses as descriptive and thus clarifying of the brokenness of the community which regularly provided the context and the language for articulating typologically such brokenness. Vaughan thus makes clear what confronted Anglicans in the loss of their church as a living institution. His closing lines echo Paul in Romans 6:1–11, which reads in part, "we are buried with him by baptism into death . . . even so we also should walk in newness of life," which is the source for much of the language used to articulate the Anglican rite of baptism. But Vaughan turns Paul's promise into a petition, an intercessory prayer that in the absence of Anglican worship Christ will still "keep and perform" what he "promised in his gospel." Not merely lamenting what is now lost, Vaughan finds through this poem a way of articulating an experience of his historical situation as well as a way of making that articulation, even in its perplexity, lead to such a prayer.

The concluding lines of "Regeneration" thus enact a leap into the religious language of petition, a persistence in asking that Vaughan would have learned from the use of the lament Psalms in Anglican worship. In the midst of a world in which the absence of direction for concepts like journeys and for the typological interpretation of situations renders the ability to locate oneself problematic at best, Vaughan posits the beginning of asking as the way of dealing with such a new situation. He reaffirms this by ending the poem with a biblical quotation from the Song of Solomon, which is itself a petition, yet one that is markedly more confident in its tone of address than is Vaughan's speaker's. The doubling of biblical allusion here, coupled with the emergence of the poem from the ambiguities of biblical and liturgical language used earlier into the clarity of biblical quotation at the end, suggests that for Vaughan the effectiveness of biblical language has come to reside in its ability to enable such asking, rather than in its ability to provide interpretations. What results from Vaughan's distinctive use of language in "Regeneration" is a keeping open of the world that language creates and thus the world of experience that we structure and know through language use to the "wind" of the spirit of God blowing through it. Remember that in stanza 1 "surly winds / Blasted my infant buds"; the development of the poem permits the conclusion that even in a wind that turns spring to winter there is the Spirit of God at work, since the speaker at the end is able to pray through the words of the beloved in the Song, "Arise O North, and come thou South-wind." The north wind, traditionally, is the wind of winter, the "surly wind" of stanza 1; traditional glosses on the passage Vaughan quotes from the Song of Solomon identify the north wind with what Saint Augustine called "certain medicinal adversities" with which God "exercises" the church in this world "that when it is delivered from the world He may join Himself in eternity with His bride," the church, "not having spot or wrinkle, or any such thing."[24] In this light, the concluding quotation manifests a discovery that present adversity can be accepted because it still yields to the possibility of being understood typologically, even though the specifics of such a reading remain unclear. The good news, of course, is that the role of the lamenting searcher after meaning is instrumental in getting to that yielding into understanding.

In terms of Herbert's poem, we noted earlier that "The Collar" poses choices for us as readers; our process toward cognition urges us to make choices that parallel the choices made by the speaker, to accept the relationship defined at the end of the poem in terms of the eucharistic board, the Holy Communion of the Anglican church. In "Regeneration" Vaughan challenges further the whole process of cognition; the speaker, like us, winds up exhausted in his search for meaning in the events he experiences, yet we can see that the process of interpretation may blind us to knowledge of what is really going on in the world to which the poem is addressed. Experiencing the frustration of interpretation, the frustration of human understanding, is thus a necessary part of being open to recognizing the course of the wind that blows. Lacking the language resources open to Herbert, Vaughan can create in "Regeneration" a poetic experience that articulates and replicates the frustration of living in a world without such resources. Yet such frustration finally becomes the way toward a renewal of the use of biblical language, not to achieve regeneration but to ask for it.

Rather than choose another version of Christian vocabulary or religious experience to overcome frustration, Vaughan remains true to an Anglicanism without its worship as a functional referent. If God moves *"Where I please,"* then Vaughan raises the possibility that the current Anglican situation is also at the divine pleasure, so that remaining loyal to Anglican Christianity in such a situation is to seek from God an action that would make the old Anglican language of baptism again meaningful, albeit in a new way and in a new setting. The confidence with which Vaughan's speaker moves to the quotation from the Song of Solomon thus becomes part of his persuasive strategy to encourage other Anglicans to persevere in making this petition to God their own. One way it does this, of course, is by raising the possibility that the use of such language may lead to retrieving the usefulness of gardens as metaphors (as in the Song and in Herbert), purged of the problematic quality they have in Vaughan's poem.

Vaughan's "Religion" is another poem which poses the problem of typological uses of language in the new historical situation characterized by the absence of that institution which gave both the occasion and the meaning to applied typology. Separated from "Regeneration" by poems which again use the confident tone of selected biblical quotations to support their problematic exploration of "Death," "Resurrection and Immortality," and "Day of Judgement," "Religion" stresses the source of the problem in the discontinuity between past events which reveal divine entry into human history and present events which have traditionally been revealed as part of the divine action through their relationship to such past events. The significance of this problem is underscored by the eschatological emphasis of the intervening poems. "Death" and "Resurrection and Immortality" present themselves as body-soul dialogues in which a divided speaker finds comfort in the face of human limitation in the Christian promise of future union in resurrection. "Day of Judgement" finds its speaker making the kind of discovery made by Donne's speaker in Holy Sonnet 4 that at the Last Day " 'Tis late to aske aboundance of thy grace":

> O then it wil be all too late
> > To say, *What shall I doe?*
> *Repentance* there is out of date
> > And so is *mercy* too;
> Prepare, prepare me then, O God!
> > (Ll. 25–29)

Indeed, as we will see, one way to characterize *Silex I* as a whole is to see it as an articulation of Vaughan's historical situation in terms of a desire to understand that situation as a preparation for the fulfillment of God's promises. But if that be the case, the problem of "Religion"—the absence of an ongoing liturgical context for making the Bible a living and transforming speech to the present—becomes even more pressing. Without what the speaker of "Religion" calls "Conf'rence" between God and humanity now, the preparation that will make the divine promises of resurrection and everlasting life valid for the speaker can hardly take place.

Thus, a pivotal point in the poem is the contrast between the frequency of divine action in the biblical past and the sense that "We have no Conf'rence in these daies." Such a juxtaposition between a sense of divine discourse in the past and absence in the present raises a fundamental question about whether or not typological language is still valid, whether or not it still has the power to proclaim the ongoingness of divine action even in the present.[25] In the opening stanza, Vaughan's speaker defines himself as walking in the biblical world, the landscape created by the Word, through the action of the Spirit:

> My God, when I walke in those groves,
> And leaves thy spirit doth still fan,
> I see in each shade that there growes
> An Angell talking with a man.
>
> (Ll. 1-4)

There, "thy spirit doth still fan"; those groves, in opposition to the groves and shades of the contemporary world, as articulated in "Regeneration," feel the wind of the Spirit, which is apparently now lacking.[26] There, as opposed to the world of present-day experience, angels talk with men; the presence of the Spirit is an ordinary experience. In that distant biblical, Spirit-blown world, the specific saving events of the past exist in a simultaneous present, equally accessible yet equally remote. Vaughan's stress is on *then*, on the sense that the age of the Spirit, the narrative of God's saving actions making him present to his people, is over. Both the simultaneity of such events observed by the "walker" in the Bible and their remoteness from the present-day world from which he speaks are factors of a sense of their being "past" in the sense of being over, of being no longer a part of the present from which the speaker observes them, so that they become "leaves" only, bearing no fruit. Jacob (l.9) and Elijah (l. 10) can precede Abraham (l. 12) in this account because these events, at least in this portion of the poem, have no relationship with the present of the speaker's experience; God "Speak'st *there* so much, that I admire / We have no Conf'rence in *these* daies" (emphasis mine). In the light of present experience for the speaker, these are events with no afterlife, part of an irretrievable past, irrelevant to the present except to define the present as a falling-away from the past. Vaughan is here articulating the experience of the Bible as object, as a book to be walked through rather than as a text for use in Anglican worship in which, in Herbert's terms, "This verse marks that, and both do make a motion / Unto a third, that ten leaves off doth lie . . . / These three make up some Christians destinie" ("The H. Scriptures II," ll. 5-8). What Vaughan explores here is the way in which a change in the use and thus experience of the biblical text changes what kind of thing it is understood to be and thus creates problems for those who have looked to the Bible as received through Anglican worship to be about issues like "some Christians destinie" in the present rather than about events long past.

The next two stanzas pose two solutions to this issue, which is as much a problem of language as it is a problem of theology. Stanza 6 poses two solutions: (1) "Is the truce broke?" or (2) " 'cause we have / A mediatour now with thee, / Doest thou therefore old Treaties wave / And by appeales from him decree?" Both these "solutions" raise further issues. If the "truce" is broken, then all that remains is separation between God and his creatures. If the "problem" is our having a "mediatour," then that raises numerous questions. The phrase "we have / A mediatour now with thee" is a combination of two phrases from the Prayer Book communion service. In what are called the "Comfortable Words," the priest in the service quotes 1 John 2:1–2: "If any man sin, we have an advocate with the Father, Jesus Christ the righteous, and he is the propitiation for our sins." At the end of the prayer "for the whole state of Christ's Church militant here in earth," the priest prays, "Grant this, O Father, for Jesus Christ's sake, our only mediator and advocate." To affirm this solution would be to argue that the experienced *absence* of God is the result of his action in Christ rather than his ongoing redemptive involvement in the world; such an interpretation turns Christian proclamation on its head. Yet it does allow Vaughan to test one way of using Prayer Book language to go on articulating contemporary experience no matter how difficult the situation.

In stanza 7, the speaker poses yet another solution, that "as some green heads say / . . . now all miracles must cease," but he also states the problem with this solution—"thou hast promis'd they should stay / The tokens of the Church, and peace." This really leads us back to the first explanation—if "miracles must cease," which are a "token of peace," then indeed the "truce" is "broke," since the church has ceased to be available as a bearer of God's promise. The image of "green heads" evokes the possibility that Vaughan is undercutting the claims of the religious leadership in England after the victory of the forces of Parliament and the abolition of episcopacy. Laud lost his head; the "green heads" in his place claimed the status of "church" for the new forms of worship and organization instituted to take the place of his church. If their argument for the legitimacy of their new institutions can be undercut, then their claims to authority can also be denied.

There are two ways of coming to grips with Vaughan's "solutions" to the problem that events no longer seem to have an afterlife, so that the Spirit is visible there in the Bible's leaves and not here, so that we may "flourish not with leafe only, but with . . . fruit also." One is to note that the definition of such "solutions" is rooted in the human faculty of knowing, the very process of trying to deal with experience in verbal terms, so that solutions that seem to refute the authority of God's actions because they deprive his saving actions of an afterlife are themselves problematic because of the limitations of their source. The other is to note that all these solutions seem to blame God for the problem; God, acting "Where I please," is the one who may have broken the treaty, used the Christ-event as a substitute for his presence, or ceased the activity of miracles, even though he promised to keep them up. But these two are really one, because it is the nature of such human activity to project the problem there, rather than accept its true origin here.

In fact, that is what Vaughan takes up in the next few stanzas, where he rejects such explanations—"No, no"—and locates the problem here by creating a vision of religion's corruption through its involvement with "the Earths darke veines":

> Religion is a Spring
> That from some secret, golden Mine
> Derives her birth . . .
>
> . . . .
>
> But in her long, and hidden Course
> Passing through the Earths darke veines,
> Growes still from better unto worse,
> And . . .
>
> . . . learnes to encrease
> False *Ecchoes,* and Confused sounds,
>
> . . . .
>
> So poison'd, breaks forth in some Clime,
> And at first sight doth many please,
> But drunk, is puddle, or meere slime
> And 'stead of Phisick, a disease;
>
> Just such a tainted sink we have
> Like that *Samaritans* dead *Well,*
> Nor must we for the Kernell crave
> Because most voices like the *shell.*
>
> (Ll. 29–48)

One source for Vaughan's imagery here is of course Herbert's "The Church Militant," which shares this vision of the church and corruption moving together, taking the church "from better unto worse." Now in a way Herbert's vision has come true, since to Vaughan the official religion of the Commonwealth, full of "False *Ecchoes,* and Confused sounds," is "a disease." But what Vaughan is about is not Herbert's solution, which would lead to the conclusion that present events mean that the true church has now left England for America. Instead, Vaughan is seeking here for a way of articulating his experience that will provide some hope for Anglicans left behind by the destruction of their church. The reference to not craving the "Kernell" is an allusion to Numbers 6:4, a description of the rules for members of the order of "Nazarites," who "shall eat nothing that is made of the vine tree, from the kernels even to the husk." Vaughan thus locates the problem with religion in "these daies" as originating in the "False *Ecchoes*, and Confused sounds," with the human corruptions of religion, which gives us a vocabulary for understanding how Vaughan felt about Puritanism. Yet to link Puritanism with the "*Samaritans* dead *Well*" and the "shell" of the grape liked by "most voices" is to engage once more in typological language. For the Nazarite relevant here is of course Jesus of Nazareth, who offered the Samaritan woman "water of life" instead of what she can give him out of Jacob's well (remember Jacob mentioned in line 9) in John 4; the water Jesus offers is the water of the New Testament, with all its purifying potential, not the water of the Old Testament, with all its judgmental ramifications. And of course the controlling reference here is to Jesus' self-offering in wine ("This is My Blood") and on the cross (the Eucharist, according to Paul, proclaims the Lord's death until he come [1 Corinthians 11:26]).

Vaughan thus finds it possible to use the language of applied typology, but only in such a way as to bring judgment on the human processes of understanding which would explain the present situation as a problem God has rather than as one we have with God. Instead, Vaughan would offer prayer loaded with references to biblical events and ask of God that those events again have an afterlife in the present of the speaker's experience. Such language, which overcomes the sense of divine absence through its use, must now at best recognize divine judgment on the current state of the church. The speaker can only pray that the continuity between past and present be restored; for that to happen, God must act again:

> Heale then these waters, Lord; or bring thy flock,
> Since these are troubled, to the springing rock,
> Look downe great Master of the feast; O shine,
> And turn once more our *Water* into *Wine!*
>
> (Ll. 49–52)

Typological language now comes into play not only to link the present situation with a past saving act, but to enable the speaker to give voice to the sense of his present as "that *Samaritans* dead *Well*," to describe the desperateness of that situation, and to articulate his prayer that God restore the afterlife of his past events by a new saving act. Thus, the concluding stanza again is made up of a whole array of biblical echoes. The request that God "Heale . . . these waters" aligns the speaker's plea with the events of 2 Kings 2:19–22, where Elisha pours salt into "the spring of the waters. . . . So the waters were healed unto this day." The waters that are "troubled" are the waters of Proverbs 25:26, where "a righteous man falling down before the wicked is as a troubled fountain, and a corrupt spring," or the results of pharoah's acts that "troublest the waters with thy feet and foulest their rivers." The "springing rock" is the rock struck by Moses to provide water for the Israelites, frequently used throughout both Old and New Testaments as a sign of God's saving actions, related in the New Testament to the "water of life" and Christian baptism. Christ is "Master of the feast" when he turned water to wine at a wedding in Cana, but also master/servant, served/server in eucharistic imagery, as displayed in Herbert's "Love (III)."

Vaughan concludes "Religion" with another quotation from the Song of Solomon, from chapter 4:12: *"My sister, my spouse is as a garden Inclosed, as a Spring shut up, and a fountain sealed up."* If the poem has opened possibilities for understanding the situation of the Anglican church in Vaughan's day, this quotation reinforces the interpretation that in spite of appearances to the contrary the church is still present, even if only in potential, as a source of "living water" if the "Master of the feast" will but reopen it. But Vaughan's description of the church's present situation is effective precisely because of his ability to use typological language so richly to voice his prayer for the renewal of divine action. This is itself an argument that such language is still effective and that as a result the prayer may be answered. Although the situation in which "Religion" is now to be found confuses the observer so that its origins can only be said to be "from some secret, golden Mine," it yet becomes possible to see that its present state is that of "poison," "puddle," "meere slime / And 'stead of Physick, a disease," requiring the renewed action of God to heal it; nevertheless the very fact that the old language for describing the church can be used to describe what it yet could become raises the possibility of restoration and thus encourages the reader to avoid despair by living in hope of such restoration.

Vaughan thus constantly seeks to find ways of understanding the present in terms that leave it open to future transformative action by God. His "The Search" explores this dynamic from yet another perspective. In this poem, the speaker engages in "a roving Extasie / To find my Savior," again dramatizing the sense of divine absence in the absence of that earthly enterprise where he was to be found before the events of 1645. In language borrowed again from Herbert's "Church Militant," Vaughan sees the sun, the marker of time, as a "guide" to his way, yet the movement of the poem as a whole throws into question the terms in which the speaker asserts that he would recognize the Christ if he found him.

Much of the poem is taken up with a description of the speaker's search through a biblical landscape defined by New Testament narrative, as his biblical search in "Religion" was through a landscape defined by Old Testament narrative. Yet without the ongoing life of the church to enact those narratives in the present, what the poem reveals is their failure to point to the Christ: "I met the *Wise-men*, askt them where / He might be found, or what starre can / Now point him out, grown up a Man?" (ll. 8–10). Ironically, this role in the Epiphany gospel is Herod's, who, when not told where Jesus was, ordered the murder of male children. The lack of an answer sends this speaker to the right place—"to *Egypt*"—and then back to "the Doctors"; asking to "see the *Temple*," he is shown but "A little dust." Herbert, who could build a *Temple* of words, could also find "My dearest Lord . . . in the next inne" ("Christmas," ll. 4, 6), among "a ragged noise and mirth / Of theeves and murderers" ("Redemption," ll. 13–14), or in "the common manger" ("Faith," l. 22), but such immediacy of discovery is closed to Vaughan, who lacks access to the public offering of Christ in the Eucharist. Further search leads but to "*Idea's* of his Agonie," not the awe-inspiring and voice-cancelling images of Herbert's "The Sacrifice."[27]

The next point in this night journey confronts the speaker with a graphic failure to understand and interpret the old records. Coming to "his grave," the speaker proclaims that "there was not the *Corner-stone*"; this leads him to conclude that "Sure (then said I,) my Quest is vaine" (l. 49). Just so, but not in the speaker's terms; if Christ is to be found in "his grave," then he cannot be the cornerstone of the new temple, and the speaker's quest is indeed "in vain." Yet because he expects to find Christ where the speaker's categories of expectation locate him, the speaker's quest manifests human vainness, human confidence in our powers of interpretation. Thus the speaker rejects the idea that the Christ might be found in the tomb, not because of his Resurrection, but because "So mild a Lamb can never be / 'Midst so much bloud and Crueltie" (ll. 51–52), thus rejecting the orthodox Christian affirmation that without the slaying of the Lamb there can be no human hope of reconciliation with God. In this light, the speaker's failure to perceive Christ amidst the "bloud and Crueltie" of his own day becomes a failure of his own interpretive capabilities.

Thus Vaughan's speaker demonstrates that an Anglican in 1650 who seeks a "gentle Jesus, meek and mild," is not likely to find one. A true savior now must be at home in a rougher and sterner world. The problems experienced here by Vaughan's speaker are dramatically self-created. This is confirmed by the next episode of the poem; refusing to move to the next stage of biblical narrative about Christ (the post-Resurrection experiences of the disciples), he instead backtracks to Jesus' temptation in the wilderness, "his retreat / From the fierce *Jew* and *Herods* heart" (ll. 55–56). What follows is an attempt to understand, typologically, the speaker's present situation in such terms and a proclamation that he will leave that situation, lacking hope of finding Christ in it, and seek him in "the desert," which, in terms of this interpretation, is "sanctified / To be the refuge of his bride" (ll. 63–64). It is for this proposed journey that "The Sun's broke through to guide my way" (l. 66).

Such a typological reading of his present situation appeals; it offers energy to imagine and also to write down "What pleasures should my Journey crown." Yet it is countered by another reading, one that also manifests itself as a counter-poem to the one the speaker is writing which urges, "Leave, leave, thy gadding thoughts" (l. 75), words which put us back into the world of Herbert's "The Collar." The process the speaker has modeled for us, described as the activity of one "Who Pores / and spies / Still out of Doores" (ll. 76–78), reveals only that it cannot "descry" anything within. This outer voice which intrudes into the poem at line 75—"Me thought I heard one singing thus"—argues that "The skinne, and shell of things / Though faire, / are not / Thy wish, nor pray'r / but got / By meer Despair / of wings" (ll. 81–87). This voice, conditional in its reality, even as the voice the speaker of Herbert's "Collar" thought he heard crying "Child," in effect rejects the idea that the absence of "The skinne, and shell," Anglican worship devoid of its enactment, means that Christ is absent. Instead, this voice urges, "To rack old Elements, / or Dust / and say / Sure here he must / needs stay / Is not the way, / nor just" (ll. 88–94). God can in fact make the absence of Anglicanism's ongoing life part of his saving actions; what the speaker is called to do is "Search well another world" (l. 95), to adopt an eschatological perspective on the present, seeing in light of the future promise of Christ's Resurrection and the new world to come rather than feeling the need to look elsewhere than where the speaker actually is in the historical specificity of his situation. To feel the need to escape is to "seek *Manna,* where none is" (l. 96).

However conditioned by the speaker's perception the reality of this intruding voice is, acceptance of it permits the poem to end with a citation from Acts 17:27–28, which offers the paradox that to *"seek the Lord"* is to be part of the Christian community, since *"in him we live and move and have our being."* In terms of Anglican experience, Vaughan urges here that the true way to keep faith with the community that is lost is to continue its search for Christ rather than to insist on the search for the mere forms that defined its worship in their "Dust." The times call for such a quest for a Christ at home amidst "bloud and Crueltie." It is this final position that yields once more to an authentic typological reading rather than the false one the speaker offered earlier.

If Vaughan urges us to keep faith with the Anglican community now lost through "seeking the Lord," we need also to be aware that by means of all the citations to the Song of Solomon Vaughan gives us in *Silex I* he keeps at work throughout an ongoing reference to the traditional image of the church as the bride of Christ. "Isaacs Marriage" brings this to the fore as a way of exploring once more what has been lost. The quotation from Genesis 24:63 which starts this poem evokes a moment now long past in which Isaac prayed and "he lifted up his eyes, and saw, and behold, the Camels were coming," bringing Rebekkah to him. In contrast to the situation in "The Search," the prayer of Isaac as "seeker" is answered immediately. Vaughan's speaker, however, finds himself in a place definable in terms of multiplication of language—"thou wert / An odde dull suitor; Hadst thou but the art / Of these our dayes, thou couldst have coyn'd thee twenty / New sev'ral oathes, and Complements (too) plenty; / O sad, and wilde excesse!" (ll. 13–17). Another contrast is with Herbert's "Jordan (II)," where a friend whispers, "*There is in love a sweetness ready penn'd: / Copy out only that, and save expense.*" But of course in "these our dayes" the bride does not come in spite of "wilde excesse" of language, perhaps contrasting Anglican set prayers with the extemporaneous ones of the Puritan clergy. There is an intermediate time in this poem as well, a less remote past when "All was here smooth as thy bride" (l. 23), which ended in the 1640s. As a poem that evokes a biblical scene and juxtaposes it to the absence of Anglicanism, this poem leads us to "The Brittish Church" with its "ravish'd" bride (l. 16). Vaughan's quest will have no easy ending: to "seek the Lord" requires full awareness of the consequences of a broken continuity with the past both for styles of language and for institutional life.

In Vaughan's depiction of Anglican experience, brokenness is thus a structural experience as well as a verbal theme. While Herbert "breaks" words in the context of a consistent allusion to use of the Prayer Book, Vaughan uses allusions to liturgical forms to reveal a brokenness of the relationships implicit in such allusions. For instance, Vaughan starts, early in *Silex Scintillans,* a series of allusions to the events on the annual Anglican liturgical calendar of feasts; "The Incarnation, and Passion" is followed later with "The Passion," which naturally leads later to "Easter-day," "Ascension-day" and "Ascension-Hymn," "White Sunday," and "Trinity-Sunday." His insertion of "Christs Nativity" between "The Passion" and "Easter-day" interrupts this continuous allusion. He also avoids the chance to do poems on Advent, Christmas, Epiphany, and Lent after "Trinity-Sunday" by skipping to "Palm-Sunday" only six poems later. In addition, the break Vaughan put in the text between the first *Silex* and the second, published in 1655, obscures the fact that the first poem in the second collection—"Ascension"—actually continues in order his allusion to the church calendar.

Because of his historical situation, Vaughan has to resort to substitutions; for example, in "The Morning-watch" "The great *Chime* / And *Symphony* of nature" must take the place of Anglican corporate prayer at the morning Office. In "The Evening-watch," the hymn of Simeon, a corporate response to the reading of the New Testament lesson at Evening Prayer, becomes the voice of the soul to the body to "Goe, sleep in peace," instead of the church's prayer, "Lord, now lettest thou thy servant depart in peace," or the voice of the second Collect, "Give unto thy servants that peace which the world cannot give" (BCP, p. 64). Vaughan thus finds ways of creating texts that accomplish the Prayer Book task of acknowledging morning and evening in a disciplined way but also remind the informed reader of what is lost with the loss of that book.

At the same time, other conjunctions of poems in both *Silex* collections create a specificity of reference to the progress of the Anglican calendar found rarely even in Herbert. The placing of Vaughan's paraphrase of Psalm 121 immediately after his "Easter-day," "Easter Hymn," and "Holy Communion" poems is no accident. Psalm 121 is one of the Psalms appointed to be read on the Anglican calendar on the twenty-seventh of each month; only in 1649, the year before the publication of the first *Silex* collection, did the twenty-seventh of the month fall in the week after Easter during the period between 1645 and 1650. In addition, in the second *Silex* collection, published in 1655, a paraphrase of Psalm 104 follows "Trinity-Sunday"; only in 1652, in the years between the publication of the two collections, did the twentieth of the month, the day appointed for reading Psalm 104 at Evening Prayer, follow Trinity Sunday in any close proximity, then coming exactly one week later on the Sunday called the First Sunday after Trinity.

This suggests one of Vaughan's strategies for communicating with his original audience and, through such strategies, urging them to keep faith with the community now lost in their common search for Christ. Those Anglicans still keeping up the readings of the Offices and the Prayer Book lectionary in private would recognize such allusions and feel a sense of community in that common perception. This use of references to a common experience of the biblical text shared by even widely separated Anglicans loyal to the defining acts of their faith must have come as an act of reassurance which could not be detected by Puritans. In this context, we might also want to note that "Dressing," a Eucharistic poem set just before "Easter-day" in the first *Silex* collection and stressing "Thy mystical *Communion*" (l. 14), echoes the appointed Psalms and lessons for Maundy Thursday, the Thursday of Holy Week, March 22, 1649. Vaughan argues that "Some sit to thee, and eat / Thy body as their Common meat" (ll. 37–38), a clear reference to the Puritan practice of receiving the bread and wine of the Eucharist sitting, rather than kneeling, which was the Anglican practice. On the other hand, Vaughan's poem is an attack on those who regard the Eucharist as "meere memorial," not sacramental, not "thy sacred feast, . . . / the dread mysteries of thy blest bloud" (ll. 34–35). This is given special significance when put into juxtaposition with the Epistle reading for Holy Communion on Maundy Thursday (1 Corinthians 11:17ff.), in which Paul warns that "he that eateth and drinketh unworthily, eateth and drinketh damnation to himself, not discerning the Lord's body," words which are echoed in the Prayer Book's exhortation that "the danger [is] great if we receive the same unworthily" (BCP, p. 258).

Vaughan's allusions to the specific readings for that day go even further. In lines 4 through 8, the speaker's prayer that Christ "with thy secret key / Open my desolate rooms; my gloomie Brest / With thy cleer fire refine, burning to dust / These dark Confusions, that within me nest, / And soyl thy Temple with a sinful rust" expands lines from Psalm 107 (vv. 9–16), the

Psalm appointed for Morning Prayer on that day: "he satisfieth the empty soul: and filleth the hungry soul with goodness. Such as sit in darkness, and in the shadow and out of the shadow of death: and brake their bonds in sunder. . . . he hath broken the gates of brass: and smitten the bars of iron in sunder." The image of "Open my desolate rooms" derives from the New Testament reading for Morning Prayer, John 10:2—"he that entereth in by the door is the shepherd of the sheep." Lines 17 and 18—"Let him so follow here, that in the end / He may take thee"—echo the Collect for that day: "Mercifully grant, that we both follow the example of his patience, and be made partakers of his resurrection." The image of "These dark Confusions" in line 7 derives from Daniel 9:8—"O Lord to us belongeth confusion"—appointed for Morning Prayer on that day. The image of God's "glorious conquest . . . even in babes" combines Jeremiah 31:15–17, the Old Testament lesson appointed for Evening Prayer, with the promises made in Anglican baptism about the destiny of baptized children:

> A voice was heard in Ramah . . . Rahel weeping for her children, refused to be comforted for her children . . . Thus saith the Lord, Refrain thy voice from weeping . . . for . . . there is hope in thine end, saith the Lord, that thy children shall come again to their own border.

The poem also includes allusions to conventional biblical sources of eucharistic imagery—"thou feedest among the Lillies"—from the Song of Solomon 6:3 and allusions to portions of the Prayer Book's communion rite. "The perfect, full oblation for all sin" (line 10) echoes the image of the cross as the "full, perfect, and sufficient sacrifice, oblation, and satisfaction for the sins of the whole world," from the Prayer of Consecration (BCP, p. 263). The images of the angels and saints and the speaker kneeling at the end of the poem echo Psalm 95, part of every Morning Prayer service—"O come let us worship, and fall down: and kneel before the Lord our maker," with its echoes of Isaiah 45:23 and Philippians 2:10 ("At the name of Jesus every knee should bow"), which takes us to the Te Deum and the Sanctus, songs of praise by angels and saints joined by worshippers using the Prayer Book.

What Vaughan has created here is a criticism of the Puritan communion and a praise of the Anglican Eucharist in the midst of a whole series of allusions to the specific lessons to be read on a specific celebration of Maundy Thursday, the "birthday" of the Eucharist. The result is the creation of a community thinking about the Anglican Eucharist whether or not they actually could participate in it. One can live in hope and pray that God give a "mysticall *Communion*" in place of the public one the speaker must be "absent" from; as a result of this poem, one can expect that from God, expect that he will grant "thy grace" so that "faith" can "make good." It is a plea as well that the community so created will be kept in grace and faith so that it will receive worthily when that reception is possible, whether at an actual celebration of the Anglican communion or at the heavenly banquet to which the Anglican Eucharist points and anticipates. As Vaughan has his speaker say in "Church-Service," echoing Herbert's "The Altar," it is "Thy hand alone [that] doth tame / Those blasts [of 'busie thoughts'], and knit my frame" so that "in this thy Quire of Souls I stand." God's actions are required for two or three to gather, so "both stones, and dust, and all of me / Joyntly agree / To cry to thee" to continue the experience of corporate Anglican worship. Those recognizing these allusions in Vaughan's intended audience and valuing Vaughan's attempt to continue within what had been lost without would have felt sustained in their aloneness and in their refusal to compromise and accept the Puritan form of communion, all the while hoping for a restoration or fulfillment of Anglican worship.

At the same time, the poem is a speech by "thy wretched one" which asks that "Thy mysticall *Communion*" be given "That, absent, he may see, / Live, die, and rise with thee" (ll. 13–16). There is in the Prayer Book, in the rite for the Communion of the Sick, a provision that if the person is so ill that he may not attend the Eucharist in church he may receive it at home, "absent" from the congregation. There is also the provision that if the illness is so severe as to prevent actual reception, if "he do truly repent him of his sins, and steadfastly believe that Jesus Christ hath suffered death upon the cross for his redemption . . . he doth eat and drink the Body and Blood of our Savior Christ, profitably to his soul's health, although he do not receive the Sacrament with his mouth" (BCP, p. 308). Such a provision underlies Vaughan's sense of communion here as well as later in "The Holy Communion," enabling him to make the full Anglican affirmation about the Eucharist even in its absence.

Such allusions remind us, in Vaughan's context, of brokenness and absence in relationship to the Prayer Book even as they urge their readers to remain faithful to what is lost. These characteristics of Vaughan's didactic strategies come together in "The Brittish Church," which is a redoing of Herbert's "The British Church" by way of an extended allusion to the lament Psalms, to the Song of Solomon 2:17 and 4:6, as well as to Hugh Latimer's sermon "Agaynst strife and contention" in the first Book of Homilies. In Herbert's poem, the Church of England is "deare Mother," in whose "mean," the middle way between Rome and Geneva, Herbert delights; he blesses God "whose love it was / To double-moat thee with his grace" (ll. 28–29). In Vaughan's poem, the speaker models his speech on Psalm 80, traditionally a prayer for the church in difficult times. Psalm 80 is a lament Psalm from which Vaughan takes lines for the Latin ending of this poem; it is one example of a way of articulating part of the ongoing relationship between God and his people, a form used in Job and the prophets in which the speaker pleads for relief to

God as the only source of relief. While Herbert's model is a psalm of praise and thanksgiving, the fact that Vaughan is still operating with allusions to the biblical literary forms suggests that the dynamics of biblical address are still functional. Like the speaker of Psalm 80, Vaughan's lamenter acts out his lament in the faith that God will respond in the end to the one who persists in his lament.

Vaughan's poem has two stanzas, each beginning with an alternating pattern of short and long lines which yields to short lines after a double repetition of this initial pattern. The second stanza ends with two lines of Latin spaced so as to duplicate the pattern of long and short lines with which each stanza starts. Vaughan here is playing with Herbert's tradition of shaped verse: both stanzas need ultimately to be seen in relationship to the shape of Herbert's "The Altar." Stanza 1 of Vaughan's poem forms at once a broken altar and a cross; the events of Vaughan's day are here articulated in reference both to the destruction of Anglican Eucharistic rites and to the destruction of Christ's body in his Passion. In Vaughan's poem it is the torn church that is the sacrifice rather than the speaker's heart of Herbert's poem. The second stanza offers us a completed altar shape, but the completion of that shape must rely on the quotation from the Song of Solomon at the close. Together the two stanzas juxtapose the cross and the altar in Anglican terms, for it is the altar rite which conveys "all . . . benefits of his passion" to its participants, according to the Book of Common Prayer. But the poem itself is about the loss of Christ and the crucifixion of his earthly body, for "he is fled" (l. 1) and "The Souldiers here / Cast in their lots again" (ll. 6–7); it ends with an appeal for Christ to regard "My ravish'd looks" and "hast thee so." Because the speaker, who is the Anglican church herself, can articulate her situation in terms of Christ's cross and the relationship, now lost, between that event and her altar, the poem can function as the kind of speech modeled on biblical example which, if faithfully pursued, can result in the recreation of the relationship depicted in the juxtaposition of the two stanza forms. Even as Christ's Crucifixion led to a Resurrection, so the events of Anglican history, when brought into speech in terms of that crucifixion, can be seen to have the chance of a hopeful outcome. Thus, the brokenness of Anglican history becomes a (potentially) redemptive emulation of Christ's sacrifice; Vaughan and his fellow Anglicans lament their situation in the faith that their persistence will lead to God's realizing that potential by resurrecting her.

At the beginning of stanza 2, the speaker commands, "O get thee wings," suggesting that Vaughan has in mind the doubled pattern of "Easter-wings" as well as the breaking up of the Anglican altar rites; what he asks for in "The Brittish Church" is in effect a new Easter for that institution. Hugh Latimer's homily, read repeatedly in the sixteenth and seventeenth centuries, laments the divided state of the church—"Oh howe the churche is devided. Oh howe

the cyties be cutte and mangled. Oh how the coote of Christ, that was without seame, is al to rent & torne" (sig. S3). In Vaughan's poem "[Christ] is
fled," leaving behind only his "seamlesse coat," which is "here" divided. The
English Puritans' destruction of the Church of England is a more heinous act
than the behavior of Jesus' own people present at his crucifixion, because the
"Jews touch'd not . . . / That seamlesse coat" which "These dare divide, and
stain." Vaughan's irony is, of course, that the historic division created by
"these" Puritans, when it is articulated in the way Vaughan achieves here,
recreates and perpetuates in poetry what they hoped to destroy and thus
suggests that a restoration in reality can be looked for.

The first stanza of "The Brittish Church" is an extensive compilation of
biblical allusions—the second line, "And while these here their *mists* and
shadows hatch," takes us back to Isaiah's vision of "the day of the Lord's
vengeance" in Isaiah 34:15: "There shall the great owl make her nest, and lay,
and hatch, and gather under her shadow." But, of course, Vaughan's poem
puts this image to an ironic use—to Isaiah, the natural functioning of the owl
and other animals is the start of a process of regeneration after the day of
vengeance, but for Vaughan the mists and shadows of error are hatched by the
Puritans, who exceed even the Jews in destroying the body of Christ. Yet if
Christ will respond to the speaker's lament, then the destruction of the
church's body will become "a death like his" leading to resurrection. In all
this, the "he" of the first line, who is "My glorious head [who] / Doth on
those hills of Mirrhe, and Incense watch," is clarified in an allusion to the
Song of Solomon 4:6: "Until the day break, and the shadows flee away, I will
get me to the mountain of myrrh, and to the hill of frankincense." Christ is
"My glorious head" because he is the head of the church in Paul's body analogy, traditional in Anglicanism's stress on the church effecting in its communion the discovery and creation of "the mystical body of thy Son." He is the
speaker's head because the speaker is part of that body which is the coat that is
now divided and stained. But, biblically, the watchfulness of God is not just a
passive observance but an active taking notice: "And it shall come to pass,
that like as I have watched over them, to pluck up, and to break down, and to
throw down, and to destroy, and to afflict; so will I watch over them, to
build, and to plant, saith the Lord" (Jeremiah 31:28). Part of Christ's and
Paul's injunctions to the faithful involve watchfulness: "Watch therefore: for
ye know not what hour your Lord doth come" (Matthew 24:42); "Watch ye,
stand fast in the faith, quit you like men, be strong" (1 Corinthians 16:13).
Thus Vaughan's speaker's plea, "Haste, hast my dear," becomes an expression
of that watchful expectation for Christ to return to complete the work of
redemption.

Vaughan picks up the allusion to the Song of Solomon in the second
stanza. His "Until these clouds depart, / And the day springs" evokes chapter

2:17, another version of Song of Solomon 4:6 ("Until the day break, and the shadows flee away, turn, my beloved, and be thou like a roe or a young hart upon the mountains of Bethar"). The speaker urges Christ to return with haste because of what has happened—"O get thee wings!"—but at least, if he plans to act out the role in which he is cast in the Song, "Write in thy bookes / My ravish'd looks / Slain flock, and pillag'd fleeces." The image of God or Christ as shepherd is pervasive throughout the Bible, both as an image of Israel forsaken by her God and as Israel cared for by her Shepherd. The image of the "bookes" of God also resounds through the Scriptures— note especially Revelation 20:12: "And I saw the dead, small and great, stand before God; and the books were opened, which is the book of life: and the dead were judged out of those things which were written in the books, according to their works." Here the speaker of "The Brittish Church," the Anglican church herself, cast in the role of the beloved of the Song of Solomon ("ravish'd" as were the people of Israel, according to the prophets' message [see Isaiah 13:16, Lamentations 5:11, and Zechariah 14:2] on the day of God's wrath), seeks her "dear," her "head," as she does in the Song, and urges him to "hast" to her relief.

The Latin conclusion to this poem—"*O Rosa Campi! O lilium Convallium! quonodo nuno / facta es pabulum Aprorum!* (O rose of the fields! O lily of the valleys! How you have been made food for boars!)"—combines another allusion to the Song with references to Psalm 80:13, where Israel like a "vine out of Egypt" has her "double-moat" of Herbert's poem "broken down," so that "the boar out of the wood doth waste it, and the wild beast of the field doth devour it." And the end of this Psalm is paraphrased in Vaughan's poem— "Return, we beseech thee, O God of hosts. . . . Turn us again, O Lord God of hosts, cause thy face to shine; and we shall be saved."

In this poem Vaughan is about another of his strategies—to describe his historical situation in biblical terms which seem to reverse the tone of their biblical analogues. The tone of the Song is overturned, as the hopeful longing and searching of the Song become a cry of desperation in Vaughan's poem. But, at the same time, precisely because Vaughan can use biblical language to describe the very situation that seems to deny biblical claims for God, he can raise the possibility that God is not absent in these events but that they are a preparation for a fuller realization of God's presence to his people and thus constitute a historical acting by God that actually furthers the fulfillment of his promises. The very fact that the Bible supplies the language for this enterprise while the cross and Herbert's "The Altar" supply its shapes argues that the biblical enterprise is not over, because even such devastating events can be articulated using these resources of language for address to God. Vaughan's use of biblical allusion in this poem confutes a pessimistic reading of events in favor of the biblical stance of lament, the age-old act of faith that God will respond in the end to the one who persists in holding him to his promises. For Anglicans, the fact that Vaughan recreates Herbert's "Altar" shape in a poem that laments the loss of that altar and asks for either a new Easter or for the martyrdom of that institution to be regarded as furthering the coming of Christ once more manifests visually the idea that offering the brokenness of the church to God is a way of furthering his actions to restore it.

One of the stylistic characteristics of *Silex I,* therefore, is a functioning close to the biblical texts and their language. Weaving and reweaving biblical echoes, images, social structures, titles, situations, Vaughan seeks to recreate an allusive web similar to that which exists in the enactment of Prayer Book rites when the assigned readings combine and echo and reverberate with the set texts of the liturgies themselves. Without that network available in the experience of his readers (or in private, if at all), Vaughan seeks it as the necessary source of informing and meaning-creative experience for his readers. This technique, however, gives to the tone of Vaughan's poems a particularly archaic or remote quality. It gives them a feeling of employing a private or privately understood or highly coded vocabulary that has led some readers to link Vaughan to the traditions of world-transcending spirituality or of hermeticism. But Vaughan's intention is in no such place; instead it seeks to provide a formerly public experience, now lost.

Poems after "The Brittish Church" in *Silex I* focus on the central motif of that poem, that "he is fled," stressing the sense of divine absence and exploring strategies for evoking a faithful response to the promise of his eventual return. The rhetorical organization of "The Lampe," for example, develops an image of the faithful watcher for that return and concludes with a biblical injunction from Mark 13:35 about the importance of such watchfulness. Vaughan develops his central image from another version of the Markan parable, that found in Matthew 25 concerning the wise and foolish virgins. The "lampe" of the poem is the lamp of the wise virgin who took oil for her lamp to be ready when the bridegroom comes. In a world shrouded in "dead night," where "Horrour doth creepe / And move on with the shades" (ll. 1–2), metaphors for the world bereft of Anglicanism, Vaughan uses language interpreting the speaker's situation in terms not unlike the eschatological language of Revelation 7, where the "stars of heaven fell to earth" because "the great day of his wrath is come." The light of the lamp is like the candle of Matthew 5:14–51, which is not hid but is "the light of the world" because its flame combines the elements required for keeping the faith:

> I can see
> Met in thy flames, all acts of piety;
> Thy light, is *Charity;* Thy heat, is *Zeale;*

And thy aspiring, active fires reveale
Devotion still on wing.

(Ll. 9–13)

Such an interpretation informs the claim that a mere light in the darkness can make "a full day" and inspires the speaker to assert that he will become the light when it fails: "And where thou mad'st an end, there I'le begin."

As a result, the poem can end with the Markan injunction, "Watch you therefore, for you know not when the master of the house commeth," which implies that there is a master who will return, and that remaining watchful through exemplifying charity, zeal, and devotion is part of the process of enabling his return as well as of being part of the wedding feast at his return. Indeed, in the terms of the biblical passages to which this poem alludes, the night itself is also part of that process, so that the speaker's watchfulness and the reader's response in watchfulness are what is required to become part of the larger process. For, as Herbert notes in "Love (III)," the servant who is awake when the master comes is the one whom he will serve. In consequence, the poem functions as an injunction to the reader to take the speaker's action and pledge of faithfulness as a model for his own behavior.

From another angle of approach to Vaughan's problem, "Church-Service" presents a speaker who must rely on the "Interceding, spiritual grones . . . / For dust and stones" of the "holy dove" (ll. 3–10), since the corporate intercessory prayer of the Anglican church is absent, become "dust and stones." But as a result of such intercession and support—"Propt by thy hand" in "thy Quire of Souls"—the speaker can make a community of "stones, and dust, and all of me" that "Joyntly agree" to join their voice with that of the "holy dove. . . . / To cry to thee" (ll. 9–19). Such a plea depends on those who have gone before and given their all in faithfulness—"by the Martyrs bloud / Seal'd"—but the result is that they become "good / Present, O God!" (ll. 18–20). Such a prayerful action in lieu of the absence of Anglican worship can work to make possible a play on that "Present," as the prayers of this community of the self in conjunction with the prayers of the "dove" and the "Martyrs" are offered as a present to God which in some sense makes God present to the speaker in and through and to "My sighes, and grones." Vaughan had in "The Search" tried to "see the *Temple*" but was shown "A little dust"; now this "dust" and the "stones" of Luke 19:40, together with the speaker, will "cry to thee."

In "Church-Service," therefore, Vaughan again takes up the broken stones/words of Herbert's "The Altar" and uses them to make his speaker's prayer that even though all that is left of the public utterances of Anglicanism are the speaker's "sighes, and grones" (l. 24) he can ask that they become "Musick." For Herbert, "A HEART alone / Is such a stone, / As nothing but / Thy Pow'r doth cut. / Wherefore each part / Of my hard heart / Meets in this frame, / To praise thy Name" ("The Altar," ll. 5–12); in Vaughan's poem, the "holy dove['s] / Interceeding, spirituall grones / Make restless mones / For dust and stones, / For dust in every part, / But a hard, stonie heart," while "busie thoughts . . . scatter quite" a "heap of sand": "But for thy might; / Thy hand alone doth tame / Those blasts, and knit my frame" (ll. 3–8, 11–16). The breaking up of the Anglican altar and its rites, here made emblematic in the dispersal of Herbert's words that form an altar, still can form a prayer which places the speaker, at least imaginatively, in a "Church-Service," in "this thy Quire of Souls" (l. 9), although he asks "O how" this be so, and answers that it is because he is "Propt by thy hand." Functioning here also is an allusion to the "mend my ryme" ending of Herbert's "Denial," another text dealing with a situation in which a speaker finds his "devotions could not pierce / Thy silent ears," but a persistence in lamenting petition is "mended" at the last. What will make Vaughan's articulation of "sighes, and grones" into the "Musick" of a church service are at once the intercession of the "holy dove," itself described as "interceding . . . grones," "thy Martyrs bloud" (l. 20), and God's action to "knit my frame," basing this assertion on the Pauline promise (Romans 8:26) that "the Spirit also helpeth our infirmities: for we know not what we should pray for as we ought: but the Spirit itself maketh intercession for us with groanings which cannot be uttered." The references to the "Quire of Souls" and the martyrs link this poem as "Musick" to the *Te Deum laudamus* and the *Gloria in excelsis,* hymns traditionally used to "praise thy Name" in Morning Prayer daily after the first lesson and at the end of the Anglican Eucharist. Vaughan's point is to claim that such behavior is required of God for his poem to achieve the function of *Te Deum laudamus* and *Gloria in excelsis* when those songs are not available for actual public use in the context of Prayer Book use. If God does so function, however, a form of Anglican worship can go on even in its absence.

In other poems, the absence of Anglican worship appears as one source of imagery. In "Christs Nativity (I)," for example, after urging "Awake, glad heart!" and noting that nature is awake—"heark, how th' *wood* rings, / *Winds* whisper, and the busie *springs* / A consort make" (ll. 1, 7–9)—the speaker asserts "Man is their high-priest, and should rise / To offer up the sacrifice" (ll. 11–12), yet no such liturgical offering of "our sacrifice of praise and thanksgiving" is now possible, a point to which he returns in "Christs Nativity (II)":

> And shall we no voices lift?
>
> .   .   .   .
>
> Are we all stone, and Earth

> Neither his bloudy passions mind,
> Nor one day blesse his birth?
> (Ll. 5–16)

A legitimate question, since, as we have noted, the Puritans eliminated the Christmas festival along with the rest of the Anglican liturgical calendar. The speaker's response is to request "let once more by mystick birth / The Lord of life be borne in Earth," a call for God to renew his saving actions.

"Buriall" ends with a similar plea, this time paraphrasing the end of Revelation (22:19–20): "Lord haste, Lord come, / O come Lord *Jesus* quickly" (ll. 39–40). Those events which in Puritan eyes were the working out of God's promises in English history appear to Vaughan's speaker as under judgment: "Tyme now / Is old, and slow, / His wings are dull and sickly" (ll. 33–35). In light of this view of events, it is the anticipation of time's end, bringing with it the renewed action of God, that enables the speaker to sustain his lament and his petition and move to poems like "Chearfulness," which follows "Buriall," with its affirmation that "Affliction thus, meere pleasure is / And hap what will, / If thou be in't, 'tis welcome still" (ll. 9–11), thus again reaffirming the Prayer Book's way of interpreting human ills.

What sustains Vaughan's speaker is thus a renewal of the ancient Christian emphasis on eschatology, an appeal to discourse articulating expectation of the imminent fulfillment of the divine promises.[28] Although never resorting to the apocalyptic imagery of Daniel or Revelation, Vaughan still finds open to him in his situation Jesus' parables of the need for watchfulness and readiness as well as Jesus' own "night-watch" in the Garden of Gethsemane. Like the writer of Revelation urging to faithfulness the churches to which he addressed his versions of the end-time, however, Vaughan stresses the importance of watchfulness and uses his eschatological expectation as a stance from which to understand present events. Remembering Jesus' injunction in Matthew 25:13 ("Watch therefore, for ye know neither the day nor the hour wherein the Son of Man cometh"), he asks in "The Dawning": "Ah! What time wilt thou come? when shall that crie / The *Bridegroome's Comming!* fill the sky?" (ll. 1–2). After considering several opportunities and approving most highly of morning, when the appearance of the "son" joins with the rising of the "sun," he finally gives up such speculation in favor of a prayer that in him Jesus' injunction in Luke 21:36—"Watch ye therefore, and pray always, that ye may be accounted worthy . . . to stand before the Son of Man"—may be realized:

> [L]et my Course, my aym, my Love,
> And chief acquaintance be above;
> So when that day, and hour shal come
> In which thy self wil be the Sun,

Thou'lt find me drest and on my way,
Watching the Break of thy great day.
(Ll. 43–48)

Redoing the form basic to Herbert's "The Call," Vaughan renews eschatological expectation, reading current events in terms of preparation and watchfulness for the fulfillment of that expectation, giving rise to a number of
poems stressing the experience of night as the scene for exemplary watchfulness, as in "The Shepheards," "The Pilgrimage," "The Constellation," and
"The World," or the experience of dawning as anticipatory of Christian hope,
either in the past, as in "Christs Nativity" or "Easter-day" and "Easter
Hymn," or in the future, as in "The Dawning."

Other poems which reflect this eschatological emphasis include the experience of suffering and isolation in the process of understanding present time in
terms of the end as well as in getting ready for it to come. In "Rules *and*
Lessons," for example, Vaughan redoes Herbert's "Perirrhanterium," transforming what was for Herbert instruction in the ethical life that led to church
going and "Church" reading into a poem in which the key terms are "*Watch* and
Pray, / These are the *Words,* and *Works* of life; this do, / And live" (ll. 140–
142). Jesus' instructions to his disciples in Luke 21:36 to prepare themselves
for his return at the end of things ("Watch ye therefore, and pray always, that
ye may be accounted worthy to escape all these things that shall come to pass,
and to stand before the Son of Man") become here the speaker's counsel to
himself and to his audience. As in Herbert, the Christian life is one of charity
and self-examination, but Vaughan adds the refusal to follow in "the same
steps with the *Crowd* . . . / If *Priest,* and *People* change, keep thou thy ground"
(ll. 43–48), obviously a timely allusion to the behavior of many Anglican
priests and layfolk after the Puritan victory in the Civil War who conformed to
the new religious dispensation rather than remain loyal to the old faith.
Vaughan thus offers an interim ethic of perseverance for those who would keep
the faith even in the face of adversity and social and political pressure to
conform to the religion of the Commonwealth; he holds to the central Anglican
affirmation that the heart of Christian living is to "*Love God, and Love thy
Neighbour*" (l. 140), but adds to it a strong sense of eschatological expectation.
Except for a brief mention of a desire that England become "an humble, holy
nation" (l. 55) in "The Constellation," all hope of a Christian commonwealth as
the goal for Christian living is absent; yet even here, there is the strong sense
that God must "guide us through this Darkness, that we may / Be more and
more in love with day" (ll. 51–52), strongly suggestive of the conclusion that
any sense of a coming new society is caught up in associations with the final
things and is not to be achieved short of that ultimate resolution.

In such terms, in fact, Vaughan presents his image of life here as one of loneliness, isolation, and longing for an ending seen in terms of the renewal of community now lost. In poems like "Peace" and "The World," the images of "a Countrie / Far beyond the stars" ("Peace," ll. 1–2) or of "Eternity . . . / Like a great *Ring* of pure and endless light" ("The World," ll. 1–2)—images of God's promised future for his people—are articulated not as mystical, inner visions but as ways of positing a perspective from which to judge present conditions,[29] so that human life can be interpreted as "foolish ranges" ("Peace," l. 17) or "sour delights . . . silly snares of pleasure . . . weights and woe . . . feare . . . *the lust of the flesh, the lust of the Eys, and the pride of life*" ("The World," ll. 11–12, 16, 35, 61–62). Expanding on the quotation from John 2:16–17 with which he ends "The World," Vaughan thus is able to use language for defining the world that is at the heart of the Bible's imagery for articulating what is to pass away when all is made new and is also at the center of the Prayer Book's rites of initiation and passage. Vaughan's language is that of biblical calls to repentance, including Jesus' own injunction to repent for the kingdom is at hand. In that implied promise—that if the times call for repentance, the kingdom must be at hand—Vaughan can find occasion for hope and thus for perseverance. The act of repentance, or renunciation of the world's distractions, becomes the activity that enables endurance.

In this situation, the speaker often claims that he is "Weary of this same Clay, and straw" ("The Mutinie," l. 1), "*Earth*" ("Misery," l. 29), "very brute" ("The Law, and the Gospel," l. 21), and "foul Clay" ("Praise," l. 41), prompting confession and assertion of contingency on God in the manner of the lament Psalm and the Prayer Book. His plea, "O let my Crie come to thy throne" ("Misery," l. 107) is a direct echo of the response in the Order for the Visitation of the Sick: "Lord hear our prayers. And let our cry come unto thee" (BCP, p. 300). Such existence is endurable here, although the speaker often longs for release, in terms of the ability to understand such agony as incorporated into Christ's agony as preparation for what is to come: "Blest be thy Dew, and blest thy frost, / And happy I to be so crost, / And cur'd by Crosses at thy cost" ("Love, and Discipline," ll. 7–9). It is also endurable when defined as a journey toward that future promise: "this night I linger here, / And full of tossings too and fro, / Expect still when thou wilt appear / That I may get me up, and go" ("The Pilgrimage," ll. 9–12). In other words, the situation Vaughan dramatizes in such a way that his readers would be encouraged to keep faith with those who are gone before and are yet to come is best characterized in terms of his quotation from Hebrews 11:13 which ends his "Pilgrimage": "And they confessed, that they were strangers, and Pilgrims on the earth."

"The Pilgrimage" thus represents a kind of arrival rare in *Silex Scintillans*. In this poem the motifs of indeterminancy, characteristic of "Regeneration," in which the speaker repeatedly sought for and failed to achieve a reading of locales and experiences in terms that would make them regenerative, are repeated but with a new sense of perspective. One place arrived at by the wanderer in "Regeneration" may (or may not) be *"Jacobs Bed"*; in "The Pilgrimage" the figure of Jacob becomes a role the speaker uses effectively to describe his experience:

> As travellours when the twilight's come,
> And in the sky the stars appear,
> The past daies accidents do summe
> With, *This wee saw there, and thus here.*
>
> Then *Jacob*-like lodge in a place
> . . . .
> Where till the day restore the race
> They rest and dream homes of their own.
>
> So for this night I linger here . . .
>
> (Ll. 1–9)

What has happened here is that the questing for meaning has been given up; events become merely "accidents" to be recorded, not to be pored over for significance. The "race," the journey, has become all there is; life is endured in desire for future arrival (*"O that I were but where I see!"* l. 14) sustained by petition for endurance: "So strengthen me, Lord, all the way, / That I may travel to thy Mount" (ll. 26–27). Thus arrival, indefinitely postponed, becomes the only place of meaning, and thus the journey itself as the sum of experience has become its own "arrival." By affirming the appropriateness of interpreting life as a journey, the speaker can adopt a tone of having gotten somewhere.

In such terms, praise of God can come for actions orienting this speaker toward such a future: "He one day / When I went quite astray / Out of meer love / By his mild Dove / Did shew me home, and put me in the way" ("Retirement," ll. 7–11). In another poem, endurance comes in terms of a plea that God "be pleas'd / To fix my steps, and whatsoever path / Thy sacred and eternal wil decreed / For thy bruis'd reed / O give it ful obedience, that so seiz'd / Of all I have, I may nor move thy wrath / Nor grieve thy *Dove,* but soft and mild / Both live and die thy Child" ("The Mutinie," ll. 35–42).

What Vaughan thus offers his Anglican readers is the incentive to endure present troubles by defining them as crossings which because they can be related to Christ's cross can be seen as making possible the return of the One who is now perceived as absent and by defining that endurance as part of what brings that return closer. Vaughan can still praise God for present action— "How rich, O Lord! how fresh thy visits are!" ("Unprofitableness," l. 1)—but his emphasis is on such visits as sustaining in the struggle to endure in anticipation of God's actions yet to come rather than as ongoing actions of God for the fulfillment of God's purposes here. The movement through *Silex I* which Vaughan constructs for us is from the difficulty in articulating and interpreting experience acted out in "Regeneration" toward an increasing ability to articulate and thus to endure, brought about by the growing emphasis on the present as preparation for what is to come. This is characterized by the speaker's self-dramatization in the traditional stances of confessional and intercessory prayer, lament, and joy found in expectation. Gradually, the interpretive difficulties of "Regeneration" are redefined as part of what must be offered to God in this time of waiting. In "Vanity of Spirit," a poem which redoes the "reading" motif of Herbert's "Jesu," instead of being able to construe the "peeces" to read either a comfortable message or *"JESU,"* Vaughan's speaker can do no more than sense the separation that failure to interpret properly can create between God and his people, requiring that new act to come: "in these veyls my Ecclips'd Eye / May not approach thee" (ll. 31–32). Only Christ's Passion fulfilled when "I'le disapparel, and . . . most gladly dye" (ll. 33–34) can once more link heaven and earth. A similar inability to read or interpret correctly is the common failing of the Lover, the States-man, and the Miser in "The World"; here, too, the "Ring" of eternity is held out as a promise for those who keep faith with the church, for *"This Ring the Bride-groome did for none provide / But for his bride"* (ll. 59–60).

In his characterization of the Anglican situation in the 1640s in terms of loneliness and isolation and in his hopeful appeals to God to act once more to change this situation, Vaughan thus reached out to faithful Anglicans, giving them the language to articulate that situation in a redemptive way. Forcing an opening in the world that a language of despair might create, Vaughan finds in the Bible, the Prayer Book, and *The Temple* (with perhaps a glance at Donne's *Anniversaries* in his "I walkt the other day" and its reference to "this frame / Which once had neither being, forme, nor name" [ll. 46–47]) the resources for a poetry that teaches an expectant endurance, proclaims the continuity of Anglican community, and offers itself as part of the way toward the future that makes hopefulness about endurance in the present possible. Although "Thick darknes lyes / And hatcheth o'r thy people," he claims, "what Angel cries / *Arise!*" ("Corruption," ll. 37–40). To create a community through the publication of his text, linking those who would find through it a sense of community in suffering and thus creating such a community and making that suffering and isolation redemptive for that community because of the future with God to which it will lead is Vaughan's homiletic task in *Silex I.* "All the year I mourn," he says, asking that God "bind me up, and let me lye / A Pris'ner to my libertie, / If such a state at all can be / As an Impris'ment serving thee" ("Misery," ll. 1–4). It is the oblation of self in enduring what is given to endure that Vaughan offers as solace in this situation, living in prayerful expectation of release: "from this Care, where dreams and sorrows raign / Lead me above / Where Light, Joy, Leisure, and true Comforts move / Without all pain" ("I walkt the other day," ll. 57–60).

Vaughan's intentions in *Silex I* thus come clearer the nearer we reach the end of it. His posing the problems of perception in the absence of Anglican worship early in the work leads to an exploration of what such a situation might mean in terms of preparation for the "last things." His taking on of Herbert's poet/priest role enables a recasting of the central acts of Anglican worship—Bible reading, preaching, prayer, and sacramental enactment—in new terms so that the old language can be used again, albeit to describe a new situation in which the effectiveness of the old acts with language survives even in the absence of the acts themselves. As a result, he seeks to create a community which is still in continuity with the community now lost because of the common future they share; he achieves this because he is able to articulate present experience in reference to the old terms, so that lament for their loss becomes the way to achieve a common future with them. Holding onto the old definitions by means of casting them in an eschatological perspective, Vaughan encourages a keeping of the faith by defining preparation for the "last things" in terms of experiencing the present absence of what would heretofore have been seen as the essential acts of preparation for that future.

Herbert may have "perceiv'd / I was deceiv'd" to conclude "both the way and end be tears" ("The Pilgrimage," ll. 28–30), but for Vaughan the experience of insight central to these poems is one in which the way and end are found in a lament that is only partially expressed in "tears":

> My crie not pour'd with tears alone,
> (For tears alone are often foul)
> But with the bloud of all my soul,
> With spirit-sighs, and earnest grones,
> Faithful and most repenting mones,
> With these I crie, and crying pine
> Till thou both mend and make me thine.
>
> ("Misery," ll. 108–114)

Joy for Vaughan is in anticipation of a release that makes further repentance and lament possible and which informs lament as the way toward release. But, in *Silex I* that release—"God will wipe away all tears from their eyes" (Revelation 21:4)—is always not yet, always still to come. To live aware of what is at stake in faithfulness to the promise of that release is what Vaughan calls Anglicans to in *Silex I*. Thus it is that he approaches the end of *Silex I* with the poem "I walkt the other day," a redoing of the opening "Regeneration" which parallels its motifs of the contrast between spring and winter, of light and shade. The poem does not end, however, with the request for "one breath" of the divine wind, but for the ability to endure:

> Grant that I may so
> Thy steps track here below,
>
> That in these Masques and shadows I may see
> Thy sacred way,
> And by those hid ascents climb to that day
>
> . . . .
>
> And from this Care . . .
> Lead me above.
>
> (Ll. 48–58).

In this light, it is no accident that the last poem in *Silex I* is entitled "Begging," in which the speaker, making a poem, asks since "it is thy only Art / To reduce a stubborn heart . . . let [mine] be thine!" (ll. 13–20). Vaughan thus ends not far from where Herbert began "The Church," with a heart and a prayer for its transformation. Without the altar except in anticipation and memory, it is difficult for Vaughan to get much beyond that point. So the moment of expectation, understood in terms of past language and past events, becomes the moment to be defined as one that points toward future fulfillment and thus becomes the moment that must be lived out, as the scene of transformation as well as the process of transformation through divine "Art." Vaughan, as both Spenser and Herbert before him, ultimately teaches behavior (*praxis*) rather than text (*gnosis*) as effective interpretation, but for Vaughan hopeful expectation is the behavior that redeems the failure of text (the Prayer Book) to keep Anglicanism alive. It is thus appropriate that Vaughan ends *Silex I* with praise to the God "that is able to keep us from falling" even in so precarious and yet hope-filled a situation and "to present us faultless before the presence of his glory."

The Homiletics of Expectation in Silex Scintillans (1655)

The Anglican community in England did survive Puritan efforts to suppress it. Increasingly rigorous efforts to stamp it out are effective testimony to that fact; while attendance at a Prayer Book service in 1645 was punished by a fine, by 1655 the penalty had been escalated to imprisonment or exile.[30] What role Vaughan's *Silex I* of 1650 may have played in supporting that survival we cannot know.[31] What we do know is that the *Silex Scintillans* of 1650 did produce in 1655 a very concrete response in Vaughan himself, a response in which the "awful roving" of *Silex I* is proclaimed to have found a sustaining response. Joining the poems from *Silex I* with a second group of poems approximately three-fourths as long as the first, Vaughan produced in 1655 a new collection which makes of the first group it absorbs no longer a work that is sufficient to promote its ends but a work that now becomes preliminary to a second group of poems with a substantially different tone and mood.32 His speaker is still very much alone in this second group of *Silex* poems ("They are all gone into the world of light! / And I alone sit lingring here" [ll. 1–2]), but the sense of the experience of that absence as agony, even redemptive agony, is missing. Poems like this one can still end, like so many poems in *Silex I,* in petition, but the tone of that petition is less anguished, less a leap into hope for renewed divine activity, than a request articulated in confidence that such release will come:

> Either disperse these mists, which blot and fill
> My perspective (still) as they pass,
> Or else remove me hence unto that hill,
> Where I shall need no glass.
>
> (Ll. 37–40)

In such a petition, the problem of interpretation, or the struggle for meaning, is given up into petition itself, an intercessory plea that grows out of Paul's "dark glass" image of human knowing here and his promise of a knowing "face to face" yet to come and manifests contingency on divine action for clarity of insight—"disperse these mists"—or for bringing the speaker to "that hill, / Where I shall need no glass," yet which also replicates the confidence of Paul's assertion that "then shall I know" (1 Corinthians 13:12).

In ceasing the struggle to understand how it has come to pass that "They are all gone into the world of light," a giving up articulated through the offering of the speaker's isolation in prayer, Vaughan's speaker achieves a sense of faithfulness in the reliability of divine activity that enables him to relinquish the struggle over the darkness of the glass more characteristic of *Silex I.* Building on the role of Jacob, accepted in "The Pilgrimage" toward the end of *Silex I,* in which to wrestle with God for a blessing becomes a blessing in itself, and in which the journey itself becomes accepted as the only ending a narrative of journeying can have this side the final ending of all narrative, the quest for meaning here in terms of a future when all meaning will be fulfilled thus becomes a substitute for meaning itself. However dark the glass, affirming the promise of future clarity becomes a way of understanding the present that is sufficient and is also the way to that future clarity. Vaughan's speaker does not stop asking for either present or future clarity; even though he is not to get the former, it is the articulation of the question that makes the ongoing search for understanding a way of getting to the point at which the future is present and both requests will be answered at once in the same act of God. This relationship between present and future in terms of a quest for meaning that links the two is presented in this poem as an act of recollection—"Their very memory is fair and bright, / And my sad thoughts doth clear" (ll. 3–4)—which is in turn projected into the speaker's conceptualization of their present state in "the world of light," so that their memory "glows and glitters in my cloudy breast." This juxtaposition of light and dark imagery as a way of articulating the speaker's situation becomes a contrast between the fulfillment of community imagined for those who have gone before and the speaker's own isolation. It also establishes a link between them:

> I see them walking in an Air of glory,
> Whose light doth trample on my days:
> My days, which are at best but dull and hoary,
> Meer glimering and decays.
>
> (Ll. 9–12)

Although their "light" reveals the dullness of his "days," it also bridges the gulf between them because it orients the direction which provides an ending to present circumstances. Although Vaughan resists borrowing from Revelation its apocalyptic imagery of beasts, seals opened, cataclysmic battles, and all the rest, he does use its rhetorical strategy of proclaiming to an audience in a time of great difficulty the reliability of God in fulfilling his promises in the future by means of describing that future as though it were past and thus available to the memory,[33] and by positing steadfastness in hope now as the way to participation in that future.

Faith in the redemption of those who have gone before thus becomes an act of God, a "holy hope" which the speaker affirms as God's "walks" in which he has "shew'd . . . me / To kindle my cold love" (ll. 13, 15–16). Such a hope becomes "some strange thoughts" (l. 27) which enable the speaker to "into glory peep" and thus affirm death as the "Jewel of the Just," the encloser of light, "But when the hand that lockt her up, gives room / She'll shine through all the sphaere" (ll. 31–32). The ability to articulate present experience in these terms thus can yield to confident intercession that God act again to fulfill his promise: "O Father . . . / Resume thy spirit from this world of thrall / Into true liberty" (ll. 33–36).

This strongly affirmed expectation of the renewal of community after the grave with those who "are all gone into the world of light" is articulated from the beginning of *Silex II* in the poem "Ascension-day," in which the speaker proclaims he feels himself "a sharer in thy victory" (l. 8), so that "I soar and rise / Up to the skies" (ll. 9–10). Like "The Search" in *Silex I*, this poem centers on an absence of Christ, but the difference comes in this distance between the speaker of "The Search" and its biblical settings and the ease with which the speaker of "Ascension-day" moves within them. In this exuberant reenacting of Christ's Ascension, the speaker can place himself with

Mary Magdalene and with "Saints and Angels" in their community: "I see them, hear them, mark their haste." He can also find in the Ascension a realization of the world-renewing and recreating act of God promised to his people: "I walk the fields of *Bethani* which shine / All now as fresh as *Eden*, and as fine" (ll. 37–38). What follows is an account of the Ascension itself, Christ leaving behind "his chosen Train, / All sad with tears" but now with eyes "Fix'd . . . on the skies" instead of "on the Cross" (ll. 51–52). Having gone from them in just this way, "eternal Jesus" can be faithfully expected to return, and so the poem ends with an appeal for that return.

Jesus left behind "two men in white," claims Vaughan's speaker, alluding to the account in Acts 1:10–11 used as the Epistle for Ascension Day in the Prayer Book, in which "two men . . . in white apparel" tell Jesus' disciples that he "which is taken up from you into heaven, shall so come in like manner as ye have seen him go into heaven." And so Vaughan's poem becomes an articulation of the Collect for that day: "Grant . . . that like as we do believe thy only begotten Son our Lord to have ascended into the heavens; so we may also in heart and mind thither ascend, and with him continually dwell" (BCP, p. 166). The link between "as we do believe" and "so we may" becomes Vaughan's affirmation that *"what two attest, is true."* His request "Come then thou faithful witness" to his reader to join him in making up two who ask, in the words of the ending of Revelation, "come dear Lord" thus makes possible an affirmation that expectation is *"true"* and the prayer valid. Vaughan here alludes to Jesus' promise to his disciples in Matthew 18:20 ("where two or three are gathered, there am I in the midst of them"); the restoration of Anglican community is made possible through the appeal of Vaughan's poem, at least to the extent that those who act together in memory of the normative context of their coming together in the past makes that past present for them. It is also the condition requisite for the efficacy of the prayer Vaughan's speaker asks his reader to join him in, for Matthew 18:19 reads, "if two of you shall agree on earth as touching any thing that they shall ask, it shall be done for them of my Father which is in heaven."

In part, what Vaughan has achieved here is the renewal of the Anglican significance of Ascension Day as well as the ability to articulate present experience in terms of applied typology.[34] This achieved reenactment of Ascension Day, in spite of the absence of the actual observation of that day because of the absence of the Anglican church to observe it, is affirmed as a way of re-establishing a kind of community with those who "are all gone into the world of light" so that Vaughan's speaker can expectantly look foward to a common future with them. His tone here argues for the achieving of a kind of answer to his prayer in "I walkt the other day" at the end of *Silex I:*

> Grant I may so
> Thy steps track here below,

That in these Masques and shadows I may see
>   Thy sacred way,
And by those hid ascents climb to that day
>   Which breaks from thee. . . .

(Ll. 48–53)

As a result, it represents a different strategy for encouraging his fellow Anglicans to continue to keep faith with the community that is lost and thus to establish a community here of those waiting for the renewal of community with those who have gone before.

This shift in strategy, which amounts to a move from arguing for the sufficiency of lament in light of eschatological expectation to the encouragement offered by an exultant tone of experiencing the end to come proleptically through anticipating it, is prepared for by the changes Vaughan made to the front matter of the 1650 edition in preparing this new, augmented edition. Gone, first of all, are the emblem of the stony heart and its accompanying Latin verse, which no longer serve to prepare the reader for the experience to follow.[35] In their place comes a quotation from Job 35:10–11 which rearticulates the searching motif of *Silex I* but puts it in the context of poetry and knowing: "Where is God my Maker, who giveth Songs in the night? Who teacheth us more then the beasts of the earth, and maketh us wiser then the fowls of heaven?" To this question the volume that follows comes as one kind of answer, for as we approach *Silex I* and *II* with their repeated motif of "Songs in the night," what becomes clear is that Vaughan now presents his poems as the answer to the question, "Where is God my Maker?" The God of Anglicans, as we have seen, is known in the results of his actions; Vaughan presents his poems as the results of those divine actions, so that the poems become a witness to the continuing activity of the God who might otherwise be experienced as absent. *Silex II* thus demonstrates for Vaughan's reader the effects of writing and reading *Silex I;* in effect replicating the relationship between Herbert's *Temple* and *Silex I,* it argues for the effectiveness of articulating the Anglican experience of the 1640s and early 1650s in the terms Vaughan teaches in *Silex I,* showing how this process can be a source of Anglican identity and a support for faithfulness to Anglican expectations. If these poems are effective in teaching readers to sustain their faithful expectations, they may become occasions for hope in the efficacy of God's promises because they may be seen as evidence of the continuation of divine activity in human history in spite of all evidence to the contrary.

The "Authors Preface to the following Hymns," which Vaughan also added in 1655, repeats and expands on this motif of the link between his poetry and knowledge of the whereabouts of God. The argument of this preface declares the power of poetry to affect the world to which it is addressed. It starts out with a lament for those "*Wits* . . . [who] cast away all their fair portion of time in . . . a deliberate search, or excogitation of *idle words*, and a most vain, insatiable desire to be reputed *Poets*." Such writers on profane subjects could have achieved much good had they taken "Christian-sacred" subjects, but they have instead produced "soul-killing issue," not merely for themselves but for "whole Generations," so that they *"minister sins and death* unto their readers" (pp. 388–391). This power of profane poets to corrupt themselves and their readers extends past the grave:

> It is a sentence of sacred authority, that *he that is dead, is freed from sin;* because he cannot in that *state*, which is without the *body*, sin any more; but he that writes *idle books*, makes for himself another *body*, in which he always *lives*, and *sins* (after *death*) as *fast* and as *foul*, as ever he did in his *life*. (P. 390)

The writing of *"idle books"* here is articulated as a kind of negative resurrection of the body in the perpetuation of the poet's ability to influence his audience for ill after his (personal) death through the endurance in life of the body of his text.

What is striking about this is that by the end of this preface Vaughan uses the same language, albeit in positive terms, to characterize his own experience as both poet and person in relationship to the text we are about to read. He claims that "By the last *Poems* in the book (were not that *mistake* here prevented) you would judge all to be *fatherless*, and the *Edition* posthume; for (indeed) *I was nigh unto death*, and am still at no great distance from it . . . But *the God of the spirits of all flesh* hath granted me a further use of *mine*, then I did look for in the *body*; and when I expected, and had (by his assistance) prepared for a *message* of *death*, then did he *answer* me with life: I hope to his glory . . . that I may flourish not with *leafe* only, but with some *fruit* also" (p. 392).

Indeed, the concluding poems in *Silex II* dramatize a speaker bidding farewell to this life. In "To the Holy Bible," for instance, he asks of the Bible, "how shall we part," and tells it, "Take this last kiss, and let me weep / True thanks to thee, before I sleep" before concluding, "Farewel O book of God! farewel!" (ll. 1–4, 36). But the point Vaughan makes in the preface is that we are to approach this text as having led to a kind of resurrection experience, God answering his preparation for death "with *life*." We are to experience the volume as a "body" of the poet which will survive death, made possible by a poet who has survived an expectation of death, both coming as evidence of a God who has answered preparation for death in these poems with life. Although the "body" of the church has been reduced to the body of one member, its experience has become a source of hope, since what is true for one can (potentially) be true for all, and all as "one body." The seeming death of

Anglicanism has not led to despair but to the possibility of celebration that events have yielded to an interpretation in which God is not absent but is instead using these events to bring "life," "glory," and "advantage."

Vaughan earlier in this preface has prepared us to link devout poetry with benefits both to the poet and his readers, *"fruit"* from *"leafe"*:

> The *performance* is easie, and were it the most difficult in the world, the *reward* is so glorious, that it infinitely transcends it: for *they that turn many to righteousness, shall shine like the stars for ever and ever:* . . . It is true indeed, that to give up our thoughts to pious *Themes* and *Contemplations* (if it be done for pieties sake) is a great *step* towards *perfection;* because it will *refine,* and *dispose* to devotion and sanctity. And further, it will *procure* for us (so easily communicable is that *loving spirit*) some small *prelibation* of those heavenly *refreshments,* which descend but seldom, and then very sparingly, upon *men* of an ordinary or indifferent *holyness.* (Pp. 391–392)

Giving up "our thoughts to pious *Themes* and *Contemplations*" is an activity common to writers and readers made possible by texts like this one. Writers do this in order to write; readers do so as a result of reading their writing. Yet readers who achieve such ends from writing become themselves types of writers, for they are shaped into kinds of texts by the God who makes possible such writing and the effect it has on them. For it is in the context of this discussion of writing that Vaughan offers Herbert as an example of one "whose holy *life* and *verse* gained many pious *converts,* (of whom I am the least)" (p. 391). Herbert's life (and verse) begets Vaughan's life (and verse); if "verse" were dropped out here—if the begotten does not become a Christian *poet* as a result of reading Christian poetry—the process still holds, because to readers texts and lives become interdependent so that the life lived after reading such texts becomes a kind of text to others, with a similar didactic function, like Herbert, whose "holy life" (and verse) gained many converts.

In each case there is a double kind of reward—the striving for and achieving of a kind of perfection so as to qualify as a true Christian writer and the "shining" that is the reward for writing an effective text, one that turns "many to righteousness." If texts become "bodies" that in some way resurrect the poet, for good or ill, and if good texts are good because they enable the giving up of thoughts to "pious *Themes* and *Contemplations*" that *"refine,* and *dispose* to devotion and sanctity" and thus lead to "the resurrection of the body and the life everlasting," then the text itself, as experienced by both writers and readers, becomes the scene and the impetus for such transformations and reorientations as it becomes the vehicle for divine action that answers preparation for "a message of death" with *"life"* itself. The human text, enabled by

God, prepares for one sort of divine text (a "message of death") and is answered by another divine text become life as text, gift, and future reality, for the Church of England as well as its members.

This process of interchange between text, writer, and reader manifests what Vaughan calls "a true, practick piety," without "which it was impossible they should effect those things abroad, which they never had acquaintance with at home" (p. 391). In effect, what Vaughan claims for his 1655 version of *Silex Scintillans* is that it replicates in the relationship between its parts the whole process of interaction and enactment of biblical texts in Anglican worship that was lost when the Puritans banned use of the Prayer Book in 1645. Vaughan's relationship to his text—his ability to write the preface as a textual sign of his receiving the divine answer of life—functions as a persuasive element in his case for reading his work as a way for the reader to join him in the journey toward the renewal of that life. Without this preface, he argues, we would have "judge[d] all to be *fatherless*," but with it, presumably, we can come to see that all have a father and an advocate with the Father, that the change from death to life in Vaughan is a sign that God is still to be found in his actions. In the same way, his introduction into *Silex II* of "some small *prelibations* of those heavenly refreshments" acts to reinforce his claim that in and through interaction with his body-as-text readers can achieve "a true, practick piety," participate in the body of Anglicanism even in its absence, and look toward hearing for themselves divine action as "*life*" rather than as "a *message* of *death*," thus becoming "*fruit*" of Vaughan's "*leafe*" and completing his self-proclaimed function as Herbert's heir to a prophetic role as poet/ priest.

Vaughan points to the biblical sources of this newly elaborated and developed definition of his role as poet/priest/prophet in the Psalmlike prayer/ hymn that concludes this preface. Put together by assembling quotations from Jeremiah 17:13–14, Isaiah 38:10–19, Psalm 43, and Jonah 2:6–9, this text assembles a series of addresses to God which ask for healing and mercy, praise God for deliverance from death and "the pit of corruption," and assert the speaker's determination to "worship towards thy holy temple" for "salvation is of the Lord." Continuing to draw on the textual resources provided by the Bible, the Prayer Book, and *The Temple*, Vaughan in *Silex II* assumes a full prophetic role as the witness and spokesman whose speaking in the present will become the evidence that God is not absent but can be relied upon to fulfill his promises; indeed, in the very acts that seem to deny the divine action God is at work bringing in his new recreative future. In this way Vaughan seeks to function as the ancient prophets, mediated to him by his interpretation of Herbert's role in *The Temple*.

To account for this shift in strategy and tone and to enable us to get inside Vaughan's methodology in *Silex II,* we need to rehearse the implications of

Vaughan's use of a prophetic voice. We have already noted how the role of prophets like Isaiah and Jeremiah was to proclaim that Israel should not expect God to preserve Jerusalem inviolate, but that the fall of Jerusalem would not mean that the historic enterprise created by God's actions in history was at an end.[36] In the face of such seemingly catastrophic events, the prophets asserted that God was at work once more in history to usher in the fulfillment of those promises. In the compilation of the Bible, however, it was the role of the prophets, as witnesses to that proclamation, that came to the fore; instead of narratives of the fall of Jerusalem and of the exile being added to the narratives of the history of Israel to that time, the texts that were added to the canon of scripture were the writings and the narratives of the prophets themselves. It thus becomes the witness of the prophetic writings, as evidence that in such a time someone kept the faith, that redeems the time between the collapse of the Old Israel and the creation of the New Israel in the events of the Gospel narratives.

What Vaughan is reaching for in this move is a role in which the presence of his poetic voice, in the time after the abolition of the Anglican church, is an effective witness that the promises of God still apply to those who keep the faith in his promises in such a time. That Vaughan can proclaim God at work in the events of his specific historic situation and describe them in the vocabulary of prophetic utterance becomes evidence in itself that God is not absent, that the old promises still hold, and thus that to Vaughan's readers there is even more reason to join with the community now lost in keeping faith with the God of that community.

Thus, even as in the later books of Isaiah the prophetic voice turns from proclamations of the fall of Jerusalem and begins to celebrate the renewal of God's promises, and even as in the later prophets like Ezekiel and Joel there is a turn at the end toward the joyful evocation of the "Day of Yahweh" to come, so in Vaughan there is a gathering sense that the time of release is near and that therefore the tone can lighten, the rhetorical approach becoming one of encouragement in keeping the faith by means of evocation of what is to come and celebration of it in anticipation of its imminent arrival. Even as Job provides a biblical analogue for a religious text with a movement through the process of lament from a sense of God's absence to a sense of his presence, so Isaiah and some of the other prophetic books provide a similar model for a text which moves from the exploration of a difficult historic situation to a joyful anticipation of its resolution.

In this context *Silex II* claims that it is what *Silex I* prepared us for and made it possible for us to reach, even as that toward which *Silex II* points and celebrates in anticipation is what the whole work points toward and would move us toward. Vaughan structures this in his dedicatory verses of 1655 added to the dedicatory verse of the 1650 *Silex Scintillans*. The earlier verse ends in begging "that thou wouldst take thy Tenants Rent." The later verses celebrate that "'tis finished" and proclaim the text, in Herbert's language of dedication, as "'Twas thine first, and to thee returns." Such language is available to him now because the speaker can see the events which destroyed the Anglican church as Herbert knew it as leading to the fulfillment of the promises made to that church. The speaker rehearses his life as filled with signs of divine "mercies" and "truth"; he speaks easily of God's "divinely" having "forgiven" his "relapse and wilful breach . . ./ While thy blood wash'd me white as heaven." With this confident reuse of biblical and Prayer Book language, he says he has only in return this book to give: "this thy own gift, given to me. / Refuse it not!" (ll. 15–17, 33–45). Given the speaker's tone here, clearly he has no doubt concerning God's willingness to accept it. Thus he ends, offering the book as a functional text to enable God to read the world: "for now thy *Token* / Can tell thee where a heart is broken." Quoting Revelation 1:5–7 to the effect that as result of what this text is about we can now confidently use the language of John the Divine that Christ "hath made us Kings and Priests unto God and his Father" as something that can be said in the past tense as a foregone conclusion, a past act, the speaker can confidently await his "coming with clouds" to reveal it to all.

In the brief verse that Vaughan then added to the 1655 *Silex* which in effect redoes Herbert's "Superliminare" between "Perirrhanterium" and "The Church," he tells "Vain Wits, and eyes / Leave, and be wise." So long as one remains a "vain wit," reading further would be to "Abuse . . . holy fire." But to "Abuse not" is to "shun not"; Vaughan redefines the contents of *Silex I* in terms of pentecostal "holy fire" which will, to the reader who will shed "true tears," become "an eyesalve for the blinde" (ll. 1–6). A true reading of *Silex I* will combine tears and fire, even as the original emblem did, to "cleanse and supple without fail, / And fire will purge your callous veyl." "Then comes the light!"—presumably the light of *Silex II,* which will enable the reader, Vaughan promises, to "see your nakedness thereby," so he urges, "Praise him, who dealt his gifts so free / In tears to you, in fire to me."[37] In light of Vaughan's original opening to *Silex I,* with its emphasis on tears and fire, this new opening comes as a sign that the speaker has moved beyond where a reader might begin, even where he began the original *Silex I.* But another way to read this is in terms of a reinterpreted poet/priest role; if pentecostal fire brought words to the apostles to enable them to convey the divine Word, so here the speaker adopts the word-bringing and fire-bringing role, asking the reader to adopt the tear-bringing role. Together, and only together, can they recreate a community of expectation and produce the "eyesalve" that can lead to sight and praise.

Having thus redefined the function of *Silex I* and given it an even more decided public role as the site of a meeting between poet and reader that will lead to sight and *Silex II*, Vaughan then offers *Silex I*, essentially unchanged in text. When he begins the poems of *Silex II*, it is with the decidedly more celebratory tone of "Ascension-day" we have already noted:

> Lord Jesus! with what sweetness and delights,
> Sure, holy hopes, high joys and quickning flights
> Dost thou feed thine!
>
> (Ll. 1–4)

In enacting his observance of the Anglican Feast of the Ascension in the terms that would have been appropriate if the Prayer Book had been in use, Vaughan's speaker affirms that a kind of Easter has really occurred in the space between the Easter poems of *Silex I* and the beginning of *Silex II*. "Easter-day" in effect argues that if the reader "Awake" (l. 5) and "Arise" (l. 13), then the "benefits of his passion" will be made available, for "his blood will cure thy mind" (l. 15). By "Ascension-day" and the beginning of *Silex II* his stance has shifted to suggest that such clarity of mind has been achieved, for it is now possible to proclaim that the world once more yields to articulation in terms of biblical narrative: "With these fair thoughts I move in this fair place, / And the last steps of my milde Master trace" (ll. 49–50). Unlike poems we have already examined in *Silex I* in which the journey motif leads through spaces impossible to interpret effectively, here because the speaker can "the last steps of my milde Master trace" he can find the journey leading to places that yield readily to articulation in biblical terms, if not to clarity of understanding. Providing a typological language to describe this particular remembrance and re-experiencing of the Ascension, the biblical texts appointed for that day once more function to link past visits of God to people with the present in terms of their common future. Unlike similar episodes in *Silex I*, this speaker's journey through biblical "leaves" does not flounder over a sense of distance from those events or over the absence of a "cornerstone" in the tomb. Instead, the post-Resurrection portion of the biblical narrative works to renew the world, to make "the fields of *Bethani* . . . shine / All now as fresh as Eden, and as fine" (ll. 37–38). Performance thus functions to enable poetic resolution, Vaughan's text enacting what Herbert claimed for Anglican worship.

In the third poem of *Silex II*—"They are all gone into the world of light!"—Vaughan's speaker affirms that "Their very memory . . . my sad thoughts doth clear." The ability to achieve an interpretation of Vaughan's historical situation in such positive terms, to see his situation in ways that promote effectiveness of interpretation, promotes and supports the tone of excited expectation that characterizes these poems. This is acted out in "White Sunday," a poem celebrating Pentecost itself, in which Vaughan gives a full reading of his situation in biblical terms, claiming explicitly that "thy method with thy own, / Thy own dear people pens our times, / Our stories are in theirs set down / And penalties spread to our Crimes" (ll. 29–32). Although such "Crimes" may be great, the very ability to "know which way to look" becomes evidence which enables the speaker to ask for a renewal of pentecostal fire with an exuberance lacking in the petitions of *Silex I:*

> O come! refine us with thy fire!
> Refine us! we are at a loss.
> Let not thy stars for *Balaams* hire
> Dissolve into the common dross!
>
> (Ll. 61–64)

This ability to use biblical narrative to describe the present now becomes in itself one sign of the presence of the "holy comfort" promised Christ's followers in the Pentecost event and thus a source of the speaker's confident ability to "discern Wolves from Sheep" (l. 24). In Vaughan's reading of his situation on this Whitsunday, the distinctive note of Puritan claims—"some boast that fire each day, / And on Christ's coat pin all their shreds; / Not sparing openly to say, / His candle shines upon their heads" (ll. 13–16)—is refuted by the evidence provided by a Bible which can once more be said to "Shine here below" so that "I will know which way to look" (ll. 18, 20). Vaughan's renewed sense of what God is doing in the critical events of Anglican history thus enables him to use biblical language to articulate the present with renewed confidence. Again, as in earlier poems in *Silex I,* the experience of Anglicans is redeemed through association with the cross, although here the cross functions readily to provide the terms for articulating this situation:

> Again, if worst and worst implies
> A State, that no redress admits,
> Then from thy Cross unto these days
> The *rule* without *Exception* fits.
>
> (Ll. 33–36)

This poem in fact claims that in such terms the Collect for "Pentecost, commonly called Whitsunday," with its petition for "a right judgment in all things, and evermore to rejoice in his holy comfort" (BCP, pp. 168–169), is being fulfilled, so that "in this last and lewdest age, / Thy antient love on some may shine" (ll. 39–40). The invitation to the reader here is to identify himself with the speaker as included in the group on whom "Thy antient love . . . may shine" because of their common faithfulness to the tradition which runs from "the Apostles" through Anglicanism to a future in which "some" will share in the speaker's prayer that God "let thy grace now make the way / Even for thy love" (ll. 57–58) and praise God as the one who "Art still the same" and "canst unlock / Thy waters to a soul that pines" even in such times as these.

In situating this poem on Whitsunday, the traditional birthday of the church and the day Cranmer chose for introduction of the first Prayer Book, Vaughan thus finds in biblical and liturgical language the terms to articulate a condemnation of Puritan claims, an assertion of the possibility of divine action yet, and a joyous plea for a renewal of the church in the terms in which Vaughan understood it. As a result of this sense of renewed expectation of divine action, argued for through the renewal of Anglican claims about the ability of language to articulate experience, the speaker's tone throughout *Silex II* is one of joyous impatience: "make no delay, / But brush me with thy light, that I / May shine unto a perfect day, / And warme me at thy glorious Eye! / O take it off! or till it flee, / Though with no Lilie, stay with me!" ("Cock-crowing," ll. 43–48). Or, again, "So hear that thou must open; open to / A sinful wretch, A wretch that caus'd thy woe, / Thy woe, who caus'd his weal; so far his weal / That thou forgott'st thine own, for thou didst seal / Mine with thy blood, thy blood which makes thee mine, / Mine ever, ever; And me ever thine ("Love-sick," ll. 17–22). The aggressive confidence of such appeals, their insistent and urgent tone, again mark what Vaughan's speaker argues has been, and thus can be, achieved by the kind of faithfulness to Anglicanism enacted in *Silex I*.

This does not mean that Vaughan achieves the ability to articulate truth in the sense that his poems contain a verbal equivalent of reality. Instead, the radical future orientation of his speaker's anticipation indicates that what is claimed for *Silex II* is the achievement of a successful way of reaching that future, found through persisting in a mode of discourse. Use of language here continues to be functional rather than referential; Vaughan's claim is to be performing the language that is, or will be, successful in its functioning. Part of Vaughan's argument is thus that Anglicanism itself persists, even though it is hidden. In "The Palm-tree," traditional language for describing the Anglican church and the Christian life as a tree is evoked to depict the church in its present suppressed state.[38] At once it is "prest and bow'd" (l. 3), although it once "had equall liberty / With other trees"; now it "thrives no where" (ll. 4–6). Yet that is not the end of the story, because "the more he's bent / the more he grows" (ll. 8–9), since "Celestial natures still / Aspire for home" (ll. 9–10). Indeed, "This is the life which hid above with Christ / In God, doth always (hidden) multiply . . . / A Tree, whose fruit is immortality" (ll. 13–16). In this redoing of Herbert's "Colossians 3:3" it is the Church Triumphant, where "Spirits that have run their race . . . meet to receive their Crowns" (ll. 17–20), but it is also the Church Militant in its current situation, made up of "the patience of the Saints . . . water'd by their tears" to whom Christ is still present, for "One you cannot see / Sits here and numbers all the tears they shed" (ll. 21–24).[39] In this image of the church in oppression, linked with its past and future, Vaughan evokes a sense of the ongoingness of Anglicanism, insists on the continued presence of Christ in and to it, and, finally, invites the reader's participation in it:

> Here is their faith too, which if you will keep
> When we two part, I will a journey make
> To pluck a Garland hence, while you do sleep
> And weave it for your head against you wake.
>
> (Ll. 25–28)

It is still through faithfulness to the Church of England, even in its hiddenness, that one can join in a community of faith with its saints by taking part in their lament for it and thus know that one is in Christ and that Christ is present to those in it and receive, through keeping the faith of its saints, the Christian hope of needing a garland for the post-resurrection celebration God promises his people.

The sense of confidence manifested by Vaughan's speaker here is revealed in the way in which this poem redoes Herbert's "Love Unknown." Beginning with the same opening ("Deare friend sit down"), Vaughan makes the speaker of the poem both teller of the tale and interpretation of the Christian life as it is defined in relationship to the Sacraments of the church provided by Herbert's "Friend." In Vaughan's poem, the "friend" is the one to whom the speaker must explain the way to find the church in its current state, reading confidently the landscape of trees, shade, and fruit in sharp contrast to the difficulty exhibited by Herbert's speaker, or by Vaughan's speaker in *Silex I.* Indeed, one way this life is read is in terms of the text "hidden" in Herbert's "Colossians 3:3"; lines 12 and 13 of Vaughan's poem point out "This is the life which hid above with Christ / In God," remaking Herbert's emphasis on "That / Is / My / Treasure" into the goal of "The Palm-tree." To lament with tears for the church that is hidden is thus to join in a community of weepers who thereby make up a kind of community here to whom Christ is still present, even in its sorrow and its hiddenness, and to understand the present, even of one's lament, as sharing in the future "Crowns."

A similar argument is articulated in "The Seed growing secretly." The "prelibation" of the heavenly feast Vaughan mentioned in the preface to the 1655 *Silex* and which he celebrates as available to faithful Anglicans in the poems of *Silex II* here becomes a part of his persuasive argument for understanding present experience as the arena for continued growth in the Christian life:

> If this worlds friends might see but once
> What some poor man may often feel,

> Glory, and gold, and Crowns and Thrones
> They would soon quit and learn to kneel.
>
> (Ll. 1–4)

They would return to Anglicanism, since kneeling was a distinctive posture for receiving the Eucharist among Anglicans to which the Puritans objected.[40] They would also "praise thee," as Herbert's speaker in "The Temper (I)" would "If what my soul doth feel sometimes / My soul might ever feel" (ll. 3–4), yet Vaughan's concern here is loss, not the abundance of "one place ev'rywhere" in Herbert's poem. Part of this poem is a lament for the loss of the availability of Anglican worship and a demand that the "eternal Dove" (l. 7) respond to make up what is now lost:

> Somthing I had, which long ago
> Did learn to suck, and sip, and taste,
> But now grown sickly, sad and slow,
> Doth fret and wrangle, pine and waste.
>
> O spred thy sacred wings and shake
> One living drop! One drop life keeps!
> If pious griefs Heavens joys awake,
> O fill his bottle! thy childe weeps!
>
> (Ll. 9–16)

At the same time, however, the effects of such divine assistance can function as incentive—"Let glory be their bait"—and the poem ends on a note of encouraging hidden Anglicans to keep faith with the life that leads to glory:

> Then bless thy secret growth, nor catch
> At noise, but thrive unseen and dumb;
> Keep clean, bear fruit, earn life and watch
> Till the white winged Reapers come!
>
> (Ll. 45–48)

Again, the injunction to "watch" which is so much a motif of *Silex I* appears, but here it is part of a larger context in which the experience of watching for the return of the master is defined as a positive, growing experience rather than that which gives meaning to what is otherwise darkness. The by now ancient Cranmerian injunction to reveal one's "true and lively faith" through the fruit of good works becomes an acceptance of Herbert's speaker's willingness for God to "take thy way; for sure they were his best" (l. 20).

In "Trinity-Sunday" the speaker asserts that his ability to use language typologically can, through divine aid, now take the place of the former sacramental activity of the church. In a redoing of Herbert's "Trinitie Sunday," Vaughan borrows the same device of having three stanzas of three lines, each line in each stanza rhyming with the other lines in that stanza; here, however, the speaker asks,

> O holy, blessed, glorious thee,
> Eternall witnesses that be
> In heaven, One God in trinitie!
>
> As here on earth (when men with-stood,)
> The Spirit, Water, and the Blood,
> Made my Lords Incarnation good:
>
> So let the *Anty-types* in me
> Elected, bought, and seal'd for free,
> Be own'd, sav'd, *Sainted* by you three!
>
> (Ll. 1–9)

That time "when men with-stood" and sacraments of water and blood conveyed the Spirit is not now. Through "the *Anty-types* in me," however, the speaker asserts that he can still ask to be "own'd, sav'd, *Sainted*"; the kind of language that distinguishes *Silex II* thus serves as a sign that God is now active in human history and is thus still available to hear such an appeal. God was never limited to the Sacraments as vehicles of his grace; as a result, the speaker can now ask for divine aid, even though those more ordinary conveyances are absent and the language of "*Anty-types*" must suffice.

A different twist on that sense of divine activity occupies the speaker of "The Jews," a poem which offers hope that God will not forever neglect his original chosen people, but will eventually "thaw . . . that long frost which now benums / Your hearts" with "the fair year / Of your deliverer" (ll. 1–4). Still another redoing of a poem by Herbert, "The Jews" finds its speaker no longer expecting Christ's return to confront "the Church." Instead, to Vaughan's speaker, his present situation—"Our fulness too is now come in" (l. 27)—parallels that of the Jews in exile, and he hopes that he "Might live, and see the Olive bear / Her proper branches" (ll. 15–16), the renewal of God's promises to the Old Israel made in Isaiah 65:17–25. If this parallel holds, however, the promise of divine compassion that will eventually "From your dark hearts this veil remove" (l. 37) also holds hope that the speaker's own situation will be put right at the same time.[41] I think it not too much to see in Vaughan's reference to the way a "righteous Father" deals with "Brutish men" (ll. 46–47), a play on "Brutus' men," a way of promising that the sufferings of Brutus' English descendants will also be relieved.

In other poems in *Silex II* the hopeful and expectant tone is achieved by distancing the lament posture of many poems in *Silex I,* going beyond that stance to articulate the anticipation of its promised result. The speaker in "Palm-Sunday" thus asserts that though he "lose all, and must endure / The proverb'd griefs of holy *Job*, / I care not, so I may secure / But one *green Branch* and a *white robe*" (ll. 43–46). This poem thus asks what the Collect for Palm Sunday asks, "that we may both "follow the example of [Christ's] patience," and also "be made partakers of his resurrection" (BCP, p. 118), through its reference to the "proverb'd" patience of Job and to "Thy bright solemnities [which] did shew, / The third glad day through two sad nights" (ll. 33–34). The speaker in the two poems entitled "Jesus Weeping" finds the lament posture in the example of Jesus' weeping over Jerusalem in Luke 19 and his weeping over the dead Lazarus in John 11; this posture brings the assertion that "the starv'd earth groans for one tear" (I, l. 16) and that if the speaker joins his own grief with Christ's, "A grief so bright / 'Twill make the Land of darkness light; / And while too many sadly roam, / Shall send me (*Swan-like*) singing home" (II, ll. 50–53). Such distancing of the lament from the stance of the speaker and the finding of it joined with Christ's own response to the sufferings of this world enable the speaker to assert in "Providence" that "thou hast made thy Arm my fold" (l. 48) (echoing the Magnificat's claim that God has "showed strength in his arm") and in "The Knot" that the role of Mary makes possible the assertion that "We are his body grown / . . . a Knot . . . / Which us in him, and him in us / United keeps for ever" (ll. 10–16). In these terms, therefore, Vaughan has found a way to make the fundamental Anglican claim that through the Eucharist "we [are] in him, and he in us," in spite of the absence of that Eucharist.

Vaughan's tribute to "Saint Mary Magdalen" juxtaposes her with those Puritans who, though they "Saint themselves, they are no *Saints*" (l. 72). Indeed, the speaker of "Saint Mary Magdalen" describes her in terms that summarize the strategies of *Silex I* and comments on her in terms that summarize the strategies of *Silex II*. Herbert's poem on Mary Magdalene focuses on the episode in which she "wip'd her Saviours feet" (l. 1); Vaughan, like Crashaw in "The Weeper," shifts the focus of his speaker's narrative to depict her persistent weeping in spite of her transfiguration into a saint. Her weeping thus becomes "her Art of love," in response to Christ's "interceding, meek and calm / Blood" (ll. 39–40, 49). Her tears of contrition and joy at the Passion thus subsume the lament posture of *Silex I*, with her "Art" giving biblical precedent for Vaughan's art. Yet the speaker goes on to claim that her "pensive, weeping eyes . . . / now are fixed stars, whose light / Helps such dark straglers to their sight" (ll. 57–60), recapitulating the light and fire that function in *Silex II* as "prelibations" of the eschatological banquet to come. Vaughan's speaker's claim about the Magdalene thus functions to point out the reward for lament as well as lament as the way to that reward:

> Learn, *Ladies,* here the faithful cure
> Makes beauty lasting, fresh, and pure;

Learn *Marys* art of tears, and then
Say, *You have got the day from men.*

(Ll. 45–48)

Thus the private devotion forced upon Anglicans by the abolition of their
normative public worship achieves a kind of approval here, because through
analogy with the weeping of the Magdalene it actually becomes public. To be
able to use biblical figures to articulate present experience again functions to
inform the present in a traditional way and to place it in a narrative with the
past event the end of which posits for both events a common future. Such an
ability thus becomes compensation enough for the loss of Anglican public
worship to allow for the celebratory tone of the speaker. If we must put up
with this situation, Vaughan seems to argue, we might as well use all the
resources we have at our disposal to make the best of things.

In general, therefore, Vaughan's tone in *Silex II* is radically more confident
and joyously expectant than it was in *Silex I*. This tone, itself part of Vaughan's
rhetoric of persuasion to keep the faith, is achieved by asserting that old signs
still reveal the faithfulness of God in his promises, as in "The Rain-bow," in
which the ancient sign reveals "my God doth keep / His promise still, but we
break ours and sleep" (ll. 19–20). The lament of *Silex I* is evoked in the way
"Fair and yong light!" is transformed into a "holy Grief"; "How am I now in
love," the speaker claims, "with all / That I term'd then meer bonds and thrall,
/ And to thy name, which still I keep, / Like the surviving turtle, weep!" (ll. 7–
10). Yet such a change in tone functions as a divine answer to the lament of *Silex
I*, a renewal of the promise that God will ultimately respond to the one who is
faithful in his lament. What was then a sense of divine absence is now seen as a
failure of interpretation; in "The dwelling-place," where God was when he was
experienced as "shrowded" by the speaker, "I do not know / What lodgd thee
then, nor where, nor how" (ll. 11–12). But that does not matter anymore: "I
am sure, thou dost now come / Oft to a narrow, homely room, / Where thou too
hast but the least part, / My God, I mean *my sinful heart*" (ll. 13–16). In "The
Men of War," the speaker interprets Luke 23:11 to mean that "Thy Saints are
not the Conquerers," another rejection of Puritan claims; what conquered
Anglicans must do is be "patient, meek, and overcome / Like thee" (ll. 9–10).
Such a stance leads to a prayer that Jesus "give me patience here, / And faith to
see my Crown as near / And almost reach'd" (ll. 37–39). The sufferings of
isolated and outlawed Anglicans themselves become the signs of hope that their
"Crown" is "near." Vaughan's ability to make faithful affirmations in *Silex II*
now becomes proof that the faithfulness sought in *Silex I* is efficacious in
surviving the interim time between Anglican abolition and restoration.

In "The Night" another reversal takes place; the darkness in which the
speaker had to struggle to find hope in *Silex I* becomes "A deep, but dazling

darkness . . . / in God" (ll. 49–50) which the speaker can pray for: "O for that night! where I in him / Might live invisible and dim" (ll. 53–54).[42] Pain is not absent from *Silex II;* in "Anguish" the speaker links writing poetry with true lament:

> O! 'tis an easie thing
> To write and sing;
> But to write true, unfeigned verse
> Is very hard! O God disperse
> These weights, and give my spirit leave
> To act as well as to conceive!
> O my God, hear my cry;
> Or let me dye!
>
> (Ll. 13–20)

Yet by this point the reader is aware of the paradox implicit in such a conclusion; for God to let the speaker die is also a way of hearing his cry, for death will put him unequivocally in God's presence. In the midst of this poem on poetry we need also to note that the syntax of *Silex II* lacks the convolutions of *Silex I,* in Vaughan's terms yet another way of pointing up the contrast between concern for divine absence in the former group, with the interpretive difficulties that brings, and the faith in the divine presence now and to come which promotes clarity of articulation in *Silex II.*

Vaughan's final treatment of the figure or role of Jacob in *Silex Scintillans* reinforces this point. In "Jacobs Pillow, and Pillar," the regress of Anglican experience from the public, communal, and "Catholick or Universal" to "the meek heart" where "The first true worship of the worlds great King / . . . did spring" and where now "the milde Dove doth dwell / When the proud waters rage" is accepted but lamented (ll. 11–12, 15, 28–29). It may be told in terms of Jacob's experience, since "thy sad distress / Was just the same with ours" (ll. 41–42). Such a retreat is not to the essence of anything, but necessitated, as in Jacob's case, by "a brother, and blood-thirsty too" whom it was necessary to "flye" into "solitude and grief" and "cold relief" on stones (ll. 43–46). We thus meet *"Jacobs Bed"* once more ("Regeneration," l. 28), but now we are sure, according to this speaker, that we know where we are and whose role we are playing and its function in the narrative of the salvation history. In fact, we are better off than Jacob, since he only had a "Day-star" from which he stood "a long way"; we have "a healing Sun by day and night," who is the "substance" for which Jacob's pillow was "but type and shade at best" (ll. 47, 49–54). Thus the language of typological depiction can function confidently once more, bringing true "rest" on the journey for "we" who form a community in exile yet who understand ourselves as a wayfaring people.

This new sense of textual and interpretive clarity is made explicit in "The Agreement," in its contrast between a former state in which the speaker's own writing was obscured so that "I read it sadly oft, but still / Simply believ'd, 'twas not my Quill" (ll. 5–6) and the present state in which "lifes kinde Angel came . . . / Scatt'ring that cloud" (ll. 7–9). If the book obscured is in some sense *Silex I,* and it might be since the speaker says that its subject was "my mid-day / Exterminating fears and night" (ll. 13–14), then *Silex II* is the record of the result of the angelic visit, in which he was pointed "to a place / Which all the year sees the Suns face" (ll. 11–12).

"The Agreement" ends with a prayer and an affirmation of faith that God will continue to act, both in regard to the speaker and to his book:

> Wherefore with tears (tears by thee sent)
> I beg, my faith may never fail!
>
> . . . .
>
> So thou who didst the work begin
>
> . . . .
>
> Wilt finish it, and by no sin
> Will thy free mercies hindred be.
>
> (Ll. 61–70)

This marks as good a place as any to begin to end my account of Vaughan and of the tradition of didactic Anglican poetry he participated in. For the point here is that he cannot end his book; only God can do that. (Having other goals than Vaughan, I hope to be in more control of *this* book's ending.) In bringing the Anglican calendar into *Silex II,* Vaughan resumes the progress to Easter and beyond he halted at the end of *Silex I* by including the Ascension, Whitsunday, and Trinity Sunday poems. With "Palm-Sunday" he heralds the beginning of allusion to a new Holy Week, but he gives us no Easter poems. *Silex II* ends, in effect, in anticipation of the final Easter, its instigation to faithfulness residing in its claim to lead to that Easter.

The last poems in *Silex II* Vaughan wants us to believe were written while he feared he was near death—one sure way, in Vaughan's terms, to get to that final Easter. His emphasis here is on "False life" as both "foul deception" and also "*A quickness, which my God hath kist*" ("Quickness," ll. 1, 3, 20). It is also on "that glad place / Where cloudless Quires sing without tears, / Sing thy just praise, and see thy face" ("The Wreath," ll. 17–19). What Vaughan has achieved in *Silex II* is a poetic strategy in which a renewed sense of divine activity is claimed through a mix of syntactical clarity, renewed typological relationships, and the speaker's own (claimed) awareness that God is at work in his experience of the absence of Anglican community. Coming after *Silex I,* it serves as a response to the struggles of that volume yet one which still functions within the ongoing allusion to Anglican Prayer Book experience, since the beginning "Ascension-day" poem resumes the allusion to the Prayer Book calendar begun in *Silex I*. Vaughan, in these poems, casts the present in eschatological terms, enacting an articulation of the present lived in light of future promise. His discoveries are of the dimensions and complexities of that life (its terms of existence), describing how one can live by the Word without the ongoing mediation of that Word through liturgical enactment. This means that one's search must be for the Word outside that enactment, for signs of its presence confirming future promise, and in light of appeal for its coming soon. In terms of language, the emphasis is on keeping language open so that the Word can be experienced, known, and recognized when it acts, when it breaks in. There must be a silencing, a breaking down of the clamor of human voices, a keeping open of human categories of knowing if the Word is to be heard when it comes, for "Thy . . . *Effects* no tongue can tell" ("To the Holy Bible," l. 35). As a result, the witness to his aloneness by Vaughan's speaker finally becomes yet one more manifestation of God's saving acts in history to bring about the fulfillment of his promises. Vaughan's echoes of the Prayer Book and its use, although to something lost, finally reassure because they do not anticipate merely the restoration of that use but the fulfillment of the promises implicit in that use. The reader's experience of *Silex II* thus comes as an affirmative answer to the issues raised and struggled with in *Silex I* and a further encouragement to keep faith with the community now broken and dispersed.

As a result, it is appropriate that the final shaping of poetic experience in *Silex Scintillans* comes once more in terms of an allusion to Herbert. At the end of "To the Holy Bible," Vaughan repeats the opening words of the *Gloria in excelsis*, as Herbert does at the end of "The Church." He follows this with a poem called "L'Envoy," as Herbert does at the end of "The Church Militant." He then replicates Herbert's trinitarian close, although he gives it in Greek, by way of Saint Basil's *Liber de Spiritu Sancto*.[43] As Herbert's self-appointed successor to the role of poet/priest, Vaughan ends by again aligning his work with the work Herbert undertook, the moving of God's people through his empowering action toward participation in the fulfillment of God's promises:

> Dear Lord . . . let grace
> Descend, and hallow all the place.
> Incline each hard heart to do good,
> And cement us with thy sons blood,
> That like true sheep, all in one fold
> We may be fed, and one minde hold.
>
> . . . .
>
> So shall we know in war and peace
> Thy service to be our sole ease,

> With prostrate souls adoring thee,
> Who turn'd our sad captivity!
>
> (Ll. 43–48, 59–62)

There is more than a glance here at Puck's speech at the end of *A Midsummer Night's Dream* blessing and hallowing the lovers in their beds, and at the ending of Spenser's *Epithalamion,* with its linking of the wedding night with the communion of saints. Now, however, the blessing desired is bestowed in that place to come, when the church as community is to be recreated, so "like true sheep, all in one fold, / We may be fed" (ll. 47–48). In some ways we must find Vaughan demonstrating the strength of the Anglican poetic tradition in his ability to find in wedding hymns an appropriate way to conclude a poem about a search for a spouse who is yet to be found.

And yet there is a difference which is marked by the fact that when Vaughan here quotes the *Gloria in excelsis* he does not quote the Prayer Book version but the King James version of Luke 2:14, which differs slightly but significantly from the line at the beginning of the Gloria in the Prayer Book.[44] "Our sad captivity" had exacted a price; when use of the Prayer Book was restored in 1662, it would not immediately become again the normative source of Christian identity, "the means of grace and the hope of glory." In noting that subtle shift in Vaughan's allusion and by taking a closer look at one of the last poems in *Silex II,* we can begin to see the cost of that absence. Vaughan's final interpretation of the events of the 1640s and 1650s is that in them God is acting to bring about not a restoration of the pre–Civil War Anglican church but the future fulfillment of his promises made in the past to that church. In those terms, the sufferings and deprivations of Anglicans in that time have meaning in biblical terms as the way of the cross they must walk in faithfulness to the God of those promises if they are to further their fulfillment and become citizens in the coming kingdom. In light of the significance this proclamation gives to the situation of Anglicans in the Commonwealth period, Vaughan can find available the celebratory language of confident expectation he employs in *Silex II.* As a result, although the language familiar to Herbert about the church he knew is still available to Vaughan, it is now used to create images of the final end of things rather than to lament what is lost or to further the restoration of what is lost.

Vaughan's "The Feast" is a poetic celebration of the Eucharist, but one that stresses its importance more in anticipation of being part of it than in actually being a part of it. It thus stresses more the Eucharist's eschatological dimensions than its this-worldly participation or community-building or identity-giving functions. In contrast to Herbert's "Love (III)," in which the speaker is called to the table to be served even though he feels unworthy, Vaughan's speaker calls the feast to come to him because he is now ready for it: "O come away, / Make no delay, / Come while my heart is clean & steddy" (ll. 1–3).

The Eucharist in this world is defined in transitory terms ("No bliss here lent / Is permanent, / Such triumphs poor flesh cannot merit; / Short sips and sights / Endear delights, / Who seeks for more, he would inherit" [ll. 7–12]), although the reception is defined here in classic Anglican terms as a conveyance of "all benefits of his passion":

> O drink and bread
> Which strikes death dead,
>   The food of mans immortal being!
> Under veyls here
> Thou art my chear,
>   Present and sure without my seeing.
>   (Ll. 37–42)

Vaughan's images of the Eucharist derive from their situational context, as a culmination of a book-long search for a persuasive language and poetic of endurance, becoming now a preparation for fulfillment rather than restoration, in a situation in which that central Anglican act was absent, "without my seeing." What Vaughan gives us is an affirmation of his speaker's readiness for the Eucharist as well as of the importance of the Eucharist even when it was not actually available to him. At this point in *Silex II* he anticipates the resumption of eucharistic reception in the terms used in the Prayer Book, since all its language of the bread and wine as conveyance is displayed. In anticipation of such an event, "My soul and all, / Kneel down and fall / And sing his sad victorious story" (ll. 58–60); the poem is one of preparation for one who, in Vaughan's terms, must see his life of isolation from the eucharistic community as, finally, a preparation for fulfillment of that life. Yet when he wrote this Vaughan could not be sure that such would ever happen here; he had faith only that it would happen eventually, at the last.

> Some toil and sow,
> That wealth may flow,
>   And dress this earth for next years meat:
> But let me heed,
> Why thou didst bleed,
>   And what in the next world to eat.
>   (Ll. 73–78)

Indeed, the invitation to the Eucharist to come, to "Spring up, O wine, / And springing shine / With some glad message from his heart" (ll. 25–27) in response to "the spilt dew, [which] / Like tears doth shew / The sad world wept to be releast" (ll. 22–24) suggests that the coming of the Eucharist once more is still far off, although it is richly anticipated.

In its context this poem gives voice to the situation of the isolated Anglican, the situation Vaughan has been addressing throughout *Silex Scintillans,* to help him define his experience as part of preparation for eucharistic reception and thus to redeem that time by defining it in ways that make it part of Anglican worship, echoing as it does at some points the exhortations to preparation for the Eucharist that Cranmer made part of the Prayer Book. Yet in contrast to Herbert's poem it speaks to a situation in which the only sure place of such experience is in the world to come, hence Vaughan's concluding quotation from Revelation 19:9: "Blessed are they, which are called unto the marriage Supper of the Lamb!" Preparation thus makes one an invited guest at the eschatological banquet, whether or not use of the Prayer Book was ever resumed short of that final celebration. The speaker has prepared; he is ready, and one sign of his readiness is the call for that banquet to come. Thus, the function of this poem in *Silex Scintillans* is part of Vaughan's strategy toward the close of the work to celebrate the anticipated fulfillment of God's promises and encourage the faithfulness of his intended audience in spite of whether or not Prayer Book worship was ever restored this side of the establishing of the kingdom of God.

Yet the poem also lends itself to a reading in terms of which the only important Eucharist is the one at the last and for which individual preparation is what is demanded. In Herbert's "Love (III)" Love itself makes the speaker ready who would otherwise never be ready; in its context, this poem furthers the intention of the Anglican Reformers from Cranmer forward to make the Eucharist the normative Christian activity. Vaughan's poem, in its historical context, makes sense as an argument for the importance of the Eucharist to the orientation of Christian living when regular reception was impossible and is thus not out of keeping with Herbert's position. Yet one of the ultimate costs of the Commonwealth period for Anglicans was the loss of any impetus to make the Eucharist the center of Anglican worship in universal fact as well as theory. The struggle to realize more and more frequent communions, started by Cranmer and continued through the period of Laud, was, after the Restoration and until the nineteenth century, effectively abandoned.[45] The path to such a loss is down the road opened by Vaughan's poem, for in its terms the only one who can come to the Eucharist is the one who is "clean & steddy," echoing the medieval emphasis on extensive sacramental preparation for Mass that resulted in a single annual reception as normative. The confidence of such a speaker, intelligible in the context of the progress of *Silex Scintillans,* ironically served as a barrier to frequent receptions when that context was removed. For Herbert, only "groaning" to be holy, pure, and clear made one eligible to enter *The Temple* or the church; Vaughan's claim to be beyond such an aspiring interpretation of self would ultimately create images of a Christian elite in relation to the Eucharist. As the preserve of those willing to make such a claim, the Eucharist would again seem distant from the lives of ordinary Englishfolk. Vaughan's final achievement in creating a way to continue in relationship with Anglican community in its absence was thus to create the possibility of a Christian life construed primarily apart from the creative acts of that community even when they were recovered.

Epilogue: Toward a Poetics of Restoration

That absence of Anglican religious life which Vaughan lamented in his religious poetry came to an end when the restoration of the Stuart monarchy in 1660 led to the Act of Uniformity of 1662 and the adoption of a new Prayer Book, albeit one changed only in minor ways from the Prayer Books of 1559 and 1604. Nevertheless, the intervening years had wrought a fundamental change in the religious climate in England which profoundly affected the ways in which the old texts would be used and understood in the new situation. At the outset of this study I noted that the understanding of religion manifested in Samuel Johnson's discussion of religious literature, with its dichotomy between didactic works which defend doctrine and lyric works which describe experiences of personal piety, is not one which would have been recognized by pre–Civil War Anglicans. Johnson's assumptions are, however, strongly indicative of the understanding of Christian life that developed in Restoration and eighteenth-century England. My task in this epilogue is to bring my account of religious literature in the English Renaissance to a close with a brief description of that new religious situation and its implications for religious literature in the last four decades of the seventeenth century.

I want to do so with special attention to the writings of Thomas Traherne and John Dryden, each of whose work in this period suggests in different ways the fate of the complex of religious assumptions and the didactic literature written to further those assumptions which have been the subject of this study. The English Reformers understood church and society as coterminous; they sought reformation of that society through its involvement in the Eucharist at which people were enabled by instruction and reception of "spiritual food" to promote the reign of charity. Their goal being the support of this transforming work, the writers of the Reformation risked much to bring about change. After the Restoration, however, the cost of recovering and maintaining an official Anglican church was paid through a new posture of caution, creating an institution whose primary social function was conservation of the political order necessary to its continued existence. Fully aware that their church was still vulnerable, that its continued existence was no longer a foregone conclusion, Anglican writers made fewer demands on their audiences. With the political and social arena no longer available as a context in which religious language could seek transformation and with England still divided between fundamentally different images of the conduct of religious life, personal and interior human experience became increasingly the realm in which the language of religion was seen to have its meaning, since individual change did not of necessity demand societal changes.

The continuing influence of the Middle Ages is apparent here, even in a society increasingly "protestant" in a superficial sense. There is little difference, finally, between mass-priest and preaching divine when both function as public repositories of authority and behavior for the people who look to them to define and exemplify the "holy" or "Christian" life so that no one else has to be very concerned about it. In this distribution of authority in a society, the role of layfolk is reduced either to private repetition of the rosary or to externally disciplined lives of personal rectitude. In both cases, clergy perform and layfolk watch; in both cases, no one moves beyond a very immature social structure of a small dominant group surrounded by a large passive and dependent one.

The medieval church tolerated the reluctance of layfolk to participate, except privately and vicariously, in the Mass by requiring communion but once a year; it may have, in fact, discouraged participation by requiring extensive preparation through the Sacrament of penance before reception. Even though Cranmer had brought the penitential rite within the Eucharist, the post-Restoration Church of England did little better by finally acquiescing to quarterly receptions, a poor substitute for Cranmer's desired weekly communion of all Englishfolk. The Christian life as private journey, characteristic of much medieval piety, flourished in the later seventeenth century and the eighteenth, supported as it was by the interpretations of Calvinism which made subjective signs of inner stirrings and outward signs of personal success proof of individual election. Milton, from a different kind of disappointment, spoke for many Englishfolk of whatever tradition when he staked his justification of God's ways on the possibility of "a paradise within thee, happier far" (*Paradise Lost*, XII.876).

This process of reemphasizing the individual as the locus of divine action and the context for meaning in religious language was of course furthered by the development of science's seeming ability to provide more reliable knowledge about the world than that previously derived from biblical and traditional sources. In the Middle Ages, Christianity attacked the ability of animist religion to explain the world and make it dependable; it did so by elevating Scripture and tradition to the authoritative level of external absolutes as arbitrated through the agency of the papacy. In the Reformation period those who rejected papal authority over the acceptable definition of Christianity were able to use the accepted authority of Scripture as a basis from which to attack tradition, including the tradition of papal authority; such an understanding of the nature of scriptural authority and the areas in which such authority held sway served the church poorly, however, when science was able to demonstrate knowledge on the basis of a source of authority independent of Scripture. The church's initial, and defensive, reaction was to see the basis of its authority challenged by such developments and to accelerate its retreat from the public arena into the realm of individual spirituality where its authority could not be questioned. A basis for resolving these issues was not available until the historic study of Scripture and the cultures which produced it, began in the sixteenth century but not really developed until the nineteenth,[1] enabled biblical claims about human life to be distinguished from the cosmology in which they were originally articulated.

In the late seventeenth century, however, these developments meant that the cultural situation of the Middle Ages was recreated, so that human life began to be understood once more in terms of separate realms of sacred and secular concerns. In the same way, the liturgical life of the Prayer Book lost its centrality and became increasingly an adjunct to the private devotional life of believers. Bifurcation between sacred and secular, public and private, liturgical and pietistic thus became increasingly the context in which religious language and the use of texts like the Bible and the Prayer Book came to be understood. Such is the situation Johnson assumes and describes; each in his own way, Traherne and Dryden point us in that direction.

Thomas Traherne and the Poetics of Recovery

Traherne was born in the fall of 1637; he was thus eight years old when use of the Prayer Book was banned in 1645.[2] Although he is conventionally linked with Herbert and Vaughan, this association obscures the fact that he was actually a younger contemporary of John Dryden who sought Anglican orders after the Restoration and wrote all his surviving works after that date.[3] Even though Traherne is in some sense the heir to the didactic methodologies of his predecessors and, as a priest, was one of those to whom fell the task of resuming the corporate worship of Anglicanism, his education for ministry was conducted at Oxford during the period of the Commonwealth and the full experience of Anglican worship was for him an adult discovery. In this light Traherne is the poet of restoration, the celebrator of what had finally been restored, what was again possible, what there was to applaud in the return of king and Prayer Book and the church of that king and Prayer Book. Vaughan lamented the "reverend and sacred buildings (however now vilified and shut up)"; Traherne could celebrate, after his ordination as an Anglican priest in 1661, "Those stately Structures . . . / fill'd with Christian Family!" ("Churches I," ll. 1, 5) and so Traherne can find once more in the Word delivered in the context of that gathered community formed through the use of the Prayer Book the actions of God in his time. After reciting, in his "Thanksgivings for the Wisdom of his WORD," the narrative of God's saving acts, Traherne asserts,

> All these hath my God given me with ten thousand times greater
> Profit and Advantage than if he had given them to me alone.
>> Multitudes of Publishers,
>> Nations of Admirers,
>> Ages of Adorers,
>>> Increase my Joys.
>
> Had they come in me in a ⎧ Hidden, ⎫ Way
>   ⎨ Private, ⎬
>   ⎩ Narrow ⎭
> I might fear some Dream,
>> Or worse Illusion.
>
> . . . .
>
> But now I see him in all Kingdoms Glorifying his Name,
>   shewing his Goodness to many Thousands,
>   ⎧ Me
>   Making ⎨
>   ⎩ Every one besides
>   The Heir of it all.
> I know him to be God.
>
> . . . .
>
> And see his Oracles exaulted on the Desks
>> In many Temples,
>> Countenanced by Kings,
>> Ratified by Parliaments,
> Joyfully Sounded from many thousand Pulpits.

(Ll. 343–373)

Traherne's use in these *Thanksgivings* of extensive quotations from the Bible along with echoes of the language, rhythms, and cadences of Prayer Book texts makes of these pieces a joy-filled celebration of and thanksgiving for the renewal of Prayer Book worship. They are in fact modeled on the way the celebratory Psalms and the Psalms of divine praise had become once more the language of public worship through Prayer Book use.

In addition, Traherne's *Centuries* and his *Poems* seek to function didactically. Answering Herbert's question, "Is there in truth no beautie" from "Jordan (I)," Traherne asserts the incarnation of Christ in the gathered Body of the Church: "The naked Truth in many faces shewn . . . / a Strain / That lowly creeps, yet maketh Mountains plain, / Brings down the highest Mysteries to sense / And keeps them there" ("The Author to the Critical Peruser," ll. 1, 3–6). In these terms he defines his task in what follows: "Our Excellence: / At that we aim; to th'end thy Soul might see / With open Eys thy Great *Felicity,* / Its Objects view, and trace the glorious Way / Wherby thou may'st thy Highest Bliss enjoy" (ll. 6–10). And in the opening verse of the first *Century,* he defines a didactic intent for what is to follow:

> This book unto the friend of my best friend
> As of the Wisest Love a Mark I send
> That she may write my Makers prais therin
> And make her self therby a Cherubin.
>
> (P. 2)

We know that Traherne wrote these prose *Centuries,* and perhaps his poetry as well, for Susanna Hopton, a noblewoman who became the center of a small community devoted to enriching its understanding of Prayer Book worship.[4] We also know that, in the words of an early biographer, Traherne became as devoted as Herbert to the daily discipline of the Prayer Book Offices:

> [Traherne] became much in love with the beautiful order and Primitive *Devotions* of this our excellent Church. Insomuch that I believe, he never failed any one day either publickly or in his private Closet, to make use of her publick Offices, as one part of his devotion.[5]

It is thus in the context once more of the ongoing "publick" worship life of the Anglican church that we should read the *Centuries* and the *Poems* and see them as homiletic of involvement in that life as the way toward "Highest Bliss." As in the case of writers we have examined heretofore, Traherne defines his use of language in functional or incarnational terms, to bring "down the highest Mysteries to sense . . . to th'end thy Soul might see . . . and . . . thy Highest Bliss enjoy." We are thus not to expect in Traherne's works to find descriptions of reality, even the reality of his experiences, but for experiences with words that seek to move the reader toward the ends viewed desirable by the writer. As he notes in *The First Century,* "I will . . . advance you to Glory . . . by the Gentle Ways of Peace and Lov," moving the reader toward "The fellowship of the Mystery . . . the End, for which we are Redeemed: A Communion with Him in all His Glory" (p. 4). And his *Centuries* end unfinished, leaving both blank space and ninety sections of *The Fifth Century* for his reader to "write my Makers prais therin," to take up the process initiated in the first four and continue it both in terms of writing religious prose and "writing" the process of growth in the Christian life.

Indeed, the methodology of Traherne's use of language is, again, to disrupt conventional interpretations so as to open the reader to new ways of seeing and understanding his experience. Traherne's word for this is "felicity"; it is what "you love, but know not" which refutes the claims of human logic that "there is no Lov of a thing unknown" (p. 3). Traherne's images of felicity have baffled many; in the context of a society recovering use of the Prayer Book's proclamation about infant baptism, one function of his depiction of felicity is to encourage his reader to take that proclamation seriously:

> We yield thee hearty thanks, most merciful Father, that it hath pleased thee to regenerate this Infant with thy Holy Spirit, to receive him for thine own Child by adoption, and to incorporate him into thy holy Church. And humbly we beseech thee to grant that he being dead unto sin, and living unto righteousness, and being buried with Christ in his death, may crucify the old man, and utterly abolish the whole body of sin; that, as he is made partaker of the death of thy Son, he may also be partaker of his resurrection. (BCP, p. 275)

Such radical claims for infant baptism—the child without self-knowledge is by water and Spirit made "partaker of his resurrection"—are articulated by Traherne through his exploration of all the ways "felicity" can mean for his speaker.

Traherne's pattern for the development of a sense of felicity also recapitulates his experience of the Anglican church in his lifetime, since it was available to him as the church in England when he was born, then forced into exile when he was a child, and finally restored when he was in his early twenties. From Traherne's perspective this restoration is the new act of God which opens the world to all the possibilities Traherne celebrates and gives thanks for and teaches how to partake in:

> But now we Churches have
> In ev'ry Coast, which Bounty gave
> Most freely to us; now they sprinkled stand
> With so much Care and Love,
> In this rich Vale, nigh yonder Grove
> That we might com in ev'ry Land
> To them with greater Eas
>
> . . . .
>
> Ungrateful We with slower hast do com
> Unto his Temple, 'cause 'tis nearer home.
> ("Churches II," ll. 33–48)

Traherne can now celebrate the renewed possibility of urging his readers, with Herbert, to "Pray with the most: for where most pray, is heaven" ("Perirrhanterium," l. 402). The temple that existed for Vaughan only in Herbert's text is now available again as an ongoing activity to which Traherne's text can point.

Nevertheless, Traherne was a man of the Restoration and not of Herbert's Church of England; although he does presuppose participation in the ongoing worship of Anglicanism as the context for growth in the Christian life he seeks to teach in his writings, his poems and his *Centuries* do not exhibit the allusory references to use of the Prayer Book we found in Herbert and also, albeit in a different way, in Vaughan. Traherne has only one poem for a feast day on the Anglican calendar ("On Christmas Day"), perhaps noting it especially because it was now possible to celebrate Christmas once more. "Bells" call "many Families to sing / His publick Praises, and rejoice" (ll. 3–4), but the attention Herbert devotes to aspects of church architecture and furnishings is absent here. And although Traherne writes a few poems with the same titles as Herbert's (notably "Nature," "The World," "The Odour," and "Love"), *The Temple* does not function for Traherne as an allusory frame as it did for Vaughan.6

There is a sense in which Herbert's church was receding in time, the new situation of the Church of England functioning as such a surprise that the old situation seemed more remote. In Walton's writings, Herbert, Hooker, and Donne achieved the status of ideal types, a burden for younger clergy like Traherne who were asked to live up to their images. In such a situation, Herbert's *Temple* seemed unneeded, since the real temples of God were "nearer home," open, and available for use once more.

Traherne did explore in writing the Anglican church year, but he did it in a separate work, *The Churchs Year Book,* which contains prayers, meditations, and poems on the various feasts, Sundays, and seasons from Easter to All Saints' Day. In this division between his poems homiletic of the Christian life and his writings on the church year, Traherne in fact inscribes the growing sense of a division between the public life of the church and the private lives of its members. Since Traherne could not have begun to use the Prayer Book in public worship until only a few years before writing these poems he was perhaps not yet sufficiently familiar with it to create the subtle interweaving of Bible, Prayer Book, and poem we have found in Spenser, Herbert, and Vaughan. Also, he had for fifteen years sought to live a Christian life without the daily public use of the Prayer Book; he could not resume that practice without reflecting the habits of the intervening years in some discernable ways in his text. Restoration after absence retains the signs of absence in restored practice through changes in assumptions about practice; no matter how much missed and longed for, the use of the Prayer Book when restored could not be the same as it was when absence had not been experienced.

In that and in the fate of Traherne's work lie signs of the new religious situation in England. Although Traherne reflects many of the same homiletic strategies we have learned to expect from our examination of the pre-Restoration poets, his work was addressed to a small community within the larger church and not to the church as a whole. After his death it disappeared almost completely, not to be published until the twentieth century. One sign of the way we have learned to read religious writing from Samuel Johnson is that *The Churchs Year Book* remains unpublished even at this writing. In a fundamental way, the religious climate of the late 1600s and 1700s was not congenial to religious writing that grounded itself in the ongoing worship of the Christian community, centered in the enactment of sacred narrative through Bible reading and sacramental participation. In Traherne's own work the bifurcation between the liturgical and the pietistic suggests that, however deeply he valued use of the Prayer Book and assumed it as the context for the functioning of his didactic writing, he had begun to conceive of growth in personal religious experience apart from the social emphasis of the Prayer Book itself. In this context, use of the Prayer Book becomes an enricher and enabler of that experience rather than the other way around. Traherne's concern for the cultivation of religious feeling locates him as a way station toward the emphasis on describing personal religious experience in poetry which Johnson was to claim as its only proper function.[7]

John Dryden and the Reasonableness of Religion

John Dryden was born in August of 1631; he was thus in his fourteenth year when use of the Prayer Book was banned. His ability to write poems in praise of Cromwell (*Heroique Stanza's,* 1659), in defense of Anglicanism (*Religio Laici,* 1682), and in defense of Roman Catholicism (*The Hind and the Panther,* 1687) suggests that Dryden was a man whose views on religion developed over time. Yet even if we discount charges of political opportunism in Dryden's religious progress,[8] what must remain clear is that Dryden reflects a new religious situation in which different Christian traditions represent -*isms,* definable institutions among which personal, individual choices can be made, whatever the grounds of those choices. Anglicanism's days of aspiring to be the sole expression of Christianity in England were over; it now could be evaluated in terms of its functioning in society in relationship to other traditions as to how well it met personal or social needs not necessarily related to its traditional sense of its own mission. Dryden's stance in *Religio Laici* is what concerns me here, although similar questions could be addressed to his other poems on religion. I want to suggest that in his defense of Anglicanism Dryden shifts the terms of discussion from discovery of self within a context of liturgical participation to an analysis of Anglicanism from the perspective of a self outside its worship community in whose personal terms it must be justified.

Dryden's illuminating preface to his *Religio Laici* seems to raise a contradiction; on the one hand, it attacks the powers of human reason—"They who wou'd prove Religion by Reason, do but weaken the cause which they endeavor to support"—while claiming that it is the power one must use to move people—"A Man is to be cheated into passion, but to be reason'd into Truth."9 This contradiction is repeated in the poem itself; Dryden claims, in lines 10 and 11, that "So pale grows *Reason* at *Religions* sight; / So *dyes,* and so *dissolves* in *Supernatural Light,*" yet the poem itself moves according to rational progression with a listing of points, a consideration of arguments, a refutation of objections, and all the appearances of rational, reasonable discourse. Indeed, he argues that

> those who follow'd *Reasons* Dictates right;
> Liv'd up, and lifted high their *Natural Light;*
> With *Socrates* may see their Maker's Face,
> While Thousand Rubrick-Martyrs want a place.
>
> (Ll. 208–211)

What Dryden is after is a labeling and locating of those who disagree with his position in terms that undercut their claims to attention and value. Dryden, both in the preface and through the poem, addresses a situation in which the differences which divided Englishfolk from each other earlier in the century still persisted into the Restoration period; through this poem Dryden seeks to deny legitimacy to those who persist in affirming their differences from Dryden's position. He at once lists those differences in terms of a private/public dichotomy:

> after hearing what our Church can say,
> If still our Reason runs another way,
> That private Reason 'tis more Just to curb,
> Than by Disputes the publick Peace disturb.
>
> (Ll. 445–448)

What in public terms concerns Dryden is not the building up of Christian community but the establishment and preservation of domestic tranquility: "*Common quiet* is *Mankind's concern*" (l. 450). His stance is therefore exclusivist rather than inclusive in its approach to difference.

Dryden's goal is thus to undercut the claims of a differing view of religion; indeed, he challenges the legitimacy of difference. Much of the poem turns on the question of how Scripture is to be interpreted: in arguing for a limited view of the human capacity of reason, however, he is not seeking to enact or incite a pushing beyond the limits of human reason to seek echoes of a new song but to undercut the claims to truth speaking of all who disagree with the established orthodoxy. At stake here is the right to claim to be "true Englishmen" and "true Protestants"; like the sixteenth-century struggles over the ability to claim the word *church* for one's Christian group, Dryden's rhetorical stance seeks to deny those who do not obey the king and do not conform to the disciplines of the established church the right to be thought of as truly English (against Catholics) or as truly Protestant (against the remaining Puritan sympathizers).

His approach to this argument is to try to expose the limitations of both Catholic and Puritan opposition to the Anglican establishment by suggesting they cannot speak the truth, since reason fails before "Supernatural Light," and to espouse the reasonableness of a position of quiescent acceptance of a bare minimum of belief. What he achieves is the appearance of reasonable argument for abandoning the activities of the human mind in matters of religion in favor of acceptance of "The things we *must* believe," which are "*few, and plain*" (l. 432). "Reason" supports Anglican claims while "Supernatural Light" undercuts rival claims; in this polemic use of the claim to "Supernatural Light" we have truly entered a new age.

Part of what we need to note here is what Dryden leaves out. Missing in this poem are allusions, either directly or through verbal echoes, to use of the Prayer Book, except perhaps in his reference in the preface to the need to "conform to the Church discipline" (p. 281).[10] Twenty years of public disuse had caused a shift in understanding about where the central activity of Christian life was to be found as well as an impoverishment of religious language for articulating historic situations. In Dryden, public worship has become a "Discipline"; that is, it is something conducted and attended because it is required for the furthering of "publick Peace," not the promotion of the reign of charity. The importance placed by Cranmer on the verbal delivery of God in public worship through the enactment of Bible reading and sacramental action is not among the things Dryden considers important; in fact, in his attack on Catholics and their stress on the importance of tradition, Dryden rejects the importance of oral language altogether: "*If written words* from time are not secur'd, / How can we think have *oral Sounds* endured?" (ll. 270–271).

Part of what lies behind Dryden's point here is the Anglican-Puritan controversy about the value of set prayers. Dryden comes down on the side of the Prayer Book with its "*written words*" as opposed to the spontaneous prayer favored by Puritans, but the manner in which he formulates the argument sets up a dichotomy between oral and written that did not apply earlier, when the written was viewed as the facilitator of the oral, the enabler of enactment, the extender of the homiletic voice. In Dryden's world the written takes on an authority over the oral; the Prayer Book is on the way toward becoming a book significant in itself as a printed object rather than as a text for use. Further, there is no sense of ongoing divine action in Dryden's view of English society; God's actions are here all safely past and therefore do not threaten to change anything.

Although the enactment of the Prayer Book was once more going on in the world around him, Dryden invokes no sense of it, for his goal is not the opening up of human awareness to make way for participation in a sense of ongoing divine action but the closure of interpretation in favor of subservience to yet another human agency for the preservation of "common quiet." This attitude is manifest both in the preface and in the poem. In fact, Dryden seems to oppose the whole activity of the Reformation itself; he argues, "Reformation of Church and State has always been the ground of our Divisions in *England*" (p. 281). Order as a static principle of social conduct is Dryden's goal. Catholics, he asserts, "should . . . joyn in a publick Act of disowning and detesting those Jesuitick Principles; and subscribe to all Doctrines which deny the Popes Authority of Deposing Kings, and releasing Subjects from their Oath of Allegiance" (p. 278). Puritans should "desclaim their Principles, and renounce their Practices. We shall all be glad to think them true Englishmen when they obey the King, and true Protestants when they conform to the Church Discipline" (p. 281). In other words, the only way for those who disagree with Dryden to be considered really English is to cease being what they are and become Englishmen like Dryden.

In such a view the function of religion has ceased to be transformational and become instead the preservation of an established political and social order. Anglicanism is no longer a procedure for living corporately, a conversation aimed at opening human conceptual frames to new ways of thinking and doing, or a communal life in which meaning is discovered through enactment of readings; instead, it has become a fixed set of verbal statements to which one must give assent to be included among Dryden's category of "true Englishmen." Dryden's attack on reason functions to undercut the abilities of others to come up with counterstatements with any claim to truth; since truth is so hard to determine, the safest course is to give up its pursuit in favor of adherence to lowest-common-denominator statements:

> The things we *must* believe, are *few,* and *plain:*
> But since men *will* believe more than they *need;*
> And every man will make *himself* a Creed:
> In doubtful questions 'tis the safest way
> To learn what unsuspected Ancients say:
>
> . . . .
>
> If after all they stand suspected still,
> 'Tis some Relief, that points not clearly known,
> Without much hazard may be let alone.
>
> (Ll. 432–444)

In the name of "common quiet," Dryden argues, believe the oldest or give up the quest. Such a stance manifests a need to affirm that human words can speak the truth to the extent to which it is necessary to do so; formularies of the faith gain power through age and the assent of the church and thus can be said to be equal to the truth without struggle or disquiet. Dryden, believing that his society was unable to tolerate the copiousness of interpretation sought earlier as a way of seeking to articulate the boundless grace of God, emphasizes instead personal adherence to past verbal formulations; such formulations become refuges in the face of truth's complexity and elusiveness rather than verbal tools to enable the quest for meaning in the present.

Indeed, Dryden claims to be profoundly distrustful of inquiry into religious subjects; to him wide distribution of the Bible has resulted in multiplicity of interpretation, to the great unrest of society:

> The Book thus put in every vulgar hand,
> Which each presum'd he best cou'd understand,
> The *Common Rule* was made the *common Prey;*
> And at the mercy of the *Rabble* lay.
>
> (Ll. 400–403)

Dryden's perspective is one in which the Bible has ceased to be a book for use and become once more a sacred icon, a holy object which is defiled by the kind of acquaintance with it Cranmer hoped would be the result of its publication in English. In the terms articulated at the beginning of this study, Dryden finds religion's ability to be reassuring to be sufficiently problematic and yet so necessary that he makes it the central task of religion, one he is willing to sacrifice all others for.

In *Religio Laici,* therefore, a discussion of interpretation becomes an attempt to quell the process of interpretation, to restrict it to the repetition of established formularies, in the name of what is to Dryden a higher good, namely "common quiet." Indeed, the arguments given early in the poem about the importance of revelation to supplant the deficiencies of faulty reason are actually aimed at those who would argue about interpretations. Dryden's sole biblical citation is from Paul's Epistle to the Romans, in which Paul argues that Gentiles who obey the law are better than Jews who do not; Dryden uses this text to argue that pagans who are obedient have a better chance to "see their Maker's Face" than contentious *"Rubrick-Martyrs"* among the English. After all, "private Reason 'tis more Just to curb, / Than by Disputes the publick Peace disturb" (ll. 447–448).

At the same time, however, Dryden creates in his speaker a model of one formed in the midst of contention who has no mean appreciation of his own opinions. He begins his preface with an attempt to disarm some possible objections to his work: "if it be objected to me that being a *Layman,* I ought not to have concern'd my self with Speculations, which belong to the Profession of *Divinity;* I cou'd Answer, that perhaps, Laymen, with equal advantages of Parts and Knowledge, are not the most incompetent Judges of Sacred things" (p. 273). Having made that disclaimer, he goes on to take it back in a show of humility: "But in the due sense of my own weakness and want of Learning, I plead not this." He then says, "I submit [my opinions] with all reverence to my Mother Church, accounting them no further mine, than as they are Authoriz'd, or at least uncondemn'd by her."

Yet he also claims he took the further precaution of having the poem read by one who is an authority in such matters and who objected to a few things. "I am sensible enough that I had done more *prudently* to have follow'd his opinion," notes Dryden, but of course he does not: "But then I could not have satisfied my self, that I had done honestly not to have written what was my own" (p. 274). Absent here is any sense of truth as that which is sought in communal engagement with Bible and Sacraments, a pursuit in which clergy and laity can join. At once granting authority to the church ("I submit with all reverence to my Mother Church") and also taking it back ("I could not have satisfied my self . . . to have follow'd his opinion"), Dryden posits a bifurcated structure of ordained and lay deciders about issues defined in terms of the "Authoriz'd" and "uncondemn'd" positions and their opposite which presupposes both that such decisions can be made, and made official, and that Dryden reserves the right to make his own decisions in spite of whatever the official position might be. What Dryden defines here is a sense of self against authority, a self that reserves the right to evaluate "Mother Church's" positions in terms of that self's own standards, in spite of his claims to the contrary. The doctrinal stance of various Christian groups who claim to speak for all Christendom thus finds its answer in a speaker whose position, however professedly subservient to Mother Church, actually is one of reserving judgment until his own criteria for significance are met. The value of the Church of England is affirmed, not because of any claims it may have over the speaker, but because it meets the speaker's standards. With the speaker Dryden creates we are well on the way toward our contemporary situation in which individuals select this or that Christian denomination, or no tradition at all, on the basis of personal preference or the meeting of narrowly conceived criteria.

Dryden takes a similar approach later in the preface when he describes how one ought to go about didactic writing:

> If any one be so lamentable a Critique as to require the Smoothness, the Numbers and the Turn of Heroick Poetry in this Poem; I must tell him, that if he has not read *Horace,* I have studied him, and hope the style of his Epistles is not ill imitated here. The Expressions of a Poem, design'd purely for Instruction, ought to be Plain and Natural, and yet Majestick: for here the Poet is presum'd to be a kind of Law-giver, and those three qualities which I have nam'd are proper to the Legislative style. . . . Instruction is to be given by shewing them what they naturally are. (Pp. 281–282)

In Tompkins' and Fish's terms, Dryden is engaged in pure rhetoric here,[11] "shewing them what they naturally are" and not doing what Herbert defined as setting up through questioning a situation in which an audience could discover who it is. Didactic poetry ("design'd purely for Instruction") in Dryden's view "ought to be plain," presumably because what it might teach is also held to be expressible plainly. Note here Dryden's overall authoritative pose; any who might question his style in *Religio Laici* clearly have not read their Horace, who gives the rules for such poems. But there is a connection; only in a world in which religion has devolved into a set of already-articulated texts believed to express the truth in a clearly defined signifier-signified relationship could one claim rules from Horace so obviously beneficial in expressing that truth. Nor, except in a culture in which a religious tradition can be proclaimed valuable for a reader simply because the writer considers himself the authority on what is best for the reader, could such a claim be made. In such a situation, authority resides in following the rules, using the right models, being enough of an imitator of classical precursors because those are the places where truth is believed to reside, and not in open-ended interactive encounters in conversation with a tradition and its texts in present moments the intent of which is to promote the reign of charity. If Dryden realized that to refer to himself as a "Law-giver" is to echo a biblical reference to Moses he gives no sign of it; certainly he seeks no biblical language in which to make his case or understand his situation.

Unlike Spenser, for whom the classical world provided generic resources to be used and "overgone," Dryden finds in Horace a source of rules and standards by which poetic performance can be judged. It is a classical and not a biblical model; Dryden manifests a situation in which adherence to the educational experience of a social class and not the biblical text available to all becomes a code of expectation by which qualities of Englishness and religious devotion can be judged. As a result, Dryden articulates in this poem a new kind of religious self, for whom preservation of a social group within the larger society (here defined in relationship to Horace as a cultural figure whom the group will know and accept as a setter of standards for works such as this one) is the proper work of religion. The practice of religion is thus to be engaged in by all for the preservation of a social order favoring a few. Dryden does not express any sense of Christianity as participation in a larger community which transcends social distinctions or any need to position oneself in relationship to that community in an attitude of humility or self-effacement. The poet in *Religio Laici* has become a "kind of Law-giver" in the sense that he is in possession of laws that can be articulated—brought into words that bear an equivalent relationship to that to which they point—and that he can claim subservience to his position so articulated as what is required of his reader. The function of the established church is to meet the needs of individuals in a society or of a particular class of that society as the poet defines them; absent here is any sense of a need to be attentive to divine requirements of humanity which might require a change in the speaker's definition. The perceptions and articulations of a self outside community have here become standards by which to judge, define, and create membership in that community. Nor is there any sense that "*Sacred Truth*," what Dryden later defines as the subject of his poem, requires what Herbert called "all possible art"; "while from *Sacred Truth* I do not swerve," says Dryden, "*Tom Sternhold's*, or *Tom Shadwell's Rhimes* will serve." We know, of course, what Dryden thought about Tom Shadwell's rhymes; he had made that perfectly clear five years earlier in *Mac Flecknoe*.

In other words, Dryden's poem comes out of an age in which division over religious issues has become so serious a problem that at least to a man like Dryden "common quiet" is the chief issue. Yet as a man of that age Dryden exhibits a closing of ranks around a single interpretive posture, a codification of that posture into "*Sacred Truth*" and an equation of certain verbal formulations with that truth. As a result, the way to make an appeal to public response that seems appropriate to him is in terms of the abandonment of interpretive processes in favor of individual allegiance to those formulations of truth. In the process, Dryden does not avail himself of the richness of biblical and liturgical allusion, the language of process and discovery, the sense of divine activity as ongoing—in short, all the things that served as poetic resources for religious poets from Spenser to Vaughan. For them he substitutes a personal voice, an imitation of Horace as a process of following rules of discourse, and a self-presentation of his own claimed subservience that seeks power through overpowering the reader. What Dryden gives us is not a text that would ever actually change anybody's mind, much less his behavior, but could serve either to antagonize dissenters from the established religion or confirm its supporters in their sense of rightness. *Religio Laici* is an exercise of power intended to further Dryden's own career and give comfort to those who enforced acquiescence to the state's demand for religious conformity by demonstrating the "reasonableness" of their position and the appropriateness of their repressive actions. It creates a community around it by confirming some readers in the rightness of positions already held and consigning other readers to the ranks of "vulgar . . . Rabble," not by confounding conventional opinion on the part of all readers and seeking to make of them questers after an as yet unarticulated future.

From another perspective, *Religio Laici* reveals a situation in which the Church of England was forced to rely on the state for its existence. Having been disestablished with the defeat of Charles I, it could return only with the restoration of Charles II. Thus forced into a position of political dependency it could only take a subservient role in society by lending itself to the support and preservation of that political and social structure on which it was now dependent. The stage was set for the parade of foolish, affected, and ineffectual Anglican clerics who populate the pages of English literature in the eighteenth and nineteenth centuries; these images of the Anglican church at once locate the Christian life as the activity of religious professionals but also suggest that they usually achieve whatever power they might have ironically, in spite of themselves, since most of what they do is tangential to the real issues faced by those to whom they minister. In the history of the Church of England it took a hundred years to begin to recover sufficiently from the effects of the Civil War and to have once more a significant impact on English society. Only with the movements of the late eighteenth and nineteenth centuries, first led by the Wesleys and then later by the Oxford reformers and the Ritualists, did the Church of England begin to take a stance toward English society more vigorous than merely holding the hand of the powers-that-be.

In the meantime, the direction of literary expression and the course of religious history took other paths. The figure of Milton dominated the religious imagination of the English. Approaching biblical texts from a radically individualistic position, finding in mythic revisions of biblical narratives a clue to the ways of God,[12] Milton prepared the way for romantic subjectivity and private apocalyptic vision. It takes nothing from the poetic achievement of *Paradise Lost* to see it as manifesting the literary and religious triumph of Puritanism just when it failed politically. But the emergence of Milton's cultural role is another story.

Elizabeth and the English Reformation (Cambridge: Cambridge University Press, 1968), esp. p. 219, and Paul S. Seaver, *The Puritan Lectureships: The Politics of Religious Dissent, 1560–1662* (Stanford: Stanford University Press, 1970), pp. 15–22. Failure to recognize the Church of England's early desire for improvement of clerical education and the political situation in which one expression of that desire was repressed has led some scholars to identify support for a preaching clergy as a Puritan position, an understandable but historically untenable interpretation. The Church of England did not believe it ought to have an uneducated or ignorant clergy.

5 · For a discussion of Grindal as Algrind, the "shepheard great in gree" of *The Shepheardes Calendar,* "July," see Paul E. McLane, *Spenser's Shepheardes Calendar: A Study in Elizabethan Allegory* (South Bend: Notre Dame University Press, 1961), pp. 140–157.

6 · Citations from Petrarch's *Rime sparse* are from the edition of Robert M. Durling, *Petrarch's Lyric Poems* (Cambridge, Mass.: Harvard University Press, 1976), esp. poem 366 (pp. 574–583).

7 · Citations from Sidney's poems are from the edition of William J. Ringler (Oxford: Clarendon, 1962).

8 · A point anticipated by Paul Alpers in his *The Poetry of "The Faerie Queene"* (Princeton: Princeton University Press, 1967), p. 14 "An episode in *The Faerie Queene* . . . is best described as a developing psychological experience within the reader, rather than as an action to be observed by him."

9 · In theoretical terms, my argument here parallels to some extent that of Maureen Quilligan in her *The Language of Allegory* (Ithaca, N.Y.: Cornell University Press, 1979). Note her comment on p. 28: "allegory works horizontally, rather than vertically, so that meaning accretes serially." I would go further to see allegory, at least in Spenser, as infolding the meaning of culturally available abstractions into the text, so as to bring the pressure of their implications to bear on the world of the reader in the moment of his reading, rather than requiring an "unfolding" of meaning into its abstract components. Such a strategy enables the text to comment on that which it infolds while invoking its cultural authority for Spenser's text.

10 · Two recent studies of *The Faerie Queene,* however, have begun to use historical material once more in effective ways. Michael O'Connell's *Mirror and Veil: The Historical Dimension of Spenser's "The Faerie Queene"* (Chapel Hill: University of North Carolina Press, 1977) is closest to my point when it asserts that "through the active strength of men, the earthly participant of [the New Jerusalem's] glory could be achieved, however imperfectly, in England's green and pleasant land" (p. 68), but O'Connell is primarily concerned to point out that "the victory was achieved by the English people . . . in the fires of Smithfield, [when] England was finally reunited with the reformed church in its bethrothal to a virgin queen" (p. 67). In other words, although Spenser "was [a poet] far from complacent about what had been and what was yet to be achieved" (p. 68), Book I is primarily about something that has already occurred which it celebrates. I would argue that Book I to the extent that it praises what has already happened does so to move things further along. Thomas H. Cain's focus on *Praise in "The Faerie Queene"* (Lincoln: University of Nebraska Press, 1978) also stresses the poet's use of historical material as a reflection of what has happened

Notes

Prologue

1 · In *Miscellaneous Prose,* ed. Katherine Duncan-Jones and Jan van Dorsten (Oxford: Clarendon, 1973), p. 77.

2 · There persists a problem in knowing what to call the Church of England. The problem centers around the adjective "Anglican." Like the term "Roman Catholic," the word is a seventeenth- and not a sixteenth-century term, although the official name of the English church was *Ecclesia Anglicana* from the Henrican Act of Supremacy of 1534 and appears in Bishop John Jewel's *Apologia Ecclesiae Anglicanae* (1564). The matter is complicated by the development of English church historiography in the nineteenth century. The development of Oxford Movement Anglo-Catholicism to challenge the eighteenth-century low church establishment led to a scramble for the ability to claim the sixteenth-century Church of England as a precursor. Through the filters of nineteenth-century concerns, the Anglo-Catholic party saw a link between the Prayer Book of 1549 (which still referred to the Mass), the liturgical program of Archbishop Laud, and their own eagerness to recover a medieval theology of the Mass, the use of elaborate ceremonial, and an elevated theology of the priest as the performer of the Mass for lay observers. The low church party saw its predecessors among Elizabethan Calvinists and Puritans and imagined that *they* were dominant. Both were wrong, but the low church side of the debate persists in distorting our view of the sixteenth-century church. Patrick Collinson, for example, claims that there were only two churches in England in the sixteenth century and Anglicanism was not one of them (in *The Elizabethan Puritan Movement* [Berkeley: University of California Press, 1967], p. 13). What is really going on here is that the reformed Church of England and English Christians loyal to the pope were in the sixteenth century fighting to use the word "church" for their groups; thus the issue is much more fundamental than which of two churches is the "true" church. That is a development of the seventeenth century and is reflected in the appearance of "Anglican" and "Roman Catholic" as descriptive terms. When those terms became current, what had changed

was not the creation of Anglicanism but the recognition on both sides that each would go on existing, no matter how little (or how much) each liked the other. In the sixteenth century there could be only one church; the other was nullified under words like "heretic" or "Antichrist." For present purposes I will use "Church of England" or "English Church" for the sixteenth-century church and reserve "Anglican" for the seventeenth-century church, but I do not guarantee complete consistency. I do not think that George Herbert thought his church was different from Edmund Spenser's.

3 · Jaroslav Pelikan, *Reformation of Church and Dogma, 1300–1700* (Chicago: University of Chicago Press, 1984), p. 184 (volume 4 of Pelikan's five-volume *The Christian Tradition*).

4 · Thus, for example, Barbara Lewalski's claim that "Calvinism provided a detailed chart of the spiritual life for Elizabethan and seventeenth-century English Protestants, and that this map also afforded fundamental direction to the major religious poets." In *Protestant Poetics and the Seventeenth-Century Religious Lyric* (Princeton: Princeton University Press, 1979), p. 14.

5 · For an example of Herbert scholarship that describes an "Anglo-Catholic" tradition and locates itself within a tradition of Protestantism as defined by Luther and Calvin, see Richard Strier, *Love Known: Theology and Experience in George Herbert's Poetry* (Chicago: University of Chicago Press, 1983).

6 · I am indebted to a splendid study, *The Dynamics of Religion: Process and Movement in Christian Churches,* by Bruce Reed (London: Darton, Longman and Todd, 1978), a highly successful attempt to understand the functioning of religion in human societies over time.

7 · In *VOICE TERMINAL ECHO: Postmodernism and English Renaissance Texts* (London: Methuen, 1986), p. 7. Goldberg's work is among the first to apply vocabulary as well as concepts from poststructuralist theory to the study of Renaissance texts. Starting from a different place (rhetorical and homiletic theory), I have recently found areas of common concern which are illuminated by poststructuralist approaches to literature, perhaps because Goldberg and others are moving away from the almost mythic reductionism and static descriptive modes of structuralist thought, a move not unlike the English Reformation's move away from the linguistic, liturgical, and theological structures of the medieval church toward a rhetorical mode which undercuts the fixity of structure and seeks new as yet unspoken discourse.

8 · (Columbia: University of Missouri Press, 1970).

9 · (Chicago: University of Chicago Press, 1952).

10 · See Martz's *The Poetry of Meditation* (New Haven: Yale University Press, 1954) and *The Paradise Within: Studies in Vaughan, Traherne, and Milton* (New Haven: Yale University Press, 1964). We are closer to the Anglican viewpoint when we think of the "inner" workings of the Spirit as taking place within the Body of Christ on earth, which is "the blessed company of all faithful people," and not in individual members of that Body. (*The Book of Common Prayer, 1559,* ed. John E. Booty [Charlottesville: University of Virginia Press for the Folger Shakespeare Library, 1976], p. 265).

11 · Especially her *Protestant Poetics and the Seventeenth-Century Religious Lyric* (Princeton: Princeton University Press, 1979), but see also her *Donne's "Anniversaries" and the Poetry of Praise* (Princeton: Princeton University Press, 1973), which offers both

an earlier exploration of what she deems a "Protestant poetics" and an application of it to the discussion of major seventeenth-century poems.

12 · Fish's major statement is in *Self-Consuming Artifacts: The Experience of Seventeenth-Century Literature* (Berkeley: University of California Press, 1972), especially pp. 1–77.

13 · See Fish's *The Living Temple: George Herbert and Catechizing* (Berkeley: University of California Press, 1978).

14 · For a helpful discussion of this tradition, see Helen Gardner, *Religion and Literature* (London: Faber and Faber, 1971), especially pp. 121–142.

15 · In "Religion and Literature" (1932; repr. Grand Rapids, Mich.: Eerdmans, 1975), in *Religion and Modern Literature: Essays in Theory and Criticism,* ed. G. B. Tennyson and Edward E. Ericson, Jr., p. 23.

16 · An incomplete review of publications from 1981 and 1982 reveals two major studies of Herbert (Heather Asals, *Equivocal Predication: George Herbert's Way to God* [Toronto: University of Toronto Press, 1981] and Barbara Leah Harmon, *Costly Monuments: Representations of the Self in George Herbert's Poetry* [Cambridge, Mass.: Harvard University Press, 1982]) two overviews of religious literature in this period (Sharon Cadman Seelig, *The Shadow of Eternity: Belief and Structure in the Poetry of Herbert, Vaughan, and Traherne* [Lexington: University Press of Kentucky, 1981] and Ira Clark, *Christ Revealed: The History of the Neotypological Lyric in the English Renaissance* [Gainesville: University Presses of Florida, 1982]) one study of Crashaw (Robert V. Young, *Richard Crashaw and the Spanish Golden Age* [New Haven: Yale University Press, 1982]) one study of Donne's *Satyres* in their religious context (M. Thomas Hester, *Kinde Pitty and Brave Scorn: John Donne's "Satyres"* [Durham: Duke University Press, 1982]) and only one study of Donne's early poetry (Patricia Garland Pinka, *This Dialogue of One: The "Songs and Sonnets" of John Donne* [University: University of Alabama Press, 1982]).

17 · Quoted from Izaak Walton's "Life of Mr. George Herbert," reprinted in *Lives* (London: Oxford University Press, 1927), p. 302.

18 · *English Reformation Literature: The Tudor Origins of the Protestant Tradition* (Princeton: Princeton University Press, 1982). See also David Norbrook, *Poetry and Politics in the English Renaissance* (London: Routledge and Kegan Paul, 1984), which builds on and acknowledges its indebtedness to King's work. Norbrook is raising the right kinds of issues in his study; had it arrived at an earlier stage in the writing of this book it might have played a larger role in my own account.

19 · Reprinted in *Lives of the Poets* (1781; repr. London: Dent, 1925), pp. 173–174.

20 · At this point we need to rethink our premises about the relationship between literature and religion. Most studies in this area privilege theological writings as though they formed a simultaneous present behind literary texts and thus establish a fixed point of reference from which decisions about the literary texts can be made. If we have learned anything from contemporary theory, however, it must be that theological texts come out of developments in culture and that those who write them are implicated in the developments of their times. The writings of a Calvin, say, cannot be quoted as though Calvin never changed his mind or developed in his thought from early to later writings; nor can those writings be cited without reference either to the

writings of an earlier age or to the context to which they were addressed. For the best discussions of these issues as they relate to doctrinal matters, see Jaroslav Pelikan, *Historical Theology: Continuity and Change in Christian Doctrine* (New York: Corpus, 1971) and the volumes in Pelikan's series *The Christian Tradition: A History of the Development of Doctrine* (New Haven: Yale University Press, 1971–).

21 · "Life of Waller," p. 174.

22 · Discussions of sixteenth- and seventeenth-century doctrinal and theological divisions rarely do justice to the actual flux of thought manifest in that age. Certainly, when the Council of Trent affirms that "we are said to be justified by faith, because faith is . . . the root of all justification" (*Dogmatic Canons and Decrees,* trans. Waterworth et al. [New York: Devin-Adair, 1912], p. 33), it is clear that easy reference to the appearance of certain "key words" in a given writer does not allow his being aligned with any one camp quite so readily as many scholars are willing to claim. The non-English theologian most closely associated with the Elizabethan church is John Calvin. Certainly, Calvinist thought, more comprehensive and systematic than Luther's, was readily available in England in this period and as a result set the tenor of much theological discourse because it offered an accessible vocabulary without the (possible) taint of medieval Christianity. To go so far as H. R. McAdoo, in *The Spirit of Anglicanism: A Survey of Anglican Theological Method in the Seventeenth Century* (New York: Scribner, 1965), to conclude that "hardly one of the Elizabethan bishops . . . was not a Calvinist" (p. 5), is simply not warranted, however. For other arguments along this line, see Norman Pettit, *The Heart Prepared: Grace and Conversion in Puritan Spiritual Life* (New Haven: Yale University Press, 1966) and Charles and Katherine George, *The Protestant Mind of the English Reformation* (Princeton: Princeton University Press, 1961). The chief exponents of this view among literary scholars include Barbara Lewalski in *Protestant Poetics and the Seventeenth-Century Religious Lyric* and Andrew Weiner in his *Sir Philip Sidney and the Poetics of Protestantism* (Minneapolis: University of Minnesota Press, 1978). The result of such an approach is the distorting of what actually takes place; Weiner, for example, discusses Sidney's religious position without reference to a single Anglican religious writer. This position must be set in juxtaposition to studies like that of J. F. H. New, *Anglican and Puritan* (Stanford, Calif.: Stanford University Press, 1964), J. Sears McGee, *The Godly Man in Stuart England: Anglicans, Puritans, and the Two Tables, 1620–1670* (New Haven: Yale University Press, 1976), and R. T. Kendall, *Calvin and English Calvinism to 1649* (New York: Oxford, 1979). Literary studies in this area desperately need an account of Calvin which clarifies his distinctive reinterpretation of the predestinarian strains in Christian thought and locates that doctrine in the broader contexts of his intellectual backgrounds, his theological pronouncements on other issues, and the larger shape and thrust of his writings. In any case, the basic English Reformation texts were written and in use before Calvin was more than one among many Protestant voices coming to England from Europe, with all of which the English Reformers sought common ground at one time or another. The English Reformation was certainly "Protestant" in that it was antipapal, but beyond that the person who desires a more precise definition goes at his peril unless he takes into account the full complex of political, social, and intellectual interactions then under way. Above all, he must take seriously the integrity of the English Reformers and their concerns as manifest in their own documents. For example, Article XVII, "Of Predestination and Election," from

the *Thirty-Nine Articles of Religion,* often referred to as a key text in making the case for Calvin's domination of Anglican theological discourse, in fact reveals a quite different situation. This article is a pastoral statement, aiding those who find that many of their parishioners think of their situation before God in terms of predestination; it encourages the use of the term with those who feel among the elect because this is comforting and encouraging, but it discourages use of the term among those who do not share this perception as a "dangerous downfall, whereby the Devil doth thrust them either into desperation, or into wretchlessness." In England, Puritan theology tends to be much more subservient to Calvinism than does Anglican. Robert K. Faulkner, in his *Richard Hooker and the Politics of a Christian England* (Berkeley: University of California Press, 1981), suggests aptly that fascination with Calvinism and Puritanism among American scholars may derive from the fact that the Puritan heritage is seen as the source of much that is valued about American culture (p. 7).

23 · As though anything *could* be outside the realm of concern of the God of Judeo-Christian tradition. Thus F. G. Robinson, *The Shape of Things Known: Sidney's "Apology" in Its Philosophical Tradition* (Cambridge: Harvard University Press, 1972), pp. 100–107, and Weiner, *Sir Philip Sidney,* p. 50.

24 · In his *Donne, Milton, and the End of Humanist Rhetoric* (Berkeley: University of California Press, 1985), Thomas O. Sloane echoes this reading of Erasmus and links it to the Church of England through his application of it to Donne. Sloane's work, which reached me after this study was essentially complete, describes the influence of humanist rhetoric on Renaissance England and its decline. I find that we are telling much the same story and regret that I could not take fuller advantage of his special perspective.

25 · For an account of the expansion of discussion and publication in the early years of the reign of Edward VI, see King, *English Reformation Literature,* pp. 76–94. Since this freedom of the press occurred during the same years as the basic documents of the English Reformation were being published, the impetus behind both publishing phenomena would appear to be the same. Tighter restrictions were enforced only when this freedom produced attacks on the reforming documents themselves, setting the stage for the arguments about the Prayer Book and its attendant texts which would be the center of religious controversy in subsequent generations.

26 · "A Confutation of Unwritten Verities," reprinted in *Cranmer: Miscellaneous Writings,* ed. John Cox (Cambridge: Cambridge University Press, 1846), p. 63.

27 · Jasper Ridley, *Thomas Cranmer* (Oxford: Clarendon, 1962), p. 266.

28 · In his *The Shape of the Liturgy* (1945; repr. London: Dacre, 1978).

29 · In *Theology as Thanksgiving* (New York: Seabury, 1981), pp. 212–213.

30 · Hooker's *Of the Lawes of Ecclesiasticall Polity,* often cited as an example of Anglican systematic theology, should be read instead as a work seeking to persuade English Puritans of the importance of participation in Prayer Book worship. The word "persuasion" occurs with almost metronomic frequency throughout the *Lawes,* especially in the prefatory sections. See *Works,* ed. W. Speed Hill (Cambridge: Harvard University Press, 1977–), esp. vol. 1, pp. 1–53. Hooker's concern with persuasion and persuasiveness reminds us of the concern with "teaching, delighting, and moving" that motivated writers of both poetry and prose, of both fiction and philosophical writing, in the Renaissance.

31 · In *Lives,* p. 314.

32 · On Herbert and Anglicanism, see John E. Booty, "George Herbert: *The Temple* and *The Book of Common Prayer*," in *Mosaic* 12 (1979): 75–90, and the introduction to my edition, *George Herbert: "The Country Parson," "The Temple"* (Ramsey, N.J.: Paulist Press, 1981), as well as Part III below.

33 · See her *Equivocal Predication: George Herbert's Way to God* (Toronto: University of Toronto Press, 1981), p. 42. Asals' brilliant reading of Herbert anticipates a number of the positions I have taken in this study; I can only hope to explore more fully her demonstration of the Anglican context of Herbert's work.

34 · In the preface to the 1655 edition of *Silex Scintillans*, reprinted in *Works*, ed. L. C. Martin, 2nd ed. (Oxford: Clarendon, 1957), p. 391. All further quotations to Vaughan's work will be from this edition and cited in the text.

35 · For a summary of how the worshipping community of both the Old and New Israels produced the "canon" of Scripture, see Guthrie, *Theology as Thanksgiving*, pp. 181–216.

36 · Lewalski, *Protestant Poetics*, p. 4. One outgrowth of recent studies in historical psychology has been the recovery of a sense that concepts of the individual, privacy, and the self have undergone radical changes since the middle of the seventeenth century. In the Elizabethan and Jacobean households, life was lived in public; as a result, definitions of personality and the self were far less distinctly drawn than they are for us. Our tendency to think instinctively of the self in terms of a "private mode" and individual uniqueness is one inheritance of the individuating tendencies of Puritanism. See Lawrence Stone, *The Family, Sex, and Marriage in England 1500–1800* (New York: Harper and Row, 1977), pp. 224–227. See also Robert R. Hellenga, "Elizabethan Dramatic Conventions and Elizabethan Reality," *Renaissance Drama* n.s. 12 (1981): 27–49; Stephen Greenblatt, *Sir Walter Raleigh: The Renaissance Man and His Roles* (New Haven: Yale University Press, 1973); J. Leeds Barroll, *Artificial Persons: The Formation of Character in the Tragedies of Shakespeare* (Columbia: University of South Carolina Press, 1974), and Thomas F. van Laan, *Role-Playing in Shakespeare* (Toronto: University of Toronto Press, 1978) for application of this insight to Renaissance literature.

37 · Martz, *The Poetry of Meditation*, pp. 118–144.

38 · In *Sermons*, ed. G. F. Potter and Evelyn Simpson, 10 vols. (Berkeley: University of California Press, 1953–62), vol. 1, p. 291. Further references to Donne's sermons will be to this edition, unless otherwise noted, and citation by volume number and page will be given in the text.

39 · *Donne's Prebend Sermons*, ed. Janel M. Mueller (Cambridge: Harvard University Press, 1971), p. 91.

40 · Wilson, in *The Arte of Rhetorique*, defines the end of rhetoric as "to perswade with reason all men to societie" and sees it as a divine gift to enable "men . . . to live together in fellowship of life." In *The Boke Named the Governor*, Sir Thomas Eliot defines evil as the pursuit of "ambition, . . . covertise and desire of treasure or possessions" and "good" as the functioning of the various degrees of society in harmony with each other. Even the Primers of the reign of Edward VI drop the private emphasis of late medieval works for private devotion and stress the uniting of society in a single process of devotional exercise, based on Morning and Evening Prayer, in which the prayers emphasize asking for divine aid in living out one's appointed role in society.

As the prayers in the Primers focus on individuals, they emphasize asking for help in developing those personal attributes which subordinate private concerns and promote the ability to fulfill societal roles. On the Primers, see David Siegenthaler, "Religious Education for Citizenship: Primer and Catechism," in Booty, *The Godly Kingdom*, pp. 217–249. In his "History, Liturgy, and Point of View in Protestant Meditative Poetry," *SP* 77 (1980): 67–83, Martin Elsky argues for the importance of Protestant liturgy as supportive of distinctly meditative styles of lyric poetry, but he fails to note the essentially supportive role of private and subjective poetic activity. Reading the plurals of the Prayer Book—"we offer and present unto thee . . . ourselves, our souls and bodies"—as singulars, he can conclude that "the real sacrificial action of the Lord's Supper is the self-sacrifice of the communicant" (p. 71), thus ignoring the social context of that language. Leonard Barkan treats some of these issues in his *Nature's Work of Art: The Human Body as Image of the World* (New Haven: Yale University Press, 1975), although I find him fundamentally misreading the evidence when he argues that the "English Renaissance picture of world order was above all a defense of the hierarchical *status quo*" (p. 77). In a world coming out of the disruptions of social order created by the Wars of the Roses and the outbreaks of plague in the fifteenth century, the organically functioning hierarchy was seen as a goal to be reached rather than as a given reality to be defended. In early Tudor biographies like that of Cardinal Wolsey by George Cavendish and that of Richard III by Thomas More, the source of their misfortune is described in terms of "the end and fall of pride and arrogancy of man," again a way of locating evil in the pursuit of individual, selfish ends and locating good in the pursuit of the good of the society as a whole.

41 · In *George Herbert: His Religion and Art* (Cambridge: Harvard University Press, 1968), p. 95.

42 · Thus Marjorie O'Rourke Boyle, *Erasmus on Language and Method in Theology* (Toronto: University of Toronto Press, 1977), p. 115. Boyle's study of Erasmus, one of the few works to discuss sixteenth-century theology in terms of process rather than stasis, as discourse aimed not at static description but at change in the world and thus as dialogue aimed at engagement, has done much to direct and inspire what follows in this study.

43 · Donne, *Sermons*, vol. 1, p. 288. See this sermon, preached on April 19, 1618, for a full discussion of Donne's sense of the importance of preaching, for persuasion to "the application thereof in particular," for "hearing is but the conception, meditation is but the quickning, purposing is but the birth, but practising is the growth of this blessed childe . . . that Gospell which is peace to my Conscience, and reconciliation to my God, and Salvation to my Soul" (p. 294), and "when we have Faith, he would not have us stop nor determine there, but proceed to works too" (p. 295), because "the best and fullest acceptation is . . . to prove that thou hast accepted [the Word] by thy life and conversation."

44 · For a fuller description of the issues involved here and their background, see Richard E. Palmer, *Hermeneutics: Interpretation Theory in Schleiermacher, Dilthey, Heidegger, and Gadamer* (Evanston: Northwestern University Press, 1969), esp. pp. 66–71 and 223–253.

45 · Although John King does document the appearance during the reign of Edward VI of a "gospelling" literature intended to make the texts of the English

Reformation, including the Bible, more approachable to an audience accustomed only to hearing them in Latin and to further the reforming intentions as they applied to society, I am concerned with that phase of Reformation literature that appeared after time and use had made the Reformers' texts sufficiently familiar so that verbal echoes and allusions to them would have been readily identifiable by a literate audience. See King, *English Reformation Literature*, pp. 209–270.

46 · For fuller discussion of the aims of the English Reformers, see the essays in John E. Booty, *The Godly Kingdom of Tudor England: Great Books of the English Reformation* (Wilton, Conn.: Morehouse-Barlow, 1981), esp. my essay " 'Godly and Fruitful Lessons': The Great Bible, Erasmus' *Paraphrases,* and the Book of Homilies," pp. 45–135.

47 · Macklin Smith's *Prudentius' "Psychomachia": A Reexamination* (Princeton: Princeton University Press, 1976) explores the essentially imperialistic relationship between Christian writing and classical literature in the early centuries of the Christian era. Eric Auerbach, in *Mimesis: The Representation of Reality in Western Literature,* trans. Willard Trask (Princeton: Princeton University Press, 1953), explores the ways in which the Bible expresses its God's absolute claim on his creatures through style as well as content.

48 · From the opening stanza of "Perirrhanterium," in *Works,* ed. F. N. Hutchinson (Oxford: Clarendon, 1941), p. 6. All further quotations from Herbert will be taken from this edition and cited by title and line number in the text.

49 · For the concept of "myth" among scholars of comparative religions, see Rudolph Otto, *The Idea of the Holy: An Inquiry into the Non-Rational Factor in the Idea of the Divine and Its Relation to the Rational,* trans. John W. Harvey (London: Oxford University Press, 1923) and Mircea Eliade, *The Sacred and the Profane,* trans. Willard Trask (New York: Harper and Row, 1959). For an example of the use of the idea of myth in the interpretation of Renaissance texts, see Michael Lieb, *Poetics of the Holy: A Reading of "Paradise Lost"* (Chapel Hill: University of North Carolina Press, 1981).

50 · Thus, in his *The Great Code: The Bible and Literature* (New York: Harcourt Brace Jovanovich, 1982), Frye argues that the Bible is myth in Eliade's sense of the word, but he immediately goes on to specify the uniqueness of the Bible as myth: "the typological structure and shape of the Bible make its mythology diachronic, in contrast to the synchronic mythology characteristic of most of the religions outside it" (p. 83), although he does not mention another diachronic mythology to permit the qualifying "most" of the statement. This is not to say that the Bible does not use myth, notably the myths of the ancient Near Eastern cultures which were the language of power and explanation available to the Hebrews; when it does so, however, it changes them in ways that undermine their claim to truth speaking. For instance, the opening of Genesis retells a myth of creation but adds the key words "In the beginning," thus undermining the essentially synchronic nature of myth. The distinctive ways in which the Bible uses myth are keys to its particular, and particularizing, claims.

51 · See his *Sacred Discontent: The Bible and Western Tradition* (Berkeley: University of California Press, 1976), esp. pp. 50–173.

52 · See his *Of Grammatology,* trans. Gayatri Chakravorty Spivak (Baltimore: Johns Hopkins University Press, 1976), esp. pp. 3–26.

53 · The Christian struggle against *logos* as transcendent idea in either its philosophical or gnostic forms dates at least from the opening of John's Gospel with its assertion that the One who is truly worthy to be referred to as *logos* is important to us not in his independence as being but in his becoming flesh, pitching his tent among us, thus entering the conditions of historical and temporal existence.

1. Toward a Poetics of Persuasion

1 · In *Desire in Language: A Semiotic Approach to Literature and Art,* trans. Leon S. Roudiez (New York: Columbia University Press, 1980), pp. 113–114.

2 · In Walton's *Life of Herbert,* p. 320, describing his compliance with canons requiring all clergy to read the Daily Offices in public.

3 · See especially *The Family, Sex, and Marriage in England 1500–1800* (New York: Harper and Row, 1977). Stone has been criticized for minimizing the depth of affection which parents could feel for children even though they knew that there was a great risk of mortality among the young. On this, see Linda A. Pollock, *Forgotten Children: Parent-Child Relations from 1500 to 1900* (Cambridge: Cambridge University Press, 1983), and Steven Ozment, *When Fathers Ruled: Family Life in Reformation Europe* (Cambridge, Mass.: Harvard University Press, 1983). I suspect that parental concern for children was real (the source of Pollock's and Ozment's evidence) but also that denial of grief was also real (the source of Stone's evidence), since denial is a common enough mode of coping with loss even today.

4 · See Frank Whigham, *Ambition and Privilege: The Social Tropes of Elizabethan Courtesy Theory* (Berkeley: University of California Press, 1984), pp. 162–169.

5 · Cited from M. St. Clare Byrne, *Elizabethan Life in Town and Country* (London: Methuen, 1925), p. 25. Byrne's is still one of the most helpful introductions to Elizabethan culture. See also the helpful survey by Joyce Youings, *Sixteenth-Century England,* in the Pelican Social History of Britain Series (New York: Penguin, 1984).

6 · The most interesting recent study of the image of royalty in this age is Jonathan Goldberg, *James I and the Politics of Literature* (Baltimore: Johns Hopkins University Press, 1983), although Goldberg seems at times to believe, with James, the official rhetoric that the king truly held all power. I find that royal power in the Renaissance was a very nebulous thing, compounded of tradition and necessity as well as pretension and self-delusion. Tudor and Stuart monarchs never had the ability to control people and their flow of information that modern totalitarian rulers can muster.

7 · For the conditions of life, especially among women of child-bearing years, and the state of knowledge of premodern medicine, see Edward Shorter, *A History of Women's Bodies* (New York: Basic Books, 1982).

8 · See in addition to Stone, Alan MacFarlane, *Marriage and Love in England 1300–1840* (Oxford: Blackwell, 1986).

9 · In *Religion and the Decline of Magic* (New York: Scribner's, 1971).

10 · For a romanticized version of life in rural England when the knowledge on which survival was based was passed on from parents to children in often experiential and nonverbal ways, see Dorothy Hartley, *Lost Country Life* (New York: Pantheon, 1979).

11 · Unless otherwise specified, quotations from the Book of Common Prayer are taken from the edition of the 1559 Prayer Book edited by John E. Booty (Charlottesville: University Press of Virginia for Folger Shakespeare Library, 1976)) and are cited by page numbers in that edition. Occasionally, I need to cite texts from the editions of 1549 or 1552, or from the 1604 edition, or lectionaries and Prayer Book supplements printed at other times, and I will note such appropriately. In general, however, the basic texts of the Prayer Book as experienced by Spenser, Herbert, and Vaughan are the texts of the Prayer Book authorized by the Elizabethan Settlement of Religion.

12 · In his *The First Urban Christians: The Social World of the Apostle Paul* (New Haven: Yale University Press, 1983), p. 164. Meeks points out that when Christian writing is removed from its original setting or placed in a different one, it "is liable to mean something quite different" from what it meant originally. I understand the function of interpretation as recovering original meaning not to limit meaning but to give us access to meaning we would not otherwise have.

13 · Use of the English Litany, required on Wednesdays and Fridays, is not a beginning, because, of course, it is an interpretation of what the beginning of English worship in the vernacular could be. What interests me is precisely how Cranmer interpreted that beginning in this, his first vernacular liturgical text.

14 · Quotations from the English Litany and documents related to it are from F. E. Brightman, *The English Rite: Being a Synopsis of the Sources and Revisions of the Book of Common Prayer* (London: Rivingtons, 1921), pp. lviii–lxviii and 174–191.

15 · Ibid.

16 · In spite of the differences separating their editors in matters of theology and ceremonial, all later Renaissance translations of the Bible (with the exception of Douay-Rheims) are based on the Great Bible. See F. F. Bruce, *History of the Bible in English,* 3rd ed. (New York: Oxford, 1978).

17 · Puritans in *The Second Admonition* to Parliament, for example, would object to time "spent in praying for and praying against the (commodities and) incommodities of this life, which is contrary to all . . . of the Prayers of the Church set down in Scripture," all major elements of the Litany.

18 · For details of the history of the Litany, see *Liturgy and Worship: A Companion to the Prayer Books of the Anglican Communion,* ed. W. K. Lowther Clark (London: SPCK, 1959), pp. 148 ff., and Francis Procter and Walter Howard Frere, *A New History of the Book of Common Prayer* (London: Macmillan, 1965), pp. 31–33 and 405–429.

19 · Brightman, *The English Rite,* p. lix, thinks Cranmer himself wrote this document.

20 · *Sermons,* VIII, 310.

21 · See my introduction to Erasmus, *The Paraphrases on the Gospels and Acts* (Delmar, N.Y.: Scholars' Facsimiles and Reprints, 1976).

22 · *The Machiavellian Moment: Florentine Political Thought and the Atlantic Republican Tradition* (Princeton: Princeton University Press, 1975).

23 · *The Renaissance Discovery of Time* (Cambridge: Harvard University Press, 1972).

24 · Pocock, *Machiavellian Moment,* p. 4.

25 · Charles Trinkaus notes Erasmus' concern with "the specific, never the gen-

eral," a consequence of his "philological and historical . . . approach [to] the interpretation of the Scriptures," as "characteristic of his humanism and the direct consequence of his extensive Biblical studies," making up his *theologia rhetorica;* see "Erasmus, Augustine, and the Nominalists," reprinted in *The Scope of Renaissance Humanism* (Ann Arbor: University of Michigan Press, 1983), p. 290.

26 · For a detailed examination of this development, see John E. Booty, ed., *The Godly Kingdom of Tudor England: Great Books of the English Reformation* (Wilton, Conn.: Morehouse-Barlow, 1981), especially my essay " 'Godly and Fruitful Lessons': The English Bible, Erasmus' *Paraphrases,* and the Book of Homilies," pp. 45–135. See also my essay "The Book of Homilies of 1547 and the Continuity of English Humanism in the Sixteenth Century," *Anglican Theological Review* 58 (1976): 75–87. See also Sloane, *Donne, Milton, and the End of Humanist Rhetoric,* pp. 65–144, although I disagree with Sloane about the degree of (potential) opposition between rhetoric and (at least the English) Reformers.

27 · Kristeva, *Desire in Language,* pp. 113–114.

28 · *Sermons,* VIII, 219–220.

29 · Studies of Donne's sermons include John S. Chamberlin, *Increase and Multiply: Arts-of-Discourse Procedure in the Preaching of John Donne* (Chapel Hill: University of North Carolina Press, 1976); Winfried Schleiner, *The Imagery of John Donne's Sermons* (Providence: Brown University Press, 1970); William R. Mueller, *John Donne: Preacher* (Princeton University Press, 1962), and T. A. H. McNaron, *John Donne's Sermons Approached as Dramatic Dialogues of One* (Ann Arbor: University of Michigan Press, 1964). W. Fraser Mitchell's *English Pulpit Oratory from Andrewes to Tillotson* (London: Russell and Russell, 1932) is still the standard overview. A helpful introduction to Donne's sermon technique is found in Janel Mueller's edition of *Donne's Prebend Sermons* (Cambridge: Harvard University Press, 1971). The early seventeenth-century sermon as an open-ended work is explored by Stanley Fish in *Self-Consuming Artifacts,* pp. 43–77, in regard to Donne, and in "Structuralist Homiletics" (1973; reprinted in *Is There a Text in This Class: The Authority of Interpretive Communities* [Cambridge: Harvard University Press, 1980], pp. 182–196), in regard to Lancelot Andrews.

30 · *The City of God,* trans. Henry Betterson (London: Pelican, 1972), p. 379.

31 · See Boyle, *Erasmus,* p. vii. See also Sloane, *Donne,* pp. 67–84.

32 · In the 1549 BCP; the BCP of 1552 dropped all reference to the Mass, reflecting and enacting a widening rupture between medieval worship and the emerging Anglican church.

33 · Thus William Tyndale: "The Scripture hath but one sense, which is the literal sense. . . . The Scripture indeed useth proverbs, similitudes, riddles, or allegories, as all other speeches do; but that which the proverb, similitude, riddle, or allegory signifieth is ever the literal sense." In *Works* (London: Palmer, 1831), vol. 1, pp. 303–304.

34 · Erasmus, *The Godly Feast,* trans. Craig R. Thompson, in *Colloquies* (New York: Bobbs-Merrill, 1957), pp. 133–134.

35 · See Boyle, *Erasmus,* p. 94; see also Charles Trinkaus, "Erasmus, Augustine, and the Nominalists," in *Scope,* pp. 274–301, for a discussion of Erasmus' "pastoral and rhetorical" theology.

36 · Boyle, *Erasmus,* p. 140.

37 · In "Anglican Spirituality: An Ethos and Some Issues," in *Anglican Spirituality*, ed. William T. Wolf (Wilton, Conn.: Morehouse-Barlow, 1982), p. 6.

38 · In Walton's *Life of Herbert*, p. 320.

39 · In his preface to the BCP of 1549, Cranmer asserts, "Now from henceforth all the whole realme shall have but one use." See *First and Second Prayer Books*, p. 4.

40 · For a more extensive discussion of this, see Guthrie, *Theology as Thanksgiving*, pp. 31–70.

41 · The fullest discussion of the Primers to date is Helen C. White, *The Tudor Books of Private Devotion* (Madison: University of Wisconsin Press, 1951), p. 121. Because White views medieval piety as liturgical rather than extraliturgical, she sees the Primers of Anglicanism as manifesting a development "away from the liturgical" (p. 237), a precise reversal of what actually transpired. Medieval primers are "liturgical" only in that they supplied the faithful with something to do while the priest said the Mass in Latin; otherwise, they have nothing to do with liturgy. On the other hand, the Anglican Primers make possible the orientation of worship alone or in families to the ongoing public worship of the church. For more on the Primers, see David Siegenthaler, "Religious Education for Citizenship: Primer and Catechism," in Booty, *The Godly Kingdom*, pp. 217–249.

42 · "A Confutation of Unwritten Verities," reprinted in *Cranmer: Miscellaneous Writings*, ed. John Cox (Cambridge: Cambridge University Press, 1846), vol. 1, p. 63.

43 · For a fuller discussion of this departure from patristic practice in the Middle Ages, see Dix, pp. 546–612. Dix's *Shape of the Liturgy* is one of the fundamental documents in the development of modern liturgical theology and practice; the only place at which he is now seriously faulted is in his reading of Cranmer's eucharistic theology, pp. 613–734. For a more recent view, see Booty, in *Godly and Fruitful Lessons* and in *The Elizabethan Prayer Book*.

44 · In "An Answer by the Reverend Father in God Thomas Archbishop of Canterbury," in *Writings*, vol. 2, p. 11.

45 · See Cranmer's attack on late medieval piety in the Book of Homilies (London: Whitchurche, 1547), sigs. J3–Klv.

46 · One of the great achievements of recent liturgical scholarship is the recovery of the patristic theology of the Eucharist, in light of which the Reformation controversies over the definition of "real presence" appear as distractions from the central issue. What is now also clear is that, if we pay attention to Cranmer's Prayer Books and his comments on his eucharistic theology, they were distractions for him as well. For modern discussions of liturgical theology, see *Anglican-Roman Catholic International Commission: The Final Report* (Cincinatti: Forward Movement, 1982), pp. 11–25, and J. D. Crichton, "A Theology of Worship," in *The Study of Liturgy*, ed. Cheslyn Jones, Geoffrey Wainwright, and Edward Yarnold, S.J. (New York: Oxford University Press, 1978), pp. 3–29. For application of these insights to the English Prayer Book, see John Booty, "Communion and Common Weal: The Book of Common Prayer," in *Godly and Fruitful Lessons*, pp. 137–216.

47 · "Mimesis and Representation," trans. David Pelauer, *Annals of Scholarship* 2 (1981): 17.

48 · On contrasts between Anglican and Puritan views on the relationship be-

tween preaching and sacraments, see Paul S. Seaver, *The Puritan Lectureships: The Politics of Religious Dissent* (Stanford: Stanford University Press, 1970), pp. 15–54.

49 · Hooker, *Lawes*, I.2, in *Works*, ed. W. Speed Hill (Cambridge, Mass.: Harvard University Press, 1977–), vol. 1, p. 57.

50 · The history of interpreting Hooker is rife with examples of those who look to the *Lawes* to know what Hooker believed rather than for what he felt his audience would find convincing. We miss the import of Hooker's intent if we overlook the extent to which the word "persuade" and the motif of seeking a common ground with those whom he would persuade to remain loyal to Anglicanism rather than follow the Presbyterian opposition dominate the presentation of his argument. See especially F. J. Shirley, *Richard Hooker and the Contemporary Political Ideas* (London: SPCK, 1949), and, more recently, Robert K. Faulkner, *Richard Hooker and the Politics of a Christian England* (Berkeley: University of California Press, 1981). For an assessment of other works on Hooker, see the essays and bibliography in W. Speed Hill, *Studies in Richard Hooker* (Cleveland: Case Western University Press, 1972).

51 · Hooker, *Lawes*, p. 57.

52 · The reading of texts "in order" is an important directional motif in Anglican documents, from the Book of Homilies (to be read "in suche ordre, as they stande in the boke") to the Prayer Book, suggesting the functioning of such texts in relationship to the directing of experience and the shaping of time as well as for the development of meaning, as the opening sermons in the Book of Homilies on reading of Scripture, faith and works come to have their full meaning in terms of the later sermons on specific works to do and sins to avoid. See BOH, sig. A 2v.

53 · Always interpretations already, each providing through the use of certain forms in specific ways an interpretation of the events they describe or the injunctions they seek to act out. Thus, the Prayer Book is an interpretation of Christ's injunction to "do this for the remembrance of me."

54 · From "Perirrhanterium," ll. 5–6. Quoted from *Works*, ed. F. E. Hutchinson (Oxford: Clarendon, 1941), p. 6. All further citations to Herbert's works will be from this edition. See also my own modern-spelling edition of Herbert (1981; reprinted New York: Paulist Press, 1984).

55 · *A Defence of Poetry*, in *Miscellaneous Prose*, ed. Katherine Duncan-Jones and Jan van Dorsten (Oxford: Clarendon, 1973), p. 77. All further quotations from Sidney's *Defence* will be from this edition and will be cited by page numbers in the text.

56 · (London: Thomas Woodcocke, 1579), sig. A4ᵛ.

57 · For a review of the relationship between the *Defence* and Gosson, see Arthur F. Kinney, "Parody and Its Implications in Sidney's *Defence of Poesie*," *SEL* 12 (1972): 1–19.

58 · For a review of the various recent approaches to Sidney's *Defence*, see W. L. Godshalk, "Recent Studies in Sidney (1970–77)," *ELR* 8 (1978): 212–233.

59 · In his book of the same name (Princeton: Princeton University Press, 1970).

60 · *Schoole*, sig. B3.

61 · In *Sir Philip Sidney: A Study of His Life and Works* (Cambridge: Cambridge University Press, 1977), p. 120.

62 · In "'Metaphor' and Sidney's *Defence of Poesie*," *John Donne Journal* 1 (1982): 117. In his fine discussion of Sidney's concept of metaphor, Heninger stresses the

ways in which Sidney draws on many traditions of theory and brings them together to achieve a sense of poetry that will achieve his goals. Especially in Heninger's sense of metaphor as a word stressing verbal action ("to carry over," "to transfer," p. 130) I find support for my own argument.

63 · *Schoole,* sig. D1ᵛ.

64 · Ricoeur, "Mimesis and Representation," p. 4.

65 · Discussions of Sidney's *Defence* that explore his debt, or lack of it, to Aristotle's definition of poetry as mimetic, or imitative, usually adopt a Platonic notion of mimesis and impose it on Aristotle. As Paul Ricoeur has pointed out, however, the Platonic sense of mimesis, "a redoubled presence, [in which] works of art and of language [are] taken for weakened copies of things," is not Aristotle's. Thus, a work of art is mimetic to the extent to which it produces "an augmentation of meaning," not to the extent to which it mirrors a preexisting reality. For a review and evaluation of the more traditional approach to this matter, see Lawrence C. Wolfley, "Sidney's Visual-Didactic Poetic: Some Complexities and Limitations," *JMRS* 6 (1976): 217–241.

66 · Ricoeur, "Mimesis and Representation," p. 10.

67 · Sidney includes the rhetorician in this list, thinking, presumably, of the rhetorician who uses language to reinforce what is already present, rather than the rhetorician of Wilson's treatise who uses rhetoric to bring into being the new relationships he posits through persuasion.

68 · See, for example, Heninger, *Touches of Sweet Harmony* (San Marino: Huntington Library, 1974), pp. 298–301, and Hamilton, *Sir Philip Sidney,* pp. 111–113.

69 · Failure to be fully aware of Anglicanism's emphases produces unusual interpretations at this point in many accounts of Sidney's argument. Thus, Geoffrey Shepherd notes that "In Sidney's circle of acquaintains Psalm-singing Christians must have been numerous" (in his edition of *An Apology for Poetry* [New York: Barnes and Noble, 1973], p. 161), but the use of musical settings for the Psalms was practically universal in Anglicanism, making Shepherd's remark a gross understatement at best. Hamilton finds that in his discussion of the "first kind" Sidney "allows only that the divine poet may cheer the merry and console the troubled" (p. 112), which, if one takes the moral emphases of Anglicanism seriously, is precisely the point. Forrest Robinson, in *The Shape of Things Known: Sidney's "Apology" in Its Philosophical Tradition* (Cambridge: Harvard University Press, 1972), accepts a dichotomy between nature and grace as being so fundamental to Sidney that he could not conceive of poetry's having a place in the economy of salvation (p. 101). Robinson is right in identifying an essentially gnostic strain in the hermetic tradition, but his reading of Sidney in this tradition ignores the fundamental ways in which Anglicanism locates salvation as being through this world, the emphasis being on "all such good works" achievable by faith through grace. Andrew Weiner, in *Sir Philip Sidney and the Poetics of Protestantism: A Study in Contexts* (Minneapolis: University of Minnesota Press, 1978), objects rightly to Robinson's conclusions (p. 45) but then in effect resurrects them (p. 50) as a result of his uncritical overreliance on Calvin's emphasis on a dichotomy between faith and works. Leigh DeNeef's discussions of the *Apology* are among the most helpful, however; I am in complete agreement with him that for Sidney and Spenser the goal of poetry is "societal and religious reform" (*Spenser and the Motives of Meta-*

phor [Durham, N.C.: Duke University Press, 1982], p. 10). See especially his "Rereading Sidney's *Apology*," *JMRS* 10 (1980): 155–191 for a discussion of Sidney's "fore-conceit" as an infinitive, with the suggestion that by this Sidney means a potential for action which comes to have meaning when it is realized in the behavior of the reader.

70 · Book of Homilies, sig. F4.

71 · See Heninger, "'Metaphor,'" p. 130.

72 · Among the many studies of rhetoric in the English Renaissance, Marion Trousdale's *Shakespeare and the Rhetoricians* (Chapel Hill: University of North Carolina Press, 1982) is one of the few that emphasizes the point that "it is the effect of discourse that matters" (p. 23). Most studies focus on the use of figures of rhetoric in poetry and other writing—essentially the use of verbal devices to further the text's effectiveness—or on the concept of invention as a way of talking about the relationship between the world the poet addresses and the work he creates to address that world.

73 · Northrop Frye, in an address to the American Academy of Arts and Sciences, quoted in *Context: A Commentary on the Interaction of Religion and Culture* (June 1, 1982), p. 1.

74 · In his *The Arte of Rhetorique* (1550), reprinted in *English Literary Criticism: The Renaissance,* ed. O. B. Hardison (New York: Appleton Century Crofts, 1963). Wilson says, "The end of Rhetorique" is "To teach. To delight. And to perswade" (p. 30). Links in the rhetorical tradition are explored helpfully by Sloane, *Donne,* pp. 67–144, and Heninger, "'Metaphor,'" pp. 124–146.

75 · Robert L. Montgomery's *The Reader's Eye: Studies in Didactic Literary Theory from Dante to Tasso* (Berkeley: University of California Press, 1949) provides a helpful discussion of Renaissance didacticism from another perspective, that of Renaissance psychology and the clues it provides us as to how didactic poets understood what human capabilities enabled their readers to respond to the didactic poem. My own procedure is to assume that such response was possible and then to explore those verbal strategies in the works themselves which give them "that same forcefulness or *energia*" needed to provoke their readers' responses.

76 · "A Letter of the Authors to Sir Walter Raleigh," reprinted in *The Faerie Queene,* ed. A. C. Hamilton (London: Longman, 1977), p. 737. Further quotations from *The Faerie Queene* will be from this edition and will be cited in the text according to book, canto, and stanza number.

77 · In *Works,* p. 140.

78 · For helpful discussions of attitudes toward the efficacy of language in the sixteenth and seventeenth centuries, see Margreta De Grazia, "Shakespeare's View of Language: An Historical Perspective," *Shakespeare Quarterly* 29 (1978): 378–388, and "The Secularization of Language in the Seventeenth Century," *JHI* (1980): 319–329. The self-revealing inadequacy of the purely human language act has been a particular concern of Stanley Fish; see his "Letting Go: The Dialectic of the Self in Herbert's Poetry," in *Self-Consuming Artifacts,* pp. 156–223, and *The Living Temple: George Herbert and Catechizing* (Berkeley: University of California Press, 1978). See also Barbara Leah Harmon, *Costly Monuments: Representations of the Self* (Cambridge: Harvard University Press, 1983).

79 · Among a number of studies, see especially Joan Simon, *Education and Society in Tudor England* (Cambridge: Cambridge University Press, 1966); James K. Mc-Conica, *English Humanists and Reformation Politics in the Reigns of Henry VIII and Edward VI* (Oxford: Oxford University Press, 1965); Arthur B. Ferguson, *The Articulate Citizen and the English Renaissance* (Durham: Duke University Press, 1965), and Joel B. Altman, *The Tudor Play of Mind: Rhetorical Inquiry and the Development of Elizabethan Drama* (Berkeley: University of California Press, 1978). See also Sloane, *Donne*, pp. 64–144, for an analysis of English humanist rhetorical theory and its sources.

80 · For an application of this phenomenon to literary study, see Altman, *Tudor Play of Mind*, esp. pp. 31–106.

81 · *Arte*, p. 27.

82 · Ibid., pp. 27–28.

83 · For a fuller discussion of the use of rhetoric in the Book of Homilies, see my "The Book of Homilies of 1547 and the Continuity of English Humanism in the Sixteenth Century," *Anglican Theological Review* 58 (1976): 75–87.

84 · In "A shorte declaration of the true, lyvely and christian faythe," one of the twelve sermons in the Book of Homilies, sigs. B4–B4^4.

85 · This shift is perhaps nowhere more visible than in the controversy over the doctrine of transubstantiation. Cranmer's shift of emphasis highlights a new sense of the function of liturgical language. According to the medieval doctrine against which Cranmer reacted, the saying of the words *hoc est einum corpus meum* by the priest made the *res* what the *verba* said it was in an objective, static, atemporal sense. Cranmer's move from a priest-centered Mass toward a community-centered rite of Communion stresses the rite as a verbally enacted means of coming to participate in the divine action in the world. The priest's saying "this is my body" informs the community of the relationship between God and his people and offers the words, the bread, and the offerers to God for his use in furthering his reconciling work in the world. To "do this in remembrance of me" becomes a use of language and bread to enable their use by God to establish a typological relationship with the particular action of God in Christ, orienting through use the present moment to the future with God proclaimed and promised in that event. In this way, the self-revelation of God through Christ in human time, orienting all time toward his future, gained not through a denial of time but through the very medium of time itself, becomes the focus of the rite. For a fuller discussion of this departure from patristic practice in the Middle Ages, see Dix, *Shape of the Liturgy*, pp. 546–612.

86 · See especially Herbert's discussions of preaching and catechizing in *The Country Parson*, pp. 232–235 and 255–257 of *Works*.

87 · Trousdale explores the rhetorical backgrounds and didactic implications of the desire for copiousness in *Shakespeare and the Rhetoricians*, pp. 39–64.

88 · See Jane Tompkins' discussion in "The Reader in History: The Changing Shape of Literary Response," in *Reader-Response Criticism: From Formalism to Post-Structuralism*, ed. Jane P. Tompkins (Baltimore: Johns Hopkins University Press, 1980), pp. 201–232.

89 · Against those who would see a continuity not only of method but also of world view between the classics and Christian writing that makes use of the classics, see Macklin Smith, *Prudentius' "Psychomachia": A Reexamination*, esp. pp. 234–300.

90 · I am indebted to the Reverend Lloyd Patterson, W. R. Huntington Professor

of Historical Theology at the Episcopal Divinity School, for guiding me through the basic premises of the discussion which follows.

91 · For discussions of mythic consciousness, see Schneidau, *Sacred Discontent*, pp. 50–103, and Charity, *Events and Their Afterlife* (Cambridge: Cambridge University Press, 1966), pp. 13–20.

92 · In Fish, *Self-Consuming Artifacts*, pp. 5–21.

93 · See especially Yates, *Giordano Bruno and the Hermetic Tradition* (Chicago: University of Chicago Press, 1964).

94 · For a reading of Renaissance allegory in these terms, see Michael Murrin, *The Veil of Allegory: Some Notes toward a Theory of Allegorical Rhetoric in the English Renaissance* (Chicago: University of Chicago Press, 1969) and *The Allegorical Epic: Essays in Its Rise and Decline* (Chicago: University of Chicago Press, 1980).

95 · Such a position would seem fundamental to the mythologizing approach taken to *The Faerie Queene* in Angus Fletcher, *Allegory: The Theory of a Symbolic Mode* (Ithaca: Cornell University Press, 1964) and James Nohrnberg, *The Analogy of "The Faerie Queene"* (Princeton: Princeton University Press, 1976).

96 · In Tompkins, "The Reader in History," pp. 203–205, and Fish, *Self-Consuming Artifacts*, pp. 17–20.

97 · As Tompkins points out, this is especially apparent in the Renaissance in the works of Ben Jonson, where the goal of poetry is the acquisition of power "for what it can do for the aristocracy it serves" (p. 208). For a fuller discussion of Jonson as a poet dependent on conventionally held values, see Manley, *Convention: 1500–1750*, (Cambridge: Harvard University Press, 1980), pp. 193–199.

98 · For discussions of the prophetic in Spenser and Milton, see William Kerrigan, *The Prophetic Milton* (Charlottesville: University of Virginia Press, 1974) and Joseph Anthony Wittreich, Jr., *Visionary Poetics: Milton's Tradition and His Legacy* (San Marino: Huntington Library, 1979). Both writers identify the prophetic figure with the visionary or inspired speaker, Wittreich especially identifying the prophet with apocalyptic writing, an identification which few modern biblical scholars would accept. The defining prophetic figures in the Bible are Isaiah, Jeremiah, and Christ, whose central act is the proclamation of the Word to a specific historical situation, calling people in that situation to judgment, relationship, and promise and whose presence performing that function becomes itself a sign of the ongoing involvement of God in history. Apocalyptic writing, like that found in Daniel and Revelation, is at best a subgenre of prophetic discourse called for in certain extreme situations, such as the Diocletian persecution, where the use of violent and vivid imagery in foretelling the future becomes a means of urging that the community so addressed keep the faith in the face of events that seem to deny the efficacy of divine promises. See Gerhard von Rad, *Old Testament Theology*, vol. 2, pp. 301–315.

99 · Wright, *God Who Acts: Biblical Theology as Recital* (London: SCM, 1952), p. 3.

100 · See Charity, *Events and Their Afterlife*, pp. 29–30.

101 · Guthrie, *Theology as Thanksgiving*, pp. 212–216.

102 · The term "applied typology" is that of A. C. Charity, in *Events and Their Afterlife* (Cambridge: Cambridge University Press, 1966), pp. 148–164, coined to distinguish the present-oriented existential functioning of biblical and biblically based typology from the traditional use of the term to mean simply the anticipation of

New Testament events in the Old, or a more symbolic usage as adornment of the text with biblical references. I am deeply indebted to Charity's splendid summary of biblical scholarship throughout this section. For discussions of typology as a mode of symbolism rather than as a mode of defining time and relationships, see Earl Miner, ed., *Literary Uses of Typology from the Late Middle Ages to the Present* (Princeton: Princeton University Press, 1977), and Barbara K. Lewalski, "The Biblical Symbolic Mode: Typology and the Religious Lyric," in *Protestant Poetics and the Seventeenth-Century Religious Lyric*, pp. 111–144.

103 · In Schneidau, *Sacred Discontent*, pp. 1–103.

104 · See Auerbach, *Mimesis*, pp. 8–18. See also Schneidau, *Sacred Discontent*, pp. 266–267.

105 · See Wright, *God Who Acts*.

106 · In *Works*, vol. 2, pp. 67–110.

107 · By this I do not mean that the Bible held for these writers the status, in the term of Geoffrey Hartman, of a "great Original" to which interpretation cannot be applied. See his *The Fate of Reading* (Chicago: University of Chicago Press, 1975), esp. pp. 16–17. Thomas Greene is right that such an attitude cannot lead to a literature that functions "transitively," or "open a window in the prison house of culture." He is also right in stating the issue in terms of a reaction against "the liturgical repetitions of an age lacking historical consciousness"—the Middle Ages—against which the Prayer Book as text for use in an age of heightened historical consciousness was created. See his helpful discussion of these issues in *The Light in Troy: Imitation and Discovery in Renaissance Poetry* (New Haven: Yale University Press, 1982), esp. pp. 28–53. The central issue here is the English Reformers' recovery of *anamnesis*, as in "Do this for the *anamnesis* of me." In the context of Anglicanism, the Bible comes to be understood as the text that is read in church by means of its relationship to the ongoing life of the church defined and identified by use of the Prayer Book, thus deriving its authority from that use and what that use enables. Its authority does not stand outside of that use, through which the events of the past it records are "remembered" through recitation of those events in the present. The Bible provides the narratives through which the significance of the present can be understood, providing now "all benefits of his passion." Nor by describing the Anglican sense of a sacramentalized view of language do I mean the Puritan emphasis on the Bible as the Word and on preaching as the quintessential Christian act, as described most recently in John R. Knott's *The Sword of the Spirit: Puritan Responses to the Bible* (Chicago: University of Chicago Press, 1980) and by Georgia B. Christopher in *Milton and the Science of the Saints* (Princeton: Princeton University Press, 1982). Verbal discourse, whether sermon or poem, was to Anglicans to be understood in the context of the action of language with water and bread and wine in sacramental enactment; the Bible conveys God's Word. Again, use of language comes to mean in relationship to a process and does not stand independent of that process.

2. Edmund Spenser

1 · In part because of the "nature-grace" debate, which turns on seeing Book I of *The Faerie Queene* as dealing with the realm of grace and the rest of the poem as dealing

with the realm of nature, first articulated in this form by A. S. P. Woodhouse in his influential "Nature and Grace in *The Faerie Queene*," *ELH* 16 (1949): 194–228. Although Woodhouse does suggest a coming synthesis of a higher to a lower order, a more rigorous division is argued by Lewis A. Miller in his "A Secular Reading of *The Faerie Queene*, Book II," *ELH* 33 (1966): 154–169. In any case, *The Faerie Queene* is not included in Lily B. Campbell's consideration of Spenser's religious poetry in her *Divine Poetry and Drama in Sixteenth-Century England* (Cambridge: Cambridge University Press, 1961). This approach to Spenser has had sufficient acceptance to allow Carol V. Kaske to assert more recently that "the philosophical point of view in *The Faerie Queene* somehow shifts from the exclusively Christian in Book I to the broadly humanistic in the later books"; see her "Spenser's Pluralistic Universe: The View from the Mount of Contemplation," in *Contemporary Thought on Edmund Spenser*, ed. Richard C. Frushell and Bernard J. Vondersmith (Carbondale: Southern Illinois University Press, 1975), p. 122. Implicit in this approach is the claim that there is a fundamental separation in the Renaissance world view between nature and grace, so that sacred and secular realms can be conceived and sustained as distinct entities. Although no one would deny that Renaissance texts use such a distinction, I would claim that it is a functional distinction, not an ontological one, which is used to distinguish the position of the Christian speaker from that which he would change, but that the Anglican attempt to function through the whole arena of human activity undercuts the finality of such a distinction. For a recent discussion, see Anthea Hume, *Edmund Spenser: Protestant Poet* (Cambridge: Cambridge University Press, 1984), pp. 59–66. Hume reaches conclusions similar to mine ("The poem's subject is nothing less than the spiritual, moral, emotional and social life of man," p. 68) but from very different premises. For Hume, the sixteenth-century Church of England was Calvinistic (p. 4) and at least the early Spenser was a Puritan (p. 9), two positions which I find untenable.

2 · See *FQ*, IV.xi.8ff. Hamilton notes, after Holinshed, that the Medway was so named because "the course therof is midwaie in a manner betweene London and . . . Canterburie," the seats of English legal and religious authority. The Church of England as a "*via media*," or "middle way" between Rome and Geneva was a commonplace of polemic in the sixteenth century. On the history of the English church as a *via media*, see H. C. Porter, "Hooker, the Tudor Constitution, and the *Via Media*," in *Studies in Richard Hooker*, ed. W. Speed Hill (Cleveland: Case Western Reserve University Press, 1972), esp. pp. 90–100. James Nohrnberg points out the importance of this episode for Books III and IV of *FQ* in his *The Analogy of "The Faerie Queene"* (Princeton: Princeton University Press, 1976), p. 66. The concept of the *via media* was not a position to which Anglicans aspired; it emerged in the controversies of the sixteenth century among Catholics, Anglicans, and Puritans as a way of articulating a position for the Church of England in apologetic writing aimed at Anglican opposition. It is therefore not correct to use it as a way of interpreting the Church of England, as in for example the commonplace that Anglicans had a Catholic liturgy and a Protestant theology. The Prayer Book was not recognized as being Catholic by Catholics, nor was its theology recognizable as Protestant by Puritans.

3 · Cited from Peter Milward, *Religious Controversies of the Elizabethan Age* (Lincoln: University of Nebraska Press, 1977), p. 77.

4 · For a discussion of the prophesying controversy, see William P. Haugaard,

("true belief leads England to the accession of Elizabeth; or the queen guides the Christian believer to redeem a nation" [p. 58]), again turning from an examination of the function of praising Elizabeth in moving an audience which included her.

11 · All quotations from *The Faerie Queene* are from the edition of J. C. Smith (Oxford: Clarendon, 1909) and will be cited in the text by reference to book, canto, and stanza numbers.

12 · From Spenser's "Letter to Raleigh," reprinted in *The Faerie Queene*, ed. A. C. Hamilton (London: Longman, 1977), p. 737. The importance of this letter for grasping Spenser's purpose in *FQ* has recently been reaffirmed by Ronald Horton in *The Unity of "The Faerie Queene"* (Athens: University of Georgia Press, 1978), although the terms in which Horton makes his case are quite different from my own.

13 · Connecting, presumably, Archimago's image making with the image of "that towre of glas" in Spenser's own "ditty." For a helpful discussion of the relationship between Spenser and Archimago, see A. Leigh DeNeef's *Spenser and the Motives of Metaphor* (Durham: Duke University Press, 1982), esp. pp. 92–102.

14 · Hooker, *Lawes*, I.57. Hooker's *Lawes* was written in response to the same crisis in Anglican history that concerned Spenser in the 1580s. Far from being an Anglican *summa*, the *Lawes* is a rhetorical work intended to persuade Puritans to participate in Prayer Book worship.

15 · Although, as we will soon see, to "read" *The Faerie Queene* is to engage in an activity not limited to the personal and mental processes of intellection.

16 · For a helpful discussion of "reading" in Spenser that parallels to some extent my own discussion, see DeNeef, *Spenser and the Motives of Metaphor*, pp. 142–156. I am deeply indebted to DeNeef's remarkable work here and at other times.

17 · James E. Phillips, "Spenser's Syncretistic Religious Imagery," *ELH* 36 (1969): 110–130.

18 · Thus especially James Nohrnberg, who sees at this moment of the poem Red Crosse's adherence "to a spiritual ideal," in *The Analogy of "The Faerie Queene,"* p. 73. Nohrnberg's sense that Spenser's poem is symbolically a zodiac (p. 761) in which all analogies are equally significant, even as the zodiac has twelve equally significant signs, is the high point of a school of interpreting Spenser to which this study is a kind of reply. The weaving of references to biblical and classical sources and analogies into an equisignificant display creating a self-contained world of the poem denies the fundamental significance of biblical reference as seeking to control the field of discourse and thus undercutting the rival claims of classical texts.

19 · Although in *The Prophetic Moment: An Essay on Spenser* (Chicago: University of Chicago Press, 1971) Fletcher does see Spenser as using biblical references and prophetic models, his scheme for understanding the Bible itself is a mythic scheme in which temple and labyrinth together create "sacred space," the threshold between which gives "the sense that great deeds contain within their forms the seeds of great truths" (p. 75), he gives away his mythic conception of the poem in references to its being a "timeless circle of continual change" (p. 57) "whose aim is to unfold states of being" (p. 54). Fletcher does approach my argument, however, when he sees *FQ* as picking "up an immense surplus of literary energy which comes through as a steady allusive recollection of the Bible" (p. 69).

20 · See his *The Veil of Allegory: Some Notes toward a Theory of Allegorical Rhetoric in the English Renaissance* (Chicago: University of Chicago Press, 1969) and *The Allegorical Epic: Essays in Its Rise and Decline* (Chicago: University of Chicago Press, 1970).

21 · My descriptions of mythic consciousness here are drawn from Charity, *Events and Their Afterlife*, pp. 13–56, and Schneidau, *Sacred Discontent*, pp. 50–102. See also G. Ernest Wright, *God Who Acts: Biblical Theology as Recital*, pp. 3–16.

22 · In *When the Gods Are Silent*, trans. J. W. Doberstein (New York: Harper and Row, 1967), p. 9. See also the analysis of Lévi-Strauss in Schneidau, *Sacred Discontent*, pp. 50–103.

23 · Maureen Quilligan makes a similar point; see *The Language of Allegory*, pp. 27–31.

24 · Thus, for example, Mark Rose, *Spenser's Art* (Cambridge: Harvard University Press, 1975), pp. 129–130, and Douglas Brooks-Davies, *Spenser's "Faerie Queene": A Critical Commentary on Books I and II* (Manchester: Manchester University Press, 1977), pp. 101–102, where Cleopolis is compared to Rome. Robert Kellog and Oliver Steele, in the introduction to their edition of Books I and II (New York: Odyssey, 1965) also allude to Augustinian dualism in this context but read the House of Pride as the City of Man. Robert Horton, in his *The Unity of "The Faerie Queene,"* pp. 54–55, juxtaposes Cleopolis and the New Jerusalem in terms of the active versus the contemplative life, a stance also evoked by Brooks-Davies.

25 · Among recent critics two especially avoid drawing a simple dichotomy between Cleopolis and the City of God. Michael O'Connell notes, in his *Mirror and Veil: The Historical Dimension of Spenser's "The Faerie Queene"* (Chapel Hill: University of North Carolina Press, 1977), that Spenser here "suggests that Britain's history has itself become a partaking of sacred myth" (p. 43). Thomas Cain, in his *Praise in "The Faerie Queene"*, while defining the relationship between the two cities in terms of active versus contemplative styles of living, points out that Gloriana's role in the passage "makes it possible to transcend the basic opposition of heaven and earth" (p. 113). Neither critic, however, indicates the essentially sequential link between citizenship in the two cities established by Red Crosse's guide. Both these books remind us of the importance of the historical dimension in *The Faerie Queene*, a subject neglected in recent Spenser studies; my own debt to O'Connell and Cain is considerable. My point of departure from their work, however, centers on our differing sense of the relationship between the fictional world of the poem and the real world to which it alludes. For both Cain and O'Connell, the fictional world is a static description of, or praise of, or commentary upon, the real world, itself seen in static terms. In my view, *The Faerie Queene* presents its images of the real world to us to incite us to engage in an active process of transforming that world into what it "may be or should be" (to borrow terms from Sidney's *Defence of Poetry*). Thus, to Spenser's reader, his praise of Queen Elizabeth's England is always seen as ambivalent, since the reader is as aware of its distance from reality as he is of its validity. Yet because such praise is "true" in the fictional world of the poem, it becomes a living possibility in the real world to which that fictional world alludes.

26 · But also found in Book XI of *The Odyssey* and Book XIV of Tasso's *Jerusalem Delivered*, to mention two of the epic models Spenser posits for his poem in the "Letter to Raleigh." Perhaps the closest parallel to Red Crosse's vision, however, is found in

Canto 34 of Ariosto's *Orlando Furioso*. Here, Astolfo acts out both the classical journey to Hades and the biblical journey to the mountaintop. Astolfo's visionary city on the mountaintop is described in terms which anticipate Spenser's language of Cleopolis and the New Jerusalem, but the city itself is identified by his guide as the earthly paradise, not the New Jerusalem. Astolfo's "aged sire" turns out to be St. John the Evangelist, who, like Red Crosse's guide, says he is present to equip Astolfo to continue his earthly mission. Ariosto, however, unlike Spenser, makes no clear link between Astolfo's earthly quest and his eventual citizenship in the mountaintop city.

27 · A readily accessible version of the Legend of St. George is found in Jacobus de Voraigne's *Legenda Aurea,* published in eight editions in England before 1527.

28 · On the economy of biblical narrative and its implications, see Auerbach, *Mimesis,* pp. 11–23.

29 · Could Spenser be alluding to the specific celebration of All Saints' Day on November 1, 1584, the month in which Convocation approved Whitgift's Articles reinforcing observance of the Prayer Book? In that year, All Saints' Day was also the Twentieth Sunday after Trinity, on which the priest prayed that "we being ready both in body and soul, may with free hearts accomplish those things that thou wouldst have done." The lessons for that day include Ephesians 5, with its injunction that people "walk circumspectly, not as unwise, but as wise men, redeeming the time," and Matthew 22, with its parable of the kingdom of heaven as a wedding, all texts which have their relevance for Book I of *The Faerie Queene.*

30 · Among the various candidates noted by Brooks-Davies, Kellog and Steele, and A. C. Hamilton are Westminster Abbey, Greenwich Palace, and Windsor Castle.

31 · This does not contradict my earlier claim that the landscape of Faerieland is not England. Historically oriented critics of Spenser tend to see Faerieland as a description of England under the veil of allegory, so that the poem can tell us what happened there. My point is that Faerieland is an instrument for seeing England, not a mirror of it. The consequence of seeing England by means of *The Faerie Queene* is to be freed from preconceptions and to discover possibilities of making things new.

32 · In a paper delivered at the Southeastern Renaissance Conference, 11 April 1980, at Duke University, Durham, N.C.

33 · Quoted from P. F. Tytler, ed., *England under the Reigns of Edward VI and Mary* (London: R. Bentley, 1839), vol. 1, pp. 114–117.

34 · See, for example, Richmond Noble, *Shakespeare's Biblical Knowledge* (1935; repr. New York: Octagon, 1970); Alfred Hart, *Shakespeare and the Homilies* (1934; repr. New York: Octagon, 1970); and Naseeb Shaheen, *Biblical References in "The Faerie Queene"* (Memphis, Tenn.: Memphis State University Press, 1976).

35 · See, for instance, C. J. Stranks, *Anglican Devotion: Studies in the Spiritual Life of the Church of England between the Reformation and the Oxford Movement* (London: SCM, 1961) for a discussion of this point.

36 · This thesis is convincingly argued in Heiko Oberman's *The Harvest of Medieval Theology: Gabriel Biel and Late Medieval Nominalism* (1963; repr. Grand Rapids, Mich.: Eerdmans, 1967). For a discussion of individualism in the eucharistic theology of the late Middle Ages, see Dom Gregory Dix, *The Shape of the Liturgy,* 2nd ed. (Naperville, Ill.: Allenson, 1945), pp. 546–612.

37 · In *Certayne Sermons,* sigs. E1v–E2.

38 · Ibid., sigs. +2–+3.

39 · This is a constant theme of Cranmer's three great sermons in the Book of Homilies on salvation, faith, and works.

40 · This collapse of "sacred" into "secular" means that the virtues explored in *FQ* II–VII must be understood as defining the "sacred" in the realm of behavior, not opposing it.

41 · *Certayne Sermons,* sigs. Nl–Nlv.

42 · Ibid., sig. Plv.

43 · Ibid.

44 · My disagreement with D. Douglas Waters' argument in *Duessa as Theological Satire* (Columbia: University of Missouri Press, 1970) is thus a fundamental one of interpreting Book I in terms of Spenser's didactic purposes rather than as a dramatization of theological controversy or as an act of anti-Catholic polemic. His effort to understand the Church of England's eucharistic theology is marred by his desire to read the statements of Cranmer and others in terms of categories of thought rather than as enabling utterances aimed at furthering a sense of corporate participation in the Eucharist. Cranmer's eucharistic theology is informed by the enactment of the Prayer Book rites rather than the other way around.

45 · Letter to Jean Desmarez, in *The Correspondence of Erasmus,* trans. R. A. B. Mynors and D. F. S. Thompson, 2 vols. (Toronto: University of Toronto Press, 1974), vol. 2, p. 81. See also *The Education of a Christian Prince,* trans. Lester K. Born (New York: Columbia University Press, 1936), pp. 162–163.

46 · See my "The Book of Homilies and the Continuity of English Humanism in the Sixteenth Century," pp. 76–80. Robin Headlam Wells, in *Spenser's "Faerie Queene" and the Cult of Elizabeth* (London: Croom Helm, 1983), reaches a similar conclusion about the importance of Erasmus' *Enchiridion* for English reforming efforts, apparently without knowing of my work; see *Cult,* pp. 41–43.

47 · See Hume, *Spenser,* p. 105, for a recent argument of this position.

48 · (Baltimore: Johns Hopkins University Press, 1981). Goldberg explores some of the issues I have raised in this study, although he focuses on Books III and IV of *The Faerie Queene.* I find Goldberg's study "endlessly" fascinating and stimulating, especially in his discussion of the issues of the poet and the power of language, but I find Spenser more altruistic and didactic and less concerned with self-advancement than does Goldberg.

49 · All quotations from the *Epithalamion* are from the edition of Enid Welsford (Oxford: Basil Blackwell, 1967) and are cited by line number in the text.

50 · Thus the "key concept in the poem" is not "harmony," as A. R. Cirillo argues in his "Spenser's *Epithalamion:* The Harmonious Universe of Love," *SEL* 8 (1968): 20, but may at best be said to be a *hope* of harmony to be achieved in part through the events of the poem and their afterlife in the response of the reader. Forcing us to see the post-wedding party, where wine is poured out "by the belly full," and the speaker's references to shortness of his wedding night as a part of a harmonious picture reveals Cirillo's myth-making process of interpretation. An essentially mythic interpretation of marriage also colors Max Wickert's reading in his "Structure and Ceremony in Spenser's *Epithalamion,*" *ELH* 35 (1968): 135–157.

51 · See his *Spenser and the Motives of Metaphor,* esp. pp. 157–173.

52 · At least for the time being; on the "failure" of Puritanism in the 1590s, see M. M. Knappen, *Tudor Puritanism* (Chicago: University of Chicago Press, 1939), pp. 283–302. For a recent argument for 1595 as the date for composition of the fragments of Book VII, see Russell J. Meyer, "'First in heavens hight': Spenser, Astronomy, and the Date of the *Cantos of Mutability*," *SS* 4 (1983): 115–130.

53 · In *Short Time's Endless Monument: The Symbolism of the Numbers in Edmund Spenser's "Ephithalamion"* (New York: Columbia University Press, 1960).

54 · Ibid., pp. 80–81.

55 · Note that Hieatt quotes, approvingly, D. H. Lawrence: "The old Church knew best the enduring needs of man, beyond the spasmodic needs of today and yesterday . . . the religious and ritualistic rhythm of the year, in human life. . . . Mankind has got to get back to the rhythm of the cosmos, and the permanence of marriage" (pp. 80–81).

In his account of "The Decline of the English Epithalamion," Paul Miller quotes Herbert Weisinger approvingly on marriage: "they are both the defence against disorder and the guarantee of order." And, on myths in general, Clyde Luckholn: "Myths and rituals are reinforced because they reduce the anticipation of disaster." In his essay, Miller describes a "myth of marriage as expressed in the Renaissance epithalamion" in terms of affirmation "that the marriage being celebrated is part of the divine and natural order. It also idealizes the bridal pair and the married condition, and insists upon the strict, sequential observance of the prescribed marriage rites and customs." To Miller, Spenser's poem "represents the zenith of the tradition in English" (in *TSLL* 12 [1970–71]: 405–416). In such a view, the immediate, specific moment of marriage as a means of proclaiming to a specific situation the God who acts in specific moments has lost all meaning, for it has been subsumed into the cycle of mythic religion. Christian marriage is not permanent—Jesus said, "they which shalbe counted worthie to enjoie . . . the resurrection from the dead, nether marie wives, nether are maried," which the Geneva Bible interprets to mean that marriage will be unnecessary after the resurrection, since it is "to mainteine & increase mankinde, when we shal be immortal, it shal not be in anie use" (Luke 20:34–36). It is, for the couple in the specifics of this temporal existence, a way of dealing with those specifics and of participating in God's specific actions for their redemption.

56 · Ibid., p. 405. Miller would have us read *epithalamia* as celebrations of marriage as "part of the natural order" (p. 410). To the extent to which we can speak of an objectively existing natural order in this age, instead of order as that which is sought, and listen to the reasons the Prayer Book gives for marriage ("a remedy against sin" as well as for mutual comfort and procreation), we can just as easily say that a marriage rite is a sign of human alienation from the order of things.

57 · For an earlier discussion of epithalamic conventions and Spenser's departure from them, see Thomas M. Greene, "Spenser and the Epithalamic Convention," *CL* 9 (1957): 215–228.

58 · Thus Welsford, *Epithalamion*, p. 180.

59 · Quoted from the translation of Roy Arthur Swanson (New York: Bobbs-Merrill, 1959), pp. 52–59.

60 · As Welsford, *Epithalamion*, suggests, p. 180.

61 · For a more traditional view of the role of Orpheus in this poem and of mythic

material generally, see Richard Neuse, "The Triumph over Hasty Accidents. A Note on the Symbolic Mode of the *Epithalamion*," *MLN* 61 (1966): 161–174.

62 · Thus Welsford, *Epithalamion*, p. 173.

63 · See Alexander Dunlop, "Calendar Symbolism in the *Amoretti*," *N&Q*, n.s. 16 (January 1969): 24–26, and O. B. Hardison, Jr., "*Amoretti* and the *Dolce Stil Novo*," *ELR* 2 (1972): 208–216.

64 · "'Fruitfullest Virginia': Edmund Spenser, Roanoke Island, the Bower of Bliss," *Renaissance Papers 1984*, pp. 1–17.

65 · In "Spenser's *Amoretti* and the Art of the Liturgy," *SEL* 14 (1974): 47–61.

3. George Herbert

1 · In poems written to his mother, *Works*, p. 206.

2 · In *The Country Parson*, reprinted in *Works*, pp. 237–243, under the headings "The Parson's state of Life" and "The Parson in his house."

3 · In *Apology*, p. 84.

4 · The matter turns on whether or not one reads poems such as "Christmas," "The Holy Communion," and several others as having two parts or constituting two poems; see discussions of individual poems in my edition (New York: Paulist Press, 1981).

5 · In applying this Pauline emphasis to Herbert, I will depart sharply from those Herbert scholars who view him primarily as the poet of "the individual Christian." For an exposition of this position in its fullest form, see Barbara K. Lewalski, "Typology and Poetry: A Consideration of Herbert, Vaughan, and Marvell," in *Illustrious Evidence*, ed. Earl Miner (Berkeley: University of California Press, 1977), pp. 41–69. See also her *Protestant Poetics*, esp. pp. 13–27. See also Richard Strier, *Love Known*, for an extreme view of Herbert's individualism in which "the religious life [is] entirely a matter of the 'heart'" (p. 163). Stanley Fish also claims that Herbert seeks a "spirituall Temple" and locates it "in the heart of the reader"; see *The Living Temple: George Herbert and Catechizing* (Berkeley: University of California Press, 1978), p. 54. My larger argument is indebted to Fish for inspiration, as further notes will make clear, but I find his perspective on Herbert misleading and partial at this point.

6 · In *Works*, ed. Hutchinson, pp. 224, 236, 255. All further quotations from *The Country Parson* will be from this edition and will be cited by page number in the text.

7 · *Prayer Books of Edward VI*, p. 446.

8 · From the Latin *aedificare*, "to make a building," a usage now rare but common in the seventeenth century.

9 · Attempts to find a metaphor for Herbert's poetic structure in *The Temple* are legion; what all have in common is the substitution of a static and closed model, whether architectural or psychological, for the Pauline image of constant openness to growth and copiousness of method. See, for example, John David Walker, "The Architectonics of George Herbert's *The Temple*," *ELH* 29 (1962): 289–305; Annabel (Endicott) Patterson, "The Structure of George Herbert's *Temple*: A Reconsideration," *UTQ* 34 (1965): 226–237; Sara William Hanley, CSJ, "Temples in *The Temple*: George Herbert's Study of the Church," *SEL* 8 (1968): 120–135; John R. Mulder,

"George Herbert's *The Temple:* Design and Methodology," *SCN* 31 (1973): 37–45; and Robert Higbie, "Images of Enclosure in George Herbert's *The Temple*," *TSLL* 15 (1974): 627–638. My concern is not to offer yet another static model or a scheme with a predetermined outcome, but to find Herbert's poems informed by their on-going relationship to yet another open-ended enterprise, the public worship of Anglicanism in the early seventeenth century. John Booty, "George Herbert: *The Temple* and *The Book of Common Prayer*," *Mosaic* 12 (1979): 75–90, and Heather Asals, *Equivocal Predication: George Herbert's Way to God* (Toronto: University of Toronto Press, 1981), with their paradigmatic images of "contrition-absolution" and the "breaking of the word," both echoing motifs of the Prayer Book, seem far closer to the mark, for both point to facilitating rather than delimiting actions of the poet.

10 · From *The Temple*, in *Works*, ed. Hutchinson, p. 198.

11 · For a review of idealistic social visions held by Puritans in the seventeenth century, see the works of Christopher Hill, especially his recent *Milton and the English Revolution* (New York: Viking, 1977). See also, of course, William Haller's classic *The Rise of Puritanism* (New York: Columbia University Press, 1938).

12 · Contained in *Liturgies and Occasional Forms of Prayer set forth in the Reign of Queen Elizabeth*, ed. W. K. Clay (Cambridge: Parker Society, 1851), pp. 288–289.

13 · This section of *The Country Parson* is found by Stanley Fish to be central to Herbert's strategies in *The Temple;* see *The Living Temple*, esp. pp. 1–53. My argument is not that Fish is wrong, but that *The Country Parson* also provides many other strategies to enable the parson's role, and that those suggested in this section do not exhaust either the parson's task or his methods or the choice of them exemplified in *The Temple*.

14 · The poet/priest's role of showing forth Christ through "breaking" words into double predicates is explored in richly illuminating detail in Asals, *Equivocal Predication*. Her brilliant study shares with my work a common effort to recover the significance of Anglicanism for our understanding of Herbert; although my approach and choice of emphasis are somewhat different, I hope that in the long run our work is mutually supportive.

15 · See his extremely important essay, "Letting Go: The Dialectic of the Self in Herbert's Poetry," in *Self-Consuming Artifacts: The Experience of Seventeenth-Century Literature* (Berkeley: University of California Press, 1972), pp. 156–223.

16 · The relationship between "The Church-Porch" and catechetical instruction has been rightly stressed by Stanley Fish (*The Living Temple*, pp. 128–129). In the context of Anglicanism's emphasis on the universality and significance of baptism, Summers' thesis that "The Church-Porch" is "pre-Christian," in his introduction to *The Selected Poems of George Herbert* (New York: 1967), p. xxii, and that of Stephanie Yearwood that it is "non-Christian," in her "The Rhetoric of Form in *The Temple*," *SEL* 23 (1983): 132, are not tenable. For links between "The Church-Porch" and baptism, see Patterson, "The Structure of George Herbert's Temple," p. 357; or between it and an entry way into the church, see Mary Ellen Rickey, *Utmost Art* (Lexington: University of Kentucky Press, 1966), p. 6. Such studies create an artificial distinction between Christian and non-Christian life in seventeenth-century England. The life described in "Perirrhanterium" is not one that could be lived "through [one's] own efforts" (Rickey), because anyone addressed by this poem in Herbert's day was already baptized and thus a recipient of grace. One did not need preparation "for entering the

church proper" since through baptism one was already a member; what confirmation marked was a new stage of life within that church.

17 · In her classic study, *A Reading of George Herbert* (Chicago: University of Chicago Press, 1952), esp. pp. 19–99, in which she finds Herbert's "The Sacrifice" informed by his knowledge of the Sarum rites for the Good Friday Liturgy, not used in England since 1558.

18 · See *Equivocal Predication*, esp. pp. 11, 18–37. Asals' treatment deals with the interplay of words in Herbert's text; I extend her central insight to larger units.

19 · *Living Temple*, pp. 168–169.

20 · See his *The Shape of the Liturgy*, esp. p. 2 on the corporate nature of the Eucharist and the need for common agreement on what one is doing rather than on what it means, pp. 48–102 for the fourfold shape, and pp. 735–753 for an eloquent summary of its significance.

21 · Mary Ellen Rickey argues that the altar depicted here is not a Christian but a pagan or Hebrew sacrificial altar (*Utmost Art*, pp. 14–16). She is right in noting that Anglicans aggressively opposed the theology of the Mass as a resacrifice of Christ, but does not see the Eucharist as an offering "of our selves, our souls and bodies, to be a reasonable, holy, and lively sacrifice," as the Prayer Book puts it and which would seem to be Herbert's point here. Rickey sunders the link between the altar referred to in the poem and the visual shape the poem presents.

22 · Vendler sees a similar kind of incompleteness which she construes as requiring "a priest, to repeat on the altar [Christ's] own original sacrifice in offering himself on the Cross." See *The Poetry of George Herbert* (Cambridge: Harvard University Press, 1975), p. 62. But this will not accord with Herbert's eucharistic theology either, for Christ's sacrifice was "a full, perfect, and sufficient sacrifice, oblation, and satisfaction for the sins of the whole world," according to the Prayer Book.

23 · In seeking to see Herbert as giving all art to God, Stanley Fish notices the split between the altar referred to in the poem and the visual shape but credits God as the shaper of the poem (*Self-Consuming Artifacts*, pp. 208–215). This is of course true in one sense, but I want to introduce the poet as didactic writer here and thus find it more helpful to see the divine action as a larger field which includes the agency of the poet as one who would pose possibilities for understanding and assenting to divine action by using the shaping of the poem as a way of raising those possibilities. In Sidneyan terms, we are called here to "praise the Maker of that Maker."

24 · Robert B. Shaw, *The Call of God: The Theme of Vocation in the Poetry of Donne and Herbert* (Cambridge, Mass.: Cowley, 1981), p. 104.

25 · See her extremely important *Costly Monuments: Representations of the Self in George Herbert's Poetry* (Cambridge, Mass.: Harvard University Press, 1982), p. 83.

26 · For a convenient summary of these arguments, see Harman, *Costly Monuments*, pp. 86–87.

27 · Ibid., pp. 82–83, although I would stress that the loss of self-identity enables not merely a giving up of self but a reception of a new kind of self in relation to that context, that of *"Child/Lord."*

28 · Since C. A. Patrides argued that the "Eucharist is the marrow of Herbert's sensibility" and that if *"The Temple* is indeed a 'structure,' it is an eucharistic one," others have expanded on this claim. See Patrides, ed., *The English Poems of George Herbert* (London: Dent, 1974), pp. 17–18. See also Elizabeth McLaughlin and Gail

Thomas, "Communion in *The Temple*," *SEL* 15 (1975): 111–125 and most especially Heather Asals, *Equivocal Predication,* which is the fullest effort to date to explore the poetic significance of Herbert's eucharistic concerns.

29 · I believe these lines are actually the text of another poem; see my edition of *The Temple,* p. 153. See also John Shawcross, "Herbert's Double Poems: A Problem in the Text of *The Temple,*" in *"Too Rich to Clothe the Sunne": Essays on George Herbert,* ed. Claude J. Summers and Ted-Larry Pebworth (Pittsburgh: University of Pittsburgh Press, 1980), pp. 211–228, who arrives at a similar position, although independently of my own research.

30 · Asals, *Equivocal Predication,* p. 14.

31 · Fish, *Living Temple,* p. 161.

32 · For a discussion of Herbert's attitudes toward love from a more traditional perspective and for a review of patristic and medieval versions of love, see Rosemond Tuve's famous essay, "George Herbert and *Caritas*" (1959; reprinted in *Essays by Rosemond Tuve,* ed. Thomas P. Roche [Princeton: Princeton University Press, 1970]). Tuve's view is that the issues in Herbert come down to a conflict between *caritas* and *cupiditas.* She defines the latter as love of self rather than erotic desire.

33 · On Herbert's relationship with the Sidney family, see Summers, *Selected Poems,* pp. 31, 146.

34 · Citations from Sidney's poems will be from the edition of William Ringler (Oxford: Clarendon, 1962).

35 · Chana Bloch's *Spelling the Word: George Herbert and the Bible* (Berkeley: University of California Press, 1985) arrived too late to be much of a presence here. I am pleased to see her concern with Herbert's use of the Bible; I find that the role of the Prayer Book in use as the context for Herbert's reading of the Bible is less central to her understanding than it is to mine, although she does understand, at least in part, the Prayer Book's importance, especially in its version of the Psalms and in its difference from medieval liturgies.

36 · The implications of the Bible as a "closed" book are explored in James Nohrnberg, "On Literature and the Bible," *Centrum* 2 (1974): 5–43. Nohrnberg's remarks need qualification in terms of the relationship between Protestant views of the Bible as icon and Anglican views of the Bible as a text-in-use to facilitate the opening of salvation-history in the present.

37 · See the extremely helpful reading of "Affliction (I)" in terms of its relationship to autobiographical narratives in Harman, *Costly Monuments,* pp. 89–105. A fuller version of this discussion, especially as it concerns autobiographical elements, is found in *ELH* 44 (1977): 267–285.

38 · See Charity, *Events and Their Afterlife,* esp. pp. 158–164. Charity notes on p. 159, "Typology . . . can be seen as an encouragement to acting rightly in relation to God's acts by assisting the hearer to hear rightly the message of God's act (or his new act). It is 'applied' because it is a means of producing an existential confrontation between man and the action of God." In his *Christ Revealed: The History of the Neotypological Lyric in the English Renaissance* (Gainesville: University Presses of Florida, 1982), Ira Clark discusses the use of types in Herbert and other poets of this period "in order to be saved by Christ" (p. 2). By not noting the source for Anglican views of the Bible and by not noting Charity's sense of the didactic functioning of typology, Clark's discussion is more limited and less helpful than it otherwise might be.

39 · For a helpful discussion of this motif, see Robert Higbie, "Images of Enclosure in George Herbert's *The Temple*," *TSLL* 15 (1974): 627–638.

40 · Or so claims Walton, *Lives*, p. 302.

41 · For another discussion of this poem in relation to Simias' poems, see C. C. Brown and W. P. Ingoldsby, "George Herbert's 'Easter-Wings,'" *HLQ* (1972): 131–142.

42 · I am grateful to my former student, Jana McCallum, for pointing this out to me.

43 · In his "'Lord, in thee the *Beauty* lies in the Discovery': 'Love Unknown' and Reading Herbert," *ELH* 39 (1972): 560–584, Ira Clark argues that these interjections "teach [the speaker] to reappraise his situation" (p. 580), yet the speaker's responses are more in keeping with one who sees the second speaker's remarks more as interruptions than as meaningful interpretations. In each case, he quickly gets back to his "long and sad" tale, forcing the second speaker to interrupt again and again and finally to take over the poem.

44 · Stanley Fish reviews the history of interpreting "The Church Militant" in *Living Temple*, pp. 142–145. I agree with Fish that those who have either rejected the place of this section in *The Temple* (especially Patterson, p. 236) or found it a conclusion have done so for the wrong kinds of reasons. Stanley Stewart, for example, in "Time and *The Temple*," *SEL* 6 (1966): 97–110, argues that "The Church Militant" is an apocalyptic poem in which the speaker views time from a position outside it in a timeless realm from which past, present, and future are visible. It is not an apocalyptic poem, since it lacks the cataclysmic imagery such a genre requires, although it is eschatological in the sense that it does posit the fullness of meaning in the end of things. Nor is it written from a perspective outside of time; the speaker is fully *in* time, although through memory, interpretation, and eschatological expectation he can review time past and present and set both in the context of a future expectation. I agree with Fish that *The Temple* ends with the work of the poem unfinished, but not because "The Church Militant" is an "anticlimax" (*Living Temple*, p. 161). Instead, the work is unfinished because the movement through "The Church Militant" is toward a future that is as yet unclear, and because the speaker ends in prayerful expectation and contingent petition that God end things in a way favorable to the claims made for God in *The Temple* as a whole, not with anything finished or over.

45 · For an assessment of the evidence concerning this matter, see Hutchinson, *Works*, p. 547.

46 · In *Praise in 'The Faerie Queene'* (Lincoln: University of Nebraska Press, 1978), p. 97.

47 · For an examination of this in more detail, see the introduction to my edition of Herbert, pp. 21–25.

4. Henry Vaughan

1 · In *Works*, ed. L. C. Martin, 2nd ed. (Oxford: Clarendon, 1957), p. 392. All further quotations from the works of Vaughan will be from this edition and will be cited by page numbers (for prose) or line numbers (for poetry).

2 · In his *Life of George Herbert*, p. 302. David Novarr does not mention the possibility, but I strongly suspect that Walton's picture of Herbert is influenced, to some measure, by Vaughan's interpretation of Herbert and his language for talking about both Herbert's life and work and his own. Novarr does demonstrate that Walton was writing about Herbert in the early 1650s (in *The Compleat Angler*) and was gathering material by 1650 which would ultimately result in the *Life*. See Novarr, *The Making of Walton's 'Lives,'* pp. 302–304. Granting this, I believe it not too much to conjecture that Walton would make use of Vaughan's praise of Herbert, published in 1652 (*The Mount of Olives*) and 1655 (second edition of *Silex Scintillans*).

3 · Quoted in Horton Davies, *Worship and Theology in England from Andrewes to Baxter, 1603–1690* (Princeton: Princeton University Press, 1965), pp. 147–148.

4 · In the introduction to my edition of George Herbert I argued that Vaughan and Traherne, in contrast to Herbert, seek a "paradise within" along the lines sketched out by Louis Martz in his *The Paradise Within* (New Haven: Yale University Press, 1964). I here retract that reading, and thus I position my reading of Vaughan in opposition to Martz and also to R. A. Durr, who stresses mysticism as the key to Vaughan in *On the Mystical Poetry of Henry Vaughan* (Cambridge: Harvard University Press, 1962). I agree with Frank Kermode that Vaughan converts mystical language (and hermetic language, too, for that matter) "to his own purposes," although my argument about what Vaughan's purposes were is not that of Kermode. See his "The Private Imagery of Henry Vaughan," *RES*, n.s. 1 (1950): 206–225. As James D. Simmonds points out in his *Masques of God: Form and Theme in the Poetry of Henry Vaughan* (Pittsburgh: University of Pittsburgh Press, 1972), p. 10, the origin of the traditional view of Vaughan lies in "the belief that Vaughan's sacred poetry was inspired by a single radical experience—conversion or spiritual awakening—and that this experience was essentially characterized by a withdrawal of his mind from ordinary human experience into a reflexive preoccupation with its solitary self." In this group fall Durr, Itrat Husain, *The Mystical Element in the Metaphysical Poets of the Seventeenth Century* (Edinburgh: Oliver and Boyd, 1948), and E. C. Pettet, *Of Paradise and Light: A Study of Vaughan's 'Silex Scintillans'* (Cambridge: Cambridge University Press, 1960). Although I disagree with his conclusions, Ross Garner in *Henry Vaughan: Experience and the Tradition* (Chicago: University of Chicago Press, 1959), pp. 128–161, helps point out what is at stake. For Garner, authentic religious experience, because it is of God, is by definition mystical, which then opens to the interpreter of Christian poetry the categories of medieval mystical assent. As I have been at pains to point out, Anglican spirituality is pragmatic and in opposition to the individualizing tendencies of the disciplines of mental prayer and private devotion; it is based on the possession of the Book of Common Prayer by both clergy and laity, the doing of which makes possible the entry of all into the corporate life of the church (see Guthrie, "Anglican Spirituality," p. 5). That is what Vaughan experienced as lost in the 1640s, and the experience of the loss of that sense of corporate identity is what is at issue in *Silex Scintillans*. For the best discussions of Vaughan's poetry, although for my purposes they underemphasize his professed didacticism and the public role he sought in publishing *Silex*, see Simmonds and Jonathan F. S. Post, *Henry Vaughan: The Unfolding Vision* (Princeton: Princeton University Press, 1982). The work of these writers should allay for good charges of looseness and lack of poetic skill in Vaughan.

Post especially is helpful in pointing to the importance of Anglicanism for Vaughan; I am pleased to confirm and extend his insights in my own argument. Although I focus on *Silex Scintillans,* I hope I do not do so at the implicit expense of his other works, as Post suggests others do who share my perspective (*Unfolding Vision,* p. xvi). I do not share with others who focus on *Silex* any belief that Vaughan experienced a conversion in the 1640s. Anglicans, generally, do not have conversion experiences; they claim that at baptism they are reborn by water and the Holy Spirit. They do have experiences of growth and development in their faith, "daily increase in . . . thy manifold gifts of grace" (BCP, p. 288). I agree with Post that historical circumstances, along with the discovery of the role *The Temple* could play in the writing of didactic religious poetry under Puritan rule, had much more to do with Vaughan's writing of *Silex Scintillans* than any personal conversion experience. If we read into Vaughan's desire in the 1655 preface to *Silex* to *"turn many to righteousness"* in terms of nineteenth-century evangelical practice, we seriously misread Vaughan's situation. Puritans rejected Anglican Christian life as Christian; Vaughan, in turn, saw that life as what defined righteousness. We must read Vaughan's didactic intent as a call to faithfulness to the Anglican definition rather than what we now call a change from non-Christian to Christian. How Vaughan sought to turn many to righteousness by refusing to conform to the new religious situation or by refusing to lapse into inactivity, but instead to find in the death of Anglicanism for the time a sign of God's ongoing activity and to find in that the incentive to keep faith with Anglican definitions of righteousness is what I seek to demonstrate in this chapter.

5 · Quoted in Davies, *Worship and Theology,* p. 143.

6 · Thomas Richards, *A History of the Puritan Movement in Wales* (London: National Eisteddford Assn., 1920), pp. 120–122.

7 · F. E. Hutchinson, *Henry Vaughan: A Life and Interpretation* (Oxford: Clarendon, 1947), pp. 118–120. See also Post, *Unfolding Vision,* pp. 121–123.

8 · Sharon Cadman Seelig points to this in Vaughan when she notes that Vaughan's poems "characteristically contrast a former positive state—either in his own personal experience or in that of mankind as a whole—with his present unhappy one," although her concern to show *Silex Scintillans* "as the record of the poet's inner struggles" leads her in directions I do not wish to follow. See her *The Shadow of Eternity,* pp. 48, 73.

9 · For other accounts of Vaughan's debt to and use of Herbert, see Pettit, *Of Paradise and Light,* pp. 51–70, Mary Ellen Rickey, "Vaughan, *The Temple,* and Poetic Form," *SP* 59 (1962): 162–170. Seelig, *Shadow of Eternity,* pp. 44–46, and, especially, Post, *Unfolding Vision,* pp. 70–162. Post's is the most detailed and helpful account, and I am pleased in this study to extend and confirm his insights.

10 · Seelig, *Shadow of Eternity,* pp. 44–45.

11 · *Works,* p. 186.

12 · In his *Life of Herbert,* p. 315.

13 · On this, see E. L. Marilla, "Henry Vaughan and the Civil War," *JEGP* 41 (1942): 514–526, Simmonds, *Masques of God,* pp. 39–41, 85–116, and Post, *Unfolding Vision,* pp. 117–124.

14 · See "The Form and Manner of Making and Consecrating Bishops, Priests, and Deacons," in *Liturgical Services in the Reign of Queen Elizabeth,* ed. William K. Clay (Cambridge: Cambridge University Press, 1847), pp. 288–289.

15 · Ibid., p. 289.

16 · Ibid., p. 291.

17 · Vaughan's use of "Oblation" as a description of what he offers here also ties together Christ's own self-offering, described in the Prayer Book as "a full, perfect, and sufficient sacrifice, oblation, and satisfaction for the sins of the whole world" (BCP, p. 263), and the action of the communicants, who offer themselves, "our souls and bodies, to be a reasonable, holy and lively sacrifice unto thee" (BCP, p. 264), language also used in the ordination rite to describe the action of self-oblation performed by the candidates for the priesthood.

18 · Post notes the deferral of poems specifically about the Eucharist in *Silex I* until after what he deems a "self-confirmation" by Vaughan in "The Match" (see *Unfolding Vision,* p. 118, n. 6), because Anglicans had to be confirmed before they could receive the Eucharist. But Vaughan actually refers to receiving the Eucharist in "The Passion" ("Most blessed Vine! / Whose juice so good / I feel as Wine, / But thy faire branches felt as blood" [ll. 15–18]), four poems prior to "The Match," suggesting that Vaughan is moving through "The Match" from the role of communicant to officiant who can use Herbert's opening lines from "The Banquet"—"Welcome sweet and sacred cheer, / Welcome deare"—to begin "The Holy Communion" with "Welcome sweet, and sacred feast; welcome life," thus placing himself in a position to replicate Herbert's priestly office as a writer of poems to the Eucharist.

19 ' I disagree with Post, *Unfolding Vision,* p. 125, that Vaughan "reinstates a version of the Book of Common Prayer"; there was for Vaughan only one Prayer Book, and his efforts are toward enabling and persuading his readers to maintain faithfulness to that book by reminding them of it and the sense of the Christian life it creates, not toward any other "version" of it.

20 · Understanding Vaughan's relationship to Herbert here helps us correct the readings of Seelig, *Shadow of Eternity,* p. 71, who sees in *Silex II* an emphasis on "the inner light of faith rather than a vision or an external event," or Post, *Unfolding Vision,* p. 211, who sees an experience of "a still point of eternal communion with God that will be his future." Post, unlike Seelig and other writers on Vaughan, does appreciate Vaughan's sense of the workings of God in history but is far more ready to see an achievement of a divine-human union already rather than a constant struggle to keep faith with the God of history in light of loss and an expectation of fulfillment even in the face of evidence to the contrary.

21 · My quotations from Vaughan's Latin poem are in reference to the translation of Ross Garner, quoted in *Major Poets of the Earlier Seventeenth Century,* ed. Barbara K. Lewalski and Andrew J. Sabol (New York: Odyssey, 1973), pp. 407–408.

22 · As in the case of many of Herbert's poems which end asking that God act as a way of taking part in the divine process of making things new, many critics read "Regeneration" as finishing something rather than getting it started. Fundamental to this approach is the positing of a regenerative pattern which the poem is seen as acting out. Louis Martz, for example, finds such a pattern in Augustinian meditation (*Paradise Within,* p. 23), R. A. Durr finds it in "the stages of . . . spiritual life" (*On the Mystical Poetry of Henry Vaughan,* p. 82), and E. C. Pettet (*Of Paradise and Light,* p. 104) finds it in a "recovery . . . and discovery . . . of religious faith." In these and other interpretations such a pattern is used to bring clarity to the poem's syntactical and imagistic confusions, confusions which I find deliberate *as confusions* rather than

problems which conceal a rational solution which can be discovered if one only has the key. Thomas J. Wyly's "Vaughan's 'Regeneration' Reconsidered," *PQ* 55 (1976): 340–353, reveals the consequences of taking Anglican writers on regeneration out of the Prayer Book context, because he believes that the New Testament views renewal "exclusively as a change within the sinner" rather than in relationship to the church as body of Christ. While I agree with Claude J. Summers and Ted-Larry Pebworth that what they term the "religiopolitical context" of the poem is important, they too argue that the poem marks "a traditional spiritual quest" in their "Vaughan's Temple in Nature and 'Regeneration,'" *JEGP* 74 (1975): 354. They are delighted to find in "Regeneration" the architecture of the Anglican church building discovered in a natural setting, but such a reading rationalizes Vaughan's play between the physical setting of the speaker's narrative and his experience in that setting. Sharon Seelig is closer to the point when she argues that "'Regeneration' does not end in vision, in complete revelation, but only in the hope of it"; see her *Shadow of Eternity,* p. 82.

23 · Post suggests other parallels in Herbert for the formal poetic elements in "Regeneration"; see *Unfolding Vision,* p. 84.

24 · In *On Christian Doctrine,* p. 16.

25 · I thus disagree with Post, who sees in Vaughan a blending of past and future so that "the present [shrinks] into an almost nonexistent moment between the two" (*Unfolding Vision,* p. 99). Vaughan's concern in *Silex Scintillans* is always an exploration of the present in relationship to past and future, specifically the new kind of present which lacks the old liturgical bridge between past and future. Nor do I see in the opening of "Religion" Vaughan's "praise of God for the opportunity to walk among His sacred leaves" (p. 104).

26 · Thomas O. Calhoun, in his *Henry Vaughan: The Achievement of 'Silex Scintillans'* (Newark: University of Delaware Press, 1981) makes a similar point about "Religion," although I disagree with his conclusion that "Vaughan's only restorative hope lies in private prayer" (p. 147). Vaughan's hope lies elsewhere than in any human activity, and the "private" element in his poems is always in the context of the experience of losing public prayer. In general I agree with Post's assessment of the interpretation of Vaughan based on concern with his supposed hermeticism, the approach taken by Calhoun. See *Unfolding Vision,* p. xii.

27 · Calhoun notes, appropriately, that "The voices informing the measure of Vaughan's lines bind the poet to a tradition of sacred literature through which he must firmly and consciously have wished to express himself in the act of revealing, to all, the bond" (*Achievement,* p. 74), but, at the same time, Vaughan wants us to see the creation of his situation in verse in juxtaposition to what could be assumed about the use of "sacred literature" in the past. He is not out to create a timeless present—Calhoun says, "all time at one time"—through a "mosaic synthesis."

28 · Post also argues for Vaughan's growing sense of living in the Last Days, although he puts too much emphasis on the role of eschatology in *Silex II* and too little on its role in *Silex I.* He also equates apocalyptic with eschatology, a common but unwarranted confusion about two modes of biblical discourse. *Unfolding Vision,* pp. 186–211.

29 · I thus find Leland H. Chambers' "Vaughan's 'The World': The Limits of Extrinsic Criticism," *SEL* 8 (1969): 137–150, a far more helpful discussion than that

of Maren-Sofie Rostvig's "Syncretistic Imagery and the Unity of Vaughan's 'The World,'" *PLL* 5 (1969): 415–422.

30 · See *A New History of the Book of Common Prayer,* by Francis Procter and Walter Howard Frere (London: Macmillan, 1965), p. 156, and Davies, *Worship,* p. 147.

31 · Post argues, in *Unfolding Vision,* that Vaughan was to his friends "a source of continuity amid turmoil" (p. 124). The edition of *Silex Scintillans* published in 1655 incorporated unsold sheets of the poems in *Silex I.* Assuming that *Silex I* was printed in an edition of one thousand copies in 1650, if enough of the sheets from that edition survived to remain usable in the edition of 1655, then we must conclude that only Vaughan's closest friends may ever have seen a copy of *Silex I.*

32 · The more positive and celebratory tone of *Silex II* has been noted by Pettet, *Of Paradise and Light,* pp. 202–203. Post also distinguishes between *Silex I* and *Silex II* but sees *Silex I* as characterized by an emphasis on beginnings and dawnings and *Silex II* by an emphasis on endings and "invading darkness" (pp. 198–199), although he notes that these foci are not exclusive (p. 191). He thus argues that *Silex II* is an apocalyptic work with an emphasis on the imminence of the Last Things. One reason for the shape of Post's reading is his desire to make the whole of *Silex Scintillans* correspond to an interpretation of the Bible as a book that "moves from Genesis to Revelation, beginning to end, light to darkness" (p. 190). One could, of course, just as easily say that the Bible moves from beginning (of creation) to beginning (of the kingdom) and from light ("Let there be light") to light ("there shall be no night there" [Revelation 21:25]). More important, my argument is that eschatological (not apocalyptic) elements are present in both *Silex I* and *Silex II;* what changes is the function of those elements in Vaughan's persuasive poetic, from *Silex I's* use of them to enable the speaker to define his situation as one not outside the history of divine saving activity to *Silex II's* celebration of the "prelibation" of the eschatological banquet available here to the one who sees the world from an eschatological perspective, which serves as a further persuasive force encouraging the reader to keep the faith in difficult times.

33 · Vaughan's highly selective use of the language and rhetorical stance of Revelation is appropriate for an Anglican in the midst of a world in which many Puritans were more enthusiastic about describing events in terms of true apocalyptic (see Post, pp. 187–188). The early Reformers, from Luther forward, had questioned the canonical authority of Revelation, and Cranmer reflected at least some doubts about the value of its more lurid imagery of divine retribution by excluding those sections of the work from use in the Anglican church by leaving them off the calendar of lessons.

34 · Lewalski finds here "Christ's ascension typologically recapitulated in his own spiritual experience, raising him to a new plateau of spiritual assurance above the turmoils of Part I" (*Protestant Poetics,* p. 322). On the one hand, Vaughan here is closer to the kind of meditative tradition articulated by Louis Martz, in which a mediator places himself, through the memory, in the midst of a biblical event, than he is to the kind of meditation advocated by Lewalski, in which the mediator sees a biblical motif repeated inwardly, for Vaughan clearly here imagines himself present so that "I see them, hear them, . . . move amongst them." I see Vaughan here as finding in the texts for the Anglican eucharistic celebration of the Ascension the language to articulate what it means to experience how "Lord Jesus . . . / Dost thou feed thine!" In the

absence of a literal feeding in an Ascension Day Eucharist, Vaughan can proclaim the possibility of feeding "by thy Spirit" because he can use the biblical account of the Ascension as the language to articulate his experience and thus open the possibility that he in the present shares a common future with those present at the actual ascension of Christ. See Martz, *Poetry of Meditation*, p. 30.

35 · For more on *Silex* 1655's missing emblem, see Calhoun, *Achievement*, pp. 220–225.

36 · For more on the role of the prophets as effective witnesses to the reliability of God and to the ongoing acts of God even in the destruction of Jerusalem, see Guthrie, *Theology as Thanksgiving*, pp. 71–109.

37 · Vaughan is not really laying out a paradigm of the Christian life here, as though there were a lock-step pattern which must be followed, although many critics have seen such a pattern in Vaughan and in Herbert as well. Instead, Vaughan's purposes are much more experiential and promissory; to persist in "tears" of lament and contrition will lead to "light" and praise. Vaughan's point is to encourage the reader to accept self-definitions in relationship to God that will lead to tears by offering the promise of a reward for that effort in spite of the cost. To argue for a fixed pattern in Vaughan is to lose most of the point of the experience he constructs.

38 · For a discussion of the ways in which the early Anglican Reformers took over the medieval use of the tree as an image of the individual Christian life and made it a metaphor for the Anglican corporate church state, see my "Godly and Fruitful Lessons," in Booty, *The Godly Kingdom*, pp. 52–56.

39 · Lewalski notes that "Vaughan's speaker seldom experiences the direct encounters and developing relationship with God or Christ so important to Herbert" (*Protestant Poetics*, p. 319). Just so; the absence of that community which proclaimed that in its worship life it became "very members incorporate in the mystical body of thy Son" creates Vaughan's central problem, which is to find how to keep faith with that body in its absence. His affirmation here of Christ's continued presence to that body in its weeping is one of the great achievements of *Silex Scintillans*.

40 · And were still arguing about in 1660; see Francis Procter and Walter Howard Frere, *A New History of the Book of Common Prayer* (London: Macmillan, 1965), pp. 166–167.

41 · In arguing for the supposed apocalypticism of *Silex II*, Post says that "The Jews" is a poem which "responds to the traditional millenarian belief in the conversion of the Jews as a signal of the Second Coming," a subject "that even the most untutored in apocalyptic prophecies would recognize as appropriate to the hour" (*Unfolding Vision*, p. 200). While it is true that the conversion of the Jews was a part of millenarian belief, it was not exclusively so, and Vaughan's treatment of this motif is totally lacking in the tone and schemes of millenarian expectation, which offers a "precise" calendar of events for the end-time, of which the conversion of the Jews was only a minor part, and an emphasis on divine vengeance against the anti-Christ and the personified forces of darkness. In Vaughan's poem, on the other hand, the expectation of the conversion of the Jews is a sign of divine love extending to "the lost Son by the newly found," not a sign of retribution, and is hereby a sign of hope for the speaker as well.

42 · For a very helpful reading of "The Night," see Post, *Unfolding Vision*, pp.

201–211. My only disagreement with Post is in his equation of the speaker with the opinion of the "men" of ll. 50–52, who "Say it is late and dusky, because they / See not all clear." What Vaughan sets up in this poem is a contrast between Nicodemus, who saw Christ as light in the darkness, and the speaker's present situation in which night is seen as "this world's defeat," and the world is characterized in terms of its "ill-guiding light" where the speaker claims to "Erre more then I can do by night." In such a world, a "sight" of Christ "can never more be done." For the speaker, hope lies in the possibility ("some say") of "A deep, but dazling darkness" in God, a reversal of God-as-light in Nicodemus' night, in which the speaker can live, instead of in the "ill-guiding light" of this world which leads men who "See not all clear" to say "it is late and dusky." Vaughan is playing here with divine light/darkness versus human perception of light/darkness and asks for incorporation into the divine rather than the humanly constructed version. To see clearly now would be to see God as "deep, but dazling darkness," not as "late and dusky," which suggests further obscuring of sight.

43 · See the note in Martin's edition, p. 751.

44 · The Prayer Book begins the *Gloria,* "Glory be to God on high," while Luke's version in the King James Version is as Vaughan quotes it here—"Glory be to God in the highest."

45 · So much so that on one Easter Sunday in the early nineteenth century only six persons received Communion at Saint Paul's Cathedral.

Epilogue

1 · See Jerry H. Bentley, *Humanists and Holy Writ: New Testament Scholarship in the Renaissance* (Princeton: Princeton University Press, 1983), for a convincing argument that modern critical study of the Bible began with the work of Valla and Erasmus.

2 · For a convenient summary of what is known of Traherne's life, see the introduction to H. M. Margoliouth's edition, *Thomas Traherne: Centuries, Poems, and Thanksgivings* (Oxford: Clarendon, 1958), xxiii–xxxviii. All quotations from Traherne's works are from this edition and will be cited by page numbers (for prose) and line numbers (for poems) in the text.

3 · It is thus incorrect to argue, as Leah Sinanoglou Marcus does in her *Childhood and Cultural Despair: A Theme and Variations in Seventeenth-Century Literature* (Pittsburgh: University of Pittsburgh Press, 1978), p. 153, that Vaughan and Traherne "faced the same dilemma: how to regain the traditional Anglican vision of order when the traditional governmental and ecclesiastical hierarchies had disappeared," a small issue in the midst of an otherwise intriguing book. Traherne faced not the disappearance of traditional hierarchies, but their restoration.

4 · See Margoliouth, *Thomas Traherne,* pp. xxxiv–xxxv.

5 · Ibid., p. xxxii. This quotation, from an unsigned preface to the reader in Traherne's *A Serious and Pathetical Contemplation* (1699), notes that Traherne "had the misfortune to come abroad into the World, in the late disordered Times when the Foundations were cast down, and this excellent Church laid in the dust." This writer's emphasis on Traherne's doing of the Daily Offices echoes Walton's similar remarks about Herbert and suggests that they shared a common intent to underscore the importance of the Offices for building up "this excellent Church."

6 · The best recent discussion of Traherne is Stanley Stewart's *The Expanded Voice: The Art of Thomas Traherne* (San Marino: Huntington Library, 1970). See also Richard Douglas Jordan, *The Temple of Eternity: Thomas Traherne's Philosophy of Time* (Port Washington, N.Y.: Kennikat, 1972) and A. L. Clements, *The Mystical Poetry of Thomas Traherne* (Cambridge: Harvard University Press, 1969).

7 · This tendency would culminate in the eighteenth century in what David B. Morris has called a pursuit of sublime feelings in the religious poetry of private devotion; see his *The Religious Sublime: Christian Poetry and Critical Tradition in 18th-Century England* (Lexington: University Press of Kentucky, 1972).

8 · Dryden's religious pilgrimage, as well as the history of its interpretations, is carefully discussed in G. Douglas Atkins' *The Faith of John Dryden* (Lexington: University Press of Kentucky, 1980).

9 · Cited from the edition of James Kinsley, *The Poems and Fables of John Dryden* (London: Oxford University Press, 1970), pp. 275, 282. All quotations from *Religio Laici* will be from this edition and will be cited by page numbers (for prose) or line numbers (for the poem itself).

10 · Although Dryden has only a few pages earlier disagreed with "the Church Discipline" in expressing his difficulties with the Athanasian Creed and the Nicene Creed. The latter was the creed appointed for use at all celebrations of the Eucharist, while the former was appointed by the Prayer Book of 1662 to be read instead of the Apostles' Creed on fourteen feasts of the church year, including Christmas and Easter, at Morning Prayer.

11 · See Tompkins, *Reader-Response Criticism,* p. 203, and Fish, *Self-Consuming Artifacts,* pp. 5–21.

12 · On Milton's use of myth, see Michael Lieb, *Poetics of the Holy: A Reading of Paradise Lost* (Chapel Hill: University of North Carolina Press, 1981). For Milton and the end of Christian humanism, see Sloane, *Donne.*

Index